FRITZ HENNIG

Tapping Hitler's Generals

Tapping Hitler's Generals

Transcripts of Secret Conversations, 1942–45

SÖNKE NEITZEL

Translated by Geoffrey Brooks
Introduction by Ian Kershaw

Frontline Books
MBI Publishing, St Paul

Tapping Hitler's Generals
Transcripts of Secret Conversations, 1942–45

First published in 2007 by Frontline Books, an imprint of Pen & Sword Books Limited,
47 Church Street, Barnsley, S. Yorkshire S70 2AS
and
MBI Publishing Co., Galtier Plaza, Suite 200, 380 Jackson Street, St Paul,
MN 55101-3885, USA

Copyright © Ullstein Buchverlage GmbH, 2005
Translation © Pen & Sword Books Limited, 2007
Foreword © Ian Kershaw, 2007

Publishing history
First published in 2005 by Ullstein Buchverlage GmbH as *Abgehört: Deutsche Generäle
in britischer Kriegsgefangenschaft 1942–1945*. This edition, published by Frontline
Books, includes an updated Introduction, Notes and Biographies, and a new Foreword by
Ian Kershaw.

The right of Sönke Neitzel to be identified as the author of this work has been asserted
by in accordance with the Copyright, Designs and Patents Act of 1988.

All rights reserved. No part of this publication may be reproduced, stored in or
introduced into a retrieval system, or transmitted, in any form, or by any means
(electronic, mechanical, photocopying, recording or otherwise) without the prior written
permission of the publisher. Any person who does any unauthorized act in relation to
this publication may be liable to criminal prosecution and civil claims for damages.

British Library Cataloguing-in Publication Data

Tapping Hitler's generals : transcripts of secret conversations, 1942–45
1. Germany. Heer – General staff officers 2. World War, 1939–1945 – Prisoners and
prisons, German 3. World War, 1939–1945 – Military intelligence – Great Britain
I. Neitzel, Sönke
940.5'48641

ISBN: 978-1-84415-705-1

Library of Congress Cataloging-in Publication Data available

Typeset by MATS Typesetters, Essex

Printed and bound in Great Britain by Biddles Ltd, King's Lynn

CONTENTS

Foreword

Long after 1945, what has been called 'the legend of the "unblemished" Wehrmacht', which claimed to have remained largely detached from the criminality of the Hitler regime and the atrocities attributable to the SS, still survived. This was to some extent an indication of the limited state of research (and a tendency to separate the military history of the war from the structural analysis of the Nazi state). The legend was shored up, too, by the postwar memoirs of leading military figures, who sought to uphold the honour of the Wehrmacht – and at the same time to exculpate themselves. But the sustenance of the legend also had political and social underpinnings. It fitted the interests of the young Federal Republic of Germany (especially when it acquired its new army, the Bundeswehr, in 1955), and of the Western Allies in the early years of the Cold War. And, not least, it accorded in part with a readiness (in some ways perhaps a necessity) among many ordinary people to believe that the deep stain of Nazism had not permeated absolutely everything, that the armed forces in which fathers, brothers, uncles and friends had served, had fought honourably for their country.

Over time, the legend was certainly eroded. Few specialist historians of the Third Reich had ever fully subscribed to it, and their work had at the latest since the 1960s started to implicate the Wehrmacht in the worst crimes against humanity perpetrated by the Nazi regime. But little of this had penetrated far into public consciousness. In the 1990s, however, one of the heated and emotional public debates about the Nazi past that periodically punctuated the politics and culture of the Federal Republic exploded the myth completely. A major exhibition on the Wehrmacht, entitled 'War of Annihilation. Crimes of the Wehrmacht, 1941–1944', which started its tour of major German cities in 1995, completely broke the image of an army which had kept its hands clean. Much in the exhibition was new, and shocking, to the wider public. The controversy that arose spawned a flood of publications, ranging from specialist research monographs to magazine articles, from written eyewitness accounts to television documentaries, which now made it impossible for a younger generation to hold on to notions of a blameless

Wehrmacht that had fought a 'normal' war while Nazi organisations, above all the SS, had perpetrated the crimes. These younger Germans had to face up to the unpleasant fact that their grandfathers, serving in the regular army, not the SS, might well have been implicated in terrible barbarities.

Sparked in part by the 'Wehrmacht Exhibition', a great deal of research in recent years has immensely extended and clarified an understanding of mentalities and patterns of behaviour within the Wehrmacht during the Nazi era, and especially during the World War II. How far the Wehrmacht accepted or rejected Nazi ideological aims has been at the centre of a good deal of the work. Much of the attention has focused on the complicity of the Wehrmacht in the Nazi regime's gross crimes against humanity, notably in Eastern Europe and on the territory of the former Soviet Union, and quite especially in the genocide against the Jews. A central question has been how much guilt the Wehrmacht, from its commanders-in-chief down to ordinary soldiers, carried for these crimes. And, related to these themes, the question of the stance of the Wehrmacht in the dying phase of the Nazi regime, when it was obvious that the war was lost, has been a key issue. Why, even in these last terrible months of the war, which cost the lives of such a relatively high proportion of the total numbers of victims, did the Wehrmacht continue to fight so doggedly in a patently lost cause? What was the attitude within the armed forces towards Hitler and the Nazi leadership, and to those who tried to put an end to the regime (most notably in the bomb-plot of 20 July 1944)? These questions still invite no easy or black-and-white answers.

If anything, answers are even harder to come by with regard to those who held command positions in the armed forces, carrying a high share of responsibility for the Wehrmacht's actions in the Third Reich, than they are for ordinary soldiers. German generals were in their postwar memoirs unsurprisingly anxious to distance themselves from Hitler and the Nazi leadership, to demonstrate their 'unpolitical' concern to carry out their duty as soldiers, and often to underline their own 'resistance' credentials (or at the very least criticism of the actions of the regime while emphasising their powerlessness to alter them). Personal papers, diaries and letters have, of course, often proved valuable, where they survive, in casting light on the contemporary attitudes of specific individuals. But in most cases they do not survive. And official military records for the most part betray little of the genuine political stance of those who compiled them. So it is probably true to say that fewer notable advances in research have been made into the mentality of higher officers of the Wehrmacht than in the case of rank-and-file soldiers.

This is why this impressive edition put together by Sönke Neitzel is so valuable. He has uncovered and examined an unusual, and most revealing, source: the transcriptions of the bugged private conversations of high-ranking German officers in British captivity made by the Combined Services Detailed Interrogation Centre at Trent Park, near Enfield in Middlesex, and now kept in the National Archives (formerly the Public Record Office) in London. Unlike the countless postwar interrogations, in which those being interrogated could conceal or distort a great deal in the answers they gave to specific questions by their captors, these were unstructured conversations freely held among Germans themselves, touching upon most sensitive issues relating to attitudes towards the German leadership and knowledge of war crimes. And, as Professor Neitzel demonstrates, the conversations were openly carried out without any awareness that they were being overheard and recorded. Moreover, the bugging of the German officers' conversations dates back to 1942. That is, their recorded views derive not from a time when Hitler's Germany already lay in ruins. They were not retrospective assessments of a fallen regime made with a careful eye on avoiding incriminating statements that could be used in a court, but were contemporary comments among more or less equals which offer a unique insight into the thinking of German generals and other officers of high rank long before the regime collapsed.

Professor Neitzel points out that the prisoners of war whose views he has assembled for us are not a representative sample of German officers. The first prisoners were taken in North Africa in 1942–43 and there was a continuing influx after the D-Day landings in June 1944 and the subsequent battles in Normandy, down to the push into the Reich itself. The experience of the Eastern Front, where of course the worst of the fighting and worst of the atrocities (including the slaughter of the Jews) took place, was limited for many of the prisoners whose words are recorded here. Even so, most of those captured had served on various fronts, often including the east, and some of them were ready and able to speak of terrible atrocities which they witnessed. If not representative in any scientific fashion, the German officers' views reproduced in this volume are certainly indicative of a wide spectrum of opinion, ranging from diehard Nazi attitudes to long-held, outrightly oppositional stances.

The polarisation of attitudes towards Hitler and the Third Reich is most plainly demonstrated, as Professor Neitzel shows, in the strongly maintained views of the very first two prisoners, General Thoma (anti-Nazi) and General Crüwell (an ardent supporter of the regime). An interesting facet of the edition is the way these two became the focal points of cliques, dividing largely on political or ideological lines. Professor Neitzel's findings indicate that no obvious sociological or denominational differences determined the shaping of Nazi or anti-Nazi stances, but that the crucial factor was the specific experience of the war, coupled with a varying readiness among the individual officers to reflect critically on the recent past.

The fact that, down to the very end of the Third Reich, such strong divisions between the captured German officers about their attitude towards the Nazi regime, and towards Hitler personally, could be sustained highlight the impossibility at crucial earlier stages, before the war, of building any reliable base of opposition within the Wehrmacht. The isolation of the then Chief of the General Staff, Ludwig Beck, when he resigned during the Sudeten crisis of 1938, or the hesitancy and ambivalence of his successor, Franz Halder as the crisis brewed to its climax in the weeks before the Munich Conference, become all the easier to understand when we see the attitudes represented in this edition of the military elite several years later, and after all that had transpired in the meantime.

It was not just a matter of expressly Nazi opinion among the generals. Nazified officers were, in fact, in a minority at Trent Park, as they surely were generally by this phase of the war. Strong antipathy towards the regime was far more commonplace. But most strikingly prevalent is the evidence of strong German patriotic and Prussian values. These had been a characteristic feature of the officer corps throughout the Third Reich. Though distinct from fully-fledged pro-Nazi views or sympathy with the regime, they overlapped to the extent that they disabled, or at least hindered, moves to direct oppositional action. Reflections of this could still be registered among the prisoners of war in Trent Park. Though, for instance, some expressed regret that Stauffenberg's attempt on Hitler's life had failed, others disapproved of the bomb-plot and saw it as irreconcilable with their sense of honour. Another indication was the lingering imprint of the oath taken to Hitler in 1934. And even when the generals in British captivity took the view that Hitler's subsequent actions had relieved them from their oath, they still felt bound by a sense of Prussian honour to continue the fight. Almost all still took the view that it was an officer's duty to fight to the last bullet (though few actually adhered in practice to their own prescribed code of ethics in this regard). So they not only for the most part strongly criticised General Paulus for his surrender in Stalingrad, but, even when claiming that it was madness to continue the war, rejected out of hand the notion that commanders on the Western Front should cease fighting and thereby open the way for the advance of the Anglo-Americans. Here, the plain implication was that the fight against the Soviets should not be given up, but would proceed with western help, another idea that had gained ground in leading Nazi circles in the latter part of the war. And the captured officers refused to contemplate taking part in BBC broadcasts or other anti-German propaganda, which they still regarded as treasonable. Even in the regime's very last days, the generals struggled to reach agreement on a letter they eventually sent to Churchill only after Hitler's death, offering (of course, in their own interest) to help bring about a 'renewal' in Germany 'in the spirit of western Christianity'.

This edition also makes clear that knowledge of atrocities on the grand scale in Eastern Europe was extensive among Germany's military elite – even those who found themselves in British captivity long before the end of the war. The transcripts of the bugged conversations include first-hand descriptions of the mass shooting of Jews (and no shortage of Nazified parlance betraying deep anti-Jewish sentiments). They also reveal recognition of the scale of the killing of Jews, and also of Poles, Russians and others. One account, and dating from as early as the end of 1943, indeed reckoned that three to five million Jews had already been wiped out. General von Choltitz, captured at the fall of Paris (where he had presided as city commander), even admitted, something not previously known, that he had systematically carried out orders for the liquidation of Jews in his area (probably the Crimea in 1941–42). For the most part, however, the blame was attached squarely to the Nazi leadership, and above all to the SS. The draft of the letter written to Churchill at the end of April 1945 acknowledged the need for punishment of those guilty of the regime's crimes – atrocities, it was claimed, committed almost exclusively by the SS, crimes of which only a small portion of the German people were aware, and then merely through rumour. One general, when the draft letter was being discussed, accepted that that it was useful to put it that way and that they were looking for a scapegoat. It shows that the 'legend of the "unblemished" Wehrmacht' was also being created by German generals even in captivity, and even before the Third Reich fell.

It is the great merit of Professor Neitzel's research that it opens up to us these previously untapped rich sources for exploring the mentality of representatives of Germany's military elite in the phase when the war had turned irredeemably against the Third Reich, and down to the collapse of the Hitler regime. For this excellent edition, we are very much in his debt.

Ian Kershaw, 2007

Introduction

1. Observations on Research and Sources

After World War II, the German generals largely rejected criticism of their role in the Third Reich and sought refuge in an alibi which said that they had fought an honourable war, had either scant or no knowledge of major atrocities, and that the military defeat was due mainly to Hitler's meddling at High Command level. The extent to which publications by former generals[1] shaped the image of the Wehrmacht for German post-war society remained, until recently, unexplored empirically. It emerges now, however, that as early as the 1950s public opinion and individual officers held a view of the Third Reich generals which did not coincide with that of 'an unblemished Wehrmacht'.[2]

The work of the Personnel Special Studies Committee of the Bundes-wehr demonstrates that from the earliest days of the Federal Republic the military has been more critical of its past than have judges, doctors or government administrators, while avoiding any major autopsy on its ranks. This is hardly surprising in view of the wartime devastation and the prevailing unsympathetic attitude of the public towards the Wehrmacht generals.

The historical research of the 1950s and 1960s was obliged to rely on accounts, primarily memoirs and approximately 2,500 reports dating from 1946–48, the result of an invitation by the US Army Historical Division to high-ranking Wehrmacht officers to write about their experiences at the front.[3] Only when the official documentation was returned to West Germany in the 1970s[4] was an evaluation of the role of the Wehrmacht and its senior commanders during World War II possible. Despite the great bulk of files, no comprehensive picture of the generals emerged, for the papers related mainly to military operations. Insight into the commanders of an army, or into Army-Group Staff, is rarely to be gained from official war diaries, operational planning and situation analysis. Private opinions on directives from 'above', about political convictions or pretended 'military necessities' are not documented in official papers and thus remain hidden from the historian.[5]

To get round this impasse the historian must fall back on letters and diaries. Such material tends to be scanty and by reason of being in private

hands is often of only limited accessibility.[6] The extent to which a
military commander saw through the tangled web of politics and war
crimes, what he knew, what he suspected, what he refused to face up to,
these remain misty to the present day, and only in the odd individual
case can one get to the truth of the matter.[7] Our knowledge of what
senior military personalities thought and knew is thus restricted.
Admiral Dönitz, for example, knew from naval officers' reports about
mass shootings on the Eastern Front but how he dealt with this information, how he interpreted it and what inferences he drew from it can only
be surmised.[8]

The London Public Record Office (PRO), since recently home to the
British National Archive, is the repository of a vast wealth of material on
the Wehrmacht and Third Reich which awaits thorough research, the
transcripts relating to the secret monitoring of private conversations
between German senior officers in British captivity being a case in point.
In contrast to the *interrogation* of prisoners of war, in which the truth-
fulness of the subject's replies may be doubtful,[9] the private unguarded
conversations of German prisoners provide a true insight into their
world of thinking and experience, since their guard was down.

The reproduction of this fascinating source allows us to clarify many
important questions. How did German generals judge the general war
situation? From what date did they consider the war lost? How did they
react to the attempt on Hitler's life in July 1944? What knowledge did
they have of atrocities, either through their own experience or based on
the reports of others? What importance did these explosive themes have
on camp life? Were there differences of opinion, or enmity between
individuals, perhaps conflict between the generations? To what extent
was rank or front-line experience important?

The Combined Services Detailed Interrogation Centre (CSDIC UK)
transcripts declassified in 1996 have been virtually ignored by researchers.
Occasionally the monitored conversations of U-boat crews are
mentioned in naval studies[10] but the files relating to Staff officers are
practically untouched.[11] The author first drew attention to these in the
Vierteljahrsheften für Zeitgeschichte where, for reasons of space, a
selection of only 21 documents was reproduced.[12] The 167 reports
reproduced in this book are the transcripts of conversations between
German generals in British captivity from the late summer of 1942 to the
autumn of 1945. With four exceptions they were all recorded at Trent
Park, the special centre set aside for German Staff officers. Documents
76, 77 and 135 recall conversations of generals Walter Bruns and
Maximilian Siry overheard in April and May 1945 at Latimer House,
Buckinghamshire, a time when for accommodation reasons not all
captured Staff officers could be settled at Trent Park. Document 152, also
from Latimer House, is the record of a conversation between two
General Staff majors captured in August 1944 in France who speak

out on the general war situation while still influenced by the attempt on Hitler's life. This report is very valuable in that there exist few extracts of conversations concerning general political questions[13] at the time of the fighting in Normandy and so provides an interesting contrast to the opinions of the generals already in custody.

The contents of the book have been separated into three categories, each set individually in date order. The first treats the reflections of the generals on the National Socialist State, the progress of the war and the internal differences resulting from these discussions (Documents 1–82). The second category documents conversations on war crimes (Documents 83–144), the third those conversations which refer to the 20 July Plot (Documents 145–67). In selecting documents, the author has been at pains to provide a representative cross-section of material split into the ratio in which they occur overall in the source. The transcripts are reproduced from the original archive. Since the conversations are verbatim, some may appear stilted or disconnected. Where portions have been omitted this is indicated by elipses, where a name or location is uncertain it is followed by an interrogation mark. Some abbreviations are indicated by square parentheses. In the original protocols, speakers were identified by initials.

Each SRX, SRM and SRGG document is headed: 'This report is most secret. If further circulation is necessary, it must be paraphrased so that neither the source of the information nor the means by which it has been obtained is apparent.' Most GRGG transcripts have at the head an extensive list of all prisoners overheard during the period of the report, identified by name, rank and date of capture. For reasons of space herein such lists have not been reproduced.

SRX, SM and SRGG documents each cover only a single conversation. The more comprehensive GRGG papers contain several conversations. The start of a new conversation is indicated by an extra line space in the text. As a rule only extracts of GRGG documents have been published here, but where they are the extract is in full.

The WO 208 protocols exist in the original German text accompanied always by an English translation. Documents 142–4 in this book are only available in the archives in English translation.

The book concludes with short biographies of all 85 personalities who lend their voice to the protocols. These biographies give brief career notes together with an assessment of character and political stance which the CSDIC prepared on most of the German officers at Trent Park. German Army assessments of the time were not particularly useful: in June 1943, Generalleutnant Rudolf Schmundt, Head of the OKH Personnel Office, complained that the frequent employment in personnel files of expressions such as 'he stands on National Socialist ground' were so vague as to be virtually useless for making judgements of an officer.[14] The CSDIC (UK) character studies[15] were probably elaborated by Lord Aberfeldy, but this is not absolutely certain. It should also be noted that from the British point of view a 'Nazi' might be a general whose position in the political spectrum was not known but whose conduct or appearance was overtly Prussian. Aside from this reservation, the CSDIC (UK) assessment is important for being of a neutral character based on week- or month-long observations of a personality at Trent Park who for most of the time was off his guard.

2. Secret Monitoring of Prisoners of War in Great Britain and Trent Park PoW Centre

During World War II probably all the belligerents listened-in secretly to their prisoners. The general rule seems to have been that the interrogation of selected prisoners was documented, but not the private conversations. Richard Overy has published the protocols of National Socialist leaders under interrogation in 1945–46.[16] Other trials were run by the United States, Great Britain, Germany and the Soviet Union.[17] As far as is known, it was the British who perfected eavesdropping as a method of intelligence gathering. At Farm Hall in Cambridgeshire, the conversations of the interned German nuclear physicists were secretly recorded in the attempt to discover how far Germany had advanced towards building an atomic bomb,[18] but the British did not disclose their practice of having listened-in systematically to selected prisoners of war for several years before that.

The British intelligence service began planning to use the method from the beginning of the war. On 26 October 1939, orders were given to set up the Combined Services Detailed Interrogation Centre. Initially under MI9, from December 1941 it fell within the ambit of the British Army's newly formed MI19 Department at the War Office under Lt-Colonel A. R. Rawlinson. All reports originating at CSDIC were to be distributed to the three arms of service for collation with other information, e.g. signals intercepts and air reconnaissance photographs, to compose a specific intelligence picture.[19] The CSDIC organisation in England was complemented later by a centre in North Africa (CSDIC Middle East) and from the autumn of 1944 another in France/Germany run by the US Army (CSDIC West).

The UK interrogation centre had modest beginnings: in September 1939, only six officers (three Army, two RAF and one RN) had been appointed to question German prisoners at the Tower of London. In December that year the centre was relocated to Trent Park, a large mansion with extensive grounds near Cockfosters, north of London. German prisoners of war – in the early years a manageable number of Luftwaffe and Kriegsmarine men – together with Italian prisoners were 'pre-sorted' in transit camps by the PoW Department and those believed to have important knowledge were sent to Trent Park for comprehensive questioning and the secret monitoring of their conversations.

CSDIC (UK) used a variety of refined tricks to tap the required knowledge. 'Cooperative' prisoners and German exiles were used as stool pigeons to get conversations moving along the desired track[20] while prisoners of equal rank but from different units or arms of service would be bunched together. This method paid off: U-boat men would air their experiences at length, airmen would explain the technology of their aircraft and combat tactics in great detail to naval comrades. Army men arrived at Trent Park relatively quickly after capture – from a few days to a couple of weeks. They would often still be suffering the dramatic effects of their capture, perhaps having narrowly escaped death – and would be anxious to talk about their experiences.

On 5 October 1940 it was decided to increase CSDIC (UK) staffing levels to enable two camps to be run simultaneously. Trent Park could house only a limited number of prisoners and space for the constantly growing number of assessors was inadequate. It was also considered prudent to have two centres in order to reduce the risk of losing everything in a Luftwaffe air raid.

On 15 July 1942 CSDIC (UK) moved with its entire staff into the new interrogation centre at Latimer House at Chesham, Buckinghamshire (No. 1 Distribution Centre) with a maximum capacity of 204 prisoners. On 13 December a second new centre ten miles away at Wilton Park, Beaconsfield (No. 2 Distribution Centre) was opened with room for 142 prisoners, mainly Italians.[21]

The opening of the two new institutions allowed Trent Park to be converted into a long-term centre for German Staff officers. In the relaxed atmosphere it was hoped that its high-ranking population would reveal secrets in their private discussions.[22] The first new prisoner was General Ludwig Crüwell. He had been captured in North Africa on 29 May 1942 and arrived at Trent Park on 26 August after a long sea voyage. He was joined on 20 November 1942 by General Wilhelm Ritter von Thoma, a prisoner of the British for the previous two weeks.

For the sake of variation and to initiate fresh themes in conversation, from time to time selected prisoners were transferred to Trent Park. These included Kapitänleutnant Hans-Dietrich Tiesenhausen[23] and Major Burckhardt, von Thoma's former adjutant during the Spanish Civil War. They remained only a few weeks before being shipped out to Canada.[24] Following the capitulation of Army-Group Afrika in May 1943, 18 senior officers ranging from the rank of Oberst to Generaloberst came to Trent Park. From the end of June 1944 there followed permanent prisoners picked up by the Allies during their push through France, Belgium and into Germany,[25] and by April 1945 the number of generals at Trent Park exceeded the capacity. The overflow went to other camps including Latimer House and Grizedale Hall at Hawkshead, Lancashire

(No. 1 Camp). From August 1942 to its closure on 19 October 1945, 84 German generals made stays at Trent Park. To these must be added at least 22 officers of the rank of Oberst and an unknown number of other ranks, mostly adjutants and valets.[26] The total number of generals held until October 1945 temporarily in British interrogation centres was 302 of whom 82 per cent (248) arrived in England after April 1945.

After the Normandy landings in 1944, interrogation camps at Kempton Park (Sunbury-on-Thames, Middlesex: British Army) and Devizes, Wiltshire (US Army) were opened to receive German prisoners captured in France, while at Kensington the 'London District Cage' was set up for prisoners suspected by the British to be implicated in, or to have guilty knowledge of, war crimes.[27] At the latter the incumbents were subjected to psychological torture.[28]

Following the German capitulation the work of CSDIC (UK) turned to obtaining information on German war crimes. On 19 November 1945 the interrogation centre in England was closed, its work being transferred gradually since summer 1945 to the new CSDIC in Germany.[29] A month before, when Trent Park closed its doors, the remaining prisoners were sent to other camps and no longer monitored.[30]

In general, all German prisoners of senior rank were brought to England for interrogation irrespective of which Allied forces had captured them. A few were shipped to the United States after brief questioning, so that many Trent Park generals did not spend the whole war in England. 31 went in several batches to the enemy generals' camp at Clinton, Mississippi, providing the United States in the spring of 1945 with the opportunity to obtain information from an approximately equal-sized number of senior German military officers as the British had.[31] There does not seem to have been any special guidelines for selection for transfer to the USA: almost all ranks and political standpoints were represented. The British clearly liked a broad sweep of characters and opinions in their camps to keep the conversations flowing.

The expense incurred in maintaining the three eavesdropping units at Trent Park, Latimer House and Wilton Park was enormous: at the beginning of 1943, 994 persons staffed the units and evaluated the monitored conversations, 258 of these being from the intelligence services.[32] From September 1939 to October 1945, 10,191 German and 567 Italian prisoners passed through these centres; between 1941 and 1945 64,427 conversations were recorded on gramophone discs. CSDIC prepared 16,960 protocols from German, and 18,903 from Italian prisoners,[33] varying in length from half a page to 22 pages.

From May 1943, special reports were introduced on German Staff officers: 1,302 protocols coded 'SRGG'[34] and 326 comprehensive reports of a general nature coded 'GRGG'.[35] The latter documented all pertinent information over two- to five-day periods. A synopsis of monitored and recorded conversations was included with any other data which the

British intelligence officer beyond the range of the microphones had picked up through listening to discussions or from his own talks with prisoners. To these must be added the recorded conversations coded 'SRM' between von Thoma and Crüwell prior to May 1943 filed amongst the Army protocols[36] together with protocols coded 'SRX'[37] of their conversations with Luftwaffe and Kriegsmarine officers. The generals' protocols run to about 10,000 pages, approximately 20 per cent of the total inventory of the monitored protocols of German prisoners.[38]

Eavesdropping Strategies

CSDIC (UK) decided against interrogating von Thoma and Crüwell, believing that the men were not in a frame of mind to divulge information. Instead, immediately after their arrival in England, they were brought to Trent Park in order that their conversations could be eavesdropped. Initially a German 'stool pigeon' was used 'very success-fully' as a prompt[39] after which an even better strategy was found in having Lord Aberfeldy[40] live in the camp with the generals from December 1942. He acted as interpreter and his role was ostensibly to see to the comforts and wishes of the prisoners, accompanying them on long walks, making purchases on their behalf in London and always being on hand as a generally valued conversational partner. Very soon he had gained the trust of most prisoners, none of whom suspected that he might be anything other than a 'welfare officer'. In reality, Aberfeldy worked for MI19, his job being to steer conversations along the lines desired by British Intelligence. A protocol (Document 147) of a conversation immediately after 20 July 1944 demonstrates that the German generals were not inhibited by his presence, a fact which enabled him to gather important information beyond the range of the microphones. A similar 'trusted man' had also inveigled himself with the Italians.[41]

Some of the generals captured in Tunisia were questioned before being brought to Trent Park. Confronting them with the usual system of intelligence gathering, it was hoped that they would discount the possibility of secret microphones at Trent Park – a hope fully realised. A number of generals did answer questions under direct interrogation, especially shortly before the war's end. All generals captured from the summer of 1944 onwards were held for a few days at Wilton Park, or exceptionally Latimer House, before being transferred en bloc to Trent Park.

At Trent Park 12 rooms were bugged including the common room. Latimer House and Wilton Park each had 30 bugged rooms and six interrogation rooms equipped with microphones. At the earphones were mainly German and Austrian exiles.[42] As soon as something important was said a gramophone recording was started. A recording would last seven minutes. A long, interesting conversation would therefore be 'apportioned' over several records. Thus for example the first conversation between generals Crüwell and von Thoma on the evening of 20 November 1942 was documented in 27 parts.[43] From these records a protocol in German language was prepared. The average consolidated recording lasted 90 minutes although some were substantially longer. The most experienced member of the monitoring team would then read through the transcript and hear the record again where a part of the text was doubtful. Ambiguous words or passages of text would be indicated by editorial marks. Following the translation of the protocol into English the manuscript would be sent to MI19 at the War Office and the intelligence departments of the Admiralty and Air Ministry. After two months the records would be returned to the Post Office research unit for erasure but recordings of special interest, mainly in respect of war crimes, were kept.

The interrogation centre had begun with a modest staff of specially trained monitoring officers who worked in the so-called M-Room. When Trent Park began work in December 1939, a staff of six listened-in to conversations. With the increase to three camps, and these were occasionally bursting at the seams, the M-Room staffing levels expanded and by 1944 had risen to a complement of 100. It was no easy matter to find qualified operatives. British people, even those with very good German language skills, were unsuited to the work, and even many persons with German as their mother tongue failed to meet requirements. To resolve this problem it was decided at the end of 1942 to employ exclusively German and Austrian exiles for the task. A three-month training period was found necessary to familiarise candidates with military vernacular and to help them develop a feeling for conversations which ought to be recorded.[44] Only political and military matters were considered relevant. Talk about the weather and the food, or intimate matters personal to the speaker, were not wanted.

Life in Trent Park

Set amongst cow pastures, plough-land and ancient woods, Trent Park was a magnificent estate located in the low hills around Enfield, in the north of London. 'Great lawns with marble statues, glorious woodland with cedars and great oaks. A golf course, large swimming pool, a fine pond with wild duck', was how detainee Generalleutnant Erwin Menny described the centre in his diaries.[45] The history of Trent Park can be traced back to the reign of Henry IV. In 1399 the king converted a huge park-like area of Enfield into a game reserve. In 1777 Sir Richard Jebb took over a part of it and built on the property a small country house, which was greatly enlarged in 1893. In 1908 Sir Edward Sassoon, a descendant of wealthy Baghdad Jews, bought the estate. After his death in 1912 it passed to his son Sir Philipp Sassoon (1888–1939).[46] A doyen of

*Above are a selection of sketches of Trent Park produced by the prisoner
Lieutenant Klaus Hubbuch in autumn 1943*

London society, there was nobody of rank or influence in Great Britain
who had not been invited to one or other of his country houses. Members
of the royal family and Winston Churchill numbered amongst the pre-
war guests at Trent Park. When Philipp Sassoon died unexpectedly in
1939, Trent Park could be used by the government.[47]

The German prisoners were lodged in the second floor of the mansion.
Generals occupied two rooms, a Generalleutnant would have his own
suite, ranks below this shared two to a room. Sources indicate that the
prisoners were 'very satisfied' with the accommodation.

> Besides a bed, cupboard, commode, table and chair, each room has a
> comfortable sofa. This sofa and the hot running water are things which
> make captivity considerably more pleasant. Bassenge, a do-it-yourself
> enthusiast, was kind enough to make me a reading lamp which he hung
> over my bed. All rooms are decorated with pages from a German art
> calendar stapled to the walls,[48]

Erwin Menny noted in his diary. There was a common area equipped
with radio, reading room, a study for painting and music and a dining
room. On the first floor was a hall in which table-tennis and billiards were
possible. 'Unfortunately there is no tennis court' General Cramer wrote
in a report to relatives of prisoners at Trent Park on 8 June 1944. All the

windows were barred but the prisoners had freedom to be in the open in the courtyard on the south side and on a 120 x 70-metre lawn on the west and north side of the mansion. These areas were surrounded by barbed wire fencing. The generals noted with pleasure that the British guards patrolling between the two barbed wire fences saluted them smartly. Oberst Lex noted in his diary: 'These guards were always very well disciplined and would greet you, e.g. at Christmas and New Year with "Merry Christmas, Sir, a Happy New Year, Sir." We really enjoyed the guard change at 0900 each morning which was carried out in the presence of an officer with typical British stiffness and pedantry. It was militarism in purity' (Franz Lex, diary, p. 19). Four days per week the prisoners were accompanied by a British officer on a ramble through woods and fields on the estate, which they quickly christened 'Little Hyde Park'. Oberst Hans Reimann ran a small shop selling smoker's requirements, beer, writing utensils, soap and other minor necessities. The prisoners received their monthly pay in pounds sterling equivalent and used it to buy personal items in modest quantities. Laundry and matters pertaining to dress were attended to by a London tailor who visited the camp fortnightly. Small everyday items not sold by the shop such as mirrors, cigar snippers, pipes and books would be obtained on request by Lord Aberfeldy on his weekly trip to London. This service increased the prisoners' trust in him.[49]

The catering at Trent Park was simple but ample, although of poorer quality than in the transit centres behind the front and at Latimer House, where the fare was highly praised but 'to our German way of thinking too abundant' as Erwin Menny observed.[50] A precise daily routine was followed. Reveille was at 0800[51] and the day ended 12 hours later with evening rounds. For entertainment and education, cards and board games were supplied and the very good library of the former German Embassy in London placed at their disposal.[52] Two British officers and prisoners Konteradmiral Meixner and Hennecke gave language tuition. Films were screened from time to time.[53]

The Geneva Convention allowed the prisoners to exchange correspondence regularly with relatives through the Swiss protecting power. The prisoners could send letters or postcards. These would take between two weeks and four months to arrive. Since they were censored, the old German script was not permitted. It was rare for any political or military information to be passed in them because the communications were read by the British and German controls. Georg Neuffer complained to his wife on 26 August 1943 that his letters 'in the manner of things so lack content that they finish up always saying the same things'. Thus the generals wrote mainly about the camp's lovely surroundings and their daily occupations. Only a few varied from this practice: on 10 July 1943 Generalleutnant Gotthard Franz wrote to his wife: 'All will be well. The nation which produced Luther, Kant, Goethe and Beethoven, will never die' (TNA, DEFE 1/339).

The longer the war went on, the worse the air raids on German cities became, the more did concern for the well-being of those at home tend to dominate the mails. Generalleutnant Friedrich von Broich wrote on 4 October 1944 to his wife: 'We are now hanging around here, debarred from playing our parts as soldiers and husbands and you women have to suffer for it and experience the war in its most dreadful form. That is such a paradox. One can go off the deep end over it and can find no peace at nights on account of one's thoughts' (TNA, DEFE 1/339).

The British suspected generals Arnim, Crüwell and Hülsen, Konteradmiral Meixner and colonels Buhse and Wolters of passing military information to Germany by means of secret codes. It is certain that in a letter to his wife dated 15 July 1944 Konteradmiral Paul concealed a message in which he relayed his grave belief that 'the enemy has all the codes' (NA, RG 319, entry 745001, Box 10).

Trent Park offered many comforts which the generals sorely missed when they arrived at other camps in October 1945.[54] The contrast to the ghastly reality of the battlefields of Europe could scarcely have been greater: 'Peace, beauty, life here – war, devastation, death [there] . . .' The only reminders that a war was in progress at all were the German air raids on London in February and March 1944.[55] From June 1944 to March 1945 the inmates had the opportunity to experience the V-weapons offensive on London. In January 1945 a V-1 flew over Trent Park and exploded two miles away. A V-2 hit only a mile away from the main camp buildings. 'It was depressing to see the daily departure of the powerful bomber formations, which returned, from our number counts, with hardly their plumage ruffled,' Franz Lex noted (Franz Lex, diary, p. 22). These were, however, the only 'occurrences' in the tranquil life at Trent Park. 'It is as if we were living in a quite unreal world,' Generalleutnant Ferdinand Heim wrote of the atmosphere at the centre:

> What we heard probably penetrated our consciousness, like the distant surf of a spring high tide, but our lives remained untouched by it. We took our meals each day when the gong sounded, every day we saw the same faces, the same English countryside, the same sky: we read, we played, we wrote, we meditated day after day as if there were nothing more natural in the world.[56]

The calm, peaceful atmosphere of the estate, combined with endless free time, allowed the generals time to reflect on the war and their experiences of it.[57] For the first time in their lives the majority were associating with many colleagues of equal rank who had shared much the same experiences and it was not humanly possible to remain silent on major subjects of common concern. How would the war turn out? How could the defeats be explained? Had the Germans brought upon themselves a special guilt?

Heim wrote of Trent Park:

We often shook our heads about our people, who seemed to be committing suicide, and at times we raged over a leadership without
accountability which was leading this people to annihilation, riding to
the death the mad idea of their intense heroism . . . accordingly we saw
from a distance the horrifyingly irretrievable situation, apparently with
no way out. Then we would retire once more to our 'monastic cells', or
into the 'monastery garden' – pious brothers who had once been
warriors . . . We tried to understand how it had come about, where its
origins and errors lay, who was responsible. One thing we saw clearly:
to lose two World Wars in a lifetime seemed like a judgement of God.[58]

It is natural to ask whether the inmates of Trent Park, and at the other
two centres, knew that they were being spied upon. The authenticity of
the protocols might be doubted if the generals suspected that the British
were actively tapping their knowledge, for it would then be plausible for
them to lace their conversations with disinformation. British methods of
information gathering were by no means unknown in Germany. Before
his transfer abroad in October 1940, the fighter pilot Franz von Werra
was for a short time at Trent Park. After his escape from Canada, he
reported extensively on British interrogation methods.[59] On 11 June 1941
Ausland-Abwehr issued guidelines for the conduct of Wehrmacht
personnel in British captivity, warning expressly of stool pigeons
masquerading in German uniform, and hidden microphones. It was
pointed out emphatically that the enemy had succeeded in obtaining
valuable information by such means.[60] The British protocols show that
most German prisoners disregarded these warnings very quickly,
irrespective of how hard it had been drummed into them, and gossiped
habitually with their colleagues about military secrets.

The conversations of NCOs contain repeated reference to the National
Socialist propaganda film *Kämpfer hinter Stacheldraht* ('Warriors behind
Barbed Wire')[61] aimed at preventing careless talk. Yet in the same breath
they would then proceed to enlighten their colleagues on what they had
deliberately withheld from the interrogation officers,[62] thus dictating
their secrets directly into British microphones, so to speak. Most
German PoWs gave no thought to the possibility of their being
overheard, or they would not have incriminated themselves by discussing their involvement in war crimes.[63] Only in a single case is it
known for certain that prisoners discovered hidden microphones.[64]
Officers were no different to other ranks in this respect. Oberst Kessler
said that he had withheld from the intelligence officer at an interrogation
centre details of his attitude to Nazism, then told Oberst Reimann what
his attitude was (Document 28). There are numerous such examples
which show that even senior officers at Trent Park fell into the craftily
designed CSDIC (UK) trap.

To prevent the monotony of camp life causing the flow of talk to dry up, the British supplied falsified newspapers and magazines to provoke ever-more lively debate. Trent Park intelligence officers took selected prisoners on long excursions. This method succeeded in making General Crüwell more forthcoming. He had been initially 'singularly un-communicative' but after a day out sightseeing he spoke for the first time about his impressions, then on general matters and finally on military questions.[65] In the course of time he opened up to 'one of our best interrogators'. Especially valuable were Crüwell's conversations with Oberleutnant zur See Wolfgang Römer, commander of U-353 sunk in the North Atlantic on 16 October 1942. Roemer responded to his enquiries by describing U-boat tactics which the British found to be of inestimable value.[66] When General von Thoma was made Senior German Officer in June 1944, he made it his custom to get new arrivals to speak out on their experiences. No stool pigeon could have done it better.

Generaloberst von Arnim tried in vain to instil a greater degree of watchfulness over private discussions at Trent Park. On 9 July 1943 in his capacity as Senior German Officer (Document 12) he urged caution in what was said – Trent Park was a former interrogation centre and one had to take into account that microphones might be hidden there. For this reason alone one should not hold conversations which might be of propaganda value to the enemy. On 15 August he renewed his appeal. He suspected that Lord Aberfeldy listened-in to prisoners' conversations from his window, and that some of the personal valets were collaborating with the British (neither true), and that one must therefore exercise the greatest caution.[67] His appeal fell on deaf ears. The prisoners would not be muzzled and chatted gaily about politics and military affairs. Generalleutnant Neuffer considered 'the stories about eavesdropping' to be 'utter stupidity'[68] while Oberstleutnant Köhncke was of the opinion that the prisoners had the right 'to talk about political things – we are, after all, not children.' One should be grateful to find oneself amongst one's peers, amongst people with some experience of life, with different points of view, he went on, and this was not the same kind of thing at all as gossiping with young lieutenants.[69] Thoma concluded, 'They have such a good intelligence service that they don't need to listen to us chatterboxes.'[70]

Further convincing evidence that the German prisoners were unaware of being eavesdropped on is contained in General Crüwell's diaries. In captivity he had consciously avoided making notes on political and military matters. In conversation with colleagues he abandoned caution and spoke out at length on the war situation in February 1944, providing MI19 with a precise strategic analysis. If he had suspected that microphones were hidden in the walls at Trent Park he would certainly have exercised discretion as with his diary notes.[71]

After reading hundreds of protocols, one is left with the impression that the generals were holding nothing back in conversation, not even von Arnim. Those who wanted to talk did so frankly at Trent Park. In the main, tactical details of operations, absent from the generals' conversations, were discussed by Wehrmacht other ranks while with a few exceptions the generals discussed more general matters. This was attributable to the higher degree of education, age and the higher military rank they held. It is this fact which makes the CSDIC (UK) protocols so interesting for historians, an insight into the thinking of a chosen circle of senior German officers during World War II beyond detailed military information.

To what extent Trent Park fulfilled its purpose and the British obtained a concrete military advantage from the practice of listening-in to long-term prisoners is only evident in a few cases. The information gleaned from a conversation on U-boat tactics between General Crüwell and Oberleutnant Röhmer has already been mentioned. At the end of March 1943 the War Office received definite information about the development of the V-2 rocket from a conversation between Crüwell and Thoma,[72] but otherwise it was only officers captured on the Channel coast who spoke extensively about military tactics. From the latter the Allies may have learned that Cherbourg was not sown with long-term mines.[73]

The *direct* military value of eavesdropping on German Staff officers may have been limited. Far more successful was the activity directed against junior officers and NCOs of the Luftwaffe and Kriegsmarine. These leaked a wealth of secret information about new weapons, operational tactics, radio and radar equipment of great value for Allied front troops.[74] The *indirect* gain, however, was enormous, for the British obtained intimate insight into the Wehrmacht, whose organisations, structure and personalities were now known to the minutest detail. The German prisoners also spoke openly about situation analyses, enabling the British to discover a great deal about how the Germans saw the overall strategic situation.

Social Profile of the Staff Officers

Not all officers who were at Trent Park speak in the published transcripts. From April 1945 CSDIC (UK) recorded far fewer conversations, and for reasons of space here a selection has had to be made to provide a broad spectrum of very senior officers with a spread of character types and biographies. Sixty-three generals, 14 Obristen (colonels), four Oberstleutnante, three majors and two lieutenants appear in the protocols. Most of the 86 were Army officers, 11 were Luftwaffe, four Kriegsmarine and one Waffen SS.

The predominant group at Trent Park was the 63 generals. These divide by rank into Generaloberst – 1: General – 8: Generalleutnant – 23 and Generalmajor – 23. The British were therefore listening-in to the second layer at the top of the Wehrmacht command structure. At first glance it is a reasonably heterogeneous group. At one end of the scale is 56-year-old Generalmajor Alfred Gutknecht, whose social background was the Kaiserreich and who since 1939 had held only administrative posts; at the other the youngest divisional comander of the German land forces, highly decorated SS-Brigadeführer Kurt Meyer, 34 years old, who since 1939 had been at the front in the thick of the fighting. The breadth of the band is what makes the protocols especially valuable, making it possible to see how differing social circumstances and war experiences had a bearing on the content of conversations.

The generals were all born in the years between 1882 and 1910, but the majority (24 generals) were born in 1894–95. The religion is known in only two-thirds of cases: the relationship of 41 Protestants to 10 Catholics may possibly represent the religious split of the whole group. All regions of the 1914 German Reich feature amongst the places of birth, although the majority of officers were Prussian born.[75] Most of the generals came from upper-class origins, although only 18 were actually of noble birth plus three amongst the lower officer ranks. Only eight of the 63 generals had seen long service with the General Staff.

Kroener[76] suggests that the social profile and make-up of the Wehrmacht officer corps should be distributed in the following manner:
 – General Staff officer of WWI
 – Front officer of WWI
 – Reichswehr officers without war experience
 – Soldiers trained before September 1939 but who became officers in wartime.
The generals should be grouped into those who rose to general rank:
 – before September 1939
 – between 1939 and 1943
 – from 1944 onwards.
Following this system, it will be seen that almost all 63 generals served at the front in WWI and were appointed to the rank of general between 1939 and 1945 (one prior to 1939, 52 between 1939 and 1943, 10 between 1944 and 1945). Put another way, the military career path of the *majority* was generally similar until the outbreak of war in 1939. In WWI they had served at the front as young officers, most of them being senior lieutenants and company commanders at its conclusion: they were then accepted into the Reichswehr and by the outbreak of war in 1939 were as a rule regimental commanders. For further progress technical quali-fications and especially achievement at the front were decisive. Of the 33 officers born in 1894–96, six were of the rank of Oberst when captured, 12 Generalmajor, 12 Generalleutnant and four General. Only two of the 63 continued into the West German Bundeswehr.

Experiences in World War II differed widely: whilst one group had made a career at the front, the other 'also served' behind the lines. The decorations awarded highlight the division as according to fighting experience. Of the total of 86 officers, 48 had awards for bravery, 26 wore the Knight's Cross (of whom five had the Oak Leaves, two the Swords and one the Diamonds), 13 had as the highest award for bravery, the German Cross in Gold. In other words, nearly all very senior officers who had been at the front over a long period were decorated. If a general lacked a decoration it was a sure sign either that he had not been at the front long, or that he had been on a quiet section of front, or had not proved his fighting abilities adequately, or he had served at a front base where little opportunity presented itself for distinguished activity.[77] Thus the undecorated general had as a rule experienced a different war to one who had won the Knight's Cross.

The question may be posed whether the protocols, at least for the generals appointed between 1939 and 1943, are representative. The great diversity of careers appears to suggest this conclusion at first glance, but the material does not lend itself to judgements about the group.

Neither age, rank, branch of service, regional origin nor religion indicate whether a man was likely to have attached himself to the pro- or anti-Nazi clique. Political leaning was personal to the officer, in combination with front experience. Living through a military disaster might lead to extensive reflection on politics, strategy and the character of the National Socialist system. The 'Napoleon winter' before Moscow in 1941, the catastrophe at Stalingrad, the defeat in Tunisia or the struggle in Normandy left many with a critical view of the leadership and the Nazi State. Such an experience was not necessarily a pre-condition for an anti-Nazi stance. General der Panzertruppe Heinrich Eberbach had never been a Party member, but was considered before his capture to be a convinced National Socialist, 'brave, loyal and firm', according to Guderian. He spent almost the entire war in the Führer-Reserve or as a field-commander in France. He experienced no great defeats, but at Trent Park spoke out against the war and Nazism. CSDIC (UK) held Eberbach to be 'a strong personality with clear opinions' who now believed that the Nazi regime was a criminal organisation and so no longer considered himself bound by his oath of allegiance.

3. The Main Subjects of Discussion

3.1 Politics, Stategy and the Different Camps at Trent Park

When Wilhelm Ritter von Thoma arrived at Trent Park in November 1942, the only other inmate was Ludwig Crüwell, captured five months previously. Both were of about the same age, highly decorated and each had commanded a panzer division on the Eastern Front and in 1942 with the Afrika Korps. The first evening they sat up talking until 2 a.m. Further long conversations followed in the next few days. After a week the first differences of opinion made themselves felt. Crüwell accused Thoma of being 'negative'. 'Frankly,' Crüwell said, 'talking to you, one gets the impression that you accept all the criticisms of Greater Germany, and that if it had been left to you from the very beginning, everything would have been done so much better.'[78] From the outset, Thoma had condemned the overall situation because the economic resources of the Allies were increasing while those of the Axis powers were diminishing. He had criticised the decision to attack the Soviet Union,[79] denigrated Hitler and the Party,[80] described in drastic terms dreadful German war crimes committed in Russia (Document 83) and reported on the programme by which the Jews were to have been removed from Europe by the end of 1942. It was a 'tragedy of obedience'[81] that German soldiers had gone along with the National Socialist regime. They had let too much go unchallenged, said von Thoma. Of course, no general could simply rebel by himself but the three C-in-Cs could have acted jointly against the outgrowth of the National Socialist State, particularly at the time of the Fritsch affair.[82]

Crüwell however had another opinion. He was proud that the Army generals of the Third Reich had served so loyally.[83] He emphasised that he had not gone through life blinkered, but considered it impossible that a German soldier could commit a foul deed.[84] It was obvious to him that the war could last very much longer yet,[85] but in the final analysis it had to be won, for otherwise it would be 'Finis Germaniae'.[86] Crüwell was thinking of his four children and their uncertain future,[87] but also of the hundreds of thousands of Germans who would have fallen in vain should the war be lost.[88]

How did these two generals, whose military careers at first sight ran such similar courses, manage to develop such divergent points of view? A closer look at their lives may provide the clue.

Thoma ended World War I as Oberleutnant in No. 3. Bavarian Infantry Regiment. On the Eastern Front during the Brossilov offensive in 1916 he won the Military Order of Max Josef, the highest Bavarian decoration for an officer. The award brought with it a title. Between 1936 and 1939 he led the Legion Condor ground forces in the Spanish Civil War. In the Polish campaign he commanded a panzer regiment; from March 1940 to July 1941 he served as General der Schnellen Truppen (motorised units). During this latter appointment at OKH he obtained a comprehensive overview of the general war situation and associated with the most senior military commanders.[89] Thoma met Hitler on numerous occasions and got on very well with him, since they conversed in the same Bavarian dialect. Thoma's assertion that he knew Hitler in the Great War cannot be confirmed, but seems unlikely.[90]

Thoma commanded a panzer division from July 1941 and received the Knight's Cross for his efforts during the Soviet winter offensive. At Rommel's request he arrived in Egypt in September 1942 as CO, Deutsches Afrika Korps. Bachelor Thoma was a military man through and through, personally brave and always to be found in the front line.[91] Wounded on numerous occasions, he was undoubtedly an inspired soldier. British military theoretician Liddell Hart described him as a tough but loveable character, an enthusiast who loved battle for its own sake, who fought without hate and respected all his enemies. In middle age he had found contentment as a knight-errant. His critical mind enabled him to see beyond his own backyard and to analyse politics and strategy.[92] As a result of his analysis of tactical experiences during the Polish campaign, in November 1939 he warned that it had not yet been proved that panzer divisions could reach their objectives against a modern well-equipped and well-led enemy in the absence of air supremacy.[93]

At a commanders' conference on the Eastern Front on 21 March 1942 when General Friedrich Materna reported Hitler as saying recently that Britian was taking giant strides towards its Bolshevisation, Thoma countered immediately, 'We will be ripe for bolshevisation ten times sooner than the British.'[94]

The memoirs of Generalleutnant Theodor von Sponeck, CO, 90th Light Division in North Africa and an inmate at Trent Park with Thoma, mention a meeting on 2 October 1942 on the El Alamein front:

General Thoma, a typical Bavarian, engaged me at once in a long conversation from which I inferred that he took a very black view of the future. Clever and open-minded, but in many things blinkered, he was consumed by a raging hatred for the Hitler regime which he could barely conceal. At the time this was dangerous, but not in the African desert, surrounded by colleagues who thought highly of his personal bravery.[95]

Thoma's front-line experience was forged not only from German victories, but also by the catastrophe before Moscow in the winter of

1941 and the oppressive material superiority of the British at El Alamein. Nevertheless his critical assessment of the war situation was based not only on these major reverses. When Thoma was captured on 4 November 1942 during the hard fighting for a hill in the Egyptian desert,[96] the Wehrmacht held most of the Caucasus and the Volga, while all of Libya and half of Egypt were in German hands. Very few Wehrmacht commanding generals of the time can have had such a pessimistic and – as we now know – realistic vision as Thoma who, according to his own admission while at OKH, was denounced as a defeatist.[97] He thus had the capability to analyse the general situation shrewdly, and this explains his efforts in August 1942 to resist his transfer to Egypt, where he considered the situation unpromising.[98]

From the time preceding his capture there is unfortunately little material on Thoma. A 16-page memorandum to Army C-in-C (ObdH) von Brauchitsch composed in October 1940 and in which he 'foresaw the whole thing' (Document 14) can be found neither in the rudimentary files of General der Schnellen Truppen nor those of the ObdH. Similarly, the two-page letter to OKW in which Thoma allegedly protested against the mass shootings in White Russia (Document 84) also appears not to have survived.[99]

In his pocket calendar, Thoma made notes daily. For 1941–42 one finds no entries about politics or the war situation. Most notes are about the weather and describe where he is.[100] Only in captivity did he become more expansive. Here he noted in his diary that he had 'a bad feeling' when the preparations for the Russian campaign began in October 1940 – a sentiment in which he was not alone.

> When the war had not been brought to a successful conclusion by the autumn of 1941, I used every opportunity at conferences to make known my opinion that the whole situation for Germany was becoming extremely critical since time was against us and America would certainly come in on the other side once the USA had made the necessary economic preparations. When we had successes but still no victory in the East in 1942, I knew then that the war was unwinnable.[101]

Apparently the preparations to attack the Soviet Union ignited in Thoma a process of reflection which culminated over the next two years in the certainty that the war was lost. Captivity played no part in his 'awakening'. The notes in his diary made at Trent Park coincide precisely with the CSDIC protocols. Thoma noted on 17 January 1943:

> . . . It is, when one considers the war potential of all those in the world against us, only a postponement, no prevention of the outcome. A long war is – measured against the war situation – impossible for little Germany, and since we have already been fighting for several years, it cannot end happily for us. I felt that when America entered the war, and the situation is very similar to when they came in during World War I.[102]

Three days later he wrote,

The spectre of this war must be exorcised from the world once and for all. The State-philosophy of the Axis Powers is based principally on contempt for the individual, freedom and free speech. If we ever make this philosophy our own, our victory would become a defeat for all people . . . I cannot predict when the war will end, but I can say one thing: the year 1943 will bring us a good way back along the road to Berlin, Rome and Tokyo.[103]

Crüwell's military career began in the Prussian Army, and at first sight it is similar to that of von Thoma. Crüwell also ended World War I as an Oberleutnant, but from then until September 1939 ascended more speedily. Both in the Reichswehr and the Wehrmacht it had been his ambition to become a Staff Officer, but he was only at OKH in 1936 and 1939, and then never more than a few months. From October 1939 he was Senior Quartermaster, 16 Armee, in August 1940 he took command of 11 Panzer Division, with which he experienced the conquest of Belgrade and penetrated deep into the Ukraine in the first seven weeks of the Russian campaign. He arrived in North Africa on 15 August 1941 and was captured there on 29 May 1942. Unlike Thoma he was never long a senior military commander. After fighting at the front in Russia only during the lightning advances of the opening weeks, he was then part of the North African 'sideshow' from August 1941. When captured, German and Italian troops were on the verge of overrunning the British defences at Gazala near Tobruk and ejecting the British 8th Army from Libya.

Crüwell's war was a war of German victories, favourable promotions and high decorations (Knight's Cross with Oak Leaves). He had had no experiences resembling those of Thoma at OKH, neither the 'Napoleon Winter' at the gates of Moscow, nor the struggle for supplies at El Alamein. Although reports from the front gave him worries and doubts, he did not infer from them that the war was lost (Document 8).[104] Even after Stalingrad he believed in a German victory and comforted himself in the face of Thoma's many complaints with observations such as 'The German Army is still the best in the world.'[105]

His political convictions can be seen more clearly from earlier in his career. Of the murder of General Kurt von Schleicher in 1934 he wrote in 1958 that it remained for him 'incomprehensible and always shameful that the senior generals of the time accepted this murder . . . on that day Hitler lost his respect for the Wehrmacht.'[106] He told Thoma in their first conversation at Trent Park that he had become resigned after the Röhm-Putsch. He had never been a supporter of the system and had not been able to emulate Blomberg's fast turn-around to accommodate the Third Reich. Being unable to change anything, from then on he had attended to his military duties only.[107] His indignation at the murder of Schleicher

did not lead to his adopting an attitude of reservation towards the Third
Reich, however, nor to condemn Hitler as being responsible for
injustices and murders.[108]

Crüwell remained constant in his loyalty to the regime. In his Trent
Park notes his closeness to National Socialist thinking is often apparent.
On 2 July 1942 he gave the following advice to his four children born in
the 1930s:

> Love for the Fatherland is to some extent the religion of our time. Love
> this Greater Germany so that the struggle continues to the end, never
> allow yourself to be alienated from this love by pacifist and weak talk.
> This love demands sacrifices which you must always feel obliged to
> make unconditionally. Never, under any circumstances, marry a
> foreigner. You were all born in the era of Germany's greatest upheaval.
> Never forget that your father fought in two wars for Germany for your
> future, he served the Third Reich and Führer, fought for him and was
> highly decorated by him.[109]

He wrote of the philosopher Schopenhauer that his theory of the
preservation of the sub-species inherited from nature had 'very much in
it'.

From here the leap to the world political view of the Third Reich is not
a large one.[110] From Oswald Spengler's *Preussentum und Sozialismus*
(published in 1920), he noted that he had not been aware of the menace
of Bolshevism, but 'it fostered the grand idea of the Third Reich. The
thinking is partly timeless, correct and definitely very interesting.'[111]

His positive attitude to National Socialist geopolitics and racial theory
is also frequently evident in his entries. The smallness of the Reich was
in his opinion responsible for the rise of National Socialism,[112] a high
spiritual and cultural standard for *Volk* and family could only be attained
through closeness to Nature, simplicity of life, adversity and struggle,[113]
and racial equality was 'not the right path'. He believed that it would
come to 'a definite battle of the races'.[114] Sacrifice had an especial
significance for Crüwell: from the proclamation by the Führer of 9
November 1944 he jotted down 'that life only acknowledges the highest
worth in him who is willing and ready to sacrifice his life in order to
preserve it'.[115]

The protocols confirm the sketch created by Crüwell's notes. If
anybody attempted to lambast the Führer, he would spring to his
defence even though he admitted that ultimately Hitler was the man
responsible for everything, including the military disasters.[116] Undoubtedly Crüwell had succumbed to Hitler's aura, and he reported as if
spellbound on his two meetings with him (Document 3). Even in 1958 he
identified 1 September 1941, the day when he received from Hitler's
hand the Oak Leaves to his Knight's Cross, as the 'culminating moment
of my life as a soldier'.[117] He evaluated 'the Führer as higher' than

Roosevelt. Hitler would be received by history in a different light, 'there is no doubt about it', he said in autumn 1942.[118] His thoughts while in the American camp for generals at Clinton prove that he never really understood Hitler's intentions. On 3 September 1945 Crüwell wrote:

> Not until after his great foreign policy successes early on did he (Hitler) lose the right course and, disappointed that Britain would not go along with his proposals, then began slowly and gradually more swiftly to depart from his originally cherished plans for peace and finally jettisoned them on 1 September 1939. But even then he was determined and convinced that the war with Poland could be contained.[119]

By burying his head in the sand, Crüwell ignored the painful realities which would have called his world picture fundamentally into question. Crüwell kept up the attitude of not wanting to know during all his captivity in England and also later in the United States. His differences of opinion with Thoma, who considered him a good soldier but 'not spiritually strong enough' to remain independent, therefore never changed.[120] Since both, with the exception of a few other prisoners, were alone together at Trent Park until May 1943, Crüwell was apparently prepared to tolerate Thoma beyond normal limits even though he 'hated' him.[121] Occasionally the pair even discovered points of mutual agreement. Both considered Goebbels's speech of 18 February 1943 at the Sportpalast as 'negative' (Document 6), and both were at a loss to understand why Paulus surrendered at Stalingrad. Crüwell remarked, 'I would have put a bullet through my head. So, I am bitterly disappointed!' Thoma concurred and said that it was a dreadful thing that so many generals had been captured at Stalingrad.[122]

The Structure of the Groups

The semi-tolerable life changed abruptly when Army Group Africa prisoners began to arrive at Trent Park from mid-May 1943. By 1 July 1943, 20 senior officers and three adjutants had been added. Initially their thoughts were focused on the defeat in Tunisia and the question of whether they had been responsible for it. After a few days they concluded that the disaster was not their fault.[123] Some blamed the Italians, who had kept their fleet at anchor, others doubted the strategic sense of having defended Tunisia for so long. Arnim even believed that his reports on the catastrophic situation had never been placed before Hitler. After about a week these conversations dissipated and the new arrivals began to group into the respective camps around Crüwell and Thoma so that their personal smouldering conflict now developed its own 'group-dynamic explosive potential'.

Arraigned on Thoma's side were von Broich, von Sponeck, von Liebenstein, Cramer, Luftwaffe generals Neuffer and Bassenge, and

Inmates of Trent Park, November 1943: (standing, left to right) von Glasow, Boes, Hubbuch, Buhse, Schmidt, Borcherdt: (seated, left to right) Egersdorff, Crüwell, von Arnim, Meixner, von Hülsen

colonels Reimann, Schmidt, Drange and Heym. Köhncke and Ernst Wolters could also be counted as members of the 'Thoma group'. Thoma himself was astonished that so many Luftwaffe officers – besides Neuffer and Bassenge, also Schmidt, Drange and Köhncke – spoke out critically against the regime and the course the war was taking.

Crüwell sought allies, for Thoma's 'eternal griping' was 'getting on his nerves' and he was determined to stick by 'the Prussian point of view', defending Fatherland and Führer against all comers (Document 10). He found supporters in von Hülsen, Frantz,[124] Buhse and in Konteradmiral Meixner,[125] who was deeply disappointed at the lack of military bearing of the Trent Park officers. 'Our generals are for the most part broken men. It is appalling what small people they are' he noted in his diary on 7 August 1943 (there are similar entries on 6 July and 17 November 1943). The adjutants also divided: von Glasow inclined towards Thoma, while Boes and Hubbuch were apparently convinced National Socialists. Both were still of the opinion in 1993 that Thoma was a military disgrace and believed that he had gone over to the British in North Africa in 1942.[126] Most of the NCO valets took no sides and remained loyal to their general. When offered paid work in the Trent Park vegetable gardens they refused tenaciously because nothing would make them support the British war effort, no matter how small.[127] Finally Bassenge's intervention put an end to this farce.

It can be summarised that while the 'Thoma group' considered the war lost, condemned the atrocities in the East and spoke detrimentally about Hitler and Nazism, the 'Crüwell people', though critical of the war situation, considered it by no means hopeless,[128] attempted to justify war crimes either by minimising their scale or doubting whether they had ever happened at all, and additionally defended Nazism. The groups were not organisations but rather a loose association of independent characters whose views on many matters coincided. Only a few shared Thoma's radical outlook. Few spoke as openly as Thoma did. Some changed their opinions in time and others drifted between the groups, or eventually preferred to spend the time in other activities such as painting.[129] Graf Sponeck made such a good copy of Rembrandt's 'Man in a Golden Helmet' that it was hung in the dining room.[130] Whereas the differences in opinion did not have the same significance as they did for Thoma and Crüwell, from the beginning they impregnated decisively the climate at Trent Park.

Crüwell urged Generaloberst von Arnim as Senior German Officer into action against the 'evil spirit' of von Thoma in order to stop 'defeatism'.[131] On 9 July 1943 Arnim urged the prisoners to discontinue all 'conversations which are in any way harmful to colleagues'. Looking on the dark side would not help bear captivity. Additionally it was one's duty to the homeland to exude confidence and so help the people at home (Document 12). Arnim was therefore working to preserve fortitude in the camp and bolster the 'rather shaky' morale.[132] His talk did not have the desired effect and deepened the divisions.[133]

After Arnim's intervention, literature critical of National Socialism such as Otto Braun's *Von Weimar zu Hitler* was no longer read only secretly.[134] Many inmates enjoyed the free access to books, periodicals and radio broadcasts. Only Crüwell, Hülsen and Lt Hubbuch continued to read the *Völkischer Beobachter*,[135] and were anxious to prevent other prisoners listening to the BBC German Service news bulletins. Crüwell, Franz and also Arnim were infuriated that Thoma, Broich and others tuned in to this propaganda, but Arnim did not have the personal authority to forbid it.[136]

In another call to reason to the Thoma group, Arnim addressed the inmates again on 15 and 16 August 1943, demanding that they refrain from 'defeatist talk': in the propaganda war, the British should not be given 'the means and the weapons'. He was unaware of course that recordings of conversations had given the British a richer fund of propaganda material than ever he could have dreamed. Besides, Arnim said, he wanted to 'safeguard' officers in the event of the German victory, he would not want to see officers being court-martialled for their behaviour in captivity.[137] Probably aware that Arnim's words were directed primarily at him, Thoma responded, 'To think it right that we should accept your laborious assessment of the situation as gospel – No! [. . .] It has been our misfortune at home that full-grown generals, enchanted by Hitler, let themselves be told off like snotty-nosed schoolboys. It doesn't change me, absolutely not.'[138]

Undoubtedly too much was asked of von Arnim in his role as Senior German Officer (SGO). Even as he arrived at Trent Park, most generals did not think of him too highly. Some held him responsible for the disaster in Tunisia and considered him no better than a good divisional commander. He lacked the charisma to arbitrate on differences and strengthen the cohesion. Even the group around Crüwell was estranged from Arnim, for whom as SGO he never succeeded in banning the BBC German Service. Finally, at a loss, he would take charge of the wireless and re-tune it to a German station, thus making himself look completely ridiculous. From then on he was an outcast, so unloved that nobody would accompany him when he wanted to take a ramble, and finally Crüwell saw himself obliged to order somebody to walk with him.[139] Arnim spent most of his time alone in his room staring at nothing for hours, making appearances ever more rarely in the officers' mess.[140]

Arnim's political opinions were not without their ambiguities. General Cramer soon came to the conclusion that although Arnim thought he was obliged to defend the National Socialist regime outwardly, his personal opinion about it was different.[141] The protocols confirm this picture. He made adverse references to the war situation, the National Socialist system[142] and German war crimes (Document 96). He often conversed freely with Lord Aberfeldy, thus ignoring his maxim that one should always remain silent in the presence of the British.[143]

The smouldering conflicts at Trent Park continued into the subsequent months.[144] Crüwell protested at Thoma's glee over German defeats[145] while Thoma took Arnim and Crüwell ever less seriously. They were like the three monkeys: 'Hear no evil, see no evil, speak no evil'.[146] On 12 September 1943 Thoma observed to Oberst Rudolf Buhse that he regretted 'every bomb, every scrap of material and every human life that is still being wasted in this senseless war. The only gain that the war will bring us is the end of ten years of gangster rule' (Document 14). 'For that reason I am seen by others as a criminal,' he said, adding that one 'should put Adolf Hitler in a padded cell.' He was clear, of course, that his open rejection of Nazism and his firm belief in the defeat of Germany was not shared by many of his prisoner colleagues who, as a rule, expressed their criticisms in a more moderate manner. Officers like Crüwell and Meixner were firmly convinced that Germany would win the war if it succeeded in fighting off the invasion. (Paul Meixner, diary, 31 March and 18 April 1944)

'One can only wonder,' Thoma wrote in his diary on 17 February 1944, that

> the majority still expect a miracle and feel slighted whenever one offers a sober and unfavourable judgement of the situation. They take it as a personal insult and feel as if struck a blow on the head. What type of

Inmates of Trent Park, November 1943: (standing, left to right) Reimann, Neuffer, Krause, Köhncke, Wolters: (seated, left to right) von Broich, von Sponeck, von Liebenstein, Bassenge

blow to the head will it be when the war ends? The lack of civilian courage, which is rarer than bravery, is responsible for the concern shown by anti-Nazis. I laugh about it and give everybody my opinion about the bitter end. My opinion is completely opposite to that of Goebbels who every week is more stupid and insolent about it in his articles in *Das Reich*: people do not seem to notice how stupid he thinks we all are.[147]

Despite all differences of opinion the Trent Park community remained intact in some respects. At Christmas 1943 all prisoners sat together for an excellent dinner with plum pudding and red wine before re-uniting in their small groups to spend Christmas Night in silent contemplation.[148]

Even on Hitler's birthday on 20 April 1944 no such scene as feared by Crüwell eventually occurred. He expected that Thoma would not raise his glass to toast the Führer and was anxious to have acting-SGO Bassenge ejected from the officer corps in case he deliberately avoided making any preparations for the special day. The 'defeatists' abstained from making trouble, however. A toast to the Führer was proposed – to Crüwell's disgust in British beer – after which Arnim made a short speech to the generals in the valets' dining room.[149]

Crüwell's situation at Trent Park became intolerable after he failed to unseat Bassenge as acting-SGO and was not approached to nominate the

Head Valet, appointed for all kinds of important organisational tasks. Besides his political tussles, Crüwell found captivity in itself an especially heavy burden. In June 1942 he wrote in his diary, a few days after his capture:

> I am completely cut off from the great struggle of our Fatherland. For me there was nothing more honourable and fine than to fight and work for our final victory. I always feared that my health would not hold out and now it has turned out completely differently [. . .] My military career with its rich prospects was very abruptly broken off on 29 May 1942. It is very harsh.[150]

On dark days his mood alternated between depression and rage 'that I am no longer there to fight.'[151] From summer 1943 he became increasingly nervy and tired. He gave up physical activities and concentrated on learning English. On 10 August 1943 he wrote:

> I have lost a lot of weight. In May 1943 I weighed 71 kilos after being 83 kilos in March. I am now conserving my energy, the best way to handle the lack of food. I think of myself as a horse in winter, getting a lot of hay and not much oats and therefore cannot do much work. But one can handle it, the spiritual burden of captivity is more onerous.[152]

Finally in mid-January 1944 he asked Lord Aberfeldy if it would not be possible to be interned in Sweden on his word of honour.[153] When this was rejected he took cold baths and scratched the eczema on his legs in an attempt to obtain repatriation on medical grounds. This was also unsuccessful.[154] On 22 February 1944, however, General Hans Cramer, who had severe asthma, and 34 German soldiers from other camps, were repatriated.[155] Cramer became important since it seemed likely that he would be closely questioned in Germany about the events in North Africa and in captivity. Crüwell then asked him to suggest to Hitler's Wehrmacht ADC Schmundt that he should be exchanged for General Richard O'Connor who had been captured in North Africa in 1941. Since O'Connor had escaped in September 1943, Crüwell's idea had no prospect of success from the beginning (SRGG 761, 14.1.1944, TNA, WO 208/5625). Arnim tried to present himself to Cramer in the best possible light as well. Arnim was certainly only the scapegoat for Rommel: ultimately he was merely a desk general who had made a fool of himself in North Africa, according to Cramer. Whether he achieved his stated aim of telling Hitler 'the Truth' about Arnim is not known.

Before his departure Cramer thanked the British Commandant at Trent Park for the excellent treatment. Whenever he had seen the alert sentries from his window he had been proud of his British blood (he had an English grandmother, Emma Dalton). Lord Aberfeldy returned to him his 'Afrika' cuff-band as a gesture of thanks. Cramer returned home from captivity doubtless bereft of any illusions about the hopeless war situation. He was even anxious to put his Wehrsold savings into a British bank before he left. A few days before his journeyed home, he also requested that should he die before being repatriated, his coffin should not be draped with the Nazi flag.[156]

Cramer left England for Algiers aboard the hospital ship *Atlantis* and arrived in Barcelona from there with the Swedish ship *Gipsholm*. A special OKW aircraft flew him to Berlin, where he arrived on 12 May 1944.

Although the exact details of what Cramer reported on his return are not known, he did at least retain a critical outlook. 'It was also not easy,' he wrote in his diary, 'to re-engage in the German morale and outlook on the war. I had lived through too much, I knew too much from the other side. In Germany they spoke of total war [. . .] over there it had been a fact for some time.'

Surprisingly after his return nobody wanted to know about Cramer. Only with great perseverance did he finally obtain an invitation for discussions at Führer-HQ, Berchtesgaden. The half-hour personal talk with Hitler and Schmundt went off 'very disappointingly', as Cramer wrote, 'and I could not disabuse myself of the impression that I had been written out of the war.' There followed a short reception with Ribbentrop and Goebbels, who had little understanding for 'my concern which

Hans Cramer, the third commander of the Afrika Korps to be captured by the British and brought to Trent Park

stemmed from my knowledge of the enemy and the view I had of our Fatherland from the outside. They didn't want to hear the truth.' Keitel and Jodl, as OKW and Wehrmacht Command Staff chiefs respectively, and as such responsible for the disaster in Africa, did not wish to meet Cramer. At the beginning of June he travelled to France where he met Rommel,who treated him 'initially with reservation but then became very comradely'.[157]

They spoke about the war in Tunisia and the imminent invasion. In the Army Group B files one finds an entry that even General Cramer expected the main thrust of the Allied landings to be either side of the Somme Estuary (BA/MA, RH 19 IX/93, 4.6.44). After the war it was always maintained that Cramer had been deliberately used by the British to spread disinformation (see Ose, *Entscheidung im Westen*, p. 90), but there is no proof, of course.

In June Cramer returned home to Krampnitz near Berlin where he met Claus von Stauffenberg on several occasions. He knew him from the Kavallerie-Schule at Hanover and from his time at the General Staff. They had also met in Tunisia in 1943. It was through Stauffenberg that Cramer was put in contact with General Olbricht, who let him into the secret of the assassination plot. Cramer agreed that should the plot succeed he would ensure that local troops occupied the area around the Victory Column. On the morning of 20 July he went to the panzer training school and ensured that the troops were ready as planned and were occupying the correct areas. After the failure of the plot Cramer quickly came under Gestapo scrutiny. He was interrogated for the first time on 23 July, was arrested on 26 July and taken to the Gestapo prison on the Prinz-Albrecht-Strasse. He was accused of being a liaison man between the Resistance and the British. The flame of suspicion was fanned when his son, a Leutnant in Normandy, disappeared on 26 July (he had been seriously wounded). The interrogations lasted 10 days. Finally Cramer was brought to the Security Police School at Fürstenberg north of Berlin as an 'arrestee against honour' since there was nothing else to be found against him. He was discharged from the Wehrmacht in September 1944 on the grounds of his asthma and hospitalised at the Berlin Charité. He was sent home on Christmas Eve 1944 and remained there under house arrest until the end of hostilities.[158]

At Trent Park he had assured Lord Aberfeldy in the course of his repatriation that he would do everything possible to discover what plans there were for a coup, which would have his full support.[159] He had kept his promise.

'Now it Should be Brought to an End, it is Simply Madness' Reflection on the Final Battles, 1944–45

When the Allies landed in Normandy on 6 June 1944 and began the closing phase of World War II in Europe, the camp community at Trent

Inmates at Trent Park, November 1944: (standing, left to right) von Choltitz, Wilck, Ramcke, Eberding, Wildermuth: (seated, left to right) von Heyking, von Schlieben, Daser

Park had remained little changed for a year. In August 1943, four officers had been transferred out to the United States, and General Cramer had been repatriated in February 1944. In January 1944 Oberstleutnant Wilfried von Müller-Rienzburg[160] had arrived. The invasion undermined the monotonous and semi-monastic existence fundamentally: from the end of May to the end of September 1944, most 'Afrikaner' were transferred to America, only the two seniors, Thoma and Bassenge, shop manager Reimann, and the generals Broich and Neuffer remained behind to greet the stream of new prisoners from France.

The first new arrival was Oberst Hans Krug. His regimental HQ had been overrun by British troops on 7 June 1944. At the end of the month the defenders of Cherbourg arrived, at the beginning of August those overwhelmed by the American offensive west of St Lô, and finally the survivors of the Falaise pocket. They came from surrendered fortifications or had simply fallen into enemy hands during Wehrmacht retreats gone awry. By the end of 1944, 32 generals and at least 14 colonels had been settled at Trent Park.[161] Many of the newcomers would be transferred out after a period ranging from a few days to several months. By the year's end, the five 'Afrikaner' had been joined at Trent Park by 20 further high-ranking prisoners.

Despite the new personnel, the basic conflicts remained unmellowed.

Some lacked interest in politics and strategy or distanced themselves in varying degrees from Hitler, Nazism and the war crimes, recognising that the war was lost and hoping for a quick end to the now senseless fighting. The BBC German Service conflict flared up from time to time (Document 43).[162] General Menny was relieved to be transferred to the United States after a four-week stay at Trent Park. 'The spirit in the Generals' Camp (Clinton) is excellent, and morale exudes confidence despite our difficult situation. Above all conduct here is respectful and decent. Unlike Trent Park one does not have to get all worked up over worthless generals, who kow-tow to the British and worship everything English and drag everything German through the mud. I remember with reluctance the foul, hate-filled atmosphere which prevailed at Trent Park under the leadership of the characterless General Thoma.'[163]

The constant comings and goings brought fresh information and impressions to the centre.[164] Most officers were troubled by the oppressive material superiority of the Allies: they had looked on helplessly as their units were crushed by the enemy war machine, watched the old cultural landscape of northern France collapse in ruins as thousands of German soldiers died in it. The collapse on all the fronts now seemed unstoppable; Germany had lost the war. Most were agreed on this fact (Document 26).[165] Only Konteradmiral Kähler, who had been captured by the Americans at Brest, said that he still believed in final victory (Document 41).[166] When in autumn 1944 the Wehrmacht sprang a surprise by holding the Allied advance at the German frontier, it generated a seed of hope within a number of generals that the enemy coalition might break asunder, and there could be, as in 1762, another 'miracle of the Brandenburg Dynasty'.[167]

Generalleutnant Menny noted in his diary:

> When the front in the West collapsed, when France and Belgium were lost in a few weeks, we all believed that the end of the war was near. Oppressed by the grim encirclements in France we considered that a long resistance along the Westwall was no longer possible. But it turned out differently, for a miracle has occurred. Hope now revives for a possible victory, and we wish for it with all our hearts even if it means that we must spend an age in captivity. I stick firmly by my old theory that the political differences and diverse interests between British and Russians will bring a favourable change [. . .] we must wait![168]

Generalleutnant von Heyking now saw room to manoeuvre for negotiations. One had to hold out, he said in December 1944, for 'the Americans have no idea what they are fighting for.' If they suffered very heavy casualties, one could get them to the negotiating table – or the enemy coalition would break up (Document 51).[169] The Ardennes offensive had fuelled these hopes (Document 52),[170] but General Ramcke was alone in his belief that the German divisions could drive the Allies

Inmates at Trent Park, November 1944: (standing, left to right) Elfeldt, Heim, Bassenge: (seated, left to right) von Broich, Eberbach, Neuffer, Reimann

back across France and into the sea. A negotiated peace seemed to many a possibility as the result of such a successful offensive, however (Document 75).

The optimists held on to their hopes for a happy outcome to the war while the realists were of the opinion that it was already decided long ago, and Germany's only possibility was unconditional surrender. 'We entered the New Year with awful morale' wrote Generalmajor Paul von Felbert in his diary. 'That Germany was totally beaten was totally clear to all of us with exception of the incorrigibles such as Ramcke and cronies' (Felbert, diary, p. 71). The differences came clearly into the light in a long conversation between General Heinrich Eberbach and his son Oberleutnant zur See Heinz Eberbach on 20 and 21 September 1944 (Document 37). The 23-year-old U-boat commander was still convinced that 'miracle weapons' would turn the tide while his father considered the whole thing 'hopeless'. He had reached the final stage of a long process of acceptance. In December 1943, the general was still believing it possible to 'crush the Russians', and in June 1944 he still would not admit that the war was lost. After beating off the invasion 'we will have our heads above water,' he hoped (Document 64).[171]

Once it had proved impossible to halt the Allied divisions, not to mention repel them, 'there was no more point to it', General Eberbach said in February 1945. Extracts from his letters from Normandy show this: 'How can it go on without the V-2 or other miracle weapons?' he asked on 11 July. Five days later he wrote: 'Heavy fighting – spearhead not large – questions in the eyes of my soldiers – we still lack the great decision.' And on 20 July: 'Hold out! Hold out! 116 Panzer Div. not for another five days! No way out.' Shortly afterwards the US 3rd Army broke through the German lines west of St Lo and near Avranches, and on 3 August 1944 broke out from the hard-fought bridgehead. The German defences were at the end of their strength, and now Hitler ordered an extravagant counter-attack which plunged the Western Army into catastrophe. On 5 August Eberbach wrote home: 'Situation remains extremely tense. All commanders exhausted. I often think of Bismarck's greatness.' Finally, on the 17th: 'No great decision. I can no longer see a way out.'[172]

Eberbach therefore had his road-to-Damascus experience at Normandy in the high summer of 1944.[173] By 1942 Thoma had had no illusions about the situation, other – perhaps not all – Afrika Korps generals followed in 1943. Even those prisoners with knowledge of strategy were obliged to acknowledge after the failure of the Ardennes offensive and the push into Reich territory by the Allied armies in January and February 1945 that the war was lost. In the early spring nobody believed in final victory or even a negotiated peace. Nevertheless the *inferences* drawn varied. Should one capitulate or fight to the bitter end? Even far from the tentacles of the regime the deeply anchored concept of military honour remained firm. The comparatively critical Generalmajor Wahle observed in February 1945 that 'the most elementary military honour' demanded that one should keep fighting (Document 64).[174] The German people must lose the war honourably by fighting to the last gasp, General Choltitz said in March 1945. The honourable struggle would prevent the people going under and having their spirit broken (Document 66). Ramcke, paratroop general and a convinced National Socialist, admitted it to be his heartfelt wish that the German people would have the strength to defend every bridge, every hill-ridge, every town, to the last. The victorious powers could then allow the Germans to quietly die out, but they would at least have gone down fighting (Document 38). In September 1944 Ramcke had defended the French port of Brest until out of ammunition, and his stubborn resistance must be the model for the Battle for Germany. That he had previously taken steps to ensure that he would be the only man to escape from Brest by air demonstrates the deceptiveness of such images of *Götterdämmerung*. That Ramcke actually believed the Allies were intent upon the biological extermination of the German people can be assumed. This kind of propaganda was mouthed by other pro-Nazi generals such as SS-Brigadeführer Kurt Meyer and Luftwaffe-Generalleutnant Heyking (Document 51).

At Clinton Camp, USA, there was an internal court martial of

Generalmajor Botho Elster for surrendering to the Americans with 20,000 men,[175] but he was able to get the charge dropped. Generalmajor Paul von Felbert was sentenced to death in his absence on 3 January 1945 for capitulating in a parallel situation in September 1944. His family was arrested. 'Nevertheless I am shocked', Generalleutnant Menny noted in his diary at the end of 1944,

> how few of the more than forty generals I have known in captivity *personally* fought to the end. It is of course simply right that every soldier and naturally a general should try everything, even the impossible. Even the impossible can be achieved by the general who has luck. How often have I escaped encirclements and other hopeless situations with my men after we had all long since abandoned hope of surviving.[176]

Not until the Allies had crossed the Rhine on a broad front did the majority think again about the 'honourable' struggle to the end. 'I always used to consider it wrong to surrender, our people might have cracked badly and that might perhaps have proved disastrous in the future. But now we *must* give in, it's simply madness,' Ferdinand Heim acknowledged in March 1945 (Document 69). Two weeks previously he had received news that his wife and youngest son had been killed at Ulm on 17 December 1944 during a British air raid.[177] New arrivals provided the Trent Park community with ever-gloomier reports about the fighting, and reinforced the pessimists. 'The bloody stupidity surrounding the German defeat is revealing itself as ever more grotesque and miserable,' noted Eberhard Wildermuth in his diary on 18 May 1945 after listening to Generalleutnant Holste's account of the fighting on the Elbe.[178]

General Kirchheim, who arrived in mid-March (Document 77), provided some interesting ideas on laying down arms. General Höhne had confided to him in the spring of 1945 that he considered all further resistance useless. Since the German people did not have a clear picture of the causes of the defeat, it was necessary to fight on to prevent another 'stab in the back' legend taking root – only in that way would the scale of the defeat and the failure of the National Socialist system become blatantly obvious to most Germans.[179]

Whatever insight they may have had into the approaching defeat, or lack of enthusiasm for a fight to the last, nevertheless the pro-Nazi generals maintained their morale. In mid-March 1945 several of them expressed indignation at a report by Oberstleutnant Kogler describing the devastating course of the air war and especially the defence of the Reich. As Wing Commander JG6, Kogler knew what he was talking about, but an Oberstleutnant did not have the competence to deliver such a wide-ranging criticism, or so Ramcke, Vaterrodt and Kittel believed.[180]

After listening to Goebbels's speech on the occasion of Hitler's birthday on 20 April 1945, one of the officers rose to his feet halfway through the playing of the national anthem and switched off the radio. General-leutnant Kittel was outraged: how could one sink so low as not to stand for the national anthem, and leave the room while it was playing? They were riff-raff and cowards, he told the assembly. It was better to fall at the front than finish up at Trent Park.[181] Eight days previously he had considered it essential to report to Germany by secret code 'how these people such as Bassenge, Thoma and Co. behave. I think the admirals [Schirmer and Kähler] have done something like that already' (Extract from SR Draft 3137/45 (GG), 12.4.1945, TNA WO 208/5622).

One of the valets was appalled to see the generals drinking wine on 8 May 1945 as if celebrating their own funerals. This was not the German spirit, it was a disgrace, and it merely proved, as General Bodenschatz remarked,[182] that the Führer was quite right when he described the generals as a 'pack of filthy swine'.[183]

Whilst a number of the Trent Park inmates, at least until the spring of 1945, were in favour of fighting to the last bullet, and remained loyal to Hitler, another group condemned any further bloodshed as senseless from the outset. 'Something has to happen, one simply cannot fight to the last soldier,' Generalleutnant von Schlieben said on 3 July 1944. The eradication of the German people by National Socialism must eventually be stopped, Oberst Wildermuth declared. The 'Afrikaners' at Trent Park were of the opinion that it was time to surrender. For Hitler, however, capitulation was unthinkable; it was all or nothing, and he was ready to accept the consequences. His willingness to drag Germany down into the abyss was the consequence of people upsetting his world view. If Hitler as Head of State could not see the writing on the wall after the defeat in Normandy, nor when the Ardennes offensive collapsed, nor even when the Allies had crossed the Rhine, how was the bloodshed to be brought to an end? Calls for responsible action by the commanders-in-chief, from a man like von Rundstedt for example, were heard repeatedly at Trent Park from the summer of 1944 onwards. The front in the West should be parted or – less striking – 'a man like von Rundstedt' had to transfer 20 divisions to the Eastern Front and so hasten the occupation of Western Germany (Document 64). Eberbach was of the opinion in February 1945 that the moment had come when Army commanders in the West had to convince themselves to lay down their arms for the common good. 'I should spend the whole time thinking: "What can I do to bring about the fall of the Hitler clique? [. . .] What can I do [. . .] to bring about, somehow, the entry of the Western Powers in?"' (Document 66). Eberbach spoke as a widely respected and known C-in-C – but what should a ranking general do? Broich suggested that as divisional commander one could simply leave gaps and so enable the Western Allies to break through along the front.

The protocols reveal that most generals declined such tactics on the basis that it did not accord with military honour: 'that couldn't be reconciled with their honour [. . .] If I, as CO of a "Division" say to my men "tomorrow we surrender", they'll say the old boy has gone crazy overnight; he's overworked; he's ill."' Generalmajor Bruhn reflected in January 1945 (Document 56). Generalmajor Hans Schaefer agreed: 'You can't persuade an officer simply to say: "we'll arrange with the Americans: 'You attack and we won't fire.'"' (Document 57). Although he considered the war to be lost as commander of the Marseilles fortifications, he had not given in: he would not fight to the last round but resisted until orderly defence collapsed.[184]

As front commanders, Broich and Eberbach might have acted as they claimed they would from the security of captivity, but a glance at how the final battles were fought suggests it was mere dreaming. Responsible steps taken *against* Hitler's orders were practically non-existent amongst the Army Group and Army C-in-Cs, except for isolated cases in the very last days of the war.

As regards the lower-ranking commanders of towns, battle groups or divisions, the failure to stick to the letter of instructions was a major exception. Generalleutnant Graf von Schwerin was the first general to have refused to participate in 'an artificially lengthened war on German soil [. . .] which would only destroy Germany'.[185] He returned from Aachen, was discharged immediately from the Wehrmacht but was not court-martialled because of his reputation and was later found re-employment. Oberst Wilck followed in Schwerin's footsteps. As the old Kaiser town descended into chaos and destruction, he defended it until orderly resistance collapsed and then – as did Schaefer at Marseilles – sent out some heroic radio messages before accepting captivity.[186]

The example of Aachen shows that a number of factors were required to undermine Hitler's final struggle fantasies: the correct assessment of the situation by the military commander of the district, the prudence of the Allied forces and often the courageous intervention of prominent civilian dignitaries. Withe the help of Swiss Consul-General Franz-Rudolph von Weiss and acting Bürgermeister Heinrich Ditz, General-leutnant Richard Schimpf, CO 3 Fallschirmjäger-Division, succeeded in surrendering Bad Godesberg to the Americans on 8 March 1945 without a fight. This was done knowing it was contrary to the orders of Feldmarschall Model. Schimpf created a situation in which Army Group B could neither remove him nor take counter-measures.[187]

Such initiatives never came from the highest levels, however, and even the involvement of divisional commanders was a rare exception. It was mostly junior officers and even simple soldiers who would ignore orders from above to prevent the greater ill. 'The troops are not insubordinate but they carry out what you might term "sit down strikes",' General Edwin Graf von Rothkirch and Trach reported in March 1945 (Document 67).

In all this the generals faced only a comparatively slight personal risk to themselves[188] while their orders to the men under their command meant death for thousands. In 1945, 1.2 million German soldiers fell – more than in 1942 and 1943 combined. Only very few generals were prepared to follow their troops to death or, as SS-Brigadeführer Kurt Meyer nicely put it, 'to peg out with the Führer'.[189] Model was one of the highest-ranking commanders to take his own life: Generals Wilhelm Burgdorf (Hitler's Wehrmacht ADC) and Hans Krebs shot themselves on 1 May 1945 in the Führer bunker in Berlin, Generaladmiral Hans Georg von Friedeburg and Generalfeldmarschall Robert Ritter von Greim followed them a few weeks after the capitulation. Yet this attitude remained exceptional, and most preferred captivity to suicide.

The picture we have of the highest generals in the closing weeks and months of the war is not a flattering one: to avoid falling victim to a flying court martial for the premature laying down of arms, or not obeying orders to hold out (Document 76) was for many generals the foremost consideration in their planning. They would rather sacrifice their men than endanger their own lives by disobeying orders from the Führer. Oberstleutnant Josef Ross's description of the fighting on the Wesel in March 1945 (Document 72) speaks a clear language in this regard.

'However highly we may esteem bravery and steadfastness in war, there is however a point beyond which holding-out in warfare can only be described as the madness of despair, and can therefore never be approved,' Clausewitz wrote in *Vom Kriege*.[190] The German generals of World War II rejected the Prussian military theoretician in favour of Hitler.

Complicity? Thoughts on Politics, Ideology and Personal Responsibility

In the quiet and seclusion of Trent Park the captured generals also reflected on general political questions. Even if this theme was not central to their conversations, the differing attitudes to the Third Reich, the role of the military in the State and the problems of personal responsibility can be clearly seen in the protocols. In retrospect, Crüwell saw no negative side to Hitler's political system. It had been the aim of the Führer to seize mastery of the independent states of Europe and so save Western culture (Document 2). The war had been necessary for Germany to recognise itself as the most important State on the continent. Crüwell was certain in addition that the Germans were the most human of the races, the few SS atrocities being only the 'outpourings of the concerned'. These remarks from 1942 are obviously set against a quite different background to those expressed by other generals in 1944–45. Whether Crüwell changed his opinion following the military collapse and the reports about the death camps is not known, but during his stay at Trent Park until his departure in June 1944 he did not depart from his pro-Hitler and pro-Nazi position.[191]

Many others went through a purification process at Trent Park, however, and confessed their fault: 'Of course, we let ourselves be taken in, too, there's no doubt about that [. . .] During the time that I was laying alone in hospital, a lot of things became clear to me,' Oberst Kessler agreed (Document 28). Some prisoners admitted freely to having been pro-Nazi in the past or to have seen the system as 'ideal' (e.g. Ludwig Krug, Walter Köhn). It had, after all, 'done some good, lifted us up out of the mud and also got rid of the scourge of unemployment. Moreover the State had made us officers what we are. Correspondingly, one had to remain loyal to it. Irregularities had been dismissed per the maxim "You cannot plane a plank without shavings falling." ' 'It had not been so bad in 1933–34,' Oberst Müller-Römer said: after a decent beginning, however, the whole movement had degenerated. 'It was rotten at the core, they had evil intentions,' Oberst Reimann concluded (Document 28).

Hitler's central role in the Nazi Movement had not always been recognised. Generalmajor Gerhard Franz, long active in the General Staff and assessed by the British as highly intelligent, saw injustice and crime as originating from within Hitler's entourage rather than from Hitler himself (Document 79). The image of Hitler as the victim of his advisers was not shared by many at Trent Park. Thoma doubtless spoke the harshest words against Hitler: he was inwardly simply evil, a Mephistopheles who belonged in a padded cell. Johannes Bruhn admitted, 'One must shake one's head in disbelief that we all followed this madness' (Document 73).[192]

Yet if Hitler was so transparently a criminal, as Generalleutnant von Schlieben thought, why did the Wehrmacht buckle under him? The High Command, so it is widely held, had failed completely, and its complacent dealings had led to the 'inner slide'[193] of the Wehrmacht. The Luftwaffe and Kriegsmarine C-in-Cs, the Army Groups and the Chief of the Army General Staff should have kept Hitler in check (Document 60).[194] Another widely held belief was that Hitler could have been controlled by warnings from a clear consensus of the senior generals challenging his war plans (Köhn, Müller-Römer). This merely goes to show how little about Hitler's personality many officers were able to understand.

It is scarcely surprising that the responsibility for Germany's military defeat should be blamed on the Party and the spineless OKW generals who had executed the Führer's absurd orders. Thoma noted in his diary on 11 February 1945: 'And what will history say of the immense cowardice of the accomplices and hangers-on?'.[195] Even if one distanced himself from the generals, there was still a united front to reject the accusation by Hitler and the National Socialist leaders, expressed ever more vehemently with time, that the generals had failed, and sabotaged the war (e.g. Documents 30, 148).[196]

In the open atmosphere of Trent Park, a few generals did admit to their personal responsibility. 'There is not one of us, who is not to blame for this human tragedy. This time for thought which I have enjoyed here was very necessary for me. The Bible, Sophocles, Goethe, Shakespeare, they all helped. And nature, too' wrote General Heinz Eberbach in a letter to his wife in July 1945 (TNA, DEFE 1/343). General von Choltitz even confessed, that he had misled his men into believing 'this shit' and had motivated people who still saw the officer corps as 'something worthy' to go along with the regime unthinkingly. 'I feel thoroughly ashamed!' he said, 'Maybe we are *far more* to blame from those uneducated cattle who in any case never hear anything else at all.' (Document 44). Of course, such self-criticism never found its way into a general's memoirs, including Choltitz's. Despite his remarkable statement, Choltitz did not go so far as to align himself with Thoma, whose verdict was that the German people and Army had lost their honour. Here Thoma was out on a limb.

Finis Germaniae? The Inmates of Trent Park Reflect on the Future

When the prisoners at Trent Park considered the future, their main concerns were about themselves and their families. Rumours about how long captivity would last, forcible transfer to the Soviet Union or the threat of war crimes tribunals featured prominently.[197] Others lamented the loss of property. General Holste complained: 'I was a man who had three estates, all of that is now gone. I have nothing but the shirt I stand up in.'[198] Similar observations do not recur frequently in the protocols, and one assumes that it was preferred to confide them to diaries and letters.[199] All prisoners shared a primitive fear that Germany could turn Communist, either because the German people would take refuge in it willingly in the chaos and collapse of National Socialism, or because the Red Army would occupy the Reich before the Allies did so. Using the style of Nazi propaganda, Ramcke compared the 'Red Peril' to the threat to the West presented by Genghis Khan.[200] Even if all did not quite see it so bluntly, it was held unanimously that Communism would mean slavery, oppression and death. A few would have been happy to make common cause with Britain against Bolshevism.[201] Only Georg Neuffer, and to some extent Müller-Römer, thought about the Russians in a more positive way. Neuffer was the only inmate at Trent Park who could read and speak Russian and frequently remarked that the propaganda picture of the primitive, retarded Soviet was not a true one.[202]

Apparently little thought was given to the medium- or long-term future of Europe. The overwhelming events of recent years were too difficult for military minds to assimilate and so see a way forward for

Europe and Germany in the future. One of the few exceptions was Eberhard Wildermuth, who had been active politically pre-war. At the end 'of our Thirty Years' War' he said,

> we have not only lost the war and our independence as a State, but our self-respect and honour. We will be under foreign masters for the foreseeable future. These masters will split Germany into several parts – but the worst is that for years the great dividing line between East and West will run through Germany. It may be a permanent division. Before these major questions there are others, more urgent, more in the present: how many millions will starve to death? How will it be possible to rebuild agriculture, industry and transport communications? How are we to rebuild a political structure with self-administration and accountability? Schools? Universities? It seems that the German administration will not be uniform under the various victors – it seems to me doubtful then that the problem can be solved at all.[203]

Thoma, too, was thinking in concrete terms about postwar Europe. Many of his ideas were nebulous and not well thought through, but on some points he saw developments astoundingly clearly: there would be no reparations, German industry would work for the Allies. He doubted if Britain would succeed in building a new Poland because the Soviet Union was leaning heavily towards the West. This antagonism 'had the seeds of World War Three in it'. It could happen that, shoulder to shoulder with British and French forces, even German formations might be 'let loose' against the Russians.[204]

3.2 'We Have Tried to Exterminate Whole Communities'. War Crimes in Trent Park Conversations

The protocols document a number of German war crimes: the deportation and internment of Jews in ghettoes, the murder of Jews in concentration camps and by mass shootings in the East, euthanasia, the shooting of hostages in Belgium, Serbia and Greece, the mass deaths of Russian PoWs, the liquidation of the Political Commissars, the shooting of German soldiers after quick court martials at the front and very occasionally rape.[205] At first sight it may be surprising to find that atrocities were given such coverage in the conversations.

The prisoners at Trent Park had been captured by the Allies exclusively in North Africa, France and finally in Germany, therefore in the theatres of war where the fewest infringements of international law were committed and utterly different from the way things had been done in Poland, the Soviet Union and the Balkans. Most generals fought on most of the fronts, especially in the East. Their knowledge of the crimes of the Wehrmacht and the National Socialist regime were comprehensive – the relevant protocols prove it. Naturally one must differentiate here betweeen who knew what and who was personally involved in which crimes.

Several generals reported having borne personal witness to war crimes: in words which have lost nothing of their horror after sixty years, Walter Bruns and Heinrich Kittel described the mass shooting of Jews at Riga and Däugavapil (formerly Dvinsk) (Documents 119, 135). Thoma, Neuffer and von Broich had also seen similar massacres on the Eastern Front.[206] Others saw the deaths of multitudes of Soviet prisoners (Neuffer, Reimann). Of death camps equipped with gas chambers, Kittel, Rothkirch and Trach, von der Heydte and Thoma[207] knew from reliable sources. It is noticeable that many crimes had been made known by acquaintances or relatives. Oberst Reimann was told of the Berditschev massacre in Ukraine by a police officer (Document 93). Eberhard Wildermuth learned of the euthanasia programme from his brother, a doctor at an asylum.

The protocols prove that knowledge of the atrocities was widespread in the upper echelons of the military command structure and reached those who would have remained ignorant of them in their particular service occupations.[208] This is not to say that in the end everybody knew everything. In the summer of 1945, discounting the assertions of Broich and Neuffer that every senior German officer knew all about the concentration camps since 1935,[209] it seems probable that many knew the dimensions of the Holocaust, for example, at least by rumour (Document 125).[210] Watching a newsreel film of the death camps at the end of September 1945, most prisoners reacted with honest shock (Document 143),[211] although some rejected the reports as Allied propaganda[212] indicating that by no means all prisoners condemned discrimination against, and the murder of, the Jews. On the contrary, even those prisoners whom the British considered 'anti-Nazi' on the basis of their political attitude supported the Jewish policy of the Nazi State. Reimann declared: 'The business with the Jews in Germany was quite right, only it should have been done quietly' (Document 40). Eberbach could accept the extermination of 'a million Jews, or as many as we have killed', although he drew the line after adult males: with respect to Jewish women and children, 'that (was) going too far'. To this his son replied, 'Well, if you're going to kill off the Jews, then kill the women and children too, or the children at least' (Document 37).

Racial-political discourses appear only rarely in the transcripts. Occasionally key words would crop up in the conversations such as 'Jewish Commissar', 'Jewish Bolshevism' or condemning Jews as 'the plague of the East'.[213] Crüwell used National Socialist racial terminology.[214] He was certain that the United States was motivated by 'the Jewish poison', and this poison was behind the devastating bombing raids on Hamburg in July 1943. He also had proof, so he said, 'that it is the *Jews*, who want to destroy us *down to the last man*' (Document 13). When

Thoma objected that in World War I highly decorated Jewish soldiers had been deported, Crüwell replied, 'Such things are of course appalling, but one should not [. . .] forget how the Jews have plagued us [. . .] have been a miserable rabble [. . .] how they exploited us. Therefore it came to pass that no Berlin city hospital had an Aryan doctor in a leading role.'[215] He added that 'the step against the Jews had to happen legally.'[216]

The Trent Park generals attempted to conceal their own involvement in war crimes for understandable reasons. Nearly always they would point to the SS as the perpetrators:[217] the culpability of the Wehrmacht – and therefore their own person – was only touched upon exceptionally. The demarcation line between Wehrmacht and SS became tangible when SS-Brigadeführer Kurt Meyer was given an icy welcome by his fellow prisoners at Trent Park (Document 114).[218] Protests were also made against Anton Dunckern, former leader of SS and police at Metz, being brought to the centre (Document 115).[219]

On the day of his arrival at Trent Park, Graf Rothkirch hit the nail on the head by admitting that in everything he said, he made sure to put it in such a way that the officer corps came out clean.[220] Only very few generals admitted at Trent Park to their own war crimes, and where they did they provided the justification for it as well.[221] Generalleutnant Menny, for example, admitted the immediate court martial and execution of men on the Eastern Front after the Russians broke through a gap created by troops leaving positions without authority. The executions were performed 'there and then' as an example to the others (Document 103). Freiherr von der Heydte admitted once having shot dead Allied prisoners in Normandy when his Fallschirmjäger-Regt. 6 needed to cross a river and the prisoners would have hampered their progress.

General Ramcke stated that he had completely demolished Brest (Document 112); General Spang was uncomfortable with having signed a number of death warrants during actions against partisans in Brittany (Document 101).[223] General von Choltitz told von Thoma that the heaviest burden which he had to discharge was 'the liquidation of Jews' (Document 106). His involvement was unknown to researchers before this protocol came to light. The executions must have taken place in the Crimea. Unfortunately nothing further is known due to the poor documentary source.

The mixture of crimes, guilt, denials of responsibility and explanations is especially clear in conversations about the Commissar Order. Thoma alleged that Brauchitsch and Halder had raised strong protests against it, but the files show the opposite.[224] He also swore on oath that no Commissars had been shot by his units (Document 6). In Halder's *War Diary* this attitude appears confirmed initially. On 21 September 1941 he wrote: 'General von Thoma: Report about the engagements of 17.Pz.Div. on the Desna. Interesting here [. . .] (d) attitude of the unit towards Commissars (are not being shot)'.[225]

The files of 2.Pz.Gr. and XXXXVII Pz.Korps show however that shootings did occur in Thoma's unit. It is certain that on 27 and 28 August 1941 respectively a Commissar was tried by Ic (No. 3 Staff Officer) at Divisional HQ and executed.[226] It is hardly likely that Thoma as divisional commander could have remained ignorant of this. Also on 21 September 1941 the files contain execution reports which cannot be doubted. On 27 September 1941 17.Pz.Div. reported having shot nine Commissars and Politruks over the previous five days.[227]

On 30 September 1941 Thoma left 17.Pz.Div. and took over 20.Pz.Div. a fortnight later. On 20 October he arrived at divisional HQ and took up his duties next day. The Ic delivered his situation report to Thoma, and it seems unlikely that the execution of a Commissar on 19 October would have been glossed over. On 23 October, the Ic's interpreter executed the next Commissar to be captured.[228] It is therefore certain that the Commissar Order was at least occasionally carried out within Thoma's jurisdiction, but Thoma's statement at Trent Park that he advised Commissars to remove their insignia to prevent identification and execution is not necessarily false (Document 6). He was no more than half truthful on the whole, however.[229]

General Crüwell was equally economic with his powers of recall. He alleged that his 11.Pz.Div. had only executed a single Commissar, which he thought was not bad going (Document 88), whereas a report by his Ic dated 14.7.1941 indicates that the figure at that time was 10.[230]

Undoubtedly the majority of Trent Park inmates had knowledge of war crimes but kept the actual extent of their own involvement to themselves.[231] The nature of the war being fought was obvious to the group around von Thoma at the latest by the time they entered captivity. Georg Neuffer was already aware of the extent of the Holocaust and by the end of 1943 was estimating the number of murdered Jews at between three to five million (Documents 94, 95). Others doubted the reports of atrocities and attempted to create some kind of perspective. One reason for not wanting to admit them was one's own war experience. A man like Crüwell, who by August 1941 had been transferred out of Russia, obviously knew far less about war crimes than many of his compatriots who remained there. That he refused absolutely to accept the reports of atrocities as true[232] and drew the corresponding conclusion was the result of his loyalty to the National Socialist State and his belief in the allegedly 'clean' Wehrmacht. Therefore he saw nothing indecent in the current practice of executing innocent hostages as a reprisal for the murders of German soldiers, and even argued thast the practice was allowed under international law.[233] Major Boes reacted similarly. When von Broich confronted him with the information in October 1943 that the Germans had attempted 'to exterminate whole communities', he squirmed like an eel to avoid having to recognise this unpalatable fact.[234]

3.3 The Insurrection of Conscience. Reactions to 20 July 1944

The protocols provide new information about the German Resistance Movement.[235] The close links between General Choltitz and the conspirators was not known previously (Documents 151, 153). The most important are undoubtedly those statements about General-feldmarschall Erwin Rommel. Researchers continue the debate on whether Rommel knew about the planned assassination and whether he considered the *murder* necessary. David Irving, David Fraser and latterly Ralf Georg Reuth share the view that Rommel was not a party to the plans of the conspirators nor did he advocate killing Hitler, since he was opposed to political assassination. Although they vary on the details, all three agree that Rommel's aim was an armistice in the West in pursuit of which he was prepared if necessary to abandon his duty and throw open the Western Front.[236] Maurice Remy argues to the contrary in his book that Cäsar Hofacker informed Rommel on 9.7.1944 about the intended asassination and that Rommel was in agreement with it.[237] This conversation doubtless had a key function in the assessment of Rommel's knowledge and conduct with regard to 20 July, yet the transmission is problematic and leaves no unequivocal conclusion. The British protocols (Documents 37, 155 and 157), ignored until the present, supply indications but no final proof, although they tend to support Remy. General Heinrich Eberbach mentioned on several occasions in captivity his conversations with Rommel on the 16th, and in particular on 17 July 1944 when the latter came out strongly against Hitler and said in conclusion that the Führer had to be '*umgelegt*'. The separable verb '*umlegen*' has several meanings, e.g. transferred, re-allocated etc., but is often a euphemism for 'killed'.

After the war, Eberbach referred frequently to this conversation but toned down the verb.[239] What he said at Trent Park is more authentic: he was speaking only weeks after the event. His remarks about Rommel are confirmed from other documents: on 30 January 1945 von Thoma wrote in his diary a long passage about Rommel's citicisms of Hitler and the way the war was going. He mentioned that Rommel had said 'The Führer must be *beseitigt*.'[240] The verb *beseitigen* can mean 'eliminate', 'dispose of' but also 'remove' and 'set aside', a way of putting things which must have come from Eberbach, with whom Thoma shared very long conversations at Trent Park. Thoma's version seems to indicate that Rommel preferred that Hitler be assassinated rather than arrested. A further indication is found in the memoirs of Ferdinand Heim, completed in May 1945, in which the author quotes Eberbach as saying that Rommel knew of the planned assassination.[241]

Even Feldmarschall von Rundstedt appears in a new light in the protocols. As the most senior of Hitler's generals he had always been thought of as the best man to lead the peace negotiations.[242] Broich stated that Rundstedt confided to him as early as May 1942 that a German victory was out of the question.[243] Eberbach had been of the opinion that Rundstedt intended to conclude an armistice with the Western Allies (Document 37). Since it appears unlikely that Eberbach and Rundstedt could have met in Normandy, the statement is probably hearsay. Moreover it seems improbable that the 69-year-old field marshal, a lack-lustre personality to judge by the source material, wanted the job of bringing the war to an end all by himself. Eberbach's observations suggest of Rundstedt an attitude much more critical than that assumed hitherto. It now seems possible that his reported answer to Keitel's question, what else should one do besides hold the front – 'Give up the war, you idiots' – was actually what he said.[244]

In addition to the new information about Choltitz, Rommel and Rundstedt, the great value of the protocols is that from a cross-section of generals meeting again more or less by chance in a British PoW institution, it is possible to glean more about their private attitudes to the Resistance Movement, an area of interest which has suffered to date from a poor documentary source.

The events of 20 July 1944 took the British Government by surprise and at first no exact picture of the occurrence could be formed. CSDIC (UK) therefore presented the generals at Trent Park with news of the bomb plot immediately and paid careful attention to their reactions to radio and press reports. Most generals had come up through the Reichswehr officer corps, a relatively small elite circle where everybody knew everybody else well.[245] Useful targets for the British eavesdroppers were Broich and von Thoma in particular, who knew Stauffenberg personally. Broich revealed his exchange of ideas with Stauffenberg in Tunisia in 1943: the latter had been unsuccessful in winning over senior generals for a coup; in particular, Manstein had refused (Document 146).

Naturally the Trent Park generals had no knowledge of the events in East Prussia and Berlin, and all the more interesting is it therefore to see how they received the few reports which got through to the London centre. Thoma, Broich, Graf von Sponeck and others showed a positive reaction and regretted Stauffenberg's failure. Broich brooded: 'I cannot understand it. Stauffenberg was always such a reliable man. To have used such a small bomb.' The more they thought it over, the more they doubted it had been a straightforward bomb attempt. The generals could not understand how the majority of those attending the situation conference could have escaped without injury, and finally many concluded that the attempt had been rigged by the Nazi leadership. Probably, they reasoned, the Gestapo had discovered that Stauffenberg belonged to the Opposition and, as before with the Röhm Putsch, had planned a refined plot: a bogus bomb attempt, aimed at the publicity value of the Mussolini visit, would now serve as the pretext for the elimination of all undesirables and to demolish the last Army bastion of power.

No doubt mishearing a word in a radio broadcast, they thought that Himmler had taken over as C-in-C, Army and Guderian was his Chief of Staff. (Hitler had announced in a radio speech that he was appointing Himmler commander of the Heimat (i.e. Homeland) Army. For the generals, the idea that a man like Himmler should now lead them was almost unbearable, and they found it hard to accept that Guderian should have accepted the post of his Chief of Staff (Document 145).

The generals were deeply shocked to learn of the trials before the People's Court and the first executions, particularly that of Feldmarschall Erwin von Witzleben. That he would be sentenced to death had been clear to the majority, but many could not come to terms with his being hanged and not shot by firing squad as their concepts of military honour demanded. 'Whoever continues to defend this Nazi system is either stupid, a coward or a characterless person with ambition,' Thoma wrote in his diary on 8 August 1944.[246]

Unfortunately not all the reactions expressed by the Trent Park generals regarding the events of 20 July 1944 are available,[247] so that the breadth of reactions is based on relatively few documents. Heinrich Eberbach considered that Stauffenberg and Olbricht acted from idealism but belittled the apparent amateurishness of the conspirators' plan. Generalleutnant Spang criticised the plotters for acting too late. It had long been clear that nothing more could be achieved and all that remained was for the fronts to collapse. Spang emphasised that the attempt had had no effect on his own unit – 266.Inf.Div. (Document 149).[248]

In December 1944 General Elfeldt criticised the attempt because if successful Germany would have given up the war. The Allies were not fighting the Nazi Party, however, but the German people, and therefore any such conspiracy was senseless. Two junior Staff officers, Major Rudolf Beck, a cousin of Ludwig Beck, and Major Hasso Viebig, were appalled by the plot. 'I could not reconcile it with my honour,' Viebig remarked (Document 152). The violent fighting in Normandy in which both had taken part had not led them to reconsider.

The question as to whether the attempt was genuine or staged was determined at the end of August 1944 when General Choltitz arrived at Trent Park. The last Wehrmacht Commandant of Greater Paris reported to the prisoners in astonishing detail about the upheaval and subsequent events in the Bendler-Strasse, information which he had probably picked up from one of his Staff officers in Paris. Now the British were also in the picture. Whether the original scepticism of some generals that the assassination attempt was genuine influenced the British Government in any way, and strengthened their reservations about the German Resistance Movement, is not known.

4. Concluding Observations

The CSDIC (UK) transcripts are an important resource for researching the Wehrmacht and Third Reich. They allow us to enter the mind of the German soldier in a way that service files and private documents such as diaries and letters seldom can do so comprehensively. The documents published here provide a more colourful and detailed picture of the generals. The protocols do not only add to our knowledge of the Wehrmacht elite, but provide new information: a bridge stretching from the involvement of Choltitz in the mass murder of Jews, to his contacts with the 20 July conspirators, to the experience of General Pfuhlstein under Gestapo arrest in Berlin.

This edition shows for the first time the extent of British military eavesdropping practice. At enormous expense CSDIC (UK) succeeded in tapping the knowledge of their German captives. Despite all warnings, neither the Staff officers nor their NCOs and men were aware that their conversations were being overheard systematically. Involuntarily for the most part they became one of the most important sources of information for the British secret service: the lower ranks mainly for tactical and technical details, the generals above all for their political and strategic assessments of military situations.

The sources in this volume are 64 generals and 14 colonels who attained their respective ranks primarily between 1939 and 1943. Even if the conversations of this group are not representative of all the generals, they provide a broad and convincing spectrum of opinion for the intermediate layer of the Wehrmacht elite, embracing front-line and administration officers as well as men of general rank and equivalent of the Luftwaffe, Kriegsmarine and Waffen-SS.

The transcripts reproduced here originate almost exclusively from the Special Camp at Trent Park for high-ranking German prisoners. They felt themselves to be 'as if in an enchanted mountain cut off from real life', wrote Eberhard Wildermuth.[249] While the war raged on the continent, the generals took walks through the old woods of the park, chatted with their comrades and had plenty of time to relax with a book or newspaper. They found themselves in the unique situation of spending a long period of time with many men of equal rank and similar experience of life. Many of the senior Staff officers at first had difficulty in coming to terms with the circumstances of their captivity. General Hans Cramer wrote defiantly in the first letter from Trent Park to his mother: 'I left Africa erect and proud, for there is nothing else you can do with the sea at your back.'[250] But to many, their military careers were destroyed: 'Not only had we lost our freedom for a long time,' General-leutnant Menny noted in his diary at the end of August 1944, two days after his capture, 'but one's own future was lost for ever too. All hopes – the imminent appointment to Commanding General, the Oak Leaves – vanished like soap bubbles. At least I can look forward to the life of a pensioned-off general after the war, providing nothing worse comes.'[251]

Most faced up to the reality of the situation after a few weeks. Rank, uniform, decorations lost their importance and from behind the former military structure the personality emerged more distinctly. Some found it difficult to adjust. General Ludwig Crüwell complained in a letter to his brother at the end of 1943: 'This waiting and inactivity is sometimes scarcely bearable'.[252] A post-capture decoration or promotion was decisive for many to preserve their self-respect.

Soon after capture, the inmates of Trent Park began to reflect on their memoirs, the war and the future. They thought more freely than before: their bond to a Third Reich condemned to defeat had for many dissolved visibly, while others realised the nature of the war fully in captivity. A reorientation lay ahead but undiscovered. After the capitulation on 8 May 1945, the war crimes trials, public persecution and the worry about how one was to reintegrate into West German society bred in the generals a defensive attitude which overshadowed further reflections of their personal role in the Third Reich.[253] It is thus fortunate for the historian that the British documented the conversations of the generals in the singular interim phase of their captivity at Trent Park.

The protocols give an idea of their thought patterns in three major areas: the wide field of politics and strategy, war crimes and the 20 July plot. They showed clearly how diversely the generals reacted to extremely difficult political amd military situations, and how wide was the cross-section of conclusions they drew from comparable experiences. At least some of the Trent Park inmates knew the criminal nature of the war and political system. The group centred around von Thoma referred repeatedly to the criminality of the National Socialist State, welcomed the assassination attempt on Hitler and were even ready to collaborate with the British under certain conditions. Even if only a few acknow-ledged their personal guilt, this circle was more disposed to self-criticism that the Crüwell clique, which refused stubbornly to recognise any substantially negative side to the system and its leadership, and harshly condemned the conspirators against Hitler.

Membership of either group bore no relationship to age, rank, arm of service, regional origins or religion. In both of these loose associations one finds a great breadth of military socialising from the young Oberst-leutnant with several years' front-line experience to the 'old' general in supply. Decisive for the group towards which the Trent Park prisoners revolved was the capacity for reflection on the part of the individual and his front-line experience. Immediate experience of military disaster played a central role in developing wide-ranging insight into politics, strategy and the nature of the Nazi system. The fighting in Normandy led Heinrich Eberbach to see the National Socialist state and its leaders in a more critical light than hitherto. With others the experiences at the front confirmed a pre-existing dubious outlook, as with von Thoma. The composition was decided individually in every case but always consisted of the two factors of ability to reflect and the front-line experience.

Although Trent Park inmates had different views of the Nazi state, its prospects in the war and its war crimes, the front-line officers at least were unanimous on one point: their concept of military honour prevented them from laying down their arms prematurely. Thus pro-Nazi paratroop General Ramcke and the former bank director and reserve officer Wildermuth, later a minister in the Adenauer Cabinet, were both similarly impregnated with the idea of fighting to the last bullet.[254]

Although Wildermuth in his summer 1944 notes considered that the July 1944 plot had been 'our last chance', he was still prepared, in September 1944, to offer resistance to the last at Le Havre. That the British could break this resistance down within two days is another matter. It was of great importance for him that he had fought 'honourably' and was not taken prisoner until wounded when British tanks encircled his command post.[255] In reality the vaunted 'heroic struggle to the last shell' was often a matter of interpreting 'heroic'. Decisive was the officer's belief that he had done his duty. The question arises here how men with higher levels of reflection would have acted if fighting on German soil in 1945. One assumes that both von Thoma and Wildermuth would have kept fighting to the war's end and never have abandoned the fight prematurely, even though they called upon others to do so when at Trent Park.

The judgment upon the German generals is confirmed by the protocols. Irrespective of the differences in their military and political dealings it is unmistakable that – with a few exceptions – they lacked the courage to do justice to the special demands of the era, to abandon ideas of military honour and, for the sake of nation and people, weigh in against a criminal state leadership. This overall judgment does not replace a differentiated and considered analysis of the individual case, for which this volume presents a wealth of material.

THE DOCUMENTS

I.
Politics, Strategy and the Different Camps at Trent Park

Document 1

CSDIC (UK), SRX 1140 [TNA, WO 208/4161]

LUDWIG CRÜWELL – General der Panzertruppe – Captured 29 May 42 in North Africa.
KRAUSE – Oberleutnant (fighter pilot Fw190) – Captured 2 Sept. 42.

CRÜWELL: If I were asked to meet HESS,[1] I should decline. Please remember, I am a man who was taken prisoner honourably and I would not (associate) with a man who – who – he is a traitor!
KRAUSE: Has the matter been clear up?
CRÜWELL: It's quite clear to me. It was officially announced at the time 'against the FÜHRER'; the adjutants were put under arrest because they allowed him to fly.
KRAUSE: Where I was it was always said that he was a hundred per cent true, that the good of the Fatherland was his sole consideration, and that he said: 'I don't believe in this Russian business; I must try to get to ENGLAND in order to save GERMANY by arranging a peace with the British in some way or other.'
CRÜWELL: I don't deny HESS's good faith in that respect but that is not my official point of view. No one but his superior officer, the FÜHRER, can decide about that. If the FÜHRER repudiates him, I also repudiate him. That's that! I am convinced of his moral sincerity in that he wanted to do good, but that does not prevent my regarding him here, in enemy country, in war time, as a traitor. There's no doubt in my mind about that.

Document 2

CSDIC (UK), SRX 1160 [TNA, WO 208/4161]

LUDWIG CRÜWELL – General der Panzertruppe – Captured 29 May 42 in North Africa.
KRAUSE – Oberleutnant (fighter pilot Fw190) – Captured 2 Sept. 42.

CRÜWELL: The FÜHRER's ideas are quite sound. If the BALKAN STATES start quarrelling among themselves the FÜHRER will decide.

KRAUSE: But CZECHOSLOVAKIA is quite a different problem.

CRÜWELL: The question of BOHEMIA and MORAVIA is difficult because that's a different race. These people will have to be transplanted, either to RUSSIA or else to the BALKANS. They hate us fanatically. We can't proclaim them an independent state. We can't allow that from a geographical point of view. But when the war is over and ten years have elapsed, everything will be settled. Even if the war ends the way I think it will, with a clear victory, these problems will not cease to exist, but I'll never live to see the day. But that's fate, and we have been born in times of violent change, like the unfortunate people at the time of the Thirty Years' War. The FÜHRER envisages a EUROPE under (our) absolute control, with a lot of entirely self-independent states like FRANCE, RUSSIA etc., and small states. I am firmly convinced that that is the only possible way in which Western civilisation can be saved; GREECE belongs essentially to the MEDITERRANEAN, and ITALY can look after her. For all I care, GREECE can go to rack and ruin – it's a filthy country.

I was six weeks in ROUMANIA with my division and four weeks in BULGARIA.[2] My division was stationed near CONSTANZ, where the bridge crosses the DANUBE, that is, in a broad strip of the DOBRUDJA. You can't imagine the appalling state their agriculture is in. The Roumanians are rotten to the core. I've seen the corruption that there is, and I can give you an instance to prove it: my 'Intendant' had the right to pay out bribes up to a large sum to the railway company. Normally the German State doesn't do that sort of thing. He said: 'Sir, if I pay so-and-so much, the truck will get through.' The country is rotten with corruption. For instance at – I can't remember the name of the damned place, my armoured regiment was stationed there – they told me how when the men were sitting in the inn drinking wine or beer on Sunday afternoon, girls walked through without a stitch on. I mean to say, that's a bit unusual to say the least of it! And in every tiny village there was a brothel. Wherever you looked, brothel, brothel, brothel, and so on. What a lot of swine! They stole like jackdaws; they stole everything you didn't keep your hands on.

[. . .]

Document 3

CSDIC (UK), SRX 1167 [TNA, WO 208/4161]

LUDWIG CRÜWELL – General der Panzertruppe – Captured 29 May 42 in North Africa.

KRAUSE – Oberleutnant (fighter pilot Fw190) – Captured 2 Sept. 42.

CRÜWELL: I consider a hereditary monarchy the best form of government there is. Only in my opinion it is finished as far as GERMANY is concerned and could only rise again if we were to lose the was completely, and I set no store by that.

KRAUSE: If we lose the war, all the FÜHRER's achievements will be forgotten.

CRÜWELL: Some things will remain for ever. They will last for hundreds of years. Not the roads – they are unimportant. But what will last is the way in which the state has been organised, particularly the inclusion of the working man as part of the state. He really has made a place for the working man in the state and no one has ever done that before. Quite apart from the fact that I am sure we shan't lose the war, supposing we were to lose it and again suffered great internal unrest, then later on the threads would always be picked up again where he (HITLER) left off. This principle of everyone working for the common cause, the idea that the industrialist is really the trustee for the capital represented by German labour and for the other capital, all sounds so easy, but no one managed it before.

I am convinced that a great part of the FÜHRER's success as Party Leader is accounted for by pure mass suggestion. It's bound up with a kind of hypnotism, and he can exercise this on a great many people. I know people who are undoubtedly superior to him mentally and who yet fall under this spell. I cannot explain why it doesn't affect me. I mean, I know perfectly well that he carries a superhuman burden of responsibility; what he said to me about AFRICA was astonishing, but I can't say that (I was influenced). One quite outstanding thing is his hands – he has beautiful hands – you don't notice it in photographs. He has the hands of an artist. I always looked at his hands; they are beautiful hands, and there is nothing common about them – they are aristocratic hands. In his whole manner, there is nothing of the little man about him. What surprised me so much – I thought he would fix me with an eagle eye – I don't mean I expected a long speech but . . . 'Allow me to present you with the Oak Leaves,' in a quiet voice, you understand. I had pictured *that* quite differently.[3]

KRAUSE: All his sections are prompted by his feelings.

[. . .]

Document 4

CSDIC (UK), SRX 1230 [TNA, WO 208/4161]

LUDWIG CRÜWELL – General der Panzertruppe – Captured 29 May 42 in North Africa.
KRAUSE – Oberleutnant (fighter pilot Fw190) – Captured 2 Sept. 42.
Information received: 21 Oct. 42

CRÜWELL: [. . .] It was impossible for us, without going to war, to give effect to the idea that GERMANY was the most important country on the continent of EUROPE.

KRAUSE: Do you think, Sir, that it would have been possible for us to gain concessions from ENGLAND, AMERICA and FRANCE, if we'd still had a man like NEURATH, one of the old regime, as Foreign Minister?[4]

CRÜWELL: I don't believe so.

KRAUSE: But why is it that GERMANY always has been hated by all the rest of the world?

CRÜWELL: That's owing to our infernal system of small states, which people still believe in even today. If we had been a united country two hundred years ago, we would have, so to speak, knocked off each other's rough edges and would have had our national require- ments, which we are now proclaiming a hundred years too late, all cut-and-dried; that would have been that, and we'd have had nothing more to ask of the world. That seems clear to me. I have no use for the type of German – he's now become a comparative rarity – who goes abroad dressed in a green coat (Lodenmantel) and carrying a ruck-sack. When you see the English walking about COLOGNE, that doesn't make a good . . . they look like butchers, cobblers, and no matter what. Nobody can deny that we are the most *humane* people in the world. Even if you consider those abortions in the S.S. . . . they are merely the product of a suffering people. The things people have accused us of! I mean, we've been bled white. Don't forget that in the first place we were swindled by those miserable Fourteen Points.

Document 5

CSDIC (UK), SRX 1537 [TNA, WO 208/4162]

THOMA – General der Panzertruppe – Captured 4 Nov. 42 in North Africa.
BURCKHARDT – Major (G.C. 1 Paratroop Battalion) – Captured 5 Nov. 42 in North Africa.
Information received: 26 Jan. 43

[. . .]

THOMA: I can tell you, you can't expect anything from the General Staff. Ninety-nine per cent of them are spineless creatures. They've always been 'yes'-men. They've never been commanders, but only 'assistants' of the commander. That is why most of them are spineless creatures. Their upbringing and so on makes them so. You can expect nothing from them.[5]

BURCKHARDT: If the Germans succeeded in overthrowing the National

Socialist Government now and then fought on, would they manage to achieve peace?

THOMA: It's not as easy as all that.

Document 6

CSDIC (UK), SRX 1587 [TNA, WO 208/4169]

WILHELM RITTER VON THOMA – General der Panzertruppe – Captured 4 Nov. 42 in North Africa.
HANS DIETRICH TIESENHAUSEN – Kapitänleutnant (Lieut. Cmdr in command of U-331) – Captured 17 Nov. 42.
Information received: 15 Feb. 43

THOMA: HITLER imagined he could break his word time and again, if you examine his political career, it has been nothing but breaches of faith. One always forgets that. The written agreements with CHAMBERLAIN[6] and all that sort of thing were all broken, so that the world has no faith in him! People shouldn't be surprised if they now say quite definitely: 'It doesn't matter what it is, right to the end, to the complete and unconditional surrender and even the least vestige of such a system must disappear,' – that's quite understandable. Of course the others are hypocrites, one should realise that clearly, because ROOSEVELT is just as much of an autocrat as HITLER[7] or CHURCHILL, but it isn't brought home to them quite so much.
[. . .]
The KAISER was as gentle as a nun in comparison with ADOLF HITLER. The former did at least let you speak your mind – the latter won't let you open your mouth. I've seen it myself, but I didn't give way, I should still be ashamed today if I had given way to HITLER. If there's any dirty business afoot I won't take part, I shouldn't dream of it. How could I bring myself to do it? How could I order my men to commit murder? I wouldn't dream of it. None of my superiors has the right to order me to do his dirty work, let him do it himself! I've said so straight out. I can swear a solemn oath that not a single man has been shot by my people,[8] but men were often brought before me. I remember once there were two or three commissars, they thought that now they would be shot. I said: 'No, take off your badges, it's better and don't let anyone else know that you are commissars.' They realised at once what was up. They took them off, too. I remember that last spring in the conferences with HQ, the army commanders were there and they told us about conversations they had had with the FÜHRER, 'THE FÜHRER is personally firmly convinced that the country in EUROPE which is nearest to communism is ENGLAND.' He actually said that last year. That's complete madness,

that's a sign that the man has never been out in the world. Then I burst out – it was with Feldmarschall KLUGE[9] – I said: 'Sir, if any country is going communist, ENGLAND will certainly be the very last to do so.' He said: 'Yes, I didn't say that, it was the FÜHRER who said it.' That's the sort of stuff the Generals are being fed on! It's a foul business, a misunderstanding of the situation.

Document 7

CSDIC (UK), SRX 1603 [TNA, WO 208/4162]

HANS DIETRICH TIESENHAUSEN – Kapitänleutnant (Lieut. Cmdr in command of U-331) – Captured 17 Nov. 42.
LUDWIG CRÜWELL – General der Panzertruppe – Captured 29 May 42 in North Africa.
WILHELM RITTER VON THOMA – General der Panzertruppe – Captured 4 Nov. 42 in North Africa.
Information received: 18 Feb. 43

THOMA: (*After listening to* GOEBBELS's *speech*): It's a scandal! It's shameful! Regarded objectively it is a speech of despair. Does anyone get a different impression of it? To me it seems to be a speech of sheer desperation.[10]

CRÜWELL: Yes, at the beginning I thought something was coming. The object of the whole speech is simply to urge the people to accept measures which are already in existence.

THOMA: Just a disgusting inflammatory speech! The net result will be that tonight – well, no, not tonight because the Jews are not allowed out – but tomorrow, when they come along wearing the Star of David, a few of them will be murdered. That's all!

CRÜWELL: What absolute rubbish! That piece at the end! He spoke too long. But it was quite senseless not to close on the note of confidence in the FÜHRER; that ought to have been the conclusion; but no, off he went again, demanding more of the women. At first I thought: 'Good Heavens, what is he talking about now?'

THOMA: I thought he was going to announce something of special importance, too.

CRÜWELL: It seems to me that if these measures are necessary, one can only ask: 'Why didn't they introduce them sooner?' But why must he *always unceasingly* stir the people?

THOMA: Absolutely disgusting! It ought to have been a short concise speech, couched in serious terms, lasting half an hour at the most, but it was a typical beer-house tirade. He's always talked like that. He's been doing it for twenty years. It's disgraceful, absolutely disgraceful! And to collect a rabble like that and compel them to go in and shout because

there's a man standing behind them. I am ashamed of the impression these fellows make on the world. I feel thoroughly ashamed.
[. . .]

THOMA: It wasn't at all a good speech. I could have imagined it in a much more dignified way. Quite apart from his digression when he stirred up hatred of the Jews again – the first half of his speech was about nothing but the Jews – the poor Jews, who have really had nothing to do with all this – and then his malicious way of saying: 'We will drive them out completely,' – what's that got to do with the present war situation? It shows a complete misunderstanding of the whole business. What can the people at home be thinking? It's sheer impudence for the fellow to reprove the middle-class – they're having by far the worst time.

CRÜWELL: Who has upheld our culture in the last hundred years, for *hundreds* of years!

THOMA: And then a typical GOEBBELS touch, 'That is all being destroyed now; but it is guaranteed that it will all be built up again immediately.' He treats the subject as though it were a house of cards. It's affrontery! He ought to realise that there are other people who give some thought to the matter and have devoted some attention to it.

CRÜWELL: Above all, people will ask why they didn't do it sooner.

THOMA: I should like to have GOEBBELS one evening in quite a small circle. I've heard a lot about how delightful and charming he can be, from people who know him well. But in those matters – no! A man who was there told me that he gave a lecture on the conduct of propaganda, at the Tank School last year, at which not only the senior officers were present but the youngest officers and women were as well. He held forth and the gist of the whole thing was: 'The masses themselves are stupid, you can do what you like with them.' That's how he talked to those people. They were amazed.

CRÜWELL: He knows something about the matter, there's no doubt about that.

THOMA: He really let the cat out of the bag, when he asserted: 'The masses themselves are stupid, you can do what you like with them.' They didn't like that at all.
[. . .]

Document 8

CSDIC (UK), SR REPORT, SRGG 5 [TNA, WO 208/4165]

LUDWIG CRÜWELL – General der Panzertruppe – Captured 29 May 42 in North Africa.
HANS CRAMER – General der Panzertruppe (G.O.C. German Afrikakorps) – Captured 12 May 43 in Tunisia.
Information received: 16 May 43

CRAMER: When we older men who have experienced the last war follow this whole business, it makes us think. I can draw such a terrible number of parallels myself, that I always say: 'It is impossible for it to turn out well, but for Heaven's sake don't let's think. . . .' Herr General, everything has turned out just as last time . . . but very gradually. If you examine the situation – AMERICA is becoming more and more powerful. I would like to be optimistic, but I don't know – and the worst part is that I have just come back from the collapse at KHARKOV; I was present at the collapse of the Rumanians, the Italians and the Hungarians, I was with the Hungarian Army as GOC(?) and now I have been through *this* business, so I have been retreating since . . . autumn(?).[11]

CRÜWELL: I don't look on the position as hopeless. It is critical but –

CRAMER: No, but hopeless. I keep on saying, one is far too apt to judge by what we remember of 1918.[12]

CRÜWELL: Yes, certainly, and it is on that that the others are counting.

CRAMER: Yes, it is really extraordinary that there should be two such wars after having really sworn after the Great War that we would never again fight the English, we all said that we wouldn't do that again. We both had the same ideas . . . these 'two white nations' etc., etc.

CRÜWELL: The English say the same.

CRAMER: But if you talk to an Englishman he doesn't quite come out into the open. I still believe that the FÜHRER honestly made proposals to the English, perhaps not quite far-reaching enough but – [13]

CRÜWELL: Well that's a question of laying the blame.

CRAMER: In my opinion there is only one possibility: we should guarantee the British Empire.

CRÜWELL: I can't imagine that the fortress of EUROPE will be overrun, I don't believe it. At any rate, if they were to try it it would be an extremely difficult job.

CRAMER: Yes, in my opinion, we have only one chance, and that is: in contrast to the Great War . . . the air force. If they were to form a bridgehead in SALONIKA it probably wouldn't matter much as we could probably hold them there or even throw them out again. But we can't hold the RAF and the RAF will attack RUMANIA and smash everything there to bits, and then we should lose the oil.

CRÜWELL: The English and American show in NORTH AFRICA was badly muddled.

CRAMER: Yes, with their overwhelming equipment, but their tactics were very bad.

CRÜWELL: But do you think, disregarding the possibility of an offensive, that the Russians –

CRAMER: We can hold that. But then comes the time, with the arrival of winter when the Russians will start again.

CRÜWELL: I believe, however, if we wee to say that we would do nothing this summer, except straighten the line . . . and build everything up and make everything ready, then they certainly wouldn't get through in the winter. For, if one looks back, their greatest successes have always been there where *no* preparations had been made.

CRAMER: Yes. Their successes were merely because of their numbers . . . infantry and tanks . . . But I'm afraid that the FÜHRER will do something . . . somewhere.

CRÜWELL: What is our position regarding personnel?

CRAMER: Not too bad. The Operations Staff Officer of the 10th Panzer Division . . . he had this . . . whole manpower business,[14] he said: 'It's not too bad.' . . . They seem to be getting more men again now, but we can't live on that for ever. Ever since the CAUCASUS affair went badly for us, TURKEY has completely turned against us.[15] Damnation, we must . . .

CRÜWELL: If we lose, then it's all up.

CRAMER: Completely finished. A short time ago I was in ITALY[16] – these completely unreliable Italians . . . but they are having a great many difficulties over the BALKANS.

CRÜWELL: What is the position in YUGOSLAVIA?

CRAMER: There is still trouble in CROATIA and we are always having a lot of trouble with the guerrillas there.[17]

CRÜWELL: If you listen to the English radio, they make up a terrific story.

CRAMER: Yes, but it's not as bad as that. We had about one to two divisions, well, let us say three divisions on a war footing . . .[18]

CRÜWELL: What's your opinion of the CHANNEL coast?

CRAMER: Perfect. They won't get in there.

CRÜWELL: All I can say is that if they land in SALONIKA, even if they have a bridgehead –

CRAMER: Yes, they'll land at . . . because we haven't got anything there.

CRÜWELL: Yes, but surely we must be in a position to send anything there.

CRAMER: We've got nothing, literally nothing. We've got as many (troops) as possible in the West and some behind the Eastern Front and that's all we've got . . . and the remainder(?) are in ITALY. We've still got very good divisions and we're getting tanks now too including the new 'Panthers'.[19]

[. . .]

CRÜWELL: Is the FÜHRER still really all right?

CRAMER: Yes, yes!

CRÜWELL: His speech especially on Heroes day – his voice sounded very – not at all so – [20]

CRAMER: Yes, but he is a man, who succeeds through his own pertinacity, who believes in his own mission, indeed he has to. Unfortunately he has somewhat . . . amongst the people . . . because he always makes the mistake of appearing only as the FÜHRER, as the great military leader – perhaps it is just tactlessness. If we are perfectly honest and judge it from the purely military point of view . . . things have gone badly ever since he took command.

CRÜWELL: Yes, we've learnt our lesson!

CRAMER: Yes.

CRÜWELL: But one doesn't know, the cause of it – but I am – there's so much time to brood over things.

CRAMER: Yes, yes!

CRÜWELL: Perhaps it was, because HALDER[21] and BRAUCHITSCH[22] couldn't get on with him properly, or was it possibly because the Russians put up a greater resistance against us than we had expected?

CRAMER: Then there's RIBBENTROP[23] with his politics.

CRÜWELL: In my opinion we had to decide either to carry on to the end with the BRÜNING system or to make a second war inevitable.

CRAMER: Yes, but I have the feelings, that . . . a bit less grasping.

CRÜWELL: . . . the Eastern campaign may last for another ten years!

CRAMER: Yes.

Document 9

CSDIC (UK), SR REPORT, SRGG 126 [TNA, WO 208/4165]

FRIEDRICH FREIHERR VON BROICH – General-major (G.O.C. 10th Panzer Division) – Captured 12 May 43 in Tunisia.
DR CARIUS – Hauptmann (ADC to M180[24]) – Captured 11 May 43 in Tunisia.
BOCK – Leutnant (ADC to BROICH) – Captured 12 May 43 in Tunisia.
Information received: 11 June 43

BROICH: After the last war it was said: 'If GERMANY wins the war, the Hohenzollern system will remain and life will be impossible.' Now we say: 'If GERMANY wins the war, the National Socialist system will remain and life will be impossible.' Our position is hopeless, there is no sense in carrying on the war any longer. It's just the same wherever we attack, we can no longer advance, and we win nothing. The quality of our troops in RUSSIA is not what it was at the beginning of the offensive. What has been lost is irreplaceable. Even if they do push forward somewhere today – drive in a deep wedge, then they are there and say to themselves: 'Our fate will be just the same as all the others; we shall be left in the lurch when things get a bit worse.'[25]

[. . .]

Document 10

CSDIC (UK), SR REPORT, SRGG 156 [TNA, WO 208/4165]

LUDWIG CRÜWELL – General der Panzertruppe – Captured 29 May 42 in North Africa.
HEINRICH-HERMANN VON HÜLSEN – Oberst (OC 21st Panzer Division) – Captured 12 May 43 in Tunisia.
Information received: 26 June 43

CRÜWELL: I believe ARNIM (PW) is frightfully well-meaning, frightfully nice. I haven't said anything to him yet, but I certainly must speak to him, he really ought to realise it for himself – but to me this eternal grumbling is terrible.

HÜLSEN: I've made up my mind, too, that if it happens again I shall have something to say about it.

CRÜWELL: Well, we can put it like this: either one says to oneself, 'Hullo, things are going wrong,' then it is not the right thing to throw all the blame on the FÜHRER, especially for those people who always used to cheer him the loudest.

HÜLSEN: And who have got the most to thank him for, because if a man jumps from Oberst to General der Panzertruppen in a single year, then he ought to mind his step; but I mean indulging in *nothing* but negative criticism and malicious grins – [26]

CRÜWELL: I mean, what happens if one adopts the attitude, as we have done, of saying that we are bound to believe in victory? I find it so unseemly to paint everything in its worst colours now. The worst one can say is that we are pursuing an ostrich policy.

HÜLSEN: Yes, of course that's what they do say, but things haven't gone as far as that yet.

CRÜWELL: It isn't like that, and besides, if things turn out differently, I shan't care a damn, but it would be shameful for me, as a General, if I had thrown in the sponge and started grumbling.

HÜLSEN: Before, when they were still there, they talked in quite a different way. I should just like to know whether those people who talk the loudest really acted according to their principles when they were in a tight corner – or whether they didn't just carry out their orders and say, 'My superiors can take the responsibility for that.'

CRÜWELL: I so often think about that at night; in the first place I don't think that things are as serious or as desperate as all that, and secondly I consider it so completely unsoldierly and unworthy.

HÜLSEN: Above all there's one thing which we must not forget, that we have given our oath. After all, he is my 'FÜHRER'. And here they are every day sitting down and pulling him to pieces.

CRÜWELL: I won't do that. I won't do that – whatever they say. But today everything now happening –

HÜLSEN: 'It's the fault of the German Reich,' . . . 'the English are all charming fellows.' There's one thing I should like to say, Sir, that, if the pessimists here are not controlled in time, we shall get two factions here. Then they will always be digging at one another, and one clique will be formed here and another clique there. In my opinion it is the Generaloberst's job to stop that, before the matter has gone past repair. It's only natural that a thing like that can gather momentum very quickly.

CRÜWELL: It would be my business to tell him, if I saw that the situation had become so serious. I have already spoken to him about it.

HÜLSEN: I believe that in general it is not so serious yet. We must try first of all to curb that among our friends, and I have decided to speak to some of them privately. Next time I'm with BROICH (PW) I shall say to him: 'Listen, BROICH, all this running down of the FÜHRER and all that won't make the slightest difference to our fate. If we adopt that attitude, then in time we shall become great friends of ENGLAND and enemies of GERMANY and after all that is our Fatherland!' CRAMER (PW) also adopts the attitude of negative criticism.

CRÜWELL: We must do something about that. Let us stick together.

HÜLSEN: Yes.

CRÜWELL: That is the only right thing to do – that is the Prussian attitude – the attitude of gentlemen.

[. . .]

Document 11

CSDIC (UK), SR REPORT, SRGG 161 [TNA, WO 208/4165]

DR PAUL MEIXNER – Kapitän (N.O. i/c LA GOULETTE, TUNIS) – Captured 11 May 43 in Tunis.
GOTTHART FRANTZ – Generalleutnant (GOC 19th Flak Division) – Captured 12 May 43 in Tunisia.
Information received: 27 June 43

FRANTZ: I should like to tell you one thing. When one hears the radio here, or reads the newspaper, one always hears such critical remarks. The circle of grumblers here is fairly large. Above all General THOMA (PW) makes such remarks. We have the misfortune to have three GOC's from AFRICA here as PW. We must see to it that these critical remarks are ignored, and that one does not become involved in discussion about them. General CRÜWELL (PW) and several others are against it. We must strengthen this circle of anti-grumblers and make a stand against these people.

[. . .]

Document 12

CSDIC (UK), SR REPORT, SRGG 204 [TNA, WO 208/4165]

HANS-JÜRGEN VON ARNIM – Generaloberst (GOC Army Group Africa) – Captured 12 May 43 in Tunisia.
Information received: 9 July 43

ARNIM: Recently morale has been fluctuating somewhat here. I know under what tremendous strain you, as commanders, and your forces were placed, and the fact that you and your men were able to carry out your duties is certainly no reason to strike a note of depression or to be sad; on the contrary, you should be proud of your troops, proud of your own achievements; it would be difficult for any other nation, any other army, to do what our troops did there. Whether the time which we were given to held out there achieved its purpose or not, is no longer a matter for discussion – I am convinced that it did. Gentlemen, the TUNIS affair cannot be looked upon as a debit but as a moral credit for us. A real ground for depression is the fact that we are now out of it and can no longer take an active part as soldiers and fighters in arms. In spite of that, we are and we remain part of the nation even if we are PW, and in spirit we are intimately bound up with the decisive battle of our Fatherland. We have perhaps more time to think things over than people at home, but we are and we remain soldiers as long as we live.

It is obvious, gentlemen, that we are still in harness as far as the war of nerves is concerned and it is clear that each one of us is worried and starts thinking: 'What will happen now? Have we sufficient means? Have we sufficient men?' It is also obvious that we ask ourselves these questions with the best will in the world, but we must consider one thing, and that is that when we continue to discuss, I might almost say 'thrash out', those problems, the fact that in our present position we are occasionally inclined to take a gloomy view of things doesn't help our people and doesn't help us to bear our lot. We must be content with the fate which is ours. Then each one of us has his own private troubles to bear, no matter what they are, and from a purely human standpoint I do not think it right for us to aggravate those by talking about them too much, although it is quite understandable. Each one of us has quite enough to bear. Quite apart from that, it is catching, and the only thing we can do to help our Fatherland is to see that our letters from here are happy, confident and optimistic, especially as we are PW. The people at home must say: 'Good Heavens, the PW have *such* confidence in us and in our Fatherland, and so the devil take us if we don't win!' We must not unload our troubles, whether they are justified or not, either onto our comrades here or onto our friends at home. The question of whether any particular anxiety is genuine or not, is justified or not, doesn't come into the question and should not be discussed. I do not want to talk about it at all. *All* that matters is how we can best help each other to bear our lot and help the people at home by improving their morale rather than by undermining it.

Then there is another matter. We are here in a former interrogation camp. None of us knows whether listening apparatus is not still installed. We must do nothing wittingly or unwittingly, whether it is justified or unjustified, true or false, which might give the enemy any weapon which he could use in the propaganda war, or the war of nerves, or in any other way to bolster up his own people and harm the moral powers of resistance at home.[27]

Gentlemen, I should like to make an urgent request – that *you should cease those conversations* if there is any possibility of their being listened to. That goes for the Mess here too. We should be ashamed of ourselves if we came home and people there were to say: 'Everything went well and the only people who caused trouble were our old Generals who were PW.' I would be the last person, gentlemen, not to sympathise with anyone who felt: 'There is something I must get off my chest.' In that case you should choose one of your comrades, whom you can trust, and say to him: 'Come here, I must get something off my chest. Let's go out into a corner of the garden where no one can listen to us and walk up and down there. I must speak to you.' There is nothing against that, and, of course, apart from that we are grown men who have the right at any time to . . . You know perfectly well what difference I mean and how to deal with it, and therefore, gentlemen, I would ask you to *desist* from conversations which might in any way incriminate your comrades. You have every reason to look with confidence into the future. We see from the newspaper reports of the English and the Russians, how they exaggerate things. We know from our own experience in Tunis how tremendously the aerial victories of the Americans were exaggerated and what the real position is. We are in the happy position of being able to listen to our own news, therefore we have a certain check.[28] I need not remind you, gentlemen, we are soldiers and soldiers we remain. I thank you.

Document 13

CSDIC (UK), SR REPORT, SRGG 342 [TNA, WO 208/4166]

Ludwig Crüwell – General der Panzertruppe – Captured 29 May 42 in North Africa.
Gotthart Frantz – Generalleutnant (GOC 19th Flak Division) – Captured 12 May 43 in Tunisia.
Information received: 12 Aug. 43

CRÜWELL: If no decision has been reached next year – and I see in that our greatest hope – the Americans will get out of the European war. After all, what do they want here? What interest have they in ITALY? What has GERMANY done to them? They've made a mass of money as usual – they've no love for the English – and above all, they recognise the Jewish poison at work among their people and realise how they are blackmailing their leaders. We see the Jewish poison in this heavy attack on HAMBURG.[29] It is the *Jews* who want to destroy us *down to the last man*. They know that the National Socialist doctrine will spread all over the world and they want to save themselves by hook or by crook from their inevitable extinction.
[. . .]

Document 14

CSDIC (UK), SR REPORT, SRGG 399 [TNA, WO 208/4166]

WILHELM RITTER VON THOMA – General der Panzertruppe – Captured 4 Nov. 42 in North Africa.
RUDOLF BUHSE – Oberst (OC 47th Grenadier Regiment) – Captured 9 May 43 in Tunisia.
A 1237 – Oberst (OC Flak) [?][30] Captured 9 May 43 in Tunisia.
Information received: 12 Sept. 43

THOMA: (*re* ITALY's *surrender*) In October 1940 I handed over a report of sixteen pages to BRAUCHITSCH.[31] I foresaw the whole thing. I also said the same thing to General CRÜWELL (PW) on 20 November 1942 when I arrived in ENGLAND. For this reason I am regarded as a criminal by the others. I regret every bomb, every scrap of material and every human life that is still being wasted in this senseless war. The only gain that the war will bring us is the end of the ten years of gangster rule. In my opinion the collapse of GERMANY is inevitable. I have been expecting it and I only hope it will happen soon. I hope that the end will come this autumn.
BUHSE: I hope that the Russians will come to an understanding with us.
THOMA: That's impossible. It's too late now. It would have been possible last year, but our so-called leaders didn't want it.[32] Every day the war continues constitutes a crime. The men at the top must realise that. KEITEL and DÖNITZ, for example, are the men. They must put ADOLF HITLER in a padded cell.[33] A gang of rogues can't rule for ever. It would be a pity if any one of them was shot. They ought to be made to do heavy work until they drop down dead. You will now see the English and Americans occupying the Italian airfields. They will occupy SARDINIA and CORSICA and then they will invade FRANCE.
BUHSE: I believe that we shall clear out of ITALY according to plan.
A 1237: I think so too.

Document 15

CSDIC (UK), SR REPORT, SRGG 615 [TNA, WO 208/4167]

ULRICH BOES – Major (Staff Officer to Generalleutnant von SPONECK (PW)) – Captured 9 May 43 in Tunisia.
BÜHLER – Unteroffizier (Batman to Generalmajor von BROICH (PW)) – Captured 12 May 43 in Tunisia.
Information received: 4 Dec. 43

BOES: In spite of the fact that we have . . . total warfare, the resources of the German people have not nearly been exhausted yet. As long as we don't use women as drivers at the front, we still haven't got total war. If our homes are at stake, if our Fatherland is at stake and if we must fight on the ODER. . . . No quarter will be given. . . . If we capitulate now, then GERMANY *will be wiped out once and for all* and you will probably find yourself in SIBERIA with me on some fine job or other, unless we perish on the way. We shall *never* hear anything of our families again. You will never be able to marry and the German people will be finished for ever. Do you believe – it makes you laugh – that a people like the damned English, of forty-nine millions or whatever it is,[34] with their supercilious but completely slow and uncultured methods, should want to dominate the German people; that's a piece of insolence which we simply cannot accept; our national pride won't allow us to be ruled by such swine.
BÜHLER: That's quite right.
BOES: We have all got to know them. We know what it looks like, the street's . . . there are a few cities, which are perhaps not bad, but the rest of it is damned awful and the people are swine and if we compare our German towns with it, or our German railways and our German traffic system and all that, then we realise that ours is a really fine country, that everything there is first class. As GOEBBELS said yesterday: 'Of course one ought to learn from the enemy, but one ought not to admire the enemy.' I gave up admiring them long ago; I admire *our* people.[35]
BÜHLER: The more I see of this business, it is really as you said just now, Sir, they have got their navy, but that is all. [. . .]

Document 16

CSDIC (UK), SR REPORT, SRGG 748 [TNA, WO 208/4167]

The following is the text of a speech by:
ULRICH BOES – Major (Staff Officer to Generalleutnant von SPONECK (PW)) – Captured 9 May 43 in Tunisia.
Information received: 7 Jan. 44

(After describing duties of NCOs while on active service, Boes sums up their duties after capture.)

BOES: [. . .] I am quite clear about it all in my own mind, and I often feel myself that the very *moderation* of our attitude in many respects – for instance, towards the English Camp Commandant[36] and senior English officers – is in many respects *totally* incompatible with my own personnal temperament, with my own personal *hatred* of the English, and may appear to many of the younger members, especially to all of you here, far too moderate – to put it mildly. And I can well understand how you, in your enthusiasm, in your patriotism enhanced by National Socialism, in your fanatical hatred of ENGLAND, which has been inflamed by tales of horror – by the air attacks which have burst on our families at home – that you, personally, would prefer a far more ruthless, a far less compromising, a far harsher attitude. That is a young man's point of view, which I myself can *well* appreciate. But when, on the other hand, you realise that neither a Generaloberst, a full General, a Generalleutnant nor a Generalmajor, nor even an Oberst can suddenly go on hunger-strike, say, because the food has deteriorated, as a young Leutnant could – and recently did – but in this place, with all these eminent personalities, famous soldiers who have commanded divisions not only in RUSSIA and AFRICA but in other theatres of war as well – and in the last war, too – who have twice fought against ENGLAND – naturally they can't start a hunger-strike or any naughty-schoolboy pranks of that kind – which is really what behaviour of that sort amounts to; that sort of thing is beneath the dignity of a General, who represents in his own person the German nation vis-à-vis the enemy. In the course of my talks with you I have often had the opportunity of reassuring myself on one point, namely that we are, at any rate, unanimous in our hatred of our hosts here. And so, in all external appearances we must give an example of German order and cleanliness, such as the English have always expected of the Germans, because we are a disciplined, orderly and organised nation.

Document 17

CSDIC (UK), GRGG 139
Report on information obtained from Senior Officers (PW) on 3 June 44 [TNA, WO 208/4363]

NEUFFER: You can say what you like, but the highest Generals did take part in that whole business, from 1941 onwards. There were certainly plenty of Generals at the FÜHRER's headquarters, who said: 'Certainly, my FÜHRER,' JODL[37] and KEITEL for a start. You can't say that they did not share the responsibility from the way in which they let FRITSCH be treated,[38] in 1934, when BREDOW was shot and SCHLEICHER.[39] Those were serious things. That was their last opportunity, in my opinion, Isn't that so?

KREIPE: Yes.

NEUFFER: If you look at it historically, everything points of course to the fact that at any rate in a Western European state – which we, after all, are – that form of dictatorship, which is pure terrorism, is impossible in the long run.

KREIPE: I consider too that all those ways which have been found of killing off the Jews are disgraceful.

[. . .]

Document 18

CSDIC (UK), GRGG 139
Report on information obtained from Senior Officers (PW) on 1–2 and 3 June 44 [TNA, WO 208/4363]

KREIPE: [. . .] We *cannot* beat the Russians. One can only hope that they may have spent themselves and will one day say: 'If the other fools don't want to, then we will just make a separate peace with HITLER.' Good. I only hope that HITLER won't be too stubborn and demand too much, but that he will be moderate. I think he will be now. That is a possibility.[40]

Document 19

CSDIC (UK), GRGG 149
Report on information obtained from Senior Officers (PW) on 22–7 June 44 [TNA, WO 208/4363]

BROICH: In my opinion the only possibility is for us to make peace, and for RUNDSTEDT[41] to march eastwards with the English against the Russians. That is the only possibility. If that doesn't happen or if chaos develops later on, we shall have pure communism.

[. . .]

KRUG: I can promise you that I'm no 110 per cent National Socialist, quite definitely not. But, I mean – I'm now talking of peace-time – we live in the State and the State has made us officers what we are. It has treated us decently and, for better or worse, that is the present Constitution.

Document 20

CSDIC (UK), GRGG 152
Report on information obtained from Senior Officers (PW) on 3 July 44 [TNA, WO 208/4363]

BASSENGE: I should be interested to know how the troops would have reacted if RUNDSTEDT had been approached (to induce him to withdraw in the West).

HERMANN: In an ordinary unit, that's to say one which is not SS, there would probably be 60 per cent in favour of it and 40 per cent against it, for at least 40 per cent of our men are old SS and SA men, etc.

HENNECKE: The Allies are convinced that they have won the war. Why are they so friendly towards us? Apparently they shrink from the idea of letting the Bolshevists into EUROPE. It seems strange to me. Sometimes I had the impression that the BAO, with all his questions about the new weapons and so on, was trying to prevent further useless bloodshed – which is really only natural.

? SATTLER: I look on all that as a cunning Jewish trick.

HENNECKE: Yes, but how often have the British made an alliance with the country which they have just conquered, against a stronger one?[42]

KÖHN: Yes, that's true, but I don't believe that they feel so sure of themselves now, that they think that victory is already theirs. They will be saying to themselves: We must try to form a strong nucleus of officers here, who will to some extent act out to be a new body of leaders, and we will use that for propaganda again.

SATTLER: That is the same story as in RUSSIA.

KÖHN: Yes, exactly the same, only that there it is perhaps done by force whereas here –

HENNECKE: I have the impression, and it is a lasting one, that the people here are afraid of the idea of Bolshevism. I keep thinking of the uneasiness which we all felt when we were suddenly told that we were allying with RUSSIA. It was something so nonsensical. The alliance which they have got with the Russians is just as nonsensical, firstly from the ideological standpoint, which means a lot of them, and secondly from the standpoint of economics, and through fear of what a power she might become.

KÖHN: That is possible, but ENGLAND has no policy of her own to formulate any longer. Her policy is formulated by the Americans.[43]

Document 21

CSDIC (UK), GRGG 154
Report on information obtained from Senior Officers (PW) on 4 July 44 [TNA, WO 208/4363]

HENNECKE: The frightful thing is that the confidence of those brave people, who have accepted one misfortune after the other, is such that they still believe – Because for a year and a half they have kept burbling about the stupendous effect of our reprisals, the nation is now clamouring for it too in their distress.

BASSENGE: When KREIPE (PW) came here I asked him: 'What are the people talking about in GERMANY?' He said: 'There is only one topic of conversation in GERMANY and that is the reprisal weapon.'

HENNECKE: It was like that a year ago, then they put an end to the talk. The reprisal weapon has come, and it's no damned good.

THOMA: Naturally, it isn't pleasant for the English, with bombs falling somewhere or other at any moment, but it isn't actually –

HENNECKE: It doesn't really count, using methods of that sort. But just think what was said about it: 'Wherever one of these things land, not a bird nor a leaf in the trees will be left alive within a radius of 6 km.'[44]

THOMA: It is our great tragedy that this German midget GOEBBELS is our military spokesman. He talks about strategic targets –

HENNECKE: Yes, he talks a great deal too much.

THOMA: He is the only one for whom I have any particular dislike, because he is crafty enough to know that he is lying. The others don't know it.

Document 22

CSDIC (UK), GRGG 156
Report on information obtained from Senior Officers (PW) on 8, 9, 10 July 44
[TNA, WO 208/4363]

KÖHN: The Bolshevists will destroy and smash everything in the path in GERMANY.

HENNECKE: Oh, I don't think they will destroy the towns.

KÖHN: They will shoot everyone. They did that in LITHUANIA and wherever else they've been.[45] Anyone who speaks his mind now will be shot immediately.

HENNECKE: Yes, if someone were to say: 'There's no point in it any more.'

KÖHN: No one says that.

HENNECKE: It's dreadful.

KÖHN: The moment that man took on ZEITZLER[46] things started to go badly. Anything more crazy – the few capable men still left to him he sends packing.

HENNECKE: They are still sending a few flying bombs over here, but they are not really doing ENGLAND any harm. When one sees what a powerful country can put up with – and ENGLAND is large too – . . . I mean, those things are mere pinpricks. It's just a pinprick compared with a single air raid of a thousand bombers.

KÖHN: Yes, if only we could send a thousand flying bombs to LONDON!

HENNECKE: A thousand isn't enough either – when you consider that just before the invasion two thousand bombs alone were dropped on the 'Batterie' on MARCOUF, in that small area.[47] Now picture the size of LONDON – thirty, forty thousand would have to fall on it. I honestly don't know what the future holds. There will probably be the most dreadful starvation; the Russians will take *everything* and eat everything up, that's the least they will do. They are insatiable, those fellows. No, it's absolutely dreadful. The best thing would be to cease hostilities in the West and join with the English in fighting the Russians.

KÖHN: Of course, but the English won't permit that, they want to march in right after us. But not in any way against the Russians; they will say: 'That's all right' – that is the false game those people are playing at and that is why I'm surprised at these poor fools who believe –

HENNECKE: You mean, they won't allow that?

KÖHN: Not the English.

HENNECKE: Well, I mean, suppose we were now to say we will cease hostilities in the West.

KÖHN: Yes, of course, if we were to suggest that; but the Western Allies don't want to. They'd say at once: 'We shall, of course, occupy the territory up to the RHINE but certainly not against the Russians. Or they'd occupy as far as BERLIN – 'We'll leave the East for the Russians.' That is the gist of what they're saying. I can't understand how the fellows here won't realise it.

HENNECKE: Yes. I recently saw a map in the 'Illustrated London News', more or less showing the old GERMANY – there was a hint of what GERMANY's boundaries will be like after the war.

KÖHN: Do they want GERMANY to be what she formerly was?

HENNECKE: Yes. I mean it was shown – of course, without CZECHO-SLOVAKIA, and POLAND had been slightly enlarged.

KÖHN: The Russians won't form a 'POLAND'; they'll make it into a 'Ukranian State of POLAND', which will extend up to the ODER.

HENNECKE: My God, what a future!

KÖHN: It will all become part of POLAND. The Allies are mad.

HENNECKE: It's ghastly.

KÖHN: We are here and our families are over there. What will happen to our families?

HENNECKE: That's just it.

KÖHN: I am convinced that the English won't oppose their victorious ally at this point – they're not dreaming of doing so.

HENNECKE: The question is what political agreement did they reach at TEHERAN; did they really set a limit to the Russians' advance?[48] The question is: will they adhere to it?

KÖHN: The Russians won't stick to it, that's out of the question. Besides,

I don't think that they will have tied themselves down to any definite agreement at TEHERAN. [. . .]

KÖHN: In my opinion things will collapse within the next few weeks.

HENNECKE: Yes, I think so too. [. . .]

KÖHN: I still won't change my opinion. Our first mistake was the war against RUSSIA.

HENNECKE: Yes.

KÖHN: I am still convinced that the Russians wouldn't have attacked.

HENNECKE: That is what we all say.

Document 24

CSDIC (UK), GRGG 159

Report on information obtained from Senior Officers (PW) [TNA, WO 208/4363]

HENNECKE: It can't go on like this. Just imagine it, in three days there have been three thousand bombers over MUNICH and so on, just imagine the damage that is being done there and how it is increasing the chaos that will come later.[49]

KRUG: That's what I say too. What did the FÜHRER say? 'And if they smash up the whole of GERMANY then we shall just live underground!'[50]

ROHRBACH: I heard that too!

HENNECKE: It's madness!

ROHRBACH: It certainly is!

HENNECKE: We didn't look at it in a tragic light then, and now everybody sees it in all its tragedy.

It says here in the newspaper that they have recently captured men on the ORNE front, who were no longer capable of working their guns, they had had practically no sleep for three weeks. It's obvious, my dear fellow, that they are bombarding the whole night through, just as they did to us at OCTEVILLE.[51] The men get no rest, they try to attack during the day, and that goes on for weeks on end. We haven't got the necessary reserves in order to withdraw the men, and they can't stand up to it. REITER[52] (Oberst, Arfü CHERBOURG) said quite rightly: 'In my opinion, a wise politician calls a halt when he sees that it is nothing but an affliction on the people; it won't gain them anything!'

NEUFFER: Well, this is the end; we can't hold the Russians now – there just isn't anything left there.

REIMANN: Do you remember, the German Army's black day on 8 August 1918?[53]

NEUFFER: But that was nothing by comparison. There's no doubt about it now, in my opinion it's just a matter of weeks.

Document 25

CSDIC (UK), GRGG 160
Report on information obtained from Senior Officers (PW) on 15–16 July 44
[TNA, WO 208/4363]

SCHLIEBEN: As I said today, why has this man HITLER never been abroad? I mean, he's seen absolutely nothing . . . HIMMLER, who's an out-and-out criminal.

THOMA: The nation can't deny that it must share the blame itself.

SCHLIEBEN: Merciful Heavens!

THOMA: If someone goes on defending the whole thing *now*, then I say he is either stupid, cowardly or lacking in character.

SCHLIEBEN: Our *poor* German people! One more thing: why have we got this impossible military leadership? Merely because that apprentice has his finger in everything! I've never met him in person.[54]

KÖHN: I should have some hope left if things weren't in such a state on the Eastern Front.

HENNECKE: I haven't the faintest hope left; on the contrary, I think it'd be wrong to be hopeful. It would only be self-deception. There is only the faint chance that at least less people will be killed . . . Just imagine it: everyone wants to get away and they will already be paying fantastic prices for any kind of small boats. They want to leave EAST PRUSSIA, LITHUANIA and all the places to which we sent our bombed-out evacuees; the same business is going on all the way down, in POLAND, LATVIA, POSEN and right down to CZECHOSLOVAKIA. Conditions will be similar to what they were in FRANCE.[55]

It would be far better for everyone to stay put, to end the struggle and to try and settle things peacefully. I don't think the Russians would carry off the women and everything there; I don't believe they would. Our stories are sure to have been exaggerated.

KÖHN: Do you think so?

HENNECKE: Of course. Everyone says that the Russians were *perfectly* –

KÖHN: But no one has been there.

HENNECKE: No, but . . . they are well disciplined.

KÖHN: Nobody has ever seen that – If you think of the way they dragged children away in SPAIN;[56] that is surely an actual fact and they apparently do the same thing in ITALY.

HENNECKE: I don't know whether that isn't one of our exaggerated stories. We have exaggerated a great deal.

KÖHN: Well, it's possible, of course.

HENNECKE: And those Spaniards we aided are well-off now. My God, something is certainly wrong somewhere. It's obvious that TURKEY will go over in the near future too.[57]

(*re newspaper article on the war situation*) It's obviously pretty bad, if the Führer is no longer convinced of the efficacy of his ideas, or rather of his ideas on *defence*. That an order to evacuate the Baltic States wasn't issued long ago is obviously due to political reasons, because they argue that in that case Finland would break away at once.[58] Those are all symptoms of a pending collapse. It's no use kidding ourselves.

Admiral Voss[58a] once appeared and went for one of us, saying: 'What do you mean by it? Things are going *brilliantly* in Russia.' That was one of those gentlemen from the Führer's HQ! We were all left speechless. How can the prospects be brilliant when we've just given up the Ukraine? After all the talk about the Ukraine in numberless newspaper articles; that this third year of her occupation was to bring the first real harvest, which would ensure our supplies for all time; the prospects can't very well be brilliant when we've just given up the Ukraine. It's all nonsense; it's just as if they were wearing blinkers! It is a *crime* against the German people – I am really becoming convinced of it. And on top of that, when, as I heard yesterday, that man actually said on the occasion of a small celebration to distribute decorations to Party members; 'German National Socialism and the National Socialist Reich are invincible,' well, it just makes you laugh. That just isn't sane any more. The trouble is that people believe it, just as we ourselves used to believe similar stories; I believed Rommel. This deceiving of the troops, too, is frightful; one doesn't know where to hide one's face. Montgelas,[59] a very sincere fellow, once said to me: 'I can't associate myself with that;' I never repeated it. Above all he was very frank in his attitude to the Party and said: 'I have experience of life and of the world and I can see that the whole thing has feet of clay. I *cannot* have things told to my men in that way; I should consider myself false and dishonourable.' I should like to know what Raeder[60] and people like him are thinking nowadays; they all share the blame. They were the people who should have taken a firm stand; they should have got together and told the Führer quite *plainly*: 'Things can't go on like this.' As Service people they should have been able to realise it. They shouldn't have been afraid of his attacks of rage, even if it had meant death for them –

Köhn: As much was required of us. Who bothered whether we would be killed when we went to the front, or even went to visit our own troops, for it was often worse for a 'Kommandeur' going to join his troops than for the men in the front line. After all, I was at Glacerie[61] the last day, when the enemy was already in the wood right in front of the 'Bataillon's' battle HQ. It was irresponsible, what they . . . there.

Hennecke: Yes, and on the other hand, those people should have had sufficient courage as citizens to tell the Führer: 'Things can't go on.'

Köhn: He wouldn't see it. However, people like Brauchitsch and Bock[62] etc. will have told him so. Whereupon he just dismissed them.

HENNECKE: The others should have done the same, until he'd dismissed them all. Then things would have been put right.

KÖHN: But then there were ambitious fellows among them who still –

HENNECKE: Yes, like KEITEL, who's a yes man.

KÖHN: KEITEL, JODL, ZEITZLER etc. – all that crowd are apparently extremely ambitious.

HENNECKE: They are the guilty men!

KÖHN: This is how ROHRBACH (PW) imagines the course of the war: first there is to be a 'General' in GERMANY who will take over the government. Secondly, he will immediately enter into negotiations with ENGLAND with the following result: the war in the West will cease immediately, the German troops will be transferred to the East at once and will take up the battle against the Bolshevists.

HENNECKE: These ideas are all prompted by THOMA (PW).

KÖHN: Yes. Thirdly, the French and English troops etc. will follow on the heels of the German troops and occupy GERMANY, so that they will remain secure in the rear at least. I said to him: 'First, there is no "General" who can suddenly take over the government. Secondly, do you really believe that the German people, with all this fighting behind them and having made some sort of peace on one front, would then start fighting again in the East? It's completely impossible.'

Document 26

CSDIC (UK), GRGG 162
Report on information obtained from Senior Officers (PW) on 23–4 July 44 [TNA, WO 208/4363]

SCHLIEBEN: I should just like to know what the outcome will be. It will result in –

SATTLER: A collapse. There's no way of stopping it.

SCHLIEBEN: I consider it to be absolutely impossible for it to be averted. Poor GERMANY! They're a pack of swine.

SATTLER: I should like to know under what conditions the Allies will make peace with us.

SCHLIEBEN: Unconditional surrender.

SATTLER: Yes, and they will get it, too. Poor GERMANY. We used to be Colonels and Generals, after the war we shall be boot-blacks and porters. We shan't get any pension.[63]

Document 27

CSDIC (UK), GRGG 164

Report on information obtained from Senior Officers (PW) on 23–4 July 44 [TNA, WO 208/4363]

[. . .]

HENNECKE: That is just what those fellows saw so clearly; they were furious about it and found themselves more and more in opposition to the attitude of the Party, but they never opened their mouths when it was necessary. The only one who possibly did it was FRITSCH and as a result he was got rid of.[64] The other said nothing. That was the *great* mistake.

KRUG: BRAUCHITSCH ought to have said: 'I beg to resign.'

HENNECKE: They were all with HITLER previously and they all co-operated. Each one of those in command at that time is equally to blame.

KRUG: I was an insignificant 'Major'.

KÖHN: Yes, we could do nothing. Moreover, I must tell you frankly that I had no idea of what was going on. I regarded National Socialism idealistically and in my opinion it offered the only possibility for the German people at that time; I also saw its successes. In my opinion nobody will deny the successes it achieved. It got rid of the unemployed for us. That was the greatest problem and were it to be condemned by world history, history would have to grant it this one achievement, that it solved the problem of unemployment.

KRUG: That is a historic fact, and we can't get away from it, that in the autumn of 1938 we ought to have lain low for twenty years and for twenty years –

KÖHN: And ruin POLAND and RUSSIA economically so that the people came to us of their own accord; that would have been the right thing. They were already economically ruined.

KRUG: The clique surrounding him is to blame for that. They ought to have said to him: 'My FÜHRER, now – '

KÖHN: Perhaps he wouldn't tolerate other opinions.

KRUG: Then they ought to have cleared out.

KÖHN: Well, a man like RUNDSTEDT could surely say to him: 'Don't take offence; you are younger, you are more adaptable, you may bring it off, but I can't take part in it. I am inwardly convinced that this is the situation and I consider it my duty to warn you, which I have done, and if you don't wish to pay attention to my warning, them I am compelled to act accordingly.' Surely he can quite easily say that. If one after the other had said that, well, I should like to see whether he wouldn't after all have begun to wonder.

[. . .]

Document 28

CSDIC (UK), GRGG 172
Report on information obtained from Senior Officers (PW) on 8–12 July 44 [TNA, WO 208/4363]

[. . .]

KESSLER (*after expressing to* Oberst REIMANN *his reluctance to speak his mind on his attitude to National Socialism when talking to a BAO*): I don't like to be told by those officers: 'Well, if that was your attitude, why didn't you speak out before?' Among ourselves, one could easily say: 'Of course, we let ourselves be taken in, too, there's no doubt about that.' Because it is only now that one sees all the mistakes which have been made. During the time that I was lying alone in hospital, a lot of things became clear to me.

REIMANN: The whole thing, the whole movement has degenerated. At the beginning it was all right, but it was rotten at the core, they had evil intentions.

KESSLER: Oh, I don't know whether one can say that – perhaps it was all planned from an ideal point of view, but in the end it was over-organised.

MUNDORFF: I won't join in all this fraternising with the English and kow-towing to them!

KÖHN: Of course it infuriates one as an old soldier and as an officer on active service, when one sees the front line left in the lurch; I mean to say, we've been left without a GAF, without artillery and without any –

MUNDORFF: But you needn't throw everything overboard immediately on account of that. My point of view is this: twice we have tried to attain power in EUROPE by waging a war and we have failed. Twice we have squared up to ENGLAND; *maybe* it wasn't a nice thing to do, but I maintain that we *must* always oppose ENGLAND. ENGLAND wants us merely as a dominion, nothing else; as a worker, a watchman in EUROPE. I can't see why, in the present circumstances, we can't have a European, Bolshevist state – that is, if Bolshevism alters a bit. It can't be prevented and it is bound to happen. Of course, *we'll* probably be the dupes; we'll perhaps be liquidated by having a bullet put through our heads. But, taking a wide view, it is GERMANY's only chance of rising again. We'd *never* rise again under ENGLAND's rule. That's out of the question! They'd see to that! Just look at the demands already – just think what that fellow DE GAULLE is demanding! The occupation of the RHINELAND for ninety-nine years, and of course POLAND will get POMERANIA and Heaven knows what else, SILESIA, up to the ODER.[65]

?HENNECKE: The victors in a war waged as ruthlessly as this one will obviously make demands accordingly.

[. . .]

Document 29

CSDIC (UK), GRGG 173
Report on information obtained from Senior Officers (PW) on 13–14 July 44
[TNA, WO 208/4363]

SPANG: I was very sorry, too, when I heard about WITZLEBEN. That is typical of National Socialism. I must tell you quite frankly that formerly I was a great friend of the National Socialists.

KRUG: So was I. They pulled us out of the mud.

SPANG: And now I *hate* the whole lot of them, because I am gradually seeing through this corruption and inferiority and the Draconic measures of these people and above all their selfish attitude. After what I've seen I am completely without hope. I know the state of our armament, I know that we have nothing at all.

KRUG: No ammunition?

SPANG: Nothing. No ammunition, no tanks, we have nothing left. There is nothing.

KRUG: . . . it is a crime to continue the war.

SPANG: They are only carrying on the war for their own sakes – for egotistical reasons, in order to prolong their own lives.

Document 30

CSDIC (UK), GRGG 176
Report on information obtained from Senior Officers (PW) on 19–21 Aug. 44
[TNA, WO 208/4363]

KLENK: I'll tell you something, the troops in the East won't hold out. Troops who are perpetually withdrawing can't hold out.

HELLWIG: They're never relieved either. They never get any rest. The people say their only hope is to be either killed or wounded. The ruthlessness was inhuman; they did two hours' sentry duty, slept for two hours and then two hours' sentry duty again – month after month in that mud and not a soul bothered about them. There's ruthlessness for you. Never have soldiers been created as we were.

KLENK: No, not so ruthlessly as we were treated. It's appalling to think of the lives being sacrificed there.

HELLWIG: The GOCs considered it criminal – criminal to continue fighting when there's no hope of success. That's my view too. A whole race can't end heroically.

KLENK: For what idea? The finest elements are being sacrificed. Most of the officers here realise fairly clearly –

HELLWIG: Yes, they all think it crazy.

KLENK: I mean, they disassociate themselves from it entirely?

HELLWIG: Completely, they call them criminals.

KLENK: They recognise no allegiance?

HELLWIG: Not an atom. SPANG may differ slightly, but he too says: 'It's criminal to continue the sacrifice.'

Document 31

CSDIC (UK), GRGG 180

Report on information obtained from Senior Officers (PW) on 25–6 Aug. 44 [TNA, WO 208/4363]

ELFELDT: I'd be the last person to deny the weaknesses in the system but I don't agree with the people here who repudiate *everything*. You can't say: 'ENGLAND is good, GERMANY is bad' – that's impossible. There was such a lot that was *so* good at home.

MENNY: If only we hadn't started this tomfool war, which wasn't necessary – After we had got CZECHOSLOVAKIA we should have stopped; everything was marvellous and we could have ordered things in peace. We could even have managed it afterwards, because I think the worst mistake we made in this war was not to invade ENGLAND after we had completed the French campaign. Even if it had meant 100,000 casualties. The Russian campaign cost us a million killed and more.

ELFELDT: The first time I heard about the Russian campaign; I think it was November –

BADINSKY: It made me quite sick.

MENNY: After all he wrote in 'Mein Kampf' about not waging a war on two fronts –

BADINSKY: 'Mein Kampf' also says that a man is either a politician or the founder of a religion; that's probably why he gave ROSENBERG[66] carte blanche. He's an ape who has ruined our people's religion. There is hardly anything we haven't attacked; we attacked the past, our religion, the Jews, FRANCE, ENGLAND, AMERICA, RUSSIA. Besides we have attacked anyone who hadn't the same political standpoint as we had – we did it in a stupid, brutal way.

Document 32

CSDIC (UK), GRGG 183

Report on information obtained from Senior Officers (PW) on 29 Aug. 44 [TNA, WO 208/4363]

MENNY: Four weeks ago at a course in BERLIN, BURGDORF[67] told the people quite frankly how desperate our position looked, how completely mismanaged – AVRANCHES(?) and so on had not happened then, it was shortly before that – and how things looked very bad for us and at the moment one could really believe that we should not pull through. He said that quite openly. But if we succeeded in holding out until September, then all the indication showed that we should manage it, because then all those things would come into action. Those were the V-2, the flying torpedoes and the U-boats and so on. So it would all depend on getting over those four weeks.

[. . .]

SCHLIEBEN: We are a thorn in their flesh.

CHOLTITZ: HITLER *hates* us.

SCHLIEBEN: Yes, he *hates* us! For how long did HITLER harangue you when you reported to him?

CHOLTITZ: Three-quarters of an hour.

SCHLIEBEN: Was he sitting at a large table, or how?

CHOLTITZ: He was standing.

SCHLIEBEN: And then they introduced the Nazi salute as a substitute for the lacking GAF, didn't they?[68]

CHOLTITZ: Yes.

CHOLTITZ: I saw HITLER four weeks ago when he nabbed me for PARIS.

BASSENGE: What kind of an impression does he make?

CHOLTITZ: Well, it was just shortly after the assassination attempt and he was still rather jaded.

BASSENGE: Is he still injured?

CHOLTITZ: He was more worn out than anything. He has put on 17 lbs!

THOMA: Mentally, he is ill, very ill.

CHOLTITZ: I went there and HITLER made me a speech for three-quarters of an hour, as though I were a public meeting.[69] He gets drunk with his own speeches! I went into the room and there he stood, a fat, broken-down old man with festering hands . . . they had been scratched a bit as a result of the attempt on his life and all the 'Gauleiter', whom he had greeted shortly afterwards, in order to gain fresh courage, all shook hands with him so enthusiastically and trustingly that he got badly festering sores. When I gave him my hand, I gave it to him very carefully, I was really almost sorry for him because he looked horrible.

THOMA: Has he got fat?

CHOLTITZ: Yes, sort of bloated.

?: He has put on 17 lbs.

?: You say he looks bloated and broken down?

CHOLTITZ: Yes. He said (*imitating* HITLER): 'Does the General know what it's about?' and BURGDORF(?) replied: 'Yes, my FÜHRER.' Thereupon he began reeling off a gramophone record like a man stung by a tarantula and spoke for three-quarters of an hour! With difficulty

I succeeded in interrupting him three times. He spoke just as loud as I am speaking now in a room that was about as large as this one, only rather longer – it was in his dug-out, because the air-raid warning had just been given outside. (*Imitating* HITLER) 'A people which does not surrender can never be defeated, such a thing has never happened in history.' Then he began talking about the Party and how he had struggled for fourteen years. (*With sarcasm*) He said some words which I seemed vaguely to remember having heard before. (*General laughter*) He trotted out all that old nonsense, so that I actually had to bite my tongue hard three times, to keep myself from bursting out. His left eye dropped a bit to the left, his right one was fixed very suspiciously on me all the time, because he hates us *all* like the *plague*. I noticed that when we – I have been commanding a 'Korps' since December 1942[70] and, in order o check up on me, I was sent again at Christmas to a course for GOCs – they have got that too, now! At the end of this course, we were all put into a marvellous train and sent to POSEN, where we were lodged for four days in an hotel, where we were actually very well off – good food and good drink – and where we were allowed to listen to speeches by prominent people on 'the greatest man of GERMANY' for four days on end. (*General laughter*).

?: SPANG was there too, wasn't he?

CHOLTITZ: SPANG was there, among others. He just accepted all these things with startled resignation. I was delighted to see that such people still exist, who are living mentally two-thirds and physically one-third on the moon. He was like a little child and always used to listen in complete wonder.

?: You will see him here, too.

CHOLTITZ: He was also the only one who took notes. (*General amuse-ment*). He took notes!

There was a terrible man there, who is a disgrace to the German Army, General REINECKE.[71]

?: Who is he?

THOMA: He was a member of the People's Court.

CHOLTITZ: I heard say that he was at the Clothing Department for a long time. (*General laughter*).

?: The very man for the job.

CHOLTITZ: (With disgust) Such a common commercial traveller, such a vulgar, horrible fellow! He always used to come on to the platform: 'Heil HITLER' – dead silence in the hall – whereupon everyone said: 'Morning', whereupon he said: 'I ought to say a few words about that!' – and that to the Commanders-in-Chief of our army! 'Anyone who doesn't say "Heil HITLER" is an outsider.' That was the gist of his speech. The next day I came down to breakfast and stood there – there were nothing but Generals all round the table – and said: 'Heil HITLER', whereupon they all began to laugh. I said: 'Gentlemen, you are on the wrong side. So is the General over there.' That was REINECKE, who had not said 'Heil HITLER' either. (*General laughter*). A really common, horrible fellow.

THOMA: Didn't anyone from the Party come then, GOEBBELS or anyone?

CHOLTITZ: That's possible. Then the best thing was a fellow from the Party, whose name I have forgotten, who came from the Party Chancellery and had the impudence to stand there and read something out for three-and-a-half hours in a completely toneless voice, just talking down to us. There was a fat brown-shirted, stupid fellow sitting on one of those narrow theatre chairs beside me and he said: 'It's intolerable, who the hell is he?' 'I wouldn't speak so loudly,' I said, 'or you will be had up there.' (*Laughter*) I said: 'Who are *you* then?' 'I am the "Gauleiter".' 'Oh, hell!' I said.

Then we all drove out from POSEN to see HITLER. This is what the lunch with Adolf HITLER was like: obviously they couldn't have two-hundred-and-fifty Generals all sitting down to table together, so half of them were there. I was among those told to come to lunch and I sat next to SCHMUNDT.[72] Adolf HITLER came into the room – looked round – dug MANSTEIN[73] in the paunch with his elbow, without saying: 'Good morning' to him. The two 'Feldmarschälle' were *not* seated beside him. He sat down at the table and looked round quite nervously, thinking he was going to be stabbed in the back any moment and was happy only when he had sat down and his SS waiter was behind him. I watched him closely and the man didn't say a word for seven minutes, he didn't speak, he just drank and incidentally ate a great deal. He had four different things to drink, including cold tea and rum (sic). I said to the fellow near me: 'The atmosphere here is unbearable. The fellow comes in without greeting anybody. What's the matter with him, he's so ill-tempered?' 'I don't know.' Then he spoke very shortly and jumped up after ten minutes and ran away out of the room, breathing fire, scared and shaking. He didn't say a word to anyone and that was what we had hurried out from POSEN for. Then came that famous speech. (*Giggling*) Adolf HITLER stood up in front of the stand and delivered a lecture – you must remember it was to two-hundred-and-fifty Generals who had all been rushed by air from the front. MANSTEIN and HOLLIDT[74] had only just arrived beforehand; they had had their lunch. As is usual with men of our age, everyone likes to have a moment's rest after a meal. Unfortunately, that clashed with Adolf HITLER's speech. We were in a barn, which was the HQ 'Quartiermeister's' Mess and the outer room where the orderlies wash the dishes, and they'd overheated the room beyond all description. We sat in that barn in the sweltering heat and Adolf HITLER talked and talked; after about seven minutes 40 per cent of the Generals were snoring. (*General laughter*). I thought, if the man's in his right mind at all he ought to say: 'Let's go out for a few physical jerks.' (*Laughter all round*). But, as usual, once he's worked up, he notices nothing.

THOMA: Well, what did he say, still the same old things?

CHOLTITZ: Except for one moment, when he said (*imitating Adolf Hitler*): 'In principle, it ought to be like this, the "Feldmarschälle" should protect my person with their sabres. In front of the "Feldmarschälle" should be the Generals, in front of them the "Divisionäre" and in front of them the "Regiments-Kommandeure" with their "Regimenter", forming an impenetrable wall.' MANSTEIN said: 'It'll probably come to that, my FÜHRER.' Whereupon Adolf Hitler, filled with hate, looked at us and said 'Feldmarschall von MANSTEIN, I accept your declaration with satisfaction. But unfortunately I must tell you that it isn't so. You need only look at RUSSIA. It's tragic, but there it is.' Actually, what with SEYDLITZ and so on, he'd . . .[75]

Document 33

CSDIC (UK), GRGG 185
Report on information obtained from Senior Officers (PW) on 3 Sept. 44 [TNA, WO 208/4363]

MÜLLER-RÖMER: I spent the entire war in RUSSIA, until last November. I can only say: it *needn't* be as bad as all that. The Russians may change quite suddenly; they are blossoming forth as Western Europeans.

HENNECKE: But you started to say that your family in SILESIA, if the Russians come there –

MÜLLER-RÖMER: If I had the choice between Russians on the one hand and English and Americans on the other, of course I should choose the people here because I know what it is like here and I am doubtful what it is like over there. Of course, it may be ghastly, but I should think that the Russians do things in an orderly manner like the Americans and English do. I don't think they'll send over Kirgizes either, because they'll want to prove to the Western European powers that they are a civilised state. They may use quite different tactics.

HENNECKE: I can only say that all repressions, everything lying dormant in people will break out the moment the war tension ends and people will be able to do as they like and no one will say anything. That's the danger. DE GAULLE is impatiently waiting to occupy the RHINELAND.[76] Whether he'll be allowed to is a different question. But revenge – that's what it will be. I am convinced that our Gestapo did dreadful things there.

MÜLLER-RÖMER: It passes all imagination what those fellows – it's not surprising if we . . . our Gestapo competed with the Russians in their bestial actions. I know the ghastly atrocities committed in POLAND since 1939, when those fellows started there!

HENNECKE: Didn't anyone oppose them?

MÜLLER-RÖMER: Yes. BLASKOWITZ did at the time but it didn't do him any good![77] The 'Wehrmacht' had no say in those matters. 'That comes under civil administration and is no business of yours.'

HENNECKE: That's the trouble; if only all senior Army leaders had unanimously said: 'We won't participate in that dirty work! It is dragging the name of GERMANY in the mud.'

MÜLLER-RÖMER: It didn't do the few who did say that any good.

HENNECKE: If they had all done it, in good time! The fact that such things were possible will puzzle world historians!

MÜLLER-RÖMER: History will hold the German Generals responsible for not having unanimously stopped all that dirty work which started at the outbreak of war, by simply protesting and laying down their arms – or something of the sort.

HENNECKE: All the Generals are protesting. I used to say to them: 'If you knew all that, I can't understand why any of you, or the entire body of Generals, didn't protest.' They all said: 'I don't want to play with fire.'

MÜLLER-RÖMER: The Generals we now have in . . . are all quite young fellows who couldn't have been more than 'Regimentskommandeure' at the time.

HENNECKE: Well, the ones before weren't young lads.

MÜLLER-RÖMER: The greatest blame falls on BOCK, MANSTEIN, LEEB[78] and RUNDSTEDT, because only the most senior officers can protest against the supreme commander.

HENNECKE: It should have been done in 1933 or in 1934 when things started.

MÜLLER-RÖMER: No, the running of the state was still all right at that time.

HENNECKE: It started with SCHLEICHER.[79]

MÜLLER-RÖMER: The German people shouldn't have stood for all the craziness of 1933.

HENNECKE: It was legally done by voting; everything was in order.

MÜLLER-RÖMER: At the outbreak of war, when POLAND had been conquered and the Gestapo had entered the country and the dirty work had started, BLASKOWITZ was the first to protest and as a result he was dismissed. All senior German Generals, from the Chief of the General Staff to the 'Heeresgruppenführer' and all that crowd, including RAEDER, should have pointed a pistol at the FÜHRER and said: 'We won't wage that kind of war!' If those dozen senior Army, Navy and GAF officers had really been prepared to risk the consequences, HITLER would have been left high and dry to get on with the war by himself.

HENNECKE: But that was the most unfavourable moment, because a stab in the back in war-time is the worst possible action, as it doesn't only affect the Party, but –

MÜLLER-RÖMER: But all that dirty work, those bestial murders, only started during the war.

HENNECKE: No, they didn't; that's the trouble.

MÜLLER-RÖMER: It wasn't so bad before the war.

HENNECKE: The civilised world was horrified at the things that went on in our concentration camps! The persecution of the Jews and all those things.

MÜLLER-RÖMER: Yes. My God – the German people should have protested!

HENNECKE: I never heard much about those things before I came here. At first I wouldn't believe them. There is such a lot of silly talk! Whenever you asked: 'Did you see it yourself?' or 'Do you really know someone?', you got the answer: 'No, an uncle of Mrs so-and-so told me.'

MÜLLER-RÖMER: The peace-time inmates of concentration camps were people who more or less were criminals and I also believe conditions there weren't so dreadful up to the outbreak of war.[80]

HENNECKE: What do you mean by 'criminals'? They were people who had been locked up arbitrarily: take FRITSCH for example. It's a scandal. There was no justice left. When FRITSCH, that very capable man, was dismissed, the *entire* Armed Forces should have risen as one man and said; 'Stop, no farther!'

MÜLLER-RÖMER: He is supposed to have planned a revolt but, of course, there's no proof.

Document 34

CSDIC (UK) SR REPORT, SRGG 1026(c) [TNA, WO 208/4168]

ALFRED GUTKNECHT – Generalmajor (Higher Commander of the Kraftfahrtruppen West) – Captured 29 Aug. 44 in Soissons-Rheims.
HEINRICH EBERBACH – General der Panzertruppe (GOC VII Army) – Captured 31 Aug. 44 in Amiens.

GUTKNECHT: Do you think that HITLER will carry on the fighting on German soil?

EBERBACH: Yes, if he has the say.

GUTKNECHT: I don't think it right, unless he can see any chance of victory.

EBERBACH: That's it.

GUTKNECHT: But if he can't see any chance, then, in my opinion, it is not right. Then everything will be smashed to bits.

EBERBACH: He always sees a chance, because he always gives way to ideas, which are not true. He has a terrific imagination and he always sees what is still to come as an accomplished fact. He sees all the new

U-boats and all the aircraft and whatever else is in process of being produced[81] as being already completed and that gives him faith and a positive attitude, which infects all those around him. You simply can't get away from the optimism, which surrounds him, when you are in his presence.

GUTKNECHT: Healthy optimism is in itself a very good thing, but there must be some limit to it.

EBERBACH: It is sheer fantasy

GUTKNECHT: I see a limit to it as soon as they penetrate from right to left, that is from the west and the east, into GERMANY proper. Then there is no longer any point in it, to my way of thinking.

EBERBACH: No.

GUTKNECHT: Because our industry too has been more or less hard hit.

EBERBACH: Yes, of course.

Document 35

CSDIC (UK), GRGG 186
Report on information obtained from Senior Officers (PW) on 4–5 Sept. 44 [TNA, WO 208/4363]

BASSENGE: I'm quite sure that General CHOLTITZ ought to be accepted with the greatest caution, because it isn't owing to any outstanding military ability that he was always with SCHMUNDT and HQ and got promoted so fast and everything.

THOMA: . . . not promoted out of turn.

BASSENGE: And how, Sir! He's younger than I am. I was 'Oberst' while he was still 'Oberstleutnant; he's been promoted out of turn time and time again.[82]

THOMA: One ought to ask him quite casually what . . . he had. It's also interesting that he's now come to me about the SEYDLITZ business. It's just the same as AULOCK (PW) did, a man who had sent HITLER telegrams of loyalty the day before his surrender.[83]

BASSENGE: And CHOLTITZ's defence of GERSTENBERG[84] yesterday was extremely significant.

THOMA: But he piped down.

BASSENGE: Yes, I shut him up all right, but this initial attempt is absolutely *typical* of the man. It would be pitiful if windbags like CHOLTITZ began gathering supporters here.

THOMA: I should tell him immediately: 'We want peace and quiet here; if you want anything, put it in writing and we will then pass it on to the Commandant.' I should take a very firm stand. It's quite out of the question that one man should appear to speak as representing the camp or otherwise.

Document 36

CSDIC (UK), GRGG 195
Report on information obtained from Senior Officers (PW) on 16–17 Sept. 44
[TNA, WO 208/4363]

CHOLTITZ: One of the Americans asked me whether all the money that
is being sent abroad at present is in preparation for a Nazi underground
movement, which is to be set up again later.

SPONECK: There's one point that needs careful consideration. Once the
war is lost, has National Socialism which, after all, was responsible for
the whole thing, got even the remotest chance? Communism has, but
National Socialism, in its present form has utterly ruined everything.

CHOLTITZ: After a time we shall hear a great deal of talk on the German
wireless about the treachery of the officers and the civilian
communities, and that's the last thing they'll . . . to the young people.

SPONECK: Yes, it may be holding now, but once the great collapse comes,
I don't for a moment believe that National Socialism will survive in
the memories of the people – will be able to arouse the slightest
enthusiasm. Communism, perhaps.

[. . .]

Document 37

CSDIC (UK), GRGG 197
Report on information obtained from Senior Officers (PW) on 20–1 Sept. 44
[TNA, WO 208/4363]

[Conversation between General HEINZ EBERBACH and his son Oblt. z.S. HEINZ
EUGEN EBERBACH]

FATHER: I can only tell you that the whole thing is hopeless. Individual
places such as BREMERHAVEN[85] and DARMSTADT,[86] have been bombed
to ruins, and so it goes on the whole time. You must realise that so far
only a quarter of their air force has been attacking us, the remaining
three-quarters having been used to attack the occupied countries. It
will all be concentrated on us now. According to the German news a
population of two million is now to be evacuated from the
RHINELAND.[87] How are you going to set about it? They are already
approaching from the other side, from EAST PRUSSIA, and they will all
meet in the centre. I was very well informed about the whole of the
STAUFFENBERG business.[88] Even when we were out at the front '
ROMMEL[89] said to me: 'GERMANY's only possible hope of getting off
reasonably well lies in our doing away with the FÜHRER and his closest
associates as quickly as possible; that will give us our first chance of
reaching a bearable peace.' ROMMEL said that!

SON: Well, that's no reason for it.

FATHER: It was the same with RUNDSTEDT. I'm really pleased that he has reappeared because he intended to conclude an armistice with the English, in order to transfer the troops from the West to the East as quickly as possible, and allow the English and Americans to march in unopposed, because it will be far better for us, if we're occupied by Americans and English rather than by the Russians.

SON: I'm quite certain of that. I simply don't believe that the English and Americans . . . so very much about the Russians.

FATHER: Yes, that's the other side of it, of course. In that respect STALIN has given very definite assurances that he will adhere strictly to the agreements. It has been laid down that the Russians will under no circumstances advance further than the ELBE.

SON: Well, that's all right!

FATHER: Yes, but if the others reach BERLIN or the ODER first, then the ODER will become the river which – it would still be much better for GERMANY.

SON: Well, actually I'm convinced of the same thing, but for the time being I still believe in V-2 – V-17.

FATHER: That's finished. V-1 would have been all right six months ago, but it's all too late now.

SON: But why? Now we are using the new weapons which are for use against aircraft, tanks and so on.[90]

FATHER: Really?

SON: And then we'll use the other things.

FATHER: It's all coming too late. Everything is being smashed up whilst it's still under construction. Three thousand bombers per day over GERMANY is too much of a good thing.

SON: Three thousand seems to be rather too many.

FATHER: You mustn't forget that a war has never yet been really decided by a new weapon.

SON: But there's one thing you mustn't forget: if we had a weapon against aircraft today, then the war would be decided.

FATHER: And do you believe that such a thing will still come in time? Those are all things which may already be known of in the world of science, but have yet to be brought into being. That is to say, it's a matter of six months, at the very least. I know how long that kind of thing takes. In practice it will be a good year before –

SON: Yes, but back in June or July it was already said that these things were in the final stages of completion.

FATHER: I've had too much experience of that kind of racket. I must say that this last period on the Western Front almost knocked the bottom out of my world. In those last hours over there, when it really did depend on our doing the right thing and leaving us to do it, it was appalling how HITLER ruined things for us by his personal interference. So that even people like Sepp DIETRICH, who really is a loyal disciple and who had just got the 'Diamonds' and 'Oak Leaves' almost turned revolutionary. That means something in the case of Sepp DIETRICH.[91] I mean the fact that DIETRICH might have adopted exactly the same attitude as we did – if he hadn't known that he would be killed in any case as soon as things began going badly for the Nazis.[92]

SON: It all depends in his case. Actually he was always a fighting man.

FATHER: Yes, but under his command the 'Leibstandarte' killed thousands of Jews.[93]

SON: What do you think about the men like HIMMLER, GOEBBELS, SPEER and so on?

FATHER: There is no doubt that HIMMLER is one of the people who has done us the greatest harm throughout the whole world.

SON: Yes, he has certainly done that, but the question is whether he hasn't achieved a hell of a lot.

FATHER: No, no, we are . . . by a certain lack of humanity and decency which one must have, because otherwise the pendulum of history swings against you. I told you that once before, in connection with that history book I always carried about with me, that that is one of the things I have learned from history. In my opinion, one can even go so far as to say that the killing of those million Jews or however many it was, was necessary in the interests of our people. But to kill the women and children wasn't necessary. That is going too far.

SON: Well, if you are going to kill off the Jews, then kill the women and children too, or the children at least. There is no need to do it publicly, but what good does it do me to kill off the old people?

FATHER: Well, simply that it is contrary to humanity, in the end it hits back at you, simply because it instils a certain brutality into the people – and there are some incidents that I have just learned about from the officers here who witnessed them themselves – the numbers of Poles we have killed, at least a million, the numbers we have killed in YUGOSLAVIA – I never knew that either, nor did I ever take part in it. The tens of thousands of Russians we have killed, not only Poles!

SON: Yes, but even if that's true, they were people who conducted guerrilla warfare against us, so there again it wasn't without justification.

FATHER: I know, too, how it was done. It was said: a hundred soldiers have been killed, therefore a thousand civilians must be shot. We were forced to do that because we are waging a war which is going far beyond our powers and it was this complete overestimation of our possibilities and our strength which led us to attempt that damn silly campaign for STALINGRAD and the CAUCASUS with forces which were quite insufficient for the job.

SON: Yes, but STALINGRAD would have succeeded all right if, at any rate, according to your opinion, the Italians and Hungarians ahead of us hadn't collapsed.

FATHER: Yes, but it was known that they would crack. Putting the Italians, Hungarians and Rumanians next to each other at the front and, what's more, up in *that* part of the front where, one look at the map and everyone said: 'That's where they will come' – those are the things that count.[94]

SON: Sometimes I have a burning desire to fight with the Russians against the English, because they have handed EUROPE over to communism.

FATHER: Yes, they really believe that Bolshevism is no longer the same and it may actually be that for the next five to ten years they will be right, as I can well imagine that the Russians would be quite glad of a breathing space.

SON: Yes, but what good is any of that to us if we make peace? Cessation of hostilities under the hardest and vilest conditions, unconditional surrender and all that sort of thing, except that we shall have another war in seven to ten years which will be fought out on German soil anyway, with the new weapons already in preparation and which will by then be ready, and one which will in any event drag in the German people either on both sides or one side; at any rate there will be a new war, so what's the good of it? Those are all things which . . . 'a frightful end', followed by 'endless frightfulness' unless a miracle occurs, and I've got out of the habit of believing in miracles.

SON (*re a future leader*): In my opinion it is a very good thing. That is what would impress me so favourably about ROMMEL in such circumstances and seems to me such a good thing, that the fellow, in the opinion of the working classes, counts as an exponent of the old regime. We must bring in people like that, otherwise you won't get the working classes round to it. The only chance the English have of winning over the working classes is not to say: 'The entire previous system was rotten to the core', but to include these men like ROMMEL and so on. A completely unknown man, a General EBERBACH wouldn't appeal to the working man *in the least*. He would say: 'He is one of the swine who took part in the 20 July affair, who wants to see which way the wind is blowing.' Only men with a name, such as ROMMEL, or even PAPEN,[95] are the ones who, to the worker, even if they don't like them personally, are capable men, recognised by the old regime.

FATHER: It will be useless to put forward proposals. The Allies will never agree to them. Where are you going to set up a 'Freikorps'?

SON: In the west, I should say.

FATHER: Under the eyes of the English and Americans, what weapons are you going to use?

SON: We'll already have them when we are demobilised.

FATHER: Where will you get your money and supplies? It's not as simple as all that. In those days after 1918, such a thing was possible in a GERMANY that was mainly unoccupied. It will be quite impossible in a completely occupied GERMANY.

SON: Well, not in big numbers, of course. It won't be a 'Freikorps' like the 'Eiserne Division' and the 'Oberland' (Post-1918 group of partisans in Eastern Germany[96]) marching through the district with bands, but groups of partisans who will support the East German population in large numbers and the refugees. In every village at the moment, and afterwards too, there will be some old 'Ortsgruppenleiter' or an old SS man, or something odd like that. There are people who will give the partisans shelter for a night and who will slip them some food. We belong to a GERMANY which is still National Socialist today, and 10 per cent of the population, or we'll say 50 per cent, will continue to be National Socialist.

FATHER: Well, I believe that when this collapse occurs their own population will beat the 'Ortsgruppenleiter' and so on to death.

SON: Yes, but those are the unsavoury elements, my dear father. I was *severely* shaken by the effect of 20 July on the German population, amongst, for instance, the work people in my father-in-law's business, where I was; they were *staunch* Nazis – that was very pleasing but showed themselves against the officers in that they said: 'We killed too few officers in 1933.' These work-people are out and out radical National Socialists, perhaps too radical. It almost borders on the National Bolshevist. But they are definitely people who would wring the necks of the small time local 'Gruppenleitern'. There are, of course, any number amongst them who would swing round purely on account of external circumstances and who would say: 'I must earn my money and support my family' – but there are others amongst them, foremen, for example, in whom I would have complete faith; not that they will make much fuss outwardly, of course, but . . . a sort of movement – active member, let's say, who will work in secret.

FATHER: What good is that?

SON: There are many farmers and so on who, in my opinion would do the same. It depends, of course, on the district.

SON (*re demobilisation of German units*): Take the best mountain 'Divisionen', take the paratroop 'Divisionen', the 'Waffen-SS-Divisionen', the better 'Panzerdivisionen', those are all units which mainly have considerable fighting spirit left, and to a certain extent still have capable, young, idealistic officers, the greater number of whom are experienced, old mountain troops, paratroops and so on, and who are mainly or exclusively volunteers. How are you going to demobilise these units when you can't even promise them decent treatment at the hands of the occupying troops? You can rely on it that

I wouldn't give up my tommy-gun either, even though I didn't know
at the moment for what purpose I needed it. I should stick a few
thousand rounds of ammunition in my dispatch case and also my
tommy-gun, nicely taken apart, and take it with me. Who knows for
what I may need it. If I were demobilised I should collect so-and-so
many Swabian soldiers from the neighbourhood and say to them:
'Come along, we don't know what's going on down there, but it's quite
possible that we can do something in one way or another, and if there
are a few tommy-guns lying around, take them along by all means. My
men would have done that.

[. . .]

Document 38

GRGG 201 (c) [TNA, WO 208/4364]
Provisional report on CS/443 Generalleutnant HEIM (Commander, Boulogne) –
Captured 23 Sept. 44 in Boulogne.

RAMCKE: We know perfectly well that if we capitulate now, we should
experience the same consequences, whether from the east or from your
side, as are expressed in the old Roman saying 'vae victis' (woe to the
conquered!). For that reason I maintain that it is better to go down with
honour, that's to say, better to fight to the end, and then you can wipe
us off the face of the earth. But in my frank opinion I should consider it
to be a mistake to *capitulate* without more ado. I did not just capitulate
in BREST, but fought to the last round of ammunition, and I hope from
the bottom of my heart that my German people at home will maintain
sufficient strength to the end to defend every foot of ground, every
bridge, every mountain ridge, and every town to the last. Then, as far as
I'm concerned you can blot us off the map and destroy us, that would
not matter, as then at least we should have gone down with honour.
That's my personal point of view. I hope that my people and nation at
home – regardless of whether they are under the leadership of Adolf
HITLER or some other statesman – will find the strength to defend
themselves to the last under these conditions, because from the
situation in 1918 we learnt the lesson that if we capitulate we are
supervised and have everything taken away from us anyhow.

ELSTER: It is time for us to make peace. What are we still fighting for?
HEYKING: I'll tell you. We are in the same position as CHURCHILL was
when the English were having such a hell of a time. CHURCHILL
couldn't make peace either, because he knew only too well that he
would be in for it then, and the Party, which does actually constitute
our command now, HIMMLER etc, can't make peace either, because
they know for a fact that they will be hanged if they do.

ELSTER: Nobody would make peace with them anyhow.

HEIM: I am absolutely convinced that we shan't get home for a long time after the war is over.

RAMCKE: That applies to me most particularly. In the eyes of the people here I am branded 'a diehard Nazi'. I wonder if I shall *ever* get home?

Document 39

CSDIC (UK), GRGG 203

Report on information obtained from Senior Officers (PW) on 26–7 Sept. 44 [TNA, WO 208/4363]

THOMA: RAMCKE is a fervent Nazi.

HEYKING: He's abusing them now, though.

THOMA: 'Now' is too late. However, he is a good soldier, a courageous NCO!

[. . .]

RAMCKE: I mean to say that, however bad things looked, and however little I might have been in sympathy with the Nazi system, in this case I was a soldier and had to fight; there was nothing for me but to by *all means* to defend the town of BREST until the last shot had been fired and only to surrender BREST to the Americans after it had been reduced to ruins. That is a fortress commander's duty. I did it until the last, according to my oath and duty and in order to uphold the honour of German arms. Whether this was right or of any advantage in view of the general political situation, no one can judge.[97]

Document 40

CSDIC (UK), GRGG 204

Report on information obtained from Senior Officers (PW) on 27–9 Oct. 44 [TNA, WO 208/4364]

REIMANN: The business with the Jews in GERMANY was quite right, only it should have been done quietly. Anyway, I'm very pleased that the English suffered a real blow at ARNHEM.[98]

[. . .]

CHOLTITZ: Have you read CHURCHILL's speech? *Appalling*, beyond all words! A Jewish brigade to go to GERMANY! Then the French will take the West and the Poles the East. The hate in that speech! I am completely shattered.[99]

NEUFFER: Don't forget that the man was probably still somewhat worked up about the ARNHEM business.

SCHLIEBEN: Well, we've known for a long time that the enemy won't present us with any bouquets.

Document 41

CSDIC (UK), GRGG 204
Report on information obtained from Senior Officers (PW) on 27–9 Oct. 44 [TNA, WO 208/4364]

SCHLIEBEN: Yes, but look, BROICH, KÄHLER (P/W), for instance, is quite sure that we shall win. KÄHLER is as firmly *convinced* that we shall win as you and I are that we *can't*.

ELFELDT: But the Navy has no insight into Army matters.

BROICH: In the first place they've no insight into the Army and, second, they form the wrong impression of tactics and war potential.

Document 42

CSDIC (UK), GRGG 209
Report on information obtained from Senior Officers (PW) on 7–10 Oct. 44 [TNA, WO 208/4364]

TRESCKOW: At LE HAVRE I had a Kapitän PALMGREEN[100] who was in command of some flotilla. He had got the Oak Leaves about 15 June, but he wasn't summoned to the FÜHRER's Headquarters until much later, in August I believe. He was one of the last to get back again from there. He arrived there and got the Oak Leaves and saw the FÜHRER in person. He said there were eight of them and they had sat at a table having tea with him for three-quarters of an hour. The FÜHRER had described the general situation in the most glowing colours. He said to them that the new weapons were just nearing completion, it could only be a matter of seconds before things got going with a swing. We were all glad to hear that and rejoiced over it. One is always ready to believe.

WÜLFINGEN: Yes, one always hopes against hope. I still do now. I can't believe that all this should come to nothing.

TRESCKOW: In my opinion, it's a question of sticking everything on one throw.

WUELFINGEN: Only I don't know on what the people are staking everything now. They are causing the German people to be completely wiped out.

TRESCKOW: Probably they are building up to a grand finale of the 'Twilight of the Gods'.

BAO: We believe we are faced with two serious problems: first, with an underground movement of the Party and secondly with an underground movement of the Armed Forces, similar to the secret 'Black Reichswehr' after the last war.

RAMCKE: I'll tell you something: imagine the tables turned, and ENGLAND had had all her towns destroyed in the same way as we have in GERMANY today; then the Germans had come over and occupied the country, for five, ten or fifteen years maybe. Imagine the country faced with great economical difficulties, etc. The German occupation authorities are in charge. What would the English do? They'd look on *every single* German in the occupation force as an arch-enemy; they'd create stumbling blocks for *every* German coming their way and either stick a knife in his ribs, poison him or bump him off in some way or another. You may rest assured of it that if the English and Americans occupy the country and even if they take French or Czechs, etc., to do it, they won't be able to annihilate a population of eighty million; they can't kill the lot of us.

You can take it from me that the German people have been convinced since the 1914–18 period to the very bedrock of their beliefs that it's the Germans who are always the victims of attack. This time RUSSIA attacked us (sic), ENGLAND attacked us and AMERICA, whom we have never harmed at all, also attacked us. War is being waged against us from all quarters.[101] It has created a feeling of *utter enmity* against *all* these powers in the *entire* German people. The Germans will say: 'Well, what do you want? Our towns are in ruins anyhow; you're welcome to come with your air force and smash them up still more, but we'll do in your men on the ground!'

BAO: No one has anything left to lose.

RAMCKE: Yes, they will say: 'We have nothing to lose! We'll stab this fat American in the back and take his coat; then at least I'll have a coat!' The Americans thought they'd enter GERMANY and penetrate up to the SIEGFRIED LINE – then they'd plaster us with bombs and a revolution would break out in GERMANY; the Germans would kow-tow and the Americans would say: 'We only wanted to fight the *Nazis* and not the German people; therefore we shall be welcomed as harbingers of peace. We'll throw the Nazis out and then we'll establish peace in no time.' That is a sadly mistaken conclusion. Just think what kind of people are in the SS. From an honest *soldier's* point of view, I personally *utterly* condemn Gestapo measures and those of the SS police organisations. It isn't German. But nowadays the SS, the *'Waffen'* SS, not those few police organisations, contains the flower of German youth. It contains Counts So-and-so, the sons of Baron So-and-so, sons of the old German, Prussian nobility,[102] real good thoroughbreds, the best youth GERMANY has, the flower of her yeomanry, etc., Anglo-Saxons, Schleswig-Holsteiners, Lower Saxons, etc., lads from STYRIA and peasants' sons from the mountains; they're all in the SS. And then you keep saying: 'The SS, always the SS!' Who is it you're hitting at? The best stock in GERMANY!

Do you know, the Americans and English and the rest made a *terrific* bloomer that time, which we *never* could understand or forget: the war was over in 1918 and the 'fourteen points' had been laid down; first of all there were the armistice conditions, then came the reparations conditions; then, from a people which had suffered from a four years' blockade, which had had to submit to having *all* its imports cut and possessed only 'ersatz' materials, with even those in terribly short supply, and which was already burdened with a catastrophically high mortality rate among old people and babies, from that people were filched during 1920 and 1921 two hundred thousand milking cows, and the blockade was kept up for three more years.[103] Those three years of blockade plus the handing-over of those two hundred thousand milking cows and of all the other things we urgently needed, especially railway wagons, to distribute at least what we had got and transfer the potato harvest quickly from the east to the west, all that cost our country five hundred thousand human lives.[104] That was the cold-blooded murder, *sheer* murder which wasn't made public. But this is blazoned out to the whole world: 'See how the Germans have treated the Jews! Look how they destroyed that village in CZECHOSLOVAKIA.' When HEYDRICH was murdered:[105] 'Look at those poor people!' But not a word was said about how those five hundred thousand people were murdered in *cold blood* during the years of 1919–20.

Document 43

CSDIC (UK), GRGG 210
Report on information obtained from Senior Officers (PW) on 11–12 Oct. 44
[TNA, WO 208/4364]

CHOLTITZ: I don't put it past HITLER to introduce the plague into GERMANY. Just imagine it: he takes half-a-dozen or so SS men and makes them wander about somewhere at the back of AACHEN, spreading the plague around. If the English and Americans catch it and don't know how or from where, I wonder whether they would stay?[106]
SCHLIEBEN: That's the question.
CHOLTITZ: Admittedly it would hit the German people as well, of course. But he's perfectly capable of it!
SCHLIEBEN: Yes.
CHOLTITZ: He has himself inoculated first, and the tiny quantity of lymph which is available, since he is the only one who has prepared for it, will go to the men in the party.
SCHLIEBEN: Yes, it's really quite a good idea.
CHOLTITZ: (*laughs*).
SCHLIEBEN: To spring a trap on those fellows with it at the end, when everything is lost.

CHOLTITZ: A *good* idea?

SCHLIEBEN: Well, I mean as a last resort, before everything – or don't you think so?

CHOLTITZ: The only thing is that our own people would be done in by it, too.

SCHLIEBEN: Yes, that's the rotten thing about it. What one ought to have are weapons to which one is immune oneself and which hurt only the other fellow.

BASSENGE: What do you think of HIMMLER's speech?[107]

WAHLE: It dates back to June. I didn't know that this morning, and then I don't understand how the man can make a speech to a 'Division' and give them tactical instructions.

BASSENGE: The whole idea is a bit of a puzzle to me too. In *that* respect I greatly regret that attempted 'Putsch', because the Party will once again use *that* to full advantage when the crash comes, the fact that the 'Generals' sabotaged and so on.

WAHLE: That's why I am very glad that the attempted 'Putsch' failed.

BAO: Now HIMMLER says that the senior German officers are to blame for everything.

CHOLTITZ: Now we are all to blame, of course, that's what they are getting at. The amazing thing is that the only people who are really capable of adjusting themselves to life after the war, with clear judgement, are the officers, and only the older officers at that, the younger ones are crazy too. We have got some completely stupid men here too, they often get up foaming with rage and leave the room if anyone listens to the English broadcasts. It just makes me roar with laughter. It is really incredible, but, you know, we must reckon with people like that, they do exist. We can't simply shoot everyone in GERMANY.

MOSEL (*re listening to BBC*): It ought to be forbidden completely here. If they wanted to hear the English news in English then I wouldn't say anything against it, but that they switch on this absolute provocative propaganda!

KÄHLER: That was the first thing I was told here: that everyone was free to do exactly as he liked.

RAMCKE: They told me we could do what we liked and so on and that here they had to hear something of the world, otherwise they wouldn't be told the truth.

KÄHLER: Of course, that's obvious: everything German is a lie, everything English is the truth. Admittedly they are inclined to say that it isn't all true, but of course it is much truer than what GERMANY reports.

MOSEL: Then that 'Lagerpost' which is always coming in.[108]

RAMCKE: Yes, that's a piece of impudence –

MOSEL: It's a *filthy rag.*

RAMCKE: What business have they got to give us such a thing? It is written by the English, I don't read it at all.

MOSEL: Neither do I.

RAMCKE: I once had a look to see what it was and then I threw it away.

KÄHLER: It's not worth it, it's better to put it straight into the fire, because it always leaves some idea behind, that is what has always happened here, which we have seen again and again.

RAMCKE: If it goes on like that for a couple of years, I shall go quite crazy.

KÄHLER: Yes.

Document 44

CSDIC (UK), GRGG 211
Report on information obtained from Senior Officers (PW) on 14–17 Oct. 44
[TNA, WO 208/4364]

CHOLTITZ: We are also to blame. We have cooperated and have almost taken the Nazis seriously. We've been on visiting terms with them, we've allowed them to greet us on railway stations and have put up with their stupidities instead of saying: 'Oh, leave us alone.' We've let those stupid cattle talk and chatter to us.

I've persuaded my men to believe in this nonsense and caused those people who still regarded the Officer Corps as something worth respecting, to take part, without due consideration. I feel *thoroughly* ashamed. Maybe we are *far more* to blame than those uneducated cattle who in any case never hear anything else at all.

SCHLIEBEN: No war was ever started or waged with as little forethought as this one, which is carried on with the slogan: 'It'll be all right.' It started like that in 1941: 'You might attack over there and break through and then go straight on to the SEA of AZOV; it'll work out all right!'

CHOLTITZ: It wouldn't be so bad if we Generals, or the generation before us, for that matter, hadn't taken part. The trouble is that we participated without a murmur; BRAUCHITSCH and those fellows.

SCHLIEBEN: Did you know that BRAUCHITSCH received money?[109]

CHOLTITZ: Yes I know that those fellows got HITLER to sack others; REICHENAU and RUNDSTEDT got BRAUCHITSCH sacked. REICHENAU quitted[110] and now HITLER is carrying on on his own; he won't let anyone lead anymore and now it can't be done. We weren't any good anymore. The moment an officer heard that BRAUCHITSCH had accepted money he should have started proceedings against the man who told him; he should have immediately demanded proof, both then and now.

Document 45

CSDIC (UK) SR REPORT, SRGG 1065 [TNA, WO 208/4169]

Generalleutnant VON BROICH (GOC 10th Panzer Division) – Captured 12 May 43 in Tunisia.
Generalmajor BASSENGE (GOC Air Defences Tunis & Bizerta) – Captured 9 May 43 in Tunisia.
Generalleutnant VON SCHLIEBEN (Commander, Cherbourg) – Captured 26 June 44 in Cherbourg.
General der Infantrie VON CHOLTITZ (Commander, Paris) – Captured 25 Aug. 44 in Paris.
General der Fallschirmtruppen RAMCKE (Commander, Brest) – Captured 19 Sept. 44 in Brest.
Generalleutnant HEIM (Commander, Boulogne) – Captured 23 Sept. 44 in Boulogne.
Information received: 16 Oct. 44

RAMCKE: I was ordered to report to Hermann GOERING. I arrived, but the one who was not there was the 'Reichsmarschall'. Where was he, then? At Karinhall.[111] Karinhall is in SCHORFHEIDE; it is the magnificent hunting lodge, the greatest German art museum we have at the moment (*laughter*). I arrived there at twelve o'clock and BRAUCHITSCH, his Adjutant, told me that there had been a stormy session about fighters on the previous day, and in that stormy session 'the milk (MILCH) had turned sour' – Feldmarschall MILCH's[112] position had been shaken, you see. He said that the session had lasted for five hours and HERMANN had stormed and raged. As a result, by midday he had not finished sleeping, so my audience was postponed until five o'clock in the afternoon. Meanwhile I walked through that wonderful wood and had a look at everything, including the entire 2 cm 'Flak-kompanie' which was stationed there as a protection, instead of being at the MÖHNE dam;[113] I looked at that, too, and at the 'Bunker' which had been built all over the wood as air-raid shelters, and also at all the young soldiers, who were brushing away the leaves with brooms and so on from the asphalt roads which have been built there. I had a look at that, too. Then I had a good lunch in a small mess in the wood there. It was built beside a small lake and was quite pleasant. It was a small mess built for the GAF constructional staff who built Karinhall.

Well, anyhow, finally I was there at five o'clock and was given tea and some small sandwiches by BRAUCHITSCH in the anteroom, and there I met that arch-fool of the GAF, Generaloberst LOERZER,[114] who is so stupid that the geese bite him and is so lazy – (*laughter*) – he is now 'head of the recruitment and national education of the GAF'; that's what he calls himself; that's his latest job, with the rank of 'Generaloberst'. Apart from that, he's too lazy to sign his own name (*laughter*). Well, there he was, sitting there, and my adjutant was there too and I had to pay my respects to LOERZER. A conversation was begun and I spoke my mind to him, first of all about personnel difficulties in the paratroops and the faulty selection of men and so on. So it went on; we had plenty of time and still we weren't called in. He said: 'Does the chief know that? You must tell all that to the chief'. Well, to cut a long story short, it was finally getting on towards seven o'clock and then they said that the art experts were there and my turn would not come until a little later; the art experts are there all day long, morning, noon and night, showing off some new Gobelin tapestry or a new picture or a new statue or a new painting which they have found in some corner of EUROPE; and then the most important service decisions are left in abeyance until the design for the new tapestry and so on has been properly settled. Well, I was in a towering rage and there I was dressed in my paratroop trousers, in field uniform!

Finally I was asked to go in. I must show you (*peals of laughter*): I came in like this, here was a long library, perhaps 18 m long, and at the side it was all filled with magnificent volumes; here was a bookcase and there some bookshelves, a globe – in the middle there was a table and here a cosy corner and there a nook for reading and there more bookshelves, and then again there was a huge great oil painting – in fact it was a magnificent library. As I was coming in, who should come in through the other door, very quietly and cautiously like a servant, but LOERZER. He didn't come in like a 'Generaloberst', but like a lackey. Then I had another look and there were two little girls playing there, KARIN and her friend.[115] Here I saw a lighted lamp and a seat, with someone sitting there – something fat was sitting under the lamp – and I came in (struts across the room) like this and said: 'Generalleutnant RAMCKE, commander of the Second Paratroop "Division", reports present and ready for duty.' Below a rather rosily shaded lamp, a figure rose and emerged from a wonderful seat with a book – a breviary, bound in red morocco with gold tooling, very handsome, with a wonderful bookplate in it – there the figure stood and I thought: is it NERO II or is it a Chinese mandarin? (*laughter*). He stood up and it was HERMANN, dressed in a large coat down to his ankles, wide and voluminous, in silky green plush, stamped with gold emblems, the sleeves gathered into many tucks, tied with a golden girdle and bound with a golden hem, and with gold tassels hanging down, with patent-leather pumps on his feet, his hair waved like this and his face rosy and shiny – not powdered white – and 'beautiful'; you could recognise the work of the hairdresser, I believe you could clearly recognise the fingerprints of the fashionable coiffeur. A cloud of all the perfumes of the orient and occident met you half-way exuding over his fat cheeks . . . 'Well, RAMCKE, how are you?' With that, he slumped back into his large chair and took up the little book again with a weary, careless, nonchalant movement of his hand and looked into it again to see how far he had read. Meanwhile LOERZER sat down – I sat down in a chair – LOERZER remained on the edge of his chair the whole time, about three-quarters of an hour (*general laughter*) and was addressed as 'du' by HERMANN, although I *never* heard him use 'du' in return. I sat like this (demonstrating).

Then it began. I had a closer look and thought: 'Good Heavens, surely I know that coat. I've got it at home on a lampshade!' That was it all right – and I couldn't help smiling to myself and thinking: 'HERMANN, old man, I know exactly where you got that silk plush coat with the printed emblems!' It was like this: At TAORMINA first the 'Fliegerkorps' and then immediately afterwards 'Luftflotte 2', LOERZER, set up their headquarters,[116] and that place TAORMINA was originally an old Norman castle of the 'Hohenstaufen' period. The former monastery, which was still standing, had been turned into a first-class foreign tourist haunt, the Hotel Domenico. That is the favourite resort of all Americans, who like to bask in the sun of ancient European culture and so on. There they are fitted out by those good business men, the Italians, with the latest wardrobes in the old European style and so on. Making the most of their opportunity, a couple of sexual perverts had settled there, Germans, and had opened one of those shops there too, a large art salon where they held exhibitions. One of them was a painter and the other was a dress designer. They had a shop in the town and I got a lamp shade there; it was printed silk stuck on a sort of parchment. It looks very pretty when the light shines through it. There are ships on it here, and then all round it stylised trees and an emperor or king mounted on horseback, with a falcon on his wrist, followed by a noble lady, also carrying a falcon on her wrist, then a falconer and a few more noble ladies scattered around, and then the whole thing repeated again. These designs which I had on my lamp, HERMANN had all down his coat –

ALL: (*Laughing helplessly*)

RAMCKE: Then silk stockings and a most beautiful clasp down here, and a bracelet dangling round his ankle.

ALL: (*Laughing*)

RAMCKE: Then *here* he had a big green emerald, matching the green of the silk, and *here* it was all platinum and diamonds – I don't know how many there were and on each hand at least two, if not three rings. Then in the centre there were gold tassels, set with stones, hanging down and tied in a knot here.

BROICH: What was it supposed to represent?

BASSENGE: That's 'costume 4', I know three already.

RAMCKE: Then the story started and I unburdened myself and said to
him: 'Herr Reichsmarschall, even during the greatest crises on the
Eastern Front in the winters of 1941/42 and 1942/43, when every man
was needed, the army with difficulty refrained, and rightly so, from
drawing on the instructional units, on the experimental reserve for the
training of future units. But we paratroopers drew on our reserves until
we'd bled ourselves white'. 'How?' he asked. I replied: '"Bataillone"
and "Stormtruppen" for the field "Divisionen" were formed from the
"Divisionen"; a whole "Bataillon" was formed from the experimental
and instructional troops, in fact they didn't even stop at the 550
transport glider pilots, who had been at the RHÖNKUPPE since they
were fifteen, being trained as pilots and stunt fliers, in order to bring
the heavy, troop-filled transport aircraft to the right places. They were
formed into *one* "Bataillon", sent to AFRICA within four days, and after
the first few days' operations those valuable people were wiped out and
annihilated in ordinary ground fighting.' He knew nothing about all
that. He had never yet seen any paratroops. Do you think he'd ever
seen a parachutist jump? Never. Thereupon he said: 'Here, LOERZER,
write this down'.

CHOLTITZ: How did he speak? In a tired voice?

RAMCKE (*Imitating* GÖRING's *nasal and high voice*): 'I knew nothing
about all that. Do you know anything about it? Well, we'll write it
down first. Now, what else?'

CHOLTITZ: Were the children playing around meanwhile?

RAMCKE: Yes, that's coming! (*Laughter*). I said: 'We haven't even got the
right foundation for the training of our paratroops; all our paratroop
officer cadets were trained at GAF battle schools; they learnt about
long-range reconnaissance operations and fighters and all that sort of
thing that we don't need at all, and what they needed to know as
"Zugführer" and "Kompaniefführer" for ground fighting, they never
learnt at all. We ought to have a training of an army nature, for
preference at the Army battle schools!' Then he blew up: (*imitating*
GOERING) 'Well, that's the last straw, if you give people an inch they
take an ell, I admit that the paratroops should really be part of the Army,
as indeed they should be, but I'm glad that I have them under my own
wing in the GAF, so that they are steeped in the spirit of the GAF. The
honour and glory and the training are not enough; it's the spirit which
counts! In the same way, for instance, the French revolutionary army
that time in PARIS simply swept away all the old French guards who'd
had years of training.' As an unimportant 'Divisionskommandeur' it
wasn't my place to point out to the 'Reichsmarschall' that he was
making a mistake in his history, and that the revolution wasn't carried
out by a young army against the royal guards, but *with* the royal guards
except for a few units, and that NAPOLEON, the greatest general of the

Revolution, had had a careful training in the old Royalist days, as had also his Generals, who carried out the revolution. But it wasn't my place to lecture him on all that!

BROICH: That wouldn't be in the spirit of National Socialism either!

RAMCKE: To cut a long story short, he flared up: 'Never! How on earth did you get that idea? For the sake of the cause I had to say that wasn't what was meant; I only meant that it ought to be like that as regards the nature of the training; as a result the best paratroop officers who have come from the Army and have a long fighting experience should have a special school for future paratroop officers, attached to a GAF battle-school – (imitating GOERING): 'Yes, I realise that, GAF battle schools – write it down at once – the best must be taken for it so as to . . . – special courses for future paratroop officers, etc.' Suddenly KARIN came running up and said: 'Daddy, my pearl necklace is all broken; look, I have found all the pearls!' He started: 'Oh dear, your lovely pearl necklace'. Everything was fixed and the child was kissed very dramatically. 'Give Daddy another kiss here', GOERING said, turning his greasy cheek towards her. After that the little 'Princess' had to go. All that happened whilst a divisional commander was making his official report and during a conference about important service matters. (Laughter).

[. . .]

Document 46

CSDIC (UK), GRGG 219
Report on information obtained from Senior Officers (PW) on 4–6 Nov. 44 [TNA, WO 208/4364]

CHOLTITZ: We can't make out THOMA any more. How can the man say the things he does and even tell us at table: 'The German people and the German Army have lost their honour'?

BASSENGE: What am I supposed to do about it?

CHOLTITZ: The two of you are like Tweedledum and Tweedledee. It's really the case that you and he are to some extent a single entity. There's nothing that can be done about that.

BASSENGE: That's nonsense.

CHOLTITZ: You must often have realised that yourself, that you are one entity.

BASSENGE: I don't know about that.

CHOLTITZ: To get down to a concrete case: recently someone told me that you had actually stated at table that the quick promotion of some Generals was probably due to their lack of character and their readiness to shout 'Heil HITLER'. You're so far removed from soldierliness that the idea no longer enters your head that a form of military ability still exists which can lead to promotion. As true as that I'm standing here, I never saw HITLER before my promotion. I did actually see him once before 1933, but I've never spoken to him. I don't know a single one of the whole crowd, and yet that man THOMA – he is the one we blame for not taking any action, for he'd been to school with them all, he was on terms of intimacy with them all, and knew that we had joined up with criminals – he's the one who gets up, and you talk about our lack of character in accepting promotion. After all, promotion usually comes only through one's superior.

BASSENGE (*to* BROICH): Then CHOLTITZ said: 'Good God, do we have to keep sucking up to the English?' I said: 'Look here, what do you mean by that?' 'These English swine are being sucked up to the whole time here', and so on. I said: 'Look here, I'm not standing that. I don't suck up to the English, but I do a whole lot of jobs in the interests of us all, and there's no question of sucking up about it. I won't take that from you.' 'Incidentally,' he said, 'you can take it from me that reports in code about THOMA are already on their way to GERMANY.' I said: 'Oh? That's very interesting,' and he added, 'and about you, too.' I told him: 'You can write what you like.' He replied: 'Certain Navy people have their code for use in letters and the reports are already on their way.'

Document 47

CSDIC (UK), GRGG 222
Report on information obtained from Senior Officers (PW) on 13–14 Nov. 44
[TNA, WO 208/4364]

REIMANN: What a sound movement National Socialism was at the beginning! We worked like slaves for the Nazis. If only they'd waited another twenty or thirty years we'd have had everything.
ELFELDT: A pity those fellows made such a mess.
REIMANN: At the start I used to think that things wouldn't turn out badly. You can't make omelettes without breaking eggs! In my opinion, the early mistakes were only superficial.

Document 48

CSDIC (UK), GRGG 225
Report on information obtained from Senior Officers (PW) on 18–19 Nov. 44
[TNA, WO 208/4364]

[. . .]
EBERDING: The FÜHRER has no eye for the right powers: we made an error of judgement over both RUSSIA and ITALY. Today of course one can say

– as quite a number here are doing – that we should never have started the war but, in my opinion, how else were we to get rid of the VERSAILLES Treaty?[117]

Document 49

CSDIC (UK), GRGG 226
Report on information obtained from Senior Officers (PW) on 20–1 Nov. 44
[TNA, WO 208/4364]

MEYER: Of one thing I'm certain, that a lot has altered as a result of my being taken prisoner . . . has altered as regards the actual facts.

BASSENGE: If I'd been as wise five years ago as I am today.

MEYER: I must say that my eyes were only opened after the FALAISE encirclement.

   If this partition plan really is put into effect then I'm afraid that the Russians will take the whole of the area east of the ELBE and the Western Powers will take the western area. I think, therefore, one can write off the area east of the ELBE.

BASSENGE: Well, they won't exterminate the people, because they won't be able to populate the area.

MEYER: It's not a question of the space, but of the people. We know that the Russians can be just as ruthless with people as they would be with the clearing of a forest.

   I'm certain of one thing, even if it's purely instinctive rather than reasoned, and that is that the fate of the German people is closely linked with that of the British people. I'll go further: I believe that one fine day not only the British people, but the so-called Western Democracies will have to stand with us against Bolshevism. I think the Democracies already have their worries on that point.

MEYER: There is no one who could take HITLER's place.

BASSENGE: Yes, but what does the *majority* of the Party, including the SS, Gestapo and whatever else there is, think about things? Are they unanimous in their outlook?

MEYER: I can judge as little as you can, because we two have been away from home for years and are not in close contact with the Party. During the few days I spent in the REICH I didn't see any signs of divergences of opinion within the Party or the Government. Everyone was abusing the next higher authority. The 'Gauleiter' groused about the Home Secretary, who was FRICK at the time[118] – HIMMLER is Home Secretary at present – they complained that the Home Office sabotaged everything, all measures; and the troops groused but you'll know that yourself. We complained as much as any other 'Division'.

BASSENGE: I didn't actually mean measures, but just in general. We are

living under a dictatorship which can only be maintained as long as
there is Praetorian guard who give it their unconditional support. It
works only within limits as is proved by history.

MEYER: They hold different views though. The FÜHRER has actually
succeeded in retaining *the faith* of the German people in him: not the
FÜHRER as much as his 'Gauleiter' etc., who have made a demi-god of
the FÜHRER and the German people – I was last on leave in May and
above all my realisation in PW camps – has utmost faith in the
FÜHRER. As long as this faith exists no-one in the REICH, whether he is
a member of the Armed Forces, an industrialist or a politician, or a
member of the Party – it makes no difference at all – is in a position to
change the system as long as the FÜHRER is alive. It's impossible.[119]

BASSENGE: That was what those, who wished to do away with the
FÜHRER on 20 July, realised.

MEYER: It is just as crazy to say that the Army would repudiate HITLER
and the 'Waffen-SS' take his part.[120] That's *utter* madness! The simple
soldier, the majority of them have faith in the FÜHRER and are prepared
to carry out any order he gives. I established that fact for myself in the
PW camps too. The people have no longer any faith in anything. We
mustn't forget that the people heard the FÜHRER's call when in the
depths of despair; they were lifted from their misery and led; all
they've ever heard is: the FÜHRER, that great man, have faith etc.; the
greatest man in our history. If someone wished to succeed *after all
that*, he'd have to have an even better gift of the gab than GOEBBELS of
the FÜHRER. It would take years, perhaps even decades, before the
masses would recognise this new personality. He might become a go-
between or an administrator for the people, but nothing more, *without*
full support of the people. After the collapse the German people will
be entirely –

BASSENGE: Yes, the most significant feature of the German people today
is their complete apathy.

Document 50

CSDIC (UK), GRGG 231
Report on information obtained from Senior Officers (PW) on 6–7 Dec. 44 [TNA,
WO 208/4364]

WILDERMUTH: The only hope is that our army will say to the enemy:
'Look here, we'll pack up now in our common interest, so that we shall
have some peace and quiet as soon as possible.'

WILCK: In my opinion that will only be possible when at least a third of
GERMANY is actually occupied, and the whole thing is carried into
GERMANY from outside, with the help of German forces. It won't work
any other way.

WILDERMUTH: We can't wait until a third of GERMANY is occupied. The commanders at the front would have to –

WILCK: No, none of them would do that. It's quite out of the question that it will come from inside. It can only come from outside.

WILDERMUTH: RUNDSTEDT would have to do it.

WILCK: No, he won't do it.

WILDERMUTH: He was quite ready to do other things! The question is rather that he won't be able to do it!

WILCK: All right, even if he wanted to he couldn't. But he won't do it. I mean the German people and the troops have been too much caught up by all our propaganda.

WILDERMUTH: Well, those from the rank of 'Korpskommandeur' upwards must see a little further now.

WILCK: Yes.

WILDERMUTH: You know, half the army knew before 20 July –

WILCK: No, no!

WILDERMUTH: Yes, that something was going to happen. Then there was incredible amount of talk about it.

WILCK: Well, I don't believe it, but –

WILDERMUTH: All the 'Armeeführer' were asked beforehand.[121]

Document 51

CSDIC (UK), GRGG 233
Report on information obtained from Senior Officers (PW) on 12–16 Dec. 44
[TNA, WO 208/4364]

MEYER: What would happen suppose we were to say now in the east and west: 'This is the end; we surrender'?

WILDERMUTH: In any case the end of the war means the occupation of GERMANY, the loss of frontier districts –

MEYER: The eradication of the German race!

WILDERMUTH: The immediate need, Herr MEYER, is to put a stop at last to the eradication of the German race which is being brought about by the wrong policy of the National Socialists.

HEYKING: Whether National Socialism would be done away with even if HITLER did abdicate now, to which we are agreeable, then the question will also arise –

WILDERMUTH: Would these people who are now in power in GERMANY – would there be any place at all left in their hearts for the Fatherland? Would this idea have any other meaning for them at all than as a phrase to be used in their propaganda?

HEYKING: Even if the Nazis did retire, do you think we would lay down our arms, we would give in? You can bet your life that they (Allies) would eradicate us just the same, and would lay down exactly the same terms. We must hold out; there's only *one* way now.

WILDERMUTH: What do you mean by 'holding out' now?

HEYKING: We don't know that a revolution won't break out among the enemy, because they have no *desire* to fight any longer. What are the Americans fighting for? They're bound to ask themselves that some time.

WILDERMUTH: All right then we'll wait for the enemy to make a peace offer, the return of the colonies, FRANCE, CHERBOURG –

HEYKING: No, not that, but to enter into negotiations –

WILDERMUTH: But no one will negotiate with *that* government, nobody could negotiate with them.

HEYKING: It's no use talking to you. I've just told you that even if our government did resign now, there would be no peace in spite of that. We shall still hold out, and the German people will go through thick and thin and won't give in at all, and then when the enemy can't get any further they'll come to us to arrange terms.

MEYER: We can see that in GREECE now;[122] don't you think that the ordinary English people and the French and the Dutch and the Swiss etc. will gradually open their eyes – damn it all, what will happen if we have communist activity all over EUROPE?

WILDERMUTH: Don't you think that the English or Swiss man-in-the-street sees that *w e* have been the most active pacemaker of communism in EUROPE?

MEYER: EISENHOWER now has broadcast daily: 'The German churches will be opened.' Where is the German church closed?

WILDERMUTH: They didn't close any churches, but that the church has been persecuted with *every* means – it's a question of the elimination of a country in the heart of EUROPE, which has carried Russian methods right into that heart.

HEYKING: Herr WILDERMUTH, you've still got one man here who thinks as a German!

WILDERMUTH: But so do I.

HEYKING: After what you've said I can no longer credit you with that.

WILDERMUTH: I was speaking from the other people's point of view, and those things are the trump card which we *ourselves* have given them.

HEYKING: We were discussing what would happen if our government resigned. Do you think the German soldiers would lay down their arms and accept the conditions?

WILDERMUTH: No, we were speaking at cross-purposes.

HEYKING: No, we've experienced the 'fourteen points' *once*, we either die or –

WILDERMUTH: We shan't be able to agree on that point.

HEYKING: Either we shall die, or they will collapse in the process too.

WILDERMUTH: The thing that I'm concerned about is that we shall no longer have a chance to rise.

MEYER: Whether we capitulate or not –

HEYKING: We shall never rise again, you can depend on that. They've drawn up quite different peace terms from those after the last World War, I'm convinced of that.

WILDERMUTH: You may be right there. But we finally destroy all chance of rising again if we continue the actual fighting too long.

HEYKING: No, no, I'm for sticking it out because I say the fellows wont stay for ever on a given frontier – the Americans no longer know what they're fighting for, and if they suffer heavy casualties they'll say: 'Well, what am I really doing here?'

WILDERMUTH: It will be over in the spring, they will get through in the spring at the latest. Then it's all over.

HEYKING: Really, Herr WILDERMUTH, opinions like that!

MEYER: For shame!

HEYKING: I mean, after all, we're still German officers.

WILDERMUTH: Well, probably I'm the person here who has suffered most for GERMANY, and for that reason I have a right to expect people to listen to my point of view.

HEYKING: I don't dispute it, but all the same, one shouldn't take that as the only possibility.

Document 52

CSDIC (UK), GRGG 234
Report on information obtained from Senior Officers (PW) on 18 Dec. 44 [TNA, WO 208/4364]

BROICH: That is the last attempt. If that comes to nothing, then it is all up. If they are attacking on a 50 km front, that can never develop into a big break-through, besides here are the ARDENNES and you can't get any further there – I don't know what the Americans there are like – perhaps if they are taken by surprise they may be able to capture 20,000 Americans, if all goes well, but all I would say is that it will cause great inconvenience but I don't think that it will make much odds in the long run.[123]

Document 53

CSDIC (UK), GRGG 235
Report on information obtained from Senior Officers (PW) on 21–2 Dec. 44 [TNA, WO 208/4364]

HEIM: It will be like this: as with all his other illusions HITLER has really put his heart and soul into this affair and has done everything to this end. Perhaps it will be the last.

EBERBACH: It won't be his last. This man will never stop having illusions. When he is standing under the gallows he will still be under the illusion that he's not going to be hanged.

MEYER: I just hope that our offensive will succeed in finally splitting the British and Americans.
EBERBACH: I fear the opposite will be the case.
MEYER: I don't consider the offensive strong enough to bring about the decision in the West, and I consider an offensive in the West which is not strong enough to undermine all the Western partnerships to be very dangerous for us.
EBERBACH: Of course.

RAMCKE (to CHOLTITZ): This offensive is enormous. The German people will not be defeated. You watch, we will pursue the Allies right across France and hurl them into the Bay of Biscay."

Document 54

CSDIC (UK), GRGG 237
Report on information obtained from Senior Officers (PW) on 21–2 Dec. 44 [TNA, WO 208/4364]

MEYER: It is like this with the FÜHRER: I was with him and he began talking: one had to watch like a lynx in order to get a word in, and at that moment he began again and talked and talked and talked until – for half an hour, three-quarters of an hour – he brings up problems and shows you that things are not right after all. You go away and say to yourself: 'That's all right, he knows better.'
CHOLTITZ: No. I went away saying: 'I'm afraid he is mad.' (Laughter).[124]
MEYER: Then I found out one thing, that KEITEL and all the people there said on principle: 'Yes, my FÜHRER!' 'Yes, my FÜHRER!' 'Yes, my FÜHRER!' No matter what he said, they replied: 'Yes, my FÜHRER!' The moment a man arrived from the front – I don't know how it was with Generals – but KEITEL and the rest tried to influence the man as to what he should say.
CHOLTITZ: No, that didn't happen to me, of course I think I would have told him where he got off. (Laughter).
MEYER: I can truthfully say that I told the FÜHRER what I considered to be right. The last time I was there was in 1943. A great part of the blame lies with the FÜHRER's immediate entourage.[125]
CHOLTITZ: My dear fellow, I know a little too much about that to be able to agree with you and I must tell you of an excellent proverb which says: 'Every man gets what he deserves.' If I dismiss seven field-marshals because they tell me the truth, if I dismiss about thirty

commanding generals because they tell me the truth – that's asking too much – If I dismiss all those who tell me the truth – and who afterwards turn out to be right, and I still won't admit – When civilians at home say to me: 'You Generals are to blame,' I say: 'We? We didn't vote for *him*, it's you who always voted for him. We can't do anything about it if he's become *legally* Supreme Commander. We can't mutiny, you know!' 'Well then, who is to mutiny?' The Army knew it wouldn't work that way. This 'Putsch' of 20 July will be regarded as an event of historic significance. Those 1,500 men, hanged by these criminals, will all get a memorial dedicated to them, for they were the only patriotic, resolute and 'ready to act' men that we had. For they foresaw the utter desolation we were being led into, if things went n as they were.

Document 55

CSDIC (UK), GRGG 242
Report on the reaction of Senior Officers (PW) in Camp no. 11 to Hitler and Goebbels's New Year speeches, 31 Dec. 44/1 Jan. 45. [TNA, WO 208/4364]

THOMA: He was remarkably quiet today; he didn't shout once.[126]
BASSENGE: One may be biased – I hardly like to put it into words, but was really HITLER?
WAHLE: Oh, yes, definitely.
BASSENGE: Everything can be faked, even his voice.

WILCK: It keeps cropping up, in fact it's become a settled there with him: 'We survive as many things: such a People and such a Leader, who has patently been preserved by Providence, can never perish.'
WILDERMUTH: Yes, that's the straw to which he clings.
WILCK: Of course, and so do the others.
WILDERMUTH: All the same one can say that our present position looks exactly like our downfall.
WILCK: That's true enough. And when he speaks of 'thousands of "Volkssturmbataillone"' –
WILDERMUTH: Of raising new 'Divisionen' out of nothing – he'd have done better to bring the old ones up to strength instead.
WILCK: Yes. Incompletely armed, equipped and trained. It means spilling the last life drops of the German people. And as for 'sweeping away the old society and system, and (preserving) the ultimate Truth, the People' –
WILDERMUTH: The people, which he holds in rein with concentration camp, torture and prison!

THOMA: He didn't speak once of the soldiers in his army: it was the people all the time.

WAHLE: The German People's State, with the middle class eliminated, destroyed and exterminated –

THOMA: That's the bait to catch the people. But not a word about the fighting men.

WAHLE: Or at most one about the armchair generals.

THOMA: Yes, but otherwise he really hadn't a word of thanks for the Wehrmacht.

WAHLE: He didn't even mention them.

THOMA: It's really rather remarkable, for there's no doubt he produced some well-turned phrases.

BASSENGE: The speech was well thought out.

WAHLE: Well, after all, he's had plenty of time for that.

WAHLE: Don't you agree that these attempts of GOEBBELS to strike the ingratiating note arise from some degree of sentimentality? A sentimental mood. There was the hope of striking a responsive note from the enemy through this offensive started for political reasons. But a victorious enemy, only five minutes off success, will, of course, never treat with him. He knows that himself now, so there's nothing left to say but 'at any rate we shall never capitulate'. The National Socialists never *will* capitulate, either. And Heaven help anyone else who does! I conclude that the whole thing is a sign of our great weakness after all. Strong terms are used to lead the people on: 'hundreds of "Volkssturmbataillone" or "Volkswehrbataillone" are being formed.'

THOMA: 'Thousands of "Bataillone".'

WAHLE: It all bears the stamp of exaggeration. Besides that, the old belief is still there that the Allies will fall out among themselves; it's the same old belief in a miracle.

CHOLTITZ: All lies and deceit!

RAMCKE: But the speech will have a terrific effect all the same. The effect of GOEBBELS's speech will also be very great.

BRUHN: Now they say the Almighty is to give them victory.

FELBERT: What impudence!

BRUHN: As the BBC commentator very rightly said at 10.00 hrs (1 Jan.): 'On the statement that "if there is such a thing as justice we are bound to win the war" any comment would be superfluous.'

FELBERT: They have God's name on their lips every five minutes.

BRUHN: Beforehand they wouldn't have anything to do with Him.

FELBERT: GOEBBELS actually speaks of 'God'. Formerly they used to speak of 'Providence'; then it gradually became 'The Almighty'; now he speaks of 'God'. God is to do it all.

BRUHN: But God doesn't help those who slit the others' throats.

FELBERT: No, and he helps only the big battalions.

BRUHN: Our people are no sort of homogeneous body; they are a morally disrupted, though outwardly solid, badly trained force of men, unused to war and terribly weakened by losses.

FELBERT: (*sighs*)

VATERRODT: HITLER's speech was certainly impressive and completely convincing.

BRUHN: The first fact of note is that he spoke at all. Secondly, he spoke with great power, and one cannot entirely escape the influence of his powerful words, his faith and his vigour. At heart one is a German and would so dearly love everything to go well for us. That makes such a speech very moving, because it always puts into words the things which to us are holy. But in spite of all that, there is much in it to which circumstances give the lie, so that one finds oneself continually torn in different directions. GOEBBELS's speech a few days ago was simply disgusting.

VATERRODT: His speech yesterday (31 Dec.) was horrible, too. It was full of repetition.

BRUHN: It was frightful.

VATERRODT: Frightful!

Document 56

CSDIC (UK) SR REPORT
Extract from SR Draft No. 85 [TNA, WO 208/4210]

Generalmajor VATERRODT (Wehrmacht Kommandantur, Strasbourg) – Captured 25 Nov. 44 in Strasbourg.
Generalmajor BRUHN (Commander 553 Volksgren. Division) – Captured 22 Nov. 44 in Saverne.
Information received: 1 Jan. 45

BRUHN: The question of all German Generals being asked to surrender has also been discussed. A Swiss proposed the matter to SCHAEFER (PW) and VON FELBERT (PW). But I told them that that couldn't be reconciled with their honour, it couldn't possibly be done: it's absolutely out of the question. If I, as CO of a 'Division' say to my men 'tomorrow we surrender', they'll say the old boy has gone crazy over night; he's overworked; he's ill. The officer corps loves its country, and believes implicitly in its own respectability and ideas of honour and lives accordingly; and like a trusting child considers it quite impossible that it is being wrongly led, and that the command is other than it says it is, and that they have stained their hands with blood etc. in the most revolting way.

Document 57

CSDIC (UK) SR REPORT
Extract from SR Draft No. 87 [TNA, WO 208/4210]

General der Panzertruppe VON THOMA (GOC German Afrikakorps) – Captured 4
Nov. 42 in North Africa.
Generalleutnant SCHAEFER (Commander 244 Infantry Division) – Captured 28
Aug. 44 in Marseilles.
Information received: 1 Jan. 45

SCHAEFER: We negotiated with that American officer VAN BERGEN, a
  German-American,[127] but they don't understand the psychology of the
  German officer. I told him too: 'How can you do that when you are CO
  of a "Division" or a GOC; when you are responsible for your troops
  you can't simply say: "I'm not going to carry on any longer; I'm
  clearing off".'
THOMA: They (the Allies) wouldn't do that either.
SCHAEFER: They probably wouldn't do it either, but they expect us to do
  it; they imply by their attitude: 'it's ridiculous to carry on fighting; the
  whole of GERMANY will be smashed to bits.' I say that I would rather
  have peace today than tomorrow, but you can't persuade an officer
  simply to say: 'We'll arrange with the Americans: "You attack, and we
  won't fire".'
THOMA: Only the Supreme Command can do that.
SCHAEFER: I told them that too, but who would do that? We discussed
  things like that for days on end.

Document 58

CSDIC (UK), GRGG 247
Report on information obtained from Senior Officers (PW) on 10–14 Jan. 45
[TNA, WO 208/4177]

KITTEL: If we could ever get so far as to make the Russians stop!
HEYKING: I personally am of the opinion that the Russians only want to
  capture and occupy what they definitely need for afterwards, and that
  then the occupation of GERMANY – they'll get in there anyway. Why
  should they fight large-scale actions now? No! They are conserving
  their forces for their later – making us their jumping-off place against
  ENGLAND. They need their troops afterwards to be able to carry
  through their further plans. They haven't the slightest intention of
  carrying on a great offensive in EAST PRUSSIA now. They won't do it.
  They will now see to BUDAPEST and the BALKANS –

HEYKING: I keep saying: 'We must just hang on for another few months, for the tension between RUSSIA and the Anglo-Saxon States is *definitely* coming!' After all, we know what's happening. The Americans are saying: For what are we waging this war?' The Russians will never . . . them in the east – do you think that the Russians will allow the nimble Americans to establish themselves in the place of the English who used to control SHANGHAI?

KITTEL: No!

HEYKING: Of course not. It isn't for nothing that the Russians have already established their communistic influence in CHINA and that CHIANG KAI-SHEK has resigned.[128] He's put in his cousin as Regent and he himself is now only C-in-C. The communistic influence in CHINA has been systematically encouraged by RUSSIA. The Russians say to themselves: 'Better to be confronted by a broken-down Jap than a hearty American.' They want to pursue their trade in the Far East. They don't want to occupy the countries in the West, they merely want friendly governments who will work for them. Hence their influence in FRANCE through DE GAULLE, in SPAIN and God knows where, everywhere, in ITALY etc. To them it's all a jumping-off ground against the English. They also want the oil-fields in the PERSIAN GULF etc., after that they'll say they've got all they want. That will give them the trade and domination of the whole of EUROPE and the English can then do what they like. The Americans will say to themselves: 'There's nothing to be made in the Far East, there's nothing in EUROPE – what are we fighting this war in EUROPE for?'

KITTEL: For nothing!

HEYKING: For nothing! It's bound to dawn on them in time!

KITTEL: It *has* dawned on them!

Document 59

CSDIC (UK), GRGG 248
Report on information obtained from Senior Officers (PW) on 15–17 Jan. 45
[TNA, WO 208/4177]

SCHLIEBEN: We shall lose everything that has been built up since the time of FREDERICK THE GREAT: SILESIA, EAST PRUSSIA, the RHINELAND. Everything on account of one Austrian corporal. A whole nation is being ruined on account of one man.

ELFELDT: It's no use any more, the end is drawing near. Even the hope that the Russians and the Allies would quarrel, which one could still have in the autumn, must be given up now. The next four weeks will be frightful; everything will collapse then.

Document 60

CSDIC (UK), GRGG 249
Report on information obtained from Senior Officers (PW) on 18 Jan. 45 [TNA, WO 208/4177]

FELBERT: When everything is over in GERMANY those Nazi scoundrels will shout at the people: 'You have to thank only the Generals for this.' They're partly right, too, as the army leaders should have said long ago: 'thus far and no further!'

Document 61

CSDIC (UK), GRGG 253
Report on information obtained from Senior Officers (PW) on 26–7 Jan. 45 [TNA, WO 208/4365]

SCHLIEBEN: I can see quite clearly that all this Bolshevism is nothing but a colossal Jewish plot.

RAMCKE: One day history will say the FÜHRER was right in recognising this great Jewish danger threatening all nations and in realising the Jewish communist threat to EUROPE from the east.[129] At one time it was GENGHIS KHAN and at another ATTILA. This time it is Jewish Bolshevism spreading over EUROPE from the Asiatic steppes, a tide we *had to* stem. Perhaps future history will say that we of the small Western European countries were so short-sighted that we did not realise it and that FRANCE, BELGIUM and GERMANY quarrelled among themselves, with ENGLAND at the back of it all because of their petty opposing interests, on account of a ridiculous little CZECHOSLOVAKIA and SUDETENLAND and a lousy DANZIG CORRIDOR and such rubbish, and that we failed to realise the threat from the east. All this will show that we failed to realise the threat from the east. All this will show that the FÜHRER's general outline of policy was absolutely . . .

SCHLIEBEN: But he did it so stupidly.

RAMCKE: To think that *we*'ve been the fools, that after we saw we couldn't persuade the others to join the anti-comintern front in the fight against Bolshevism, *we* had to be the fools who were the *first* to rush in. That's the stupid part of it. The others refused to join in and suddenly we found ourselves forced to fight on two fronts.

SCHLIEBEN: We're picking the chestnuts out of the fire for them and have probably landed ourselves with ten million wounded.[130]

RAMCKE: It'll happen like this: I believe resistance may flicker up in the east now and again –

SCHLIEBEN: I have waged war against the Russians long enough. In my opinion all is up; the men *can't* carry on any longer.

RAMCKE: No, they can't and they don't want to, otherwise the Russians wouldn't have advanced so quickly. The men are exhausted. They have no reserves left, no fuel and they are not adequately equipped for the winter. They can't man the positions in sufficient numbers. The whole show is over. The men realise and know for certain that the offensive on the Western Front, of which they've been told to expect so much, has been a flop. So this is the end.

BAO: The German government must realise that all is lost. They must think of the people.

FELBERT: No. They have never considered the people.

BRUHN: The dreadful thing is that the people believe in them. We remained in the front line until we were captured; we too were dazzled and thought that others were decent too – we loved our country as a child loves its mother. But there are no decent people in the government: that has become obvious now. If at least they'd grab a grenade and themselves try and stop the Russians; instead of that they send children and old people to face the tanks. It is a criminal fight to preserve their own lives. They know that not a soul in the world would accept as much as a piece of bread from them; they have nowhere to live and now they're just prolonging their existences instead of shooting themselves. Fighting has lost all its chivalry. No one will negotiate with our government in whose hands are all the means of pressure, the wireless and the Press. The people all believe they'll be killed and violated.

FELBERT: First of all you have to realise all that has been done. We had no idea of the dirty business, done by our people and others, the Security Service and SS. In two wars no prisoner was ever as much as beaten in my presence; I never saw a Russian prisoner of mine shot; I *never once* saw a child, woman or man shot.[131]

BAO: German propaganda made HITLER into a sort of God, and now the people expect a miracle.

FELBERT: That's just the trouble.

BAO: They expected wonders from the V-1 and V-2 and now they're expecting them from these atom bombs and all that. They believe all that sort of thing.

FELBERT: It's all no good at all.

NEUFFER: If you judge the situation objectively and from a distance, it is as follows: they can do what they like, they are coming from the west and east as deliverers from the HITLER regime. They are the only ones who can rid us of the fellow.

THOMA: That's the great tragedy in our history, that we need such a terrible, lost war as this, in order to throw out the gang at home.

NEUFFER: But that is really what always follows dictatorships.

Document 62

CSDIC (UK), GRGG 254
Report on information obtained from Senior Officers (PW) on 28–31 Jan. 45
[TNA, WO 208/4365]

BRUHN: The things he said! He more or less attacked our families this
    evening.[132]

FELBERT: Yes.

BRUHN: Do you know what that *scandalous* fellow said: he said that tens
    of thousands and hundreds of thousands are being wiped out, he found
    no expression other than 'are being wiped out in the East at present'.
    But all that doesn't count. Another forty million can be wiped out so
    long as *he* is still there at the end, and he will see to it all right that
    chaos follows.

FELBERT: He will certainly see to that.

BRUHN: The same class of people as those involved in 20 July will appear
    again. The man is crazy.

FELBERT: If his aim had been to build up a decent German state, then I
    could have understood it. But that wasn't his aim. It has been built up
    by lying and cheating, *that* is the damnable part of it.

WAHLE: These are still the same old phrases, and apart from that,
    absolutely illogical. I could make exactly the same speech myself.

BASSENGE: So far as I can remember, this of all his speeches hangs
    together least, and everything is completely confused, and, apart from
    that, there was nothing in it.

WAHLE: It was perhaps the last.

BASSENGE: I hope so.

WAHLE: It is all just bluff, and also by this time he should leave
    prophesying alone – he has so often proved wrong. Now he is
    prophesying again about ENGLAND.

BASSENGE: 'This plebeian Jewish plutocratic – '

WAHLE: The well-known phrases. They don't become any more credible
    through everlasting repetition.

CHOLTITZ: I must say that speech is most significant for GERMANY.
    Those few who have any hope left at all can't see any other hope except
    in him. Eighty per cent of GERMANY does not believe any longer; the
    other 20 per cent – and that includes the fighting youth – believes only
    in him, because it can't see anything else. Of course he is crazy. We
    have known that for a long time now.

SCHLIEBEN: Fourteen years, one wouldn't think it possible.

SCHLIEBEN: The speech said comparatively little. It began again with the
    fourteen years, and I must say, in such a situation a drowning man

clutching at a straw. I think that it will have some effect only on those people who are still sitting in a safe place, but the masses who are now in flight will be furious. Those who are still in safety will say: 'Well, it will turn out all right somehow.' That's how I judge the speech.

WAHLE: In my opinion, what you say about clutching at a straw is absolutely true. He believes that he has been chosen by Providence. That is his last hope, and I must admit that he really believes it honestly. That is the straw by which it all hangs, and all the others who can still raise any faith in this belief, clutch at it with him. The refugees from the East, they don't believe in it any longer.

SCHLIEBEN: No, no, after all they have seen the whole mess-up, and then the cold – it all has its effect on them. He can't imagine what it's like because he's never been with the troops.

ULLERSPERGER: The whole point of the speech was to show the people at home and foreign countries that we shall fight to the end. Moreover, one thing is clear, and he's quite right over that. Whatever the outcome of the war, the English will be torn to pieces by the Bolshevists. It makes no odds whether it's now or in the next ten years. They will come to grief over their social problems.

EBERBACH: I can just imagine that my wife will act in accordance with this speech and will give her last ounce of energy, and ruin herself for the rest of her life, and my fifteen-year old-boy – [133]

HEIM: Because those people just can't see the sadness of it.

EBERBACH: Since the time of NORMANDY I've always tried to make it quite clear to her from here that HITLER has been completely mistaken in several things. I've tried to send hints to her by writing 'I am of exactly the same opinion as General VON GEYR';[134] she knows what I mean.

WILDERMUTH: The basis of it is honest this time. He says: 'I have been chosen by Providence and therefore all I can do is to stick it'. On that basis the speech is honest, and for that reason will have a better effect than others of his.

EBERBACH: But only those can see it through with him who also believe that he is the instrument of Providence. Perhaps he is, but in quite a different sense.

WILDERMUTH: He is our retribution for SADOWA[135] (laughter).

BROICH: I'm convinced that as a result of this war we shall lose altogether fifteen or eighteen millions.[136] That would do away with our twenty million surplus inhabitants.

EBERBACH: I'm practically certain the Russians will wipe out all their prisoners beforehand, while they're still on the roads.

BROICH: If the figures given are approximately correct, those two-hundred-and-eighty-thousand men, then they have – we have killed a great number too, and the people said they sometimes had orders to do so. Take our 'Division', 'Gross Deutschland' that time at KURSK – they murdered everyone wholesale.[137] We said: 'That's madness!' 'Well, what can we do with the PW,' they said. 'They only hinder our advance.' It's true, sometimes we didn't bother much about them; we just said: 'There, beat it!' They went away quite calmly but then they – we said: 'Guerrilla warfare is everywhere.' They said: 'Those we leave behind will become partisans in the Russian way, therefore the tank troops will shoot in the front line, all those we can't transport away from here.'

EBERBACH: I don't think the Russians are doing it just because we did, but simply because they have a desire for revenge.

BROICH: Yes, a desire for revenge and fear of partisans of course.

EBERBACH: The 'Sunday Times' says that the Russians already report the use of hand grenades by civilians and therefore they are forced to wipe out everyone.[138] What they so bitterly resented when we did it is now being done by them as a matter of course.

BROICH: Besides they maintain that we wiped out great numbers too.

EBERBACH: Any day now you can expect someone to say of his own accord: 'I won't carry on any more, we must finish it.' Any armistice would be better than this destruction.

BROICH: You must remember that, on the other hand, there are a lot of people who are very afraid they'll be hanged immediately.

EBERBACH: That's just it.

BROICH: They don't listen to the news as much as we do, but nevertheless, if the German wireless broadcasts: 'BEUTHEN has been evacuated, there is fighting to the north of BRESLAU' – if they announce that, everyone must realise what's up.

EBERBACH: It is very difficult –

BROICH: To know where to start; it could be done by the 'Korps' if the divisional commander agrees; every divisional commander will need to have a regimental commander in his 'Division' who is utterly in agreement with him, so that he could do it by issuing false orders; it isn't as difficult as all that.

EBERBACH: The English and Americans should be made to get a move on.

BROICH: If we don't do anything else: either we must surrender or, as divisional commander, I should place my reserves at a wrong point and then when the Allies attack at that point I could always say I had made a mistake.

EBERBACH: RUNDSTEDT can do quite a lot on his own; he can say: 'I can let you have twenty 'Divisionen' for the East – I'll tie down the enemy in the West.'

BROICH: Yes. 'I'll guarantee to hold the front', etc. All he has to do then is to move his troops to the wrong place and all is up. I can't understand why they don't set about it.

[. . .]

HEIM: It isn't true that all our leaders are spineless.

EBERBACH: No!

HEIM: Who creep and crawl to him the moment they come before him, as one likes to picture it, but on the contrary he has a *remarkable* hypnotic power.

EBERBACH: Yes, that's it. Incidentally it must have been similar with NAPOLEON and people like that.[139]

HEIM: Does he obtain this influence consciously or is it always there, or partly one, partly the other?

EBERBACH: Partly one, partly the other.

HEIM: He knows it and makes full use of it. He probably doesn't quite know wherein it lies, but he is conscious of it and uses it. Do you think that there are some people who do not come under his hypnotic influence?

EBERBACH: Yes, there are.

HEIM: I didn't actually take that man Thomale[140] particularly seriously, he is so extraordinarily obliging, but I only knew him at the school at DRESDEN.

EBERBACH: (*Laughing*) A man who has had the face to make jokes about the FÜHRER, all premeditated, in order to win him over on to his side. He has tremendous powers of deliberation, a free and independent man. In some respects they are perhaps similar. THOMALE is another of those people who won't let anyone else get a word in, he's enormously effervescent, of tremendous vitality and it is a question of vitality against hypnotic influence and a man like that is not easy to get the better of!

HEIM: But GUDERIAN is effervescent too.

EBERBACH: GUDERIAN is older, he is not a person who has that inner vitality.

HEIM: In my opinion, as soldiers and comrades of GUDERIAN,[141] there's one thing we must keep saying: GUDERIAN is not spineless, GUDERIAN is no fool, on the contrary, there are other forces at work here.

EBERBACH: Well, I don't think GUDERIAN should have agreed to the offensive in the West, which drew off quite considerable forces from his front.

HEIM: I don't believe he was asked, he had the Eastern front, and it's a principle of HITLER's who saw this problem coming – of choosing either the East or the West – to say: "I won't have anyone here who is to have any say beside me in these matters, so I shall send GUDERIAN to the East."

EBERBACH: But GUDERIAN has the East and was bound to say: "I can't spare one 'Division' here, on the contrary, I must have additional 'Divisionen', because the Russian offensive will start, and we know what that looks like."

HEIM: Do *you* know for certain that he didn't say that? We don't know!

Document 63

CSDIC (UK), GRGG 259
Report on information obtained from Senior Officers (PW) on 11–13 Feb. 45
[TNA, WO 208/4177]

CHOLTITZ: How do you picture your life in the future?

VATERRODT: I have no idea at all at the moment. After all, they can't turn all the officers out on to the street! That's impossible! Because the Americans – and the English – have at least an interest in seeing that they are not all idling on the streets.

CHOLTITZ: The civil service has to a large extent been Nazified. It must be replaced in some form or other. I should not be surprised at all if they used at least some of us for minor posts.

VATERRODT: I can well imagine, too, that they are interested in allowing us at least some pension on which we could live, if not the pension which would be due to us in the normal way. I am not too pessimistic about that. At any rate, even if they don't give us *that*, they must find some sort of occupation for us, where we can do something for the Fatherland.[142]

CHOLTITZ: Well, of course, some of us will be sent to RUSSIA.[143]

VATERRODT: We don't know that; where does it say that?

CHOLTITZ: They have announced it: the war criminals will immediately be brought to justice.

VATERRODT: Who *is* a war criminal?

CHOLTITZ: The governments are deciding that.

VATERRODT: Where does it say that every General is a war criminal?

CHOLTITZ: No, not every one, but they will demand those they want.

VATERRODT: They can only be quite isolated cases, those who have behaved particularly badly.

CHOLTITZ: I have never had a town burnt down or anything like that, but suppose I had given orders to my 'Korps' that such-and-such a place was to be burnt down, so that the Russians should not get in, I should then be a war criminal.

VATERRODT: Would they know that General so-and-so did it?

CHOLTITZ: Yes, because they have the order. They have got all the 'Korps' orders.

[. . .]

Document 64

CSDIC (UK), GRGG 260
Report on information obtained from Senior Officers (PW) on 14–15 Feb. 45
[TNA, WO 208/4177]

BROICH: If we got another treaty of VERSAILLES today we'd jump for joy.

WAHLE: If you were a GOC at the front today, and hadn't been here, would you fight or not?

EBERBACH: I would fight, but I would do everything in my power to influence all those with whom I came into contact to get the thing finished.

WAHLE: That's different, that's quite another matter. Would you be prepared to offer your powers of leadership to the full, and your own person?

EBERBACH: Yes, of course.

WAHLE: Everything else is, in my opinion, purely theoretical.

EBERBACH: But all the time I would be thinking: wouldn't it perhaps be better if I, together with my neighbouring army commander, were to come to some sort of terms now? I should have to consider, of course, whether it could be done and what the effects might be. Particularly as regards the Western Powers; not the Russians, there's no choice there.

WAHLE: I asked, because at table THOMA said that we couldn't understand what people like HALDER etc. could be thinking of to carry on fighting! I said: 'What else can they do?' They have to. The most elementary military honour demands that. Nobody in the front line, not even the C-in-C, can even consider whether or not he should carry on fighting.

EBERBACH: Yes, he can, now is the time for that.

WAHLE: No. You said yourself that, as regards the Russians, it's a matter of course.

EBERBACH: But I should spend the whole time thinking: 'What can I do to bring about the fall of the HITLER clique? Have I any possibilities in that line? What can I do, as soon as I'm in the West, to bring about, somehow, the entry of the Western Powers?'

WAHLE: You would be so wound up in the whole business –

EBERBACH: All the same I *already* found time for thoughts like these while I was in the West. But it was like this: I was in command of the 5th 'Panzerarmee', or 'Panzergruppe West', as it was next called, for a bare four weeks. Then I commanded for a fortnight or three weeks that 'Panzergruppe EBERBACH', quite different units again. Then I commanded the 7th 'Armee' for a week. One didn't have time to do anything about it. But despite that I allowed myself to think all those treacherous thoughts and I discussed them with some of the GOCs. It had got as far as that already. We Swabians are revolutionaries. For instance, I'm convinced that someone like GERSDORF,[144] who's an eminently clever and brave man, would never think about such things. It would be out of the question for him. He's a Prussian. Obeying orders is the only thing which matters to him, whereas we inclined far more to such rebellious thoughts. In BERLIN, however, such thoughts seldom came to me.

WAHLE: But to put it into practice! Think it, yes!

EBERBACH: In BERLIN one always said to oneself: 'First the invasion must come; if we repulse that then the tide has turned.' As long as the invasion hadn't started the war hadn't yet been lost. But the moment the invasion succeeded, the only way one could judge the situation was to say to oneself: 'There's no further point in it now.'

I am convinced that if THOMA were at the front now he would swear like a trooper, but he would do his job honourably and bravely.

WAHLE: Then my fears are set at rest.

Document 65

CSDIC (UK), GRGG 262
Report on information obtained from Senior Officers (PW) on 18–20 Feb. 45
[TNA, WO 208/4177]

CHOLTITZ: Isn't it a typical sign of a declining world that they are governed by a man who can't even walk properly?

MEYER (*reporting a conversation with* EBERDING): I said: 'If the Bolshevists succeed in conquering GERMANY, then it means the extinction of our people.' He replied: 'That's *nonsense*! We have lost so many wars; we lost in 1918, we lost against NAPOLEON and so on.'

ULLERSPERGER: There's no comparison at all!

MEYER: I said: 'What you are saying is senseless. That was an alteration in *system*, but nothing more than that. If Bolshevism triumphs today, then it will be a question of the biological *annihilation* of our people.' He can't see that.

ULLERSPERGER: Obviously, because only a convinced National Socialist can understand that.

MEYER: Afterwards he said: 'I can't refute what you told me; I don't know where you learnt it – ' The fact is, there's one thing I must say. Mistrust of our Generals is in my opinion, and I realise it more and more – in some ways by no means entirely groundless, because they have not accepted National Socialism as a *religion*, as *we* have, but only as a system of government obtaining for the moment.

ULLERSPERGER: Yes, of course.

MEYER: For instance, he said to me: 'It is the third system which I have experienced.' That's wrong, a man can only give himself *once*; I have *breathed in* National Socialism as a religion, *as my life*, no matter whether it is called National Socialism or has some other designation. I have realised that that is the only right life for our people, that otherwise our culture would go to the devil. This National Socialism stands for the conditions of life and for the things which are essential for our people for the preservation of our race, our people and our culture. He said: 'What do you mean by culture?'

Document 66

CSDIC (UK), GRGG 267
Report on information obtained from Senior Officers (PW) on 2–3 Mar. 45 [TNA, WO 208/4177]

CHOLTITZ: 'We shall not go under!' But you know,any decent nation may lose a war, that means that it has been led in a stupid manner or has been put in a totally crazy political situation; they *can't*, however, lose the war if they fight on to the end honourably. That is what the enemy is afraid of!

ELFELDT: If the Allies had gone on to BERLIN in one fell swoop after NORMANDY –

CHOLTITZ: Our spirit would have been broken!

ELFELDT: Yes. Actually the military fame of the German Army cannot be destroyed, *whatever* defeats they may yet suffer, this nation *can only go down with honour*.

CHOLTITZ: Lose the war with *honour*. It will never go under!

BRUHN: Now that the bombs are raining down the simple worker, the ordinary 'Regierungsrat', the 'Major', the German housewife etc. take it as the proof of what HITLER and GOEBBELS have always said: i.e. That you with devilish baseness want to destroy *everything German, no matter* whether woman or child. It's a lie and a complete distortion of the facts.

BAO: Do you think this hatred will continue after the war when we're occupying Germany?

BRUHN: No, we must see to that; it will be a difficult task. I don't think so, although there is a danger. It'll have to be tackled with great strictness but also with a great deal of understanding for this tortured people. You can't hang everyone; that is impossible as you'd be sowing the seeds of further massacres. The younger generation will have to be watched very carefully and we'll have to take a firm stand with them. *All that* is well and good once we have fuel and the possibility of providing sufficient food for the population, so that they won't steal, murder and pillage and take everything they find.

CHOLTITZ: We no longer know the meaning of the word 'national'. There's no mention at all of it being a matter of honour. It has become a matter of *plunder*! These damned criminals!

RAMCKE: I only know that stealing went on in the RHINELAND in 1922.[145]

CHOLTITZ: You don't know *anything at all* about it: you've merely read that in the 'Völkischer Beobachter'. How do you know about it?

RAMCKE: Leutnant HAMM lived in the RUHR district. One night there came a knock at the door and his parents were told that they had to clear the house, it was requisitioned. Leutnant HAMM arrived home on return from ENGLAND and wanted to go into his house; a French sentry stood in front of it. All the silver was missing.

CHOLTITZ: Excuse me, but haven't you yourself taken silver? Isn't that also requisitioned privately owned silver?

RAMCKE: No!

CHOLTITZ: What is it then?

RAMCKE: I got it from a naval officers' mess.

CHOLTITZ: But that's private property, that has been pinched too!

RAMCKE (*continues his story*): The upholstery was slashed open, the pictures had been taken away or slashed and destroyed. There was nothing left in the whole house which could be used. And that happened not to one, but to 100,000 families all over the French-occupied RHINELAND.[146]

CHOLTITZ: I'm not talking about what gets smashed up, I'm saying that we *steal*! We collect the stuff up into stores, like proper robbers, in guarded stores, that's the frightful part of it. This *revolting* business of engaging in *organised* robbery of private property.

RAMCKE: Where has that happened?

CHOLTITZ: Throughout the whole of FRANCE. The damned GAF has taken away whole train-loads, that man, that HIMMLER. Whole train-loads of the most beautiful antique furniture from private houses! It's frightful; it's an indescribable disgrace! Any people can lose a war; that's no disgrace, it's just political folly to lead a capable and brave people into such a situation. But to cover ourselves with the *shame* of carrying out organised robbery under the supervision and help and encouragement of the state, no, my dear fellow, that's a different matter! It's ridiculous for an army suddenly to drive away a train full of furniture in peace-time. You have seen the destruction wrought by the soldiers; they all do that. No, this stealing just because the other poor unfortunate people have been conquered; the so-called victorious state goes in and *robs*! No, my dear fellow, we are *steeped* in materialism, we have ceased to wage war as idealists.[147]

Document 67

CSDIC (UK), GRGG 270
Report on information obtained from Senior Officers (PW) on 9 Mar. 45 [TNA, WO 208/4177]

BASSENGE: The attitude of the troops to the officers is quite different from what it was in 1918, or has that changed, too?

ROTHKIRCH: In 1918 we experienced more open *revolutionary* tendencies. As the end drew near, the men were already behaving in a very insolent fashion.[148] They don't do that now. On the other hand one must take into account the fact that the Party is carrying out *terrific* propaganda against us, especially against the Generals. The troops are not insubordinate but they carry out what you might term 'sit down strikes'. They don't act against the officers, as they used to in the last war, but, as commanders are now reporting, when one leaves them alone on sentry duty or on piquet one part will cross over to the other side, all 25 of them; or else they just sit there and do nothing when the Americans arrive.

THOMA: Yes, that is just a physical collapse.

ROTHKIRCH: Yes, but it's not a revolution. But the *civilians*, they call us 'strike-breakers', 'war prolongers', etc. The civilians dig up the mines and cut the wires behind our backs. You see that in official reports. I read in a report which my 'Armee' passed on that the civilians yelled 'prolongers of the war' and dug up mines. The civilian population in the RHINELAND, west of the RHINE, is saying: 'It's all quite useless now, so why do they heap these additional unpleasantnesses on us, why blow up the bridges and dig tank traps and so on?' They won't lend a helping hand. And some of the bridges didn't blow up either, the TREVES bridge didn't blow up,[149] then there are RHINE bridges –

[. . .]

ROTHKIRCH: I've had practical experience of it. It was at TREVES and it simply turned tail and ran. And the men in the 'Volkssturm'! I had some of them in my village. I was living with a priest. There were two members of the 'Volkssturm' there, they got up at 0800 or 0830 hours and shaved until 0930 hours. Then I asked them what they were going to do that day. They replied that they were going to chop wood for the priest. Then they were told to dig a few positions. They said no, they couldn't do that. They had received different orders from their 'Bataillonskommandeur', they couldn't do that.

   Then I wanted to have some of the 'Volkssturm' on the KYLL.[150] There are very steep hills there and positions had been dug in them. I said: 'Now let us put a 'Volkssturmbataillon' here. The Americans won't notice whether it's a member of the 'Volkssturm' there or not.

The main thing is that they think that this stretch is manned.' But that wasn't possible either.

CHOLTITZ: Who gives the orders then?

ROTHKIRCH: The 'Volkssturm' come under the 'Gauleiter'.

CHOLTITZ: Don't they come under any military direction whatever?

ROTHKIRCH: You will never believe the funniest thing of all: when I left BOLITHA(?) I was sent up to EAST PRUSSIA[151] and my orders were to guard against the possibility of a Russian break-through via TAURAGE. I got the orders from Gauleiter KOCH! That's not an exaggeration, it's absolute fact.

ROTHKIRCH (*re guerrilla warfare*): We will set it in motion. I know that for a fact, because I was in command of a guerrilla school in RUSSIA where men were trained by us in guerrilla warfare. They have been taken over now and they are now training partisans themselves. That is how I know.

HEIM: Do you think it will really help at all?

ROTHKIRCH: Yes, they are already staying behind now. There were some in my villages. They were SS men who, after the third cognac, told my intelligence officer exactly what they were supposed to do. Of course, they weren't suppose to do that. But they told him just the same. They were there and were supposed to spy out everything. Most important of all, they were supposed to enlist other supporters. These SS men said that it was exceedingly difficult as there were no volunteers. Besides which – like us all – though they had explosives, they had no fuses. That was why they approached my intelligence officer.[152]

HEYDTE: So it was really more for purposes of sabotage?

ROTHKIRCH: Yes, just like the guerrillas do. But it's a scourge for the civilian population.

HEIM: So these SS men were very pessimistic, were they?

ROTHKIRCH: The civilian population will hand them over at once.

HEIM: If they don't hang them themselves.

BASSENGE: In addition to which every stranger in the locality is shadowed as soon as there's an L of C commandant there, etc.

ROTHKIRCH: Your view is quite correct. But that again is overshadowed by yet another factor. There are the many badly bombed towns. Naturally enormous numbers of people have fled from the towns into the villages. Then, of course, they have to decide: who is a partisan? The evacuees blur the picture badly.

HEIM: Then there is also the question whether the population will participate.

ROTHKIRCH: I don't think they will west of the RHINE. But I believe that there may perhaps be more wild, fanatical people east of the RHINE.

Document 68

CSDIC (UK), GRGG 273
Report on information obtained from Senior Officers (PW) on 16–19 Mar. 45
[TNA, WO 208/4177]

ROTHKIRCH: While I was there you had to report and give the number whenever you wished to withdraw from a 'Bunker', for they all had numbers; every 'Bunker' in the west has a number. There are special maps with all the numbers. Each 'Bunker' had to be reported by number as a retreat of any description was forbidden. No general was authorised to order a withdrawal and on several occasions when whole 'Divisionen' were encircled, enquiries were made and we were informed at 4 o'clock in the morning that we were *not* to withdraw. Everyone had, however, gone in the meantime.

CHOLTITZ: It was exactly the same at AVRANCHES.

ROTHKIRCH: When I left we were still strictly forbidden to give any order to withdraw. The 'Divisionskommandeur' simply wasn't in command any more. You could really no longer say the men were fighting. The only unit still putting up a bit of a fight was the 2nd Panzerdivision. They *actually* only had two tanks left. That will go down in history.[153]

BASSENGE: It's high time now, yet the Allies are still stuck on the RHINE and if the Russians open the door, within forty-eight hours GERMANY will be Communist as far as the west. It's no problem, for the key positions, the communications, are all controlled by the Nazis; if HITLER orders it, it will be done. Such an organised Bolshevism will progress far more quickly in GERMANY than one which grows out of chaos; the whole thing will be settled in forty-eight hours. Then the 'SEYDLITZ Club' will arrive, with or without recognition from HITLER or the Nazis or the new party, whichever it is. Something of the sort will certainly happen. Peace will certainly happen. Peace will certainly not come the way one imagines, i.e. the rest of the German Army being sandwiched on the ELBE and then surrendering and that then being followed by a beautiful, generous peace. My convictions are still the same as ever; I say: it no longer depends upon whether HITLER's GERMANY survives or not, or what is going to happen to GERMANY, or all the various questions of peace; those are all unimportant questions in comparison to the main question: where will the line of Western civilisation run? If it extends only as far as the RHINE at the end of this year, in 1950 it will be back on the Spanish border or at the gates of GIBRALTAR and then the English policy of the balance of power in EUROPE – quite apart from civilisation – will be completely impossible; it won't exist any more.

If one wants to avoid future chaos and all resulting political consequences one can only do so by a national coup d'état. I can see no other possible way but with each day it drags on that grows more difficult, of course.

Document 69

CSDIC (UK), GRGG 276
Report on information obtained from Senior Officers (PW) on 25–7 Mar. 45
[TNA, WO 208/4177]

HEIM: I always used to consider it wrong to surrender, our people might have cracked badly and that might perhaps have proved disastrous in the future. But now we *must* give in; it's simply madness.
SCHLIEBEN: It's sheer suicide.
HEIM: The absolute *suicide* of a race of millions, such as has never before occured in history, because it is in the hand of a *madman*, a *criminal*.

Document 70

CSDIC (UK), GRGG 278
Report on information obtained from Senior Officers (PW) on 30 Mar.–2 Apr. 45
[TNA, WO 208/4177]

HEIM: The German people deserve no better – this business of 'Werewolves' is absolute madness.[154]
WILDERMUTH: In the first place it's simply a repetition of the 'Patriotic Formations' after the last war, secondly the people are standing with their backs to the wall. It's not the people who are doing it but the Party members and the fanatical youth. I had certainly reckoned with it, but I'm amazed that they've started so soon; from experiences in the BALKANS I had counted on it starting six months after the occupation. But they are starting at once. It's just their madness again. But I am convinced that there are people who really believe in it.
HEIM: It's impossible to say. But it serves the German people right. It's unbelievable.
WILDERMUTH: It will, of course, reduce everything to ruins and rubble and will lead, after a short space of time, to barbaric counter-measures on the part of the others.
HEIM: The Allies will have to set up a counter-movement.
WILDERMUTH: That's been one of my ideas for a long time, but that is not to say, of course, that a vague possibility will become a reality. One can only suppress guerrilla warfare with strong units formed from the population of the country. After a year or two they will be forced to arm us themselves. It's dreadful, of course, another civil war.

Document 71

CSDIC (UK), GRGG 280
Report on information obtained from Senior Officers (PW) on 7 Apr. 45 [TNA, WO 208/4177]

HEYKING: I can't imagine it lasting much longer.

JÖSTING: Out of the question – a fortnight or three weeks maybe. It's amazing! The whole front line must be bent all over the place.

HEYKING: Oh well, strong armoured spear-heads have broken through everywhere and fighting continues in the rear. Wherever resistance is shown they destroy everything, as they did at EISENACH yesterday.[155] They'll do the same to all the towns.

JÖSTING: Yes, they said the same to me *too*, when I was captured, i.e.: 'If we hadn't got MAINZ today, six hundred aircraft would have attacked it, and then the requisite number of tanks.' We hadn't got anything. Our 'Panzerfäuste'! The need a man who has handled them ten or twelve times before.

HEYKING: Yes, otherwise he's afraid.

JÖSTING: I had a hundred 'Panzerfäuste'. I was never allowed to fire more than twenty-four of them.

HEYKING: Oh well, we haven't enough to practise with!

JÖSTING: Yes, and you need young and efficient men to handle them, not the old creatures I had. They were willing but incapable! They were 45–47-year-olds from the 'Flak' and the searchlights. They scraped everyone together and threw them into the fight.

Document 72

CSDIC (UK), GRGG 282
Report on information obtained from Senior Officers (PW) on 10–13 Apr. 45 [TNA, WO 208/4177]

ROSS: Before I was captured everyone realised that it would be madness to continue the war but none of the higher authorities had the courage to take a firm stand.

BRUHN: But they didn't know how many people have been shot and what has gone on in concentration camps. We have sinned, not you and I personally, but all of us as representatives of this system which has broken every moral code in the world. If you admit life is ruled by a great moral code you must condemn yourself.

ROSS: I hold the view, which is perhaps very strict, that people in leading positions who did know about it must be blamed for failing to oppose the Party. Even if you merely consider the last phase of this struggle at WESEL,[156] all from the highest to the lowest, always said 'yes' and 'amen' to everything, because their convictions were outweighed by the thought: 'My own neck is at stake.' No one said: 'I'd rather go to the dogs if it helps the people at large.' All they did was to say 'yes' to everything.

[. . .]

DASER: In contrast with the army of occupation which you experienced – when we regarded them as an enemy power – the Germans today give them an enthusiastic reception; they don't only hang out white flags but welcome them and say: 'You're a thousand times preferable to the Nazis, to our own people.'

ROSS: Quite right.

?: 'Please help us to kill off the Nazi bosses.'

ROSS: Quite right. Only with the great difference, over which we must not have the least doubt, that this enthusiasm and all those things are the swing from one condition to another, but once this war is over –

DASER: No, I disagree with you there; the white flag does not only indicate: 'Hands up, I surrender, please don't bomb us any more' etc., but 'I greet you and ask you to help me to . . . the last of the Nazi bosses and all that goes with them.'

ROSS: That remains to be seen.

DASER: Things have already come to that today, and you may say that's typically German, I admit that; perhaps another people might behave differently in a situation like this, but only a people which from its own self, from the fundamental ethical conceptions which, either from religion or education, or from their whole outlook are still latent in the people –

ROSS: There is no doubt, sir, that every decent-thinking person in GERMANY cannot take strict enough action, in the interests of the German people as a whole, against all these underground movements and all these reactionaries, whether they are National Socialists or some other elements. They must *all* disappear. We must accept the consequences of a lost war and clear up and cooperate in reconstruction. Anyone opposing that must be got rid of. This fact *cannot* be stressed enough. Are you of a different opinion?

BRUHN: No, but I should like even to add something: unfortunately during the last few years the German people has realised that in spite of love of country and patriotism they have to turn to their enemies in order to rid themselves of the growth inside them. I'm convinced that the majority of even the lowest working classes as well as the other classes are not only ready to welcome their enemies but also to give them the fullest cooperation because they have come to realise that their greatest enemy is in their own country. Despite that fact, thousands of fanatics will be against it and we ourselves shall have to annihilate them in the end.

ROSS: Yes.

BRUHN: But this 'Werewolf' movement is directed first and foremost against the enemy and as a result the Anglo-Americans will have to take steps against it too.

Ross: Those 'Werewolves' will operate against anyone inclined to co-operate with the enemy on a reasonable basis.

Bruhn: Yes, but we'll soon track them down. I must say that, after the damage done as regards the education of the younger generation, we shall have no alternative but to shoot thousands, perhaps tens of thousands of people in cold blood, maybe even one's own brother, if they oppose the rehabilitation of the German people. If we don't do that we're lost for centuries to come. The workmen feel that too.

Document 73

CSDIC (UK), GRGG 284
Report on information obtained from Senior Officers (PW) on 16–18 Apr. 45
[TNA, WO 208/4177]

Fischer: Such criminals! I have no other expression for these people at the head of our government; they're rogues and criminals in my eyes, no matter what anyone here says about his oath of allegiance.

Bruhn: Oh, that oath is rubbish. Hitler has released us from our oath by his whole behaviour. One is only constantly astounded that we all ran after this will o' the wisp as we did.

Fischer: Why was that? Because our officers were so unpolitically minded, and believed the government to be just as respectable as the officers. Had it been a democratic government we would never have believed that. Had the 'National' been missing from 'National Socialism' we would never have believed it either. It was the 'National' which did it; it was under that cover that he deceived us and also destroyed the middle class as such.

Bruhn: From the negative point of view, from the criminal one, they certainly did their job well by using such logic.

Document 74

CSDIC (UK), GRGG 286
Report on information obtained from Senior Officers (PW) on 19–21 Apr. 45
[TNA, WO 208/4177]

Heim: Pfuhlstein, do please answer just *one* question which has always puzzled us beyond solution: what are the German people doing now? Why are they still fighting as they are?

Pfuhlstein: I will tell you exactly – exactly is saying too much, perhaps. I went through the battle for Wertheim.[157] I was retired out of the service and without the right to wear uniform etc. The fact is that any man who runs away – there are regimental courts martial everywhere – anyone found in the rear is shot. Orders now are always worded as follows: 'I order this and that. If it should not succeed, you will be shot.' The people know, therefore: 'It's no good retreating, I shall be caught and killed. Therefore I shall have to stay at the front and act as if I am fighting. I shan't fight, because it's pointless. I won't open fire, or I might fire my rifle once or twice, but there's no point in it. Perhaps I shall be wounded, a slight wound, that would be a stroke of luck.'

Then, around WERTHEIM, the civilians were literally hostile to the German soldiers and yet had the greatest sympathy for the fellows, as, of course, they had no more reinforcements and supplies or rations. All those who were giving the orders – they know all that – what was dashing around was no more than a rabble. There were no vehicles and there was no artillery; there was absolutely nothing left there, so the civilians feel the greatest pity for those troops. On the other hand, they were outspokenly hostile, saying: 'You idiots, what's keeping you here? As long as you stay here the place will be attacked. If you start pooping off your silly popguns our town will be shot to pieces. You will be out anyway within a couple of hours or a day. Our town is still standing now, but then it will be destroyed. Give up this stupid idea and go away!' They actually tried to defend WERTHEIM with, I believe, two 'Kompanien'. They delayed things for twenty-four hours, with the result that the Americans heavily shelled the, till then, completely undamaged town and caused a tremendous amount of destruction.

Then our engineers blew up two bridges over the TAUBER and one over the MAIN, but in such a stupid way that the houses over a wide area left and right of them collapsed, the hospital – no windows left, roof gone and everything else imaginable. But in the bridge itself they blew a hole measuring only 4 m! Then the Americans arrived, threw a few planks over it and two hours later their tanks were driving across.

HEIM: That bridge business is a perfect symbol for the whole German nation: self-destruction!

PFUHLSTEIN: Of course it had to be a large hospital, full to the brim with wounded and sick from the town! The town was smashed through the demolitions of our own engineers; on account of our stupid popguns the little half-timbered town was subjected to twenty-four hours' artillery fire. Then they withdrew and the Americans arrived and two hours later the tanks were rolling across.

HEIM: Why aren't the Americans advancing more quickly?

PFUHLSTEIN: Because they still continue to overestimate us. They don't realise what miserable remnants they are. They just don't believe how miserably off the men are and how low is their fighting value.

HEIM: What did you do during the fighting for WERTHEIM?

PFUHLSTEIN: Watched it through my field-glasses. I sent my own and other children down into the cellar.

Document 75

CSDIC (UK), GRGG 289
Report on information obtained from Senior Officers (PW) on 27–8 Apr. 45 [TNA, WO 208/4177]

HEIM: May I ask one question which interests us all very much? I would like to refer back to a remark you made earlier on: 'We thought, it's a good thing, if the fellows desert, for then we are rid of the swine.' At that time we, here, considered it would be more to the point if everyone were to desert. We even went so far as to say that a commander who didn't do so was was either a fool or a scoundrel, afraid either of being shot or of the SS. Now we are interested to know whether such thoughts were entirely impossible to German commanders?

VIEBIG: The desire to terminate hostilities is, I think, not yet acute. As I saw from my own troops, even if comparisons with the spring offensive of the great battle in FRANCE (1918) were inevitable: 'This is the final attempt,' the troops and junior officers attacked with tremendous fervour, just because we were finally advancing again. Each man told himself that everything had been saved up for this, we, too, were told at the conference with the FÜHRER[158] that everything that we have had now been scraped together, there were so-and-so many tank 'Korps' there, the plan simply must succeed. It was clear to me that it had been very hurriedly arranged and in many respects badly prepared, the artillery preparation for instance. They had staked everything on one card, placing all their hopes on the element of surprise. But even I hadn't reckoned with supplies breaking down so completely that eventually the artillery had no ammunition and the tanks no petrol.

HEIM: Did you think that if things had worked out as you expected, it would have resulted in a reversal of the war situation?

VIEBIG: No, I didn't believe that, nor did I consider it possible that there would be a definite change in the course of the war.

EBERBACH: But perhaps you thought that as a result of it the way for political opportunities would be opened up again?

VIEBIG: Well, that under certain circumstances a compromise peace might have been arranged.

HEIM: In other words, it didn't seem entirely without point to you.

VIEBIG: Not as far as I could foresee, no.

BASSENGE: When you say a compromise peace had you reckoned on the enemy negotiating with the Nazi regime at all? That is one question which was quite clear to us here: there never was a basis for negotiating. Unconditional surrender was the only basis for negotiation.

VIEBIG: Our government would *never* have been prepared to do that, even if they had only had the most meagre success.

HEIM: You mean, therefore, that up to December there was hardly a person who said that we really ought voluntarily to make peace, rather here in the West than in the East.

ROTHKIRCH: Perhaps I should remark here that just as the attack started I was with the 'Heeresgruppe', with Generaloberst REINHARDT, who, as High Priest of the 'Heeresgruppe' was bound to be in the know. He had learnt about the attack twenty-four hours before, through conversation with the OKH, and was of the same opinion as VIEBIG, in the sense that it was believed that it could bring about a decisive turning point in the war; that if the attack succeeded in reaching the objective they had in mind it would be possible to win a basis for concluding a bearable peace.[159]

HEIM: And REINHARDT is without doubt one of the most sober and sensible men that we have.

VIEBIG: Things became very different after the end of January/February of course. After that every 'Divisionsführer' and 'Regimentskommandeur' told himself that it was madness what we were being forced to do.

Document 76

CSDIC (UK) GG-REPORT, SRGG 1171 (C)

CS/1952 – Generalmajor BRUNS (Heeres-Waffenmeisterschule 1, Berlin) – Captured 8 Apr. 45 in Göttingen – and other Senior Officers (PW), whose voices could not be identified.
Information received: 28 Apr. 45

FRANZ: I had just crossed the RHINE and reached SPEYER and then I telephoned the C of S of the 'Armee'.[160] He asked: 'How many men have you left?' 'Only a few officers,' and with them I was to form a 'Kampfgruppe FRANZ'. We went on to KARLSDORF(?) and collected about forty men from the surrounding villages. At half-past nine the telephone rang: 'OBERMEYER(?) speaking: I belong to the FÜHRER's court martial. General HÜBNER[161] is in the village here and has orders to see you tonight.' I knew there was something of the sort and also what it meant for me. Well, I lit a good Havana cigar, sat down on the sofa and waited for him. Suddenly there was a knock and General HÜBNER entered and said to me: 'I am the FÜHRER's flying court martial.' (Laughter) 'and have authority to shoot officers, including Generals, on the spot, if I ascertain that anything has been neglected or not carried out.' The moon was shining and it was quite light out-of-doors. (Laughter). Thereupon I said to him: 'Sir, I am at your disposal; you can shoot me on the spot if you wish.' He said: 'I have brought everything along; two officers and a firing squad consisting of twelve men, but first I want to discuss with you the fighting at Treves, along the Moselle and up to the Rhine.'

I had something with which he hadn't reckoned. I had a map scale 1 : 300,000 which showed the Battle HQs of my 'Division' up to the Rhine – the whole thing took place within twenty-eight days – none of them were farther apart than 2 or 3 cm, which is equal to 8–9 km on a 1 : 300,000 map. This showed that we must have fought at least a day in each of them along this line, else there would have been a big jump. I laid down the map on the table in front of him and said: 'Sir, would you like me to hold a long lecture or shall I tell you in a few words?' He said: 'Make it short.' Very well, I started: 'Here are the HQ's. This is how we fought.' Then he suddenly exclaimed: 'But that is *totally* different from what we assumed at OKW. We thought it had been a major catastrophe, at which everything was swept away in a body. That is a most interesting report you have given me. We thought a mess had been made. You will not be shot. (*Laughter*). I only have one request: have this map copied immediately. I shall show it to the Führer myself in order to show him how the troops have actually fought.' Then he looked for a second culprit: General Utz(?)[162] whom he had also intended shooting. I had explained everything to him within an hour. He said I should not be shot, whereupon I said: 'Orderly, bring me a bottle of champagne!' I thanked him for allowing me to live (*laughter*) and gave him the map. In the meantime a teleprint message arrived, saying I was to take over the Taunus front near Wiesbaden forthwith. I said to him: 'Yours is a very difficult task, having to institute proceedings of such a nature with Generals.' He answered: 'Believe me, it gives me great satisfaction to shoot a General who has been proved to have neglected his duty.'

?: Wait till he arrives as PW at this camp!

?: We should like to meet him!

Franz: For example: he also shot the Remagen people.[163] He didn't do it just out of blind obedience to an order but because of a fanatical faith in the cause. The Führer had so much faith in him that he personally entrusted him with this difficult task.

Document 77

CSDIC (UK) GG-REPORT, SRGG 1171 (C) [TNA, WO 208/4169]

Generalleutnant Siry (Commander 347 Infantry Division) – Captured 10 Apr. 45 in Friedrichsroda.
Generalleutnant Kirchheim (Führerreserve OKH) – Captured 12 Apr. 45 near Quedlingburg.
Information received: 30 Apr. 45

KIRCHHEIM: Do you consider yourself bound by your military oath?

SIRY: Well, really, the military oath is valid as long as the FÜHRER is alive.

KIRCHHEIM: Do you consider the FÜHRER to be mentally normal?

SIRY: It isn't for a subordinate to lay down whether his superior is mentally normal or not.

KIRCHHEIM: If the fate of the nation hangs in the balance, then yes.

SIRY: Picture the time when FREDERICK THE GREAT, in the now ever-quoted speech to his generals at LEUTHEN, saying that he would ignore all the rules of the game,[164] then any number of his generals could also have said: 'The man is mad,' and could have broken their military oath.

KIRCHHEIM: Surely *we* have seen now that *all* resistance is hopeless. In the last years we have always been up against superior forces; we have always gone backwards, and now our army is completely routed and in the meantime the others have become much stronger, so that the ratio in strength has changed to our disadvantage, and when they have advanced to the heart of our Fatherland and smashed all our industries – well, how can the tide be turned –

SIRY: Naturally there will be no turning of the tide now, but it is possible that political developments are to be expected. I hope that the business has come to an end, that in the next few days HIMMLER really –

KIRCHHEIM: It has come to an end.

SIRY: But it is a very, very different chapter.

KIRCHHEIM: To ease my mind I confided in one man – a thing I usually never do, and which I afterwards regretted having done – that was General HÖHNE, with whom we lived.[165] HÖHNE told me the following – a point of view of which I thoroughly disapprove – he said: 'You are right in everything; I also agree that all resistance is senseless, it is utterly useless. I also admit that in the next few weeks the *last* of our remaining national wealth will be destroyed. I also agree that hundreds of thousands more perhaps millions, will die and also stocks and dwelling places will be destroyed, but,' he said, 'I would urge you most emphatically not to do anything, as over there they are looking for just such a one on whom they can put the blame. Afterwards they will, although our army has now already completely collapsed' – he said, 'as in the last months I commanded a "Korps", I know a complete collapse has already occurred and it is hopeless to continue to fight. But,' he said, 'people in general don't know it. It will be twisted round, just as they did it on 20 July, to mean that it was *you* who stabbed our army in the back and you are dishonoured to the end of your days.' I said: 'If that is the only danger, if, as you say, perhaps millions of lives might still be saved, then from fear of being accused of that, should I watch these millions being annihilate? No, I won't do that.' Thereupon I asked the six Generals, of course in quite an unobtrusive way: 'Gentlemen, I'd like to hear your opinion. Don't you think it is right for the Army commanders, now that they can see the seenselessness of resistance, simply to stop the fighting and offer the surrender of their Armies of their own accord?' No one said it was *not* right. They then suggested one didn't know whether the families of those concerned might not be in the hands of the FÜHRER. But I said: 'No – I'd like to know whether you consider such action as dishonourable or necessary.' All six of them said it was the only possible thing to do.

SIRY: A point like that, of course, was perfect for a debate, because no one person was obliged to make the decision for himself.

KIRCHHEIM: That's why I didn't bring the subject up any more, because, when anyone says to me: 'Your suggestion is the right one but you must look out for yourself' – well, I won't argue with such men. A man that considers that to be the right course but is afraid of the consequences –

SIRY: It's not so much fear as the natural dread of a falsification of the facts of history, a thing which had already become widespread.

Document 78

CSDIC (UK), GRGG 292
Report on information obtained from Senior Officers (PW) on 1–2 May 45 [TNA, WO 208/4177]

SCHLIEBEN: DÖNITZ is such a damned fool.[166]

FISCHER: After the announcement: 'The FÜHRER is dead,' the 'German Hymn' was played, then came the Order of the Day, of which we heard only the end, saying that the oath of allegiance which all members of the forces had taken, was now carried over to his successor.

SCHLIEBEN: Well, that's not binding.

FISCHER: No, by no means. It seems that the foreign powers didn't want to continue negotiating with HIMMLER after all; that's why DÖNITZ and BUSCH have taken over.[167]

PFUHLSTEIN: I wonder whether he will do anything at the last minute?

FISCHER: A blessing if he does.

SCHLIEBEN: It's quite clear to me now what a tragedy it was that 20 July didn't come off.

REIMANN: That hysterical fool DÖNITZ!

HEYDTE: That charlatan!

BASSENGE: Are we supposed to say 'Heil DÖNITZ' now?

BROICH: Can I transfer my oath to anyone else? Can one swear allegiance to DÖNITZ over the telephone?

WILDERMUTH (*re* HITLER's *death*): I think it means someone just has to give the order.

BROICH: Above all HIMMLER wants to keep out of it.

BASSENGE: That young ass DÖNITZ.

WILDERMUTH: Well, he is senior to BUSCH.

BROICH: Next to KEITEL he is the most senior one and KEITEL has probably said: 'For God's sake not me!'

FISCHER (*after* DÖNIT'S *radio address*): DÖNITZ has gone haywire!

BROICH: It's as if 'Little HITLER' were speaking.

FISCHER: Now it will be: 'FÜHRER's HQ speaking' – it's daft!

ELFELDT: I don't by any means believe the whole business.

FISCHER: I wonder whether HIMMLER will recognise it?

HEYDTE: There ought to be some statement issued concerning the formation of a government now.

FISCHER: DÖNITZ will form one out of Nazis and create a military dictatorship.

BROICH: In order to get special (peace) offers again. With those fellows anything and everything is possible.

WAHLE: The condition would have to be that we were no longer National Socialists. Then they could say that a new government has been set up, but it hasn't now.

FISCHER: He's following the same course. It's a one-day government. It needn't be in the least true that the FÜHRER is dead.

BASSENGE: No, it needn't.

HEYDTE: Anyone who says: 'I will conquer the Russians,' must, logically, be thinking of the other side of the question too.

ELFELDT: He still believes that he will screw better conditions out of them, that the Allies will be split, that the English will suddenly announce: 'That is our man; we will negotiate with him.'

[. . .]

HEIM: I tell you, I know DÖNITZ: where's the *logic* of it? How does he think he'll do it? By saying: 'Those who don't fight to the end are cowards and traitors!'?

NEUFFER: Nothing's impossible. We still don't know yet – the same thing applies to GUDERIAN for instance – whether the man isn't speaking under compulsion. You mentioned GOEBBELS and HIMMLER?

HEIM: Strangely enough GOEBBELS didn't speak. GOEBBELS has, therefore vanished, too, and HIMMLER has also vanished from the public eye.

NEUFFER: If DÖNITZ were simply speaking under pressure it would explain things. Otherwise there would be much in GUDERIAN's attitude which couldn't be explained. In these extraordinary times, there are situations where a man for some motive or other – we'll say in order to save his wife or children –

HEIM: The English will naturally say: 'One realises now that you are all crazy. Not only HITLER, but all of you.' It's such madness!

NEUFFER: There's nothing solid left.

HEIM: DÖNITZ surely won't be blind to the fact that the moment HITLER's gone, even though he does maintain the oath is automatically transferred to him, everyone will naturally say: 'It's finished now.' That's obvious.

NEUFFER: Southern GERMANY is completely finished, from the military point of view as well. ITALY too. Practically speaking there's only DENMARK and NORWAY left.

HEIM: How can a reasonable being, in possession of his five senses, say such a . . . !

NEUFFER: We don't know what led up to it. We can't form any picture of what means have been used. I think anything is possible today. I even think it's possible that GOEBBELS too has been speaking under pressure for a considerable time.

HEIM: But after all, since HITLER is officially dead and has therefore vanished from the public eye, what point is there in his successor still following the same crazy policy?

NEUFFER: One can't judge that from here. I can imagine that with GOEBBELS too, it was a case of 'must', just as it was with DITTMAR.

HEIM: He said: 'We shall go on fighting until the people in the East are freed from slavery and destruction.' The German people can only laugh bitterly and say: 'That man in mad, too.'

NEUFFER: Well, in the east, in SILESIA, EAST PRUSSIA, that is, east of the ODER, there will only be those Germans left who were overrun, because a great number got out. It's a puzzling piece of folly.

HEIM: How a man can say a thing like that! Because if you hold it up to the light, what he said was absolute nonsense. 'And if the English and Americans hinder me in doing so, then I am compelled to continue the fight against them too!'

NEUFFER: In the present situation it's ridiculous, because he has no basis left.

HEIM: A man like DÖNITZ, who knows perfectly well what HITLER did, for instance, with the Generals and the officers, the COs, has painted him today as an absolute angel. Fancy DÖNITZ saying that of HITLER.

NEUFFER: One must remember one thing, of course, that the Navy never had anything in common with the GAF and Army.

HEIM: But DÖNITZ, in his position, knew what was happening. He must know enough to realise that it's an appalling business. If one reaches such a decision as DÖNITZ's, one must see some sort of possibility.

NEUFFER: That's no decision. Either he is crazy himself – and one can hardly think that. He appears to have spoken quite sensibly, at any rate his articulation was clear and military-like. But either he's under pressure or – one just doesn't know. How is one to explain it? I mean if this madness is to be carried on to the end, the rest of the people's eyes will naturally be opened. I believe all this present horror propaganda has a very positive effect, as opposed to the hatred propaganda of the last war, the only explanation of which lay in the perpetual danger policy of the KAISER. This time the English have seen themselves what has been done. They couldn't have expected that. I've been reading English newspapers for two years and one could tell from them that they were completely without any realisation of the matter. Since you've been a PW you yourself have also experienced the fact that the people simply couldn't grasp what was going on.

The troops will also try and back out if they can. The moment they can, they will go home or surrender. The tragedy is that they will still be taken by the Russians.

HEIM: This business about the oath automatically being transferred is grotesque.

NEUFFER: Yes.

GOERBIG: I believe DÖNITZ will avoid signing his name under the capitulation and is boasting, although he has nothing behind him, saying someone else will have to sign it.

BROICH: I've got the idea that the FÜHRER perhaps arranged all that as a legacy, and DÖNITZ had to promise him . . .

GOERBIG: Of course, the FÜHRER said –

BROICH: 'You've got to do it now.'

GOERBIG: HITLER said: 'Grossadmiral DÖNITZ, I have confidence that, after my death you will (continue) the fight – will you promise me that, as man to man?' 'Yes, my FÜHRER!' 'It is my dying wish.'

BROICH: And he announced that yesterday, 1 May – it's 1 May intentionally – to be the date to mark HITLER's death.

GOERBIG: The peace offer has fallen through.

BROICH: Probably we shall hear soon that HIMMLER has killed DÖNITZ.

GOERBIG: Of course.

WILDERMUTH: It's a Party swindle with DÖNITZ, to push the blame for defeat on to the Armed Forces. HIMMLER is the man who negotiated about the 'surrender' and plenty of people in GERMANY will say: 'Heavens, at any rate he had the sense to do that; I'll forgive him a lot for that. Now HIMMLER's gone and DÖNITZ appears. Needless to say the Armed Forces can never get enough blame.' It makes you sick!

SCHLIEBEN: So stupid.

WILDERMUTH: The man isn't authorised at all to lead or speak.

Document 79

CSDIC (UK) GG-REPORT, SRGG 1176 [TNA, WO 208/4170]

Generalmajor Dr REITER (9th Infantry Regiment) – Captured 16 Apr. 45 in Rechlingen.

Generalmajor FRANZ (Commander 256 Volksgrenadier Division) – Captured 8 April 45 in Birnfeld.
Information received: 2 May 45

FRANZ (re HITLER's *death*): There has never been such a collapse of a nation.

REITER: Frightful.

FRANZ: With so many resulting problems and concomitant symptoms.

REITER: The FÜHRER is by no means the greatest scoundrel, the greatest criminal.

FRANZ: I am sure he is not. (*Emphatically*) He is certainly not.

REITER: He is a tragic figure, surrounded by incompetent, criminally disposed people.

FRANZ: They made him into one themselves in the end. Naturally he had a certain leaning that way. They would not have succeeded with any other, normal person.

REITER: No.

FRANZ: If a quiet sensible man were President of GERMANY – they could not have turned old HINDENBURG into a criminal so easily. But then there should have been people who would say to him: 'My FÜHRER – '

REITER: So we are not entirely blameless.

FRANZ: Where GOERING was concerned, for example, someone should have gone to him in the early days and said: 'My FÜHRER, we would like to point out – '

REITER: The people he had round him! That waster RIBBENTROP, that pathological morphia addict, GOERING. That was the type of person he had. HESS has gone.

FRANZ: He was perhaps the best of the lot.

REITER: I should have said this evening . . . should have stood up and said: 'Gentlemen! (*Dramatically*) Our former FÜHRER is dead. I request, let us break up the meeting.'

FRANZ: That would have been the best thing, so that no great discussions – I have met the FÜHRER personally a few times. His nose rather put me off. His eyes and the way he looked, and his nose and that bristly moustache which gave his face such a stern appearance – rather a fanatical expression. That made one rather suspicious about him. But I am convinced that if the man had fallen into the right, into sensible hands – for instance he should have been made 'Reichskanzler' under old HINDENBURG – then things would not have turned out as they did.[168] There should have been someone above him – not only God Almighty, whom in any case he did not recognise.

REITER: To sum up, today I would say: the man has certainly done the Germans some good services. I would say: he is a tragic figure, a centre of contention and a tragic personality, surrounded by an incompetent circle of criminals.

FRANZ: Yes.

One gets one shock after another. They are all things which it was impossible to reckon on.

REITER: It's all dreadful, absolutely dreadful.

FRANZ: HIMMLER and DÖNITZ will now wage war on each other!

REITER: They say that the FÜHRER designated DÖNITZ to be his successor. How did he visualise it all? It has to be acceptable to the people. How can he pick on that man? It's out of the question.

FRANZ: Actually the German people shouldn't put up with it.

REITER: DÖNITZ wants to carry on the war just as the FÜHRER would have done.

FRANZ: I simply don't know what to say.

REITER: The moment the FÜHRER's eyes close, a new government should be set up; it must be approved by the people.

FRANZ: It should be elected. Yes, they are doing all the things they shouldn't do all over again. The German people could flatly announce: 'It's out of the question! I must be consulted as to whether I agree or not.' It's just another dictatorship now. From one dictatorship to another. The FÜHRER was the only man with character. He impressed us. Actually, he once had very good ideas.

REITER: He was a historical figure; only history will be able to give him his proper due; one must first hear all that happened; we have heard nothing. Those incompetent fools who never told the FÜHRER that he was being lied to in reports etc.! We, too, shall be blamed for that, you can be sure of that.

FRANZ: At the moment we are under no military oath.

REITER: No – well yes. If the FÜHRER handed over – I really don't know.

FRANZ: I don't care a damn, I swore allegiance to *him*. I never swore allegiance to DÖNITZ.

REITER: We shall have to take a new oath now.

FRANZ: I wouldn't dream of swearing allegiance to just anyone now.

REITER: Anyway, it's out of the question for PW.

FRANZ: At any rate, I owe allegiance to no one now, at least, that's what I'm telling myself. I don't know if I'm right or not.

Document 80

CSDIC (UK), GRGG 300

Report on information obtained from Senior Officers (PW) on 16–17 May 45 [TNA, WO 208/4177]

MASSOW: We Generals must be put into circulation again, we must assist in the reconstruction, we must cooperate again, and it would therefore be absolutely incomprehensible if we were kept here indefinitely for a long period.

[. . .]

Document 81

CSDIC (UK), GRGG 301
Report on information obtained from Senior Officers (PW) on 18–19 May 45
[TNA, WO 208/4178]

DITTMAR: If they adopt the HANOVER-HERSFELD line as the Russian–
  Anglo-American demarcation line GERMANY will go red.
THOMA: Yes.
DITTMAR: We must be extremely careful to see that we are not backing
  the wrong horse, if we enter into dealings with the Anglo-Americans.

FRANZ: These English and Americans are a sanctimonious crowd. The
  things they are carrying out now, with high-sounding words. First they
  kill the German population with their bombs etc., and then they just
  leave them to die. With all their fine speeches and so on, they are doing
  exactly what they want to do: eradicate twenty million Germans. To
  support their actions they bring up the concentration camp business
  and leading Party men, etc. They bring that up and say: 'That is our
  permit for doing what we do.'

Document 82

CSDIC (UK) SR REPORT, SRGG 1271 [TNA, WO 208/4170]

The following is a lecture on conditions on the Russian front given by:
CS/443 – Generalleutnant HEIM (Commander, Boulogne) – Captured 23 Sept. 44
in Boulogne – to his fellow officers (PW) on 23 May 1945.

HEIM: Could the war have been won at all, even if no military mistakes
  had been made? My opinion is: no. From 1941 onwards *at the latest* it
  was just as much lost as the Great War because the political aims bore
  no relation whatsoever to GERMANY's military and economic
  possibilities.[169] The only thing HITLER's particular method of waging
  war cost the German people, was millions too many people killed.
  That's the only thing – the war could not be won. The remarkable
  thing is this, a thing about which I am always thinking: how is it that
  a country like GERMANY, which is situated in the middle of the
  continent, has not developed politics to an *art*, in order to maintain
  peace, a sensible peace, in this much more difficult situation, than, for
  instance, the English situation; that on both occasions we were so
  fatuously stupid as to think that we could challenge the world – which
  is of course what it eventually amounts to when the war has been lost
  – without seeing that that is absolutely impossible in the situation in
  which we find ourselves in GERMANY. What are the reasons for it? Is it
  lack of political understanding, is it lack of political experience – I am

no politician, I am no historian, I don't know, I only see the question. We never could have won the war. Only in my opinion this method of conducting the war cost us millions too many lives, and secondly the complete plundering and looting of GERMANY in all directions. Had the war been conducted differently, it might have lasted another six months or a year but the outcome would have been exactly the same.

The Russians are excellent soldiers. Even FREDERICK THE GREAT admired their toughness.[170] I have seen various Russian Generals being interrogated; they included the most varied types. Young men between 30 and 40, for instance, who were originally labourers at MOSCOW and who then attended these military academies and were trained there, men with plenty of brains and sense, extremely clever. Others, the older ones, whose roots go back to the Czarist time, who were young men at that time and were then taken over. They were more or less people who were good soldiers, but who were not Communists at all at heart, whereas these young people were out-and-out Bolshevists, they made no bones about it, on the contrary, and one must admit that the Russians are extraordinarily quick to learn. They have learnt a tremendous amount from all the fighting, from all the campaigns in FRANCE etc., and knew how to pass on to the officer corps quickly the lessons they had learned from the fighting, and then gradually, under the very strict and energetic leadership of STALIN, got things so much in hand in time, that, together with their material superiority – for you must never forget that RUSSIA only had a war on one front, and that she was able to turn her whole military might towards the West – so at the same time as our warfare was becoming more and more stupid, they finally gained superiority, and then got on not only through this superiority, but then undoubtedly also very ably commanded in the course of the years 1942, 1943 and 1944.[171] I am convinced that if their command had been as good in the winter of 1941/42 as it was later, there would probably have been a collapse on the Eastern Front then. The fact that we did succeeding holding them up on the Eastern Front was on the one hand due to HITLER and the brute-force which he brought to bear behind the front with this victory slogan: 'Hold out at all cost' – and on the other hand it was perfectly clear that the Russian command from top to bottom didn't quite recognise their big chance or see the big gaps there which could have been taken advantage of by quick action.

The Russians did not carry our a 'Blitzkrieg' quite to extremes. They adopted a great many things we used in our 'Blitzkrieg': the use of tank corps, the idea of large encircling movements, the formation of pockets etc., they adopted those, but in contrast to us they were commanded in a much more reasonable, substantial way, and did not set themselves such *enormous* aims[172] which were fulfilled in FRANCE in a way which no soldier would have believed possible. That was one of HITLER's ideas,[173] and he was right about it. The Russians took from us the idea of fighting with large tank armies, and how to carry out large outflanking movement, but they did it more slowly and carefully; with us it always immediately overran all bounds and that was because HITLER's ideas were always like that: in FRANCE he was right, in RUSSIA he made the fundamental mistake of thinking that it was only necessary to attack the enemy properly and penetrate his front, and that we should then have more or less complete freedom of movement. In FRANCE that was the case![174]

It was incredible what the Russians achieved in the way of reserves. We realised that in the winter of 1941/42 when the roads were just mud tracks. If I remember right we had about a hundred different types of trucks manufactured by a variety of firms,[175] each having its own special spare parts; so the spare parts of one couldn't be used for others, and those were vehicles naturally intended for use on European roads; the Russians only had three types of Ford trucks, a small one, a medium one and a large one; consequently all spare parts could be used for any of them.[176] One of the most amazing features is that the Russians were an out-and-out peasant nation up to the outbreak of the World War; they were an agricultural people; Bolshevism transformed their Soviet Nation of peasants into a nation of technicians within a period of 20 years; so the Russians must possess a natural technical talent. People who knew RUSSIA well told me that the Russians, even the peasants were always very handy craftsmen who used their primitive means to fabricate things, motivated by an inner urge to create. For instance in RUSSIA, at the time of those large pockets when thousands of their trucks and vehicles were either completely destroyed or damaged, two or three Russians used to be got together and told to make one vehicle from the wreck of four others. They achieved it too. One reason of course was that any part of one vehicle could be used for another and because they had a natural talent and were undoubtedly trained for the job. It was one of the major surprises. The Ford vehicles probably with cooperation from FORD, were constructed along entirely different lines from the ordinary ones in EUROPE. They were higher off the ground, giving them more freedom of movement; they all had two rear wheels and two rear tyres each side, besides which they had a special peculiarity; you know the so-called snow-chains used here; they had similar mud-chains which were somewhat different; the Russians, knowing what their winter is like, had organised them accordingly. We didn't do that. We went there with absolutely normal central European vehicles and consequently we got stuck everywhere.

Our Air Force made terrific efforts to destroy enemy transport by attacking big railway marshalling yards or railways in narrow valleys. Undoubtedly these attacks were effective for quite a time but it was incredible how quickly repairs were carried out; our recce aircraft reported that the entire population of the neighbourhood was being collected, given spades and pickaxes and everything was put in order again. Sometimes our pilots were quite desperate because they realised that the damage they had once more caused would be repaired within two or three days, and the trains would be running as usual everywhere. In this respect the Russians had recognised the meaning of total warfare, and put it into practice to a far greater extent than we had, we who talked such a lot about it.

Russian women are far better and more reliable workers than Russian men. For that reason the Russians usually recruited great numbers of women to carry out road work. This system was capable of coping with the circumstances; our system as it gradually developed would have been equally efficient if it had gone the whole way and regarded human beings as cyphers. It was exactly the same under the Czars. The terrific problems of road and rail transport were thus solved by the Russians throwing in *all* their forces with relentless energy.[177]

From the point of view of actual fighting the German soldier always felt superior to the Russian on account of his knowledge, his efficient handling of weapons and his tactics. Tactics on both sides were probably equal but German soldiers were more highly trained in the various things and knew more about them. Especially after 1941, the great shortcomings of rapid training became apparent in the Russian soldiers, besides which Slavs are doubtlessly not as intelligent or receptive as Germans. However the Slavs have one *immense* advantage over Western Europeans: death means nothing to them, nothing at all! This attitude towards death is entirely different from ours, even the European Slavs. He inclines towards the oriental attitude and consequently is incredibly steadfast. He'll fight until the last as a matter of course much more readily than we Western Europeans. We used to shout and shout about it but in practice it was difficult to carry out. It wasn't so hard for the Russians; they really did allow themselves to be slaughtered. In addition the so-called commissar system which meant there were commissars in every army branch, right down to the individual companies,[178] proved a great main-stay. Even if a simple soul, a peasant who doesn't know much more about Bolshevism than we do, faltered, there was always someone who, by iron energy, persuasion, punishments or rewards, was able to save the situation. Thus, on the whole, the Russians were quite excellent soldiers.

German arms were superior to Russian ones in 1941. From 1942 onwards the Russians came along with their masses of T-34s – which were the best tanks in the world for a long time, there's no doubt about it in spite of their many disadvantages.[179] Above all these tanks had the advantage of a slanting shape which caused shells to bounce off them unless fired under *exceptionally* favourable conditions. Its disadvantage was its relatively poor field of vision which was much worse than ours. However, they produced them in large quantities. In that respect we also made a huge mistake. We didn't believe Russian industry capable of holding out – I can't judge to what extent they were aided by ENGLAND and AMERICAN – and of recuperating so quickly from their collapse in 1941 when they lost the whole of the DONETZ basin, STALINGRAD etc. which contained gigantic factories. This was probably due to the fact that no one knew what was going on beyond the URALS. We only realised later, in retrospect, that they must have a terrific industrial area there which enabled them to produce such quantities of war materials in spite of everything.[180] Then they brought out their so-called STALIN 'Orgeln', rocket-launchers, 'Katuschkas'. At any rate they were most unpleasant as new weapons. Gradually we grew accustomed to them. They're like this: contrary to artillery shells they approach so slowly you can't hear them; in the case of artillery fire you can usually hear each shell being fired and can throw yourself down and take cover but you cannot do that in the case of these rockets because they approach so slowly they make no noise; suddenly they land all round you in the field where you happen to be standing, driving or riding, all in the course of a minute. First and foremost is their moral effect! Their actual effect wasn't as great. We also had a rocket-launcher but it couldn't be thrown in on that scale. The principle was the same. As regards anti-tank weapons, they hadn't any more than we had, the so-called 'Pak-Kanone', but they were mainly on the defensive then and were forced to bring out a slightly larger calibre than we had. We had the '3.7' which proved *completely* useless after some time. The Russians soon switched over to '5.6'; nowadays '7.5s' are preferred as a rule. You never use anything smaller than '7.5' nowadays.[181] They were very effective as they penetrated everything. The Russian campaign was interesting in as far as one observed the continual battle between tanks and defence weapons. When the Russian brought out their new weapon we had to alter our tank tactics. We could no longer dash into an attack in a straight-forward manner as we used to do, reckoning that we might lose a tank or two; we couldn't do that but we had by cautiously creeping forward to try and locate the weapons and attempt an attack from the side. That was the continuous struggle. The Russians then developed a new method of using their weapons; they attempted to form 'Pak' nests in order not be be surrounded; that sort of thing is always in a continuous state of development.

The Russians were extremely clever at forming army corps without us noticing it. I was told an example of that – it must have been in 1944 – when we realised, and it was also mentioned in the press, that a large strategic concentration was moving down near ODESSA, so an attack there was expected. Then, much to our surprise, it was made in the centre. What had the Russians done? They had originally assembled in concentration areas. They had set up the whole WT network in the normal way, then left this WT network standing and sent the troops northwards on short night marches. That took a fortnight. They made short marches by night, so that in the morning when it was light and the reconnaissance aircraft made their early morning patrol, everything was hidden away and not a soul was to be seen on the roads.[182] Then there was this point: sometimes it was noticed, but our forces were already *so* weak, that even when we did notice it, we could take no decisive action against it. The Russians have such a huge population, they can keep on forming new divisions. Just imagine that huge country! The latest figures for the population are probably 200 million. Then millions of Chinese coolies were fetched as well[183] and are doing armament work at the front. Also in that respect HITLER kept on deceiving himself – nobody knows where he actually got hold of the idea – into thinking that this Russian industry was nearly at an end and that their transport system was breaking down. Certainly I believe that the Russian High Command was for a time anxious about their transport system, but there couldn't have been any question at all of a complete collapse.

Russian low-level command wasn't as efficient as ours – in my opinion this is also due to their being Slavs; they are somewhat lacking in middle classes such as the Western Europeans have:[184] consequently their successes were only achieved with far greater sacrifices. Once I saw some very unbiased statistics compiled from a great mass of troops experiences; in general you can reckon on three Russians killed to one German.[185] However, they can afford it whereas one is already too much for us. That's the difference. A Russian division consists of from 10 to 14 thousand men.[186]

I was only in the UKRAINE, in the southern territory. There were no partisans there at all. That is because there are no woods there. There were no partisans where there were no woods. They couldn't live in the villages as the population would have objected. They reasoned: 'If we allowed partisans to live here we'll be the ones to suffer. Take them away!' As a result there were no partisans there at all. You found them wherever there were woods.[187] They did it along *completely* revolutionary lines. In time they dropped entire *armies* etc. by parachute.[188] Of course we had to *pay dearly* as our forces were already fairly thin and we had to think a long time whether to throw a man in to the North, Centre or South. Immense forces were swallowed up merely in protecting ourselves against the partisans, without our even contemplating fighting them.[189] The partisans got their supplies by air or by organising looting raids in the neighbourhood – they plundered all the villages and took along everything they found, cows etc.[190] They hadn't many tanks but if they were in a forest through which lead important communication roads which constitute the *life lines* of armies, and stay there for a few days they caused untold damage.[191] It tied down an immense number of our forces and it was a very nerve-racking and exhausting kind of war for the troops in those parts, as a partisan in the forest is like a wild animal. A peasant nation like the Russians which is far nearer to the soil than we are has a natural sense of direction. Only when fighting a people of that sort do you realise to what extent you've become townsmen.

The partisans didn't make propaganda among our troops. Not whilst I was there, which was until 1942. Later on when we suffered those heavy collapses, they made more use of it. They didn't do so until then. I met a very interesting man, General POPATOFF(?). He was commander of the 5th Russian Army[192] which was facing us in the KIEV region. He was one of the former – he called himself a MOSCOW labourer and probably came from the working classes but changed over to a military career at the age of 17. He will have been between 35 and 40 years of age. His answers to interrogation were very clever; we asked his opinion of the Russian and German artillery. Finally he was asked: 'What do you think is the reason we have managed to reach KIEV?' He thought for a moment and said: 'It's not surprising as a matter of fact. You had the initiative – we hadn't.' A very clever and accurate answer. Not because of the difference in arms or because one or the other had rather more but it depended on the initiative. That became apparent the moment the initiative went over to the Russians.

Two of HITLER's sayings were circulated with a purpose at the time. First: 'The bubble which I shall prick', and secondly: 'the colossus with feet of clay'. Both sayings proved to be quite wrong. Now one can ask: could that mistake have been avoided? If you wage war you must try and put everything you can into it; I have no doubt about that. I know General KÖSTERING who was military attaché. He was a German, born at LENINGRAD and practically at home in RUSSIA; Russian was his mother tongue, and he was highly esteemed there and in our innermost hearts we said: 'No!'[193] even if we didn't realise the extent of it; but we all knew that things were different from what HITLER imagined them to be. HITLER didn't sense it as he has the remarkable peculiarity of always having preconceived ideas about everything. Once he said: 'I don't give a damn for intellect, intuition, instinct is the thing.'[194] He had a certain instinct – Heaven only knows where he got it – and he put greater faith in that instinct than in any intellect. It is psychologically quite comprehensible that as he believed his intuition was right, he distrusted all figures which seemed to contradict his intuition and rejected them. A twirp like RIBBENTROP, who was only a jobbing assistant of course knew it would all miscarry. I'm also convinced that KÖSTERING and that lot were *entirely* in the picture as to what was happening in the background. However, one might have known it wasn't a mere soap bubble. The man responsible for making decisions either didn't know or didn't want to know. And that, as CHURCHILL recently said quite rightly, was 'the great act of folly of a tyrant'.[195] From then on all sensible people realised the war was lost.

The Russians were very clever pupils. However it was apparently known before, that the Russians were not great industrial inventors but very receptive learners. It was very interesting: in 1927 and 1928 we had various military institutions in RUSSIA, air-training schools, tank-training schools, everything which was forbidden by the Treaty of VERSAILLES.[196] We had people over there – for instance *I* myself had several friends – who anyway had been to RUSSIA. If you asked them: 'What is RUSSIA *really* like?' they always produced two categories of people according to how they let themselves be influenced. Some said: 'It's a great big swindle!' Others said: 'RUSSIA will prove an *immense* danger! Don't let us close our eyes to that!"

I can tell you how PW were treated; they were usually set to work at the front straight away. *One* thing is certain. My documents contained a huge number of cases, confirmed by numerous witnesses, of *excessive* cruelty at the moment of capture.[197] That is partly due to the Slav character which doesn't fear death but is afraid of torture. The following happened: at KIEV where we were stationed a long time[198] the Russians had agents consisting of men and women in civilian clothes who roamed the streets allegedly on a visit to some aunt of theirs. Some of these people were taken and discovered to be agents; they were to find out military secrets. These people were interrogated not by the SS according to SS methods but by my intelligence men as is the proper military way. If they refused to talk we threatened to beat them. Then they talked. If you said: 'You'll be shot!' they didn't say a word. But if you hinted there were other methods besides shooting etc. – that we had learnt a lot from the Russians in that respect! A completely different way of looking at things. For instance, eyes put out, cut off noses, ears and genitals – it was difficult to tell whether this took place before or after death – but a great number of thus mutilated corpses were found. Now comes a peculiar fact: Russian PW were well behaved and quiet, they didn't grumble – that's typically Slav too. When they get excited, become angry, also in the fury of battle, they become cruel. When they are conquered or when they are left in peace and you don't want anything from them they are the most reliable, useful and placid people I know. Undoubtedly we Western Europeans are up against a mentality foreign to us. In retrospect, when looking back at BUCHENWALD etc., we must come to the conclusion that HITLER didn't respect and even envy STALIN for nothing. They had something in common, with the difference that on the one side it was the actual expression of a completely different national character and with us just something pathological.

II.
'We Have Tried to Exterminate Whole Communities.' War Crimes in Trent Park Conversations

Document 83

CSDIC (UK) SR REPORT, SRM 145 [TNA, WO 208/4165]

LUDWIG CRÜWELL – General der Panzertruppe – Captured 29 May 42 in North Africa.
WILHELM RITTER VON THOMA – General der Panzertruppe – Captured 4 Nov. 42 in North Africa.
Information received: 5 Dec. 42

THOMA: In November or December the order came down from the Army Group HQ that the (Russian) Regimental Commissars were to be taken prisoner.[199] Of course that very soon became known and therefore everyone was after these Commissars and they got to know about it too, they were absolute fanatics – they said: 'Then I shall hold out to the last and drive my men on, because I shall be killed in any case.' I had one who had been in BERLIN in TUKHACHEVSKI's time.[200] He called himself liaison officer between the encircled Army Group, the Corps which we had there, and the man in command of the partisans, that was General BELOW(?),[201] and this particular colonel was the liaison officer. He spoke a little German and I said to him: 'You've been in GERMANY, do you really believe that we kill people? Look out of the window' – a crowd of Russians happened to be going past at that moment – we had Russian workmen, whom we treated well and they worked hard. I said: 'Take a look out of the window, those men aren't at all badly off.'[202] Then he said: 'Yes, that may be, you need them for labour, but you shoot the Commissars, we've got some of your orders.' I denied it, or course, and said: 'You're wrong there.' He said: 'No, we can't be wrong there, because a number of such orders have been found.'[203] Then I said: 'But we haven't got any Commissars.' 'Yes, your officers and Commissars are one and the same,' he said. I reported it at the time. Then a few weeks later we lost two captains, both splendid leaders who had advanced too far from an excess of zeal and had been captured. And we didn't retake this village until some weeks later, it was near VLASITCHI(?),[204] and we asked the peasants about them immediately and they said they had been taken to the next village. We sent the interpreter to make enquiries in the next village: 'Yes, they were brought here by sledge and were shot here behind the barn.' And then they uncovered the grave and there they were in it, they had all been shot in the back. 'Yes,' he said calmly, 'your officers are also Commissars.' I know that HALDER, BRAUCHITSCH and everyone were absolutely opposed to that order.[205]

CRÜWELL: You must have been at the FÜHRER's Headquarters at that time?

THOMA: Yes, just at that time.[206] The matter was discussed for a long time – those are the famous FÜHRER's orders. Those are the things for which I blame Field Marshal KEITEL above all. He should have said: 'My FÜHRER, let's sleep on that till tomorrow morning,' because those are only spontaneous ideas of his. 'If we do this, our people will be treated in the same way and then on grounds of discipline – our men will become "rowdies".' If it had been put to him in that way he might have been convinced, even if against his will. But as it is they simply obey. And the orders that came through latterly were enough to make you sick and they were all signed 'KEITEL, Field Marshal'.

CRÜWELL: And what were they?

THOMA: For example, there is the order that a man can only get further promotion, if it has been thoroughly investigated whether he is a 150 per cent true National Socialist, and there has to be this thorough investigation and he has to furnish proof. How is a soldier to produce proof? And our 'First Soldier' issues orders like that! That caused very bad feeling especially among the older officers.[207]

CRÜWELL: What were NEHRING's[208] orders?

THOMA: NEHRING is stupid. He re-issued extracts from those orders. He issued some stupid orders which came down in the form of leaflets. One of these so-called orders was: 'We are so short of material that every cartridge case is of the greatest value at home, and if material continues to be wasted as it is at present, we will have to stop the war in the autumn.' He issued orders like this, signed NEHRING, thousands of them were sent down.[209]

Document 84

SRX 150

CRÜWELL – General der Panzertruppe – Captured 29 May 42 in North Africa.
THOMA – General der Panzertruppe – Captured 4 Nov. 42 in North Africa.
BURCKHARDT – Major (C.C. 1 Paratroop Regiment – Captured 5 Nov. 42 in North Africa.
Information received: 26 Jan. 43

THOMA (*re explains about atrocities*): '. . . so that I am actually ashamed to be an officer.' And then he said: 'Why are you telling me this?' I said: 'Whom else should I tell it to?' He said: 'That's a political matter, it's got nothing at all to do with me.' I've never forgotten that of HALDER.[210] Then I went and put it into writing and gave it to BRAUCHITSCH. And BRAUCHITSCH didn't say much, but I could read in his eyes what was up – he said: 'Do you want to take it further?' He said: 'Listen, if you take it further, anything may happen.' Then I said: 'Of course, because I am ashamed to have experienced a thing like that.' The good people say: 'The FÜHRER doesn't know about that.' Of course he knows all about it. Secretly he's delighted. He says: 'Things – went – badly – for – so – many – years.' and now he's getting his own back, and thereby, by that attitude, he has thrown away the inner respect of the honest decent people. Of course, people can't make a row, they would simply be arrested and beaten if they did. But he says – he just ignores it, he's not in the least interested in it. (He just says) 'Let the hooligans remain in power' – and so they do and it's obvious what you said to me recently. 'It mustn't happen again that they go about with the red flag. Of course it won't happen because it's a dictatorship, but that doesn't mean that the idea has been uprooted completely, that's why they are all the more likely to blow up. Or, worse still, we may get passive resistance – that's much more dangerous. In a company it doesn't matter if there are rows now and then, but when there's a passive resistance in a company – there is such a thing too.

Document 85

CSDIC (UK) SR REPORT, SRM 175 [TNA, WO 208/4165]

LUDWIG CRÜWELL – General der Panzertruppe – Captured 29 May 42 in North Africa.
WILHELM RITTER VON THOMA – General der Panzertruppe – Captured 4 Nov. 42 in North Africa.
Information received: 14 Feb. 43

THOMA: A Staatsanwalt from MINSK came to see me in March; he was really a BERLIN Staatsanwalt. He was a man in the forties and he begged me to do everything in my power to enable him to join up as a soldier in any capacity – he was a NCO on the reserve. He said: 'I can't stand the things that are going on here any longer.' Then he told me the kind of thing that happened. I know myself that there were actually savage, brutalised louts there, who trampled on the bellies of pregnant women, and that sort of thing.
CRÜWELL: Yes, but those are very isolated cases for which even the SS can't be blamed. I can't believe that Germans would do such a thing!

THOMA: I don't think I should have believed it either, if I hadn't actually seen it. I made two written reports about it. I feel that no one can accuse me of having been in any way responsible for it.

CRÜWELL: What did you report in writing?

THOMA: The atrocities perpetrated by the SS and the shootings and the mass executions at PSKIP(?) and at MINSK – two pages of typescript which I sent to the OKW.[211] I received no reply. I established that no soldiers were ever involved, only a special detachment of the SS. They introduced the name 'Rollkommando.' It's no good denying it. Of course, these people have become completely brutalised by months of such conduct.

CRÜWELL: I am the last to want to defend such atrocities but, taking the broad view, you must admit that we were bound to take the most incredibly severe measures to combat the illegal guerrilla warfare in those vast territories.

THOMA: Yes, but the women had nothing whatever to do with it. Orders were actually given that all Jews were (to be cleared out of) the occupied territories – that is the great idea, but, of course, there are so many in the east that you don't know where to start.[212]

Document 86

CSDIC (UK) SR-REPORT, SRGG 209 [TNA, WO 208/4165]

GEORG NEUFFER – Generalmajor (GOC, 20th Flak Division) – Captured 9 May 43 in Tunisia.

GERHARD BASSENGE – Generalmajor (GOC, Air Defences Tunis/Bizerta) – Captured 9 May 43 in Tunisia.

Information received: 10 July 43

NEUFFER: What will they say when they find our graves in POLAND? The OGPU[213] can't have done anything worse than that. I myself have seen a convey at LUDOWICE(?)[214] near MINSK; I must say it was frightful, a horrible sight. There were lorries full of men, women and children – quite small children. It is ghastly, this picture. The women, the little children who were, of course, absolutely unsuspecting – frightful! Of course, I didn't watch while they were being murdered. German police stood about with tommy-guns, and – do you know what they had there? Lithuanians, or fellows like that, in the brown uniform,[215] did it. The German Jews were also sent to the MINSK district, and were gradually killed off, so far as they survived the other treatment. By treatment I mean housing and food and so on. It was done like this: when Jews were taken away from FRANKFURT – they were only notified immediately beforehand – they were allowed to take only a little with them, a hundred marks, otherwise nothing, and then the hundred marks would be demanded from them at the station to pay the fare.[216] But these things are so well known – if that ever gets known in the world at large – that's why I was so surprised that we got so frightfully worked up over the KATYN case![217]

BASSENGE: Yes.

NEUFFER: For that's a trifle in comparison to what we have done there.

Document 87

CSDIC (UK) SR REPORT, SRGG 303 [TNA, WO 208/4166]

KURT KÖHNCKE – Oberstleutnant (Commander, 372 Heavy Flak Battery) – Captured 8 May 43 in Tunisia – and a number of German Senior Officers (PW) one of whom may be:

HANS REIMANN – Oberst (Commander, Panzer Grenadier Regiment 86) – Captured 12 May 43 in Tunisia.

Information received: 12 Aug. 43

KÖHNCKE: Oberst HEYM (PW)[218] says: 'If I were commander of the German troops I would set alight every village and every town in ITALY and withdraw slowly to the BRENNER, as a reply to the fact that the Italians have now apparently sent divisions to the BRENNER in order to guard the railway there.' That's a fine idea, completely senseless, but just like us.

?: Yes. (*laughing*)

KÖHNCKE: Just like us: 'I am going to destroy everything now and withdraw.'

?: That's the old Vandal spirit.

? REIMANN: If we do that, these people will promptly declare war on us.

?: Just like in the campaign in the west the Württemberg engineers said: 'Shall we just set the village on fire a little, Sir, or shall we destroy it completely?' (*laughter*)[219]

?: I keep thinking of the people at REGGIO when we were there how they hated giving up quarters to us – that finished me off.

?: Then when we were in ITALY proper the attitude of everyone was altogether against us.

?: It was divided into three parts throughout ITALY.

KÖHNCKE: Fascism?

?: Yes, and the Fascists were not the best of the bunch.

KÖHNCKE: No, Fascism and the Church . . .

?: The Fascists were just people who had nothing to lose.

?: Anyhow, the royalists were very decent people, they didn't want to have anything to do with that crowd. 'We must hold our tongues and we quite like you, but why are you at war? We don't *want* any war, our people want to have their families, they want to live for their children, they are very modest in their demands.'

?: We don't want war either; I didn't want it and I wasn't asked either.

?: The feeling in GERMANY at the beginning of the war was: anxious, but determined.

?: Anxious, but determined – we must be honest about it.

Document 88

CSDIC (UK) SR REPORT, SRGG 422 [TNA, WO 208/4166]

LUDWIG CRÜWELL – General der Panzertruppe – Captured 29 May 42 in North Africa.
HANS-JÜRGEN VON ARNIM – Generaloberst (GOC Army Group Africa) – Captured 12 May 43 in Tunisia.
Information received: 15 Sept. 43

CRÜWELL (*Re shooting of Russian PW by Germans*): LIEBENSTEIN (PW)[220] made a fuss at the dinner-table again today because we had shot so many Russian prisoners. Our people only shot one Commissar – was that so awful?[221]

ARNIM: The SS have shot a lot of people, which was very stupid. Because except for the first two who were still convinced communists, they were just soldiers under orders, and not even members of the party.

CRÜWELL: Was it chiefly only commissars or was it also . . . any sort of P/W . . . ?

ARNIM: Oh no, only the Commissars.

CRÜWELL: He behaves as if all the prisoners had simply been shot.

ARNIM: Well I wouldn't swear to it that when PW were taken away and one of them collapsed on the road, someone didn't give him a shot in the back instead of dragging him along.[222]

CRÜWELL: I think all this is so ridiculous and *quite* monstrous, that one should go around grumbling like that – and light a cigarette – and throw mud like that at one's own people whilst in a prison camp. Don't you think so? But if things turn out differently then we'll talk about it again, Sir. Then the others will pretend they have not said anything. Then they'll only be annoyed that the FÜHRER doesn't say to all the generals 'en bloc': 'You are all the most charming people.' When you see these people you have to admit the FÜHRER is *quite* right to have his suspicions.[223]

Document 89

CSDIC (UK) SR REPORT, SRGG 495 [TNA, WO 208/4166]

FRIEDRICH FREIMERR VON BROICH (GOC 10th Panzer Division) – Captured 12 May 43 in Tunisia.

EGERSDORF – Oberst (Commander, TUNIS) – Captured 8 May 43 in Tunisia.
ULRICH BOES – Major (Staff Officer to Generalleutnant von SPONECK (PW)) –
Captured 9 May 43 in Tunisia.
Information received: 21 Oct. 43

?: We can't complain if they ever stand on German soil and simply raze
   . . . *completely* to the ground, or deport the people into concentration
   camps and make them work. We have done *exactly* the same sort of
   thing.
?: If anyone had any doubts about it, he was enlightened in no uncertain
   manner by our behaviour in all the occupied territories – I witnessed it
   in GREECE too.[224]
?: The soldiers . . . the best propaganda *for* the THIRD REICH that you
   could possible imagine. These people in FRANCE and in the BALKANS
   whom I met were enthusiastic about the discipline of the Germany
   army. And the very *moment* the Party and the SS took over the
   control, even the most harmless citizens became fanatics – *against* us.
   I mean, is that wise or is it part of the creed? If that were really a part
   of National Socialism, then National Socialism would be the greatest
   crime there is. But it isn't so by any means – National Socialism is
   actually a *wonderful* creed. The people who are at present playing first
   fiddle aren't National Socialists at all; they are *criminals*.
?: If GERMANY is destroyed in this war, so that even our private lives
   cease to be our own, do you think that generations to come will curse
   these people?
?: I have to admit that mistakes have been made.
?: That is quite beside the point. Mistakes have been made in every age
   by every nation. The point is that the men in authority are *bad*
   characters of a *low* type; *that* is the criminal part of it. That is vastly
   different from 'making mistakes'.
?: I don't want to accuse the government, but I think the manner in
   which we have behaved towards the rest of the world is so *shameless*
   that even our children will blush. In my opinion no greater outrage to
   civilisation than this mass murder of innocent people who have done
   nothing beyond the fact that perhaps they had been circumcised or had
   belonged to some other race . . . Are there any pure races left now?
?: BAYERLEIN once told me about the ghettos in WARSAW;[225] he was taken
   round at the time. He said it makes him shudder to think of it.
   Twenty-four people living in one room, and the bread ration so
   calculated that 1 per cent and 2 per cent were *bound* to die every week.
?: In the long run we owe the fact that we got out of the mess again
   entirely to National Socialism. Nobody else brought it off; we tried all
   ways – with Herr BRÜNING and Herr –
?: But after all we too witnessed it; if it hadn't been the FÜHRER it would
   have been someone else, who might have done it in a different way.

?: You can't say that. We can only say that he was the one – all the rest is theory.

?: Of course everything else is theory, but what you are saying isn't entirely devoid of theory either; because, if he hadn't turned up, it would probably have developed more slowly and a slow steady development is often better than a blow-up of that sort. I should feel happier at any rate and the German people too, I feel sure.

?: At any rate I don't believe that a hundred years hence history will say: 'We have the FÜHRER to thank for our resurrection after 1918'; but it will unfortunately have to say: 'We have him to thank for the loss of our independence.' That will be the final judgment.

?: Yes, and above all it will . . . as a step back into the darkest ages . . .

?: Yes – barbarity.

?: There has never been anything like it except the Thirty Years' War. In the Thirty Years' War it wasn't so conspicuous because conditions were different then, but nowadays it is damned conspicuous.

?: We have shown clearly that we are *completely* incapable of ruling other people.

?: Yes, such a 'ruling class' . . .

?: How could a thing like that last? And quite apart from states further away, just think of BOHEMIA and MORAVIA alone – do you think that could have gone on for a few more years?

?: POLAND – they would continually have killed off our local leaders.

?: We can't compare ourselves with ENGLAND in the slightest degree. Ask the people in South-West (AFRICA). They think they're very well off under English rule.

?: I mean, at the beginning ENGLAND used quite different means when establishing her world empire, from those she uses now.

?: Yes, we wanted to establish a world empire only four years after we had introduced general conscription!

?: No, this is how I look at it. Owing to the war there is no doubt that measures have become more severe – but they *had* to.

?: Well, nobody objects to the fact that everybody plays his part in the war and so on, but I am convinced that *no* educated, thinking person considers it right the way we have behaved towards the Jews, the Poles and the Czechs and towards the people of opposite views in the concentration camps.

?: But that German-speaking Germans at DANZIG should be *forbidden* to join GERMANY simply because some arrogant English government forbids it – that they feel unhappy there and –

?: Quite right, but that is very different from trying to exterminate whole peoples.

?: Well, I don't think that was our intention.

?: Well, perhaps we didn't intend it, but we have done it. When somebody tells me that at LODZ or the devil knows where, eighteen thousand

Jews have been killed in one morning –

?: Well, say its eighteen hundred. Do you think that's right – or even one-hundred-and-eighty? Even if it's eighteen, if they haven't committed any crime! What right have we to indignation about the massacres of KATYN? Heaven forbid, if the Russians ever open these mass-graves! They are now claiming – of course it can't be checked up – that we killed seventeen thousand at KIEV alone.[226] The Russians are thirsting for revenge.

?: Well, at any rate the Russians who are in our service consider themselves well off, because they are treated decently, as human beings.[227]

?: The Germans are decent fellows; that's the tragic part of it. The unfortunate thing is that the Germans show themselves to others in quite a different light and not as they really are. Quite the contrary, make enquiries in the former occupied territories that we held in the years 1914–18. The people there still hold the German soldiers in high esteem, as I was able to prove time and time again when we were there this time. But I shouldn't like to go twenty years hence to the districts which have been . . . by the SS and the SA. These press-gangs – oh, no! A *tragedy* to live to see such things!

BOES: On the other hand you only need to ask our people in the RHINELAND how they were treated.

?: But that's quite different! I admit they shot SCHLAGETER, because he carried out sabotage on the railway but he's the *only* one we can produce.[228]

?: Yes, but there are sure to have been others who weren't executed but . . . in prisons.

?: Good God, but we've massacred people in their thousands. There's no comparison. At least there were proper courts, before which they appeared. In my opinion, if hundreds or thousands had been shot, we should certainly know about it, they would be . . . as martyrs. Those six or seven or twelve martyrs of the movement![229]

BOES: The point is that one is the struggle for a new order in EUROPE – opposing it stands a world empire, that won this world empire for itself perhaps hundreds of years ago. The one has still to win its empire; that costs sacrifices; while the other one has already passed that stage.

?: We shall never win it by these means; on the contrary, by these means we have shown that if it's possible for anyone to have the leadership in EUROPE, it must in no circumstances be us. Then the whole of EUROPE would rise as *one* man against us as far as they have any feelings of decency left – *that* is what we have achieved. For that is what they are without any doubt, EUROPE's birth-pangs – whether the child will be still-born, we do not yet know; this uniting of great areas into a single empire – that is in process of creation and will come one way or the other. *Who* will predominate is not yet known. *I* am afraid that we have shown, unfortunately that we could *never* exert a predominance like that because we are simply not morally in a position to do so – *no longer* in a position, because everything which used to be admired in a German has been changed to the opposite in the course of the last fourteen, or rather ten years. There is no longer any *justice*, there is no longer any *decency*; there is nothing but force and brutal suppression of opinion and of the right to live and think and so on. A tyranny such as ours has hardly *ever* existed before, and I am *convinced* that, however the war had ended, the next generation, *at least* would, figuratively speaking, have gone about with daggers in their pockets. The young people would not have put up with it in the long run either, for no country has *ever* had a tyranny like this. To modify it – that can't be done, because that is the curse of the wicked deed – they could no longer do that because by then there would be many too many who wanted to avenge themselves.

BOES: Have you experienced this tyranny yourself, Sir, or your family?

?: Well, comparatively little, because I am a soldier and they have not dared to come near us. In one small case I have experienced it, where such difficulties and scenes were made for an officer's wife, simply because she had unwittingly bought a few glasses from a Jewish household, and was then denounced by a maid. She was said also to have criticised the regime at home, while in fact she was an ardent National Socialist – she won't be one any longer.

?: We soldiers are *by far* the best off in this respect. From what I have heard from my friends who have not enjoyed the protection of being a soldier, their treatment is *very* different. Even *now*, I am still a good National Socialist, but in the . . . sense. *Those* are no National Socialists.

?: The FÜHRER's greatest fault is that he does not think like normal people do.

?: Oh, I think he does, but he believes that people are too good.

?: If any man tells me that he prays to God that, if a war must be waged, he should be there to wage it, that in itself is a sign of megalomania.[230]

?: One is always trying to find reasons why things aren't going well now. One has a perfect right to do so, for in the long run you can't live on faith alone. The only people who work on 'faith' – but far more skilfully than the National Socialists – are the Roman Catholic Church. While *here* they always want to prove to me that what has turned into its opposite within three or six days must still be believed in, I can't have any part in that. For that purpose God gave me a mind. It may, perhaps show a lack of character, but I cannot overcome my reasoning. When I see everything that – not in the newspapers, but what I personally *know* because I have *seen* it personally, if I put all *that* into the scales and weigh it, then I am compelled to say: 'Nothing can excuse it, *nothing at all*.' If you . . . a pact of friendship, quite apart from the political side – the way we have broken our pact with RUSSIA is in my opinion scandalous.[231] That is something else that had never happened before. You will argue: 'In wartime only *that* is right which is of advantage to the people!' In the long run that is no advantage. The shooting of the Commissars – I have not been able to discover in any war, except in the dimmest past, that orders like that have been issued by the highest authority. I have seen (?) these orders personally.[232] That is a sign that like a God, that man has simply disregarded everybody and all pacts which exist, and exist on both sides – that is megalomania. We saw the result in the fury with which the Commissars have fought.

?: Don't you believe, Sir, that the English would have broken a pact with just as few scruples, if it had been to the advantage of their people?

?: Certainly; but they would choose a much more skilful reason. In general they don't go in for unnecessary cruelties – that was reserved for us. The English think further ahead. We always think only how to get material for the next speech.

Document 90

CSDIC (UK) SR REPORT, SRGG 520 [TNA, WO 208/4167]

LUDWIG CRÜWELL – General der Panzertruppe – Captured 29 May 42 in North Africa.
HANS-JÜRGEN VON ARNIM – Generaloberst (GOC Army Group Africa) – Captured 12 May 43 in Tunisia.
Information received: 3 Nov. 43

CRÜWELL: If you listen to the gentlemen here, we've done nothing else but kill off everyone. But if you ask anyone, they were never present themselves. They heard about that from THOMA (PW).

ARNIM: I've never spoken to an eye-witness either.

CRÜWELL: It's THOMA, he's seen them all, the eye-witness.

ARNIM: Hasn't THOMA seen it himself?

CRÜWELL: No, no, but he's at any rate supposed to have seen people who did it.

ARNIM: I don't believe that either.

CRÜWELL: No, but he's on friendly terms with all those swine. That's the crazy part! He's almost on terms of 'du' with Sepp DIETRICH.

ARNIM: Charming! And then he curses the whole thing.

CRÜWELL: Yes, that's just what I *mean*. Where's he going to find all this circumstantial evidence(?) if people don't trust him blindly? No one would tell me about it, because they would say: 'This man may be quite a passable soldier, but we don't want to have anything to do with him otherwise.'

ARNIM: They haven't told him either.

CRÜWELL: Well, I don't know.

ARNIM: He may have heard somewhere or other about some case.
I don't like it either, when hostages are killed, when ten Frenchmen are killed because a few Germans have been killed somewhere.

CRÜWELL: But, Good God, in a case of *necessity* – that's *military* law – it's international military law.[233]

ARNIM: I must honestly say in that case I'd carefully pick out the people I was going to take, we'll say criminals or people like that.

CRÜWELL: Well, yes, but you take some of the good ones as well, so that it acts as a deterrent. You *can't* object to that, although I should have a horror of it, too, I am glad that I am not Governor of PARIS. But what would you do then, Sir? If you didn't kill *any*, then *we* should be killed.

ARNIM: Yes, I would get hold of those who had actually committed the murder, those who had committed the *first* murder, with the help of the police or of police troops.

CRÜWELL: Yes, if you *could* do that, then there would be no need for all this business of hostages, but that's how it is. I have never in my life had any hostages killed because I have not been in a dilemma – I have taken hostages, but, thank God, I have not needed to have them killed, but that is in accordance with military law. That's typical again of the English, they say: 'Those Huns – the things they do!' and on the quiet they say to the others: 'You must make a firm stand against them, you must do everything underground, secretly.'

ARNIM: They incite the underground people and if we defend ourselves against them, then there's a great outcry. Incidentally, they are doing the same themselves in INDIA as they are reproaching us with.[234]

CRÜWELL: Yes, certainly, they are letting all the . . . die.

ARNIM: They don't even publish an account in the newspaper when they kill hostages from among Indian nationalists.

Document 91

CSDIC (UK) SR REPORT, SRGG 647 [TNA, WO 208/4167]

HANS CRAMER – General der Panzertruppe (GOC German Afrika Korps) – Captured 12 May 43 in Tunisia.
KLAUS HUBBUCH – Leutnant (ADC to Generalmajor BOROWIETZ (PW) – Captured 9 May 43 in Tunisia.
Information received: 10 Dec. 43

HUBBUCH (*re executions in* POLAND *and* RUSSIA): They are these bands that are taken prisoner and are then put beside their graves and shot – and moreover all of them. None of them are taken prisoner and treated as soldiers, but they are shot.

CRAMER: Yes, that's what I always say too. Outrages have certainly been committed, so-and-so many Jews have been killed and Heaven only knows what, but so far I have never found anyone who has admitted to me that he has witnessed it in person. I am firmly convinced that *terrible* atrocities . . . but at present I haven't any proof of it.

Document 92

CSDIC (UK) SR REPORT, SRGG 666 [TNA, WO 208/4167]

WILHELM RITTER VON THOMA – General der Panzertruppe – Captured 4 Nov. 42 in North Africa.
GERHARD BASSENGE – Generalmajor (GOC, Air Defences Tunis/Bizerta) – Captured 9 May 43 in Tunisia.
Information received: 16 Dec. 43

THOMA: [. . .]
In the paper today there are details of the mass poisonings, that gas business. I know it's true, because the people who did it told me about it themselves.
BASSENGE: I don't know, but I presume it is . . . 100 per cent correct.
THOMA: Yes, I heard of it from a man who had to do it. It was SS men and Gestapo youths who rounded up the Jews and so on, and as they had no technical experts amongst their own numbers, chemists who were in the gas department of the Ordnance Branch, had to work with them.[235] One man told me himself with horror that that time in RUSSIA was the most appalling time of his life; I said I wouldn't have done it.
THOMA: When I've got both the German and English news service I can roughly sift out what's true.
BASSENGE: Obviously everyone lies like a trooper in war-time and here one has the opportunity of hearing both sides –
THOMA: We get a clearer picture than the Generals in command at the front.
BASSENGE: We were never so well-informed as we are here.

Document 93

CSDIC (UK) SR REPORT, SRGG 666 [TNA, WO 208/4167]

HANS REIMANN – Oberst (Commander, Panzer Grenadier Regiment 86) – KURT KÖHNCKE – Oberstleutnant (Commander, 372 Heavy Flak Battery) – Captured 8 May 43 in Tunisia.
Information received: 19 Dec. 43

REIMANN (*re atrocities in* RUSSIA): It's *true* this time. Tell me one thing, in the 1914–18 war did you ever believe in your own mind that a German soldier was capable of doing things like that?

KÖHNCKE: Never.

REIMANN: Never – do you really believe it now?

KÖHNCKE: I have heard so much about it, that I have to believe it. I myself haven't been there so I can't pass an opinion.

REIMANN: A senior police official actually told me about it in the train, that they had shot thousands of Jewish men, women and children at BERDICHEV and ZHITOMIR[236] – he actually told me about it without my asking and he gave such a horrid and vivid description of it that I brought out a bottle of vodka from my bag on the rack and changed the conversation to something else and drank with the fellow. And I've also heard about it from other people. He told me about it with the businesslike calm of a professional murderer.

Document 94

CSDIC (UK) SR REPORT, SRGG 676 [TNA, WO 208/4167]

GEORG NEUFFER – Generalmajor (GOC, 20th Flak Division) – Captured 9 May 43 in Tunisia.

GERHARD BASSENGE – Generalmajor (GOC, Air Defences Tunis/Bizerta) – Captured 9 May 43 in Tunisia.

Information received: 19 Dec. 43

BASSENGE (re BBC midnight news in German[237]): They dished up the mass executions of Jews in POLAND. They estimate here that altogether five million Jews – Polish, Bulgarian, Dutch, Danish and Norwegian – have been massacred.

NEUFFER: Really? Not counting the German ones?

BASSENGE: Including the German Jews, during the whole time. They furnished evidence that an enormous number from camp so-and-so between such-and-such a date, fifteen thousand here, eighteen thousand there, twelve thousand there, six thousand and so on – I must say that if 10 per cent of it is correct, then one ought to –

NEUFFER: I should have thought about three million.

BASSENGE: You know, it really is a disgrace.

NEUFFER: This trial, which has been going on at CHARKOV is really very unpleasant for HITLER too.[238]

BASSENGE: Yes, The Generaloberst[239] (PW) was talking today about the SEYDLITZ people.[240] He said that we must understand that it was only human that those people, who have been through it, should now try to find the reasons and the people responsible for it. If they, in their state of mental depression, adopt that attitude, we mustn't judge them too harshly, even though one is bound to condemn it. He was trying to gloss it over.

NEUFFER: He is frightfully uncertain.

BASSENGE: The first man here to join the SEYDLITZ . . . will be von BROICH (PW). That's dead certain. He said today: 'I would join them at once.'

Document 95

CSDIC (UK) SR REPORT, SRGG 681 [TNA, WO 208/4167]

WILHELM RITTER VON THOMA – General der Panzertruppe – Captured 4 Nov. 42 in North Africa.

GEORG NEUFFER – Generalmajor (GOC, 20th Flak Division) – Captured 9 May 43 in Tunisia.

GERHARD BASSENGE – Generalmajor (GOC, Air Defences Tunis/Bizerta) – Captured 9 May 43 in Tunisia.

Information received: 20 Dec. 43

THOMA: In ATHENS two years ago, Sepp DIETRICH told me personally – I have known him for twenty years. I said to him: 'That's a nice business! Civilians are simply shot, are they? It's the same psychosis as we . . . in 1914 when everyone was just shot – people seeing spies everywhere and so on'; He said: 'I don't care; once they've been shot, I shall be left in peace.'[241] 'Yes,' I said, 'but that is a very dangerous solution, particularly for those who order it.' He replied: 'That doesn't worry me, I'm keeping the last bullet for myself.' He himself is a remarkably energetic man. I hardly think that he would let himself be taken alive. If they captured him, it would only be by accident – and he'll take good care to prevent that. But it is a dreadful thing when one thinks that the men in (military) uniform are ordering things like that.

NEUFFER: I don't believe it. I don't believe that the army has anything to do with it. It is all propaganda . . .

THOMA: It is propaganda too, but, of course – firstly there are the notices, signed by the town major. They know here who the town major is, they know it is so-and-so and there they have it. But it is a scandalous business. There are no end of cases.

NEUFFER: Yesterday evening we reckoned that, according to all reports, five million Jews must have been killed by us up to date.

THOMA: I mean, it's a psychological disease which has spread throughout the Party, not the Army, that everything Jewish must be exterminated – they have orders to do it. I remember in the spring of 1942, when their airmen were always dropping that 'Freedom Pamphlet' with a facsimile in it of the order signed by HITLER about shooting of Commissars, etc. I wasn't there – I asked the GSO I, Ops: 'Have we still got the order?' He replied: 'No, we had to destroy it.'[242]

Document 96

CSDIC (UK) SR REPORT, SRGG 739 [TNA, WO 208/4167]

FRITZ KRAUSE – Chief Artillery Officer (German Army Group Africa) – Captured 9 May 43 in Tunisia.

FRIEDRICH FREIMERR VON BROICH (GOC 10th Panzer Division) – Captured 12 May 43 in Tunisia.

FREIHERR KURT VON LIEBENSTEIN – Generalmajor (GOC, 164th Division) – Captured 13 May 43 in Tunisia.

GERHARD BASSENGE – Generalmajor (GOC, Air Defences Tunis/Bizerta) – Captured 9 May 43 in Tunisia.

Information received: 1 Jan. 44

?BROICH: In this war I once had to have men shot. They were two men who were arrested as spies and active ones at that, according to statements of the inhabitants, and so we said: 'All right, they must be shot.' . . . these men (the firing squad) were fine honest people, some of them were fairly experienced Gefreite and they were pale as death, the job was so hateful to them. Then the adjutant came up and said he was all in for that day, he was running about in circles and was almost crazy because it had got on his nerves so much.[243]

?KRAUSE: . . . often attacked the DRs on these long roads between SALONIKA and SOFIA and when that happened the neighbouring(?) villages were immediately razed to the ground and everybody, men, women and children were herded together and slaughtered. The 'Regiment' commander, BRÜCKELMANN told me about it too. He told me once how horrible it was. They were driven into a pen and then the order was given: 'Fire on them.' Of course there was a terrible screaming as they fell – the children too – and of course they weren't killed outright. Then an officer had to go along and put a bullet through their heads. Another time they dragged them all into the church and took them out singly. They always shot them in threes. The ones inside could hear this and they barricaded themselves in and put up resistance; then they had to burn the church down because they couldn't get in. He said this massacring was horrible, although . . .[244]

?: There were others there too . . .

?: No, no, . . . Greek(?) villages.

?: But did the order come from the Army . . .

?: Yes.

Document 97

CSDIC (UK) SR REPORT, SRGG 815 [TNA, WO 208/4167]

GEORG NEUFFER – Generalmajor (GOC, 20th Flak Division) – Captured 9 May 43 in Tunisia.
GERHARD BASSENGE – Generalmajor (GOC, Air Defences Tunis/Bizerta) – Captured 9 May 43 in Tunisia.
Information received: 2 Feb. 44

NEUFFER: The Russians haven't reached the spot yet where those large-scale mass murders took place.
BASSENGE: Were they on such a large scale?
NEUFFER: Yes, Russian and Polish Jews. That was what I was telling you about, how they did away with thousands of them, with all sorts of accompanying horrors. KATYN was child's play in comparison.
BASSENGE: Oh, were the numbers so much higher?
NEUFFER: Yes, of course. That is not even counting the German Jews. That hasn't all been brought to light yet. I mean to say, they sometimes talk about it in their propaganda, but – . For instance, for fun they would drive train-loads of Jews out – in the winter – and in a wooded country – I know it from v. BROICH (PW), you can ask him yourself – OPPENHEIM,[245] that famous FRANKFURT Jew, who had those racing stables, they stopped the train, made him and the others get out and chased them into the woods in the bitter cold. I mean to say, when all *that* is found out. The trouble is that unfortunately it is nearly all true. On the contrary, they (Allies) have no idea of what *really* happened.
BASSENGE: That OPPENHEIM was the man who, during the Great War, established one of the largest military reserve-hospitals we had in GERMANY, at FRANKFURT; I happen to know that.
NEUFFER: That makes no difference.
BASSENGE: His wife is an 'Aryan' and she is a school-friend of my mother's. She and my mother went to school together at FRANKFURT.
NEUFFER: I don't suppose she is alive now, is she?
BASSENGE: Well, I never heard of her again.
NEUFFER: Their pretext in the case of the Polish and Russian Jews – and undoubtedly it was to some extent justified – was that the Jews would have assisted the partisans or had done so already. Good Heavens, for one thing the Jews are afraid, and for another thing you can't blame them for working against us. But things are always like that with us; sheer mass murder.[246] Our Luftgau hadn't much room at SMOLENSK; therefore two-thirds of them were stationed at MINSK, among others also all the workshops, tailors, shoemakers and so on. All the craftsmen there were Jews, and sometimes they failed to appear – they had been shot by the Gestapo. As a result, those people didn't want to

leave their workshops any more.

BASSENGE: And couldn't your Luftgau commander have kept some craftsmen for himself?

NEUFFER: Well, FISCHER[247] was a perfect fool in that respect. I have nothing against him otherwise, but that man hasn't the *faintest idea* of military matters. Then he was so stupid in the things he said, he told his driver when they encountered large crowds of people at SMOLENSK: 'Oh, just drive on at full speed, it doesn't matter if you run over a few of them.' etc. He had no conscience in that respect.

Document 98

CSDIC (UK) SR REPORT, SRGG 839 [TNA, WO 208/4168]

HANS CRAMER – General der Panzertruppe (GOC German Afrika Korps) – Captured 12 May 43 in Tunisia.
KURT KÖHNCKE – Oberstleutnant (Commander, 372 Heavy Flak Battery) – Captured 8 May 43 in Tunisia.
Information received: 15 Feb. 44

CRAMER (*re* GERMANY's *war guilt*): The worst thing is that we are very much to blame for the way things have gone.

KÖHNCKE: Yes, of course.

CRAMER: In the Great War we could say: we were the decent ones and were dragged into it, and cheated, and deceived,[248] and we fought decently; but in *this* war it's *all* the other way round. We are the attackers, the blusterers, we started everything, we have behaved like *beasts*.

KÖHNCKE: That's the depressing thing, Sir!

Document 99

CSDIC (UK), GRGG 153
Report on information obtained from Senior Officers (PW) on 3 July 44 [TNA, WO 208/4363]

[. . .]

SCHLIEBEN: You have some remarkable experiences with these young 'Leutnants' who come from the Hitler Youth![249] During the Yugoslavian campaign I had a few Serbian officers in the vicinity of my battle HQ who were PW. They were standing about; there were carts there so I said: 'Let them sit down.' Suddenly one of my staff officers, a fanatical Nazi, a GSC I (Ops) actually came up and said: 'Sir' – I was an 'Oberstleutnant' at the time – 'shall I shoot them?' It's crazy! They had learnt those methods in POLAND. Once, in RUSSIA, I was woken up one night by an extraordinary sound of firing; it was my 'Adjutant' who, with the clerk or somebody, had suddenly shot about seven Russians in the night. We were quartered in a sort of school and I thought – I suddenly heard a sound of tommy-guns and afterwards I found out that they'd shot these people. They were civilians . . . The number of people they killed in POLAND alone!

SATTLER: I heard that, too!

SCHLIEBEN: They have become completely brutalised. I remember once visiting a 'Batterie' in RUSSIA as 'Regimentskommandeur'; the 'Batterie' was in my immediate neighbourhood. A Russian soldier who had just been taken prisoner was standing there. I said: 'What's up with him?' 'Well, we're just about to shoot him.' I asked why. 'Well, he fired at us.' 'But he is a soldier and has every right to shoot.' If I hadn't turned up that man would probably have been dead two minutes later.[250]

Document 100

CSDIC (UK), GRGG 169
Report on information obtained from Senior Officers (PW) on 2–4 Aug. 44 [TNA, WO 208/4363]

SATTLER: Yes, we have shot people. That began in POLAND back in 1939. The SS is said to have wreaked terrible havoc.

?SCHLIEBEN: That was probably the reason why BLASKOWITZ was dismissed.

SATTLER: Yes, of course, and KÜCHLER, too, because he severely punished a few SS men who had murdered people. Thereupon there was the hell of a row and after that the SS got their special court, that is, SS men could be had up only before SS courts martial, not ordinary service ones, whereas up to then the SS was supposed to come under the armed forces. That followed on the disgraceful behaviour of the SS in POLAND, because the military authorities said: 'This dirty scoundrel goes around shooting women and children; it's the death sentence for him.' Then HIMMLER came along and said: 'That's out of the question.' I had actual experience of that myself.[251]

SPONECK: But even before that business we were not allowed to take proceedings against them. I know the case of the Director of Music of the 'Leibstandarte' whom we dragged off his band-wagon, because he had shot so many Jews in a mad lust for blood. We had him brought before HOTH's court martial. The man was immediately taken out of HOTH's jurisdiction, sent to BERLIN and came back again, still as Director of Music.[252]

SATTLER: Was that in peace-time?

SPONECK: It wasn't in peace-time; it was during the war before WARSAW.

SATTLER: Yes, that's just what I mean. The SS intervened and said: 'No.' KÜCHLER had stopped in, too. In 1939 those fellows were shooting like mad and the higher authorities, like KÜCHLER, for example – he had a row, too – stepped in and wanted to condemn the fellows to death, but the SS came along and said: 'No, we have our own courts; that's out of the question.' Thereupon, in spite of the fact that the SS came under the armed forces, and in war-time was actually a part of the armed forces, the SS suddenly got its special courts. Instead of getting shot, those fellows got promotion and that was the end of the matter.

NEUFFER: In 1941 the FÜHRER issued an order to the effect that as few Russian prisoners as possible were to be left alive and as many as possible killed.[253]

REIMANN: What barbarism!

NEUFFER: That transporting of the Russians to the rear from VYASMA[254] was a ghastly business!

REIMANN: It was really gruesome. I was present when they were being transported from KOROSTEN to just outside LVOV. They were driven like cattle from the trucks to the drinking troughs and bludgeoned to keep their ranks. There were troughs at the stations; they rushed to them and drank like beasts; after that they were given just a bit of something to eat. Then they were again driven into the wagons; there were sixty or seventy men in one cattle truck! Each time the train halted ten of them were taken out dead: they had suffocated for lack of oxygen. I was in the train with the camp guard and I heard it from the 'Feldwebel', a student, a man with spectacles, an intellectual, whom I asked: 'How long has this been going on?' – 'Well, I have been doing this for four weeks; I'll not be able to stand it much longer, I must get away; I can't stick it any more!' At the stations the prisoners peered out of the narrow openings and shouted in Russian to the Russians standing there: 'Bread! and God will bless you,' etc. They threw out their old shirts, their last pairs of stockings and shoes from the trucks and children came up and brought them pumpkins to eat. They threw the pumpkins in, and then all you heard was a terrific din like the roaring of wild animals in the trucks. They were probably killing each other. That *finished* me. I sat back in a corner and pulled my coat up over my ears. I asked the 'Feldwebel': 'Haven't you *any* food *at all*?' He answered: 'Sir, how could we have anything, nothing has been prepared!'

NEUFFER: No, really, all that was incredibly gruesome. Just to see that column of PW after the twin battle of VYASMA–BRIANSK, when the PW were taken to the rear on foot, far beyond SMOLENSK. I often travelled along that route – the ditches by the side of the roads were full of shot Russians. Cars had driven in to them; it was really ghastly!

Document 101

CSDIC (UK), GRGG 173
Report on information obtained from Senior Officers (PW) on 13–14 Aug. 44
[TNA, WO 208/4363]

SPANG: These fellows in the French Patriot movement! It will be my fate to be handed over to those people later.

KRUG: Why?

SPANG: Well, it stands to reason. You can well imagine that, as 'Divisionkommandeur' I signed so-and-so many death warrants.

KRUG: Oh, well –

SPANG: I had to sign a certain number of death warrants against Terrorists. My sector in BRITTANY was the one where there was the heaviest terrorist fighting and moreover some very ugly incidents happened where I was. There were *hundreds* of Maquis, etc. there – I had a certain number of losses every day, one loss after the other. They seized my officers from Staff headquarters. They simply took out one 'Bataillonskommandeur', Hauptmann NISKER(?), three terrorists went in . . . gone! They made surprise attacks – previously I had gone out every day, but it was no longer possible for me to drive out so often – I drove out two or three times – behind every wall, behind every wood –
    I said: 'I have only one request, and that is for you to shoot me. Give me that opportunity. I was taken prisoner by American troops – shoot me. I don't want to be handed over to that French resistance movement.' Then the IO said: 'There is no question of that.'

KRUG: I agree with him.

SPANG: It will come. They will go now and examine the documents. Then there'll be the interrogation – my troops have been taken prisoner, etc. – then they'll say: 'The "Divisionskommandeur" issued the following instructions, to carry on with ruthless severity, etc.', which of course, for me – quite obvious – 'so-and-so many men have been killed.'

KRUG: I don't think that the French will have much say in it here.

SPANG: That's where you are mistaken! That will be my fate – I know that already. I have already considered whether I couldn't procure some sort of poison. I wouldn't take it now, but just when I am being taken away. But how could I do it? I have no weapons.

KRUG: But in my opinion it is absolutely out of the question.

SPANG: Yes, yes, it will come. There is *no* doubt! It will certainly come. The French will . . . the so-called war criminals . . . 'Divisionalskommandeure' who gave those orders. Moreover I signed death warrants.[255]

Document 102

CSDIC (UK), GRGG 176
Report on information obtained from Senior Officers (PW) on 19–21 Aug. 44
[TNA, WO 208/4363]

HELLWIG: I am not of the opinion that the FÜHRER is a criminal and that his intentions were evil.

KLENK: No, let's put it like this: the ideas are all right and the ideas are all you can wish for but the executive organs are definitely criminal.

HELLWIG: Yes, that's true enough.

KLENK: I mean to say that their methods, for instance, are criminal.

HELLWIG: Yes, their behaviour towards the Jews and the Poles.

KLENK: We didn't know any figures, but my God, when you hear the approximate figure! Gosh! Of course the enemy will have a right to say: 'Men who condone such things must be evil.' A very simple formula. A world order exists and we have sinned against it.

HELLWIG: Well, our world order is really based on faith, on religion.

KLENK: We have all repudiated that!

HELLWIG: That is stupid; I mean to say that it makes no difference which religion it is, whether it's Roman Catholicism or the Evangelical faith; they are all based on faith, belief, goodness etc.

KLENK: In the last resort this is the foundation of any world order; whoever goes against these laws of world order will be held responsible by a world tribunal. That behaviour of ours towards English officers was dreadful too.

HELLWIG: Have you ever spoken to Americans? I never knew they could be as cordial.

KLENK: Yes, they're ready to help any good fellow. You can't say they've any hatred.

HELLWIG: No hate at all! How badly we've been brought up! Hatred! The manner in which we treated the Jews was wrong.

KLENK: Those methods were quite wrong.

HELLWIG: They should have been allowed to leave the country with all their money.

KLENK: Why not? Send them out of the country; get rid of them in a decent way, but not . . .

HELLWIG: Children have been shot!

KLENK: The numbers must have been colossal.

HELLWIG: I was at GOMEL . . . at RYECHITSA; there is a wood with sand dunes where hundreds of Jewish men, women and children lay buried. I wouldn't believe it; it was behind our lines in RUSSIA. I thought it was an exaggeration until I myself saw children of four or five, girls of fourteen, fifteen and sixteen . . .[256]

KLENK: It's shattering!

HELLWIG: One thing strikes me: The individual counts for nothing in

National Socialism. You never hear a friendly word spoken; you never hear our losses mentioned; everything is just thrown in ruthlessly as a matter of course by the higher commander and the most ruthless commander gets the Knight's Cross, the 'Oak Leaves' and the 'Swords'. It's dreadful! I breathed a sign of relief after being with the Americans; they're *human beings*.

Document 103

CSDIC (UK), GRGG 182
Report on information obtained from Senior Officers (PW) on 27–8 Aug. 44
[TNA, WO 208/4363]

MENNY (re SCHLIEBEN's *order not to surrender*): I once issued an order like that in RUSSIA and it succeeded in restoring a position. I had just taken over a 'Division' there, which had newly come from NORWAY, so that it was as yet fresh, and still good. The enemy broke through, simply because a few fellows had run away. Immediately I insisted on fetching the deputy judge advocate general from the Q(?) Staff(?) at the rear and brought him to the front – his knees were knocking together with fright – and we tried the men directly behind the place where the enemy had broken in and sentenced them immediately and shot them at once, on the spot. That went round like wildfire and the result was that the main defensive line was in our hands again at the end of three days. From that moment on there was quite good order in the 'Division'. It acted as a deterrent, at any rate no one else ran away *unnecessarily*. Of course a thing like that is contagious, it is demoralising when everyone runs away.

ELFELDT: Where was that.

MENNY: It was on the DNIEPER at KORTIZA – afterwards the 'Division' was wiped out down to the last man.[257]

ELFELDT: In the KIEV district, or where?

MENNY: Near ZAPOROZHE. Opposite ZAPOROZHE[258] there is a large island 3 km long, called KORTIZA.

BROICH: On the Eastern Front at . . . we passed a camp[259] where there were 20,000 PW. At night they howled like wild beasts. They hadn't got anything to eat. It wouldn't have been possible to give them anything even if we had wanted to, because we had scarcely anything ourselves. Everything was in such a mess at that time. Then we marched down the road and a column of about 6,000 tottering figures went past, completely emaciated, helping each other along. Every 100 or 200 m two or three of them collapsed. Soldiers of ours on bicycles rode alongside with pistols; everyone who collapsed was shot and thrown into the ditch. That happened every 100 m.

SCHLIEBEN: I spoke to a Russian General, who said to me: 'You know, those who were taken prisoner at STALINGRAD will have had just the same fate as the prisoners you took that winter.' In practice it was quite impossible suddenly to feed such a haul of prisoners at STALINGRAD.

? BROICH: I once spoke to Oberst von GRAEVENITZ,[260] he will be 'General' now, who was PW Inspector from the Ministry. He told me that he had travelled round those camps in POMERANIA, where the PW came straight from RUSSIA and had never seen such a thing. The men had no buttocks left at all, but only an orifice. They were complete wrecks, just skin and bone. Besides that they had dysentery all that sort of thing.

HENNECKE: I know that when they were sent to factories, they had to be nursed back gradually before they were fit for any work at all.

BROICH: Besides that they had no clothes to wear and nothing –

SCHLIEBEN: STALIN will have plenty to say about that.

BROICH: I should think that if we have got 3½ million PW, 1 million will certainly have died.[261]

SCHLIEBEN: Yes, that's quite certain.

[. . .]

Document 104

CSDIC (UK), GRGG 183
Report on information obtained from Senior Officers (PW) on 29 Aug. 44 [TNA, WO 208/4363]

CHOLTITZ: I have witnessed some *dreadful* things! They put us in such a *disgraceful* light. The highest SS official arrived and said: 'Sir, I am handing over this camp.' I asked: 'What sort of camp is it?' He answered: 'All of my camps were emptied, but I still have a prisoners camp.' 'Who are imprisoned here?' 'Thirty women who have to be taken away, they are all pregnant.' 'What am I to do with them?' 'Oh, let . . . I don't care a hoot. . . .' The next morning I remember the fellow had said something to me. They had *all* made off. Not a *single* SS or policeman was there. I went there (and discovered) that they were thirty *ladies*, the wives of the *very* industrialists who had run our war industry in PARIS for the last two years. They had been arrested as hostages. They were *ladies*, just like 'Frau' THYSSEN and 'Frau' – .[262]

BASSENGE: VÖGELER[263] and that kind.

THOMA: What were they doing there; why were they imprisoned there?

CHOLTITZ: They had been imprisoned there as hostages for *several* years, I set them free at once, offering profuse apologies. We then found the corpses of four naked women, whom they had violated shortly before they left.

THOMA: Yes, that is known here. The only consolation for the Army is that the papers here always lay stress on: SS and Gestapo. Why did they leave those dead women lying about down there?

CHOLTITZ: Well, they were violated – they just felt like it.

THOMA: Of course the Americans and English turned up there.

CHOLTITZ: The French found it and they reported it to me. No, it was the Swiss ambassador who was still there. Those swine made off at night without telling me, they left their quarters open, full of arms and a cellar filled with explosives and a picture of HITLER as its only guardian! They left it for my opponents the French communists to seize. They simply drove off!

THOMA: Who were those?

CHOLTITZ: The Gestapo.

THOMA: Are the names –

CHOLTITZ: Yes, of course. He visited me and negotiated with me.

Document 105

GRGG 187 [TNA, WO 208/4363]

Provisional report on CS/223 – General der Panzertruppe EBERBACH (GOC 7th Army) – Captured 31 Aug. 44 in Amiens – before his arrival in Camp No. 11. This report contains information from a conversation between the above officer and a junior British Army Officer [BAO]

EBERBACH: That evening I spoke to HIMMLER. He had given a lecture and in the evening he sat down at our table. I told him that I couldn't understand the general inhuman treatment of the Jews. It was rather risky, but actually one can say a thing like that to HIMMLER and discuss it with him. He replied that I ought to realise what the situation was: If there were still Jews in all the large towns today, with the bombing raids, then it was perfectly obvious that by them spreading rumours and inciting against the government, the present good behaviour of the population would pretty certainly come to an end.[264] One had to agree with that up to a point. It wasn't advisable to tell him that if the Jews had been treated differently, they could have been made to have quite a different attitude towards the government.

BAO: And how often did you have the honour of hearing a speech by the FÜHRER himself?

EBERBACH: Never. He was supposed to speak there but it was cancelled on the last day. We were supposed to go over from SONTHOFEN to the BERCHTESGADEN district to see him, but that was cancelled, because some foreign diplomats had arrived, with whom he had to confer. At the whole session at which I was present, there were many less so-called noted speakers taking part than there were at the former one.

ROSENBERG, too, for instance, who was said to have spoken always was not present and neither was GOEBBELS.

Document 106

CSDIC (UK), GRGG 189
Report on information obtained from Senior Officers (PW) on 29 Aug. 44 [TNA, WO 208/4364]

CHOLTITZ: The worst job I ever carried out – which however I carried out with great consistency – was the liquidation of the Jews. I carried out this order *down to the very last detail.*[265]

THOMA: The whole thing is done on HITLER's orders. EBERBACH said yesterday again: 'HITLER has no idea that the people have been hanged.' Ha! Ha! Ha! It's a good thing that you can now produce such unimpeachable proofs.

Document 107

CSDIC (UK), GRGG 195
Report on information obtained from Senior Officers (PW) on 16–17 Sept. 44 [TNA, WO 208/4363]

THOMA: The men were sitting together one evening in December in a peasant's cottage at ALEXANDROWKA – that was about 20 km from my HQ – there were the 'Hauptmann', the tank 'Oberleutnant' and the 'Unteroffiziere', all together in the only warm room. They were drinking their miserable wine ration together. That was all established in the court proceedings. Each man probably had about half a field cup of 'Schnapps'. You *can't* get drunk on that, and the Commandant himself strongly denied that they were in the least bit drunk. He said that they were completely sober, which is the extraordinary part of it. Anyway, the following occured: The 'Hauptmann' said to the 'Oberleutnant': 'I can't stand the sight of these peasants' faces!' . . . pulled out his revolver and shot down the peasant over the table to which he himself had invited him.

EBERBACH: But the 'Hauptmann' received a heavy sentence.

THOMA: Yes, but just wait till you hear the rest: He then told one of the orderlies to take his body away. His wife screamed and howled and ran with their children – a little girl, a little boy and a two-month-old baby – into the farthest corner and sat down on the top of the stove, where she cried, which, after all, is only very natural. He then said to the 'Oberleutnant': 'I want my peace; clear them out from up there!' And he drew his revolver and shot down the woman. She was likewise dragged outside. That left the little girl, a ten-year-old boy and a two-month-old baby. In the meantime, they got in a fellow who was a musician by trade and he played the accordion and they went on drinking. Suddenly he said: 'She must go, too!' So the ... said: 'Shoot the other one!' Whereupon he shot the girl. Then there was the ten-year-old boy. The 'Hauptmann' said: 'Take him out and shoot him outside.' He was taken outside and he, too, was shot in the neck. The two-month-old brat was lying up there yelling and he said: 'Away with the little beast.' They knocked it off the stove, picked it up by its foot and threw it out into the snow. Of course, the people reported it the following day. I immediately sent a Judge Advocate there. 'I must take a psychiatrist along with me,' he said. They completely denied that they were in the least bit drunk and said they were absolutely sober. During the proceedings they were asked why they had done it. He said: 'They weren't human beings, they only count as animals; nothing at all can happen to us.' 'They are certainly human beings who go about their business like anybody else!' 'Sir, the FÜHRER says they are not human beings, we do not admit the fact that we can be charged with murder, for they are not humans.' That was their defence. Then came the findings of the court martial and one was sentenced to be degraded and to penal servitude and the other, the 'Hauptmann' – because he took part in the shooting as well – got more because he was responsible, and was sentenced to several years' penal servitude.

I didn't sign the findings. All the troops were up in arms over that terrible affair. I tell you, the Germans have kind hearts. I demanded the death penalty for both and, what's more, that they be shot publicly by the troops. But, because they were officers, the Judge Advocate said I was not permitted to shoot them before the FÜHRER had given his consent. Then a week later notification arrived that: 'The FÜHRER confirms that it is absolutely in order for the men to be punished. But he refused to authorise the death sentence, because according to his standards, the Russians are not human beings.' They were not punished. They were sent to a sort of penal 'Kompanie'.[266]

Document 108

GRGG 198(C) [TNA, WO 208/4363]

Provisional report on information obtain from CS/382 – General der Fallschirmtruppen RAMCKE (Commander, Brest) – Captured 19 Sept. 44 in Brest.

[...]

RAMCKE: When I took over the command at BREST, I first of all brought four high officials up for trial by court martial, and officers; then I immediately had six men shot for defeatist talk, and for going over to the enemy and desertion; in fact I had them shot after I had called up representatives from each unit – 300 men in all. After that there was order![267]

Document 109

GRGG 199 [TNA, WO 208/4363]

Provisional report on information obtained from Generalmajor BOCK VON WÜLFINGEN (Oberfeldkommandatur, Liege) – Captured 8 Sept. 44 in Liege.

SEYFFARDT (*re Russian PW*): They had to kill them all.
?HEYKING: The Commissars etc.?
SEYFFARDT: No. 'No prisoners are to be taken!' stated the order.
?: That was so for a time.
?SEYFFARDT: They were all killed, all of them. They were killed in *thousands*. They captured about 600,000 prisoners in that one pocket near GSCHATSK,[268] and, of those 600,000, 400,000 were said to have died on the march from GSCHATSK to SMOLENSK alone.[269]
?TRESCKOW: Whose idea was that, and what was the reason for it?
?SEYFFARDT: The FÜHRER, that was one of the FÜHRER's orders.

Document 110

GRGG 201(C) [TNA, WO 208/4364]

Provisional report on information obtain from CS/443 Generalleutnant HEIM (Commander, Boulogne) – Captured 23 Sept. 44 in Boulogne.

HEIM: HIMMLER does an incredible amount for his SS; a man has only to do like this and everything he wants is there.
ELSTER: Well, why doesn't he take steps to prevent these swinish tricks that the SS and Security Service have done?
HEIM: He's supposed not to have been in favour of that.
?HEYKING: The SS and Security Service in general are blamed for all the Jewish massacres and so on. On the other hand, HIMMLER is supposed to have said at a big CO's conference – he was asked about the Jewish question and he merely replied: 'Well, gentlemen, as to this "Jewish question" I can only say that the orders were given and I carry out orders.' He wasn't giving them a chance. In the end everyone merely says that they haven't the final word in these matters.[270]
[. . .]

Document 111

CSDIC (UK), GRGG 210
Report on information obtained from Senior Officers (PW) on 11–12 Oct. 44
[TNA, WO 208/4364]

CHOLTITZ: The orders arrived to shoot the Commissars.[271] We all objected strongly to doing this and said it was a really dirty job and a mistake, because if we considered them as proper soldiers and told them that we were taking them prisoner and sending them to GERMANY to show them the social conditions, then their resistance would be less. I was in front of SEBASTOPOL and SCHMUNDT, who was HITLER's adjutant, came to me. I didn't know him, but he knew me, and he remained in my dugout for a few days and watched me at work. I said to him: 'My dear SCHMUNDT, don't make that mistake, leave it now, give up that order so that we may stop having that strong opposition.' What do you English do? You say: 'All Nazis will be killed, they will all be hanged!

[. . .]

BAO: The French said that to me too.

CHOLTITZ: That's all very well, but it shouldn't be said openly. You incite – the Nazi says to himself: 'It doesn't matter what happens, even if GERMANY is smashed, I may *perhaps* save my life that way, whereas otherwise I certainly shan't save my life!' A thing like that is madness.

BAO: We come back to the point again, Sir, that there are two factors of which we are afraid: first a Nazi underground movement after the war and secondly an underground movement of the Armed Forces, like the 'Black Reichswehr' and so on after the last war.

CHOLTITZ: Our best men have gone, because HITLER began the war. Those were the ones who were hanged. It is certainly untrue that the officers' corps agitated for war – we were all talking about it the other day and I asked them all what they knew from their people. We knew exactly how weak we were, there were fifteen annual classes which we hadn't trained, we as experts, wouldn't agitate for war, because we knew perfectly well that fifteen annual classes were not ready and they could never be trained afterwards. Our best men left. The generals fought tooth and nail against the French campaign,[272] incidentally, as we were able to see later, they were wrong, because HITLER happened to be right that time. Because he was right, that man usurped the leadership on the Eastern Front and wouldn't let anyone get near it any more. We are getting a terrible state of affairs in EUROPE; the Russians are taking HUNGARY and the whole of the BALKANS, it can't go on like that.

Document 112

CSDIC (UK), GRGG 215
Report on information obtained from Senior Officers (PW) on 23–4 Oct. 44 [TNA, WO 208/4364]

CHOLTITZ: Did you destroy BREST?

RAMCKE: Yes.

CHOLTITZ: The town and everything else?

RAMCKE: Yes.

CHOLTITZ: Why on earth did you destroy the town?

RAMCKE: Well, for one thing Allied bombing destroyed the harbour installations and naturally hit the town as well. I had evacuated the population. The Americans bombarded the town ruthlessly too, and I said to myself: It's as much their blame as ours; those swine must not be allowed to establish themselves here on any account; they mustn't be allowed to use the town as a harbour and must be prevented from quickly establishing quarters for reconstruction personnel. Well, I set fire to it and burned it down. I was furious because 75 per cent of my hospital cases who were lying in field hospitals . . . on the 8th, before the siege started, had been caused by terrorists; I was livid with rage.

CHOLTITZ: How did you manage it? I should be interested, because of PARIS. How do you set a town on fire?

RAMCKE: For one thing I didn't allow any fires caused by bombs or artillery fire to be extinguished, on the contrary, we fed the fires.

CHOLTITZ: How is that done?

RAMCKE: You enter a neighbouring house and throw in some kindling material. Then you open doors and windows, creating a draught.

CHOLTITZ: Yes, you can do that with one house, but you can't set the whole town on fire that way, can you?

RAMCKE: We were stationed all around BREST; we had a defence zone in depth and our main defence installations were in BREST; we had to blow up houses to give us a field of fire; we had to clear a space for the 'Bunker' and above all we had to prevent the narrow streets being blocked by bombing or artillery-fire. We therefore blew up any houses standing at dangerous corners, so as to keep the streets clear.

CHOLTITZ: Who did all that for you?

RAMCKE: There was a 'Pionierzug' at the Garrison HQ and then there were naval personnel, a demolition squad from the fortress garrison; I fetched them all from their 'Bunker' and formed them into 'Kompanien'; then there was a railway 'Kompanie', which demolished the entire railway; then there were all the military police, consisting of 163 men, who had arrived there from the field HQ; I ordered them to do it and thus had a really large detachment operating.

CHOLTITZ: Did you destroy the town completely?

RAMCKE: It was entirely wiped out!

CHOLTITZ: But that's a *war crime*!

RAMCKE: No. I demolished the electric railway . . .

CHOLTITZ: No one worries about that, that's obvious. But why did you destroy civilian houses?

RAMCKE: I told you the reason; I blew them up whenever they were an obstruction and whenever military necessity called for it.[273]

CHOLTITZ: But RAMCKE, *that*, of course, is a war-crime!

RAMCKE: Of course! But I was only following the example of the English round about 1793, when NELSON burned down the whole of TOULON.[274]

CHOLTITZ: Why did he do that?

RAMCKE: Because he didn't want the French to have the use of the harbour.

Document 113

CSDIC (UK), GRGG 221
Report on information obtained from Senior Officers (PW) on 10–12 Nov. 44
[TNA, WO 208/4364]

ELFELDT: When we were in the KIEV district, my CO of signals(?) came back quite horrified . . . spoken . . . it was an engineer 'Bataillons-kommandeur' – and this engineer 'Bataillon' had the task of blowing up that . . . in which were these 32,000 Jews including women and children.

HEIM: Even if the figures are not correct, I mean, there are things which can absolutely be characterised as criminal, or even as completely crazy and mad.

ELFELDT: In just the same way as I have obligations towards my family and my nation, so have we of course, as a nation, certain rules which we must observe towards the rest of humanity, there's no doubt at all about that. I can't behave like a wild beast.[275]

Document 114

CSDIC (UK), GRGG 225
Report on information obtained from Senior Officers (PW) on 18–19 Nov. 44
[TNA, WO 208/4364]

BASSENGE: I've got the impression that MEYER will not be in the least in the way here.

WILDERMUTH: No, he won't. But one never knows what a man like that has done in the past.

BASSENGE: No, he must be treated with reserve.

WILDERMUTH: One is never sure with a man like that whether he may not have done things which are not in keeping with the code of behaviour of an officer.

BASSENGE: I shall not make a point of seeking his company but he mustn't get the feeling that he is being boycotted here.

WILDERMUTH: No, we can't boycott him if he behaves correctly.

BASSENGE: I agree. That is my personal impression.

WILDERMUTH: He doesn't make a good impression on me.

BASSENGE: No.

WILDERMUTH: His face! Would you like a face like that in your regiment?

BASSENGE: No, I know that type well and I always go by their fingers; I look at their hands.

WILDERMUTH: In carrying out the mass executions the SS did things which were unworthy of an officer and which every German officer should have refused to do, but I know of cases where officers did *not* refuse, and *did* do them, those mass executions. I know of similar things which were done by the army, and by officers. I personally always adopted the attitude that I wouldn't obey an order like that because it's against my honour as an officer; I'm not an executioner, I'm an officer. The question arises; are the majority of us of the view that the SS did things which some people possibly consider necessary from a political point of view, but which we, as officers, would never have done and therefore purposely left to people who are not officers. I don't know whether one could get away with that attitude. It would be a very good thing politically if the German officers' corps were to say: 'We dissociate ourselves in that way from these people,' but they could immediately confront us and say: 'But if you please, in this instance the German Hauptmann So-and-so, or the German Oberst So-and-so did exactly the same thing as the SS.'

Document 115

CSDIC (UK), GRGG 226
Report on information obtained from Senior Officers (PW) on 20–1 Nov. 44
[TNA, WO 208/4364]

MEYER: Do you know that I had an NCO shot at CAEN because he raped a girl?

EBERBACH: No.

MEYER: The fellow did the following: He was drunk and then went . . . where there were several women; he picked out a girl and forced her to guide him to the next village. The girl ran away and he re-entered her house, locked the girl in and finally raped her. The girl died. Thank God we succeeded in establishing the . . . the following morning and I had the fellow shot; I ordered the mayor and several municipal councillors to attend the execution. They had to watch it. Whereupon the mayor sent me word that he thanked me on behalf of the local population for the expeditious way in which the case had been handled. He regarded it as an offence committed by a criminal, not by a German soldier. He repeated those words at the funeral so that relations with the population were on a perfect footing once more and that matter had been cleared up.[276]

EBERBACH: (*laughing*) That's something speaking in your favour.

But I believe that the FÜHRER issued an order for the East that the raping of women and girls should not be . . . as a criminal offence, but only as a disciplinary – as terror was part of the rules of war.

MEYER: I never heard that.

EBERBACH: You haven't been in the East for a long time. I don't know that order either as it is a long time since I was there, but officers who were there recently, said that such a FÜHRER-order existed.

MEYER: That is . . . by that we undermine all that is best in the troops.

EBERBACH: That order wasn't issued for the West, merely for the East.

MEYER: On the other hand, I know several officers who had Ukrainian girls during the winter of 1941–42 at TAGANROG – there were marvellous girls down there. Those officers, after having been before a Court of Honour, haven't been promoted until this day.[277]

EBERBACH: I can't make HIMMLER out at all; on the one hand, because he decided to have all the Jews massacred, consciously . . .

MEYER: Do you know why? HIMMLER is the most faithful executor of the FÜHRER's orders. The FÜHRER used to say: 'Should the Jews succeed once again in involving EUROPE in a war, it will not mean the destruction of the German people, but the annihilation of the Jewish race.'[278]

WILDERMUTH: A leader of the SD and police officer is not a real officer. I refuse to have anything to do with the SD.

THOMA: It occurs to me, because it said in the newspaper today that that man (Generalmajor DUNCKERN (PW))[279] is from the SD – perhaps I should ask for him to be sent somewhere else. I refuse to associate with those swine.

WILDERMUTH: So do I.

THOMA: All those who occupied any position of authority in the SD are nothing but murderers.

WILDERMUTH: They are all murderers.

THOMA: Perhaps the Waffen-SS is a little better.

WILDERMUTH: In the Waffen-SS there are men who did nothing beyond fighting bravely. One never knows what a man may have been involved in. That is the reservation I feel with regard to MEYER (PW). How do I know what crimes he may have committed?

THOMA: He was in RUSSIA and was picked out by the 'Leibstandarte'!

BROICH: Anyone who is CO of the 'Hitler Youth Division' in 1944 must be a Nazi, that's obvious. That man would be the first to shoot our wives and us if he were given the order to do so, just like all the others, and he'd do it with glee. Just like RAMCKE (PW), he is pretending to know nothing about it all.[280]

WILCK: His whole expression –

BASSENGE: He behaved quite sensibly today –

BROICH: That man is clever and knows the lie of the land exactly: he is reticent and pretends not to know anything.

WILCK: Of course he'd like to become one of us now.

BROICH: It was sheer cowardice on his part to pretend to be an Army 'Oberst'. Suddenly the Army is good enough for him.[281]

WILCK: Yes, all of a sudden.

[. . .]

MEYER: Do you know that our education has resulted in a certain amount of brutality, which is partly quite unconscious to us – for instance, the execution of those involved in the 20 July 'Putsch', and above all, the liquidation of their families.

EBERBACH: Were you present?

MEYER: No, I only heard about it recently.

EBERBACH: Were you present at that RÖHM business, those executions as LICHTERFELDE, etc.?

MEYER: I was present in MUNICH but took no part in the shooting. That business was clean though. They were shot like soldiers, but the majority of those who performed the executions at the time are no longer alive. Only Sepp DIETRICH is still alive and . . . the others have all been killed.[282] It puzzles me today. The next-of-kin of those shot on 30 June 1934 have been *excellently* cared for; their wives and children etc. were given plenty of money. They came under the FÜHRER's *protection* etc. I don't know what happened afterwards – whilst this time they even shot pregnant women. If I imagine my wife stood up against the wall with her children by her side . . . bumped off![283]

EBERBACH: Yes, what a dreadful life!

MEYER: Yes. We have gained our personal strength and endurance from our faith in the purity of our ideas . . . from our belief in our race, from our belief in a healthy, clean family-life and now suddenly! The fact which depresses me so much is that we are represented as being *swine*. You are told to your face the exact opposite of what you were fighting for and what you have striven for.

EBERBACH: Chin up!

Document 116

CSDIC (UK), GRGG 227
Report on information obtained from Senior Officers (PW) on 22–3 Nov. 44
[TNA, WO 208/4364]

MEYER: I must say that I heard about large-scale massacres of the Jews for the first time at COMPIÈGNE and after that LUBLIN business was made public.[284]

EBERDING: I just heard tales about it too. I don't know anything positive. CHOLTITZ (PW) was present at the capture of SEBASTOPOL and one of the officers of his 'Regiment' was actually invited to be present when thirty thousand Jews were shot.[285]

MEYER (*incredulously*): Thirty thousand?

Document 117

CSDIC (UK), GRGG 232
Report on information obtained from Senior Officers (PW) on 8–11 Dec. 44 [TNA, WO 208/4364]

WILDERMUTH: If only ours were a young immature people, but they have been infected to the depth of their moral fibre. I must tell you that I have considered this question really seriously; a nation which has accepted such a rule of lies, brute force and crime, in the main without raising any objection, is simply not a people; a people in which the murder of mental defectives was possible and where intelligent people could still say: 'That wasn't at all a bad idea of theirs' should be liquidated. Such bestiality has never been seen in the world before. One might just as well get rid of all consumptives or all suffering from cancer.[286]

WAHLE: I wanted to hear your opinion about the following: if one accept as a premise that the Germans are the most immature people in the world, that they were forced by BISMARCK into unity and that after BISMARCK, came that crazy fellow ADOLF and wanted to force them into –

WILDERMUTH: Into mastery over EUROPE.

WAHLE: Yes, into becoming a world power, do you think that an intelligent or redeeming deed could be performed now by anyone who has been infected by this National Socialist poison? I don't think so.

WILDERMUTH: Well, it depends to what extent he has been infected: RUNDSTEDT has perhaps not been infected to such an extent; I don't know him.

WAHLE: All the same, he sat in that court and condemned a large number of innocent men along with that group. RUNDSTEDT and SPECHT. He condemned innocent men like WITZLEBEN and BECK.[287]

Document 118

CSDIC (UK), GRGG 237
Report on information obtained from Senior Officers (PW) on 21–2 Dec. 44 [TNA, WO 208/4364]

WILDERMUTH: Hans von GRAEVENITZ was head of PW welfare. He told me GOEBBELS had to speak so that the people should stop agitating that the Russians should be left to perish as second-rate human beings and he actually hinted to me that one-and-half million PW were left to perish, partly whilst being transported and partly later on in GERMANY.

ELFELDT: I spoke to GRAEVENITZ in the spring of 1942 when the greater part of the prisoners was being brought in. On that occasion he told me: 'The majority of them are in such a miserable condition as you wouldn't believe could be possible.' A greater number of them died afterwards in GERMANY as as a result of complete exhaustion. Those immense losses occurred when that mass of PW was suddenly transported from the front to the German PW camps, right at the beginning too, and, of course, when they were suddenly put into PW camps which hadn't adequate accommodation. Subsequently all efforts were made to right matters but as a result of those weeks of under-nourishment –

WILDERMUTH: Probably to some extent the thing was unavoidable.

ELFELDT: At BRIANSK later on there was a commandant who managed to put the PW to work in the fields and by the spring conditions had become bearable. But it is indescribable how many of them perished during the winter up to that period. If a capable commandant had been on the spot in the autumn and had had the fields reaped, then it wouldn't have been . . .

WILDERMUTH: You can't feed them properly if you keep them on the march; they'd eat too much. Some of the deaths are a direct consequence of the war and we can't be held responsible for them.[288]

Document 119

CSDIC (UK), SR Report SRGG 1086(C) [TNA, WO 208/4196]

Generalleutnant SCHAEFER (Commander, 244 Infantry Division) – Captured 28 Aug. 44 in Marseilles
Generalmajor VON FELBERT (Commandant of Feldkommandatur 560 Besançon) – Captured 5 Sept. 44 in Landresse.
Generalmajor BRUHN (Commander, 553 Volksgrenadier Division) – Captured 22 Nov. 44 in Zabern.
Generalleutnant KITTEL (Commandant, Metz and Commander, 462 Volksgrenadier Division) – Captured 22 Nov. 44 in Metz.
Information received: 28 Dec. 44

KITTEL: (*re administration in* RUSSIA) I quarrelled with every Security
Service chief, because I would brook no . . . in my affairs. I had the
sentences prepared for me, then I had them brought to me and signed
them personally from the very beginning, from a certain level of
severity upwards. That's to say I wasn't interested in two years'
imprisonment; the people could demand that themselves, but ten
years' hard labour or six years' penal servitude or a death sentence – I
said: 'I'm going to sign those myself,' having regard alone to the
political consequences. I had town majors who have straight away
hanged a Russian for the theft of a piece of soap. The very first thing I
did if I arrived somewhere and got a town major's office under my
control was just to say to my operations officer: 'Please issue order No.
so-and-so.' That set out what sentences he could inflict and what he
could not inflict and stated that I reserve for myself the right of
confirmation of all death sentences and that they were to be confirmed
by me.
? BRUHN: But surely those 'Wehrmachtskommandanten' were always
army officers –
KITTEL: Yes.
? BRUHN: Reserve officers, or were they SS officers?
KITTEL: They were a great many regular officers among them.
? FELBERT: Can the officers be classified by saying that the very young
ones who went through the Hitler Youth Movement and became
'Bannführer' etc. were particularly strict?
KITTEL: No. The people in control there were nothing but old crocks.
There were some queer fish among them. I'll just pick out one case: I
had one town major who was at MACHAJEWKA(?)[289] near STALINO.
MACHAJEWKA(?) was a fairly large place, with 300,0000 inhabitants. He
was a regular officer and had now finally been discharged with the rank
of 'Oberstleutnant'.
? FELBERT: But didn't have anything at all to do with politics?
KITTEL: He had nothing to do with politics. When he was in ordinary
uniform he looked tolerable. He had had a summer tunic made out of
drill, evidently to his own specifications, and one day a few soldiers
came to the town major's office at MACHAJEWKA(?) and presented in
front of my desk a man they were holding by the scruff of the neck.
'I've got a Russian spy here.' (*laughs*) It was the town major himself!
He had asked a few soldiers where they came from and where they
were going, so they had seized him by the scruff of the neck and
marched him into his own office. And that swine had hanged more
than anybody else. I put an end to his activity then. He was an
Austrian, funnily enough, for the Austrians were extraordinarily
lenient otherwise. I always said I was glad if I didn't have a fire-eater
as town major, who always thinks that everyone is a bandit and is
bound to get the wrong man in the end. A charming Austrian like that,

who occasionally drank a vodka with them and got on very well with the major, and in that way slowly collected people he could trust; one like that has . . . far better service than one who bangs on the table and says: 'Eight horses were stolen tonight; I'm going to burn down this village.' They did that, too.

? FELBERT: So the crimes of which we are being accused there, these murders etc., can be grouped: one group consists of political crimes carried out by the SS and Security Service; but then there is also a second group of crimes committed by town majors who have overstepped the mark in an obvious failure to recognise a just verdict.

KITTEL: All these matters could very quickly be rectified by the mere fact that they came to light.

BRUHN: Was action taken against these gentlemen?

KITTEL: Yes. Those town majors had complete freedom of action. The paragraphs on the rights and duties of the military administration were drawn up so loosely that that was perfectly possible. He said: 'That is an act against the Armed Forces.' The penalty for an act against the Armed Forces is death, so he gave the death sentence. To begin with, my military police confiscated goods, and I said: 'I shall punish any man who confiscates anything. Whatever is confiscated goes to a hospital.'

FELBERT: Have you also known places from which the Jews have been removed?

KITTEL: Yes

FELBERT: Was that carried out quite systematically?

KITTEL: Yes.

FELBERT: Woman and children – everybody?

KITTEL: Everybody. Horrible!

FELBERT: Were they loaded into trains?

KITTEL: If only they had been loaded into trains! The things I've experienced! I then sent a man along and said: 'I order this to stop. I can't stand it any longer.' For instance, in LATVIA, near DVINSK, there were mass executions of Jews carried out by the SS or Security Service.[290] There were about fifteen Security Service men and perhaps sixty Latvians, who are known to be the most brutal people in the world. I was lying in bed early one Sunday morning when I kept on hearing two salvoes followed by small arms fire. I got up and went out and asked: 'What's all this shooting?' The orderly said to me: 'You ought to go over there, Sir, you'll see something.' I only went fairly near and that was enough for me. Three hundred men had been driven out of DVINSK; they dug a trench – men and women dug a communal grave and then marched home. The next day along they came again – men, women and children – they were counted off and stripped naked; the executioners first laid all the clothes in one pile. Then twenty women had to take up their position – naked – on the edge of the trench, they were shot and fell down into it.

FELBERT: How was it done?

KITTEL: They faced the trench and then twenty Latvians came up behind and simply fired once through the back of their heads. There was a sort of step in the trench, so that they stood rather lower than the Latvians, who stood up on the edge and simply shot them through the head, and they fell down forwards into the trench. After that came twenty men and they were killed by a salvo in just the same way. Someone gave the command and the twenty fell into the trench like ninepins. Then came the worst thing of all; I went away and said: 'I'm going to do something about this.' I got into my car and went to this Security Service man and said: 'Once and for all, I forbid these executions outside, where people can look on. If you shoot people in the wood or somewhere where no one can see, that's your own affair. But I absolutely forbid another day's shooting there. We draw our drinking water from deep springs; we're getting nothing but corpse water there.' It was the MESCHEPS spa[291] where I was; it lies to the north of DVINSK.

FELBERT: What did they do to the children?

KITTEL (*very excited*): They seized three-year old children by their hair, held them up and shot them with a pistol and then threw them in. I saw that for myself. One could watch it; the SD had roped the area off and the people were standing watching from about 300 m off. The Latvians and the German soldiers were just standing there, looking in.

FELBERT: What kind of SD people are they, then?

KITTEL: Nauseating! I'm convinced that they'll all be shot.

FELBERT: Where were they from, from which formation?

KITTEL: They were Germans and they were wearing the SD uniform with the black flashes on which is written 'Sonder-Dienst'.

FELBERT: Were all the executioners Latvians?

KITTEL: Yes.

FELBERT: But a German gave the order, did he?

KITTEL: Yes. The Germans directed affairs and the Latvians carried them out. The Latvians searched all the clothes. The SD fellow saw reason and said: 'Yes, we will do it somewhere else.' They were all Jews who had been brought in from the country districts. Latvians wearing the armband – the Jews were brought in and were then robbed; there was a terrific bitterness against the Jews at DVINSK, and the people simply gave vent to their rage.

FELBERT: Against the Jews?

SCHAEFER: Yes, because the Russians had dragged off 60,000 Estonians. But, of course, the flames had been fanned. Tell me, what sort of an impression did these people create? Do you ever see any of them shortly before they were shot? Did they weep?

KITTEL: It was terrible. I once saw them being transported but I had no idea that they were people who were being driven to their execution.

SCHAEFER: Have the people any idea what is in store for them?

KITTEL: They know perfectly well; they are apathetic. I'm not sensitive myself but such things just turn my stomach; I always said. 'One ceases to be a human being; that's got nothing more to do with warfare.' I once had the senior chemist for organic chemistry from IG FARBEN as my adjutant and because they had nothing better for him to do he had been called up and sent to the front. He's back home now, though he got there quite accidentally. The man was done for weeks. He sat in the corner the whole time and wept. He said: 'When one considers that it may be like that everywhere!' He was an important scientist and a musician with a highly strung nervous system.

FELBERT: That shows why FINLAND deserted us, why RUMANIA deserted us, why everyone hates us everywhere – not because of that single incident but because of the great number of similar incidents.

KITTEL: If one were to destroy all the Jews of the world simultaneously there wouldn't remain a single accuser.

FELBERT (*very excited and shouting*): It's obvious; it's such a scandal; it doesn't need to be a Jew to accuse us – *we ourselves must bring the charge*; we must accuse the people who have done it.

KITTEL: Then one must admit that our State system was wrongly built.

FELBERT (*shouting*): It is, it's obvious that it's wrong, there's no doubt about it. Such a thing is unbelievable.

BRUHN: We are the tools –

FELBERT: That will be marked up against us afterwards, as though it had been we who did it.

BRUHN: If you come along today as a German General people think: 'He knows everything; he knows about that, too,' and if we then say: 'We had nothing to do with it,' the people won't believe us. All the hatred and all the aversion is a result purely and simply of these murders, and I must say that if one believes at all in divine justice, one deserves, if one has five children, as I have, to have one or two killed in this way, so that that may be avenged. If one sheds blood like that, one does not deserve victory; one has deserved what has now come to pass.

? FELBERT: I don't know at whose instigation that was done – if it came from HIMMLER then he is the arch-criminal. Actually you are the first General who has told me that himself. I've always believed that these articles were all lies.

KITTEL: I keep silent about a great many things; they are too awful.

FELBERT: Do you think it all comes from HIMMLER?

KITTEL: Naturally. It someone at the top says: 'Exterminate those cattle' – off they all go. I had rows about the thing with every single chief of police. The chief of police in WEIMAR[292] came to me, an unparalleled DON QUIXOTE, wearing the uniform of a 'Generalleutnant' – I was 'Generalmajor' in LAMMERSDORF(?).[293] I said: 'What do you want to discuss with me?' – 'Well, well, etc., the whole situation here displeases me, it will be fundamentally altered immediately, it's disgraceful,' etc. – 'I'm sorry if you do not agree with some of my measures; you can naturally tell me that quite calmly but not in this way. I will send for my "Kriegsverwaltungsrat".' – 'Who is that?' I said: 'You shall meet him directly.' It was Dr SCHMIDTHUBER(?), a MUNICH notary. Well, he came in and the General turned round and said: 'So that's what the fellow looks like.' I said: 'Excuse me, General, this is my "Kriegsverwaltungsrat". I do not wish my subordinates to be spoken of in that tone in my house.' – 'I've already heard all kinds of things about him.' SCHMIDTHUBER(?) smilingly stood in front of him and said: 'Sir, I would point out that I am senior in SS rank to you.' He is the only SS man whom I have met who managed things charitably and sensibly. The man was worth his weight in gold to me. I was still inexperienced in all those things. How should I know all about the administration of the town; how should I know about the administration of a province half as large as BAVARIA? He knew something about it, for in BAVARIA he was the big man for concluding contracts. He drew up government contracts and so on. He, too, always said: 'Sirs, everything will have its revenge; let us keep clear. Let us accept no invitations from the SD; let us accept no invitations to houses where Jewish loot is to be found; let us never remove furniture from Jewish homes; instead we will live simply and modestly with whatever we happen to find.' I could go on telling you things for days on end.

FELBERT: What happened to the young, pretty girls? Were they formed into a harem?

KITTEL: I didn't bother about that. I only found that they did become more reasonable. At least they had concentration camps for the Jews at CRACOW.[294] At any rate, from the moment I had chosen a safe place and I built the concentration camp, things became quite reasonable. They certainly had to work hard. The women question is a very shady chapter.

FELBERT: If people were killed simply because their carpets and furniture were needed, I can well imagine that if there is a pretty daughter who looks Aryan, she would simply be sent somewhere as a maid-servant.

KITTEL: You've no idea what mean and stupid things are done. You can't get at the people concerned. If you go for a fellow like that, he'll hang a political . . . on you. I have politically a . . . because I have made trouble about various things.

FELBERT: What happens to the people who complain?

KITTEL: They are simply undermined. They can't maintain their position. Some dirty work is started, an anonymous letter is written 'Semper aliquid haeret'. Now and again you are compelled to take drastic measures to catch one of those fellows. At every attack which you make upon a certain class in our State administration, you get in return three or four *unfounded*, either anonymous or somehow raked together, counter-blows.

I had an Oberst BIERKAMP(?)[295] as head of the Security Services at CRACOW.

BRUHN: What sort of people are they?

KITTEL: They are Party members and civilians; they are Security Service people. When HIMMLER formed his state within the state, the Security Service was founded like this: they took 50 per cent good police officials who were not politically tainted, and added to them 50 per cent criminals. That's how the Security Service arose. (*Laughter*) There's one man in the criminal department in BERLIN, in that famous 'Z' section whom I frequently used when espionage cases were being held by us in the Ordnance Branch; and the question then arose of nationality and of whether they had not already got a file, whether the man had not cropped up somewhere before. There is the so-called 'Z' section for foreigners. I don't know what 'Z' means. It was called 'Z' section 'K'. After 1933 he said to me: 'We have been sifted through now. The politically tainted officials of the State Police have been got rid of and have either been pensioned off or put into positions where they can no longer do any harm. The sound nucleus of police officials, which every State needs, is now intermingled with people from the underworld of BERLIN, who, however, made themselves prominent in the movement at the right time. They have now been put to work with the others.' He said straight out: '50 per cent of us are decent people and 50 per cent are criminals.'

SCHAEFER: I think, if such conditions are permitted in a modern State, one can only say that the sooner this pack of *swine* disappear, the better.

KITTEL: We fools have just watched all these things going on. Did you never know that HIMMLER is a state within the state?

SCHAEFER & BRUHN: No.

KITTEL: I've often sat up all night discussing with people how the THIRD REICH came into existence. I had pangs of conscience as to whether I should in those circumstances remain in the Army at all.

FELBERT: It wasn't possible to remain in the Army in this State of ours; one was compelled to take measures against it.

SCHAEFER: At the time when you saw those murders at DVINSK, surely you had someone in authority over you?

KITTEL: The 'Heeresgruppe'.

SCHAEFER: You must have gone to official lectures about the construction of field works, etc. – was not a position like yours important enough for you to report the murders and add an expression of your horror?

KITTEL: I told the people that.

SCHAEFER: How do our C-in-Cs react to that?

KITTEL: 'We can't do anything about it; it's nothing to do with us.' It's a matter of organisation. In the POLAND that remains there is the Generalgouverneur Dr FRANK,[296] who is personally a right-thinking man, and he said to me quite clearly – although I'm actually of the opposite school of thought: 'If what I want to do here is carried out, there will be no bands in POLAND. My powers have a certain limit which you yourself know.' It is like this: the Generalgouverneur at the present moment has Obergruppenführer KOPPE, with the rank of a GOC, in the position of a Secretary of State, with unlimited police authority at the same time.[297] So I said to myself that KOPPE has creative power in the whole of POLAND under FRANK. Some stupid question about competence cropped up. I went to KOPPE and said: 'I have a case which comes under your jurisdiction and that of the Generalgouverneur.' So he said: 'The Generalgouverneur is not the competent authority for that, but Herr HIMMLER in BERLIN. I only come under the Generalgouverneur to the extent that he has the *right* to give me *directions* but I come under *HIMMLER*.' KOPPE was appointed as successor to Obergruppenführer KRÜGER,[298] and he (KRÜGER) did everything he could to annoy FRANK. If FRANK considered it necessary to take some sort of governmental measures, then KRÜGER, via HIMMLER, would simply muck it up for him through official police channels. He was continually throwing a spanner into the works.

BRUHN: Then HIMMLER must be the man responsible.

KITTEL: He *is* the man. There is *no* other man in GERMANY who has a word to say on questions of executive powers to a man in the Security Service, in the Police, the Traffic Police, the Gestapo –

BRUHN: And the Waffen-SS –

KITTEL: Well, the position in the Waffen-SS may be a little different.

FELBERT: Only HIMMLER's organisations have any say.

KITTEL: Yes. One can name umpteen cases. Someone may be acquitted by the court, and on leaving the court is arrested for being a public danger, and then doesn't get out.

BRUHN: Yes, one simply doesn't know about all that.

KITTEL: But you must know it. I once wrote a letter to the Minister of Justice, GÜRTNER, who once commanded a 'Bataillon' of mine, about a case like that in which someone was acquitted by the court and –

FELBERT: Then arrested again in spite of that.

KITTEL: The prison sentence which the prosecution had demanded was then simply carried out by the six months' imprisonment which had been demanded being –

BRUHN: Turned into six months' protective custody!

KITTEL: Six months' protective custody.

BRUHN: But that is no longer the rule of law.

KITTEL: Oh, you must surely have realised that.

SCHAEFFER: We *should* know that, but we have been carefully kept in
ignorance.

[. . .]

? BRUHN: Yes, but then, suppose we win the war tomorrow, there would
be a catastrophe!

KITTEL: It wouldn't be a catastrophe, but –

? BRUHN: Because we represent a different standard of honesty, we shall
be disposed of sooner or later anyhow. Things will reach such a pitch
that when they no longer have any Jews left to shoot, they will
probably shoot the relations of the officers.

SCHAEFFER : That's why it will be a catastrophe if we win.

BRUHN: For – whoever has once started that bloodshed, it becomes as
much of a necessity to him as our lunch to us; he won't be able to stop
it – or he will go crazy.

KITTEL: Oberst BIERKAMP(?) the head of the Security Service at CRACOW
told me that when he sees that a man enjoys shooting others, he gets
rid of him.

BRUHN: Does he shoot him himself?

KITTEL: No, he doesn't do that – he transfers him to another job.

BRUHN: In other words – one can see it from dozens of examples – it's
their orders which turn the men into sadists.

KITTEL: Of course. Tell me, will it never be possible to get such things in
GERMANY right again?

BRUHN: You mean a return to decency? That can only come about by our
losing the war, i.e., only by scrapping this whole system of government.

FELBERT: We should never get things right again after a victorious war.

SCHAEFFER : You are amazed that we don't know all that. Do you think
HITLER knows it? And he is our supreme commander.

KITTEL: No. Those things are not passed on to HITLER.

SCHAEFFER : But HIMMLER knows it, doesn't he?

KITTEL: HIMMLER knows all right.

Document 120

CSDIC (UK), SR Report, SRGG 1093 (C) [TNA, WO 208/4169]

Generalleutnant SCHAEFER (Commander, 244 Infantry Division) – Captured 28
Aug. 44 in Marseilles
Generalleutnant KITTEL (Commandant, Metz and Commander, 462
Volksgrenadier Division) – Captured 22 Nov. 44 in Metz.
Information received: 28 Dec. 44

SCHAEFER: After the stories you've told me one might think one was
really no longer bound to the FÜHRER.

KITTEL: We can't think that.

SCHAEFER: I mean in our hearts; when one goes over all the crimes that have been committed, it makes one's hair stand on end.

KITTEL: 18,000 people were shot in ROSTOV, there are about 60,000 people in mass graves near LUBLIN.[299]

SCHAEFER: One can only say that if GERMANY is destroyed it is justice and nothing else. It is a tragedy that so many millions of decent people should be wiped out, and towns too, for the sake of men who are leading a gangster existence – there's no other way of describing it. I simply cannot swallow it.

KITTEL: In UPPER SILESIA they simply slaughtered the people systematically. They were gassed in a big hall.[300]

SCHAEFER: When was that done?

KITTEL: Up till the spring, then it was stopped.

SCHAEFER: Who are the people concerned?

KITTEL: I don't know. There's the greatest secrecy about all those things.

SCHAEFER: One can hardly believe that such a thing could happen in the world.

[. . .]

Document 121

CSDIC (UK), GRGG 245
Report on information obtained from Senior Officers (PW) on 5–7 Jan. 45 [TNA, WO 208/4364]

WILDERMUTH: I'm thinking of something which I only came to realise fully here, that is those famous GERMAN atrocities. People didn't know about them. Most of the officers here just can't understand the most well-known ones. They *didn't* know about them. They said: 'Oh, well, that is atrocity propaganda, things like that don't really happen!' People in foreign countries can hardly believe them. I can only say: they *did* take place. There's that famous story about the mentally deficient; I know about it because my brother was a doctor in a lunatic asylum. Thank God he is in charge of a military hospital during the war and is not involved in that business. Through him I know exactly what happened. When I told my colleagues at the bank in BERLIN, it must have been in 1941, they laughed at me and said: 'What you say is nonsense, things like that don't happen, that isn't possible.'

Document 122

CSDIC (UK), GRGG 254
Report on information obtained from Senior Officers (PW) on 28–31 Jan. 45 [TNA, WO 208/4364]

KITTEL: I told the American IO: 'Our first response to what you intend doing with GERMANY will be to massacre whatever Jews remain.' Eight hundred thousand out of the nine hundred thousand are still sure to be alive. We had a Jewish concentration camp at CRACOW – it was grotesque but we had one there. A camp containing five thousand men and five thousand women, kept strictly separated; the discipline here was incredible; they had a department for criminals. I often had Jews to dig trenches; I asked for two thousand Jews for trench-digging.

RAMCKE: What sort of an impression did they make in those concentration camps? Did they partly administer themselves; or what?

KITTEL: The camp authorities lived inside the camp which is a sign they felt secure. Of course it was strongly guarded outside; it was even guarded by live wire, but on the whole you did not get the impression that the inmates were in such a bad way.

RAMCKE: I don't believe that Jews will dare to show themselves openly in GERMANY in business or as tools under the protection of the Americans and British in the future.

KITTEL: I hope not.

Document 123

CSDIC (UK), GRGG 256
Report on information obtained from Senior Officers (PW) on 3–5 Feb. 45 [TNA, WO 208/4177]

BRUHN: I must assume, after all I have read about the FÜHRER, that he knew all about it.

FELBERT: Of course he knew about it. He's the man who is responsible. He even discussed it with HIMMLER.

BRUHN: Yes, that man doesn't care a hoot if your relatives are annihilated.

FELBERT: That man doesn't care a damn.

BRUHN: They distribute their 'Oak Leaves' and decorations and whatever else they have, solely according to who can guarantee them their lives longest. He is directing the resistance fight in such a manner that he causes chaos and will be able to say afterwards that it's the Western democracies who've caused chaos in GERMANY. In reality cause and effect will be mistaken for each other. And we're to put up with that kind of thing! I never saw through it; I don't mind if they shoot me, but they can only shoot me for stupidity, not for any dirty business. Nevertheless they must grant me extenuating circumstances, inasmuch as I acted in good faith. You must usually believe what official representatives tell you. No one would have imagined it possible for a *criminal* to get into the government.

Don't you think that our 'Armeeführer' or our 'Heeresgruppenkommandeure', when reporting about us to KEITEL and RUNDSTEDT said: 'A last point I have to mention is those massacres in SOUTH POLAND – shouldn't we protect our officer corps against being blamed for such actions?' Do you think discussions on those matters took place? What did they do about it?

FELBERT: You can see for yourself.

BRUHN: They've probably given them money and an estate, and tied their hands in that way.[301] Or else the people have got annoyed and said: 'That's nothing to do with me; leave me in peace!'

FELBERT: You see it in the case of BLASKOWITZ. They simply got rid of him.[302]

BRUHN: Did he actually bring a thing like that up? With whom?

FELBERT: He brought it up in the OKW, I believe. As a result the man was simply sacked; he went immediately.

BRUHN: Then we who are regular officers must advocate that men be shot who are themselves wearing our uniform.

FELBERT: Naturally you must.

BRUHN: We must even disassociate ourselves from our *own* superiors, who are also regular officers.

FELBERT: Yes, because they knew. They knew about it without any doubt.

BRUHN: Well, give me a motive.

FELBERT: What do those people call a motive?

BRUHN: To get promotion? That makes it even *worse*. To get a decoration? That makes it worse still. They were so well off that they lacked for nothing – they were even better off than that.

FELBERT: Those people all miscalculated. They all said to themselves: 'The war is nearly over anyway.'

BRUHN: Yes, but surely I can't miscalculate on questions of honour?

FELBERT: Oh, *those* people have no honour.

BRUHN: But they must have. We've always preached it; after all we were 'Bataillon' and 'Regimentskommandeure.'

FELBERT: We have no honour either. We have ambition, filthy ambition, filthiest ambition, but nothing more.

BRUHN: Do you believe then, that, not with individuals but with the mass of people, their ambition is so great that even if they are regular officers – I'm speaking only of those and not of the SS – they shrink from no measures whatever, just to serve their ambition?

FELBERT: I don't know what was behind it all. Of course, it's also possible that pressure was brought to bear on them.

BRUHN: But there was always the possibility of simulating illness and saying: 'I can't do it any more.' Do you really think they soberly said to themselves: 'Might is Right' and 'we'll win the war and then no one will worry about that.' But in that case those people can have no conscience at all.

FELBERT: They haven't.

Document 124

CSDIC (UK), GRGG 260
Report on information obtained from Senior Officers (PW) on 14–15 Feb. 45
[TNA, WO 208/4177]

WAHLE: Once, in 1941, we liquidated a Russian Commissar[303] who had
   been captured on his way *back* to the East in the company of another
   Russian. He had quickly managed to throw away his map and all kinds
   of things. He appeared as a handsome, immaculately dressed officer
   who first of all feigned innocence, saying he'd lost his way when
   looking for supply vehicles and stating he was an officer. I had seen the
   map and noticed it had indications of how they intended by-passing us;
   during the night also something had occurred: some cavalry had
   broken through in the rear. Whilst my adjutant and I were examining
   his maps and papers he continued his tale in an extremely self-assured
   manner. Suddenly . . . passed me a slip of paper and whispered: 'Here
   is a Commissar's identity card.' The man broke down on the spot; he
   knew his fate was sealed. We packed up the things and sent him back
   to the 'Division', where he was then put to death . . . It happened at the
   time the Russians were dropping those pamphlets containing that
   CLAUSEWITZ quotation which had been got up very well, and which
   said: 'It is impossible either to hold or to conquer RUSSIA', in
   November 1941.
ELFELDT: In what area did it happen?
WAHLE: It occurred near PRTEMOVSK;[304] do you know the place, it's near
   BACHMUT. The town used to be called BACHMUT and lies between
   ROSTOV and KHARKOV.

Document 125

CSDIC (UK), GRGG 264
Report on information obtained from Senior Officers (PW) on 24–6 Feb. 45 [TNA,
WO 208/4177]

KITTEL: I forbade that at DVINSK and the immediate result was that it
   stopped at once. I didn't have any say in the matter at STALINO, that's
   to say the tragedy had already taken place, and it had also already taken
   place at ROSTOV; the people had already been killed there, but it was
   put down to my account. I shall certainly be named as a war criminal.
   18,000 Jews were killed at ROSTOV. Of course I had nothing to do with
   the whole affair! But it is down on my account because I was the only
   known 'General' there.[305]
EBERBACH: Who is really responsible for the affair? There's no doubt at all
   that the FÜHRER knew all about this massacre of the Jews.
KITTEL: Well, those Jews were the pest of the east! They should have been

driven into one area and employed on some useful occupation. By the way I'm going to hold my tongue about what I do know of these things, until such time as they pick me out. After the fall of ROSTOV the Russians accused me, in a great official solemn declaration on the radio, of having poisoned 18,000 Russians. As regards that I can only say: until then I knew nothing whatsoever about the whole affair in which so many people were killed, and was actually not under the impression either that so many people had been removed from there. They were probably carried off. I don't know. Anyhow I'm certainly one of the best nominees for a war criminal – although there are quite a number of them – WILDERMUTH (PW) also told me in the strictest secrecy that he has signed about forty sentences of death in his official capacity as 'Feldkommandant'.[306] Yes, I have some anxiety on that score!

I deprived the Security Services people of *every* possibility of maltreating the population, but I could not overcome the fact that my own superiors made arrangements with the Police General which simply knocked me off my feet. I said to General von ROTHKIRCH who played a part down there in the defence of the DNIEPER line in the winter of 1941/43:[307] 'Well, Sir, with the signing of this agreement with the police you are handing over *all* your executive power, and *we* are responsible for it!'[308] And now this is what happens! I wrote that quite clearly to the Supreme Command of the Armed Forces too. This government by HIMMLER and his men who received personal instructions, is intolerable. Just look at FRANK,[309] one of the personalities who does not have a very good press, he is stationed at CRACOW and has an SS-Obergruppenführer in charge of the German police in POLAND. The whole of POLAND forms a completely autonomous government under FRANK. Now comes the strange part of it. I went to FRANK and said to him: 'We will have to make some changes in the distribution of labour forces.' So he said: 'I'm not authorised to do that. Hasn't the Secretary of State told you that already?' I said: 'Who is in charge of that in POLAND then?' He said: 'I have an administrative job! You go and see SS-Obergruppenführer KOPPE, and see to it that you reach an agreement with him!'[310]

EBERBACH: Didn't he come under FRANK?

KITTEL: FRANK merely had the right to give instructions, and KOPPE got his orders from BERLIN. It turned out from that mess that the police did what they liked and FRANK was over them in administrative matters. So just what a State needs, namely a legislative power and an executive power, was lacking, and that was lacking in the whole of the east, and that's the secret of our whole failure. When I think of that 'Don Quixote' we had at ROSTOV, General HENNECKE(?), Chief of the Police of WEIMAR, and then subsequently Chief of Police at ROSTOV,[311] although admittedly he only used his authority very little – then one can only say that this man with his pushing ways: 'This is the SS, this is Heinrich HIMMLER, room will be made here; this house will be a Police Station, and later there will be a leaders' headquarters here.' That was set up first of all. He brought a completely separate electric power station from GERMANY, electric stoves, huge radios and everything. I said to him: 'If you take over the executive power here I shall have to submit to the orders of my superiors; the police are here – 800 Russian police with whom we have so far kept the town in order; there is no German policeman over them, but it is done on a certain basis of trust; the people have such-and-such weapons.' 'What, they have weapons, that's unheard of, that's contrary to all the FÜHRER's orders.' The first thing was that they disarmed the police – trouble started from that day. Then they disbanded the police and picked people out from the rabble. All that work of the last five months was completely undone and destroyed in one month. Then one affair occurred – the SS shot all the prisoners in the civil prison at ROSTOV. They set fire to the prison and it didn't burn. The Russians captured it in that state, and can put it all down to my account, because at first I had the executive power in my hands.

Document 126

CSDIC (UK), GRGG 265
Report on information obtained from Senior Officers (PW) on 7 Feb.–1 Mar. 45
[TNA, WO 208/4177]

BRUHN: I do believe that shootings and all sorts of things were carried out there on a large scale, and as a matter of fact KITTEL (PW) told me that. He was an eye-witness of it at Lvov and CRACOW when hundreds and thousands of people were shot; he knows it for a fact, but I didn't know it. I've never spoken to an eye-witness of a thing like that. I've heard it, but it was impossible to establish the truth of things like that. KITTEL is on the list of criminals, and one must not forget that such people are subconsciously obsessed with the idea that they must go in the direction through thick and thin, because they'll fall anyhow, whereas people like ourselves are much more conscious of the fact that we can go everywhere, wherever we like. Of course, they can stand us up against the wall, but then it would be judicial murder. But I asked KITTEL: 'What did you do on that Sunday morning when the hundreds of people were shot near your house?' Then he said: 'Everyone knew about it.'[312] (Cf. SRGG 1086(C)). So in a certain sense he was implicated in it, and one must not forget – I believe ULLERSBERGER (PW) is also afraid of a similar fate, and MEYER (PW) will say to himself anyhow: 'They will have their knife into me, because so-and-so many PW were shot by my "Division".' Those people know for a fact that they probably haven't a chance of returning to their own country. So on the one hand it leads to complete agreement and co-operation with all these ideas expressed by GOEBBELS, or on the other hand it leads to personal rows like we have here. KITTEL described it to me like this: he had a house at some place or other, and then one Sunday morning he was woken from his beautiful sleep by intermittent rifle-fire. So he asked someone to go and see what was happening. After a time this fellow returned and reported to him that a few hundred Jews were assembled there and were just being shot. That was in the area south-east or south-west of RIGA. He experienced the same thing again at CRACOW. Then he said that soldiers were under his command who were off duty on Sunday morning and who were stationed in that village, had all gone there and watched it. Then they dug their graves and then they picked up the children by their hair and then simply killed them. The SS did that. The soldiers stood there, and besides that the Russian civilian population stood 200 m away and watched as they were killed there. He proved how vile the whole thing was by the fact that an out-and-out SS man who was employed on his staff later succumbed to a nervous breakdown and from that day onwards kept saying that he couldn't carry on any longer, it was impossible; he was a doctor. He couldn't get over it. That was his first experience of such things actually being done. A cold shudder ran through SCHAEFFER (PW) and me when we heard that, and then we said to KITTEL: 'What did you do then? You were lying in bed and heard that, and it was only a few hundred metres away from your house. Then surely you must have reported that to your GOC. Surely something was bound to be done about it?' He replied that it was generally known and was quite usual. Then sometimes he also inter-spersed remarks such as: 'There wasn't anything particularly bad about it either,' and 'they were to blame for everything anyhow,' so that I almost assumed at that time, that it hadn't even mattered very much to him personally.

SCHLIEBEN: We are doomed to bloodshed.

BRUHN: It's simply like this, that if we, as decent people were asked today: 'What should be done to a government like that, what should become of a people like that which has carried out such things on a large scale?', one can surely only say that for the sake of humanity a people like that should *not* win the war, but should be pushed back to its frontiers. In that way one becomes an accuser of one's own country.

SCHLIEBEN: This is the situation into which those people have brought us. And then he (GOEBBELS) quotes the Almighty!

BRUHN: GOEBBELS drags up all sorts of things which he has no right at all to say. This is the scourge of God which is now overtaken humanity. That's what happens if you look upon life solely for eating and drinking.

SCHLIEBEN: Such a thing does exist and it is coming too! 'And I will visit the sins of the fathers upon the third and fourth generation!'

BRUHN: For the same reason I believe that when the policy of extermination overtakes us, which we have actually merited by our shedding of blood, the blood of our children will have to be shed too, or perhaps that of our relations.

Document 127

CSDIC (UK), GRGG 270
Report on information obtained from Senior Officers (PW) on 9 Mar. 45 [TNA, WO 208/4177]

ROTHKIRCH: The IO said: 'You were in the military "Kommandantur" in RUSSIA. You were at LVOV; what did you do there?' 'I was in command of the local "Kommandanturen" there.' 'A large number of crimes must have been committed in your area too?' Yes, of course they occurred but military administration hasn't the slightest connection with civil administration. On the contrary, there was usually a fair amount of animosity between us; we had the prerogative and woe to anyone who dared carry out executions in my area. Whereupon he said: 'We act on the principle that anyone who witnesses a crime and does nothing to prevent it, is an accessory.' Then he asked me about MINSK. I said: 'I was GOC there but my instructions were quite clear: I had to fight the partisans as GOC of security troops of the "Heeresgruppe Mitte".'[313] Well, then he interrogated me fairly thoroughly. What can he do? Of course I said I had nothing to do with all that business. I said: 'Not only I, but none of the Generals had anything to do with it, on the contrary, we turned it down in the most definite way. Many a General was dismissed as a result of his refusal.' Then the IO said: 'Incidentally, the Russians will demand the handing over of a lot of officers.' Of course those officers who held those administrative jobs should be among them. If you're handed over, it's all up.

CHOLTITZ: There's a man here, General KITTEL, who was the subject of a whole evening's broadcast.

ROTHKIRCH: He was at LVOV. He had some sort of local 'Komman-danturen" –

CHOLTITZ: Surely he didn't permit executions to take place, did he?

ROTHKIRCH: If you're in charge of villages and towns and the SS comes along and takes the people away, what can you do? Of course masses of people were shot at LVOV. Thousands of them![314] First the Jews, then Poles who were also shot in thousands, non-Jews, the whole aristocracy and great landed proprietors and masses of students. It's all very difficult.

CHOLTITZ: How dreadful!

Document 128

CSDIC (UK), GRGG 271
Report on information obtained from Senior Officers (PW) on 10, 11, 12 Mar. 45
[TNA, WO 208/4177]

BRUHN: If you were to ask me: 'Have we deserved victory or not?' I
    should say: 'No, not after what we've done. After the amount of
    human blood we've shed knowingly and as a result of our delusions
    and also partly instigated by the lust of blood and other qualities, I now
    realise we've deserved defeat; we've deserved our fate, even though I'm
    accusing myself as well.' Even if you take the indubitable courage and
    achievement of the population into account, we are not suffering an
    undeserved fate; we are being punished for letting a national
    resurrection which promised so well, go to the devil.

BROICH: We shot women as if they had been cattle. I was at ZHITOMIR the
    day after it happened, while moving forward when the second offensive
    was about to start. The 'Kommandant', an Oberst von MONICH(?)[315]
    happened to be there and he said, quite appalled: 'We might drive out
    afterwards; there is a large quarry where ten thousand men, women and
    children were shot yesterday.' They were all still lying in the quarry.
    We drove out on purpose to see it. The most bestial thing I ever saw.

CHOLTITZ: One day after SEBASTOPOL had fallen – whilst I was on my way
    back to BERLIN – I flew back with the Chief of Staff,[316] the CO of the
    airfield was coming up to me, when he heard shots. I asked whether a
    firing practice was on. He answered: 'Good Lord, I'm not supposed to
    tell, but they've been shooting Jews here *for days* now.'

BROICH: The most ridiculous story is the one WILDERMUTH (PW) tells
    about CROATIA when he was there. Some incident had happened in a
    factory somewhere or other; maybe someone was shot; in any case
    nothing of any importance. The 'Bataillonskommandeur' had the six
    hundred workers shot, *including* the German foremen, without
    establishing their identity! Just imagine it! It all came out afterwards.
    The man concerned, who was in charge of it all, came along and said:
    'Good gracious, they have shot my son as well!' WILDERMUTH
    experienced that incident himself.[317]

CHOLTITZ: Once I went to OLDENBURG and visited Gauleiter RÖVER[318]
    who said to me on parting: 'I must congratulate you, Sir, on your
    "Regiment". You are now in command of the "Oldenburger
    Regiment". How are things in the field?' I said: 'Well, the soldiers'
    morale is high, everything is in order. It's just the *home front* that
    doesn't satisfy our men.' He asked why ever not. 'Well, we can't stand
    this shooting of Jews.' The man couldn't understand that. 'And we
    cannot stand – I stress this fact in the name of my men – we won't
    stand the persecution of churches and religious houses.' In SOUTH

OLDENBURG, which is Catholic, nuns and monks were being turned out of their houses and were not permitted to remain within a radius of 60 km, to prevent them from being assisted by the population.[319] He looked very amazed and then started shouting like a madman, saying: 'What! Is that what your men are concerned about? It's incredible! The FÜHRER gave orders, shouting at me furiously, that a report be sent him every day in which not at least a thousand Jews were shot.'

ROTHKIRCH: Only in GERMANY, or where?

CHOLTITZ: No – everywhere. I presumed he meant POLAND. 36,000 Jews from SEBASTOPOL were shot.

Document 129

CSDIC (UK), GRGG 272
Report on information obtained from Senior Officers (PW) on 13–16 Mar. 45
[TNA, WO 208/4177]

ROTHKIRCH: All the gassing institutions are in POLAND, near LVOV.[320] I know that there are large gassing centres there but I don't know any more. Let me tell you though, the gassings are by no means the worst.

RAMCKE: I first heard about all those things here in this PW camp.[321]

ROTHKIRCH: I'm an 'Administration General' and the people here have already interrogated me. It was near LVOV. Actually we washed our hands of it all because these atrocities took place in a military area. At LVOV in particular I was always receiving reports of those shootings and they were so bestial that I wouldn't care to tell you about them.

RAMCKE: What happened?

ROTHKIRCH: To start with the people dug their own graves, then ten Jews took up their position by them and then the firing squad arrived with tommy-guns and shot them down, and they fell into the grave. Then came the next lot and they, too, were paraded in front of them and then fell into the grave and the rest waited a bit until they were shot. Thousands of people were shot. Afterwards they gave that up and gassed them. Many of them weren't dead and a layer of earth was shovelled on in between. They had packers there who packed the bodies in, because they fell in too soon. The SS did that, they were the people who packed the corpses in.

RAMCKE: Were they 'Waffen-SS'? What did the Security Police do?

ROTHKIRCH: I believe they were Security Police.

RAMCKE: Where were they recruited from?

ROTHKIRCH: I can't tell you that, they were typical – they were SS men. There are photographs in this newspaper, you can see them. We received a description. I don't know to this day why I got it. The SS leader wrote that he had shot the children himself – women were shot as well – because it was so repulsive; they didn't always die immediately; he actually *wrote* that, I have the thing at home. He described how he grasped the children by the neck and shot them with his revolver because that way he had the greatest certainty of their dying instantaneously. This thing, which I had not asked for at all, I sent home.

The Governor at Lvov, a Dr LASCH,[322] invited me to go to the opera with him. After the long interval he suddenly said to me: 'You know, Graf ROTHKIRCH, it was terrible. It's *so* dreadful it's indescribable. Just imagine what I have done. If only I hadn't done it. I attended one of those shootings today.' The man was *completely* out of his mind. A year ago I was in charge of the guerrilla school where men were being trained in guerrilla warfare; I went on an exercise with them one day and I said: 'Direction of march is that hill up there.' The directors of the school then said to me: 'That's not a very good idea, sir, as they are just burning Jews up there.' I said: 'What do you mean? Burning Jews? But there aren't any Jews any more.' 'Yes, that's the place where they were always shot and now they are all being disinterred again, soaked with petrol and burnt so that their bodies shan't be discovered.' 'That's a dreadful job. There's certain to be a lot of loose talk about it afterwards.' 'Well, the men who are doing the job will be shot directly afterwards and burnt with them.' The whole thing sounds just like a fairy story.[323]

RAMCKE: From the inferno.

ROTHKIRCH: Yes, I was at KUTNO,[324] I wanted to take some photographs – that's my only hobby – and I knew an SS leader there quite well and I was talking to him about this and that when he said: 'Would you like to photograph a shooting?' I said: 'No, the very idea is repugnant to me.' 'Well, I mean, it makes no difference to us, they are always shot in the morning, but if you like we still have some and we can shoot them in the afternoon sometime.' You can't imagine how these men have become completely brutalised. Just think of it some of these Jews got away and will keep talking about it. And the craziest thing of all: how is it possible for pictures to get into the press? For there are pictures in this paper (Weltwoche?[325]). They even filmed it and the films, of course, have got abroad; it always leaks out somehow. In Lvov, just like people catching fish with a net, ten SS men would walk along the street and simply grab any Jews who happened to be walking along. If you happened to look Jewish, you were just added to their catch (*laughs*). Sometime the world will take revenge for that. If those people, the Jews, come to the helm and take revenge, it will of course be terrible. But I think it doubtful whether the enemy will permit them to get there, for most of the foreigners, the English, the French and the Americans, are also quite clear about the Jews. It won't be like that. They've allied themselves with the devil in order to beat us; just as we concluded that alliance with the Bolsheviks for a time, they are doing the same thing. The important question is: which ideology should gain the upper hand in the world? And whether they will trust us? One must now work to that end so that they will trust us and we must steer clear of everything which will arouse them afresh so that we first show them: 'Friends, we want to cooperate in creating a sensible world.'

Document 130

CSDIC (UK), GRGG 272
Report on information obtained from Senior Officers (PW) on 16–19 Mar. 45 [TNA, WO 208/4177]

HEYDTE: There's another camp which is even worse than LUBLIN; it's in CZECHOSLOVAKIA. Half-a-million people have been put to death there for *certain*. I know that *all* the Jews from BAVARIA were taken there. Yet the camp never became over-crowded.[326]
WILDERMUTH: Yes, I've heard of that too.
HEYDTE: But I don't only know that all the Jews from BAVARIA were taken there, I know that all the Jews from AUSTRIA were taken there, and still the camp wasn't over-crowded.
WILDERMUTH: From all over GERMANY. It appears that most of the Jews from GERMANY were either sent to LUBLIN or to that place.
HEYDTE: I was also told that the Jews are simply gassed in a gas-chamber there. They gassed mental defectives too.
WILDERMUTH: Yes, I know. I got to know that for a fact in the case of NUREMBERG; my brother is doctor at an institution there. I've seen one of those transports myself. The people knew where they were being taken.
HEYDTE: Yes, and then they've also done it with old people.
WILDERMUTH: Not with old people!
HEYDTE: Homes for old people! Yes, that is so.

Document 131

CSDIC (UK), GRGG 275
Report on information obtained from Senior Officers (PW) on 24 Mar. 45 [TNA, WO 208/4177]
[. . .]

ROTHKIRCH: Look how brutalised we've become: I drove through a small Polish place where students were being shot merely because they were students, and Polish nobility and estate owners were all being shot: it was not out in the fields, it was in the town, in front of the Town Hall, you could still see the bullet marks on the thing. I went to BOCKELBERG

(VOLLARD-BOCKELBERG?)[327] and told him about it. He said: 'Listen, we can't do anything else, it has to be done, because students are the most dangerous people of all, they must all go, and as for the nobility, they will always work against us. Anyway, don't get so worked up about it, if we win the war, it won't matter.' I replied: 'Sir, that may be, but new principles like that take some getting used to.'

Document 132

CSDIC (UK), GRGG 276
Report on information obtained from Senior Officers (PW) on 25 Mar. 45 [TNA, WO 208/4177]

DASER: I tried to restrict it all the time and as a result the number of shootings decreased *considerably*, not only in my area but in the entire area

THOMA: Well, who ordered those shootings?

DASER: FALKENHAUSEN. I protested against it very successfully as those mistakes had been made before – they shot two or three at LILLE; an officer and civil servant were shot in the street by civilians at BRUSSELS. They used to throw hand grenades at the crowds streaming out of cinemas. They shot either a 'Hauptmann' or a 'Major', besides a uniformed official and a paymaster. Whereupon three or four hostages were shot.

THOMA: Who were the hostages?

DASER: People who had been handed over to us for working against us; people we could lay hands on, who were in possession of arms, although that was forbidden, or people who had made attempts to sabotage railways. If they were caught red-handed they were shot on the spot anyway. I was able to achieve two things: firstly I managed to prevent five or six hostages from being shot immediately the next day whenever one of our men was shot; I ordered them to wait a fortnight or three weeks in case the perpetrator was found, as on some occasion three or four hostages were shot because one of our men had been killed and a week later we caught the culprit. I never signed a death-warrant; they always went up to BRUSSELS. I became well known on that account with the 15th Armee, who reported to FALKENHAUSEN that the troops were being molested and cables were being cut. They asked him to have more hostages executed. He called us to a conference where I objected against those measures. I said: 'It's no use, we are only creating martyrs. The way it has been done up to now is wrong.' He then said: 'All right, I agree with your ideas and your argument.'[328]

Document 133

CSDIC (UK), GRGG 277
Report on information obtained from Senior Officers (PW) on 28–9 Mar. 45
[TNA, WO 208/4177]

WILDERMUTH: In SERBIA I too was given orders to have a hundred people shot for every German killed and fifty for every German wounded. However, I never carried out these orders. One 'Kommandant' of some Serbian place, after a skirmish 10 or 20 km away in the mountains, during which two Germans had been killed and three wounded, used to have three hundred and fifty Serbs shot, two hundred for the two Germans killed and a hundred and fifty for the three wounded. About two thousand four hundred people were shot there. The reaction came when he had six hundred people from an aircraft factory shot in one day, including the German foreman. These are things which shouldn't happen. I never even dreamt of carrying out that order.[329]

A few months later General BADER asked me: 'Why didn't you carry out that order?' I told him that no one could order me to do something opposed to my honour as an officer and beside, that that order was frightfully stupid as it caused every Serbian to take up arms. That was our difficulty: we received orders which made us feel morally obliged to oppose. The ethical principle is *quite* obvious. Take an extreme case: you are ordered to torture your mother. You should rather die than carry that out. That's obvious. Just as when you are ordered to shoot a hundred innocent Serbs, which is just as stupid and dirty; it's a question of ethics. If I, because I passed that order on – or possibly one of my 'Bataillonskommandeure' may have carried it out, and the Allies charge me on that account and say: 'You passed that order on.' I'll answer: 'Well, I had to, otherwise I'd have been shot.' That is my defence, but it doesn't excuse me morally.

HEIM: The only question is: what shall be our attitude when we are put before one of those Courts of Inquiry? In my opinion our conduct must be *uniform*, we must uphold the principle of only having carried out orders. I don't know what I should have done in your case. I should probably have acted in the same way. Today, however, I think we *must* stick to that principle if we are to create a uniform basis which would provide us with a more or less effective defence and, above all, prevent the Allies from playing us off against each other in the *worst possible manner*. There are soldiers too, among those holding the Court of Inquiry. When they retire for the verdict, they'll say: 'There's nothing you can say against that point of view.'

WILDERMUTH: They certainly *won't* say *that* because they go by completely different standards from ours.[330]

HEIM: They may say it in very serious cases like *that* one, for instance.

WILDERMUTH: That field order was valid for the whole of SERBIA. Now it becomes interesting: when BADER heard about that incident at BELGRADE, he wanted to go for that commander.[331] The 'Division' shielded him, by saying: 'Excuse me, those were orders, which he carried out. Think before you issue orders.' Then everything petered out in the usual way, apart from some minor repercussions, just as if the order had never been issued.

HEIM: You can't even imagine all the examples which occurred in practice.

WILDERMUTH: I'll tell you of another instance in which I intervened. It concerned the well-known order issued in 1942, regarding activities by saboteurs and commandos, who were to be shot immediately. I read that order when in hospital at home. After I got out again, the order was mentioned during an officers' conference in the 43rd 'Regiment',[332] and I said it naturally only concerned people not in uniform, although it was quite obvious that the order had a different intention.

HEIM: At the time HITLER at any rate, thought those terror measures would frighten his opponents.

HEYDTE: I quite agree with you, Sir.

HEIM: We ought to discuss these matters at a larger gathering in order to create a basis of defence, and a fairly *sound* one at that.

WILDERMUTH: Then there were things which hadn't been ordered, but which gradually became customary. At LE HAVRE I once had thirty people, including some who had collaborated with us, arrested. There they were in prison. A terrific air raid took place.[333] We couldn't very well leave them there and I didn't know what to do with them. One of my staff suggested: 'Let's shoot them!' Whereupon I said: let them go and join the resistance movement outside the town. Thirty people make no difference. But at other places other measures were adopted.

HEIM: You must give different examples to the English, because they and especially the Americans do not think along the same purely military lines as we do.

WILDERMUTH: I meant to warn you against that. The Allies are much fussier in some matters than we were. I remember that from the last war. They shot many more men for refusing to obey orders and deserting than we did.

HEIM: Don't you think that during the Boer War many a British officer received an order which he didn't consider fair.

Document 134

CSDIC (UK), GRGG 278
Report on information obtained from Senior Officers (PW) on 30 Mar.–2 Apr. 45
[TNA, WO 208/4177]

BROICH: I visited DACHAU once in 1937. We were taken round everywhere. At that time there were 5,000 people there, 35,000 had passed through.[334] They said enormous buildings were going to be put up. Things were to be such that about 30,000 could pass through each year. They said 'Some come here with a ticket "Never to be released". Some remain three months, they are harmless birds of passage, who are simply to be sand-papered down a bit, and with some it's a question of! Well, if they're all right in a year or two and have been properly broken, they can come out. The 'Oberst' told us all that.'[335]

BRUHN: Was that a conducted tour for Army officers?

BROICH: No, it was quite private. I was in MUNICH for the 'Brauner Ball' festivities and ... said to me: 'W ALDECK' – that's the 'Ober-gruppenführer', the old fellow, the hereditary prince, an utter fool – 'asked me today if I wouldn't like to go along there. It's too gruesome going alone and I don't like that kind of thing.' He said: 'It's quite amusing.' I said: 'It doesn't attract me very much, on the other hand, it's quite interesting to go once.' So we went, there was HASSE ... , myself and WALDECK.[336] In civilian clothes. WALDECK was in SS uniform.

REIMANN: LEX[337] said recently that ULLERSPERGER had made the following remark: 'What do I care about Good Friday? Because a filthy old Jew was hanged umpteen years ago?'

Document 135

CSDIC (UK), GG REPORT, SRGG 1158(C) [TNA, WO 208/4170]

Generalmajor BRUNS (Heeres-Waffenmeisterschule 1, Berlin) – Captured 8 Apr. 45 in Göttingen – and other Senior Officers (PW) whose voices could not be identified.
Information received: 25 Apr. 45

BRUNS: As soon as I heard those Jews were to be shot on Friday I went to a 21-year-old boy and said that they had made themselves very useful in the area under my command, besides which the Army MT park had employed 1,500 and the 'Heeresgruppe' 800 women to make under-clothes of the stores we captured in RIGA; besides which about 1,200 women in the neighbourhood of RIGA were turning millions of captured sheepskins into articles we urgently required: ear-protectors, fur caps, fur waistcoat, etc. Nothing had been provided, as of course the Russian campaign was known to have come to a victorious end in October 1941! In short, all those women were employed in a useful capacity. I tried to save them. I told that fellow ALTENMEYER(?)[338] whose name I shall always remember and who will be added to the list of war criminals: 'Listen to me, they represent valuable man-power!'

'Do you call Jews valuable human beings, Sir?' I said: 'Listen to me properly, I said "valuable *man-power*". I didn't mention their value as human beings.' He said: 'Well, they're to be shot in accordance with the FÜHRER's orders!' I said 'FÜHRER's orders?' 'Yes', whereupon he showed me his orders. This happened at SKIOTAWA(?),[339] 8 km from RIGA, between SIAULAI and JELGAVA, where 5,000 BERLIN Jews were suddenly taken off the train and shot. I didn't see that myself, but what happened at SKIOTAWA(?)[340] – to cut a long story short, I argued with the fellow and telephoned to the General at HQ, to JAKOBS[341] and ABERGER(?),[342] and to a Dr SCHULTZ[343] who was attached to the Engineer General, on behalf of these people; I told him: 'Granting that the Jews have committed a crime against the other peoples of the world, at least let them do the drudgery; send them to throw earth on the roads to prevent our heavy lorries skidding.' 'Then I'd have to feed them!' I said: 'The little amount of food they receive, let's assume 2 million Jews – they got 125 gr of bread a day – if we can't manage that, the sooner we end the war the better.' Then I telephoned, thinking it would take some time. At any rate on Sunday morning I heard that they had already started on it. The Ghetto was cleared and they were told: 'You're being transferred; take along your most essential things.' Incidentally it was a happy release for those people, as their life in the Ghetto was a martyrdom. I wouldn't believe it and drove there, to have a look.

?: Everyone abroad knew about it; only we Germans were kept in ignorance.

BRUNS: I'll tell you something: some of the details may have been correct, but it was remarkable that the firing squad detailed that morning – six men with tommy-guns were posted at each pit; the pits were 24 m in length and 3 m in breath – they had to lie down like sardines in a tin, with their heads in the centre. Above them were six men with tommy-guns who gave them the coup de grâce. When I arrived those pits were so full that the living had to lie down on top of the dead; then they were shot and, in order to save room, they had to lie down neatly in layers. Before this, however, they were stripped of everything at one of the stations – here at the edge of the wood were the three pits they used that Sunday and here they stood in a queue 1½ km long which approached step by step – a queueing up for death. As they drew nearer they saw what was going on. About here they had to hand over their jewellery and suitcases. All good stuff was put into the suitcases and the remainder thrown on a heap. This was to serve as clothing for our suffering population – and then, a little further on they had to undress and, 500 m in front of the wood, strip completely; they were only permitted to keep on a chemise or knickers. They were all women and small two-year-old children. Then all those cynical remarks! If only I had seen those tommy-gunners, who were relieved every hour because of over-exertion, carry out their task with distaste, but no, nasty remarks like: 'Here comes a Jewish beauty!' I can still see it all in my memory: a pretty woman in a flame-coloured chemise. Talk about keeping the race pure: at RIGA they first slept with them and then shot them to prevent them from talking. Then I sent two officers out there, one of whom is still alive, because I wanted eye-witnesses. I didn't tell them what was going on, but said 'Go out to the forest of SKIOTAWA(?), see what's up there and send me a report.' I added a memorandum to their report and took it to JAKOBS myself. He said: 'I have already two complaints sent me by Engineer "Bataillone" from the UKRAINE.' There they shot them on the brink of large crevices and let them fall down into them; they nearly had an epidemic of plague, at any rate a pestilential smell. They thought they could break off the edges with picks, thus burying them. That loess there was so hard that two Engineer 'Bataillone' were required to dynamite the edges; those 'Bataillone' complained. JAKOBS had received that complaint. He said: 'We didn't quite know how to tell the FÜHRER. We'd better do it through CANARIS.'[344] CANARIS had the unsavoury task of waiting for the favourable moment to give the FÜHRER certain gentle hints. A fortnight later I visited the 'Oberbürgermeister' or whatever he was called then, concerning some other business. ALTENMEYER(?) triumphantly showed me: 'Here is an order, just issued, prohibiting *mass*-shootings of that scale from taking place in future. They are to be carried out more discreetly.' From warnings given me recently I knew that I was receiving still more attentions from spies.[345]

?: A wonder you're still alive.

BRUNS: At GÖTTINGEN I expected to be arrested every day.

Document 136

CSDIC (UK), GRGG 281
Report on information obtained from Senior Officers (PW) on 8–9 Apr. 45 [TNA, WO 208/4177]

JÖSTING: A great friend of mine whom I can trust implicitly, an Austrian, still in VIENNA, as far as I know, belong to 'Luftflotte 4', and was down at O DESSA.[346] When he arrived there some 'Oberleutnant' or 'Hauptmann' said to him: 'Would you like to watch? An amusing show is going on down there, umpteen Jews are being killed off.' He answered: 'Good Heavens, no.' He had to pass the spot, however, and witnessed the scene. He told me himself that the barn was bunged full of women and children. Petrol was poured over them and they were burnt alive. He saw it himself. He said: 'You can't imagine what their screams sound like. Is such a thing right?' I said: 'No, it isn't right. You can do whatever you like with them, but not burn them alive or gas them or Heavens knows what else! It's not their fault. They should be imprisoned and after the war has been won you can say: "This people must disappear. Put them in a ship! Sail wherever you wish', we don't care where you land but there is no room for you in Germany from now on!"' We have made enemies galore! We killed them everywhere in the east and as a result people hardly believe the real KATYN[347] story any longer, but say we did it ourselves.

No, if I hadn't several proofs of that sort of thing I wouldn't make such a noise about it, but in my opinion it was *utterly* wrong! What madness was that onslaught on Jewish homes; I happened still to be in VIENNA at the time, at BAD VÖSLAU.[348] We were then already short of glass and everything else and then we go and smash all their windows! Those people could easily have been turned out and we could have said: 'Well, this business is now taken over by a Christian, Franz MEYER. They'll be compensated, whether well or badly makes no difference.' But we were short of everything and still everything was smashed and the houses set ablaze. I quite agree the Jews had to be turned out, that was obvious, but the *manner* in which it was done was *absolutely wrong*, and the present hatred is the result. My father-in-law, who certainly couldn't stand Jews, always said: 'That will not pass unpunished, say what you like!' I'd be the first to agree to getting rid of the Jews; I'd show them the way – out of GERMANY! But why *massacre* them? That can be done *after* the war, when we can say 'We have the power; we have the right; we have won the war; we can afford to do it!' But now! Look at the British Government – who are they? The Jews. Who governs in AMERICA? The Jews. While Bolshevism is Judaism in excelsis.

Document 137

CSDIC (UK), GRGG 286
Report on information obtained from Senior Officers (PW) on 19–21 Apr. 45
[TNA, WO 208/4177]

WILDERMUTH (*re killing of inmates of lunatic asylums*): I once spoke with the director of the whole business at ANGERS(?). His name was EBERT or EBES(?).[349] In the course of a somewhat heated argument I said to him: 'You're a lawyer too, there's a certain unpleasant paragraph in the penal code called "murder". You will have to come to terms with it. It must be perfectly clear to you that you will one day have to answer for it.' That gave the man a bit of a shock.

BROICH: No more people over 70 years of age even being accepted in hospital any more.

WAHLE: Not even if an operation is necessary?

BROICH: Operations could be done, but the patients had to return home afterwards. My father-in-law – it was forbidden and was quite impossible; that was in POTSDAM and even the operation was only carried out at all because the doctor was a friend. He said: 'No, I may not take you in, it would get us into the greatest difficulties.' That was in the spring of 1942.

ELFELDT (*re killed-off mental cases*): 70–80,000 people have been put away, haven't they?

WILDERMUTH: Yes, and I arrive at that figure from my brother's figures and from that EBERT or EBES(?). I said: 'Have they killed 100,000 people there?' To which he merely replied: 'No, not 100,000.'

BROICH: Was there more?

WAHLE: No, less.[350]

Document 138

CSDIC (UK), GRGG 288
Report on information obtained from Senior Officers (PW) on 24–6 Apr. 45 [TNA, WO 208/4177]

HEILMANN: We were in the front lines and said: 'It isn't our business what they do in the rear.' Gradually it leaked out how they were treating the many PW.

FISCHER: At least three or four million of them died of starvation during the winter of 1941/42.[351]

HEILMANN: I took several Russian PW along with me; they were shoemakers and tailors. I had them at the airfield at MAGDEBURG. When we went on operations, we couldn't take them along. On that occasion the CO of the airfield told me: 'We can arrange matters. There is such a number of them here; occasionally they go and bathe and just collapse and die.' There were so many of them – they were given very little food. *That* was the great crime. They're human beings – good God, Russians are *human beings* too. Then they keep on talking about Asiatics –

FISCHER: What was our behaviour like?

HEILMANN: Even if they are Asiatics. But every human being has the right to live.

FISCHER: We have behaved like savages, not like civilised people.

HEILMANN: We have deserved the name of Huns for all time. Since BUCHENWALD – good Lord, those photographs are ghastly. It really makes you feel ashamed.

FISCHER: Then we talked about KATYN, about those 11,000 officers – how many have *we* put to death![352]

Document 139

CSDIC (UK), SR REPORT SRGG 1203(C) [TNA, WO 208/4170]

Generalleutnant SIRY (Commander, 347 Infantry Division) – Captured 10 Apr. 44 in Friedrichsroda.
Generalstabsintendant PAUER[353] (formerly of the OKH) – Captured 7 Apr. 44 in Kleinrinderfeld.
Information received: 6 May 45

SIRY: One mustn't admit it openly, but we were far too soft. All these horrors have landed us in the soup now. But if we'd carried them through to the hilt, made the people disappear *completely* – no one would say a thing. These *half* measures are always wrong.

In the East I suggested once to the 'Korps' – thousands of PW were coming back, without anyone guarding them, because there were no people there to do it. It went quite well in FRANCE, because the Frenchman is so degenerate that if you said to him: 'You will report to the PW collecting point in the rear' the stupid idiot really did go along there. But in RUSSIA there was a space of 50–80 km, that is to say a 2 to 3 days' march, between the armoured spear-heads and the following close formations. No Russians went to the rear; they lagged behind and then took to the woods left and right, where they could live all right. So I said: 'That's no good, we must simply cut off one of their legs, or break a leg, or the right forearm, so that they won't be able to fight in the next four weeks and so that we can round them up.' There was an outcry when I said one must simply smash their legs with a club. At the time, of course, I didn't really condone it either, but now I think it's quite right. We've seen that we cannot conduct a war because we're not *hard* enough, not barbaric enough. The Russians are that all right.

Document 140

CSDIC (UK), GRGG 300
Report on information obtained from Senior Officers (PW) on 16–17 May 45 [TNA, WO 208/4177]

HABERMEHL: [. . .] FELBERT (PW) told me he had been 'Kommandant' of BESANÇON; people who were found in possession of arms had to be condemned to death. They were condemned to death by the Military Court, the sentence was confirmed in PARIS, went back, and then he was the man responsible for carrying out the sentence, and he said that in this way, while he was in charge, forty people were shot. He said he couldn't do anything about it, but he is sure that action will be taken against him.[354]

Document 141

CSDIC (UK), GRGG 301
Report on information obtained from Senior Officers (PW) on 18–19 May 45
[TNA, WO 208/4178]

DITTMAR (*re concentration camps*): What did we know about them?
SCHLIEBEN: Everybody knew that dreadful things happened in them – not exactly what, but just that dreadful things happened – every one of us know that as far back as '35.
DITTMAR: To Germans?
BROICH: Primarily to Germans.
ELFELDT: We knew (what happened) in POLAND to the hundreds and thousands of Jews who, as time went by, disappeared, were sent away from GERMANY and who after '39 were said to be accommodated in ghettos and settlements in POLAND – we were told that.
SCHLIEBEN: They all disappeared.
ELFELDT: Who ever got to know that millions of these people – as the Russians now assert – perished or were burnt in AUSCHWITZ and whatever these small places are called?
BROICH: Certainly none of us.
ELFELDT: We heard about AUSCHWITZ when we were in POLAND.[355]
BROICH: I visited DACHAU personally in '37. The commandant of the camp said to us: 'If I had to spend a year here, I should throw myself on the electric wire. I couldn't stand it for longer than a year – nobody could.'
HOLSTE: Some people stood it for twelve years.
BROICH: We were quite convinced that we were only shown what we were supposed to see. I went there with the hereditary Prince of WALDECK,[356] that swine; he had two camps under his control. We spent six hours there and afterwards were absolutely overcome by what we had seen, although we did not see any of the tortures we have heard about lately.

DITTMAR: I didn't hear the name AUSCHWITZ until I went to PARIS.[357]
THOMA: That's how they led the people up the garden path.
DITTMAR: It wasn't a question of leading them up the garden path, it was a carefully thought-out secret security system.

Document 142

CSDIC (UK), GRGG 311
Report on information obtained from Senior Officers (PW) on 1–6 June 45 [TNA, WO 208/4177]

Generalleutnant FEUCHTINGER (Commander, 21st Panzer Division, captured 3

May 45 in Hamburg) – gave Generalleutnant VON MASSOW the following report about the massacre of 25,000 Jews in Pinsk:

FEUCHTINGER: When I was at Pinsk I was told that in the previous year there had been still 25,000 Jews living there and within three days these 25,000 Jews were fetched out, formed up on the edge of a wood or in a meadow – they had been made to dig their own graves beforehand – and then every single one of them from the oldest grey-beard down to the new-born infant was shot by a police squad. That was the first time I myself had actually heard and seen what happened there. I had previously not believed or considered it possible that anything like that went on. The nurse at the officers' hostel where I lived told me that: For heavens sake, don't say anything about my having told you that.[358]

Document 143

CSDIC (UK), GRGG 314
Report on information obtained from Senior Officers (PW) on 7–30 June 45 [TNA, WO 208/4178]

III. THE CONCENTRATION CAMP FILM

The senior Officer PWs have been given a showing of the concentration camp film; attendance was compulsory for all inmates of the camp. Their reactions to it were as follows:

1. In conversation between Generalleutnant v. SCHLIEBEN and Generalmajore v. FELBERT and HABERMEHL:

SCHLIEBEN: That's the only thing about the 'thousand year REICH' which will last for a thousand years.
FELBERT: Yes, we are disgraced for all time.

2. In conversation between Generalleutnant v. ORIOLA and SIEWERT:

ORIOLA: HITLER ordered all those killings.
SIEWERT: Still, it's no wonder those people starved; we hadn't anything left ourselves.
ORIOLA: Concentration camps will always remain an impossible institution, specially in countries which have a depraved government.
SIEWERT: It's a very effective film; it's a fine sort of recommendation for us! It really was like that, I saw it. The worst thing was that *anyone* could have *anyone else* put in such a camp without a sentence.

3. Generalleutnant DITTMAR and HOLSTE agreed that what the film showed was revolting, even though there was no means of comparing that with what happened in Russian camps. They could not understand why the SS had not destroyed all the damning evidence.

4. In conversation between General FINK and Generalleutnant DITTMAR and HEIM:

HEIM: This air raid on DRESDEN was a different matter after all.
DITTMAR: Certainly that was quite different from this direct torture of individuals.
HEIM: This slow, intentional, systematic murder.
DITTMAR: That's why it can't be compared.
HEIM: The other (DRESDEN) could at least be called warfare in the last analysis.
DITTMAR: You could see there that that was not the only purpose –
HEIM: But *this* is an absolute disgrace.
DITTMAR: This *is* an absolute disgrace.
FINK (*enters*): One needs to have seen a film like that.
HEIM: RÖHRICHT said that compared with the 200,000 at DRESDEN –[359]
FINK (*excitedly*): It can't be compared with DRESDEN!
DITTMAR: That's too weak an argument.
FINK: The Russian method of shooting in the back of the neck is a kindness –
DITTMAR: In comparison with this vileness.

Document 144

CSDIC (UK), GRGG 363
Report on information obtained from Senior Officers (PW) on 24 Sept.–9 Oct. 45
[TNA, WO 208/4178]

1. THE WAR CRIMES TRIALS

1. Various of the senior officer PW are expecting to be called as witnesses at the NUREMBERG War Crimes Trials. General EBERBACH is among their number. In conversation with General v. THOMA he speculated as follows upon the reasons for his being summoned:

EBERBACH: Either they want me about the shooting of the Canadian PW – I have already once proved to them that it happened before I went there.[360] Or they want to interrogate me about the transfer of the police into the armed forces in connection with preparations for the war. I joined two years before the law was enacted. Or SPEER has named me as a witness; I can tell only good of him.

2. In the following conversation with Oberst WILDERMUTH and Obersleutnant v.d. HEYDTE, General EBERBACH defined the attitude he would adopt according to whether he believed the NUREMBERG trials were genuine or merely staged:

EBERBACH: I should not like to land in trouble one of my comrades, say, Genoberst GUDERIAN or Minister SPEER, whom I consider as a comrade too in that respect because I have worked closely together with him. I really do not know why they want me as a witness; my position was not of such importance. But these people want to know something from me and I should like to be able to advise other people who will be heard. There are only two points of view possible: either I assume: 'The British are decent fellows; they do really intend to pronounce an impartial sentence and I, as a decent man myself, will try to help the British to pronounce an unbiased sentence by making objective statements.' The other attitude is: 'This whole affair in NUREMBERG is deliberately staged in order to drag the Germans who have to appear before it into the dirt and in order that a sentence which has already been passed in advance shall only contribute further to sully the German name; in such a case I can only state that I will not say anything at all as a witness, or as little as possible, for why should I lend my good name to have the German reputation dragged still further into the mud?'
WILDERMUTH: I should say as little as possible.
HEYDTE: If I may butt in, I do not believe that it will be a *staged* trial.

3. General EBERBACH spoke as below to Generalleutant HEIM, Oberst WILDERMUTH and Oberstleutant v.d. HEYDTE about the background to one incident in RUSSIA which might be looked upon as a war crime:

EBERBACH: I know of cases where the men in RUSSIA committed things in their desperation in that terrible winter which they would never have done under different circumstances. To mention one case: Our 'Bataillon' of motorcyclists had, after having attacked a village in snow 120 cm deep and having captured it with considerable loss from an enemy whose behaviour was fiendish, and having then captured the next village too, in which the Russians had laid mines, drove the Russian population over these mines. Of the thirty men who drove over them, twenty-one were blown up. The commander of the 'Bataillon'[361] told me: 'I lost so many fine fellows that I simply could not bear the responsibility towards German mothers and fathers of sending my men through those mines.'
HEYDTE: I can only say that, though I can't approve of it, I can understand it.

EBERBACH: I understood it, too, at that moment, when the whole lot was fighting desperately, but I did not approve of it, though I did not start any court martial proceedings against the CO of the 'Kompanie'.

4. The same speakers held a general discussion of the duties and obligations of a witness, v.d. HEYDTE pointing out that a witness gave evidence under oath; he gave a negative reply to EBERBACH's question whether it would be in order for him to shake hands with any of the accused whom he knew. WILDERMUTH advised EBERBACH 'not to remember' if he was in doubt as to the implications of any given answer.

5. In conversation with Oberstleutnant v.d. HEYDTE, Generalleutnant ELFELDT repeated the opinion expressed in the past that all senior officers would be tried by the Allies in due course. The speakers agreed in believing that the British and Americans wanted to annihilate the German military and academic classes. They also agreed in condemning the German use of gas chambers, but stated that in their view the Germans had already been sufficiently punished. In a conversation between ELFELDT and Generalleutnant HEIM it was stated that too much fuss was made about German maltreatment of Jews: 'after all, many more Germans died in this war than Jews died in gas chambers'.

6. [. . .]

III.

The Insurrection of Conscience. Reactions to 20 July 1944

Document 145

CSDIC (UK), GRGG 161 [TNA, WO 208/4363]

ATTEMPTED ASSASSINATION OF HITLER AND SUBSEQUENT EVENTS. This report deals with the reaction of Senior Officers (PW) in Camp No. II to the news of the above events, which they had learnt of from the radio and British newspapers.

SPONECK: Nobody was really wounded. That seems suspicious to me, I mean if it had been a real attempt on HITLER's life none of them would still be alive.

THOMA: If they had a mine in there – an ordinary anti-tank mine –

SPONECK: A hand grenade –

THOMA: It seems fishy to me.

BASSENGE: Whether it was a serious attempt on his life or only a fake, in either case it is a bad sign.

THOMA: It is supposed to have been a revolt by the generals. Graf STAUFFENBERG – I know about him – he was with me at the headquarters – he was always keenly opposed to the (Party) business; above all, he was very cool-headed and clear-thinking – an excellent fellow – really a most estimable and a very capable General Staff . . . is the man who threw the bomb. Now that a start has been made it will go on. There is a possibility that . . . very quickly, especially in the south. I could well imagine STAUFFENBERG's doing it. In the first place he had access to him, because he was there a long time.

I am shaken to the core about GUDERIAN. He knows what the end will be. If anyone thinks differently now, one can only say that he isn't quite right in the head.

KRUG: STUMPFF has the handling of the GAF at home.[362]

THOMA: If it has already started in the GAF then the fun is going to wax fast and furious. That is typical too: the Navy steps in immediately and so does HERMANN.

GUDERIAN is a decent fellow in himself. I have known him since he
was a 'Hauptmann'. He was very keenly opposed to the Nazis and
always spoke·of them as 'stupid sheep'. Then the Nazis came into
power and he suddenly swung over. Then after those winter campaigns
in RUSSIA, he allowed HITLER to treat him like a street urchin. He
swore at him and kicked him out. I was told by GUDERIAN himself that
he asked for an enquiry to be made, but it was refused; he asked to be
relieved of his command – it was all refused. He remained at home in
BERLIN for one year and eight months as a nonentity. Before I went to
AFRICA, I visited him. He told me himself: 'I am ashamed to go to the
barber's because they say: "What are you doing here?"' That's the man
who later emerges and lets that sloppy job be foisted on him,
negotiating with industry and that sort of thing, and who lets HITLER
present him with an estate in the WARTHEGAU, in spite of the way in
which he has been treated![363]

KRUG: But, Sir, after all those people are not normal. If someone shouts
at me and treats me badly, then I don't have anything to do with him,
I don't let him make me a present of anything.

SATTLER: But your point of view is not quite correct, KRUG. We are
soldiers and if we have done anything wrong in the eyes of our
superiors, our superior officer has the right to tell us so as *plainly* as he
likes. I should say: 'I won't have that, Herr KRUG; I require you to
command your regiment according to my orders!'

THOMA: Then the other man can say politely: 'I don't agree; I will go!'

SATTLER: No, there I . . . opinion, Sir. That's what my superior officer is
there for, to tell me a thing like that.

THOMA: But I wouldn't allow myself to be ordered about by a fool.
GUDERIAN, who was always against the Nazis, now lets himself be
bought, and isn't ashamed – which is a sign that, clever though he was
before, he must now have completely deteriorated mentally – ashamed
to act as Chief of Staff to HIMMLER, in a situation where everyone
knows where things are heading.

KRUG: Yes, indeed.

THOMA: SCHMUNDT[364] is a good, decent fellow, but, when he says quite
naturally to the officers at a conference: 'I have had the *blessing* of
spending the last two years in very close contact with the FÜHRER', can
you consider him normal?

(?) SATTLER: What was it he said about six months ago at an adjutants'
conference at the OKH? An adjutant who was present there told me
that he said: 'The worst people are the Generals; if they are not
promoted or given accelerated promotion and awarded the Knight's
Cross, they are discontented.' What do you think of that, that's what
SCHMUNDT says.

THOMA: Well, it's a terrible business. HITLER has so much weighing on
his mind that he simply doesn't know where to turn. His whole

outlook breeds fear in him. I know what his cars were like, they had bullet-proof glass as thick as this. They were armour-plated all over and then he always used to drive like mad in order to avoid any chance of being hit. HIMMLER said to me: 'The KAISER' – although he was very nervous too – 'didn't have a third as many people to protect him as HITLER has.' The OBERSALZBERG is covered with huge fences . . . a perimeter of 15 km.[365]

HENNECKE: Well, that's the beginning of the end.

KRUG: That may . . . revolution in GERMANY, but in HITLER's hands.

HENNECKE: Yes, that's obvious.

KRUG: How could GUDERIAN allow himself to be made HIMMLER's Chief of Staff?

HENNECKE: They're playing their last card, that's obvious.

KÖHN: But imagine the effect that will have on the front? The thing is *finished*.

KRUG: Well, you gentlemen know me, don't you? I mean you know what I think. Let's admit we'd rather bring about an end today than tomorrow.

HENNECKE: Yes, I've said that for a long time. General von THOMA (PW) said: 'There's no longer any point in it; they're wiping out our towns.' And one's seen it, too. MUNICH has vanished from the face of the earth.[366] It's senseless, and we shall lose in any case. I'm firmly convinced of that.

KRUG: *How can* GUDERIAN become HIMMLER's Chief of Staff – HIMMLER who has killed so many Generals!

KÖHN: He happens to be a vain man!

HENNECKE: GUDERIAN, the man who has been treated so badly himself!

KRUG: Undoubtedly!

KÖHN: Ambition, you see, is man's greatest driving force – it's terrible, terrible!

HENNECKE: The dreadful thing is that these gentlemen are gloating over the news and aren't considering the tragedy of it all; that's the most terrible thing about it. They think things will be all right now. On the contrary: it's the Russians that have got the advantage and *only* the Russians, not the others. They won't get there in time and will also be out of EUROPE again as quickly as possible, because they want to avoid their own Bolshevisation.

KRUG: It was because I'm so depressed I came here and not to . . . anti-National Socialist –

HENNECKE: Oh, Heaven forbid.

KRUG: Well, I wouldn't like to appear as though I were suddenly a turncoat. I am *not*. I deny that most definitely.

KÖHN: There's no doubt whatever that in its ideals National Socialism was the only salvation.

KRUG: Yes, that's perfectly true.

KÖHN: Only unfortunately human shortcomings made it work out differently. It was too idealistic in its conception. There's no doubt in my mind, either, that HITLER was the great man, who simply foundered on his own idealism.

KRUG: And also on the people who grovelled around him. I said to THOMA: 'I quite agree, as things are at present, but the chief blame does not lie with HITLER; 90 per cent of the blame attaches to those around him, from HITLER down to our German Generals.'

HENNECKE: Just the same as with the KAISER.

KRUG: It's those people who've driven him crazy. Why does he behave crazily? Because they've encouraged him; because they've led him to it.

HENNECKE: It's easy enough to say: 'There will never be another 1918!' You bet!

REIMANN: It says in the paper that HITLER made a long speech – 'Providence has once more saved him' – so thanks to providence, we're going even deeper into the mire.

BROICH: At any rate it's started!

REIMANN: Yes, it's the beginning of the end.

BROICH: The people might have breathed again. Everyone in GERMANY says: 'Only the Army can save us!'

REIMANN: It's the beginning of the end. Are the people – the officers – simply going to allow themselves to be taken into custody and killed?

KRUG: The radio said: 'It's presumed' – they presume in GERMANY – 'that Generals von BRAUCHITSCH, BECK and HALDER were also involved.'[367]

REIMANN: Things will reach the stage when the Russians, Americans and English will be hailed as liberators.

BROICH: I'm convinced of it. But STAUFFENBERG, always had the idea –

REIMANN: A fine, decent fellow, that man.

BROICH: An upright man.

REIMANN: The pattern of a decent, clever General Staff Officer and a man who cared for his troops.

BROICH: You couldn't think of a cleverer and better General Staff Officer than he was.

REIMANN: It really used to be a pleasure to work with a man like that.

BROICH: . . . had at least come off!

REIMANN: *Yes, if only it had come off!* The massacre will go on now. They'll overrun everyone now!

BROICH: Incidentally, I believe that even if it had come off HIMMLER would still have taken over.

REIMANN: Yes, undoubtedly. He'll do so next time, too.

BROICH: It will probably be HIMMLER's turn next.

KRUG: . . . revolution in GERMANY.

REIMANN: Yes, poor GERMANY, poor GERMANY!

BORCHERDT: We always believed that STALIN would be assassinated but in the meantime they assassinate (sic) HITLER.

REIMANN (*after hearing recording of* HITLER'*s speech the last words of it being* 'That we shall and must carry on our work'[368]):Yes, right into Hell itself!

REIMANN: I have felt this coming, ever since the beginning of that damned revolution on 30 June 1933 (sic). The virus blisters which then spread throughout our body politic – have now burst. I have had so much to do with the Party, with the SA, I have had countless numbers in the yearly intakes of recruits.[369] Those people have always hated us, although they have disguised it more or less, they have all, including the FÜHRER, felt distrust for and aversion to an officer. That is coming out now. You could hear it today in his speech – he spoke about the Home Army and then about the declaration of loyalty by the GAF and the Navy, but not a word about the Army.[370]

KRUG: Well, we haven't got any head – he is that himself.

REIMANN: Yes, but I assure you that in the next few days, according to the sinister law of sequence, *another* murderous attempt will come; that is the notorious duplication of events. One misfortune follows immediately upon another; you wait and see, in the next few days they will fire again either at him once more or at . . . HIMMLER or GOERING. Those people are just as damned stupid, with their silly complex about loyalty, as the German people is good and decent.

KRUG: It was stupidly done.

REIMANN: I don't believe in *anything* any more, not in *anything*. No '-ism' can ever stir me again.

BASSENGE (*after being told of 'Calais'-Sender report that a special plane was held ready to take* HITLER *to* JAPAN): If only he'd already gone!

Document 146

CSDIC (UK), SR Report, SRGG 962 [TNA, WO 208/4168][371]

The following conversation took place between:
General der Panzertruppe von THOMA – Captured 4 Nov. 42 in North Africa.
General der von SPONECK (GOC 90th Lt Division) – Captured 12 May 43 in Tunisia.
General der von BROICH (GOC 10th Panzer Division) – Captured 12 May 43 in Tunisia.
another German Senior Officer PW, and a British Army Officer.
Information received: 21 Jul 44

BAO: Who is this STAUFFENBERG?

BROICH: What happened?

BAO: He threw the bomb. A Count STAUFFENBERG, a Colonel.[372]

BROICH: That is my GSO I (Ops).

BAO: He has been shot.

BROICH: Good Heavens! It can't be true! An excellent man like that! He was my GSO I (Ops) and four weeks before he lost an eye and two of his fingers whilst flying at low level in TUNISIA. He was sent home severely wounded. We often chatted together and even in 1942 we used to go around to all the field marshals and try – he told them that if the conduct of the war wasn't changed, there was *bound* to be a catastrophe, just as actually happened. Good God![373]

SPONECK: STAUFFENBERG did the deed and was, of course, shot; some of the Generals took the other side, HIMMLER took over the Army and GUDERIAN is said to have become Chief of Staff to HIMMLER![374]

BROICH: Has HIMMLER taken over the Army?

BAO: Yes.

SPONECK: And STUMPFF the GAF. STUMPFF is a fool, the stupidest man they could have chosen.[375] What luck! (*Laughter*) They have no one left anyhow.

BAO: STAUFFENBERG has been shot. Wasn't he married to an Englishwoman?

BROICH: No. He had a charming wife.[376] He was one of the cleverest, an *exceedingly* well-educated man, a brilliantly clever fellow!

BAO: How old was he?

BROICH: He must have been about thirty-eight.[377]

BAO: The whole thing seems very funny to me. How did those people get in?

BROICH: There must have been some conference or other.[378] He belonged to the General Staff. I believe he was serving again. Maybe he was present at the conference; he was in the organisation department up at GHQ for two years. He told me a lot of things; he said that I have no idea what things were like there.

BAO: So he threw that bomb.

BROICH: Yes, I can well believe that of him; he was a sincere fellow!

SPONECK: Now a massacre will start in GERMANY, the extent of which we can't realise.

BROICH: Yes

BAO: It has already started.

BROICH: Nobody will die a natural death. I can't understand that STAUFFENBERG, who usually is such a reliable person, only took such a small bomb![379]

BAO: I heard HITLER's broadcast. He said that the bomb exploded two metres away from him. Even so, he wasn't wounded.[380]

BROICH: That's funny!

BAO: And that this 'Putsch' was instigated by dismissed Generals, who hadn't done their duty, as, for instance, RUNDSTEDT[381] and all those people. That is probably the reason for all those peculiar accidents those Generals have had.

BROICH: Well, DOLLMANN really *did* have a stroke.[382] Two years ago DOLLMANN suffered with his head; he always used to drink a lot of red wine and smoke huge cigars, and that tells in time.

SPONECK: No, that can't be so.

BROICH: And MARCKS in a car – that's true, too; MARCKS didn't commit suicide.[383]

BAO: Is STAUFFENBERG's wife still in GERMANY?

BROICH: Yes, she's in GERMANY, she is on her father-in-law's estate.[384]
[. . .]

BROICH: His father[385] was Lord Chamberlain to the King of WÜRTEMBERG.

BAO: But isn't STAUFFENBERG a famous name?

SPONECK: Yes, it is. Count SCHENCK von STAUFFENBERG, a very old family. Good God, that grand fellow – he should have at least done the thing properly.

BAO: Well, goodbye, Sir! (BAO *leaves*)

SPONECK: It means civil war.

BROICH: Good God, STAUFFENBERG! I wouldn't have believed anyone else capable of it! STAUFFENBERG is such an honest man, I always said: 'He would be the first to do it himself.' A shame, he was such a charming man.

?: Now they'll start agitating against all officers, you see if they don't.

BROICH: He said that others are supposed to be implicated, too.

?: Now, in view of this, they'll liquidate every discontented General and everyone they don't like the look of. They'll be having concentration camps for Generals next.

BROICH: It's quite possible.

SPONECK: I believe it is the end.

BROICH: I don't think so yet.

SPONECK: Unfortunately it didn't come off; I can only say I think it a great pity that STAUFFENBERG didn't succeed.

BROICH: That's the pity. Good Lord, why did that bomb have to be so small!

?: Well, he didn't want to kill the others as well.[386]

SPONECK: Yes, but that just can't be helped. It must have been a hand grenade; it can't have been anything larger.

?: But, gentlemen, surely that would have been ample if a hand grenade had exploded two metres away from him.

BROICH: Yes, but you can be unlucky with a hand grenade. Perhaps someone stood in the way or perchance the burst somehow or other went to the side. Good God, good old STAUFFENBERG. Well, he's sure to have been at OKW, he used to work there and he is in a position to get at those people. It's remarkable that the FÜHRER broadcast!

?: Did he broadcast?

BROICH: Yes. The BAO said just now that he heard him.

?: THOMA (PW) heard it just now –

(THOMA *enters*)

THOMA: It's a nasty business, gentlemen!

BROICH: Yes, it is the STAUFFENBERG who was my GSO I (Ops). I always thought him capable of it.

THOMA: Yes. Well, STAUFFENBERG – we often discussed it.

BROICH: He's the one who, in 1943, drove around to all the field marshals and army leaders and asked them whether they would take part or not. MANSTEIN is said to have been the only one who refused to take part. He said that all the others agreed to take part immediately, but they weren't prepared to take over the leadership. If, however, someone would do that, they would at once be –

THOMA: Yes, but they wouldn't take over the leadership.

BROICH: Then, I believe, the time was not yet ripe. He said MANSTEIN had said that the whole thing was out of the question.[387]

?: Yes, it was not yet ripe, because the whole of the German people would have howled like a whipped dog and would have said: 'Our beloved FÜHRER' and 'against that man of genius' and 'our Generals have landed us in this.' But I can imagine that now perhaps the workers –

BROICH: And who has been dismissed, the Generals or who?

THOMA: ZEITZLER has gone[388] and one of those who was injured is said to have died.[389] They didn't mention any names at all. The saddest thing is that GUDERIAN is to be HIMMLER's Chief of Staff.

?: That is horrifying.

BROICH: That means he's lost to us!

SPONECK: The question is whether in these circumstances GUDERIAN will not try to seize power himself.

?: Yes, because on the whole GUDERIAN was a decent fellow.

BROICH: He was a decent and energetic fellow – I can't understand it.

SPONECK: Wait and see, I could imagine him doing it.

?: What, with HIMMLER?!

BROICH: What is HIMMLER's job?

THOMA: HIMMLER is supposed to be there to clean up all the internal affairs in GERMANY, and for the GAF for GERMANY proper STUMPFF has been appointed; there must be something up, that comes from the *German* news service.

SPONECK: He is the stupidest man there is.

THOMA: He (HITLER) hasn't got anyone else. And then it has also been said the GOERING and DÖNITZ immediately made speeches of loyalty to HITLER on behalf of their respective services.[390]

?: That is of no importance.

BROICH: And is anyone else from Headquarters gone?

THOMA: Georg ZEITZLER[391] – but apart from that, nothing else has been said about the whole business.

?: But there must be something going on at home, otherwise they wouldn't . . . to the world –

THOMA: Yes, because it is from the German news service, naturally from the short-wave transmitter. I am very sorry about STAUFFENBERG. He is said to have been shot immediately.

SPONECK: My God, it's a tragedy that he missed.

THOMA: Yes, one can really say so.

?: Providence will preserve HITLER for a harder punishment.

? SPONECK: I think if HITLER were dead, this business with HIMMLER would probably have come about just the same. I am convinced now that HIMMLER will twist this whole business to his advantage. That was always the intention.

THOMA: I mean they have obviously had an inkling(?) that something like this would happen. HIMMLER has become considerably less sure of himself since HEYDRICH is dead. HEYDRICH was bloodthirsty. HIMMLER is only a . . . I have always heard from those around him that HIMMLER is a silly fool. As a boy he was . . . his father was always complaining that he should have such a stupid son.

SPONECK: I could imagine GUDERIAN[392] having done that in order, say, to try to bring in some sort of order.

THOMA: But with a man like HIMMLER?!

BROICH: GUDERIAN is an honourable man.

THOMA: Yes, certainly. But he is bound to them now. Anyone who has been cursed like that and then . . . from HIMMLER – he accepted a stolen estate, so he is bound to them.[393]

SPONECK: He couldn't refuse it.

BROICH: He couldn't refuse it, so what could he do?

THOMA: I think he should at least have said: 'I will wait until the war is over.'

SPONECK: Oh, that's frightfully difficult.

THOMA: LEEB[394] and those sort of people refused it.

?: Yes, but they have been removed.

THOMA: But they did refuse it!

SPONECK: GUDERIAN wanted to be somebody, I can believe that.

THOMA: Well, he won't be anybody now.

SPONECK: Let's wait and see, I have got confidence in GUDERIAN.

THOMA: Not with HIMMLER! They will let hell loose now on all and sundry.

?: Obviously, they will let fly at all the Generals now.

SPONECK: I would like to say that, however terribly the rage of the *Nazis* against the Generals is now, it may not be at all a bad thing for the future. One fine day the Nazis will disappear and then those people, who were hounded by the Nazis will . . .

?: Yes, that's true.

SPONECK: The officers' party. On the whole those who are being persecuted now by the Gestapo will be better off in the future. Perhaps this deed is something which the people will put to *our* credit one day.[395]

?: Yes, the people will say: 'That was our Army, we have always pinned our hopes in the Army, they tried to do something.' (*Laughter*).

Document 147

CSDIC (UK), GRGG 162
Report on information obtained from Senior Officers (PW) on 19–22 July 44
[TNA, WO 208/4363]

THOMA: Do you know who has got command of the GAF? STUMPFF.

BASSENGE: That's the best solution. He doesn't decide anything, he doesn't decide anything at all, he just dithers about until the opportunity has gone by. That is the best thing they could do; he is such an idiot. I believe I am beginning to see daylight, Sir. It was a put-up job – that attempt to blow HITLER up was a fake – it was a put-up job in order to have a pretext for getting rid of all the unwanted people at one blow!

THOMA: Yes, it may be that a second 30 June is coming, seeing that they pulled that off so well. That's quite clear to me. But at any rate the STAUFFENBERG business could be – from his nature and his ways, it is quite possible for him . . . but they make propaganda *too*.

BASSENGE: He wouldn't be so stupid as to make a plot with insufficient means; he wouldn't do that, he is certainly much too clever for that; and to plant a little bomb like that in HITLER's room, which doesn't even work, which was probably nothing but a hand grenade done up in cardboard . . . Perhaps they knew, HIMMLER knew, that STAUFFENBERG was the leader of some counter-movement.

THOMA: STAUFFENBERG held his tongue just as little as I have and spoke just as openly.

BASSENGE: They got wind of it and said: 'How can we do it? Either we suppress it completely and don't publish any communiqué at all, in which case this movement will be damned or destroyed for the moment, but that is no good because a new one will be formed immediately. We will do it like this: we will invent a story that a murderous attempt has been made by this movement, we will make a big affair out of it and in that way we can get popular support in introducing measures for suppressing any and every opposition. We will lock them all up and dismiss them all.'

THOMA: They will shoot . . . You wait and see; the SS men will come into the units and the devil alone knows – but it won't do them any good now.

BROICH: Do you know, I've though it over and I believe it was a put-up job. It's funny – that business in the 'Bürgerbräukeller' in 1939 was a put-up job too, just as the 'Reichstag' fire was.[396] At any rate, it's possible, it is also possible that they were after STAUFFENBERG, because when he came to me he already said to me: 'It's a good thing that I am going to the front for a while.' We discussed this matter from time to time and he always said: 'If it's going to be done, it must be done properly, otherwise there will be an awful massacre.' For that reason, and because he is a very clever and energetic person, I believe that if he had undertaken it he would have carried it out thoroughly. HITLER said the same things in his last speech as he did that time in the 'Bürgerbräukeller'.

BAO: LEY spoke in an armament factory, I believe, yesterday and said: 'The English Lords, the German Counts and Barons are all . . . and that we'll be annihilated, our families and all. We are all blue-blooded swine.'[397]

BROICH: We were always considered that in the eyes of the Nazis.

BAO: Now it'll start, there's sure to be a massacre. LEY and HIMMLER have always tended towards the left.

BROICH: Yes, they always have. I believe, though, that they won't publish many names, so as to make as little of it as possible, and to prevent the Army from realising: 'Hello, our field marshalls are being made away with, something must be very wrong here!'

BAO: I hope they won't start massacring their families!

BROICH: They'll have to do a lot. BECK was a fine man, the most decent man imaginable. I am convinced that he probably had nothing whatever to do with this business. I mean to say, he went at the same time as FRITSCH did, because already in 1938, he said: 'I am not joining in these politics.' When the show started we all said: 'For God's sake, has the man gone mad!' All except some opportunists, and there were quite a few of them. We obviously all wanted to free ourselves from the VERSAILLES Treaty and see a free GERMANY reinstated, but never – I remember the time when everyone was saying: 'Heavens, a war would be the greatest possible madness!' I am quite pleased to be here for the time being!

BROICH: The names of all the others – you'll only hear about it in a round-about way. They won't let anything come out, they'll disappear. They are bound to announce on the wireless: 'So-and-So and So-and-So', as at the time of the RÖHM Putsch. They say there were only four people in it, quite ridiculous! If they say, 'Marschall' So-and-So or 'Generaloberst' So-and-So, then –

SCHLIEBEN: They'd be advertising it.

BROICH: Yes. Then the army people would say: 'Oh, our "Generals" with long service behind them, can't be completely in the wrong. If *they* do that –'

SCHLIEBEN: I'm beginning to see things clearly now, I must admit.

BASSENGE: As a result of today's news and LEY's speech, I think that the whole thing is nothing but a put-up job, because that a man like BECK – he has not been on active service for five or six years, he just sits at home, he has got a little house somewhere, and grows his flowers and feeds his hens – he didn't have anything to do with it. GUDERIAN is a good tank man, terrifically impulsive and so on, but no great personality. The chief of the General Staff must be a calm, dispassionate sort of man, not a hot-head like that. I am convinced that the whole thing is a put-up job. A lot of people here know Graf STAUFFENBERG. He is a sensible man; he wouldn't have used a cigar-box full of gun-powder. I don't believe the whole story. The point of the whole thing is just the same as at the 'Reichstag' fire and 'Bürgerbräukeller'; those people have . . . as an alibi for a similar purse and LEY has expressed it quite clearly, much more clearly than the others: 'Now comes the second part of the revolution', and that is the communist part. Now the counts and barons are in for it.

KRUG: I shan't don this uniform again . . .

REIMANN: Let's hope the moment is soon here when we can tear off this damned Swastika thing. Everything is cracking up now. If someone had told us that a little time ago, we'd have asked if he'd drunk a bottle of brandy.

KRUG: Why should they shoot SPONECK's cousin, when he is a prisoner in GEROLSHEIM?[398]

REIMANN: No one knows. They've also shot Graf STAUFFENBERG's brother, the university professor.[399]

KRUG: And GUDERIAN lends himself to that!

SCHLIEBEN: I don't know what we are to do after the war. The best thing would be to buy a rope and hang oneself.

BROICH: I'd hang a few others first! Then I should have a certain feeling of satisfaction. We must see how things go, but I'm in favour of forming a 'Division' or 'Regimenter' from the PW and marching with the English against GERMANY. Now they will exterminate all officer class.

SCHLIEBEN: They still need them. They can't exterminate them at present. I hope this 'REICH that was to last a thousand years' will soon come to an end and that they will then disband these 'Ordensjunker' too. I wonder whether the stiff resistance which is being offered now in FRANCE is really the right thing?

BROICH: What is the good of it if we hold one in FRANCE and the Russians are on the ODER?

SCHLIEBEN: That's just it.

Document 148

CSDIC (UK), GRGG 171
Report on information obtained from Senior Officers (PW) on 5–8 Aug. 44 [TNA, WO 208/4383]

[. . .]

BROICH: That speech of the FÜHRER's was disgusting and TERBOVEN's still more.

SATTLER: Did the FÜHRER make a speech?

BROICH: We, the Army, had continuously sabotaged his plans ever since 1931.

BASSENGE: Let the idiot babble![400]

BORCHERDT: Funny that those traitors, who always carried on the sabotage, had all been decorated with the Knight's Cross and the Oak Leaves, etc.!

[. . .]

KRUG: One thing is unique in history – German 'General feldmarschälle' are being kicked out of the Army, the people, who were received with such acclamation . . . In the whole history of the world there's never been anything like it. I mean, there is no one in GERMANY who can – who is there in GERMANY to say: 'This is the end, peace now.' Who? He would be shot immediately!

KÖHN: They are merely fighting for their lives now, and nothing else.

KRUG: Naturally, and look, another General, STEGMANN[401] has already been killed. There's nothing else to do but die, for if you go back you are shot and die anyway . . . There can be no way out other than death. For if they are not killed up at the front then they will be exterminated at home.

KRUG: KEITEL won't know another moment's peace. He is a disgrace to every decent-thinking member of the Officer Corps.

REIMANN: You, as a decent fellow, wouldn't find rest, but they, Hermann GOERING and KEITEL, remain quite unperturbed.

KRUG: But KEITEL will go down in the history of the German Officer Corps dishonoured and disgraced.

REIMANN: Dishonoured and disgraced, yes. They are a bunch of swine, those rascals! KEITEL always says: 'Yes, my FÜHRER' to everything.

KRUG: He ought to put on an SS uniform. That's where he belongs.

THOMA: RUNDSTEDT was forced into it.[402] That is the devilish part of HITLER. The whole world knows that RUNDSTEDT's heart is on the other side. There is no secret about it. HITLER more or less forced him into it and said: 'Well, if he refuses I'll get him too.' Because so far RUNDSTEDT had always been so clever and had always acted in such a way that he could never be caught out. He kept his tongue well under control, but everybody knew his feelings. But he wasn't to be caught. Then HITLER, who is devilishly revolting in cases like that – he is an out-and-out swine.

ROHRBACH: I believe that they only included RUNDSTEDT so as to pin him down, to goad him, on the one hand, and so as once again publicly to save their face, in order to proclaim to the world: 'You see how objective we are, we even include on this Court of Honour a man who we well know is against us.'
HERMANN: Yes.
ROHRBACH: That's how I see it.
[. . .]

SPONECK: This is a unique occurrence in the history of the world.
THOMA: In the whole of history I don't know of a Field Marshal's being shot.
BROICH: Even in the French Revolution they didn't hang Field Marshals.
SPONECK: They had the guillotine then. I think that beheading is still a more honourable death.[403]
SATTLER: As common criminals, apparently.
SPONECK: Even though they didn't handle the weapon themselves.
BROICH: It would be different if it were the man who actually carried out the attempt.
THOMA: Those were actually treated better; they were at least shot.
SPONECK: Yes, but he (HITLER) is a 'God'. It is a crime against 'God'.

SCHLIEBEN: Have you heard that they have hanged eight Generals, including HOEPNER? They were hanged two hours after the People's Court passed its sentence.[404] A nice crowd! It's crazy. Fancy hanging a 'Generalfeldmarschall'! It's unprecedented in history! When a man like STREICHER[405] is guilty of fraud time and time again, the matter is hushed up. No, you wouldn't believe it possible! The whole show is beginning to collapse; there is no alternative, but public opinion all over the world will say: 'Why couldn't GERMANY out of her own strength . . . these people?'

Document 149

CSDIC (UK), GRGG 969 [TNA, WO 208/4168]

The following conversation took place between: CS/145 – Generalleutnant SPANG – Divisional Commander 266 ID – Captured 8 Aug. 44 near Brest – a British Army Officer and an American Army Officer.

BAO: Did you hear of von Witzleben in France?[406]

Spang: He's a very good friend of mine.

BAO: You know what's happened to him?

Spang: No.

BAO: He and eight others have been hanged by Hitler.[407]

Spang: Is that really true?

BAO: It was announced on the German radio.

Spang: No, really? Generalfeldmarschall von Witzleben was my superior officer before the war. I was in Cologne and built the so-called 'Führer' line. He used to fly over to visit me and always expressed his appreciation. I was 'General' in the 1st 'Armee' during the war.[408] Generalfeldmarschall von Witzleben is one of our most correct, finest, most impeccable Generals; extremely honourable and correct in his ideas and very much loved by his men and even more by his staff. We held him in very great respect. I heard something about Generaloberst Beck, too.[409]

AAO: That happened way back on 20 July. There's not doubt about his being dead.

Spang: May I add something about Generaloberst Beck, so that you have a little character sketch of him, too. Generaloberst Beck was my 'Regimentskommandeur' when I had an 'Artillereabteilung' in 1927–28.[410] Generaloberst Beck is superior in intelligence to Generalfeldmarschall von Witzleben. He's an *outstandingly* distinguished character. He's an insatiable worker, who is only satisfied with the best. He was my ideal of a 'Regimentskommandeur'. As I had formerly been on the General Staff for thirteen years, I was always brought in to help with these regimental exercises, to work out the picture and help with all the preparations, even as a 'Batteriechef'. Generaloberst Beck is a very, very fine, decent man. Once we had a trial of Ludin and Scheringer, it was a National Socialist affair before the war, in which both officers were thrown out of the army, because they had carried on national-socialist activities. Oberst Beck, as 'Regimentskommandeur' actually spoke against them both.[411] Generaloberst Beck is a really irreproachable fellow, he possesses very great ability and knowledge and is a very sincere character. I couldn't say that to you if I didn't know them both (Witzleben and Beck) so well personally.

Thank God this business has not affected the front. I called my officers' corps together and addressed them and told them my opinion. I said: 'These matters don't affect us.'

I simply can't believe that Witzleben has been hanged. A 'Generalfeldmarschall' hanged! Witzleben – if I may say so – was not so very active. He was a 'grand seigneur', a distinguished, decent man, who was very clever himself but who didn't really – one might say – go at things with a will. He didn't do that, he was more of a 'grand seigneur'.

That's why I simply can't believe that he – one thing is quite impossible, that the officers wanted to line their own pockets and do it for their own gain. It is quite impossible, too, that the officers could have done a thing like that merely as a bid for power. That's quite out of the question.

AAO: No, you know, I have travelled a lot in GERMANY. I have always stressed the difference between the armed forces and this other thing.

SPANG: It is very difficult for me to tell you . . . I can't do that. I could tell you a great deal as an army officer, but you will understand that I can't speak about it.

AAO: No, of course, you can't, we realise that perfectly well.

BAO: But for you, Sir, at this moment the war is over; and it is practically over for all Germans. That is not the fault of the armed forces, it is the fault of this man . . .

SPANG: I have a very clear opinion on it, too, but the FÜHRER is my Commander-in-Chief. I ought not to speak about it.

Generalfeldmarschall von RUNDSTEDT[412] had become President of the Court of Honour and Generalfeldmarschall von WITZLEBEN was his subordinate, the is to say, Generalfeldmarschall von RUNDSTEDT was successor to Generalfeldmarschall von WITZLEBEN. They were on excellent terms and were great friends. It was an incredible . . . for Generalfeldmarschall von RUNDSTEDT

AAO: I believe that that was why they put von RUNDSTEDT on that tribunal. Just because he was so friendly with him.

SPANG: No, because he was the most senior of all the Generals. He is sixty-eight years old, is impeccable and is also a very distinguished and honourable man. He was also recognised by the French people as a very decent fellow and always spared the French people wherever he could.[413] I can't imagine that General von RUNDSTEDT either wanted it or was in agreement with the appointment.

AAO: (Translates newspaper report of trial against rebel officers.)

SPANG: HOEPNER and I were young General Staff Officers together.[414] HOEPNER is a very capable man but he is one of those with a very strong will of his own, with very clear-cut ideas. He was previously degraded to Private. He was degraded from 'Generalobers' to Private.[415] Paul von HASE was my very best friend, he was Commandant of BERLIN. We attended the Army College at METZ together, in 1905. 'Paulchen' von HASE, who never harmed a soul, a Guards Officer – 3rd 'Garderegiment', the former 'Alexander' (Grenadier), a very handsome man, tall and slender. We were great friends and later on became General Staff Officers. He was under me in the last war. He has a Baltic-German wife and nine children, I think.[416] You know, it's very hard for me because I know all these colleagues well, and their attitude too.

AAO: Do you think that those officers actually took part in that attempt?

SPANG: In the attempted assassination, in the preparations and execution of – ? I can hardly think that the FÜHRER and the present government could condemn them unless they . .

AAO: Without grounds – I can't think that either.

SPANG: But if they did do anything like that then, in my opinion, they did it from the purest motives. They did it in the interests of our great German Fatherland. Not from self-interest or lust for power.

AAO: Their aim must certainly have been to end the war as quickly as possible and thus still save something for the German people.

SPANG: Naturally, I'm not too clear on these things, but at any rate, if they took part in it then they acted for the Fatherland from the deepest inner convictions.

I will admit to you that I have not of course often been able to meet these officers during the war and we never heard what was going on at home, and I have not been on leave since February last year, so I haven't talked to anyone and at the front we don't discuss that sort of thing. We ought not to discuss it either. I haven't spoken a word about this to my staff – all I did was to call my Officers' Corps together and condemn the attempt on HITLER's life very severely. That is still my conviction. I condemn the attempt, certainly! I condemn it – because it was made much too late, at a time when they knew perfectly well that nothing could be achieved by it any longer, and moreover an attempt like that, when we are in a crisis, might cause discord at the front, and in that way the fighting spirit might be impaired. On those grounds I condemn it as an officer and a commander. Therefore I called my Officers' Corps together and said: 'If it is our fate to be defeated, then let us hold out to the last so that we are at least destroyed honourably, but don't let us lay down our arms and have all sorts of promises made to us and then go under without honour, after all.' That is still my point of view and I would never think or act otherwise. My Officers' Corps understood me perfectly. Never for a moment was there a case where an officer spoke about it in any way, or I noticed any discontent or anything like that, because I knew my whole staff so well and there was a great feeling of confidence existing between my Officers' Corps and myself. I had splendid colleagues, who threw themselves wholeheartedly into their work. I had so many trustworthy officers who would have stuck to me through thick and thin and who had pledged themselves to tell me if any discord should arise on the staff or anything like that. Then I would straighten out the situation, because there mustn't be anyone on the staff who might go behind my back or grumble or anything like that. We are bound to give a lead in every way. That was how I trained my staff. I knew perfectly well that if there had been any case in my staff or in my 'Division', then a certain number of officers would immediately have said to me: 'You must keep a look-out there and there, Sir, such-and-such has been said or has happened.' Then I would have set to work immediately and restored order. On our front the attempt has not had the slightest repercussion.

Document 150

CSDIC (UK), GRGG 180
Report on information obtained from Senior Officers (PW) on 25–6 Aug. 44
[TNA, WO 208/4363]

LIEBENSTEIN: Did you hear any more about the attempt on HITLER's life, whether it was an actual fact or just a bogus job?

MENNY: The English and Americans here maintain that it probably was just a put-up job. In my opinion that is quite out of the question. We received a WT message saying no orders from WITZLEBEN, . . . FROMM, HALDER, STAUFFENBERG or OLBRICHT were to be executed, those were the six names mentioned. That happened immediately after the attempt; that WT message came through roughly 10 hrs after it happened. I mean the fact that FROMM and HALDER were mentioned[417] goes to prove that it wasn't just a put-up job.

[. . .]

ELFELDT: What do you say to the hanging of German marshalls?

RADINSKY: I was . . . that by all the Americans . . .

ELFELDT: It's true.

RADINSKY: My answer was always: 'What do you think of German officers raising their hand against their supreme commander for the first time in German history?' The whole thing is abnormal.

MENNY: People here are indignant too. It isn't nice to be hanged. However, you shouldn't play with murder. They could have imprisoned HITLER; assassination isn't the right way. Taking everything into consideration, you must admit that the National Socialists brought about their revolution without reverting to violence. They didn't murder anyone at the time – the RÖHM affair? *He* was among their own ranks.

ELFELDT: The thing I can't understand about the STAUFFENBERG 'Putsch' is why they didn't secure a prominent Party leader. For that HELLDORF is a nincompoop, he hasn't any influence on the people.[418]

MENNY: Did he also take part?

ELFELDT: He has also been shot.

MENNY: Really!

ELFELDT: I've seen it in black and white.

Document 151

CSDIC (UK), GRGG 180 [TNA, WO 208/4363]

Provisional report on information obtained from CS/211 – General der Infantrie Dietrich VON CHOLTITZ – Army Commander of Greater Paris – Captured 25 Aug. 44.

[. . .]

AAO: May I as a personal question? From the way you talk I could almost think that you were mixed up in it. For what reason did you not take part?

CHOLTITZ: We were in the war all the time, so how could we take part? They are all friends of mine. STAUFFENBERG once told me that I ought to take over a post.[419] I said: 'I am being hounded into action the whole time.' Whenever there was any trouble, I had to go there.

The situation with regard to the attack on HITLER's life was this: the general atmosphere among the leaders tended towards bringing about a change and there wasn't a single General who did not want it, because all of them realised that things could not go on as they were. Consequently there was no great excitement even on the day when it happened, because we were expecting it all. I said to an 'SS-Führer': 'It's a fine state of affairs at home, isn't it!' All the 'SS-Führer' said was: 'He's not quite all there.'[420] Well, I must say that's a harmless way of looking at it. We were not so frightfully moved by it.

AAO: You are not expecting a repetition of this attempt, are you?

CHOLTITZ: I could almost swear to it. I would put my hand in the fire – I look at such things, I might almost say, from the point of view of fate. Fate must will this man to go on to the end, to the bitter end, and I am dreadfully sorry that the German people will be involved in it, with endless losses, but nothing else is possible – down to the smallest boy in the Hitler Youth.

Document 152

CSDIC (UK), SR REPORT SRM 837 from 26 Aug. 44 [TNA, WO 208/4139]

Major i.G. BECK (IA, LVIII Panzer Korps) – Captured 16 Aug. 44 in Sairies.
Major i.G. VIEBIG (LXXXIV Panzer Korps) – Captured 21 Aug. 44 in St Lambert.

VIEBIG: Throughout the whole war I have conducted myself as a National Socialist, and at home too, not as a politician but mainly as a soldier. I have always held the view that as a soldier one is bound to obey one's supreme commander under all circumstances; I held, and still hold, the same view with regard to that revolt on the 20th, i.e. under no circumstances should a thing of that sort be done.

BECK: That's my opinion, too.

VIEBIG: For me to revolt against my supreme commander would be something that I could not reconcile with my honour. That has nothing whatever to do with my political views.

BECK: When I was in ITALY the people there were disgusted when we arrived because we were people who could really tell them something. But when I went to see General BREITH, CO of artillery schools,[421] in BERLIN, he said: 'I will give you a piece of good advice. Don't talk too much or you'll be the cause of your own undoing. I know of two officers who got away from STALINGRAD and who talked so much that they are now under lock and key.'

Did you know LÖFFELHOLZ-KOLBERG(?)[422]? He was completely done for. He had had tropical fever. He was totally incapable of giving a straight answer any more. They had originally intended him as GSO I (Ops) for that 'Division' in SICILY, because I was too young.

LATTMANN[423] was, for us, the epitome of decent, arch-Prussian commanders, and he, too, was infected by National Socialism in so far as his actions were similarly guided by 'blind faith'. At that time he held speeches of one or two hours' duration each week to the 'Fahnenjunker' and, in my opinion, everything that he said was absolutely his own conviction. He often used to visit me at home and each time one found confirmation of the fact that, in that respect, he was really talking from conviction. I can't imagine that the man has swung right round merely on account of his STALINGRAD experience. That's why I believe that the whole peculiar business with the liberation committee in MOSCOW isn't too clear either.

VIEBIG: SEYDLITZ was our 'Gruppenkommandeur' in the fighting to open the pocket round DEMIANSK,[424] that's how I know him well.

BECK: He's an extraordinarily decent fellow and a clever man. But even then, although he was advancing at great speed on STALINGRAD – from CHUGUEV[425] near KHARKOV[426] it went in one thrust as far as KALATCH – he was already very pessimistic about the outcome of the war, so that it's quite possible that SEYDLITZ really is speaking his own mind.

VIEBIG: I know LATTMANN, I have my doubts about him.

BECK: I spoke to LATTMANN's brother[427] who quite recently – at the beginning of July – went to the 'Heeresgruppe Bertha'. I was astonished when he told me: 'I am convinced that that's my brother and that he really does talk and think like that. For I've heard him myself on the radio and, after all, one must admit, he only says what we all think.' (Laughs) To which I said: 'Sir, it is, perhaps, not quite as you say, that we all think along those lines, as I am convinced that a large section of the Officer Corps don't think that way at all but believe, now as before, in a successful outcome, but, more than anything, I am astonished that you, Sir, should think the General LATTMANN speaks from innermost conviction because I know him as quite a different person.' But I must admit, even a man like Sepp DIETRICH,[428] with whom I spoke at great length, was standing first on one foot, then on the other, saying: 'How will it end?' But the most shattering thing of all was my visit to General SPEIDEL.[429] The whole three-hour conversation was utterly pessimistic. He said: 'Things are turning out exactly as your uncle prophesied; he always said that there would be fantastic successes during the first three years of the war, but that then there would be no more, and the thing would finally end in a catastrophe.' It's a remarkable thing, but when the happenings of the 20th were made known for the first time, I was very worried when I heard it in case my uncle might be involved in the affair, because I knew that he was always completely antagonistic. I discussed it with the Chief of Staff,[430] and with the GOC, saying that I was extremely worried, as I could imagine he would be involved in the affair in some way, even if he didn't take an active part. Whereupon General KRÜGER[431] said to me: 'BECK, I don't believe it, and for this reason: your uncle was always an extremely careful man, who never ran any risks, I can't imagine that he would suddenly adopt a different attitude, when such an enormous risk must have been attached to the affair.'

The only one who was still optimistic was BAYERLEIN, because he still had his men together.[432]

Document 153

CSDIC (UK), GRGG 183
Report on information obtained from Senior Officers (PW) on 29 Aug. 44 [TNA, WO 208/4363]

BASSENGE: Is FROMM dead, too?

CHOLTITZ: No, he didn't take part in it at all. I spoke about it before-hand[433] to OLBRICHT[434] and to GOERDELER.[435] Of course, they didn't know the actual day, or they didn't say anything to me about it, obviously in order not to incriminate me when I was going to the front. They didn't tell me that they were going to kill him, but only they wanted to render him hors de combat, they wanted to lock him up, but unfortunately STAUFFENBERG was five years too young – that was the only fault of a man who was otherwise almost a *genius*. He went to the conference with his brief-case in his hand and put it between Adolf HITLER's legs under the table and then he went out. JODL said: 'Stay here, STAUFFENBERG!' He said: 'No, I haven't had breakfast yet and I must make a telephone call, too. I shall be back again soon!' Then STAUFFENBERG waited 300 m away, near HITLER's 'Bunker'. Then he maintains that there was such a terrific explosion that he thought no one could get out alive. Then he did the most incredible thing. On the strength of the explosion he went to the guard and remained there for three-quarters of an hour, because he was not allowed to go out, and then finally he rang up and they did let him out. He got into his aircraft and flew to BERLIN and said that the attempt had been successful, without checking up whether it was true! Because of that, all those people . . .

ELFELDT: What happened to the people who were not officially –

CHOLTITZ: They were all hanged.

SPONECK: The others, too?

CHOLTITZ: Yes.

THOMA: FELLGIEBEL,[436] too?

CHOLTITZ: Yes. *All* of them.

ELFELDT: What is ZEITZLER doing?

CHOLTITZ: ZEITZLER is under house-arrest.[437] When STAUFFENBERG arrived at the airfield, he told his brother that it had been successful, whereupon they started moving. GOERDELER said to me – as true as I am sitting here – : 'Herr von CHOLTITZ, if we shut off OBERSALZBERG with *one* 'Division' and put him out of action, then the whole people will forsake him.' Whereupon I said: 'Herr GOERDELER, I *beg* of you, don't *think* such a thing. It is a *fundamental mistake*! It i s n ' t so!' But those people were so obsessed with the idea that they were going to save the Fatherland and they were so *reckless*, it was almost unbelievable. They actually did not collect even a hundred men. They took it so lightly!

HITLER said to me: 'You needn't be alarmed, it is not as though only the Army had taken part in this attempt by a few Generals to usurp power. The whole people, with its opposition, slight though it is, whether it comes from middle-class, social-democrat or communist circles, took part in it.'

?: What did he say? They did take part?

CHOLTITZ: 'The whole people, in its opposition, slight though it was. Those usurpers wanted to surrender German soil. I will not yield a single yard of German soil.'

SCHLIEBEN: That foreigner!

BASSENGE: What does his entourage say; what is the talk there?

CHOLTITZ: All I can say is that I felt as though I were in a madhouse.[438]

BASSENGE: Isn't there one sensible man there to say: 'For God's sake, where is this leading us?'

CHOLTITZ: I presented myself and said: 'My FÜHRER, the LXXXIV 'Korps' has been practically wiped out in defensive battle.' Suddenly, as though he had a mental black-out, he looked round and went on talking about something else.

SPONECK: Has there been any sort of rebellion against the FÜHRER on the part of the Party or SS, either during the 'Putsch', before it or after it; any sort of a split? There was a rumour here that HELLDORFF –

CHOLTITZ: HELLDORF has been hanged. Our Foreign Office was involved in it, too.

NEUFFER: Who among them . . . ?

CHOLTITZ: I believe Secretary of Legation von HEFDEN(?).[439]

SPONECK: Aren't the numbers known?

CHOLTITZ: Well, you know, it keeps changing; you can't tell how many people are hanged each day.

SPONECK: Ten times the number of people who appear before the court are simply bumped off.

CHOLTITZ: I'd estimate about three or four hundred people, in connection with that assassination attempt. The best people we have, of course.[440]

SPONECK: Have radical changes taken place among the personnel of HQs at home, of 'Wehrkreis' and 'Luftkreis' personnel?

CHOLTITZ: I believe there have been a *lot* of changes.

[. . .]

Document 154

CSDIC (UK), GRGG 186
Report on information obtained from Senior Officers (PW) on 4–9 Sept. 44 [TNA, WO 208/4363]

CHOLTITZ: The following happened: Generaloberst JAENECKE returning from the CRIMEA had a short, but very heated interview with HITLER. HITLER did this (*demonstrating*) and threw all the Generals out of the room field marshals KEITEL and JODL among them, and he became so angry with him that Generaloberst JAENECKE who is a decent sort of fellow –

BADINSKY: I know him.

CHOLTITZ: JAENECKE left the room and slammed the door.[441] He met the adjutant outside and said: 'Tell the FÜHRER I have left.' HITLER waited for him for some time, hoping he'd calm down. After that heated argument ZEITZLER on leaving, said: 'That scoundrel HITLER.'

GOERDELER heard about that remark. He hoped that that utterance meant the time was ripe for him to get in touch with ZEITZLER, the Chief of the General Staff.[442] A meeting between GOERDELER and ZEITZLER didn't however, come off. ZEITZLER refused, saying: 'I have no desire for it.' He wasn't in a position, in any case. I said to GOERDELER: 'What do you expect to achieve?' He answered 'I want to explain things to ZEITZLER and if, after that, the wretch still has the courage to denounce me, well, I can't help it!' I think ZEITZLER was quite capable of denouncing him.

HITLER was very suspicious of ZEITZLER and there seems to be some connection between him and 20 July. JODL said to me: 'That man ZEITZLER laid the foundations of that dirty business of the 20th by his miserable grumbling.' No interview between GOERDELER and him took place. I am glad, as it wouldn't have made any difference. I know for certain that ZEITZLER wouldn't have done it. Even if a 'Leutnant', a 'Kompaniechef' or a 'Bataillonskommandeur' were to say: 'We've arrived at the stage when we must have peace; we must rid ourselves of HITLER' a 'Kompanie' of the 'Grossdeutschland' would appear on the one hand, a 'Kompanie' of the SS 'Adolf Hitler' on the other; they'd attack the 'Bataillon' and kill them all. The time *isn't* ripe yet.

They didn't trust FROMM and he was the only one who didn't participate. FROMM really didn't take part in the 'Putsch'.[443]

BADINSKY: He'll have said: 'What do you think I am?' He had OLBRICHT shot, didn't he?

CHOLTITZ: Yes, he was killed. FROMM himself gave BECK the 'coup de grace' with his own pistol. You know, the peculiar thing is that BECK shot his own eyes out but didn't manage to kill himself even by his second shot; then FROMM gave him the 'coup de grace'.[444] HIMMLER appeared at BERLIN an hour later[445] and was bitterly sorry that they were already dead; the reason why he arrested FROMM was because he suspected FROMM had killed all his accomplices.

Document 155

CSDIC (UK), GRGG 187 [TNA, WO 208/4363]

Provisional report on information obtained from (amongst others) CS/223 – General der Panzertruppe EBERBACH (GOC VII Army) – Captured 31 Aug. 44 in Amiens – before arrival in camp No. II.
This report contains information obtained from the above PW [...] in conversation with a low-rating British Army Officer.

EBERBACH: I remember my last conversation with ROMMEL, where he stated his attitude perfectly clearly: that there was nothing else to be done but to make an armistice, at once if possible, and if necessary to take steps against the present government, in case they weren't sensible enough to give the order.

BAO: Did he really speak out as openly as all that?

EBERBACH: Yes, to me. Similarly, I knew that Feldmarschall von RUNDSTEDT would have been willing to make an armistice with you here in the West – if necessary also against the German government. For MANSTEIN any practical step was out of the question, because he no longer held his command on the Eastern Front; but I think I can assure you that MANSTEIN was and still is also one of those soldiers who thinks for himself and who is not carried along by the National Socialist Party.[446]

[...]

Document 156

CSDIC (UK), SR Report SRGG 1018 (C) from 2 Sept. 44
[TNA, WO 208/4368]

Generalmajor Alfred GUTKNECHT (Higher Commander of Kraftfahrtruppen West) – Captured 29 Aug. 44 in Soissons-Rheims.
General der Panzertruppen Heinrich EBERBACH (GOC 7th Army) – Captured 31 Aug. 44 in Amiens.

[. . .]
EBERBACH: Of those who took part in it, I know STAUFFENBERG and OLBRICHT best, and all I can say is that I am firmly convinced that STAUFFENBERG and OLBRICHT really acted out of idealism, in the belief that they were thereby doing the best thing for the REICH. Apart from that, the way they did it was undoubtedly childish and stupid.
GUTKNECHT: Yes, of course it was. It was something like the KAPP 'Putsch'.[447] There were no preparations at all, so that right from the start it was doomed to failure.
EBERBACH: One would really never expect such intelligent people as those two to be as naïve as all that.
GUTKNECHT: I wondered afterwards what would have happened, supposing the attempt had been successful. What would have happened *then*? I believe absolutely no preparations of any kind were made at all.
EBERBACH: They were so stupid that they didn't even take over the telephone exchanges, so that while it was actually going on, officers could ring up the FÜHRER's HQ from BERLIN. They had no business to tackle it so idiotically.[448]

Document 157

CSDIC (UK), GRGG 195
Report on information obtained from Senior Officers (PW) on 16–17 Sept. 44
[TNA, WO 208/4363]

CHOLTITZ: STAUFFENBERG put the question to me: 'Is it necessary for the FÜHRER to be killed or not?' I replied: 'The thing's impossible without getting rid of the root of the trouble.'
EBERBACH: ROMMEL also convinced me of that, he said:[449] 'The FÜHRER must be killed. There's nothing else for it, the man really has been the driving force in everything.'
CHOLTITZ: I was at POSEN, and saw HITLER there. He was *quite* mad. From that moment on I knew complete physical destruction was the only answer. But I shouldn't have thought that ROMMEL would have reach the same conclusion.

EBERBACH: Yes, ROMMEL was very emphatically of that opinion. He said: 'Heaven knows, I've experienced it personally in TUNIS and TRIPOLI. The man must go!' He was most emphatic. GAUSE, who was my Chief of Staff, and who was formerly ROMMEL's Chief of Staff,[450] confirmed and amplified . . . in every detail.

Document 158

CSDIC (UK), GRGG 196
Report on information obtained from Senior Officers (PW) on 18–19 Sept. 44
[TNA, WO 208/4363]

[. . .]

CHOLTITZ: When STAUFFENBERG said to me: 'I am ready; it can start for all we care,' I said to him: 'STAUFFENBERG, that sounds so flippant. Are things really prepared? Can such matters ever be fully prepared?' Incidentally there were four officers in the room whilst we were speaking.

EBERBACH: Well, except for one, who with a collection of twelve armed clerks, arrested them all, a thing which shouldn't have happened –

CHOLTITZ: Who was that? The 'Major'?

EBERBACH: An 'Oberstleutnant', who had only just been promoted.[451] I knew it from my people, who sent an officer out to me to give me all the information.

CHOLTITZ: That is sure to have been the man who always reported the situation and who was with FROMM.

EBERBACH: No. The man who did it belonged to STAUFFENBERG's staff; he was from the AHA(?). He arrived with twelve clerks, armed with rifles and hand grenades and took them all into custody.

CHOLTITZ: That 'Major' must have shot STAUFFENBERG on the spot. STAUFFENBERG was the first to be shot.

EBERBACH: No, they apparently didn't shoot them on the spot but put them into a room first. FROMM was set free and he ordered that STAUFFENBERG, MERZ and OLBRICHT should be shot immediately and that BECK should be handed a revolver. FROMM seems to have been liquidated in the meantime as well. I believe it is in one of the English newspapers. I am sorry because FROMM behaved very decently in this affair. He must have known that it would end tragically for him. In having those people shot on the spot and sending BECK a pistol he saved them a lot of suffering; he behaved like an officer and a gentleman. I never cared much for FROMM but that action of his pleased me.

CHOLTITZ: STAUFFENBERG was the *ideal* of the coming German generation. Sensible, very simple, he had a charming family circle; he was a good, honest, Christian and courageous man. He was the type of young German manhood who . . . ought to be at the head of things.

EBERBACH: That was always my opinion of him too. The first time I heard him speak about that matter – GEYR and I visited him – he opened his heart to us straight away.[452] He didn't know my views. If I had *still* been a fervent Nazi at that time, I should have had to . . . him straight away, without more ado.

CHOLTITZ: I'll admit he was *incredibly* indiscreet.

EBERBACH: Unfortunately that was probably part of his honesty.

CHOLTITZ: Why unfortunately?

EBERBACH: It was unfortunate for the cause! Do you know the reason why we officers kept out of the thing and why we didn't let fly ages ago? It is because we are far too decent to undertake the things such a 'Putsch' entails.

Document 159

CSDIC (UK), GRGG 197
Report on information obtained from Senior Officers (PW) on 20–1 Sept. 44
[TNA, WO 208/4363]

[Conversation between General HEINZ EBERBACH and his son Oblt. z.S. HEINZ EUGEN EBERBACH]

[. . .]

SON: You've no idea how adversely this STAUFFENBERG business affected the Officers' Corps. The fact that the individual soldier at the front was being killed, and that the officers at home were breaking their oath, infuriated the people. The fact that LINDEMANN, for example, through his own swinishness, let about 100,000 soldiers on the Eastern Front go to the devil – he let his whole front go to hell and went over to the other side with half his staff.[453]

FATHER: It hasn't yet been established that LINDEMANN went over to the other side. Nothing is known about him.

SON: Then GUDERIAN wouldn't have requested that he and his Chief of Staff and Major KUHNERT(?)[454] should be thrown out. At the time I was told by people in GERMANY, including an Oberleutnant, that THOMALE(?) told them a gap of 120 km had been made, and that the IV. 'Armee' was suddenly left standing there more or less leaderless, and that the 'Divisionen' had been told: 'We've been left in the lurch, the best thing is to surrender.' Part of the 'Divisionen' did so, others didn't.

FATHER: I've never heard anything about that business.

SON: Well, that there really was a gap, which suddenly –

FATHER: But it was in the centre, and it was before 20 July.

SON: Yes, the LINDEMANN business happened before 20 July. He said that people did it more or less deliberately in order to get certain sections of the army under their control and to achieve something they needed a collapse.

FATHER: Propaganda within the Army was impossible, the people could only do it amongst themselves: moreover, RUNDSTEDT who is now in command again in the West, was party to it, and so was ROMMEL and –

SON: Well, what does 'party to it' mean?

FATHER: They knew about it and were willing and agreed to it, and RUNDSTEDT wanted to arrange an armistice with the Allies and arrange with them that his 'Armee' should turn back in order to hold back the Russians until such time as the Allies had occupied the territory at least as far as the ODER. I must say that from what I've seen I can unfortunately do nothing else but admit those people were right. Actually I know for certain – I'm not sure about MODEL, I couldn't speak to those people privately – but KLUGE was also in favour of it.

SON: Well, all I can say is, why didn't the fools cooperate?

FATHER: What does cooperate mean? That STAUFFENBERG business was supposed to happen first, and then the thing was so far prepared internally that no one could expect, once the FÜHRER really was dead, the thing to go smoothly and that the Army and the fronts were to hold on. The break-through near AVRANCHES hadn't yet occurred on the 20th, and RUNDSTEDT was to make an armistice in order to turn about and hold back the Russians; that was the idea.

SON: The whole thing seems to me so criminal, at least, the way they prepared it. It would have meant civil war in GERMANY on a fantastic scale. It would have soon got around that the thing was connected with an attempt on the FÜHRER's life and the German people wouldn't stand for that. Not on any account! The German Navy certainly wouldn't have joined in. SCHNIEWIND is the only naval man who was involved and he only had a very minor job. The German Navy *wouldn't* have joined in.[455]

FATHER: Nearly all important people in the Army were involved, all except one, which is all the more surprising because he was very badly treated: MANSTEIN. He said, and I agree with him: 'No, I'll take no part in it.' He said, and I agree, that we must see this thing through to the bitter end, because that is the only chance for our people of coming out of this more or less united.[456]

SON: Besides, the entire junior officer corps wouldn't have cooperated from the moment they realised that it was connected with an attempt on HITLER's life.

FATHER: But all those junior officers would have realised what things were like, because they themselves experienced the way they were being led. It must have been obvious to them that it was a matter of putting the SS into power, and the trend in the Army is opposed to letting the SS get into power.

SON: What about GUDERIAN?

FATHER: GUDERIAN said to me long ago: 'The FÜHRER is mad!' I shared the idea he had at the time: to get hold of the FÜHRER, let's say imprison him, but at any rate keep him alive and to liquidate his entire entourage. I have changed my views in the meantime and realise that the FÜHRER is responsible for the whole thing.

SON: I can't understand why GUDERIAN is on HITLER's side in that case.

FATHER: It was like this: you could say that all the Generals were given the choice of either . . . or you are all involved; your wives and children will be shot and you yourselves will be hanged.

SON: Well, I don't think that GUDERIAN would have been given the job of Chief of Staff if he hadn't been considered very reliable.[457]

FATHER: Of course not! That man, whom they held to be so reliable told me that. I'm just waiting for the moment when GUDERIAN shoots the FÜHRER and all the others at the top.

SON: I think that is rather wishful thinking.
    THOMALE(?) showed courage in BERLIN![458]

FATHER: Of course I know people are saying it can't be done like *that*. Apart from that, THOMALE(?) said to me long ago: 'You know the FÜHRER is mad. Of course there are moments when you say to yourself "the man's a genius" but there are weeks when you say he's crazy. It can't go on like this!' For instance, he told me that HITLER is up every night until four or five in the morning because he can't sleep; then he lies down for a few hours and at 10 o'clock he is about again, but he is so shaky that he can't sign anything until 1 o'clock. He gets injections first thing in the morning. Two doctors are continually on the spot; one gives him injections against epileptic fits and the other injections against nerves and other things. I don't know what they are exactly, but at any rate he gets injections every day. By 1 o'clock he has calmed down sufficiently to be able to sign his name and see people.[459]

SON: Well, all that may be the case, but these are all more or less signs of overstrain.

FATHER: All right, let's admit they are signs of overstrain. But in that case the man should take the consequences and say: 'I can't lead the Army and the Armed Forces, an expert must do that.'

SON: We have no experts.

FATHER: What do you mean by that? Without a doubt GUDERIAN could have led the Armed Forces better than the FÜHRER did, and so could MANSTEIN.

SON: I'll admit he might have lead the Army, but the Armed Forces?

FATHER: I'm convinced that MANSTEIN has enough common sense to have had an expert put forward by the Navy, at his side, and he would have managed to lead the Combined Armed Forces. If it comes to that, JODL isn't bad, but he hasn't the moral courage to stand up to the FÜHRER in his fits of rage and say: 'No, what you say can't be done.'

SON: Of course I am not quite in a position to judge. Why is a man like

DÖNITZ out and out on his side? He's a man worthy of consideration!

FATHER: Yes, I don't know about that either. That's not my province. But the people I know – I mean, apart from those, all the ones who were connected with the affair and the ones who have been arrested and shot as a result of it, or rather hanged, the ones named are only a fraction of the number that have actually disappeared. The best people, for example, that 'Oberquartiermeister', General WAGNER[460] and General FINK,[461] who was in charge of the 'Quartiermeister' organisation in the West, had been especially brought over from the Eastern Front because he was the best man for the job. WAGNER's Chief of Staff, BUHLE's Chief of Staff,[462] in the OKW operations staff there was MEIXNER,[463] a first-rate fellow, and ZEITZLER, in fact I might almost say, everybody who was any good at all.

SON: Yes, and what does a man like Sepp DIETRICH say about it?

FATHER: Sepp DIETRICH railed against the FÜHRER and his entourage to such an extent that it became most unpleasant. Then he was sent for and he said: 'All right, that's fine, but I shall speak my mind. I shall tell ADI' – he always calls HITLER 'ADI' – 'that he is leading us all to destruction.' He went there and was awarded the Diamonds and promoted 'Generaloberst' (*chuckling*) so, of course, he kept his mouth shut. We all swore at him. Then he said: 'I shall go straight back there – you are right!' But then I got him as my 'Armee' commander. That's the state of affairs it was. Sepp DIETRICH is all right as a soldier, but not as a 'Korps' commander nor was an 'Armee' commander, and I had to hand over my 'Armee' to him. But you know me well enough to know that that wouldn't in any way make me change my opinions.

Document 160

CSDIC (UK), GRGG 201 [TNA, WO 208/4364]

Provisional report on information obtained from CS/443 Generalleutnant HEIM (Commander, Boulogne) – Captured 23 Sept. 44 in Boulogne.

HEIM: I received the following information from an extremely reliable source, from a General Staff Officer in the General Army Branch in fact. He said the last attack had come about as follows: the FÜHRER had ordered that the 'Divisionen' which were recently being formed at home and of which the date for completion of formation had been laid down as the beginning of September, were immediately to be sent into action in the East, regardless of their condition, and were to occupy the switch(?) lines on the German frontier. Then OLBRICHT and FROMM and all these people said that it was a decision born of sheer despair and would rob us of the very last troops we could throw into the balance at all, because it had long been shown by experience that all formations of that kind are lost if they are put into a switch-line. So those Generals opposed that strongly, but without success(?). So they decided that it was high time to act. It was a case of the man having no power of judgement, and a thing like that could not be done. Actually the FÜHRER withdrew this order after the attempt on his life, but it was then immediately issued again, because the issue in the West had collapsed in the meantime. The position is that we lack any proper professional military leadership, either administrative or strategical. That's the tragedy of the whole affair.[464]

Document 161

CSDIC (UK), GRGG 213
Report on information obtained from Senior Officers (PW) on 18–19 Oct. 44
[TNA, WO 208/4364]

CHOLTITZ: Would you kill HITLER, too?

SCHLIEBEN: It's very difficult to say whether he should be killed or not; it might turn him into a martyr. I should hand him over to the Russians, to work in some Siberian mine or other; that would settle the matter.

CHOLTITZ: As long as the man lives, German Youth will believe in his return and think *only* of resistance. He mustn't be surrounded by a Napoleonic halo of glory either – that is to any, exiled.

SCHLIEBEN: Would you kill him, then?

CHOLTITZ: Certainly. Death is no martyrdom. He should be killed and the whole world should be told about it; he should be photographed pleading for his life, and should be shown in a really bad light, just as they did with Feldmarschall von WITZLEBEN. He should be made to wear just a pullover, and to stand there as a criminal, with his hair cropped and so on.

Document 162

CSDIC (UK), GRGG 220
Report on information obtained from Senior Officers (PW) on 7–10 Nov. 44
[TNA, WO 208/4364]

BASSENGE: What would you say to the following question supposing a man like RUNDSTEDT, for example – knowing perfectly well that there's only one way to avoid chaos this winter or next spring – were to pack up the Army, do away with the Nazi system and finally open the gates to the enemy, what percentage of the armed forces would help him, and what percentage would not? Providing it was made known in a suitable manner and the lines of communication worked. Just the psychological question of what percentage of the Army and

the population would cooperate under present conditions, and how many would fight against it, that is, apart from SS 'Divisionen' –
DASER: One hundred.
BASSENGE: One hundred per cent would cooperate? You're convinced? Not the young officers and young people –
THOMA: They, too, have lost much of their enthusiasm I believe.[465]

Document 163

CSDIC (UK), GRGG 238
Report on information obtained from Senior Officers (PW) on 23–6 Dec. 44 [TNA, WO 208/4364]

EBERBACH: I should have had great difficulties with my 'Divisionen', if that 20 July business had spread any further. That 1st SS Division would certainly have fired. The indignation and anger among the chaps in those 'Divisionen' about the 'Putsch' was so profound that even I was amazed – not only among the SS 'Divisionen' but also among some of the infantry 'Divisionen'.
BASSENGE: Yes, I can well believe that, with the propaganda there was. When things go wrong they always blame whoever started them.
EBERBACH: Therefore it is very significant that the responsibility for that business on the Western Front was borne by the home forces only; the home forces had only enquired whether they 'Feldmarschälle' would participate or what attitude they would take.
BASSENGE: Is that actually so? What did the front-line troops say to that?
EBERBACH: I got it from ROMMEL himself who discussed the matter quite frankly with me; he said he agreed and would take part. Even ROMMEL said at the time: 'We can't start it, *we* can't start a revolution against HITLER at the front as that would cause our front to collapse. You must first pull off something at home and then we'll declare ourselves on your side.' Obviously, all except those who turned it down categorically, like MANSTEIN, took that view, including RUNDSTEDT.

Document 164

CSDIC (UK), GRGG 263
Report on information obtained from Senior Officers (PW) on 21–3 Feb. 45 [TNA, WO 208/4177]

[. . .]
HEIM: It is *incredible* cheek to shoo these people for that reason. One can only repeat that if an army and an officers' corps puts up with a thing like that –
BASSENGE: HEIM, you have always refused to countenance revolt on the

part of the officers.

HEIM: I say, if we had been there, of course we would not have revolted, but history will one day establish as a fact, that an army which puts up with things of that kind is doomed to ruin.

BASSENGE: We ought to have revolted, at the latest, at the time of the FRITSCH affair.

HEYDTE: He didn't interfere at the front, but he must be causing terrific trouble in our army at home.

HEIM: Is he killing everyone off there?

HEYDTE: Yes. Altogether most peculiar conditions across in the home army, after 20 July. I visited a friend of mine who was a recruit at the time as I was, and who is director of the 'Foreign Armies Section', and when I asked him how things were he simply replied: 'I haven't been shot yet, but it happens here that someone suddenly disappears and is gone, nobody knows where!'

BROICH: The only safe place is here in ENGLAND. (*Laughter.*)

[. . .]

Document 165

CSDIC (UK), GRGG 286
Report on information obtained from Senior Officers (PW) on 19–21 Feb. 45
[TNA, WO 208/4177]

SCHLIEBEN: Where were you actually taken from?

PFUHLSTEIN: It was done in the meanest way. I had that head wound and remained another four or five days with the 'Division'. I then went home to WERTHEIM and then I was sent for and suddenly appointed commandant of the fortified area HOHENSTEIN-ORTELSBURGER WALD – it was considered a light job – which was about 180 km in breadth, and with the help of a few other people I was supposed to fortify it. I myself lived with a small staff at ALLENSTEIN. During the night of 31 August/1 September there was a tremendous knocking on my door and in came the commandant of ALLENSTEIN, a 'Generalleutnant' who was formerly in command of the IR 7 or 8,[466] followed by an SS man, a detective. So I, in my nightshirt, said: 'What's this?' 'I have an order from the FÜHRER to arrest you.' He added – and it was a mean trick on his part – 'Arresting a comrade is the worst job I've ever had in my life. I really can't bear to watch it. You must dress. Please dress quickly, I want to get the job finished. Hurry up, be quick!' He was complaining the whole time about having to rush around in ALLENSTEIN at half-past one in the morning and forced me to hurry in a disgusting way. If he had been friendly he would have said: 'Take a change of linen and so on with you.' I was only able to dress, and when I was dressed this detective came up and manacled me. Twenty minutes after he'd told me that, I was standing in the street in the uniform of a 'General' wearing the Knight's Cross, and with manacled hands.

I was taken, manacled, in an ordinary passenger train to BERLIN, I arrived in the evening, when it was dark, and said to him: 'Listen, take off the manacles, I swear I won't run away. I will hold on to your trouser leg.' We went through BERLIN, the manacles were removed – we crossed over the Potsdamer Platz in the dark and then went inside. They took my uniform away, put me in an awful suit of drills, manacled me again, and threw me into the cell, where they left me for a week without any sort of trial. I said: 'Is one interrogated here, or is one simply hanged or shot without being interrogated, or what happens? Make an end of it! Does one remain lying here till one dies?'

I have been wounded twice in my left forearm here and I was able to pull off the left manacle – they were handcuffs. I had to try to get the handcuff on again. I could risk that when I lay in the bed, under the cover. A fellow looked through the peephole every ten minutes. I was always afraid I should drop off to sleep and that a hand would suddenly be hanging out underneath the cover.

When the air-raid warning went those condemned to death were not taken to the shelter but were chained hand and foot and thrown into bed.

ELFELDT: Tell that to KITTEL some time. He maintained that it was all just propaganda.

PFUHLSTEIN: I'd rather not, it's not particularly pleasant for me either. That was an indication to me as to who was and who wasn't condemned to death, old SCHULENBURG, the ambassador, for instance.[467]

SCHLIEBEN: How much did you say at your interrogation?

PFUHLSTEIN: I had decided on a definite limit. I admitted without any hesitation: 'I had orders to occupy a western part of BERLIN and to put out of action the SS artillery school near JÜTERBOG.' The basis of the plan was KLUGE's and BECK's intention of setting up a 'Reichsgeneralstabschef' under HITLER and creating a new army C-in-C and 'Reichsgeneralstab' and they intended to take the whole matter up with the FÜHRER and tell him that they were of the opinion that this plan simply must be carried out and that should the FÜHRER be unwilling to agree to the proposal it was then intended to get FELLGIEBEL to cut his lines of communication and by surround his HQ to exert pressure on the FÜHRER to accept the proposal. As far as this I had to – OSTER had given all that away.

EBERBACH: Was that read out to you?

PFUHLSTEIN: Yes. I was fetched from my cell and dragged into the wash-room where I had three minutes in which to wash myself. There, standing naked in front of the wash-stand, I saw OSTER, as white as the wall. He looked at me, a look which told me everything – he had admitted all that he knew.[468]

EBERBACH: Did they torture you?

PFUHLSTEIN: Not me. That one look was sufficient to tell me that I would have to admit everything OSTER knew about me. The bearing of that man told everything.

SCHLIEBEN: What was OSTER?

PFUHLSTEIN: CANARIS's Chief of Staff.

In my opinion the people released from KÜSTRIN were those who were still comparatively young and fresh. On 30th January they felt the Russians would be in BERLIN in two days. The defence of BERLIN was organised on the spur of the moment, and for that they suddenly needed hundreds of officers again. So they quickly picked out all the people who were still hale and hearty. They took SPEIDEL, KLUGE(?), the brother FELBERT, the son . . . HOEPNER and a few others.[469] In my opinion they left there all the older people over 50, of whom they couldn't expect much physically.

SCHLIEBEN: Didn't STÜLPNAGEL tell you where he was before in November?

PFUHLSTEIN: I believe he was in FÜRSTENBERG, together with Joachim(?) von STÜLPNAGEL.[470] I believe they released him again too.

SCHLIEBEN: Did they also lock up any members of princely houses?

PFUHLSTEIN: Yes I met Prince Ernst August of HANOVER in the lavatory in the cellars of the Prinz Albrecht Strasse.[471]

SCHLIEBEN: Was STÜLPNAGEL still in KÜSTRIN on 30th January?

PFUHLSTEIN: Yes and was transferred with all the rest of them, in an omnibus; it was a 'journey into the blue' without any definite destination in view. It was simply flight from the Russians, with the intention of reaching the neighbourhood of BAD KÖSEN[472](?). We had planned that when the Russians came we would all break out, either with that damned commandant or without him, it didn't matter to us, or we would do him in first.

SCHLIEBEN: Who was he?

PFUHLSTEIN: I don't remember his name. A horrible fellow. I had a 'Kriegsgerichtsrat', who was with the 'Oberste Generalrichter' in BERLIN, who was responsible for these things. I managed to send a girl to him. I smuggled a letter to her round about 15th January, and I wrote to this 'Kriegsgerichtsrat' saying: "Please go immediately to the 'Generalrichter'! What is the general intention regarding the transfer of the KÜSTRIN people further into the REICH? The Russians are coming! Please read the army communiqués. Time presses. It's a question of days. Please go to the 'Generalrichter' today. We know nothing. Time presses!" Something after that style. The girl went to BERLIN immediately and saw this man. A few days later I received a letter from him in answer: "Many thanks for your letter, which I received. A transfer of the KÜSTRIN fortress is not under consideration." Those damned fellows in BERLIN simply hadn't tumbled to it.

PFUHLSTEIN: I had been connected with the preparations – together with STAUFFENBERG – since about 1943, i.e. over eighteen months.

THOMA: Was FELLGIEBEL really hanged?

PFUHLSTEIN: Yes. I was relieved of my command at the time of the attempted assassination itself. I had first commanded a 'Division', I was then wounded and was at ALLENSTEIN, where I was arrested. I spent three months in chains in the SS gaol, the 'Reichssicherheitshauptamt', BERLIN, Prinz-Albrecht-Strasse and then two months in a concentration camp.

THOMA: How did the SS behave there?

PFUHLSTEIN: Like swine! Like *utter swine*! People were hanged right and left of me. HALDER and SCHACHT were there.[473] HALDER is still stuck in Albrecht-Strasse.[474]

THOMA: What was he accused of?

PFUHLSTEIN: I don't know.

THOMA: Were you there with them?

PFUHLSTEIN: Yes.

THOMA: Together?

PFUHLSTEIN: No. Each one was hand-cuffed in his own cell, not a word was exchanged, I only saw him. HALDER wasn't hand-cuffed.

THOMA: Who else was there? It said in the newspaper today that SCHACHT's brother had said that he was dead.

PFUHLSTEIN: I don't know. CANARIS was hanged because as former head of the 'Abwehr' he was also implicated. Afterwards I spent two months in a newly organised officers' concentration camp at KÜSTRIN, it was to have been a fortress but it was a concentration camp. There were about twenty senior and junior officers there.

THOMA: What were they there for?

PFUHLSTEIN: Some because they had participated and some because they had relatives who had, i.e. a PAULUS, a HOEPNER, a HASSELT, and FELLGIEBEL's brother, and other brothers and close relatives of those deeply involved in the 20 July affair.

THOMA: What a race of scoundrels ours has become!

PFUHLSTEIN: Finally I was released, and then came the vital point, I had to report to General BURGDORF, Chief of the Army Personnel Directorate, and he informed me that I have been discharged from the service since 14 September without the right to call myself 'Generalmajor', without the right to wear uniform, but with a pension. It was their intention to give me an opportunity to make good my offence by seeking death in the front line and their intention was to call me up as a 'Major' available for further employment so that I should still be in time to give my life for HITLER at the front. But my health was in such a bad state that they gave me a reprieve to recuperate with my family. I went to WERTHEIM AM MAIN and was with my family when the Americans arrived.

THOMA: How was it that you got off so lightly in connection with the 20 July affair?

PFUHLSTEIN: They knew that I was to occupy a section of BERLIN and that I was to carry out the disarming of the SS artillery school. They found out that much but they didn't find out that I knew that it was a matter of bringing about the death of HITLER.

PFUHLSTEIN: For three months I never left my cell except to go to the lavatory or to another part of the building. For three months I saw neither sun, nor moon, nor cloud, nor people, nor tree; I had no newspaper and, of course no clock. I never spoke to a soul, I had to do mouth exercises in my cell because I noticed that speaking had become difficult. I did tongue exercises so that I shouldn't lose the power of speech. For three months the light was on day and night. I was in a little cell underground with a high-powered bulb shining on my head. Day and night, night and day; for three months, from 1 September to 24 November, to be exact, the thing was never turned off. I didn't go mad, but I was near it, and I don't even know if I'm normal now. On either side were people who – different faces every day, new ones kept coming and the old ones went. You saw these hangmen peeping through the door – when someone was hanged they were allowed to have his toilet articles – and you saw them looking to see what they could steal. They took his washing things, we'll say he had a good piece of soap, and you saw them squinting at the soap. Then the next day the cell was empty, two hours later someone else was in it and the soap had been stolen.

Document 166

CSDIC (UK), GRGG 294
Report on information obtained from Senior Officers (PW) on 2–5 May 45 [TNA, WO 208/4177]

[Generalleutnant KIRCHHEIM on his broadcast appeal over Luxembourg Radio to Feldmarschall KEITEL to bring fighting to an end]

KIRCHHEIM: When it came to it, I told myself that there was still some point in it, because every day not only so-and-so many soldiers were dying, but also women and children. Then I said to myself: It's necessary too that it should be officially stated in public that we have really had nothing to do with these appaling horrors. We didn't know that 50,000, 100,000 – and in REVIN[475] there were two Generals, one of whom was General BRUNS, who was in the Ordnance Branch, and he said he himself had seen how 42,000 Jews were shot. He described that in the most dramatic, terrifying way. The second was a 'Generalmajor' from a Thuringian family, who had latterly been in command of a 'Panzerkorps',[476] and he said he had actually seen how 100 civilians in FRANCE were locked up in a church which was then set on fire. When I heard that I said: 'HITLER *must* know about it, I won't wear his Knight's Cross any longer.'

KIRCHHEIM: I listened at the trial of a gentleman from the Foreign Office called TROTT ZU SOLZ; he behaved *excellently*.[477] For instance when he was asked whether he knew anything about the plot, he said: 'Of course; I have admitted that on more than one occasion.' He always stuck to that. Finally the presiding judge,[478] that infamous – who managed the first proceedings so frightfully roughly and brutally, and who said to HOEPNER:[479] 'Well, you certainly are a swine' – said to him finally: 'How can you reconcile that with your obligation of loyalty to the FÜHRER?' 'Oh,' he said, 'a tie of loyalty has never existed between me and the FÜHRER.' Finally he said: 'Why, your honour, are you having all this questioning done at all? I have admitted everything and I know quite well that it is punishable by death. I was fully aware of that when I decided to take part in this plot.' Then this man, who had treated the others so roughly, said: 'Well, even if *you* refuse to continue your defence, this court, which really wants to find out the truth, will not agree to it. We want to find out the exact motives, in order that we might perhaps be able to pronounce a milder sentence after all.' Then came a 'Major' from the reserve, who was acquitted; then a third on whom judgment was deferred. Then came the Police President of BERLIN, Graf HELLDORF,[480] and then unfortunately I had to go. I didn't hear his trial.

BASSENGE: How long did the trial of each individual last on the average?

KIRCHHEIM: In the case of TROTT ZU SOLZ it lasted nearly three hours. One had the impression that it was being conducted absolutely correctly, but that was very simple because everything was proved against him.

In our Court of Honour it was KEITEL who opened the proceedings. He outlined the case quite briefly, then either KALTENBRUNNER[481] or the SS-Gruppenführer MÜLLER[482] appeared as prosecuting counsel and said to us: The charges are based on these and these facts, admitted' – I was not present at any sentence at which guilt had not been admitted. That was read out to us. PFUHLSTEIN (PW) however maintains that it was in part simply cooked. That is possible, but I must say that we did not reckon with this possibility; KALTENBRUNNER gave me the impression of an absolutely decent man. Then questions could be asked, and then we voted in order of seniority, that's to say starting with the youngest. In the case of ROMMEL's Chief of Staff, for instance, I, as most junior officer present, immediately voted against the attitude adopted by KEITEL in his introductory speech and said: 'No, he is above suspicion.' Although that wasn't quite the case, as he had heard about the plot and reported it to ROMMEL. But ROMMEL hadn't passed the information on.

BASSENGE: ROMMEL knew about it.

KIRCHHEIM: We don't know that. Suddenly I got the *dreadful* thought: 'If ROMMEL didn't pass it on then he, too, must be implicated. Could ROMMEL have had anything to do with it?'

BASSENGE: Most of us here think that he did.

KIRCHHEIM: I think so too now. If one had only asked the question: 'How much time had lapsed in between?', that would have forced the prosecuting counsel to delve deeper into the question: 'Maybe ROMMEL himself is the one to blame?' However, all I said was: 'In view of ROMMEL's character, SPEIDEL was compelled to assume that the information would not be withheld by ROMMEL. If that information was not passed through ordinary channels, it is quite possible that, taking into account ROMMEL's close relations with the FÜHRER, he may have informed him of it in some other way.' Anyway, I cast my vote for 'not guilty', but I was out-voted. Naturally, even though I regard myself as released from my oath of secrecy, I can no longer say who voted for and who against.[483]

BASSENGE: How many were there present?

KIRCHHEIM: Five 'Generals'.

BASSENGE: Any from the GAF?

KIRCHHEIM: No. It's possible that there may have been someone from the GAF, acting as deputy, at some time or other, but there was no-one from either the Navy or the GAF present at the three sessions I attended. KEITEL was always present, RUNDSTEDT and GUDERIAN were there twice. Permanent members were: RUNDSTEDT, GUDERIAN, the deputy commander of WIESBADEN, SCHROTH, SPECHT, KEITEL. SPECHT was, I think, 'Generalleutnant' in the Personnel Branch and has now become deputy GOC somewhere. KRIEBEL and I were the two deputy members.

Document 167

CSDIC (UK), GRGG 296
Report on information obtained from Senior Officers (PW) on 6–9 May 45 [TNA, WO 208/4177]

KIRCHHEIM: Now, gentlemen, I wanted to speak to you of my experiences as a member of the Court of Honour.[484] I am glad to have the opportunity, for so many false opinions have been spread about the activity of the Court of Honour that it is the duty of every member of this Court of Honour to clear matters up where he can.

I received the news that I was a deputy member of the Court of

Honour by a telephone call one afternoon from General REINECKE, who was not a member of the Court of Honour, but was the only officer on the People's Court, and I was told to be in BERLIN the following morning. I was to go at 11 o'clock to a small villa in DAHLEM which KEITEL had set up as an office, and that's where the Court of Honour sessions were held. When I arrived the first session of the Court of Honour was over. Then it turned out that I had been told to come two hours too late. That was the session at which the first victims of the People's Court were judged by Court of Honour, that's to say HOEPNER, WITZLEBEN, etc. On that occasion I found the officers extremely depressed. The members were: KEITEL, RUNDSTEDT, GUDERIAN, who was not present on that day, SCHROTH, SPECHT; and as deputies, KRIEBEL from MUNICH, and myself. The officers said: 'There is probably no hope for any of the officers who have been tried today, for they all admit that they not only knew of the plot, but also helped with the preparations.' Then the question was discussed as to whether it would be expedient or possible to refuse to accept the nomination to the Court of Honour. The officers were unanimous in saying that it would be a betrayal of one's friends to refuse. For the inevitable result would be that either the Court of Honour would be dissolved, just as a great many of the trials later took place without a Court of Honour, or else, that another Court of Honour would be appointed, in which they would select the 'Generale' with extreme care, and in which the majority of the members would probably be SS 'Generale'. I accepted this point of view, but during the following days I became doubtful as to whether I should not ask to be released from this job after all, especially after I had read the first description of the proceedings in the People's Court. Then I said to myself: 'If I have got to hand over officers who are merely suspected, but against whom nothing has been proved, but who have had to leave the service for the time being, so that they may be handed over to the People's Court – if I have got to hand these officers over to a brutal court like that I cannot square that with my honour.'

For that reason I made the request to be allowed to be present at a session of the People's Court as a spectator. This request was granted, and I attended the session at which the People's Court was to pronounce legal sentence on some of the officers on whom judgment had been passed at the first session of this Court of Honour. I only stayed there until noon. During that time a regular 'Major' whose name I don't remember; his father-in-law, a 'Major' in the reserve; and TROTT ZU SOLZ, the Counsellor to a Legation, were sentenced. It was the same day on which Graf HELLDORF was sentenced.[485] Now as regards the appearance of the accused: they appeared to be in perfect physical condition. You couldn't see any exhaustion resulting from a considerable time in prison. The Court of Honour session had taken place at least a week earlier. They looked splendid, and were not badly dressed as HÖPNER was at the first session. They were all well dressed and groomed, and everything was in order. Their behaviour was good too: the 'Major' behaved with great dignity, although I admit his father-in-law did not.[486] The judge dealt with him rather ironically.

The first thing which astounded me was the manner in which the President of the Court treated the accused – and that was the reason why I had asked to be present. I have never seen a trial at which the prisoners were treated with such politeness by the president.[487] He was such an actor and obeyed his orders so implicitly that at one time he treated the people in the most cruel and brutal manner; and then he got a tip from higher authority that the report in the newspapers had probably made an extremely unpleasant impression at home and abroad, so he adopted different tactics. To give you an example, how he treated TROTT ZU SOLZ – TROTT ZU SOLZ behaved really admirably; he conducted himself with perfect calm and pride and didn't deny anything. After he had been cross-examined for about an hour the presiding judge said to him: 'Well, accused, how do you reconcile that with your obligation of loyalty to the FÜHRER?' So TROTT ZU SOLZ said: 'I don't understand how you can say that. You know perfectly well that I have never been bound by an obligation of loyalty to the FÜHRER.' On another occasion he said: 'But don't you realise – you say that so simply – don't you realise that you are signing your death warrant?' Then he said: 'I know that perfectly well. I can't think why I'm still being cross-examined here, for I have already admitted everything so often: that I knew of the plot, that I helped in the preparations; that is sufficient grounds for my death sentence; what is the point of my cross-examination being continued any longer?' Thereupon the presiding judge –

SEVERAL: FREISLER.

KIRCHHEIM: – said in a very courteous way: 'Well, even if you have given up your case, it remains the business of this High Court to establish the truth down to the last detail, because we might perhaps still find extenuating circumstances.' Of course that was only a gruesome piece of play-acting on his part, but all the same this trial showed that if it continued to be conducted in that manner at any rate, the fear which I had, which might perhaps have caused me to ask for my release from the Court of Honour, was unfounded, for each of the accused could say what he liked. They were undoubtedly not under pressure. I also believe that as long as the Court of Honour existed, the accused were not put under pressure to force them to make statements which were untrue. The session was not open to the public, but about 250 spectators were admitted, for whom there were seats. Apart from that there were about 50 standing, packed closely together, although admittedly they were only people who had received entrance tickets, but there were, for instance, some twenty tickets placed at the disposal of the OKH in BERLIN, and they were given to the first people who asked for them.

What things were like afterwards we shall admittedly only find out later on, and I believe that when we do find out the fate of the unfortunate people who were sentenced after the Court of Honour had ceased to exist, and compare it with the fate of the others, not all of whom could be saved – that was impossible; when it had been proved and they had admitted that they had taken part in the plot, they could not be saved. But I attended three sessions. At each session several were acquitted, and at each session there was at least one who was not punished in such a way as KEITEL said in his opening speech: 'The FÜHRER is informed and believes that they are guilty, or wishes that they should be handed over to the People's Court.'

I will now describe to you the last proceedings against General SPEIDEL, the Chief of Staff to Generalfeldmarschall ROMMEL. At the beginning of the trial we were told that in the FÜHRER's opinion an investigation must be held in the People's Court, as he was at any rate guilty of negligence. At the time the Court of Honour consisted of the following: KEITEL, RUNDSTEDT, GUDERIAN, myself, KRIEBEL. The youngest had to speak first, so I had to give my opinion first. I said: 'The General made his report to his immediate superior. In the case of a personage such as Generalfeldmarschall ROMMEL, he couldn't have any doubts that the report would be passed on; therefore he is not guilty, not under suspicion.' Then it was said: 'But as Chief of Staff he must have known that the report was not passed on.' I said: 'Well, the Generalfeldmarschall, in view of his relations with the FÜHRER, might have passed on the information in a private letter.' Afterwards the sentence read – it was undoubtedly not quite watertight from the legal point of view, because as Chief of Staff he must have known, it was negligence at least – the sentence read: Not guilty! But as he must have known that the report was not passed on an investigation must follow in order that he may be cleared of all suspicion. Therefore a temporary removal from the Army is considered necessary, but the Court of Honour adds a rider that they hope and expect that he would return to the Army with full honours after a short time. I don't think more could have been done for General SPEIDEL under the circumstances. Just imagine what would have happened if the Court of Honour hadn't been available; he'd have been handed over the People's Court.

That sitting was the last one held by the Court of Honour, the reason for the disbanding of the Court of Honour being that all those arrested and under suspicion had been tried and that the task of the Court of Honour was therefore completed. But in actual fact a number of arrests were still made and a number of sentences were also passed. But how these sentences were arrived at we don't know. We don't know before what court they were brought and we don't know whether a different authority sat and dealt with the matter from their point of view. It may be that they were simply handed over to the People's Court.

PFUHLSTEIN: As regards the SPIEDEL matter I would just like to say that my impression is that the decision as to who was to appear before the Court of Honour was made entirely by the 'Reichssicherheitshauptamt', that is to say, by HIMMLER and KALTENBRUNNER. Because it was like this: I was arrested on 1 September and was immediately taken to the 'Reichssicherheitshauptamt' where those people were kept whom they considered the most compromised. The next place of imprisonment was MOABIT, and then came a much better camp – a long way outside – I don't remember the name at the moment – where the arrested officers concerned were far better off and could come and go in freedom. There, for instance, were HEUSINGER and General FALKENHAUSEN, and there were also SPIEDEL and a whole lot of other people who were far less compromised. I was very deeply compromised; I was chained and was with all those who were most deeply compromised, 90 per cent of whom were hanged. I was lucky in that I had extricated Herr KALTENBRUNNER from a nasty dilemma only a short time before[488] and that turned the scales; he told me himself – he got me out on 5 January – that as he knew me personally and that as I had rescued him from a very unpleasant situation he had decided not to bring me before the Court of Honour, nor hand me over to the hangman.

KIRCHHEIM: How was he going to save you?

PFUHLSTEIN: He simply dropped the charge entirely, reported to the REICHSFÜHRER about it, and the REICHSFÜHRER accepted his suggestion that I –

KIRCHHEIM: Was he above suspicion?

PFUHLSTEIN: Not above suspicion. That is to say, the charge against me was quite enough to send me to the gallows. But by reason of that personal matter I had the man's goodwill. 'We'll wash that out because we know each other; you helped me out of a difficulty, now I'll help you.'

KIRCHHEIM: You would have come before the People's Court?

PFUHLSTEIN: No, not even that. That was impossible. I only wanted to illustrate by that that I'm convinced that in the end the final decision lay with KALTENBRUNNER or Herr HIMMLER, who in my case decided in my favour.

KIRCHHEIM: But I don't believe KALTENBRUNNER produced cooked evidence.

PFUHLSTEIN: No, I don't think so.

Short Biographies

Generaloberst Hans-Jürgen von Arnim
Born Ensdorf, Silesia, 4.4.1889. Prot. Entered Army 1.4.1908. **WWI:** Served at Staff and front, finally Hauptmann and Battalion Cdr, Res.Inf.Reg.93. **Reichswehr:** Staff and field. **WWII:** 2.12.1939 Generalleutnant; 12.9.1939–11.10.1940 CO, 12.Inf.Div.; 12.10.1940–11.11.1941 (with breaks) CO, 17.Pz.Div.; 4.9.1941 awarded Knight's Cross; 17.12.1941 General der Panzertruppen; 11.11.1941 Cmmdg Gen., XXXIX.Pz.Korps; 3.12.1942 C-in-C, 5.Pz.Armee Tunisia; 4.12.1942 Generaloberst; from 9.3.1943 C-in-C, Armeegruppe Afrika; 12.5.1943 PoW Tunis; Trent Park 16.5.1943–16.6.1944; to USA. Repatriated 1.7.1947. Died Bad Wildungen, 1.9.1962.

On 13.12.1942, Walter Model, C-in-C, 9.Armee assessed him: 'Fully proven Commanding General in defensive fighting. Energetic and relishes responsibility. Committed himself unconditionally, unshakeable confidence even in crisis situations. Lives and leads per the National Socialist worldview.'

CSDIC (UK) opinion: He drifted between the two political cliques at Trent Park but had no clear affinity with either. Considered extremely anti-Communist and anti-Semitic but the British could find no concrete indication of active support for the Nazi Party.

Generalleutnant Curt Badinsky
Born Grebenstein/Hofgeismar, 17.5.1890. Entered Army 15.1.1910. **WWI:** Mainly commands at Jaegerbataillon 9, finally Oberleutnant, 1a, Group Staff, General Wehr. **Reichswehr:** Infantry officer; 1.8.1938 Oberst. **WWII:** 26.8.1939–6.1.1942 CO, Inf.Reg.489; 11.10.1941 awarded Knight's Cross; 1.2.1942 Generalmajor; 17.1.1942–10.7.1942 Leader and CO, 23.Inf.Div.; 1.9.1942–16.11.1942 CO, 269.Inf.Div., then Territorial Section Cdr, Bergen; 1.3.1943 Generalleutnant; from 24.11.1943 CO, 276.Inf.Div.; 20.8.1944 PoW Falaise; 25.8.1944–23.9.1944 Trent Park, then Clinton Camp USA. Repatriated 21.6.1947. Died Oldenburg/Oder, 27.2.1966.

CSDIC (UK) opinion: A professional soldier, 'having the honour of the soldier at heart'. Thought to be 'anti-Nazi', he characterised Hitler as 'an ape' and condemned his politics as 'devastating', but was not openly an enemy of the regime.

GENERALMAJOR DIPL. ING. GERHARD BASSENGE

Born Ettlingen, 18.11.1897. Prot. **WWI:** Entered Army 4.10.1914 Inf.Reg.29; April 1916 fighter pilot, Jagdstaffel 2 *Boelcke* (seven victories); 1918 Leutnant; 1919 Freikorps Lüttwitz, transferred into Reichswehr; 1922–27 Undergraduate at Technische Hochschule Hanover. **Reichswehr:** Finally Comp. Cdr, Inf.Reg.6; 1.1.1934 transferred to Luftwaffe; until 1937 Head of Weapons Development Section at Reich Air Ministry; 1938/39 Luftwaffe General Staff; 1.5.1939 Oberst. **WWII:** 30.1.1940–31.7.1940 Chief of Staff, Fliegerkorps z.b.V (paratroops and airborne forces); 1.8.1940–4.10.1940 Chief of Staff, Luftflotte 5; afterwards Chief of Staff, German Luftwaffe Mission to Rumania, served as Fliegerführer on Eastern Front, awarded German Cross in Gold 27.7.1942; 1.1.43 Generalmajor; from 1.2.1943 Commandant, Fortified Region Tunis/Bizerta; 9.5.1943 PoW Tunisia; 16.5.1943 Trent Park. Repatriated 2.10.1947. Died Lübeck, 13.3.1977.

CSDIC (UK) opinion: 'Very intelligent, a great pillar of the anti-Nazi clique with an orderly mind, which is perhaps due to his long staff training. Has offered to collaborate with us in getting rid of the Nazis and stopping the war, and his statement that no selfish motives underlie this offer may be believed.'

MAJOR I.G. RUDOLF BECK

Born Frankfurt am Main, 11.8.1908. Prot. Entered Army 29.10.1935. **WWII:** 1.9.1939–15.8.1940 Battery Cdr, 3.Art.Reg.29 (mot.); until January 1942 Director of Lectures, Artillery School Jüterbog; 15.11.1942–8.5.1943 General Staff training; 1.6.1943 Major, 1.General Staff Officer, Division *Manteuffel*, Tunisia; from December 1943, 1.General Staff Officer, LVIII.Pz.Korps, France; August 1944 PoW Normandy, spent short time Latimer House monitoring centre, west of London.

On 10.2.1944 assessed as: 'Strong, self-possessed personality with great verve, full of ideas. Energetic and determined, puts forward his views firmly but tactfully. Pronounced leadership personality who deserves notice. Clear National Socialist disposition.'

OBERSTLEUTNANT I.G. ULRICH BOES

Born Elsdorf/Lower Saxony, 30.1.1911. Prot. Entered Army 1.4.1930; 20.4.1939 Hauptmann. **WWII:** October–December 1940 General Staff course, War Academy; January 1941–September 1942 General Staff officer zbV (special purposes) at Wehrmachtführungsstab; from 28.11.1942 1a Division *Broich/Manteuffel*; 9.5.1943 as Major; PoW

Tunisia; mid-June 1943–30.1.1944 Trent Park; end 1943 Oberstleutnant; then PoW in Canada. Repatriated 13.3.1947. Entered Bundeswehr 1956, last rank Brigadegeneral.

Assessment of 21 March 1943 stated: 'Outstanding service achievements, these combined with his good human qualities elevate him to above average amongst his peers. Tactful before commanders, who esteem him highly. Played a decisive role in the expansion of the Division and was involved to an outstanding degree in its successes . . .' An earlier assessment of 10.12.1942 considered that he 'stood squarely on the ground of National Socialist philosophy'.

CSDIC (UK) opinion: 'This man is a young Nazi Regular Officer. He is fat and gross and an Anglophobe. In a lecture he once gave to the batmen he called the British "degenerate and cowardly and a filthy nation like the French". Needless to say his knowledge of Britain and the British is non-existent. Strangely enough, on social occasions, this man can be entertaining. His fund of dirty stories is immense and he is adept at telling them – especially in the Hamburg dialect.'

OBERST GEBHARD BORCHERDT
Born 18.6.1895. Prot. **WWII:** From outbreak of war to November 1941 CO, reserve infantry battalions; 1.4.1941 Oberst; 27.11.1941–8.12.1942 Führer-Reserve; from January 1943 Tunisia, first as local commandant, Bizerta; 20.2.1943 Commandant, District and City, Tunis; 11.5.1943 PoW. Only decoration Iron Cross Class II. No further details of his life are available.

Characterised in his service files by CO, 168 Inf.Div. as 'conventional, a precise and reliable personality' who was however 'as a Field-Commandant too slow and has too little verve'.

CSDIC (UK) opinion: 'He is a perpetual source of amusement and very much in need of care and attention. He definitely appears to have a "kink" and is known to his fellow PoWs as "mother's darling". How he reached his present rank is a mystery.' Though considered 'No Nazi' he inclined towards Crüwell's clique.

GENERALLEUTNANT FRIEDRICH (FRITZ) FREIHERR VON BROICH
Born Strasbourg (then German), 1.1.1896. Prot. Entered Army 2.7.1914. **WWI:** Cavalry officer; 1918 Oberleutnant. **Reichswehr:** Cavalry regiments; 1.10.1937 Oberstleutnant. **WWII:** 1.9.1940 Oberst; from end 1939–end 1941 CO, Kav.Reg.21, 22 and 1; after re-formation of 1.Kav.Div. into 24.Pz.Div., 1.12.1941–31.10.1942 CO, 24.Schuetzen-brigade; 27.8.1942 awarded Knight's Cross; 10.11.1942–5.2.1943 CO, Brigade *von Broich*; 5.2.1943 CO, 10.Pz.Div.; 15.2.1943 Generalmajor; 1.5.1943 Generalleutnant (advised in England); 12.5.1943 PoW Gombalia, Tunisia; 1.6.1943 Trent Park. Repatriated 7.10.1947. Died Leoni, 24.9.1974.

Constantly praised by his superiors as an above-average officer. Last assessment of 1.3.1943 judged him to be: 'Decent, open and upright character, good National Socialist attitude, proven in battle, forward-looking determined troop leader with good tactical feel, mentally and physically lively. Proved himself again in the fighting in the the central Tunisian mountains.'

CSDIC (UK) opinion: 'This jolly ex-cavalry man has a twinkle in his eye. He is not particularly intelligent, but is always most amusing and charming. He has travelled around Europe fairly extensively and, as a result, has a broader outlook then most of the other Generals.' A monarchist who advocated the territorial division of the Reich as it existed in Imperial times, 'he is anti-Nazi, defeatist and monarchist. He has a horror of Communism equalled only by his horror of Nazism. He writes very anti-Nazi letters to his wife, so much so that she is constantly appealing to him to be more careful, as she has had trouble with the Gestapo about it.'

GENERALMAJOR JOHANNES BRUHN
Born Neumünster, 10.7.1898. Prot. **WWI:** Entered Army 21.6.1915; as NCO wounded at front four times; 1918 Leutnant (Reserve); 1.4.1920 joined police; 1.4.1935 re-entered Army in rank of Hauptmann. **WWII:** At outbreak of war, CO, (heavy) Art.Abt.602; 28.7.1941 CO, artillery regiments; 1.3.1942 Oberst; 15.10.1942 CO, Art.Reg.113 and 149; 20.12.1943 awarded Knight's Cross; 30.9.1944 CO, 553.Volks-grenadierdivision; 1.11.1944 Generalmajor; 22.11.1944 PoW Saverne (France); 28.12.1944 Trent Park; May 1945 transferred USA. Repatriated 26.6.1947. 1951–54 CO, Grenzschutzkommando Mitte (frontier police). Died Lübeck, 20.11.1954.

Bruhn was always appraised as above average, in his last assessment on 1 March 1944 by the Commanding General V.Armeekorps he was considered 'outstanding; an especially valuable leader-type personality by character and as a soldier, never loses faith even in the most difficult situations. Outstandingly brave, wounded on six occasions. National Socialist. The best artillery commander I have come across in this war.'

CSDIC (UK) opinion: By far the most intelligent of the generals captured in the second part of 1944. A man who combined great personal charm with an air of integrity. Considered 'anti-Nazi', he became more interested in politics during captivity. In his opinion a Communist Germany was to be prevented at all costs.

GENERALMAJOR WALTER BRUNS
Born Kirberg/Limburg, 15.9.1891. RC. Entered Army 10.2.1910. **WWI:** Service with pioneer units, finally Hauptmann and comp. cdr. **Reichswehr:** Staff appointments in Ordnance and Fortifications; 1.4.1938 Oberst. **WWII:** Chief of Construction Staff, Landau; 1.4.1940

Cdr, Rhine crossings; 1.5.1941–1.5.1942 CO, Bridge Staff *Bruns*, Army Group North; December 1941 eye-witness to mass executions at Riga; 1.6.1942 Army Ordnance Warrant Officer Training School I; 20.7.1944 complicity in assassination plot, with his troop occupied the Berlin City Fort but Gestapo never discovered his involvement; 24.1.1945 Führer-Reserve; 8.4.1945 PoW Göttingen, to Trent Park; 21.2.1948 freed, gave evidence at OKW war crimes trials. Died Göttingen, 15.4.1957.

Assessed on 5 March 1944 as: 'Of unobjectionable character. Not very attractive but of passable military appearance. Highly esteemed technically and very interested. No doubts as to his National Socialist convictions.'

OBERST RUDOLF GUSTAV BUHSE
Born Graudenz, 10.4.1905. Prot. **Reichswehr:** Entered Army 1.4.1924; from 1937 Inf.Reg.47, 22.Luftlande.Div. **WWII:** Fought in France and Russia; stationed in Crete; 17.8.1942 awarded Knight's Cross; October 1942 transferred from Crete to North Africa 21.Pz.Div.; 9.5.1943 PoW Tunisia; end May 1943 Trent Park. 1956–62 Bundeswehr, Brigade-general. Died Tutzing, 26.11.1997.

CSDIC (UK) opinion: 'He is a Nazi but has the good taste (or the good sense) not to make this obvious to the British.' Considered a hero by the younger Trent Park inmates, in his spare time studied architecture.

MAJOR WALTER BURCKHARDT
Born Strasbourg, 19.2.1908. Prot. Studied law at Breslau. **Reichswehr:** 9.4.1930 entered Landespolizei; 15.10.1935 transferred into Army; 16.8.1937–15.1.1939 Oberleutnant, with von Thoma in Spanish Civil War. **WWII:** 1939 Hauptmann and Comp. Cdr, 12.Inf.Reg.458 in Poland; 1.8.1940 transferred to Luftwaffe (paratroops); May 1941 CO, II./Fallschirmjäger-Reg.1, Crete. 1.1.1942 Major, Battalion Cdr, Fallschirmjägerbrigade *Ramcke*; 5.11.1942 PoW El Alamein. 23.12.1942–2.43 Trent Park. For other details of his career, see TNA WO208/4182.

Assessed on 28 January 1942 as: 'Pronounced soldierly appearance, emphatically correct military behaviour. Of unobjectionable character, ambitious, an exemplary officer, impassioned, full of verve and ideas. Excellent instructor. Leader type. Brave and hard on himself and his subordinates. Proven in the field as battalion commander in Crete. Convinced National Socialist.'

GENERAL DER INFANTERIE DIETRICH VON CHOLTITZ
Born Wiesegräflich/Upper Silesia, 9.11.1894. RC. Entered Army 6.2.1914. **WWI:** Leutnant, Inf.Reg.107. **Reichswehr:** Infantry and cavalry units, from 1.2.1937 Battalion Cdr, Inf.Reg.16; 1.4.1938 Oberstleutnant. **WWII**: 1.4.1941 Oberst; 18.5.1940 awarded Knight's Cross; 10.9.1940–27.8.1942 CO, Inf.Reg.16; 1.9.1942 Generalmajor; 27.8.1942–12.10.1942

CO, 260.Inf.Div.; 7.2.1943–5.3.1943 CO, XVII.Armeekorps; 1.3.1943
Generalleutnant; 5.3.1943–1.10.1943 CO, 11.Pz.Div.; 1.10.1943–
15.11.1943 CO, XXXXVIII.Pz.Korps; 1.3.1944–16.4.1944 CO,
LXXVI.Pz.Korps (Italy); 13.6.1944 Cmmdg Gen., LXXXIV.Armeekorps
(Normandy); 1.8.1944 General der Infanterie; from 7.8.1944 Wehrmacht
Commander, Greater Paris; 25.8.1944 PoW; 29.8.1944–10.4.1945 Trent
Park. Repatriated April 1947. Died Baden-Baden, 5.11.1966.

Assessment on 1 April 1942 by CO, 22.Inf.Div.: 'By disposition and
ability an able soldier and officer. Has a good tactical grasp and can make
rapid decisions. Gets to the heart of a problem with few words. In battle
leads his regiment with prudence and a strong, sure hand. When he puts
his mind to it can be a personal example. Many successes are to be
credited to his personal initiative. Adept at socialising. Unfortunately
owing to the war suffers from stomach complaint. The increased
nervousness makes him very irritable at times and he then becomes very
excitable as a consequence.'

CSDIC (UK) opinion: 'PoW is a cinema-type of a German officer, fat,
coarse, bemonocled and inflated with a tremendous sense of his own
importance.' His fickle nature did not endear him to his colleagues who
spoke of him unflatteringly, see e.g. GRGG 183, 29.8.1944 and GRGG
184, 30.8.1944, TNA WO208/4363.

GENERAL DER PANZERTRUPPE HANS CRAMER
Born Minden, 13.7.1896. Prot. **WWI:** 10.8.1914 entered Army, Leutnant,
mostly Comp. Cdr with Inf.Reg.15. **Reichswehr:** Staff cavalry units;
1.2.1939 Oberstleutnant. **WWII:** From 22.3.1941 CO, Pz.Reg.8 in North
Africa; 27.6.1941 awarded Knight's Cross; 1.10.1941 Oberst; 1.4.1942
Chief of Staff, General der Schnellen Truppen; 1.9.1942–22.1.1943
General der Schnellen Truppen; 1.11.1942 Generalmajor; 20.11.1942–
10.12.1942, acting CO, XXXXVIII.Armeekorps; 22.1.1943–10.2.1943 CO,
General-Kommando zbV (special purposes) *Cramer*; 22.1.1943
Generalleutnant; from 13.3.1943 Head of German Afrika Korps; 1.5.1943
General der Panzertruppen; 12.5.1943 PoW Tunisia; 16.5.1943–
22.2.1944 Trent Park. Repatriated (severe asthma) arrived Germany
12.5.1944. Involved in 20 July 1944 plot; from 26.7.1944–5.8.1944 held
by Gestapo, Prinz-Albrecht-Strasse prison in Berlin; transferred to
satellite camp of Ravensbrück, transferred at end of September to Berlin
Charité hospital; from 24.12.1944 placed under house arrest at home;
14.8.1944 discharged from Wehrmacht. From May 1945 appointed by
British as C-in-C of all German PoWs in Holstein (Wehrmachtstab
Nord); 15.2.1946 discharged again. Died Hausberge, 28.10.1968.

On 8 April 1942 assessed as: 'Blameless, self-possessed character. Adept,
quiet type. Imposes his will. Forward looking with very good tactical sense
and ability. Quick to make decisions and give orders. Commits himself
tirelessly against the enemy. An above-average regimental commander.'

CSDIC (UK) opinion: An old cavalry man who had been forcibly motorised. Enjoyed the panzer battles in the North African desert, repeatedly emphasising that a 'true' soldier fought honourably, as in North Africa, unlike the war in Russia. Cramer's colleagues considered him incompetent. Assessed by the British as 'anti-Nazi' and a pro-monarchist in favour of restoring the Kaiserreich under Rupprecht von Bayern, Cramer spent most of his time at Trent Park alone in his room, presumably because of his severe asthma.

GENERAL DER PANZERTRUPPE LUDWIG CRÜWELL
Born Dortmund, 20.3.1892. Prot. Entered Army 6.3.1911. **WWI:** Service at front and Staff; 1918 Oberleutnant. **Reichswehr:** Mainly Staff appointments; 1.3.1936 Oberst. **WWII:** 23.10.1939 Senior QM, 16.Armee; 1.12.1939 Generalmajor; 1.8.1940–15.8.1941 CO, 11.Pz.Div.; 14.5.1941 awarded Knight's Cross; 1.9.1941 awarded Oak Leaves, Generalleutnant and Cmmdg Gen, Deutsches Afrika Korps; 17.12.1941 General der Panzertruppen; 29.5.1942 shot down on reconnaissance flight west of Tobruk, PoW; 22.8.1942–16.6.1944 Trent Park, then Clinton Camp, USA. Repatriated April 1947. In the 1950s was considered a likely prospect for the post of General-Inspekteur der Bundeswehr but declined on grounds of ill-health (see Meyer, *Heusinger*, p. 556 and letter from Adolf Heusinger to Berndt Crüwell, 27.9.1958). Died Essen, 25.9.1958.

His superiors considered him to be outstandingly positive. General Werner Kempf wrote of him on 28 October 1941: 'Outstanding person. Exemplary, brave. Great tactical knowledge and ability, very prudent, very fast to make decisions, tirelessly active. Led outstandingly and achieved great successes.' In his opinion of 12 April 1942 Rommel concurred with the foregoing.

CSDIC (UK) opinion: He headed the 'Nazi clique', and was a follower and admirer of Hitler, whom he had met twice. An 'ignorant, stupid, sentimental, narrow-minded, conceited, vain and self-satisfied type of Prussian senior officer. He seems to regard himself as a second Frederick the Great. He never tires of boasting about his capture of Belgrade five days after the invasion of Yugoslavia, and the fact that he was promoted full General over the heads of 130 Lieutenant-generals.' (see e.g. SRX 1153, 9.10.1942, TNA WO208/4161). Otherwise, his only interest besides military affairs were horse-riding and his four young children. The British do not appear to have been aware of his avid interest in reading history.

GENERALLEUTNANT WILHELM DASER
Born Germersheim/Pfalz, 31.8.1884. RC. Entered Army 6.7.1903. **WWI:** 15, 18 and 30.Bav.Res.Reg. longest period as Regimental Adjutant, finally Hauptmann and Battalion Cdr. **Reichswehr:** Comp. and Battalion

Cdr. **WWII:** 26.8.1939 Oberst, as CO, Inf.Reg.388 attached to 3.Gebirgsdivision at Murmansk; physical breakdown, 22.9.1941 reported sick; 1942/43 Feldkommandant, France, 15.12.1942–10.6.1943 Oberfeldkommandant, 670 Lille, then Feldkommandant, 454 southern sector Eastern Front; from 15.5.1944 CO, 70.Inf.Div. (composed of walking sick/stomach/intestinal problems) Walcheren Is., Holland; 6.11.1944 PoW Walcheren; 9.11.1944 Trent Park; May 1945 transferred USA. Repatriated 10.12.1949. Died Ingolstadt, 14.7.1968.

Assessed positively as regimental commander. Last assessment 24.10.1943 also good: 'Has proved himself as Feld Kommandant (district commander of occupation troops) particularly in clearance and evacuation tasks . . . stands on the ground of the National Socialist worldview.'

Generalleutnant Kurt Dittmar

Born Magdeburg, 5.1.1891. Prot. Entered Army 6.3.1909. **WWI:** Mainly Pionierbataillon.4; 1918 Hauptmann and Battalion Cdr, III.Inf.Reg.165. **Reichswehr:** Pioneer officer, field and Staff. **WWII:** Oberst, CO, Pionier-Schule II; 15.3.1940 Pionierführer, 1.Armee; 1.4.1940 Generalmajor; 20.2.1941–11.10.1941 CO, 169.Inf.Div.; from 1.4.1942 General, zbV, OKH radio broadcaster explaining Army reports; 25.4.1945 PoW; 18.5.1945 Trent Park. Repatriated 15.5.1948. Died Stadtoldenburg, 26.4.1959.

Generaloberst Johannes Blaskowitz, C-in-C, 1.Armee, summed up Dittmar on 26 February 1941 as: 'Mentally and physically active personality with good soldierly and human qualities. Fighting with 1.Armee he was extraordinarily prudent and independent. Filled the post of Army Engineer-Leader 1 especially well.'

Dittmar's radio commentaries were comparatively realistic assessments of the military situation. Goebbels considered him clever and praised his reporting skills but brought him to heel in July 1944 for speaking too pessimistically in his latest programme and having 'fallen in love with the truth'. Goebbels, *Tagebücher*, Vol. II, 14.1.1944, p. 88 and Vol. 13, 14.7.1944, p. 112.

No detailed CSDIC (UK) opinion available but was considered by Allied interrogators to be a long-winded bore whose image of himself was as the ideal Prussian officer and gentleman. His offer of collaboration was rejected as pure opportunism.

General der Panzertruppe Heinrich Eberbach

Born Stuttgart, 24.11.1895. Prot. Entered Army 1.7.1914. **WWI:** Platoon Leader, Inf.Reg.122; 25.9.1915 severely wounded, PoW (of French); 1917 returned to Germany via Switzerland; 1918 served with 8th Turkish Army in Palestine, final rank Oberleutnant. **Reichswehr:** 13.12.1919 entered police; 1.8.1935 transferred into Army; 1.10.1937 Oberstleutnant; 10.11.1938 CO, Pz.Reg.35. **WWII:** 4.7.1940 awarded Knight's Cross; 1.8.1940 Oberst; from 2.7.1941 CO, 5.Pz.Brigade; 31.12.1941 awarded Oak Leaves; 6.1.1942–25.11.1942, CO, 4.Pz.Div.; 1.3.1942 Generalmajor; 1.1.1943 Generalleutnant; 28.2.1943–14.10.1943 and 25.11.1943–1.6.44 Inspector of Panzertruppen (1.8.1943 General der Panzertruppen); 15.10.1943–24.11.1943 commander various Panzerkorps on Eastern Front; from 7.7.1944 C-in-C, Pz.Gruppe West (5.Pz.Armee); 22.8.1944 Leader, 7.Armee; 31.8.1944 PoW near Amiens; 6.9.1944 Trent Park. Repatriated 6.1.1948. Died Notzingen, 13.7.1992.

During the war Eberbach received very positive assessments from his superiors. On 1 March 1944 Guderian said of him: 'Lively, open character brimming with confidence. Convinced National Socialist active in recruitment. Outstandingly proven in battle as regimental and then divisional commander, commmanding general and leader of Army section. Gutsy, superior panzer leader able to handle the most difficult situations. One of our best, an example of effective leadership by example.' In the column 'His Strong Points' Guderian noted, 'Brave, loyal, firm'.

CSDIC (UK) opinion: 'A strong character with clear-cut views. Has kept aloof from politics. Supported Nazis some years, although never a Party member. Has realised that the Nazi Government is a criminal body to whom he feels no longer bound by his oath. Said that he was in agreement with the Generals' revolt.' Although increasingly critical of the regime he would not participate in making propaganda broadcasts to the German people or similar operations.

OBERLEUTNANT ZUR SEE HEINZ EUGEN EBERBACH
Born Esslingen, 2.7.1921, eldest son of General Eberbach. Entered Kriegsmarine 15.8.1939. **WWII:** November 1941 watchkeeping officer, U-407, eight patrols; June 1944 Cdr, U-967; August 1944 Cdr, U-230, last operational U-boat in Southern France. Attempted to attack Allied invasion fleet; 21.8.1944 grounded boat at St Mandier, destroyed boat by explosives, captured with crew (see his report SRGG 1051, TNA WO208/4168). 20.9.1944–30.11.1944 Trent Park. Repatriated 28.2.1946. 16.11.1956 entered Bundeswehr, last rank Commander. Died 20.11.1982.

GENERALMAJOR KURT EBERDING
Born Reppline/Breslau 18.12.1895. Prot. **WWI:** 2.9.1914 entered Army; 1918 Leutnant, acting Company Cdr, Jaegerbataillon 6; 31.12.1920 discharged. **Reichswehr:** 1.8.1923 reactivated; 10.11.1938 CO, II./Inf.Reg.11. **WWII:** 1.12.1939 Oberstleutnant; 1.10.1941 Oberst; 18.10.1941–20.1.1943 CO, Inf.Reg.53; 18.2.1942 awarded German Cross in Gold; 25.3.1943–14.11.1943 CO, 38.Inf.Div.; 1.9.1943 Generalmajor, transferred Führer-Reserve, various temporary command positions;

5.7.1944 CO, 64.Inf.Div., fought on south bank of Scheldt; 2.11.1944 PoW Knocke, Belgium; 5.11.1944–10.4.1945 Trent Park, then USA. Repatriated 17.8.1947. Died Erlangen, 28.6.1978.

CSDIC (UK) opinion: 'Generalmajor Eberding struck Allied officers as being rather sour, unimaginative and stiff, in fact a typical example of 30 years' service in the German Army. His philosophy appears to consist of "obeying orders" and his religion to be "the destiny of the German people". He is a Nazi type, who must be watched carefully.'

OBERST HORST EGERSDORF
Born Kiel, 15.1.1891. Prot. Entered Army 19.3.1908; 1913 police troop, German South-West Africa. **WWI:** July 1915 PoW; August 1918 exchanged and returned to Germany. **Reichswehr:** Rank at release 31.12.1920 Hauptmann; 1934 re-entered Army. **WWII:** Various administrative appointments including from 1.4.1942 Oberst, Kontroll-kommission Afrika, Morocco; 12.3.1943 City Commandant, Tunis; 8.5.1943 PoW Tunisia; 17.6.1943–16.6.1944 Trent Park, then USA.

Described on 12.12.1942 as: 'Elegant character, uncomplicated, upright personality with good understanding of the service, aware of his obligations and responsibilities. Of average talents. Energetic military comportment combined with a good social attitude, his comradely ways have won him all-round respect and approval. His soldierly nature compensates for what he lacks in the way of mental gifts.'

CSDIC (UK) opinion: An active officer with 'little brain' and 'a frightful snob'. Although claiming to be a Nazi, he read anti-Nazi literature but was more interested in himself than politics.

GENERALLEUTNANT OTTO ELFELDT
Born Sülze/Mecklenburg, 10.10.1895. Prot. Entered Army 27.6.1914. **WWI:** Fuss-Artillerie-Reg.20, finished war as Leutnant, Regimental Adjutant. **Reichswehr:** Artillery units; 1930 Hauptmann, for a time as Battery Cdr. **WWII:** 25.10.1939 Oberstleutnant, artillery Staff Officer, Army Gr.A; 1.6.1940 Oberst; 1.9.1940–19.10.1942 Staff Officer, Generals der Artillerie beim ObdH (C-in-C Army); 26.11.1942–11.11.1943 CO, 302.Inf.Div.; 1.1.1943 Generalmajor; 8.8.1943 Generalleutnant; 17.11.1943 awarded German Cross in Gold; from 27.12.1943 CO, 47.Inf.Div.; 30.7.1944 Cmmdg Gen., LXXXIV.Armeekorps; 20.8.1944 PoW Falaise; 23.8.1944, Trent Park. Repatriated 20.1.1948. Died Bad Schwartau, 23.10.1982.

On 27.9.1943 Commanding General, XVII.Armeekorps, assessed Elfeldt als 'above average'. 'Serious-minded mature personality of great value. National Socialist in word and deed. Close to his men. In the winter campaigns proved himself a brave and determined leader of his then untested Division . . . The tendency mentioned in the assessment of 20.2.1943 of allowing his commanders too much free rein has not reappeared.' In an assessment by General Hube in December 1943 it was reported that 'the depressing events involving the retreat in the East have made him rather pessismistic despite his personal bravery and he is not suitable to be a commanding general.'

CSDIC (UK) opinion: Elfeldt was the first German General to give the Hitler salute on his arrival at Trent Park. 'Although an anti-Nazi, he would not be prepared to overthrow the Party so long as the war lasts, but he has stated that he would consider cooperation with the Western Democracies after Germany's defeat'.

GENERALMAJOR BOTHO ELSTER
Born Berlin, 17.5.1894. Prot. Entered Army 28.2.1913. **WWI:** Mainly served as adjutant, final rank Oberleutnant and Brigade Adjutant, 213.Inf.Div. **Reichswehr:** 1.7.1920 transferred to police; 1.8.1935 re-entered Army as Oberstleutnant and CO, Pz.Abwehr.Abt.3; from 10.11.1938 CO, Pz.Reg.8; 1.8.1939 Oberst. **WWII:** From 2.3.1941 Occupied France; from 28.10.1941 Senior Panzer officer, Army Gr.D; 1.3.1943 Generalmajor; from 30.4.1943 Feldkommandant in France; from 1.4.1944 at Biarritz. At end of August 1944 he led a 20,000-strong force northwards towards the German lines, but was intercepted by US forces on 14.9.1944 and surrendered in the face of hopeless odds. 24.9.1944–26.9.1944 Wilton Park, then USA. Died Böblingen, 24.6.1952.

On 27.2.1943, the Chief of the General Staff, Army Group D, described Elster as 'a strong personality with elan! National Socialist, proven in the face of the enemy, mentally and physically top notch. Energetic, good organiser.' Why he was withdrawn from front-line duties in 1941 and spent the rest of his Wehrmacht career in a military backwater in France is not known.

GENERALMAJOR PAUL VON FELBERT
Born Wiesbaden, 9.11.1894. Prot. Entered Army 9.4.1912. **WWI:** Grossherzoglich-Mecklenburgischer Jägerbataillon.14 Western and Eastern Front; finally Oberleutnant and Company Cdr. **Reichswehr:** Cavalry and infantry units; 1.4.1937 Oberstleutnant. **WWII:** 23.10.1939 CO, Schützen-Reg.8; 1.4.1940 Oberst; 3.6.1940 transferred Führer-Reserve; from 20.7.1942 Feldkommandant, Besançon; 1.10.1943 Generalmajor; 10.9.1944 PoW (French); 28.12.1944–8.8.1945 Trent Park; 3.1.1945 sentenced to death in his absence for cowardice in the face of the enemy. Repatriated 3.11.1947. Died Wiesbaden, 3.2.1973.

CSDIC (UK) opinion: 'A rather weak personality, a definite opponent of National Socialism whose eyes had been opened since being taken prisoner and now believes that attempts should be made to convince Germnan commanders at the front to lay down their weapons.'

GENERALLEUTNANT EDGAR FEUCHTINGER
Born Metz, 9.11.1894. RC. Entered Army 7.8.1914. **WWI:** Artillery units, finally Leutnant. **Reichswehr:** Artillery units; 1.8.1938 Oberstleutnant; 26.8.1939 CO, Art.Reg.227. **WWII:** 1.8.1941 Oberst; 16.8.1942 Führer-Reserve; from 7.4.1943 CO, Schnellen Division West (motorised troops), formed from parts of 21.Pz.Div.; 1.8.1943 Generalmajor; 7.3.1944–15.3.1944 Deputy Leader, 8.Pz.Div. Eastern Front; 1.8.1944 Generalleutnant, from June 1944 involved with 21.Pz.Div. in heavy fighting in Normandy; 6.8.1944 awarded Knight's Cross; 5.1.1945 arrested, confined at Torgau military prison, sentenced to death for corruption and absence without leave (on D-Day, 6.6.1944, was staying with a girl-friend in Paris). Sentence commuted to service at the front as a gunner; 2.3.1945 deserted; 3.5.1945 surrendered to British forces, Hamburg; 29.5.1945–5.7.1945 Trent Park. Repatriated 23.8.1947. 1953 recruited by Soviet military intelligence GRU, betrayed West German defence secrets to the East. Died East Berlin, 21.1.1960, in unknown circumstances at a meet with his controller.

As to the corruption aspect of his death sentence the personal file contains no details. His last assessment of 23 February 1945 states: 'Very active, skilled personality happy to be in the thick of it. Enjoys responsibility. Proven at the front by his resolve and great activity. Led his Division sure-handedly and also quickly dispersed foreign units firmly in hand. Good organiser.'

GENERAL DER FLIEGER JOHANNES FINK
Born Pfullingen/Württemberg, 28.3.1895. Prot. **WWI:** 15.8.1914 entered Army, Company Cdr, Battalion and Regimental Adjutant, Inf.Reg.127, finally Oberleutnant. **Reichswehr:** Various positions, including Signals Officer, Inf.Reg.13; 1.9.1933 transferred into Luftwaffe; 1.6.1938 Oberst. **WWII:** 1.11.1938–20.10.1940 CO, KG 2 (bomber wing); 20.6.1940 awarded Knight's Cross; 1.10.1940 Generalmajor; 1.10.1942 General-leutnant; 1.11.1942–9.2.1944 CO, 2.Flieger Div.; 1.4.1944 General der Flieger; 10.2.1944–11.9.1944 Cmmdg Gen. Luftwaffe, Greece; from 3.2.1945 Führer-Reserve; 23.4.1945 PoW Heggbach (French); 30.4.1945 Trent Park. Repatriated 15.5.1948.

CSDIC (UK) opinion: Considered 'no Nazi', thought the Wehrmacht would cast him off for capitulating without a fight, which in turn freed him from his oath of loyalty. For this reason he felt at liberty to answer truthfully the questions of the British interrogators.

GENERALMAJOR GERHARD FISCHER
Born Greifenberg/Pomerania, 16.5.1894. Prot. **WWI:** 3.8.1914 entered Army, finally Leutnant, Inf.Reg.42. **Reichswehr:** Infantry officer; 1.10.1937 Oberstleutnant. **WWII:** 26.8.1939 CO, Inf.Ersatz-Reg.34; 1.4.1940 CO, Inf.Reg.478; 1.10.1940 Oberst; from 5.2.1941 to Führer-

Reserve and homeland duties because of heart condition; 1.6.1944 Generalmajor; from 2.10.1944 Wehrmacht Kommandant, Koblenz; 26.3.1945 PoW Limburg/Lahn (US); 14.4.1945–5.7.1945 Trent Park. Repatriated 15.5.1948. Died Gielgen near Bonn, 24.3.1967.

Acting Generalkommando XII.Armeekorps (Wiesbaden), where Fischer was course leader for reserve officers, assessed him on 16 March 1943 as: 'Of open, happy nature, strong personality. Good National Socialist, knows how to influence his students with its philosophy. Proven at the front. Specially proven as leader of numerous officer courses. Vigorous and competent.'

CSDIC (UK) opinion: 'A regular officer of a bluff and jovial type, but not a very striking personality. He has a very low opinion of Nazi rule and is thoroughly defeatist.'

GENERALLEUTNANT GOTTHART FRANTZ

Born Berlin, 5.5.1888. Prot. Entered Army 4.3.1907 **WWI:** Cdr, field artillery units, finally Hauptmann and Adjutant, Art.Kommandant.56. **Reichswehr:** 3.8.1921 discharged; 1.11.1937 reactivated, Luftwaffe, Flak Cdr, Oberstleutnant; 1.1.1939 Oberst. **WWII:** 6.7.1940–30.11.1941 CO, Aerial Warfare School, Bernau; 1.9.1941 Generalmajor; 20.12.1941–28.2.1942 Staff Officer, 12.Flak.Div. in Russia; 28.2.1942–20.12.1942 CO, 12.Flak.Div.; from 21.12.1942 CO, 19.Flak.Div. in Tunisia; 1.4.1943 Generalleutnant; 12.5.1943 PoW Tunisia (US); 18.5.1943 awarded Knight's Cross (advised in England); 22.5.1943–21.8.1943 Trent Park, then to USA. Repatriated to Germany 1.2.1945 on health grounds; April 1945 PoW (Soviets), released 2.11.1949. Died Bad Homburg, 21.1.1973.

Assessed on 15.3.1939 as 'A personality with clear objectives, approaches a task with skill or energy. Never idle. Gets involved successfully, based on good knowledge and experiences from current training, has a decisive, uniform influence without limiting the responsibility of the battery commanders . . . fully proven in tense situations. Dyed in the wool soldier and National Socialist, transmits National Socialist philosophy by deed and word in uplifting manner.'

CSDIC (UK) opinion: Another perfect caricature of the Prussian general: 'He is of medium height, slim, beak nose, wrinkled face, thin lips and has been seen without his monocle on only one occasion – that was when he took it out after a few minutes of emotion. He even wears it under his tropical sun-glasses and seems to sleep with it as it is always in place when he is counted in bed in the morning . . . It took him nearly three weeks to learn that it was not the duty of British officers to search the shops of London for red-brown boot-polish, not even for a German General.' He decorated his immaculate uniform with every medal he had ever been awarded, including those from the defunct kingdoms of the old Kaiserreich. His preoccupation with appearance was the source of much hilarity at Trent Park, and Frantz gradually became a totally isolated figure.

GENERALMAJOR GERHARD FRANZ
Born Bobeck, Thuringia, 26.2.1902. Prot. **WWI:** 15.10.1917 NCO, Training School, Weilburg. **Reichswehr:** With Inf.Reg.17; 1.4.1939 Major; 15.7.1939 1a Gen. Staff, 29.Inf.Div. (mot.). **WWII:** 1.4.1941 Oberstleutnant; 24.7.1941 awarded Knight's Cross; 1.1.1942–30.9.1942 Chief General Staff various Armee and Panzer Korps, Eastern Front; 1.7.1942 Oberst; August 1942 sentenced to two years' imprisonment postponed to end of the war (officer of his Staff was shot down behind Russian lines carrying plans for 1942 summer offensive in south); 1.10.1942–15.2.1943 Chief General Staff, Afrika Korps; from 1.9.1944 CO, 256.Inf.Div.; 1.12.1944 Generalmajor; end March 1945 notified of new court martial (lost contact with his Division, Rhein-Main area), 8.4.1945 sought out US forces and surrendered at Birnfeld; 5.5.1945–5.7.1945 Trent Park. Repatriated 15.5.1948. Died Bad Wildungen, 24.12.1975.
   CSDIC (UK) opinion: 'He gave the impression of being a man of above-average intelligence and a strong and outspoken anti-Nazi.'

GENERALMAJOR PAUL GOERBIG
Born Saarbrücken, 23.5.1895. Prot. **WWI:** 8.8.1914 entered Army, pioneer and mortar units; finally Leutnant and Comp. Cdr, Minenwerferbataillon 23. **Reichswehr:** Mortar and mechanised units; 2.10.1938 Oberstleutnant. **WWII:** 10.11.1939 CO, Pz.Abt.67; from 1.11.1939 General Army Office; 1.9.1941 Oberst; 1943/44 Feld-kommandant, 509, Russia; 1.4.1944 Generalmajor; 1945 CO, Sennelager Military Training Depot; 10.4.1945 PoW Bad Grund (US); 29.4.1945 Trent Park. Repatriated 1947. Died Hamburg, 17.8.1974.
   Following an anonymous accusation not proceeded with, the February 1943 character assessment considered Goerbig thus: 'Oberst G. is a very judicious, very shrewd, very well-disposed and perhaps rather mercantile-motivated man (to say trafficker would be going too far) who does favours willingly, enjoys the good life, is a good friend to everybody and by his manner at the present time could easily uplift the people's spirits . . .'
   CSDIC (UK) opinion: 'He is looked upon by officers in touch with him before his arrival at No. II Camp as a smooth, untrustworthy type, endowed with more shrewdness than intelligence and determined to treat his captors courteously in the hope of obtaining some personal advantage.'

GENERALMAJOR ALFRED GUTKNECHT
Born Badingen/Stendal, 20.6.1888. Prot. Entered Army 19.3.1908. **WWI:** April 1914–November 1917 Comp. Cdr police troops, German East Africa; 28.11.1917 PoW (British). **Reichswehr:** 1920 joined German police; 16.6.1936 transferred to Army; 1.4.1936 Oberst; from April 1938

passed over for promotion. **WWII:** 3.10.1939–5.3.1940 Staff Officer, Grenzabschnittskommando Nord (border command), various appointments as Senior Officer, Transport including Staff Officer, AOK 16 (West); 1.7.1942 Generalmajor; from 20.9.1942 Senior Cdr, Transport Troops, West; 29.8.1944 PoW between Reims and Soissons (US); 5.9.1944–25.10.1944 Trent Park, apparently repatriated and in April 1945 employed as Motor Managerial Inspector with Oberbefehlshaber Süd. Suicide, Berlin, 12.11.1946.

CSDIC (UK) opinion: 'PoW seemed to be no fervent Nazi, nor to be very politically minded, but just a patriotic German who realised the hopelesssness of Germany's war situation and who was therefore anxious to see an end made of the present useless sacrifice of lives, even if Germany must sue for peace. He strongly condemns atrocities.'

GENERALMAJOR DR RICHARD HABERMEHL

Born Lauter/Hessen, 19.11.1890. Prot. **WWII:** From 1.8.1939 ministerial adviser and Generalmajor, Luftwaffe, President of Reich Meteorological Office; 14.4.1945 PoW Hanau (US), from 9.5.1945 Trent Park. Repatriated 17.5.1948.

CSDIC (UK) opinion: 'In conversation before his arrival at No. II Camp he has expressed anti-Nazi and anti-militarist views.'

GENERALMAJOR LUDWIG HEILMANN

Born Würzburg, 9.8.1903. RC. **Reichswehr:** 3.2.1921 volunteered Army, 12-year contract NCO career; Inf.Reg.21; 3.2.1933 discharged on completion, Feldwebel and Platoon Leader; 1.7.1934 reactivated in rank of Oberleutnant. **WWII:** 17.6.1940 Comp. Cdr, infantry regiments, finally Inf.Reg.423; 1.8.1940 Major, transferred to Luftwaffe (paratroop arm) and until 14.11.1942 CO, III./Fallschirmjäger-Reg.3, operations in Crete and Soviet Union; 14.6.1941 awarded Knight's Cross; 1.4.1942 Oberstleutnant; 1.12.1943 Oberst; 15.11.1942–16.11.1944 CO, Fallschirmjäger-Reg.3, *inter alia* defence Monte Cassino; 2.3.1944 awarded Oak Leaves; 15.5.1944 awarded Swords; 17.11.1944–5.3.1945 CO, 5.Fallschirmjäger-Div.; 22.12.1944 Generalmajor; 12.4.1945 PoW Adenau; 15.4.1945 Trent Park. Repatriated August 1947. Died Kempten/Allgäu, 26.10.1959.

Assessed as 'an upstanding, reserved personality, straightforward character, is not striking but more than he seems. Rooted in National Socialism upon which his soldierly career is based. Very well proven at the front, crisis-proof, calm, strong nerve. Has proved that he can handle the most difficult situations. As regimental commander is proven as a leader of men, has mastered troop organisation, education and training in outstanding manner. Very approachable and knowledgeable. Average mentally, clear sober judgement, physically fit, tough and has endurance.'

CSDIC (UK) opinion: 'He is very intelligent and has spoken freely to

Allied officers in contact with him before his arrival at No. II Camp. He has been reported by the officers at No. II Camp as an ardent Nazi, which he doubtless was and still is; nevertheless, he justifies his willingness to work with the Allies by the hope it offers of speeding up the termination of the war and rescuing what is left of his home country'.

GENERALLEUTNANT FERDINAND HEIM
Born Reutlingen, 27.2.1895. Prot. Entered Army 24.6.1914. **WWI:** Feldartillerie-Reg.13 and 27; finally Oberleutnant and Regimental Adjutant. **Reichswehr:** Artillery units; 1.5.1935–9.3.1937 tutor at War Academy. **WWII:** 1.8.1939 as Oberst, Chief of General Staff, XVI.Armeekorps; 3.9.1940–14.5.1942 Chief of General Staff, 6.Armee; 1.2.1942 Generalmajor; 1.7.1942–1.11.1942 CO, 14.Pz.Div., involved in push on Stalingrad; 30.8.1942 awarded Knight's Cross; 1.11.1942 Generalleutnant; 1.11.1942–26.11.1942 given charge of XXXXVIII.Pz.Korps with orders to protect 3rd Rumanian Army front north-west of Stalingrad, the Red Army overpowered his weak corps and encircled 6.Armee; Recalled, arrested and imprisoned at Berlin-Moabit; April 1943 hospitalised; July 1943 discharged Wehrmacht (for a detailed description of the foregoing in a conversation with Ramcke see SRGG 1063(c), 25.9.1944, TNA WO208/4169, also Heim, *Seine Kalkulation*, pp. 49–61 and Kehrig, *Stalingrad*, pp. 139–42, 157f, 189f, 263 and 460). Following assassination attempt, on 21.7.1944 Heim petitioned General Schmundt, Hitler's Wehrmacht ADC, for a position 'as an old follower of the Führer' in a situation where 'National Socialist officers are needed'. 1.8.1944 on recommendation of Schmundt's successor, General Burgdorf, Heim was 'reinstated at the disposal of the Army' in rank of Generalleutnant and given charge of the fortress of Boulogne; 23.9.44 PoW of Boulogne; 28.9.1944 Trent Park. Repatriated 16.1.1948. Died Ulm, 14.11.1977.

After his conduct had been praised on 19.9.1944, Burgdorf observed after the fall of Boulogne that Heim had not lived up to his promises. Shortly before his fall from grace, Heim was assessed by Generaloberst Hermann Hoth: 'Cool personality, difficult to penetrate. I confirm his personal bravery and operational knowledge. His independent character needs the occasional severe prod to get him going. Then he carries a thing through to the end. A fully proven and successful panzer leader.'

OBERST EDUARD HELLWIG
Born Marienwerder/West Prussia, 9.10.1895. **WWI:** 4.8.1914 entered Army, artillery units, mainly Feld-Art.Reg.283. **Reichswehr:** 5.12.1918 discharged as Leutnant into Reserve; 15.10.1934 reactivated, Hauptmann. **WWII:** Major and CO, sArt.Abt.536 (heavy artillery battalion), Polish, French and Russian campaigns; 16.4.1942–7.3.1943 CO, Art.Reg.340; 8.3.1943 Art.Reg.661; 20.9.1943 Art.Reg.243;

30.7.1944 PoW Normandy (US); August 1944 short period Trent Park. No further details available.

Characterised by his superiors in January 1944 as 'very clear logical personality, ambitious, keen, good achiever . . . exceptional verve physically and mentally. National Socialist attitude.'

CSDIC (UK) opinion: 'Very anti-Communist.' Believed that Hitler had done great things for Germany but 'should not have involved himself in military matters'. The only hope for Germany was that the Western Allies would prevent the Russians entering the Reich. Told interrogators that he had witnessed the shootings of hostages by the SS and Gestapo in Russia.

Konteradmiral Walter Hennecke

Born Betheln/Hannover, 23.5.1898. **WWI:** 2.10.1915 entered Imperial Navy, served aboard large cruiser *Freya* and battleship *Kaiserin*, finally Leutnant zur See and watchkeeping officer, torpedo boat. **Reichswehr:** Shipboard gunnery officer and instructor; 1.8.1938 Fregattenkapitän. **WWII:** 7.11.1938–29.7.1940 First Officer, cruiser *Nürnberg*; 1.2.1940 Kapitän zur See; 30.7.1940–4.4.1943 CO, Naval Gunnery School; from 6 May 1943 Commandant, Normandy Sea Defence Region; 1.3.1944 Konteradmiral; 26.6.1944 awarded Knight's Cross; 26.6.1944 PoW Cherbourg (US); 3.7.1944–12.9.1944 Trent Park, then Clinton Camp, USA. Repatriated 18.10.1947. Died Bad Lippspringe, 1.1.1984.

CSDIC (UK) opinion: 'Gave the impression of being by no means 100 per cent Nazi. Though he may be anti-Nazi he is not pro-British and out for himself.'

Oberst Ernst Herrmann

Born Frankfurt an der Oder, 30.8.1896. **WWI:** Pioneer units; 7.5.1916 Leutnant; 1.4.1935 as Hauptmann transfer to Luftwaffe. **WWII:** Cdr, searchlight battery; 1.12.1939 Oberstleutnant; 1.12.1939–18.6.1941 CO, Flakartillerie-Schule IV; 3.7.1941 CO, Flak.Reg.30, Cherbourg; 1.3.1942 Oberst; 1.8.1944 awarded Knight's Cross; 24.6.1944 PoW Cherbourg (US); 30.6.1944–23.8.1944 Trent Park. No further details available.

Assessed on 11.3.1944 as being of 'good soldierly appearance. Mature, self-assured personality with serious, clean view on life . . . open honest character not afraid to say what he thinks, tactful before his superiors but puts his case firmly and with conviction. Stands on the ground of the National Socialist worldview and influences his men in this sense.' Herrmann was further assessed on 17 September 1944 when he had already been three months in enemy captivity: 'Imbued with National Socialism by which he has lived his life. It is thus beyond any doubt that he cannot be shaken by enemy propaganda. His high awards and previous record prove that he will commit no dishonourable or unmilitary conduct.'

CSDIC (UK) opinion: 'Not really a Nazi, though afraid to come out in open opposition he criticised Hitler's leadership and expressed the opinion that it was high time for Hitler to abdicate.'

OBERST DR FRIEDRICH AUGUST FREIHERR VON DER HEYDTE
Born Munich, 30.3.1907. RC. **Reichswehr:** 1.4.1925 entered Army; 31.8.1926 left Army as Ensign and studied Law at Innsbrück, Vienna, Graz and Berlin; 1932 Doctorate in Law; 1.3.1935 re-entered Army. **WWII:** at outbreak of war Oberleutnant, Comp. Cdr, Pz.Abwehr.Abt.6; French campaign with 246.Inf.Div.; 15.7.1940 transfer to Luftwaffe paratroops, Comp. Cdr in Fallschirmjäger-Reg.3; as Hauptmann and CO, 1.Bataillon in operations on Crete and Russia; 9.7.1941 awarded Knight's Cross; July 1942–January 1943 Major, CO, Fallschirm-Lehr-Bataillon, North Africa; 15.1.1943 No. 1 Staff officer (1a), 2.Fallschirmjäger-Div.; 15.1.1944 CO, Fallschirmjäger-Div.6 which he led in the fighting at Normandy; 1.7.1944 Oberstleutnant; 18.10.1944 awarded Oak Leaves; 23.12.1944 CO, Fallschirmjäger battle group, PoW Ardennes (US); 23.2.1945 Trent Park. Repatriated 12.7.1947. After war entered politics (CSU 1947), Professor in Law, universities of Mainz and Würzburg (1951–54), Judge, Koblenz (1954–59). Died Aham, Landshut, 7.7.1994.

The only assessment is that of 15.11.1939: 'Very impassioned officer characterised by flexibility, verve and a pronounced mental attitude for operations. Relishes independent decision making and responsibility. Open, decorous in opinions, reliable. To summarise, a personality of probably high warrior-like quality.'

CSDIC (UK) opinion: 'Von der Heydte was an enthusiastic Nazi until he was disillusioned in 1933/34, when he became strongly anti-Nazi. He is believed to be genuinely anxious to cooperate with the Allies to bring the war to an end. He gave a lot of information on the German paratroops and their part in the Ardennes counter-attack.'

GENERALLEUTNANT RÜDIGER VON HEYKING
Born Rastenburg/East Prussia, 10.1.1894. Entered Army 22.3.1914. **WWI:** Platoon and comp. cdr, Inf.Reg.85; 1918 Leutnant, observer KG 2. **Reichswehr:** Kraftfahrt.Abt.4 (mot.); 1.4.1934 transferred Luftwaffe; 1.1.1939 Oberst. **WWII:** 3.2.1938–24.2.1940 CO, Fliegerausbildungs-Reg.2 (aircrew training); 24.2.1940–1941 CO, KG zbV2; 1.11.1941 Generalmajor; 1.7.1943 Generalleutnant; 24.22.1942–4.11.1943 CO, 6.Luftwaffe-Feld-Div., then Führer-Reserve; 20.3.1944 awarded German Cross in Gold; 30.4.1944 CO, 6.Fallschirmjäger-Div.; 3.9.1944 PoW Mons (British); 26.9.1944 Trent Park; May 1945 to USA. Repatriated June 1947. Died Bad Godesberg, 18.2.1956.

Assessed on 14.4.43: 'Generalmajor v. Heyking has led the Division since 26.11.1942. He is a strong, vigorous personality, commander-type. From the first day on has held the reins of his Division very tightly. Well-liked by his subordinates. Enjoys being at the front, always well forward, quick to adapt to new situations. Master of the principles of military tactics and is able to explain them in training. Proven National Socialist.'

CSDIC (UK) opinion: 'Von Heyking is quite friendly and to a great extent cooperative in his attitude to Allied officers. He thinks the war is definitely lost and is disillusioned and disgusted by the commands of Higher HQ.'

GENERALLEUTNANT RUDOLF HOLSTE
Born Hessisch Oldendorf, 9.4.1897. Prot. **WWI:** 15.8.1914 entered Army; Feldart.Reg.62, finally Leutnant. **Reichswehr:** mainly Adjutant, Art.Reg.6; 1.3.1939 Oberstleutnant. **WWII:** 8.12.1939–11.4.1942 CO, Art.Reg.1 and 73; 1.2.1942 Oberst; 6.4.1942 awarded Knight's Cross; 1.1.1943–7.6.1943 acting CO, 14.Pz.Div.; 16.6.1944 acting CO, 4.Kav.Brigade; 27.8.1944 awarded Oak Leaves; 1.10.1944 Generalmajor; 28.2.1945 CO, 4.Kav.Div.; 20.4.1945 as Generalleutnant, acting CO, XXXXI.Armeekorps; 3.5.1945 Wittenberg PoW; 18.5.1945 Trent Park. Repatriated 10.10.1947. Died Baden-Baden, 4.12.1970.

CSDIC (UK) opinion: Of above-average intelligence and fully cooperative. He claimed to have always been anti-Nazi, but it was felt that he was merely an opportunist, and must have kept in well with the Party, otherwise he would not have risen so quickly in rank and prestige.

LEUTNANT KLAUS HUBBUCH
Born Karlsruhe, 1.5.1922. RC. **WWII:** 12.3.1940 entered Army, Pz.Reg.8/15, Pz.Div., North Africa; 1.6.1942 Leutnant, finally Comp. Cdr; March–May 1943 Ordnance Officer to Divisional Commander Generalleutnant Willibald Borowietz; 9.5.1943 PoW Tunisia; end May 1943–30.1.1944 Trent Park, then Canada. Repatriated 26.6.1947. Died Cologne, 1.4.1997.

CSDIC (UK) opinion: 'This young man is a typical Nazi product. Hubbuch has the typical lack of intelligence, narrowness of vision and overwhelming jingoism of the Nazi. He is an unpopular figure except with people like Crüwell, who find him a useful tool. His general knowledge is so limited that it is astounding – so are his manners. He thinks Boes a fine figure and worships Oberst Buhse, another Nazi and one of the early and youngest Knight's Cross winners. If Germany should lose the war, however (an inconceivable event in his opinion), he will try to join a "Freikorps" on the lines of those in existence after the last war, and strive for revenge. He would make an implacable and cruel enemy.'

GENERALMAJOR HEINRICH-HERMANN VON HÜLSEN
Born Weimar, 8.7.1895. Prot. **WWI:** 13.8.1914 entered Army, mainly Leutnant, 4.Garde-Reg. zu Fuss. **Reichswehr:** Cavalry regiments;

1.3.1938 Oberstleutnant. **WWII:** 6.8.1939 CO, Aufklaerungs-Abt.44
(reconnaissance); 1.2.1940, Oberst; 1.4.1941–17.8.1941 CO, Reiter-Reg.2;
2.11.1941 awarded German Cross in Gold; 25.5.1942–15.12.1942 CO,
9.Schützen-Brigade, 9.Pz.Div.; 25.4.1943 as Oberst, acting CO,
21.Pz.Div, Tunisia; 1.5.1943 Generalmajor; 13.5.1943 PoW (France);
26.5.1943–25.5.1944 Trent Park. Repatriated 17.2.1947. Died Celle,
6.6.1982.

Assessed 15.12.1942: 'Blameless character with noticeably elevated
view of life and duty. Correct in his National Socialist attitude. Fully
proven at the front. Has come on well tactically as troop leader. Mentally
and physically extraordinarily active. Full of ideas. Strong side: Very
agile, therefore many-sided, energetic. Combats slackness and
unmilitary conduct harshly without regard to eventual personal
disadvantage. Good instructor. Weak side: inclination to talkativeness
and egotism tends to concern himself overmuch with trivialities.'

CSDIC (UK) opinion: 'This tall, slim German General most certainly
has not the figure of his age. He is very well preserved indeed and one of
the keenest sport enthusiasts here. Hülsen is a strong supporter of the
Nazi clique and of Crüwell. He is always urging the latter to give us as
much trouble as possible, and, of course, Crüwell is only too willing to
listen to his type of talk. On practically the first day here, Hülsen advised
as many people as he could that it was their duty to annoy us and cause
us as much trouble as possible. Hülsen is a hanger-on of the worst type
and is always trying to be with Arnim.'

OBERST ERWIN JÖSTING
Born Remscheid, 30.6.1890. Prot. Entered Army 1911. **WWI:** Company
cdr, finally Oberleutnant (aerial forces). **Reichswehr:** 1920 discharged;
1934 reactivated to Luftwaffe as Hauptmann; 1935 CO, Fliegerhorst
Stade (aerodrome cdr); 1937 Major; 1938 CO, Fliegerhorst Bad Vöslau
near Vienna. **WWII:** 1941 acting CO, Special Staff Bulgaria; 1944 Oberst,
CO, Fliegerhorst Mainz-Finthen; 22.3.1945 PoW (US); 7.4.1945 Trent
Park. Repatriated 1946. Died Gütersloh, 1.6.1953.

CSDIC (UK) opinion: 'He is a Nazi of the Prussian type. To Senior
PoWs he shows himself outspokenly anti-Semitic, while decrying the
unwisdom of atrocities against Jews.'

KONTERADMIRAL OTTO KÄHLER
Born Hamburg, 3.3.1894. Prot. **WWI:** 1.4.1914 entered Imperial Navy,
served on large cruiser *Roon*; 1916, U-boats, finally as Leutnant (Reserve)
and watchkeeping officer UB-112. **Reichswehr:** served mainly aboard
torpedo boats; 1.4.1939 Kapitän zur See. **WWII:** 15.3.1940–20.7.1941
Commander, merchant raider *Thor*, successful cruise Central Atlantic,
then Staff appointments; 22.12.1940 awarded Knight's Cross;
16.10.1942–4.1.1944 Head, Shipping Division, OKM; 1.2.1943

Konteradmiral; from 29.1.1944 Cdr, Naval defences, Brittany; 15.9.1944 awarded Oak Leaves; 18.9.1944 PoW Brest (US); 23.9.1944–25.10.1944 Trent Park. Repatriated 28.2.1947. Died Kiel, 2.11.1967.

On 24.1.1944 the Naval Quartermaster-General described him as 'a personality with strong disposition. Reliable, conscientious, knowledgeable, discreet, pensive. His inner calm allows him to distance himself from all matters. His calm is conditioned by his temperament and reinforced by a philosophical attitude to life.'

CSDIC (UK) opinion: 'Nazi bearing and outlook. Disliked by his fellow PoWs at No. II Camp.'

OBERST KESSLER
CO, Grenadier-Reg. zbV.752 of 326.Inf.Div, to which two Eastern battalions were subordinated; 31.7.1944 PoW Granville, France (US); at Trent Park for a few days from 9.8.1944.

GENERALLEUTNANT HEINRICH KIRCHHEIM
Born Gross Salze/Saale, 6.4.1882. Prot. Entered Army 1.5.1899. October 1904–March 1914 Colonial police, German South-West Africa, finally Oberleutnant. **WWI:** Finally Hauptmann, CO, Jägerbataillon.10; 13.10.1918 Pour-le-Merite. **Reichswehr:** Finally Commandant, Glanz; 31.3.1932 retired; 1.10.1934 reactivated. **WWII:** 1.12.1939–31.1.1941 CO, 169.Inf.Div.; 1.3.1941–15.6.1941 *Sonderstelle* Libya as leader of Italian Div. *Brescia*; 30.4.1941–1.5.1941 led elements of 5.Light Div. in attack on Tobruk, afterwards violent argument with Rommel, who accused him of cowardice for over-protecting his troops; 15.6.1941 OKH Special Staff Tropics; 15.10.1944 Wehrersatz Inspector, Berlin; 1.4.1945 Führer-Reserve; 12.4.1945 PoW Quedlinburg; 4.5.1945 Trent Park. Repatriated 6.10.1947. Died Lüdenscheid, 14.12.1973.

CSDIC (UK) opinion: 'He gave the impression of being an old man, a typical Prussian officer, but with sensible ideas, now at least.'

GENERALLEUTNANT HEINRICH KITTEL
Born Gerolzhofen/Lower Franconia, 31.10.1892. RC. Entered Army 16.7.1911. **WWI:** Platoon/comp. cdr, finally Oberleutnant, Asia Korps. **Reichswehr:** Comp. cdr, infantry. **WWII:** 26.8.1939–30.4.1941 CO, Inf.Reg.42, found too pedantic and transferred to Führer-Reserve; 26.6.1941 Führer-Reserve, Army Gr.Nord; 15.5.1942 Commandant at Stalino, Rostov, Saporoshye, Krivog-Rog, Uman, Tarnopol, Lvov and Cracow; 8.11.1944 City Commandant, Metz and CO, Volksgrenadier Div.462; 12.8.1944 awarded Knight's Cross; in the end-battle for Metz he put himself in the front line and received a leg wound; 22.11.1944 PoW (US); 6.1.1945 Trent Park, May 1945 USA. Repatriated 1947. Died Ansbach, 5.3.1969.

Last assessment October 1944 stated: 'Open, straight character, strong-willed, enjoys responsibility, ruthless towards himself, tirelessly active, gifted organiser. Convinced National Socialist. Proven outstandingly as regimental commander in the West, as troop leader in East. Achieved great things at Cracow by powers of creativity, improvisation. Pronounced leader personality. Has outstanding knowledge of weapons. Mentally flexible. Suitable for divisional commander.'

CSDIC (UK) opinion: 'Kittel is a professional soldier of exceptional intelligence, who in the course of his career has been connected with most major political happenings in Germany. He is strongly opposed to the Nazi "State within the State" and he detests the Police, SS, SD and administration camarilla which advanced in the wake of the German Army. However, because of his oath to Hitler and what he believes to be his duty towards Germany, he will not do or say anything which might damage the war effort of the Reich. He has a strong sense of humour and takes a philisophical outlook on life.'

OBERSTLEUTNANT OTTO KLENK
Born Leipzig, 13.6.1898. **WWI:** 20.3.1915 entered Army, artillery units on Western and Eastern Fronts, finally Leutnant (Res.); 31.1.1919 discharged. **Reichswehr:** 1.10.1937 re-entry, Hauptmann. **WWII:** At outbreak, Regimental Adjutant, Inf.Reg.380; 15.12.1939 to artillery, battery cdr; 27.3.1940 CO, I./Art.Reg.215, France and northern sector, Russian Front; 1.9.1940 Major; 1.4.1942 Oberstleutnant; 11.4.1942–10.5.1943 CO, Art.Reg.305 (including Stalingrad); 6.6.1943 CO, Art.Reg.266, 10.8.1944 PoW Brest (US); mid-August 1944 at Trent Park for short period.

In spring 1942 given positive assessments, but commander of newly formed 305.Inf.Div, would not recommend Klenk as regimental commander because he tended to speak without thinking, liked making trips away and finding himself little dodges, all of which pointed to his not being 'crisis-proof'. Klenk was therefore transferred to 266.Inf.Div., these being occupation troops in Brittany.

CSDIC (UK) opinion: A defeatist and anti-Nazi.

OBERST WALTER KÖHN
Born Magdeburg, 13.1.1895. Prot. Entered Army 11.3.1913. **WWI:** Leutnant, adjutant Inf.Reg.37. **Reichswehr:** 1920 discharged, joined Prussian Landespolizei; 15.10.1935 re-entry Army; 31.12.1937 Oberstleutnant. **WWII:** At outbreak CO III./Inf.Reg.29; 11.11.1939–4.10.1940 adjutant, OKH Inspectorate of Infantry, then CO, Inf.Reg.418; 1.12.1940 Oberst; 22.10.1941 to Führer-Reserve, temporarily 7.Armee Liaison Officer to Kriegsmarine; 14.5.1944 CO, Grenadier Reg.739; 26.6.1944 PoW Cherbourg (US); 6.7.1944–23.8.1944 Trent Park.

Judged on 1.3.1944 by 7.Armee as 'mature and steady personality. Amiable nature, active, stimulating. Correct National Socialist attitude.

Proven at the front. A well-loved comrade.'

CSDIC (UK) opinion: 'A Nazi at heart and one of those who had believed in Hitler, he was badly shattered by German defeats in the West and East and by the attempt on Hitler's life. An embittered Anglophobe, he felt the time had now come for Germany to orientate herself towards Russia, as being the best way out. He strongly criticised the Party leaders and their treatment of high-ranking Army Officers and considered that the Party were now only continuing the war for the sake of prolonging their own lives'.

OBERSTLEUTNANT (RESERVE) KURT KÖHNCKE
Born Lübeck, 19.9.1896. Prot. **WWI:** 12.8.1914 entered Army, Hussar-Reg.6, Inf.Reg.162, and Staff, 91 and 81.Inf.Brigades (Western Front); 31.10.1915 Leutnant (Res.); 6.12.1918 discharged. **Reichswehr:** From May 1924 farmed family estate Frauenmark; August 1932 joined NSDAP; 1.9.1937 entered Luftwaffe as Hauptmann. **WWII:** 1.10.1939 Major; 1.4.1942 Oberstleutnant, CO, (heavy) Flak-Abt.372 Tunisia; 8.5.1943 PoW; 16.5.1943 Trent Park, probably to USA June 1944.

CSDIC (UK) opinion: 'Originated from a wealthy family with large estate in Mecklenburg. He loved his Frauenmark property and had not forgiven the Nazis for their interference in the running of the estate. He seems to have a led a gay youth and married late – only two years ago. Köhncke was an "anti-Nazi" with many interests, liked wining and dining and the high life generally. One of his favourite occupations was gossip and he and his room-mate Oberstleutnant Wolters were like two old women in this respect. All the gossip of the camp was discussed with much amusement. Their room was the nicest at Trent Park. Although a patriot, Köhncke had given a British officer to understand that he was happy at Trent Park because it gave him time to catch up on reading and drawing.'

GENERALMAJOR FRITZ KRAUSE
Born Dahme/Jüterbog, 29.1.1895. Prot. Entered Army 11.11.1913. **WWI:** Artillery; 1917/1918 Oberleutnant, battery cdr, Res.Art.Reg.9. **Reichswehr:** Artillery officer; 1.10.1936 Oberstleutnant; 10.11.1938 CO, Art.Reg.64; 1.6.1939 Oberst. **WWII:** 20.1.1941 Artillery Cdr 104; 15.12.1941 Artillery Cdr 142; 1.7.1942 Generalmajor; 16.8.1942 awarded German Cross in Gold; 1.9.1942 Senior Artillery Cdr, North Africa; 1.1943–3.1943 also 164.Light Div.; April–May 1943 334.Inf.Div.; 9.5.1943 PoW Bizerta; 16.5.1943–23.9.1944 Trent Park. Repatriated 27.6.1947. Died Ingelheim, 14.2.1975.

Assessed by Rommel on 10.2.1943 as 'Straightforward, exemplary character. Positive attitude to National Socialism. Proved himself greatly as senior artillery commander during the major offensives and retreats of summer and winter 1942 in Africa, such that he was promoted to Generalmajor after the capture of Tobruk. Mentally and physically very vigorous and active.'

CSDIC (UK) opinion: A pleasant rather unintelligent man, anti-Nazi. His main occupations at Trent Park were chess, table-tennis and bridge. He was an inspired cello player in the string quartet.

GENERALMAJOR HEINRICH KREIPE
Born Niederspier/Thuringia, 5.6.1895. Prot. **WWI:** 11.8.1914 entered Army, Leutnant, Res.Inf.Reg.237 (Western Front). **Reichswehr:** Infantry officer; 1.10.1938 Oberstleutnant. **WWII:** 26.8.1939 CO, Inf.Reg.909; 1.10.1941 Oberst; 13.10.1941 awarded Knight's Cross; 10.6.1943–24.10.1943 acting CO, 79.Inf.Div.; 1.9.1943 Generalmajor; 15.2.1944 CO, 22.Inf.Div. (Crete); 26.4.1944 Crete, kidnapped by British commandos; 25.5.1944–23.8.1944 Trent Park. Repatriated 12.1947. Died Northeim, 14.6.1976.

His superiors wrote of Kreipe as a strong, energetic personality of firm character. No mention was made in the files of his attitude to National Socialism.

CSDIC (UK) opinion: 'A rather unimportant and unimaginative anti-Nazi, possibly because events are trending that way. Rather weak character and ignorant.'

GENERALMAJOR LUDWIG KRUG
Born Berlin, 23.3.1894. Entered Army 22.3.1914. **WWI:** Leutnant and adjutant, pioneer battalions. **Reichswehr:** (Longest period) comp. cdr, Pionierbataillon.6; 1.10.1936–19.5.1940 CO, Pionierbataillon.34; 1.1.1938 Oberstleutnant. **WWII:** 1.12.1941 Oberst after various Staff appointments; 1.10.1941–7.6.1944 CO, Grenadier-Reg.736; 21.4.1944 awarded German Cross in Silver; 1.7.1944 Generalmajor; 7.6.1944 PoW St Aubin, Normandy; 17.6.1944–8.9.1944 Trent Park. Repatriated 21.2.1946. Died Koblenz, 19.8.1972.

CSDIC (UK) opinion: 'He was a Nazi, but, as he himself stated, not a 110 per cent Nazi, his Nazism being based chiefly on sentimental nationalism and on fear of the consequences for Germany if National Socialism should collapse. He approved of the Nazi ideals, but the 20 July attempt on Hitler's life shattered his morale and he became bitterly disillusioned with the Party'.

GENERALMAJOR KURT FREIHERR VON LIEBENSTEIN
Born Jebenhausen, 28.2.1899. Prot. **WWI:** 20.12.1916 entered Army, finally Leutnant, Dragoner-Reg.26 (Western Front). **Reichswehr** Reiter-Reg.18 (cavalry); 1.4.1937–1.9.1939 Assistant to Military Attaché, Paris; 1.4.1939 Oberstleutnant. **WWII:** Army General Staff; 10.1940–5.1942 Chief of General Staff, Pz.Korps *Guderian* (later Pz.Gr.2); 1.2.1942 Oberst, mid-1942 field, acting CO, 3.Pz.Div.; 19.12.1942 CO,

164.Inf.Div. (Tunisia); 1.3.1943 Generalmajor; 10.5.1943 awarded Knight's Cross; 13.5.1943 PoW Tunisia; 1.6.1943–23.9.1944 Trent Park, Deputy Senior German Officer. Repatriated 1947. 4.6.1956–30.9.1960 Generalmajor, Bundeswehr. Died Munich, 3.8.1975.

In last assessment on 1.10.1942 considered to be: 'Officer with outstanding mental abilities. Confident, clever personality with sound nerve and great inner calm. Personally very brave and ready to serve at front. Embodies the great ideas of National Socialism and the military life and knows how to pass on this worldview philosophy to others.'

CSDIC (UK) opinion: 'This is the most un-German-looking of the Generals. As a result of his travels, he has a broader political outlook than some of the others and definitely belongs to the anti-Nazi group. He also has a keen sense of humour, which is frequently applied against the Nazis. Liebenstein is a talented artist and spends a lot of his time painting very creditable water-colours. He is a great lover of horses and was most grateful when provided with some English hunting scenes for his room. He admires the British and their traditions and detests dictatorship in all its forms. He takes a sympathetic view of the Italians and is of the opinion that they are despised by the Germans more than they deserve. He also admires the culture of the French – and their women, their food and their wines. He speaks quite good English and fairly fluent French.'

GENERALLEUTNANT GERD VON MASSOW
Born Hadersleben/N.Schleswig, 13.9.1896. Prot. **WWI:** 10.8.1914 entered Army, platoon and comp. cdr, Jägerbataillon.7, finally Leutnant. **Reichswehr:** Until 1930, Inf.Reg.18, finally Hauptmann; 1.4.1935 transfer into Luftwaffe; 9.6.1936–7.3.1940 Kommodore, Jagd-Geschwader 2. **WWII:** 1.10.1939 Oberst; 19.7.1940–30.7.1944 Senior Cdr, Fighter and Fighter-Bomber Training School; 1.4.1943 General-major; 31.7.1944 Cmmdg Gen., Aircrew Training; 20.4.1945 Generalleutnant; 5.5.1945 PoW Gmund (US), Trent Park. Repatriated 1.3.1947. Died Bad Pyrmont, 29.6.1967.

GENERALLEUTNANT ERWIN MENNY
Born Saarburg, 10.8.1893. Prot. Entered Army 29.6.1912. **WWI:** Western Front, finally as Oberleutnant, squadron cdr, Dragoner-Reg.22. **Reichswehr:** Reiter-Reg.18; 20.4.1936 CO, Pz.-Abwehr.Abt.35 (anti-tank); 1.8.1937 Oberstleutnant; 31.3.1939 Oberst. **WWII:** 26.8.1939–11.5.1940 CO, Schützen-Ersatz-Reg.81; 12.5.1940 CO, Inf.Reg.69; 15.4.1941–20.7.1942 15.Schützen-Brigade and temporary acting CO, 15.Pz.Div. (North Africa); 26.12.1941 awarded Knight's Cross; 1.4.1942 Generalmajor (Eastern Front); 21.9.1942–31.12.1942 acting CO 123.Inf.Div.; 1.11.1943–30.11.1943 CO, 72.Inf.Div., then transferred to Führer-Reserve; 10.2.1944 CO 84.Inf.Div.; 21.8.1944 PoW Falaise near

Magny (Canadian); 25.8.1944–23.9.1944 Trent Park, then Clinton Camp, USA. Died Freiburg, 6.12.1949.

Assessed on 3.12.1943 as: 'Reserved, clear personality. Likeable character. Convinced National Socialist, confident of its rightness. Personally brave and of exemplary readiness to serve at front. Flexible leader-type personality with clear tactical judgement. Does not know the word "difficulty". Led his men well and surely in a difficult situation and showed understanding for coherence.' At the same time it was thought that as a divisional commander Menny had reached the limit of his capabilities as a troop leader.

CSDIC (UK) opinion: 'A Nazi'.

SS-Brigadeführer und Generalmajor der Waffen-SS Kurt Meyer
Born Jerzheim/Braunschweig, 23.12.1910. **Reichswehr:** entered Landespolizei Mecklenburg 1929; 15.10.1931 entered SS; 15.5.1934 platoon leader, SS-Leibstandarte *Adolf Hitler* (LAH). **WWII:** Hauptsturmführer at LAH regimental Staff; 1.9.1940 CO, Reconnaissance Section; 18.5.1941 awarded Knight's Cross; 21.6.1943 SS-Standartenführer; 23.2.1943 awarded Oak Leaves; June 1943 CO, Pz.Grenadier-Reg.25, SS-Div. *Hitler Jugend*; 1.8.1944 SS-Oberführer; 26.8.1944 awarded Swords; 1.9.1944 SS-Brigadeführer; 7.9.1944 PoW Liege. At first, PoW camp near Compiègne unrecognised, then to Trent Park 17.11.1944-mid-Apr 1945; 10.12.1945 at Aurich, Canadian War Crimes Tribunal; 28.12.1945 sentenced to death, sentence commuted to life imprisonment. Released 7.9.1954. Died Hagen, 23.12.1961.

On 29.4.1943 SS-Obergruppenführer Sepp Dietrich assessed him as 'outstanding, uncommonly mature and responsible personality. As a military leader he combines the greatest personal bravery with outstanding tactical understanding. The great successes achieved by his battle formations especially in the struggle against Bolshevism are unique and attributable solely to his fanatical fighting spirit and prudent leadership.'

Generalmajor Hans von der Mosel
Born Bodenbach, 3.5.1898. Prot. **WWI:** Entered Army; 28.11.1916 Leutnant, Inf.Reg.101. **WWII:** 23.5.1940–30.4.1943 Battalion then Regimental CO, finally of Grendier-Reg.548; 1.7.1940 Oberstleutnant; 1.7.1942 Oberst; 9.8.1942 awarded Knight's Cross; 1.5.1943 CO Fortress Brest; 12.8.1944 Chief of Staff to General Ramcke, Fortress Brest; 1.9.1944 Generalmajor; 19.9.1944 awarded Oak Leaves; 18.9.1944 PoW (US); 25.9.1944–25.10.1944 Trent Park. Repatriated 1948. Died Nienburg, Lower Saxony, 12.4.1969.

CSDIC (UK) opinion: 'Gave the impression that he was 100 per cent behind the Nazi regime. Underlined this fact by clicking his heels and giving the Hitler salute.'

OBERST DR RUDOLF MÜLLER-RÖMER
Born Cologne, 13.6.1895. Prot. Entered Army 22.3.1913. **WWI:** Signals branch, Western Front, Serbia and Russia, finally Leutnant, adjutant, Nachrichten-Ersatz-Abt.7. **Reichswehr:** 9.4.1920 released; 1.10.1933 re-entry, Signals Officer, Glogau Fortress Command Office. **WWII:** Polish campaign, signals officer, Grenzabschnitts-Kommando 13 and Gruppe *Schenckendorff*; 16.4.1940–20.1.1943 CO, Korps-Nachrichten-Abt.435 and 442; 15.10.1943 Signals Commandant, Paris; 25.8.1944 PoW Paris; 8.9.1944 Trent Park.

On 7.4.1943 Römer was assessed: 'Open, exemplary, correct character, military attitude and outlook. National Socialist. Vigorous, enjoys life, comradely, clear and sure in his thinking and dealing. Proven at the front. Mentally very lively with many interests, particularly music. Volunteered for front-line duty (Inf. or Pz.Gren.).' On 10.3.1944 his 'good National Socialist stance' was reported.

CSDIC (UK) opinion: 'Expressed very anti-Nazi views, wanting to see the eradication of Gestapo and SD and of higher SA and Party officials, and said that for the last two years Germany had no further chance of winning the war. He stated that he had never at any time been a follower of Hitler.'

OBERST ARNOLD MUNDORFF
Born 19.1.1898. Entered Army 4.5.1914. **WWI:** Finally Leutnant (Res.) Grenadier-Reg.119, served Eastern Front, Serbia and France. **Reichswehr:** 1.4.1920 transferred to police; August 1935 re-entered Army; 15.10.1935 Hauptmann. **WWII:** 1.10.1939 Oberstleutnant, from outbreak of war CO, infantry battalions; 10.1.1941–20.10.1943 CO, Grenadier-Reg.447, 1.3.1942 Oberst, until July 1944 in Führer-Reserve; 7.7.1944 CO, Grenadier-Reg.922, 243.Inf.Div.; 31.7.1944 PoW Normandy (US); spent first three weeks of August 1944 at Trent Park.

On 16.3.1943 assessed as a regimental commander of average ability. 'Mentally good and active. Handled the demands of the winter war despite his heart condition. On the whole his service achievements are adequate. Convinced National Socialist, reflects the philosophy to his officers and men.'

GENERALLEUTNANT GEORG NEUFFER
Born Steinbach/Oberpfalz, 18.4.1895. Prot. **WWI:** 2.8.1914 entered Army, Bavarian artillery regiments; 7.1917 cdr, AA battery. **Reichswehr:** Artillery regiments; 1.4.1935 transferred to Luftwaffe; 1937 CO, Flak-Abt.88 Legion Condor, Spain. **WWII:** From August 1939 Chief of Staff, various appointments; 1.12.1941–17.4.1942 Chief of Staff, Luftgau-Kommando, Moscow; 18.4.1942–11.11.1942 CO, 5.Flak-Div., Darmstadt; 12.11.1942 CO, 20.Flak.Div., Tunisia; 9.5.1943 PoW Tunisia; 16.5.1943 Trent Park; 1.7.1943 Generalleutnant; 1.8.1943

awarded Knight's Cross. Repatriated 7.10.1947. Died Soest (Holland), 11.5.1977.

CSDIC (UK) opinion: 'A man who radiated charm and goodwill. Well-read, intelligent and a pillar of the "anti-Nazi clique", a good listener. The only long-term officer at Trent Park ever to have a good word for the Russians. Shared several of von Thoma's aversions, e.g. was uncomfortable at wearing his decorations.'

GENERALLEUTNANT RALPH GRAF VON ORIOLA
Born Herischdorf/Silesia, 9.8.1895. RC. Entered Army 5.3.1914. **WWI:** Feldartillerie-Reg.6, Western Front, finally Oberleutnant. **Reichswehr:** Battery cdr, artillery; 1.8.1937 Oberstleutnant. **WWII:** 1.9.1939 CO, Art.Reg.252; 1.6.1940 Oberst; 20.2.1942–16.2.1943 Artillery Cdr, 7.Armee; 17.2.1943–2.5.1943 CO, 72.Inf.Div.; 1.5.1943 Generalmajor; 1.11.1943 Generalleutnant; 3.5.1943–28.6.1944 CO, 299.Inf.Div., Eastern Front; 23.12.1943 awarded Knight's Cross; 12.2.1945 acting CO, XIII.Armeekorps; 31.3.1945 PoW Althausen/Bad Mergentheim; 27.4.1945 Trent Park. Repatriated 17.5.1948. Died Nuremberg, 28.4.1970.

CSDIC (UK) opinion: 'Has impressed Allied officers as intelligent and not arrogant. He is fully cooperative and would like to be employed by the Allies in some capacity in the reconstruction of Germany.'

GENERALMAJOR ALEXANDER VON PFUHLSTEIN
Born Danzig, 17.12.1899. Prot. **WWI:** 29.3.1917 entered Army, finally Leutnant in 4.Garde-Reg. zu Fuss. **WWII:** 3.11.1938–31.3.1941 No. 1 Staff Officer (Ia), 19 and 58.Inf.Div.; 1.6.1939 Oberstleutnant; 29.7.1941–2.3.1942 CO, Inf.Reg.77, then Inf.Reg.154; 1.2.1942 Oberst; 17.8.1942 awarded Knight's Cross; 1.7.1943 Generalmajor; 1.4.1943–10.4.1944 CO, Div. *Brandenburg*; 9.5.1944–5.6.1944 CO, 50.Inf.Div., wounded; 8.8.1944 CO, Hohenstein Fortress; 1.9.1944 arrested by Gestapo, held at Prinz-Albrecht-Strasse; 14.9.1944 on recommendation of Honour Court discharged from Wehrmacht; 24.11.1944 held at Wehrmacht detention facility, Küstrin; 31.1.1945 released. Offered rehabilitation by proving himself at the front. Appointed Major and battalion cdr, but had no intention of going through with assignment and gained second spell in hospital; 2.4.1945 Wertheim (his home town) surrendered to US forces; 20.4.1945–30.8.1945 Trent Park. Died 20.12.1976.

In assessments always portrayed as mentally strong, ambitious and well-proven troop leader inclined at times to pessimism and sarcasm. Respecting his dismissal as commander of 50. Inf.Div. General Weidling wrote: 'Pfuhlstein is a pessimist. Probably brought about by his physical condition. He cannot be committed to the end. He lacks belief in National Socialist ideology. For this reason he is inclined to forgive his men for their apparent failure.' Pfuhlstein had close contacts to the military conspiracy. At the suggestion of Oster, Admiral Canaris chose him as leader of the Brandenburg Division so that in the event of a coup some part of the division would be deployed against the regime. As early as 1943 it was planned for Pfuhlstein to occupy West Berlin and the SS artillery school at Jütebog; but Oster overestimated Pfuhlstein's readiness to act (See Höhne, *Canaris*, p. 473f).

GENERAL DER FALLSCHIRMTRUPPEN BERNHARD RAMCKE
Born Schleswig, 24.8.1889. Prot. Entered Imperial Navy 1905 as officer cadet. **WWI:** Cruiser *Prinz Adalbert*; 1915 naval infantry, Flanders, finally Leutnant zur See; 24.4.1918 awarded Prussian Military Service Cross, the highest decoration for valour. **Reichswehr:** 10.3.1919 transferred to Army, between the wars service with Inf.Reg.2, finally comp. Cdr; 1.3.1937 Oberstleutnant. **WWII:** 1.3.1940 Oberst; 16.1.1940–18.7.1940 CO, Inf.Ersatz-Reg.69; 1.8.1940 transferred to Luftwaffe paratroop arm; May 1941 acting CO, Fallschirmjäger-Sturm-Reg.1 (Crete operation); 1.8.1941 Generalmajor; 1.8.1941 Generalmajor; 21.8.1941 awarded Knight's Cross; 1.4.1942–12.2.1943 CO, Fallschirmjäger-Brigade *Ramcke* (North Africa); 13.11.1942 awarded Oak Leaves; 21.12.1942 Generalleutnant; 13.2.1943 CO, 2.Fallschirmjäger-Div.; 11.8.1944, CO, Brest Fortress, where his bunker was the last to surrender on 19.9.1944. This bunker was found to contain a vast store of cognacs, liquor, enormous quantities of food and other plunder. 19.9.1944 awarded Swords and Diamonds; 27.9.1944–10.4.1945 Trent Park. December 1946 handed over to French; 21.3.1951 sentenced to five years' imprisonment for war crimes at Brest including hostage taking, murder of civilians, looting, intentional burning down of private residences, use of French persons for war work contrary to intenational law, etc. Released 23.6.1951, time served while awaiting trial. Died Kappeln, 5.7.1968.

CSDIC (UK) opinion: 'Ramcke is inordinately vain and has a most extensive knowledge of distorted history; ambitious, ruthless yet naive, an opportunist. As the Nazi Party is on the decline he is beginning to change his views. He claims to have made 800,000 Reichsmark out of his book *From Cabin Boy to Paratroop General*. When captured Ramcke was found to be in possession of a large quantity of French brandy and liqueurs, also a complete dinner service, probably looted. Ramcke makes no bones about the fact that he was determined to win the highest decorations and has described to British officers how he recommended his subordinates for high decorations, knowing full well that the High Command would have to recommend him for a higher award than they received. He was awarded the Swords and Diamonds for his defence of Brest and his last act was to send a WT message to Hitler recommending himself for the award of an estate.' (See GRGG 211,

14–17.9.1944, GRGG 214, 20–23.10.1944, GRGG 221, 10–12.11.1944, TNA WO208/4363.)

Oberst Hans Reimann
Born Wilkonice/Posen, 28.3.1899. Prot. **WWI:** 1917 entered Army; 18.10.1918 Leutnant, Western Front. **Reichswehr:** Oberleutnant Inf.Reg.6; 1.12.1938 Major. **WWII:** French campaign, CO, MG-Bataillon.1; 1.8.1940 Oberstleutnant; June–November 1941 (Russia) CO, Kradschützen-Bataillon.16 (motor-cycle rifle) and II./Schützen-Reg.64 before long period hospitalised; 1.4.1942 Oberst and CO, Pz.Grenadier-Reg.86, 10.Pz.Div.; 8.5.1943 awarded German Cross in Gold; 12.5.1943 PoW Tunisia; 26.6.1943 Trent Park.

Generalmajor Broich assessed him in March as a 'decent, exemplary character, energetic, active, practical and tactful. Especially well-loved comrade, good sociably, humorous. Good National Socialist. Trained his regiment very well and led it successfully at the front.'

CSDIC (UK) opinion: 'This Oberst is a very charming man and violently anti-Nazi, but when recently over-awed by General Crüwell, he disappointingly failed to stick to his guns although usually he makes no attempt to hide his views. He keeps on asking a British Army officer to get him a job on some Allied Commission after the war and feels he would be a successful re-educator of German youth. He is a regular officer from Silesia and is always careful to point out the differences between Silesian and the Prussian proper. He is a great lover of nature and his favourite animal is the sheep. He collects every picture of sheep he can lay his hands on.'

Generalarzt (Generalmajor) Dr med Karl Reiter
Born 1888. **WWII:** 16.4.1945 PoW (British); at Trent Park for a few weeks from end of April 1945.

Oberst Helmuth Rohrbach
Born 24.8.1895. **WWI:** 3.8.1914 entered Army, Inf.Reg.16; from 3.10.1915 Leutnant. **Reichswehr:** Inf.Reg.14; from 1937 Battalion Cdr; 1.10.1938 Oberstleutnant. **WWII:** 10.10.1941 Oberst; 15.11.1941–21.5.1942 German liaison officer to 2nd Italian Army (Yugoslavia); 27.6.1942 CO, Grenadier-Reg.729 (709.Inf.Div., France), fought with this regiment in Normandy; 24.6.1944 PoW Cherbourg (US); 30.6.1944–23.8.1944 Trent Park.

Considered unsuitable for a front-line regiment for mental irresolution – his natural pessimism often made difficulties appear larger than they actually were.

CSDIC (UK) opinion: 'Since capture made several sharp criticisms of the Party and of Hitler, realising that the game was up, although previously he had been a more ardent Nazi, having at one time held a post as liaison officer to some Gauleiter in Berlin'.

OBERSTLEUTNANT JOSEF ROSS
Born 26.2.1898. RC. **WWII:** French campaign, Regimental Adjutant;
from August 1940 Staff Adjutant, 126 Inf.Div.; August 1941 wounded,
Eastern Front, afterwards CO, Ersatzbataillon.184, home territory and
Wehrbezirkskommando Duisburg; January 1944 CO, Ersatz-Reg.416,
Osnabrück; autumn 1944, Commandant, Wesel region; 23.4.1945 PoW
(British).
CSDIC (UK) opinion: 'He has stated that he would gladly work with
the Allies for the building up of a new Germany after the war is over, but
feels strongly that any such action on his part before that moment would
be tantamount to high treason.'

GENERAL DER KAVALLERIE EDWIN GRAF VON ROTHKIRCH UND TRACH
Born Militsch/Silesia, 1.11.1888. Prot. Entered Army 1.3.1908. **WWI:**
Cavalry, Staff and field, finally Rittmeister, 91.Inf.Div. **Reichswehr:**
Cavalry units, 1932 Olympics, equestrianism; 1.10.1934 CO,
Kav.Reg.15; 1.4.1936 Oberst; 1.3.1938 CO, 2.Schützen-Brigade. **WWII:**
12.9.1939 Chief of General Staff, XXXIV.Armeekorps; 1.3.1940
Generalmajor; 25.4.1940–10.10.1940 CO, 442.Landesschützen-Div.;
11.10.1940–4.1.1942 Oberfeldkommandantur 365; 1.3.1942 General-
leutnant; 5.11.1942 awarded German Cross in Gold; 10.1.1942–
7.10.1943 CO, 330.Inf.Div., Eastern Front; 8.10.1943–31.12.1943
General, Security Forces and Military Cdr, White Russia; 1.1.1944
General der Kavallerie, acting CO, various corps, Eastern Front;
3.11.1944 Commdg Gen., LIII.Armeekorps, Western Front; 6.3.1945
PoW Neunkirchen (US); 9.3.1945–5.7.1945 Trent Park. Repatriated 1947.
Died 29.7.1980.
Assessed on 1.3.1944 by Feldmarschall Busch as: 'Eccentric character.
In the winter of 1943, despite great difficulties, rigorously organised the
new area given over to him, setting aside opposition and securing reliable
cooperation with the numerous service offices in his domain. He
handled the local partisan warfare with prudence, tenacity and bravery.
His attitude to National Socialism is undoubted.'
CSDIC (UK) opinion: 'The typical Prussian regular officer aristocrat.
His connections and manners are impeccable. To Allied officers he has
shown himself violently anti-Nazi, probably quite geninely, in view of
his attitude that his class has been ousted by upstarts from its rightful
place in the German sun'. Freiherr von Broich, a Trent Park inmate,
considered Rothkirch 'lacking the least conscience'. He was so close to
the Party and SA that 'we [the Army] were never able to get rid of him'.

GENERALMAJOR ROBERT SATTLER
Born Königshütte, Upper Silesia, 6.12.1891. Entered Army 2.12.1912.

WWI: Inf.Reg.63, finally as Oberleutnant Reichswehr Comp. Cdr. Inf.Reg.15 and 11. **Reichswehr:** 1.4.1937 Oberstleutnant. **WWII:** 1.4.1940 Oberst; 1.9.1939–19.4.1942 CO, Inf.Reg.176, Poland, France and Russia, relieved 'for not showing the necessary alacrity in defensive actions'; 21.1.1942 awarded German Cross in Gold; 1943, CO, Acceptance Office IX for Officer Applicants; 1.10.1943 Generalmajor; 25.4.1944–21.6.1944 CO, Cherbourg fortifications, afterwards CO, Cherbourg town; 27.6.1944 PoW Cherbourg, (US); 5.7.1944–23.9.1944 Trent Park. Died 7.8.1978.

CSDIC (UK) opinion: 'A dumb vain man, who felt that he ought to be a Nazi but didn't quite know what to do about it. He tried to make up for his lack of height by a certain snappishness of manner but was, nervertheless, not unpleasant.' Sattler had not been keen on fighting to the last bullet at Cherbourg. After Schlieben refused to let him sail out from the almost encircled enclave by E-boat (see SRGG 949, 4.7.1944, TNA WO 208 4168), he surrendered his force of 400 to US troops a few days later, upon receipt of their ultimatum. Naval Group West considered Sattler's conduct 'a completely incomprehensible procedure undoubtedly contrary to Hitler's instructions' (see Neitzel, 'Kampf um die deutschen Atlantik- und Kanalfestungen', p. 390).

GENERALLEUTNANT HANS SCHAEFER
Born Triptis/Orla, 3.4.1892. Prot. Entered Army 28.2.1912. **WWI:** Leutnant, including Grenadier-Reg.10. **Reichswehr:** 1.4.1936 Oberst leutnant; 1.10.1938 Oberst. **WWII** 1.9.1939–2.2.1942 CO, Inf.Reg.127, Poland, and 251, Poland and France; 3.2.1942–31.12.1942 CO, 252.Inf.Div.; 1.4.1942 Generalmajor; 1.1.1943 Generalleutnant; 1.1.1943–5.6.1943 CO, 332.Inf.Div.; 28.7.1943 awarded German Cross in Gold; 14.4.1944 CO, 244.Inf.Div. and CO, Marseilles fortifications; 28.8.1944 PoW (US); to CSDIC (West) in France, camp near Marseilles, later Revin north of Charleville; 1.1.1945 Trent Park.

CSDIC (UK) opinion: 'Created a rather bad impression on arrival at No. 11 Camp. He appears to be self-centred and self-satisfied, adopting the air of a spoilt child. He seems not to be a good mixer and is rather intolerant. He appears to be anti-Nazi. He thinks steps should be taken to induce the Wehrmacht to give up the struggle; at the same time he does not believe any such approach has hope of success as long as the Wehrmacht remains one fighting whole.'

GENERALLEUTNANT KURT WILHELM VON SCHLIEBEN
Born Eisenach, 30.10.1894. Prot. **WWI:** 11.8.1914 entered Army, Leutnant, 3.Garde-Reg. zu Fuss; 1.8.1938 Oberstleutnant. **WWII:** 16.8.1939–June 1940, adjutant to acting CO, XIII.Armeekorps; 15.8.1940–20.7.1942 CO, Schützen-Reg.108 (mot.); 1.8.1941 Oberst; 20.7.1942–31.1.1943 CO, 4.Schützen-Brigade; 1.2.1943–31.3.1943 acting

CO, 208.Inf.Div.; 17.3.1943 awarded Knight's Cross; 1.5.1943 General major; 1.4.1943–7.9.1943 CO, 18.Pz.Div.; from 12.12.1943 CO, 709.Inf.Div.; 1.5.1944 Generalleutnant; 21.6.1944 CO, Cherbourg fortifications; 26.6.1944 taken PoW at his Octeville command post; 1.7.1944–9.8.1945 Trent Park. Repatriated 7.10.1947. Died Giessen, 18.6.1964.

CSDIC (UK) opinion: 'With his pink complexion, round boyish face, huge bulk and lumbering gait he gives the appearance of an overgrown, mentally under-developed school-boy type who will bully his inferiors and toady to his superiors. At first very truculent. Polite firmness proved successful. Has more bluff that guts. Like most prisoners of war he is much inclined to self-pity. Conversation with him revealed colossal ignorance. He said the Russians were a primitive people who had really achieved little. Scotland was a completely unknown place to him. He asked if it were hilly or flat.'

GENERALLEUTNANT PAUL SEYFFARDT
Born Weilburg, 4.3.1894. Prot. Entered Army 27.1.1912. **WWI:** Inf.Reg.161, Western Front, finally Oberleutnant and regimental adjutant Reichswehr squadron cdr, Reiter-Reg.15 and 16. **Reichswehr:** 31.7.1937 Oberstleutnant, from 16.2.1939 Inf.Reg.111. **WWII:** 12.3.1940 CO, Inf.Reg.111; 17.1.1942 awarded Knight's Cross; 19.7.1942 Oberst; 12.4.1942–4.11.1943 acting CO then CO, 205.Inf.Div.; 15.5.1943 Generalmajor; 21.1.1944 Generalleutnant; from 7.2.1944 CO, 348.Inf.Div., France; 7.9.1944 PoW Marbaix; 21.9.1944–25.10.1944 Trent Park. Died Baden-Baden, 20.9.1979.

Seyffardt, who in August 1941 received the Infantry Assault Badge as regimental commander, was assessed on 7.11.1943 as follows: 'Dashing personality, of pronounced leader-type nature. Knows how to transmit National Socialist philosophy to his subordinates. Outstandingly well proven at the front. Mentally well adjusted, physically still suffers from wound received in World War I, but tireless and pushes himself hard . . . additionally, as the result of a certain imbalance has the tendency to exaggerate things and does not always express himself truthfully in service reports.'

CSDIC (UK) opinion: This cousin of Feldmarschall Bock 'now sees that one of the big mistakes made by the German Officer Corps was to have allowed themselves to become politically subservient to the Party'.

GENERALLEUTNANT CURT SIEWERT
Born Ratzeburgm 5.4.1899. Prot. **WWI:** 27.12.1916 entered Army, Grenadier-Reg.5, finally Leutnant. **Reichswehr:** 1936 General Staff Officer at OKH (including adjutant to C-in-C Army, Generaloberst von Brauchitsch); 1.4.1939 Oberstleutnant at General Staff. **WWII:** 1.12.1941 Oberst at General Staff; 1.2.1941–14.9.1943 Chief of General Staff

XXXVIII.Armee Korps; 1.12.1943 Generalmajor; 29.2.1944 awarded Knight's Cross; 1.7.1944 Generalleutnant; 15.9.1943–13.4.1945 CO, 58.Inf.Div., wounded, to Führer-Reserve; 4.5.1945 PoW Niendorf near Lübeck (British); 1.6.1945–8.8.1945 Trent Park. Repatriated 15.5.1948. 1957–30.9.1960 Generalmajor, Bundeswehr. Died Hannover, 13.6.1983

Von Siewert's only available assessment is dated 9.11.1938: 'Determined, clear leader-type personality of firm character. Tactful, practical, modest. Suitable for any post at the front or General Staff.'

CSDIC (UK) opinion: Polite and cooperative, very intelligent and decent character, for many years friend of von Thoma. Typically for General Staff officer he blamed the Party (i.e. Hitler) for all negative occurrences. Expressed his readiness to work for Western Allies. Considered 'anti-Nazi', Siewert was prepared to discuss political matters and appeared anxious to learn the true facts about the full extent of German atrocities.

GENERALLEUTNANT MAXIMILIAN SIRY
Born Parsberg, 19.4.1891. RC. Entered Army 25.7.1910. **WWI and Reichswehr:** Artillery units. **WWII:** 1.4.1940–10.1.1942 Senior Artillery Commander 125; 12.1.1942–15.5.1943 CO, 246.Inf.Div.; 13.6.1942 awarded Knight's Cross; 16.5.1943–14.2.1945 Senior Cdr, Coastal Artillery North; from March 1945 CO, 347.Inf.Div.; 10.4.1945 PoW (British), Latimer House. Died Fulda, 6.12.1967.

GENERALLEUTNANT KARL SPANG
Born Mergentheim, 22.1.1886. RC. Entered Army 21.8.1905. **WWI and Reichswehr:** Staff and field, artillery units, finally CO, Artillery-Reg.19; 1.4.1939, Commandant, Westwall Aachen. **WWII:** 24.9.1939 Commandant, Westwall Lower Rhine and CO, Div. *Spang*; 31.5.1940–15.9.1940 Führer-Reserve; 16.9.1940–15.11.1940 Stab AOK Staff, Army High Command 1; 16.11.1940–13.5.1941 CO, 337.Inf.Div. In April 1941 Spang was criticised by his 1a, Major Graf Pückler-Burghaus, as 'suffering acutely from the fact that he had got only a rearward division to command and as he did not even have the clasp to his Iron Cross First Class he felt passed over.' Also predisposed to nervousness, which led to Spang being relieved of command on 13.5.1941. 14.5.1941–7.12.1941 Führer-Reserve; 8.12.1941–30.12.1941 Commandant, Poltava; 31.12.1941–24.5.1942 Commandant, Crimean Isthmus; 25.5.1942–5.10.1942 Commandant, Rearward Army region 585; 6.10.1942–20.11.1942 Commandant, Rearward Army region, 593; 21.11.1942–30.12.1942 CO, Battle-Group *Spang*; 21.12.1942–14.1.1943 acting CO, Army Gr. Don and Commdg Gen. Security Forces; 15.1.1943–1.6.1943 Führer-Reserve; from 1.6.1943 CO, 266.Inf.Div.; 8.8.1944, PoW Brest (US); 12.8.1944–23.9.1944 Trent Park. Died Ellwangen, 29.8.1979.

Spang was considered 'a difficult man', assessed in April 1941 as being 'very nervous, almost morbidly ambitious'.

CSDIC (UK) opinion: 'Mentally deranged and showed signs of suicidal tendencies. Very anti-Nazi.'

GENERALLEUTNANT THEODOR GRAF VON SPONECK
Born Offenburg, 24.1.1896. RC. **WWI:** 12.8.1914 entered Army, Leutnant, Garde-Grenadier-Reg.1, Western and Eastern Fronts; 5.7.1916 awarded Bavarian Military Max Josef Order. **Reichswehr:** Field and Staff; 1.1.1938 Oberstleutnant. **WWII:** 1.10.1938–14.12.1940, No. 1 Staff Officer, XV.Armeekorps; then until 26.1.1942 CO, Schützen-Reg.11; 12.9.1941 awarded Knight's Cross; 22.9.1942 CO, 90.Light-Div.; 12.5.1943 PoW Tunisia; 1.6.1944–23.9.1944 Trent Park. Died Heidesheim an der Brenz, 13.7.1982.

Asessed by Feldmarschall Erwin Rommel on 11.2.1943: 'Leader-type personality with strong character, firm in his resolve and actions. Embodies as a soldier the ideology of National Socialism. Led his Division in difficult defensive actions and retreats in North Africa with prudence, skill and determination and proved himself again in the front line. Energetic mentally and physically and has élan.'

CSDIC (UK) opinion: 'This PoW is somewhat neurotic and very moody. One day he will be exceedingly talkative and amusing and the next he snoops around the place like a dog with his tail between his legs. He is a very talented painter and spends most of his time alone with his work. The ADCs say that he was the most popular General in North Africa with junior officers and the troops. He is one of the best types we have had pass through our hands. PoW is defeatist, anti-Nazi and a monarchist.'

GENERAL DER PANZERTRUPPEN WILHELM RITTER VON THOMA
Born Dachau, 11.9.1891. RC. Entered Army 23.9.1912. **WWI:** 3.Königlich-Bayerisches Inf.Reg., Western and Eastern Fronts (Serbia, Rumania, Russia), finally Oberleutnant and Comp. Cdr. **Reichswehr:** Mostly with 7.Bavarian Inf.Div.; 1.8.1936 Oberstleutnant; 1.4.1938 Oberst; September 1936–May 1939, CO Ground Forces, Legion Condor, awarded by Franco Spanish Cross in Gold with Swords. **WWII:** 1939 CO, Pz.Reg.3, 2.Pz.Div., Poland; 1.8.1940 Generalmajor; from March 1940–July 1941 General der Schnellentruppen at OKH; 17.7.1941–30.9.1941 CO, 17.Pz.Div.; 14.10.1941–21.7.1942 CO, 20.Pz.Div.; 31.12.1941 awarded Knight's Cross; 1.8.1942 Generalleutnant; 1.11.1942 General der Panzertruppen; 1.9.1942–4.11.1942 Cmmdg Gen. Deutsches Afrika Korps; 4.11.1942 PoW Tel-el-Mapsra west of El Alamein (British); 19.11.1942 Trent Park; 17.6.1944 German Senior Officer, Trent Park. 1946 at Wilton Park, leg amputated, repatriated. Died Starnberg, 30.4.1948.

Assessed by Chief of Staff Generaloberst Franz Halder on 6.5.1941 as: 'Warhorse. Front-line soldier through and through with inclination to be adventurous. Outstandingly practical with comprehensive technical knowledge and rich experience of battle. A man who knows how to help out in every situation and never loses his sense of humour. Outstandingly well proven at the front.' On 22.3.1942 General Materna added: 'A great character, energetic, independent leader-type personality, his personal commitment is an example to all and the best possible influence on officers and men. Very caring superior. A Divisional Commander upon whom one can always rely.'

CSDIC (UK) opinion: 'Very intelligent and exeedingly well read. He has a striking personality and is violently anti-Nazi. Plays neither cards nor chess, but prefers to study art, history and politics. His reminiscences are as interesting as his political views and he has had many and varied contacts with all sorts of eminent people from New York actresses to Balkan monarchs. Entirely devoid of "side" and will not suffer fools gladly. He could be a great leader if only he possessed the ability to coordinate his ideas and the courage to support them by action.'

KONTERADMIRAL HANS UDO VON TRESCKOW
Born Wohlau, Silesia 25.6.1893. Entered Imperial Navy 1.4.1912. **WWI:** Served aboard battleship *Deutschland*, then as watchkeeping officer, UB-48, finally Oberleutnant zur See. **Reichswehr:** Various appointments, ship and shore; 1.10.1937 Kapitän zur See; 12.11.1938 CO, Gunnery Section, Kriegsmarine Yard, Wilhelmshaven. **WWII:** 13.8.1942 Naval Commandant, Seine-Somme; 13.9.1944 PoW Le Havre (British); 22.9.1944–25.10.1944 Trent Park. Repatriated 13.1.1947. Died Bückeburg, 5.1.1955.

CSDIC (UK) opinion: 'He was clearly not in agreement with Nazi doctrines, but felt he must still hope for a German victory even if this could only be achieved by a miracle. He belittled the extent of atrocities with which Germans are charged, and the number of people alleged to have carried them out. He does not agree with the scorched-earth policy ordered by the Nazis, but felt helpless in face of it.'

GENERALMAJOR WILHELM ULLERSPERGER
Born Regensburg, 6.8.1894. RC. **WWI:** 2.8.1914 entered Army, Leutnant Bavarian Pionierbataillon.1, fought in France, Serbia and Rumania. **Reichswehr:** Pioneer units; 1931 CO, fortification pioneers, Küstrin, Aschaffenburg and Weisen; 10.10.1937 Oberstleutnant. **WWII:** 1.9.1939–17.4.1940 CO, Pionier-Reg.7; 1.10.1940 Oberst; 18.4.1940–31.5.1942 CO, Pionier-Reg.667; 17.11.1941 awarded German Cross in Gold; 1.6.1942–21.3.1943 Senior Pionier-Offizier 3; 22.3.1943–25.5.1943 Pionierführer, 4.Armee; 16.6.1943–25.10.1943 Pionierführer,

1.Pz.Armee; 14.12.1943 Fortifications Pionierkommandeur 1; 1.8.1944 Generalmajor; 23.11.1944 PoW Strasbourg; 19.12.1944–10.4.1945 Trent Park, then USA. Died Bad Reichenhall, 16.5.1978.

CSDIC (UK) opinion: 'A Nazi-type, but well behaved and polite. He is unpopular with his fellow PW.'

GENERALMAJOR FRANZ VATERRODT
Born Diedenhofen, 24.9.1890. Entered Army 29.11.1909. **WWI:** Leutnant, Inf.Reg.137, finally Hauptmann and comp. cdr. **Reichswehr:** 1.10.1920 transferred to Baden Police; 1.10.1933 Oberst and CO, Baden Police; 1.8.1935 transferred into Army as Oberstleutnant and CO I./Inf.Reg.55. **WWII:** 26.8.1939–31.8.1940 CO, Inf.Reg.14 and 623; 20.8.1940–16.3.1941 CO, Landesschützen-Reg. Stab zbV 56 (Staff); 1.3.1941 Generalmajor; from 17.3.1941 Wehrmacht Commandant, Strasbourg; 25.11.1944 PoW Strasbourg; 30.12.1944 Trent Park; May 1945 transferred to USA.

Six months before he was taken prisoner his assessment reported: 'Practical, very self-possessed personality. Convinced National Socialist. Proved himself as regimental commander in the crossing of the Upper Rhine. Advances the interests of the Wehrmacht with energy and flair . . . maintains good discipline in the field . . . occasionally by harsh punishment.'

CSDIC (UK) opinion: 'Vaterrodt is anti-Nazi, extremely defeatist, and hopes that the war will be over very soon. He suffers from heart trouble and is a rather nervous though pleasant type.'

MAJOR HASSO VIEBIG
Born Neubrandenburg, 21.5.1914, brother of Wilhelm Viebig (below). Entered Army 21.5.1934; 1.4.1936 Leutnant. **WWII:** Hauptmann, served in Poland, France and Russia as regimental adjutant, battery cdr; from 1.9.42 General Staff training; 1.8.1943 Major, 2. Staff Officer, 24.Inf.Div.; 1.2.1944 1. Staff Officer, LXXXIV.Korps; 21.8.1944 PoW Falaise. Repatriated October 1946. 1947 Gehlen military intelligence; 1958 entered Bundeswehr; 30.9.1970 Brigade-General, retired as Deputy CO, 10.Pz.Div. Died Owingen, 16.9.1993.

Asessed on 1.3.1943 as 'Well-integrated personality with serious outlook on life and great awareness of duty. Convinced National Socialist who knows how to disseminate his belief. Very well proven at the front . . . can think for himself, and puts over his ideas in a clear and adroit manner. A hard worker with strongly developed initiative and resolve. Rigorous military approach.'

GENERALMAJOR WILHELM VIEBIG
Born Horst, near Blumental/Ostpriegnitz, 3.6.1899 (brother of Hasso Viebig). Prot. **WWI:** 3.9.1916 entered Army, Feldart.Reg.3, Western

Front, finally Leutnant. **Reichswehr:** Artillery units; 1.1.1937 Major. **WWII:** 1.9.1939–1.12.1941 CO, Art.Reg.257; 1.4.1940 Oberstleutnant; 25.1.1942 awarded German Cross in Gold; 1.3.1942 Oberst; 11.5.1942–18.10.1942 CO, Art.Reg.23; 19.10.1942–15.5.1944 CO, Pz.Art.Reg.93; from 10.8.1944 CO, 277.Volksgrenadier-Div.; 1.1.1945 Generalmajor; 9.3.1945 PoW Nieder Lützingen. Lacking orders on the eastern bank of the Rhine, Viebig, armed only with a single machine gun, with a few infantrymen defended the town until Allied tanks pulled up outside the house he was using as his HQ. 24.4.1945 Trent Park. Repatriated 17.5.1948; from 1952 Warendorf, German Olympic Committee, military equestrian section. Died 16.1.1982.

In his last assessment before capture he was described as being of 'distinguished, blameless character, firm clear personality, a little temperamental, likeable, comradely and sociable. A good National Socialist. His regiment, well trained by him in the West, proved itself unreservedly well in the Italian campaign . . . very caring, protective commander who has successfully trained and deployed his officers on the right lines.'

CSDIC (UK) opinion: 'Like his brother, he was at first arrogant but then became very charming and talked freely. He stated that he is not a Nazi and, as a regular officer, was not a Party member, though, again as a regular officer, he "thought National Socialism". A number of his friends were connected with the 20 July "Putsch", amongst them Hoepner, Lindemann, v. Witzleben and Stieff.'

GENERALMAJOR CARL WAHLE
Born Dresden, 7.2.1892. Prot. Entered Army 25.3.1912. **WWI:** Western Front, Staff and field, mainly in the Saxon Füsilier-Reg.108, finally Oberleutnant. **Reichswehr:** Various positions, including. 10.Inf.Reg.; 1.4.1936 Oberstleutnant,; 1.10.1938 Oberst. **WWII:** 1.8.1938–14.10.1940 Military Attaché, Bucharest (SRGG 1082, 25.12.1944 TNA 4169); 15.10.1940–1.1.1942 CO, Inf.Reg.267; 1.7.1942 Generalmajor; from 1.7.1942 City Commandant, Hamburg (for his report on bombing of the city July/August 1943 see SRGG 1066, 22.8.1944 TNA 4169); 4.8.1943 awarded Knight's Cross of War Service Cross with Swords; 1.1.1944–14.2.1944 CO, 214.Inf.Div.; 15.2.1944–31.7.1944 CO, 719.Inf.Div.; from 1.8.1944 CO, 47.Inf.Div.; 4.9.1944 PoW near Mons (US); 12.9.1944–9.8.1945 Trent Park. Repatriated 30.9.1947. Died Prien/Chiemsee, 23.2.1975.

CSDIC (UK) opinion: 'PoW has been abroad a good deal and has surprisingly sane views on the general political set-up, which includes his attitude towards Russia. Although very anti-Nazi, PoW still feels a queer sense of loyalty towards his government, which, however, appears to be more of a pose, as he is afraid of possible consequences for his family if he admits his real views. An unusual trait in a German general,

PoW tried to stress his great stupidity, when, in reality, he gives the impression of a rather shrewd man of the world.'

OBERST GERHARD WILCK
Born 17.6.1898. **WWI:** 20.11.1916 entered Army, Western Front, Inf.Reg.21, finally Leutnant. **WWII:** 27.8.1939 CO, Inf.Feldersatz-bataillon.16; 1.3.1940–10.8.1941 CO, II./Inf.Reg.362; 1.7.1940 Oberstleutnant, 9.10.1941–30.9.1943 CO, Grenadier-Reg. 362; 1.4.1942 Oberst; 25.11.1943–25.7.1944 CO, Grenadier-Reg.913; from 1.9.1944 acting CO, 246.Volksgrenadier-Div. defending Aachen; 10.10.1944 PoW Aachen; 26.10.1944–31.3.1945 Trent Park.
Last assessment on 24.8.1944 stated: 'Straightforward character, especially reliable, prudent and determined, pronounced leader-personality. Led his regiment in difficult attacks and trench warfare with outstanding success. Correct National Socialist. Of good mental and physical disposition. Above average.'
CSDIC (UK) opinion: An ambiguous personality. He stated that in his opinion the defence of Aachen made no sense from a military standpoint, but his orders did not allow him to capitulate and in any case he feared retaliation against his family. Therefore he thought he had made the best of the situation and was relieved when the Allies occupied the area south of Cologne where his family lived.

OBERST EBERHARD WILDERMUTH
Born Stuttgart, 23.10.1890. 1908/9 One-year volunteer, 1.Württembergisches Grenadier-Reg. linked to study of law at Tübingen, Berlin and Leipzig. **WWI:** 1914 same reg., Western, Eastern and Italian Fronts. **Reichswehr:** 1921 at Stuttgart, attorney at Reich Institute for Unemployment Pay and Labour, ministerial adviser, Reich Labour Ministry; 1928 Director; and 1930 Board Member, Deutsche Bau-und-Boden Bank. **WWII:** 1939 Major (Res.) mobilised, CO, II./Inf.Reg.272, France; 15.8.1940 awarded Knight's Cross; 1941/42 Serbia, CO, Inf.Reg.737, 717.Inf.Div.; 1.12.1941 Oberstleutnant; 1.5.1942 CO, Inf.Reg.317, Eastern Front; 1.12.1942 Oberst; 15.5.1943 CO, Grenadier Reg.578, 305.Inf.Div., Italy; 12.8.1944 Kommandant, Fortress Le Havre; 12.9.1944 PoW Le Havre; 5.11.1944 Trent Park. Repatriated 1946. Postwar involved in domestic politics; 20.9.1949 Federal Minister for Reconstruction. Died Tübingen, 9.3.1952.
CSDIC (UK) opinion: 'Reared in the atmosphere of Württemberg liberalism, PW's outlook was fundamentally liberal but he was a staunch German patriot, a brave officer, and violently opposed to the present regime. He was anxious to re-educate the young Nazis and, to use his own words, "lead them back to the truth". In May 1944 he had expressed to his friend Goerdeler his willingness to cooperate after the latter had sounded him out on his attitude to the impending putsch against Hitler.'

As an Oberst (Res.) he considered the generals 'narrow' and 'lacking in clarity of purpose'. He enjoyed the company of von der Heydte, Eberbach and Heim (see Diary, Wildermuth, 1945 BA/MA NL 251–73 particularly entries 8.3, 6.4, 8.4 and 18.6 of 1945).

86. GENERALMAJOR DETLEF BOCK VON WÜLFINGEN
Born Kassel, 10.12.1895. Entered Army 10.2.1914. **WWI:** Various positions, including Dragoner-Reg.16; finally Oberleutnant. **Reichswehr:** 15.10.1935–28.2.1940 CO, Nachrichten-Abt.28 (signals); 1.8.1937 Oberstleutnant. **WWII:** 1.3.1940–20.12.1940 CO, Nachrichten-Reg.589; 1.6.1940 Oberst; 21.12.1940–15.4.1943 Head of Signals, 17, later 15.Armee; 1.6.1943–24.8.1943 CO, Inf.Reg.311; relieved of command by CO, 217.Inf.Div. for nervousness and repeated criticism of his predecessor, as a result of which he 'had lost respect in the regimental officer corps'. 15.9.1943–31.3.1944 Head of Signals, German Army Mission, Rumania; 1.12.1943 Generalmajor; from 1.9.1944 Feldkommandant 681; 8.9.1944 PoW Liege; 22.9.1944–25.10.1944 Trent Park.

His last assessment on 10.3.1944 stated: 'Soldier of the old school with good human qualities. Very knowledgeable and ideally industrious. His efforts to do his best, linked to a certain nervousness, make him irritable, and then he belittles the efforts of others and generally adopts quite the wrong approach. Convinced National Socialist, proven at the front. Cooperated well with the Rumanians . . . undoubtedly often exaggerates difficulties and makes life difficult for himself.'

CSDIC (UK) opinion: 'Is an egocentric and not very bright. His main interest seems to be the survival of the German nobility. He said that Nazi ideology was firstly against the Jews, secondly against the nobility and thirdly against professional officers. This may well be the reason why he joined the Party himself.'

ABBREVIATIONS

Ia	1. Generalstaboffizier (1. Staff Officer)
1c	3. Generalstaboffizier (3. Staff Officer)
AAO	American Army Officer
AHF	*Arbeitsgemeinschaft historischer Forschungseinrichtungen in der Bundesrepublik Deutschland*
AOK	Armeeoberkommando (Field Army Command)
BA/MA	Bundesarchiv/Militärarchiv
MSg	Militärgeschichtliche Sammlungen
N, NL	Nachlaß (Abatement)
Pers	Personal
RH	Reich Heer
RM	Reich Marine
RW]	Reich Wehrmacht
BAO	British Army Officer
CSDIC	Combined Services Detailed Interrogation Centre
FO	Foreign Office
GAF	German Air Force
GOC	General Officer Commanding
GRGG	General Reports German Generals
GSO	General Staff Officer
IfZ	Institut für Zeitgeschichte (Institute of Contemporary History)
IO	Intelligence Officer
KTB	Kriegstagbuch (War diary)
MGM	*Militärgeschichtliche Mitteilungen*
MGZ	*Militärgeschichtliche Zeitschrift*
NKFD	Nationalkomitee 'Freies Deutschland' (National Committee for a Free Germany)
NKVD	Soviet secret service
ObdH	Oberbefehlshaber des Heeres (Commander-in-Chief of the Army)
OKH	Oberkommando des Heers (Army High Command; Army General Staff)

OKW	Oberkommando der Wehrmacht (Armed Forces High Command)
PW, PoW	Prisoner of war
PRO	The National Archives, Public Record Office (London)
RSHA	Reichssicherheitshauptamt (Reich Security Main Office)
Sipo	Sicherheitspolizei (Secret Security Police)
SR	Special Reports
SRGG	Special Reports German Generals
SRM	Special Reports Army
SRX	Special Reports Mixed
TNA	The National Archives (Kew, Richmond, Surrey)
VfZG	*Vierteljahrshefte für Zeitgeschichte*
WO	War Office
WWR	*Wehrwissenschaftliche Rundschau*
zbV	zur besonderen Verwendung (for special use)
ZfG	*Zeitschrift für Geschichtswissenschaft*

Endnotes

Introduction

1 Of the numerous publications of this kind, one could mention for example: Siewert, 'Schuldig?'.

2 Searle, 'Wehrmacht Generals', p. 282.

3 Amongst them were more than 300 generals. For the full context see Wegner, 'Erschriebene Siege'.

4 See additionally Eckert, 'Kampf um die Akten'.

5 One is accordingly obliged to work with circumstantial evidence, which may be controversial, e.g. see recently Hürter, 'Militäropposition', and the riposte, Ringshausen, 'Paraphen'.

6 The Bundesarchiv/Militärarchiv at Freiburg has few legacies from former Wehrmacht generals providing detailed information about the war period, although the quantity of material is greater than that of the other two services. The diaries of Franz Halder were an early central source of Army history. Other important collections remain in private hands, e.g. letters and diaries of Generalfeldmarschall von Manstein.

7 See e.g. Hartmann, 'Halder', Clasen, 'Reinhardt'. Johannes Hürter discusses this problem in his collective biographical study 'Die deutschen Oberbefehlshaber an der Ostfront 1941/42'. His book 'Gotthard Heinrici' provided a very revealing insight into Heinrici.

8 Author's interview with former naval surgeon at Ijmuiden, Stabsarzt Dr Hans Lauterbach, November 1994. The difficulty here is that Dönitz left no private notes about his wartime service. For further aspects of the problem see also Ruschenbusch, 'Dönitz', Kraus, 'Dönitz'.

9 Rafael Zagovec, in 'Das Deutsche Reich und der Zweite Weltkrieg', Vol. 9/2, pp. 289–381, deals comprehensively with the Western Allies' interrogations of German prisoners. From this he shows that information about the morale of German soldiers was gained but makes no mention that the British were eavesdropping on their prisoners over a long period.

10 Gannon, 'Black May', pp. 334–83, provides a selection of eavesdropped protocols from the period March to August 1943. Blair, 'Der U-Boot Krieg', Vol. 2, p. 949, produces protocols from American camp sources.

11 Among the few to use this source are Schmidt, 'Rudolf Hess', p. 328: protocol SRGG 1236, 20.5.1945, TNA WO 208/4170 (Karl Bodenschatz on Hitler's reaction to Hess's defection) and Hoffmann, 'Staatsstreich', p. 913: protocol SRGG 1219, 15.5.1945, TNA WO 208/4170 (Karl Bodenschatz speaking to an RAF officer about the 20 July plot), both recorded at Latimer House (Luftwaffe overspill unit). Also Toliver/Constable, 'Galland', pp. 307–11; Irving, 'Tragödie der deutschen Laftwaffe', p. 373f. Irving posted Document 135 on an

internet site and refers in his biography of Hitler, 'Führer und Reichskanzler', to protocol SRGG 1133 (TNA WO 208/4169) of which he gives a summary. Graf Rothkirch has never described killing Jews himself.

12 Neitzel, 'Deutsche Generäle'.

13 Files TNA WO 208/4138 and 4139 contain the transcripts of prisoners captured at Normandy, an especially fruitful source of information for historians.

14 Schmundt's activity report, 24/25 June 1943, p. 75.

15 Unless otherwise stated, all are to be found in TNA WO 208/3433, 3504. Duplicates are filed as SRGG reports in WO 208/4363.

16 Overy, 'Verhöre'.

17 For USA see Blair, 'Der U-Boot-Krieg', Vol. 2, p. 949; for Germany see 'Report on Special Installation at Dulag North and Dulag Luft', TNA WO 208/3554. The only known German document is a general report mentioning eavesdropping installations ('Abwehrstelle im Wehrkreis VI', B No. 445/43 g II Kgf, v. 29.7.1943 in BA/MA RH 49/112), but additionally see, 'Dulag Nord Abwehrstelle. b. MOK Nordsee', B. NR.G1123/44 ET 7.6.1944 re technical interrogation of crew members of Canadian destroyer *Athabaskan*, sunk 29.4.1944: BA/MA RM 7/1261. German generals were at least occasionally eavesdropped on by the Soviets; see Leonid Reschin, 'Feldmarschall im Kreuzverhör'.

18 'Hitler's Uranium Club', see D. Hoffmann, 'Operation Epsilon'.

19 CSDIC (UK) was subordinate to the Joint Intelligence Sub-Committee, the Inter-Service Topographical Unit (RN) and the Central Interpretation Unit (RAF, air reconnaissance). The comprehensive weekly Intelligence Summaries are at TNA AIR 22 and TNA ADM 223. For the value of prisoners of war for the overall intelligence picture, e.g. in the Battle of Britain, see K. Jones, 'From the Horse's Mouth', where brief mention is made of the practice of eavesdropping on Luftwaffe crews. See also Fedeorowich, *Axis Prisoners of War*.

20 In their PoW camps the British used a total of 49 secret informers who reported on 1,506 prisoners. See Hinsley, 'British Intelligence', Vol. 1, p. 282f. Cf. CSDIC (UK), p. 6, TNA WO 208/4970.

21 Between 15.7.1942 and the opening of Beaconsfield on 13.12.1942, the interrogation and recording of Italian prisoners was undertaken at Newmarket using a mobile unit near the Italian PoW camp.

22 The usual stay in standard interrogation centres was a few days to several weeks. As soon as it was thought there was nothing more to be gained from him, a prisoner would be shipped out, before 1944, to either Canada or the Near East. Numbers to the end of 1943 were between 300 and 1,850 men, after Normandy this increased rapidly to 144,450 by the end of that year. Wolff, *'Die deutschen, Kriegsgefangenen in britischer Hand'*, p. 20f.

23 Kapitänleutnant Hans-Dietrich Freiherr von Tiesenhausen (22.2.1913–17.8.2000) was taken prisoner on 17.11.1942 when his U-boat was sunk. He arrived at Trent Park on 20.1.1943.

24 The following prisoners were with Crüwell at Trent Park for at least a few weeks from August 1942: Lt Schumann (Army), captured North Africa, 27.5.1942; Oberleutnant Faber, Fw190 pilot shot down 23.6.1942; Oberleutnant Guntram von Waldeck *alias* Krause, allegedly an Fw190 pilot claiming to have been shot down 2.9.1942, probably an informer; from 31.10.1942 Oberleutnant zur See Römer, commander U-353, sunk North Atlantic, 16.10.1942. The first German general

captured by the British, Generalleutnant Johann von Ravenstein, was never at Trent Park.

25 A list of Trent Park prisoners exists only for the period from spring 1945 onwards.

26 No complete list of the prisoners held at Trent Park is available; the names of generals have been adduced from various sources.

27 Certain prisoners of 12.SS-Panzerdivision *Hitler Jugend*, believed to be implicated in the murder of Canadian prisoners in Normandy in June 1944, were interrogated and recorded at London District Cage. Some of these reports are at TNA WO 208/4295. See also Neitzel, 'Des Forschens noch wert?'.

28 Sullivan, 'Auf der Schwelle zum Frieden'.

29 'Future Policy Regarding Interrogation Centres, Joint Intelligence Sub-Committee', Meeting, Tuesday 28 August 1945: TNA WO 208/3451.

30 A large number of generals arrived later at Island Farm Special Camp 11 at Bridgehead, South Wales opened on 6.1.1946. See website at www.islandfarm.fsnet.co.uk.

31 For German generals in American captivity see Krammer, 'American Treatment of German Generals'.

32 Until 1945 the number of personnel at the three centres remained constant. In March 1945 CSDIC (UK) employed 967 staff, 218 of these being engaged on intelligence work, 192 were guards and 28 worked on technical maintenance, War Establishment Committee Investigating Section, CSDIC (UK) 19.3.1945 TNA WO 208/3451.

33 At TNA WO 208/4136–40 there are protocols for 3,838 Kriegsmarine prisoners overheard (SRN 1–4857), 3,609 Luftwaffe prisoners (SRA 1–5836), 2,748 Army and Waffen-SS prisoners (SRM 1–1264) and 2,076 prisoners of several branches together (SRX 1–2141).

34 TNA WO 208/4165–70.

35 TNA WO 208/4363–66, 77, 78.

36 TNA WO 208/4136.

37 TNA WO 208/4161–63.

38 GRGG 243, TNA WO 208/4363 is recommended as an index for all SRGG and GRGG papers to 31.12.1944. 'The Generals – Views of German Senior Officer PoWs', TNA WO 208/5550 is a 12-page synopsis of the 1943 conversations.

39 The identity of this person is not known. In the protocols under identity code A713, the informer is an Oberleutnant Krause, *alias* von Waldeck, allegedly 'shot down in his Fw190 on 2.9.1942'. In June 1943 prisoner A713 was now a Hauptmann 'shot down in his Ju88 on 1.6.1943'. These men were the same person. See SRX 1140, 8.10.1942, WO 208/4161 and SRX 1799, 23.6.1943, TNA WO 208/4163.

40 The true identity of 'Lord Aberfeldy' is unknown. He is not listed in 'Burke's Peerage'. Theodor Graf von Sponeck stated that before the war the British officer lived in Düsseldorf and lost a leg at Dunkirk. Sponeck, 'Meine Erinnerungen', p. 143.

41 CSDIC (UK), S.8, TNA WO 208/4136.

42 At the beginning of 1943, CSDIC (UK) employed 101 foreign nationals. TNA WO 208/3451.

43 SRM 70 to SRM 96, TNA WO 208/4136.

44 CSDIC (UK) especially Appendix E, 'M-Room', TNA WO 208/4970.

45 Menny, BA/MA N267/4.

46 In World War I, he was private secretary to Field-Marshall Douglas Haig; he later became an MP and served 1924–37 as Under-Secretary of State

for Aviation in the Ministry of Transport. See Stansky, 'Sassoon'.
47 From 1947 Trent Park was an Arts Training College under the Ministry of Education. After 1974 it formed part of the Middlesex Polytechnic, since 1992 a university.
48 Menny, BA/MA N267/4.
49 For a forthright description of Trent Park see Ramcke, 'Fallschirmjäger', pp. 79–82 and Heydte, 'Muss ich sterben, will ich fallen', p. 185. Erwin Menny remarked in his diaries that anything that could still be bought in England was incredibly expensive. This was because the British converted *Wehrsold* at a ludicrous rate of 1 pound sterling to 20 Reichsmark. BA/MA N267/4.
50 Menny, BA/MA N267/4.
51 Ibid., and Crüwell Diary, Vol. 2, p. 3.
52 Between November 1942 and January 1943, von Thoma read Clausewitz, 'Vom Kriege'; Goethe, 'Briefe'; Tirpitz, 'Erinnerungen'; Langhoff, 'Moorsoldaten'; Bismarck, 'Gedanken und Erinnerungen'; Friedjung, 'Zeitalter des Imperialismus'. Diary entries, 20.11 and 27.12.1942, 1.1, 11.1. and 17.1.1943. BA/MA N2/3.
53 For example, 'Desert Victory' on 9.4.1943 which von Thoma considered well done and in no way offensive to the Germans. Crüwell thought the Germans would have made a better production of it, SRM 194, 9.4.1943, TNA WO 208/4136. At the end of November 1943 'The Gentle Sex' and a propaganda report about the 'National Kommittee Freies Deutschland' was screened. GRGG 90, 3.–9.10.1943. This was followed in the week beginning 6.2.1944 by 'A Christmas Carol' and 'God Save the King', GRGG 118, TNA WO 208/4363.
54 This applied very much to the camps in France, Belgium and to some extent Germany whence the generals were brought from the United States and Britain after 1945, although the situation deteriorated noticeably in British camps too. Thus von Thoma's bitter complaint in November 1945 about the conditions at Grizedale Hall in Lancashire. Searle, 'Wehrmacht Generals', p. 298.
55 The attacks evoked astonishingly little reaction from the prisoners, as CSDIC (UK) remarked in GRGG 123, 20.–26.2.1944, TNA WO 208/4363.
56 Ferdinand Heim, 'Seine Kalkulation', BA/MA MSg 1/3149 p. 71.
57 See Crüwell's statement, Document 8, 16.5.1943.
58 Ferdinand Heim, 'Seine Kalkulation', BA/MA MSg 1/3149.
59 Telegram 27.1.1941 No. 245 RLM Attaché Group, PAAA, R41141 (according to Rüdiger Overmans).
60 OKW A Ausl/Abw-Abt. 4091/41g, 11.6.1941, BA/MA, RM 7/3137.
61 See e.g. SRN 4677, March 1945, TNA WO 208/4157. For the various warnings not to betray information in captivity see for example 'Extract from SR Draft No 2142', TNA WO 208/4200.
62 See for example, SRN 185, 22.3.1941, TNA WO 208/ 4141; SRN 418, 19.6.1941; SRN 462, 28.6.1941, both TNA WO 208/4142; SRN 741, 10.1.1942 TNA WO 208/4143.
63 See for example SRM 741, 4.8.1944, TNA WO 208/4138.
64 'Extract from Draft No. 2148', 5.3.1944, TNA WO 208/4200.
65 Crüwell noted in his diary on 15.10.1942 (Vol. 2, p. 4) that he had had two days out with Colonel Richardson of the War Office, one to Hampton Court and the other to Windsor and Eton.
66 'Notes on the Extraction of Information from PoWs', MI19, 24.6.1943 TNA WO 208/3438. In mid-June Churchill forbade the 'nonsense' of

'enemy generals being taken on sightseeing tours'. These were then severely restricted without his prior permission. This led to a fall-off in new information, and after CSDIC (UK) complained in March 1944, the ban was relaxed. See reports 11.6.1943, 15.6.1943 and 2.3.1944 in TNA PREM3/363/3.

67 GRGG 72, 14–20.8.1943, TNA WO 208/4363.

68 'Extract from SR Draft 5915' (GG), 16.8.1943, TNA WO 208/3473.

69 'Extract from SR Draft 5917' (GG), 15.8.1943, TNA WO 208/3473.

70 'Extract from SR Draft 5914' (GG), 16.8.1943, TNA WO 208/3473.

71 See Crüwell Diary, Vol. 1, 6.6.1942, p. 22; 13.6.1942, p. 72; 27.6.1942, p. 136; Vol. 2, 15.10.1942, p. 7f. A detailed conversation with Admiral Meixner about the strategic situation is documented at: SRGG 896, 26.4.1944, TNA WO 208/4168.

72 Per Hinsley, 'British Intelligence', Vol. III, I, p. 326f. There is no transcript of a 'V-2 conversation' in the SRM batch containing the spring 1943 discussion between the two officers. In the summary of 1943 conversations there is mention of 'secret rockets'. It was probably here that Thoma made his prophecy. 'The Generals – Views of German Senior Officer PoWs', TNA WO 208/5550.

73 Another exception was a comprehensive discourse by Oberstleutnant von der Heydte regarding his parachute drop during the Ardennes campaign, probably the best detailed description of the operation in existence. To some extent the talk by Oberstleutnant Kogler, Wing Commander JG6, respecting the development of the air war in 1943/44, may have been useful to the Allies. Kogler was shot down during Operation 'Bodenplatte' on 1.1.1945. See SRGG 1131 (Heydte), 26.2.1945, also SRGG 1140 (Kogler), 15.3.1945, TNA WO 208/4169.

74 For all details see Hinsley, 'British Intelligence in the Second World War' (5 vols).

75 So far as can be determined, there were only ever three Austrians at Trent Park: Konter-Admiral Paul Meixner, Oberstleutnant Johann Kogler and Oberstleutnant Wilfried von Mueller-Rienzburg.

76 Kroener, 'Strukturelle Veränderungen'. For the whole context see also Stumpf, 'Wehrmacht-Elite'.

77 Only two generals who served within the Reich or occupied territories received a high decoration: Generalmajor Wahle the rarely awarded Knight's Cross of the War Service Cross with Swords, and Generalmajor Krug the German Cross in Silver.

78 The first long conversation, lasting into the early hours of 21.11.1942, was harmonious except for a difference of opinion on Thoma's attitude to National Socialism. SRM 99, 20.11.1942 and SRM 127, 26.11.1942, TNA WO 208/4136.

79 Thoma's attitude was already clear from a conversation he had with Air Vice-Marshall Conrad Collier during the flight from Cairo to Gibraltar. TNA PREM 3/363/3, SRM 179, 20.11.1942, TNA WO 208/4136.

80 A typical outburst of rage by Thoma is documented in SRX 1610, 28.2.1943, TNA WO 208/4162.

81 SRM 136, 29.11.1942, TNA WO 208/4136.

82 SRM 82, 20.11.1942, similar statements in SRM 102, 21.11.1942; SRX 1422, 26.12.1942; GRGG 179, 24.8.1944, all TNA WO 208/4364 and SRX 1610, 28.2.1943, TNA WO 208/4162.

83 SRM 80, 20.11.1942, TNA WO 208/4136.

84 SRM 136, 29.11.1942, TNA WO 208/4136.

85 He stated this previously in conversation with Thoma, see SRM 98,

21.11.1942, TNA WO 208/4136.

86 SRM 118, 24.11.1942, TNA WO 208/4136.

87 SRM 82, 20.11.1942, TNA WO 208/4136.

88 SRM 79, 20.11.1942, TNA WO 208/4136.

89 Confirmed by Generaloberst von Arnim in respect of both Thoma and General Hans Cramer, from April 1942 to January 1943 Chief of Staff and Commander (General der Schnellen Truppen). See SRGG 191, 4.7.1943, TNA WO 208/4165.

90 Hitler and Thoma served with different Bavarian infantry regiments (Reserve-Reg. No. 16 and No. 3 respectively) and are unlikely to have met during WWI. After his return from American captivity on 27.10.1919, Thoma served with Reichswehr units at Munich where he would have been in close proximity to Hitler and a meeting may have occurred. SRM 78, 20.11.1942, TNA WO 208/4136.

91 For his assertion that a general must lead from the front see SRX 1572, 7.2.1943, TNA WO 208/4162. A rough description of his capture appears in SRM 108, 23.11.1942, TNA WO 208/4136.

92 Liddell Hart, 'Deutsche Generale', p. 79. Liddell Hart met Thoma at the end of 1945 when the expansion of the German panzer arm was discussed.

93 Förster, 'Dynamics of Volksgemeinschaft', p. 204f.

94 BA/MA RH 27/20–97 Materna had this information from Rudolf Ruoff, C-in-C 2.Pz.Armee, who had attended one of Hitler's conferencesd on foreign affairs. To his reply, Materna allegedly responded, 'Yes, but no politics here.' SRX 1648, 11.3.1943. In his diary at the beginning of 1944, with regard to the foregoing, he wrote, 'I was appalled at such ignorance', BA/MA N2/3.

95 Spoeck, 'Erinnerungen', p. 64.

96 Thoma diaries his capture fully: 4.11.1942, BA/MA N2/3.

97 See diary entry, 31.12.1943.

98 SRX 1572, 7.2.1943, TNA WO 208/4162 and SRM 104, 22.11.1942, TNA WO 208/4163. In October 1940 Thoma had been on a fact-finding mission to Libya and provided Hitler with a totally negative impression of the Italian leadership and forces. 'Das Deutsche Reich unde der Zweite Weltkrieg', Vol. 3. pp. 202, 206.

99 No documents of this kind have been found in the files of the General der Schnelltruppen, 17.Pz.Div. (which Thoma commanded from 19.7.1941) nor the OKW.

100 Thoma made only two diary entries about the Russian campaign: on 20.1.1942 he described the cold and the breakdown of order in the front line, and next day the cold and despair in the line, 'I have never known a similar situation in my 12 years' experience of warfare', Thoma Diary, BA/MA N2/2.

101 Thoma Diary, 23.10.1943, BA/MA N2/3.

102 His 1.1.1943 entry compared the situation for Germany as being similar to that of 1917, and references to the greater economic potential of the Allies occur everywhere. Thoma Diary, BA/MA N2/3.

103 Thoma Diary, BA/MA N2/3.

104 Typical of his attitude was his spontaneous reaction to a 'Daily Telegraph' report on 5 November 1942 on the retreat from El Alamein, 'It makes you sick, but actually I had expected it.' He comforted himself with Goebbels's assurance that the war would be decided in Europe: SRX 1212, 5.11.1942, TNA WO 208/4161. For Crüwell's hopes that despite everything the war could be won by the determination of the

central leadership see SRX 1218, 31.10.1942, TNA WO 208/4161; for his reflections on the war situation see SRX 1149, 9.10.1942, TNA WO 208/4161; SRX 1535, 26.1.1943, TNA WO 208/4162; SRGG 342, 12.8.1943, TNA WO 208/4166. He remained unwavering at Trent Park. On 8.4.1944 he provided Admiral Meixner with a written comparison of the respective situations in 1917 and 1944 from which it is clear that he underestimated the Allies' resources, and overestimated those of the Axis. In view of German coastal fortification work he considered an invasion unlikely and doubted that a Russian summer offensive could succeed. 'The thing does not look hopeless', he concluded. SRGG 892, 8.4.1944, TNA WO 208/4168, see also SRGG 819, 4.2.1944, TNA WO 208/4168.

105 SRM 79, 20.11.1942, TNA WO 208/4136.
106 For note about General von Schleicher see Crüwell Papers.
107 SRX 1185, 24.10.1942, TNA WO 208/4161 and SRM 79, 20.11.1942, TNA WO 208/4136.
108 See SRM 82, 20.11.1942, TNA WO 208/4136.
109 Crüwell Diary, Vol. 1, 2.7.1942, p. 173f.
110 Ibid., Vol. 2, 10.7.1943, p. 92.
111 Ibid., Vol. 2, 26.7.1943, p. 103.
112 Ibid., Vol. 1, 26.8.1943, p. 117.
113 Ibid., Vol. 2, 7.5.1944, p. 13.
114 Ibid., Vol. 2, 1.6.1945, p. 133f.
115 Ibid., Vol. 2, 30.11.1944, p. 55.
116 See SRX 1149, 9.10.1942; SRX 1155, 11.10.1942, TNA WO 208/4161.
117 Note on Hitler, Crüwell Papers.
118 SRX 1215, 29.10.1942, TNA WO 208/4161.
119 Crüwell Diary, Vol. 4, 3.9.1945, p. 175f.
120 SRX 1408, 23.12.1942, TNA WO 208/4162.
121 GRGG 42, 15.7.1943, TNA WO 208/4363.
122 SRM 160, 4.2.1943, TNA WO 208/4165.
123 In his memoirs, von Arnim pointed to the overwhelming supply of materials to the Allied side, and the 'drying up' of supplies to the Axis forces, the latter being left finally without air cover. 'It was like being a fireman fighting a dangerous blaze and having someone shut off the water behind your back.' BA/MA N61/4, p. 8.
124 For Frantz's position in the dispute between Thoma and Crüwell see SRGG 161, 27.6.1943, TNA WO 208/4165.
125 On 27 June 1943 Admiral Meixner assured Crüwell of his support, SRGG 163, TNA WO 208/4165, but came down heavily against corruption in the Party, and a few weeks later considered the war lost. Crüwell thought of Meixner as 'an especially nice person in whose company he liked to be', Crüwell Diary, Vol. 3, 1.1.1944, p. 55.
126 For the formation of cliques and the first discussions see GRGG 57, 15.7.1943, TNA WO 208/4363, also letter dated 3.7.1993 from Dr Klaus Hubbuch to General Beckmann. Hubbuch correspondence files.
127 GRGG 113, 9–15.1.1944, TNA WO 208/4363.
128 Compare with the optimistic assessment of Boes in SRGG 428, 21.9.1943, TNA WO 208/4166.
129 In particular Kraus and Schnarrenberger (Thoma clique) and Egersdorf (Crüwell) distanced themselves from this dispute. GRGG 57, TNA WO 208/4363.
130 See Sponeck, 'Meine Erinnerungen', p. 143.
131 SRGG 191, 4.7.1943, TNA WO 208/4165.

132 For von Arnim's discourse see SRGG 204, 9.7.1943, TNA WO 208/4165.
133 See e.g. SRGG 34, 11.7.1943, TNA WO 208/4363.
134 GRGG 58, TNA WO 208/4363. In summer 1943, the prisoners were supplied with the following political books: Spengler, 'Untergang des Abendlandes'; Spengerl, 'Preussentum und Sozialismus'; Heiden, 'Europas Schicksal'; Langhoff, 'Moorsoldaten'; Lochner, What about Germany?'. See GRGG 61, TNA WO 208/4363.
135 Ibid.
136 See GRGG 67, 70, 74, 78, 85, 19–25.9.1943, TNA WO 208/4363. The normal radio programme at Trent Park was as follows: 1000 BBC German news repeated at 1205, 1705 and 2200; 1400 news from Germany; 2140, 2240 and 2330, Calais-Sender (British propaganda broadcast from Bletchley Park); 2300 music from Calais-Sender; 0030 BBC German news in full. GRGG 169, 2–4.8.1944, TNA WO 208/4363.
137 Extract from SR Draft No. 5908 (GG), TNA WO 208/3473.
138 Extract from SR Draft No. 5914 (GG), TNA WO 208/3473.
139 GRGG 106, 5.12.1943, TNA WO 208/4363. The same behaviour continued at Clinton camp in the USA. After one of his 'stupid' speeches on 31.1.1945, when he said that it was only thanks to the Party (i.e. Hitler) that Germany had not yet lost the war, von Arnim was gradually cold-shouldered by most generals. Sponeck, 'Meine Erinnerungen', p. 146.
140 GRGG 115, 23–29.1.1944, TNA WO 208/4363.
141 GRGG 90, 3–9.10.43, TNA WO 208/4363.
142 See GRGG 89, 4.10.1943, TNA WO 208/4363.
143 See GRGG 89, 4.10.1943, TNA WO 208/4363. Here he gave Lord Aberfeldy to understand that the Nazi regime had to disappear. Since 1933 they had done much good, but now had gone too far. 'Then he was asked how, in his opinion, Hitler and his gang should be got rid of, to which he replied, "By killing them".' Further proof of his attitude was a letter of 11.1.1944 to OKW chief Keitel refuting a 'Daily Express' report that Rudolf Hess had visited Trent Park. He finished the correspondence 'Filled with the deepest confidence in our leadership . . . God bless the Führer in his onerous mission!' BA/MA Pers 6/18. The failure to sign off with 'Heil Hitler!' would be seen as ambiguous.
144 See for example SRGG 661, 15.12.1943 and GRGG 107, 19–20.12.1943, TNA WO 208/4363.
145 See SRGG 654, 14.12.1943, TNA WO 208/4167. In his diary Thoma always wrote praising the military successes of the German soldier always adding the rider that they could not change the outcome of the war. See 17.2.1944, 9.4.1944, 8.8.1944. That he was pleased to hear of German defeats is not conveyed by the protocols.
146 Thoma to Lord Aberfeldy, beginning August 1943. GRGG 70, TNA WO 208/4363.
147 On 23.10.1943 Thoma remarked that although one had access to everything in newspapers and radio, there were always those who remained 'unshakeable optimists due to their fears or stupidity. A survey of the military, and above all economic situation, is impossible for them. They keep hoping – and they call it a sober assessment of the situation – as if there actually were any hope!' Thoma Diary, BA/MA N2/3.
148 GRGG 109, 19–25.12.1943, TNA WO 208/4363. Not all inmates were happy with the Christmas sermon delivered by a Swedish priest. Hubbuch wrote indignantly in his diary, 'We should look inside

ourselves and acknowledge our guilt! What does he mean by that? We
withdrew and our enemies devised the war guilt lie in the First World
War.' Hubbuch Diary, 24.12.1943.
149 GRGG 129, 10–16.4.1944 and GRGG 130, 17–23.4.1944, TNA WO
208/4363.
150 Crüwell Diary, Vol. 1, 5.6.1942, p. 18f.
151 Crüwell Diary, Vol. 1, 5.6.1942, p. 5.
152 Crüwell Diary, Vol. 2, 10.8.1943, p. 111. Crüwell is the only prisoner
known to have complained about the catering. In the USA he was
located in the military hospital at Camp Forrest (Tennessee) from
4.2.1945 to 3.5.1945 for his nerves and general debility. Crüwell Diary,
Vol. 4, 11.5.1945, p. 95.
153 GRGG 114, 16–22.1.1944, TNA WO 208/4363.
154 GRGG 123, 20–26.2.1944, TNA WO 208/4363.
155 At first Cramer was not comfortable with the idea of returning home as
a defeated general but eventually accepted that it had been for the
purpose of political prestige that the troops at Stalingrad and Tunisia
had not been extracted. GRGG 98, 1.11.1943; GRGG 106.5,
5–11.12.1943; GRGG 113.9, 15.1.1944; GRGG 123.20, 26.2.1944, TNA
WO 208/4363.
156 GRGG 122.13, 19.2.1944, TNA WO 208/4363.
157 Memoirs, 1896–1944 (written in November 1944), p. 25, 25a.
158 Ibid., pp. 29–30.
159 GRGG 98, 1.11.1943, TNA WO 208/4363.
160 Oberstleutnant von Müller-Rienzburg, 1943, CO pilot training school
A/B7, later allegedly a Luftwaffe liaison officer. According to the British
he was 'shot down in his Fw190 of II/SG4 in Italy' and spent a few
months at Trent Park in the spring of 1944.
161 The actual number of Obristen (colonels) is not known: for them Trent
Park was a transit camp. In addition to these men must be added from
the Mediterranean Generalmajor Kreipe, kidnapped from Crete by the
British, and two regimental commanders of 362.Inf.Div. captured at the
end of May 1944 in Italy and who spent a brief period at Trent Park that
June.
162 In autumn 1944, with one exception, all generals and admirals captured
at Brest (Ramcke, von der Mosel, Erwin Rauch, Otto Kähler and Karl
Weber) as well as von Wülfingen, von Trescow and von Heyking, were
all opposed to listening to the BBC news. GRGG 210.11, 12.10.1944,
TNA WO 208/4364.
163 BA/MA N267/4. Oberst Köhn spoke in similar vein about Thoma's joy
when St Malo was finally surrendered, 'This Thoma is very dangerous,
he is a man who should be hanged as a traitor.' GRGG 177, 22.8.1944,
TNA WO 208/4363. Memoirs, 1896–1944 (written in November 1944),
pp. 25, 25a.
164 For a thoughtful overview on the last battles for the Third Reich from
multi-perspectives see Kunz, 'Wehrmacht und Niederlage'.
165 The conversations were so pessimistic in character that even to the
comparatively phlegmatic Konteradmiral Hennecke it seemed he was
listening to Englishmen rather than Germans. GRGG 158.13, 14.7.1944,
TNA WO 208/4363.
166 Konteradmiral Otto Kähler was the only prisoner at Trent Park who
commented positively on Himmler's speech of 18.10.1944 proclaiming
the setting up of the *Volkssturm*.
167 Thoma rejected as eyewash the propaganda comparisons of the

desperate current military situation with Frederick the Great because the latter was a war between crowned heads and not peoples. Diary, 6.6.1944, BA/MA N2/3. On 24.1.1944 Crüwell observed *Friedrichstag*, remarking that the older he grew, the more Frederick the Great was his idol and 'in these difficult times the image of my hope', Diary, Vol. 3, p. 66.

168 BA/MA N267/4 Menny was at Trent Park between 25.8.1944 and 23.9.1944 before his transfer to Clinton, USA. These lines date from late autumn 1944.

169 See also Reimann's hopes, October 1944, GRGG 216, 26–28.10.1944 TNA WO 208/4364.

170 Fuller reactions to the Ardennes Offensive in GRGG 235, 16–18.12.1944, TNA WO 208/4364.

171 See also Salewski, 'Die Abwehr der Invasion'.

172 BA/MA, MSg 1/1010.

173 Eberbach recognised at Normandy 'that the people upstairs are crazy'. GRGG 277, 28–29.3.1945 TNA WO 208/4177. In 1979 he wrote that at the end of 1944 he had ignored the OKW order to destroy all civilian food depots in France and deport the male population for forced labour in Germany 'because it would show us up as barbarians before the world'. BA/MA MSg1 1/1079. In a report made when Cdr, 3.Pz.Korps on the Eastern Front in October/November 1943, he had stated 'During our retreat we had destroyed *too little* . . . all officers should be advised that more use is to be made of the practice than previously of shooting cowards on the spot.' BA/MA RH10/55. Apparently Eberbach underwent a *volte face* in Normandy.

174 Wahle said that in August 1943 he and Olbricht discussed the whole situation and what should be done. 'I told Olbricht there was nothing left for us but honourable defeat. He replied, "What do you want then, a people of 80 million simply cannot just go down." Then I saw that Olbricht no longer had much hope.' SRGG 1038, 10.9.1944, TNA WO 208/4168.

175 Elster reported fully on his capture to General Ramcke. SRGG 1061(c), 24.9.1944, TNA WO 208/4169. General Graf von Schwerin was accused in 1946 at the generals' camp at Neu-Ulm of having capitulated too quickly in April 1945. Searle, 'Wehrmacht Generals', p. 26f.

176 BA/MA N267/4.

177 Wildermuth Diary, 11.3.1945, BA/MA, NL 251/73. In mid-November 1944, Heim said, 'Therefore the only thing to do is carry on fighting, hold out to the last, even if that means we lose everything. A people which fights to the last moment finds the moral strength to rise again, a people which throws its weapons into the cornfield is finished for ever, history proves it.' GRGG 221, 10–12.11.1944, TNA WO 208/4364. SS-Brigadeführer Meyer spoke out similarly, but later changed his opinion. GRGG 229, 27.11.1944–1.12.1944, TNA WO 208/4364.

178 Wildermuth Diary, 18.5.1945, BA/MA NL 251/73.

179 Hildegard Hamm-Brücher, conversation at Aschaffenburg, 17.7.2004.

180 GRGG 273, 16–19 March 1945, TNA WO 208/4177. The address appears in SRGG 1140, 15.3.1945, TNA WO 208/4169.

181 GRGG 286, 19–21.4.1945, TNA WO 208/4179.

182 General der Flieger Karl Heinrich Bodenschatz (1890–1979), Luftwaffe Liaison Officer at FHQ.

183 GRGG 323, 30.6.1945–5.7.1945, TNA WO 208/4179.

184 Neitzel, 'Kampf um die Atlantik und Kanalfestungen'.

185 Henke, 'Besetzung Deutschlands', p. 155.
186 Ibid., p. 154ff.
187 Ibid., pp. 357–62.
188 Of the 3,149 Wehrmacht generals, 372 fell in the field in WWII and another 171 died as PoWs, about 17 per cent. The total of all Wehrmacht dead was 34 per cent, twice as high. Searle, 'Wehrmacht Generals', p. 17f; Overmans, 'Militärische Verluste', p. 319. The full list of dead Wehrmacht generals appears in Foltmann/Möller-Witten, 'Opfergang'.
189 GRGG 254, 28–31.1.1945, TNA WO 208/4365.
190 Clausewitz, 'Vom Kriege', p. 243.
191 By contrast he did not react positively to Goebbels's speech of 18.2.1943, see Document 7.
192 Similarly, see Konteradmiral Hennecke, GRGG 170, 5–8.8.1944, TNA WO 208/4363.
193 von Schlieben, GRGG 174, 15–16.8.1944, TNA WO 208/4363.
194 In the published protocols, remarks were made by Thoma, Neuffer, Felbert and Hennecke. There are similar expressions in the unpublished material, see e.g. GRGG 139, 3.6.1944 (Bassenge), GRGG 180, 25–26.8.1944 (Spang), TNA WO 208/4363.
195 On 23.10.1943 he wrote of the higher generals, 'None of them served the Fatherland, but were the stooges of a sick man who could not think clearly. How bitter a thing that the Fatherland will be destroyed because of it.' He criticised Hitler's advisers and adjutants in similar vein in the 30.1.1944 entry. BA/MA N2/3.
196 See also GRGG 329.6, 20.7.1945, TNA WO 208/4179.
197 In autumn 1944, Bassenge spread the rumour that all ranks from Oberst upwards would be put on trial after the war. GRGG 216.26, 28.10.1944, TNA WO 208/4363.
198 GRGG 201.18, 19.5.1945, TNA WO 208/4177.
199 Thus Wildermuth's worries about his family expressed in his diary take on a central importance. Wildermuth Diary, BA/MA NL 251/73.
200 For the general hatred of Communism see e.g. GRGG 25, GRGG 26, TNA WO 208/ 4363, SRX 1581 13.2.1943, TNA WO 208/4162.
201 See e.g. GRGG 178, 23.8.1944 (Aulock), GRGG 181, 25.8.1944 (Choltitz), TNA WO 208/4363.
202 See e.g. GRGG 12, TNA WO 208/4363.
203 Wildermuth Diary, 13.5.1945, BA/MA NL 251/73.
204 SRX 1648, 11.3.1943, TNA WO 208/4162.
205 The protocols contain few details reports about anti-partisan operations in the East. Von Schlieben told Bassenge about a large operation on the Eastern Front in which 2,000 prisoners had been shot by Russian auxiliary troops. GRGG 231.2, 6–7.12.1944, TNA WO 208/4364.
206 Thoma, see e.g. SRX 1401, 17.12.1942, TNA WO 208/4161.
207 On 3.5.1945 Thoma wrote that the 'horrors of the concentration camps far exceeded what one could accept, since one only heard the occasional rumour.' Diary, BA/MA N2/3. What he actually knew about the extermination of the Jews is unknown; the entry might have been written to cover his back.
208 Thus von Thoma talked about the mass graves of Jews at Odessa and Sevastopol, places where he had never been. SRX 1739, 7.4.1943, TNA WO 208/4163. Kreipe found 'shameful' those 'measures which had been taken to transfer the Jews out', GRGG 139, 3.6.1944, TNA WO 208/4363.
209 GRGG 323, 30.6.1945–5.7.1945, TNA WO 208/4178.

210 Generalmajor Sattler, captured at Cherbourg on 27.6.1944 and who had fought in France and Russia stated, 'When I think back on the rumours I heard about the shootings in Poland, then the Hungarian Jews, the shootings in the Balkans. In France there was a lot of truth in it – the shootings and so on. GRGG 168, 31.7.1944–1.8.1944, TNA WO 208/4363. Although he had heard of the atrocities, apparently he did not know the scale.

211 Other protocols show the horror of some inmates at the crimes against the Jews, see e.g. GRGG 231, 6–7.12.1944, TNA WO 208/4363. Wildermuth noted on 20.4.1945 about the Allied reports on the concentration camps, 'The impression is fearsome. Even here amongst the generals. It is the moral sentence of death on Germany.' BA/MA NL 251/73.

212 See e.g. Franz and König in GRGG 297, 10.5.1945, TNA WO 208/4177 or Generalmajor Dornberger, GRGG 344.8, 13.8.1944, TNA WO 208/4179.

213 See also Köhn, 2.7.1944, the Soviets did not want peace because they had fallen too far under Jewish influence, GRGG 153, 3.7.1944, TNA WO 208/4363 and Oberst Aulock, 'On balance the British have lost the war as much as we have. The American Jew has won it by the money he has made.' GRGG 178, 23.8.1944, TNA WO 208/4363.

214 For Crüwell's anti-Jewish utterances see also SRX 1221, 1.11.1942, TNA WO 208/4161: for racial discourses see also SRX 1094, 26.8.1942, TNA WO 208/4161; for Thoma's remarks to a British officer about Jewish immigration into Germany in the inter-war period see SRGG 301, 28.7.1943, TNA WO 208/4166 and in similar vein to Burckhardt SRX 1536, 26.1.1943, TNA WO 208/4162. For Thoma's, and particularly von Sponeck's remarks on the inaccuracy of Nazi propaganda respecting Jews, GRGG 175.17, 18.8.1944, TNA WO 208/4363. For Ullersperger on the degenerative Jewish influence and the dangers of mixed marriages GRGG 262, 18–20.2.1945, TNA WO 208/4177.

215 SRX 1577, 11.2.1943, TNA WO 208/4162.

216 SRX 1184, 23.10.1942, TNA WO 208/4161.

217 Crüwell, for example, see SRX 1579, 12.2.1943, TNA WO 208/4162 or König, GRGG 302, 20–23.5.1945, TNA WO 208/4177.

218 Meyer visited Eberding in his room, to the latter's disgust. Although they had long talks from time to time, Meyer mostly kept to his own quarters. GRGG 227, 22–23.11.1944, TNA WO 208/4364. Broich was concerned that the '100 per cent Nazi' in the ranks would send secret reports to the Reich about everybody's political opinions. GRGG 224, 17–18.11.1944, TNA WO 208/4364.

219 Dunckern never came to Trent Park. After long interrogations at Wilton Park he was sent to the USA.

220 SRGG 1133, 9.3.1945, TNA WO 208/4169.

221 As a precaution for possible charges by the Allies, the two lawyers at Trent Park, von der Hedte and Wildermuth, delivered talks describing what war crimes were and how one should act in proceedings as a witness or the accused. SRGG 1141, 3.4.1945, TNA WO 208/4177.

222 GRGG 371, 10–12.3.1945, TNA WO 208/4177.

223 He reported on the anti-partisan war at GRGG 172, 8–12.8.1944, TNA WO 208/4363. The 266.Inf.Div. War Diary has no valuable information about engagements between the Division and partisans. BA/MA RH26-266-9 (June–July 1944).

224 See note 205.

225 Halder, 'Kriegstagebuch', Vol. III, p. 243.
226 Ic, Interrogation Report. BA/MA RH21-2/654, pp. 250 and 253.
227 Ic, Report of 17.Pz.Div. to Pz.Gr.2, Ic BA/MA RH21-2/658 p. 222.
228 Ic Activity Report 17.8.1941–30.4.1942, BA/MA RH 27/20/189.
229 Oberleutnant Filster, adjutant, I/SR.59 of 20.Pz.Div. on 20.4.1942 drafted a memorandum on the Soviets in which he said, 'To destroy them requires the harshest, most ruthless methods with all the physically and morally destructive weapons available . . . ' His 1a, Major Stoecker approved the clarity and style of the documented but then regretted that the racial differences had been underplayed. Thoma noted on the covering sheet 'For the War Diary', but his opinion is not recorded. BA/MA RH27/20–108.
230 Ic Report 11.Pz.Div. to XXXXVIII.Armeekorps, 14.7.1941, BA/MA RH24-48/198, Anl.29.
231 The protocols provide no definite indication as to which of the Trent Park inmates were involved in which war crimes. For the problem of proof, see note 329 to documents, below.
232 SRGG 520, 3.11.1943, TNA WO 208/4167.
233 See also SRX 1579, 12.2.1943, TNA WO 208/4162.
234 SRGG 495, 21.10.1943, TNA WO 208/4166.
235 For the most recent study on the military resistance see Heinemann, 'Der militärische Widerstand'.
236 Irving, 'Rommel'; Fraser, 'Knight's Cross'; Reuth, 'Das Ende einer Legende'.
237 Remy, 'Mythos Rommel', pp. 277 and 286.
238 Irving and Fraser both rely on GRGG 1347, report of 19.8.1945 in TNA WO 208/4170, where Eberbach quoted Rommel as having said that Hitler 'must be got rid of [loswerden]'.
239 On 14.10.1952 Eberbach wrote to historian Percy Schramm, 'It was not Rommel's intention to murder Hitler, but to put him on trial.' BA/MA MSg 1/1079. On 15.5.1979 in a memorandum regarding his conversation with Rommel on 17.7.1944, Eberbach insisted he could only recall Rommel saying 'Hitler must go', BA/MA 15.5.1979 MSg 1/1079.
240 Thoma Diary, 30.1.1945, BA/MA N2/3.
241 Heim, 'Seine Kalkulation', p. 70, BA/MA MSg 1/3149.
242 GRGG 149, 22–27.6.1944, SRGG 506, 24.10.1943, TNA WO 208/4166.
243 SRGG 813, TNA WO 208/4167.
244 Researchers doubt whether Blumentritt, Rundstedt's Chief of Staff, and his 1a, Bodo Zimmermann, answered in this form. Ose, 'Entscheidung im Westen', p. 157; Ziemke, 'Des Führers gehorsamer Diener', p. 489; see also Messenger, 'The Last Prussian', p. 197f.
245 See also Kroener, 'Fromm', e.g. p. 323.
246 Thoma Diary, 8.8.1944. BA/MA N2/3.
247 Some prisoners spoke on this theme only incidentally. Hennecke remarked on 21.7.1944 that he feared the attempt might lead to civil war. If Germany were defeated, Communism might then hold the balance. SRGG 963, 21.7.1944, TNA WO 208/4168. Menny, captured 21.8.1944, condemned the attempt four days later at Trent Park, saying that a regime cannot be toppled by the murder of its leader. GRGG 180, 25–26.8.1944, TNA WO 208/4363.
248 See SRGG 975, 11.8.1944, TNA WO 208/4168.
249 Eberhard Wildermuth to his wife Marianna, 8.2.1945, BA/MA NL 251/90.
250 Diary passages from captivity, BA/MA, N267/4.

251 Ludwig Crüwell to his brother Werner, 28.12.1943 (Crüwell Correspondence). similarly in his letter of 27.3.1944 to Waltraud, Graefin von Schweinitz, ibid.
252 See, *inter alia*, Searle, 'Wehrmacht Generals'. Searle differentiates the generals' political attitudes after 1945. Meyer, 'Zur Situation der deutschen militärischen Führungsschicht', pp. 652–707.
253 Oberst Aulock, commandant, St Malo fortifications, acknowledged that the surrender of the citadel was for him one of the most difficult decisions of his life and he was still asking himself if he could have kept fighting longer: GRGG 177, 22.8.1944, TNA WO 208/4363.
254 At the end of 1945 in PoW Camp 300, Wildermuth set down a comprehensive account of the battle for Le Havre based on notes he made at Trent Park between December 1944 and February 1945. The original is in his 1945 diary, BA/MA, NL 251/73.
255 The commandant of the Cherbourg fortifications, Generalleutnant Wilhelm von Schlieben, taken prisoner on 26.6.1944, wrote on 1.7.1944, 'Purely from a military point of view I have nothing to reproach myself for, I say merely that it would have been a better outcome for me to die . . . Now I do not know if they wanted me to put myself in the path of a firing machine gun. That would have been an historical fact.' SRGG 936, 1.7.1944, TNA WO 208/4168. Schlieben probably felt that the National Socialist leadership was annoyed at Allied press reports regarding the circumstances of the surrender. In fact Goebbels stated of Schlieben, whom he described as 'a typical Schleicher-type Reichswehr creature', that one could never speak of being taken prisoner in such a way that there was some kind of heroic aspect to it, while Hitler called Schlieben a 'chatterbox'. Neitzel, 'Kampf um die Atlantik- und Kanalfestungen', p. 390f.

Documents

1 Rudolf Hess (26.4.1896–17.8.1987), from April 1933 Hitler's deputy, flew to Scotland on 10.5.1941 on his own initiative and without Hitler's knowledge with the intention of negotiating a peace deal with Britain before the attack on the Soviet Union. Schmidt, 'Hess'.
2 In January 1941, 11.Pz.Div. was at Ploesti in Rumania to secure the oilfields. The division moved to the Bulgarian western border in March in preparation for the Balkans campaign.
3 Hitler awarded Crüwell the Oak Leaves on 1.9.1941 at FHQ 'Wolfsschanze'. The second visit occurred on 19/20.5.1942, a few days after his wife's funeral. On both visits Crüwell was deeply impressed and said he would never forget the experience as long as he lived. SRX 1259, 8.11.1942, TNA WO 298/4161: Ludwig Crüwell, 'Begegnungen mit bedeutenden Persönlichkeiten. Erinnerungen und Abschiedworte für meine Kinder' (1958), pp. 19–25, (Crüwell literary bequest).
4 Konstantin Freiherr von Neurath (2.2.1973–14.8.1956) was German Foreign Minister from 2.6.1932 to 4.2.1938.
5 Similarly in SRX 1496, 14.1.1943, TNA WO 208/4162.
6 Arthur Neville Chamberlain (18.3.1869–9.11.1940), British Prime Minister 28.5.1937–10.5.1940. Negotiated with Hitler the Munich Agreement of 30.9.1938 that allowed a German occupation of the Czech Sudetenland and prevented war. By occupying the remainder of the country on 15.3.1939, Hitler made a mockery of the treaty.

7 The generals were virtually unanimous in their feelings towards Roosevelt. Luftwaffe Generalleutnant Walter Friedensburg (1889–1959) considered him 'one of the world's cruelest monsters' – 'He is perhaps the greatest criminal there has ever been' (SRGG 1154(c), 22.4.1945). Generalmajor Goerbig confessed at the beginning of May 1945, 'When the American President (Truman) said how sorry he was that Roosevelt had not lived to experience the day, I could hardly conceal my joy that this piece of shit was denied the satisfaction' (GRGG 296, 6–9.5.1945, TNA WO 208/4177).

8 See his remarks quoted in the Introduction.

9 Generalfeldmarschall Hans Günther von Kluge (30.10.1882–18.8.1944), from 18.12.1941 C-in-C Army Group Centre. Thoma refers here to a commanders' conference on 21.3.1942 in which the C-in-C, 4.Pz.Armee, General Richard Ruoff, spoke about a foreign policy discussion he had had with Hitler in which the latter had asserted that Britain was making giant strides towards 'Bolshevisation'. Thoma responded, 'Previously we were ten times more Bolshevised than the British.' The protocol does not indicate whether von Kluge attended the commanders' conference.

10 Goebbels's speech of 18.2.1943, very anti-Jewish in its opening passages, is reproduced in Heiber, 'Goebbels-Reden', Vol. 2, pp. 172–208.

11 On 20.11.1942 Hans Cramer was given command of Generalleutnant Heim's weak XXXXVIII.Pz.Korps which, together with 1st Rumanian and 22nd German tank divisions, lay behind the front line held by the 3rd Rumanian Army. The previous day the Soviets had begun their pincer-offensive on Stalingrad, after which the Don Front collapsed. Later, while commanding 'Gruppe Cramer' near Kharkov, he witnessed another great Soviet offensive. He did not participate in von Manstein's counter-offensive, which succeeded in recapturing Kharkov, because he had been transferred to the Führer-Reserve on 10.2.1943. On 13.3.1943 he arrived in Tunisia as Commanding General, Deutsches Afrika Korps, where he experienced the defeat of Heeresgruppe Afrika. The experience of two devastating defeats apparently lay behind his pessimism as to the future course of the war. SRGG 59, 22.5.1943, TNA WO 208/4165.

12 Thoma often drew this comparison with 1918 (see for example SRX 1644, 11.3.1943, TNA WO 208/4162).

13 Cramer means the two peace offers made by Hitler in the autumn of 1939 and summer of 1940 in which he proposed to guarantee the security of the British Empire in exchange for a free hand in the East. For further literature on this theme see Weinberg, 'Welt in Waffen', pp. 106–12, 173f. For Hitler's speech of 19.7.1940 see also Lukacs, 'Churchill und Hitler', pp. 223, 277. The speech is reproduced in Domarus, 'Hitler', Vol. 2, p. 1540ff.

14 Oberstleutnant Graf Schenk von Stauffenberg (15.11.1907–20.7.1944) was transferred to 10.Pz.Div. as Ia (No. 1 General Staff Officer) in February 1943 and was seriously wounded on 7.4.1943. Active from May 1940 in the OKH organisational divisions, he had insight into the tense personnel situation in the Army, but had no involvement in personnel administration. Hoffmann, 'Claus Schenk Graf von Stauffenberg', pp. 242f, 245, 253.

15 After the German defeats in the winter of 1942, Turkey became increasingly pro-British. Krecker, 'Deutschland und die Türkei im Zweiten Weltkrieg'. For the political consequences of the defeat at Stalingrad for the Axis partners see also Förster, 'Stalingrad'.

16 Cramer had no command in Italy. He must be speaking here of his

journey to North Africa, during which, in Rome in March 1943 he very probably held several conversations at Italian High Command, although no details are known.

17 In the spring of 1943 Tito's Communist partisans became stronger militarily. In the winter of 1942 the Wehrmacht failed to wipe them out in a major offensive, 'Weiss'. The Italian 2nd Army had long been incapable of controlling its appointed zone of occupation in southern Croatia. Schmider, 'Partisanenkrieg', pp. 193–261.

18 On 9.4.1943 in Yugoslavia there were five German divisions (114, 117 and 118.Jäger-Div., 187.Res.-Div. and SS-Gebirgs-Div. 'Prinz Eugen') and 369th Croatian Infantry Division. Although able to fight, they would have had only limited value in the major offensives on the Eastern Front on account of their obsolete equipment. KTB OKW 1943, p. 261. For the usefulness of these units in battle, see Schmider, 'Partisanenkrieg', pp. 535–41.

19 The new 'Panther' tanks were used for the first time in battle in Operation 'Zitadelle' in July 1943, Schmider, 'Partisanenkrieg', pp. 535–41.

20 Hitler's speech on *Heldengedenktag* (Heroes' Memorial Day), 21.3.1943 is reproduced in Domarus, 'Hitler', Vol. 4, pp. 1999–2002. It was comparatively objective and summarised the great danger that Germany had faced from the Red Army in the winter offensive of 1942, but which had been successfully withstood. Corresponding to the less favourable war situation at the time, the speech was not immoderately optimistic.

21 Generaloberst Franz Halder (30.6.1884–2.4.1972) Chief of Army General Staff, 1.9.1938–24.9.1942.

22 Generalfeldmarschall Walther von Brauchitsch (4.10.1881–18.10.1948) C-in-C Army (ObdH), 4.2.1938–19.12.1940.

23 Joachim von Ribbentrop (30.4.1893–16.10.1946), from 4.2.1938 German Foreign Minister.

24 The identity of M180 is unknown.

25 This gloomy appraisal of the situation, very close to the reality, is noteworthy because Broich was not present at the devastating Soviet winter offensive of 1942/43. He commanded a rifle brigade of 24.Pz.Div. until 31.10.1942, when he was transferred to Tunisia.

26 This observation was most probably aimed at General von Thoma, who took four and a half years to progress from Oberst to General der Panzertruppe, although the last promotion from Generalleutnant to General der Panzertruppe took only four months.

27 Apparently the inmates were unaware that Trent Park had been converted from an interrogation centre for 'normal' prisoners into a bugged centre to eavesdrop on senior officers. Even after this rejoinder the prisoners exercised no especial caution in their conversations.

28 The prisoners were also permitted to listen to the German radio programmes.

29 Between 24.7.1943 and 3.8.1943, Hamburg was bombed on four occasions by night and twice by day by British and American bombers; 41,500 persons lost their lives. 'Das Deutsche Reich und der Zweite Weltkrieg', Vol. 7, p. 40.

30 The identity of this Oberst could not be ascertained.

31 This report has not been found in the archives.

32 Stalin's readiness for a diplomatic solution was signalled through various channels, but Hitler always rejected any idea of a compromise. Hildebrand, 'Das vergangene Reich', pp. 787–806.

33 It was a forlorn hope that Generalfeldmarschall Keitel (22.9.1892–16.10.1946), head of OKW, and the C-in-C Kriegsmarine, Grossadmiral Dönitz (16.9.1891–24.12.1980) would attempt to unseat the Führer. For Keitel see Mueller, 'Keitel'. For Dönitz the latest literature is Schwendemann, 'Deutsche Menschen vor der Vernichtung durch den Bolshevismus retten', and Jörg Hillmann, 'Die Reichsregierung in Flensburg'.

34 At the 1934 census, Great Britain had a population of 48,789,000. Butler, 'British Political Facts', p. 323.

35 The draft of Goebbels's radio broadcast of 3.12.1943 appeared next day in the 'Völkischer Beobachter'.

36 The Trent Park commandant was Major Topham. Ramcke, 'Fallschirmjäger', p. 80.

37 Generaloberst Alfred Jodl (10.5.1890–16.10.1946), from 23.8.1939 Chief of the Wehrmacht Command Staff.

38 Army C-in-C Generaloberst Werner Freiherr von Fritsch (4.8.1880–22.9.1939) was accused by the Gestapo of having been blackmailed in 1936 for a homosexual act. Replaced on 4.2.1938 by Brauchitsch, he was proven innocent by the Reich Military Court the following month. Appointed by Hitler to head Art.Reg.12, he fell on the outskirts of Warsaw during the Polish campaign. There was outrage amongst senior commanders at the Gestapo allegation, a fabrication based on false identity. The best short account with sources is Mühlheisen, 'Fritsch', a detailed presentation appears in Janssen/Tobias, 'Der Sturz der Generäle'.

39 General Kurt von Schleicher (7.4.1892–30.6.1934) and Generalmajor Ferdinand von Bredow (16.5.1894–30.6.1934) were shot dead the same day by SS men during the Röhm putsch. Fallois, 'Kalkül und Illusion'.

40 Hitler never considered the possibility of a special peace settlement. See Hildebrand, 'Das vergangene Reich', pp. 787–806, Martin, 'Deutsche-sowjetische Sondierungen'.

41 Generalfeldmarschall Gerd von Rundstedt (12.12.1875–24.2.1953) was the longest-serving Wehrmacht general of World War II. He was appointed C-in-C West on 15.3.1942; a convincing strategy to repel the Allied landings eluded him. After the Allies landed in Normandy in June 1944, Hitler transferred him to the Führer-Reserve on 2 July 1944.

42 In the eighteenth and nineteenth centuries, Britain frequently took the long view by siding with former enemies against allies. An example was the difficult alliance with France following the Vienna Congress of 1815, as the result of which both fought Britain's former ally during the Napoleonic Wars, Russia, in the Crimean War (1853–56). Historical parallels to the hope expressed here that Britain might change sides to fight alongside Germany against the Soviet Union are rare, but one occurred in 1808 during the war against Spain (1796–1808) when the latter allied with Britain against Napoleon.

43 In 1944/45 the United States carried more political weight than Great Britain. Ovendale, 'Anglo-American Relations' pp. 50–70; Dobson, 'Anglo-American Relations', pp. 72–100; Hathaway, 'Great Britain and the United States', pp. 9–15.

44 A number of Trent Park inmates were visibly disappointed that the damage to London caused by the V-1 and V-2 campaign was less than expected. See Otto Elfeldt, SRGG 988, 24.8.1944, TNA WO 208/4168, and Erwin Menny, diary notes BA/MA, N267/4. Further reaction to the first wave of projectiles are reproduced in GRGG 146, 11–16.6.1944,

TNA WO 208/4363, and for expectations of the V-2 see SRGG 980, 24.8.1944, TNA WO 208/4168. For V-weapons propaganda following the defeat at Stalingrad see Hölsken, 'V-Waffen', pp. 93–114. Between 12.6.1944 and March 1945 the Germans fired 5,822 V-1 flying bombs and 1,054 V-2 rockets on Britain; 8,938 persons were killed, 24,504 injured; 31,600 buildings were destroyed, 1.42 million damaged. These effects were too slight to influence the course of the war. Ibid., p. 200f.

45 Soviet policy in the Baltic states of Lithuania, Estonia and Latvia from the summer of 1940, and Eastern Poland from 17.9.1939 was directed towards deportations, not mass killings. The most recent estimates show that the Soviets deported 315,300 to 340,000 persons from Eastern Poland up to June 1941. Applebaum, 'Gulag', puts the number of Balts deported in 1940/41 at 160,000. For Estonia see Laar, 'Estland und der Kommunismus'. In Poland, however, the Russians murdered 14,587 Polish PoWs and 7,285 civilians. For additional data see Musial, 'Schlachtfeld'; and Häufele, 'Zwangsumsiedlungen'.

46 Kurt Zeitzler (9.6.1895–25.9.1963) was Chief of the Army General Staff 24.9.1942–20.7.1944.

47 The naval coastal battery 'Marcouf', equipped with three 21-cm guns, was the heaviest in Normandy. It lay behind 'Utah' beachhead and was subjected to heavy Allied bombardment from April 1944. On the night of 5.6.1944, 101 Lancaster bombers dropped 598 tonnes of bombs on the battery. Nowadays it is a popular tourist attraction. Harnier, 'Artillerie im Küstenkampf', pp. 92–7.

48 Churchill, Roosevelt and Stalin discussed military and strategic questions at the Teheran Conference, 28.11–1.12.1943, with the aim of coordinating efforts. The Anglo-American landings in France were agreed for May 1944, while the three leaders agreed that the borders of Poland would be shifted westwards and East Prussia annexed to the Soviet Union. Most questions remained unfinalised for lack of preparation and the short period of the conference. No agreement as to the territorial extent of the Russian advance westwards was reached either at Teheran or Yalta. Eubank, 'Summit at Teheran'.

49 Hennecke refers to the three heavy daylight raids on Munich on 11, 12, and 13.7.1944 in which 2,807 B-17 bombers of the 8th USAAF dropped 5,783 tonnes of bombs and inflicted great damage on the city; 1,613 persons lost their lives, 3,955 were injured as the result of the attacks. Permooser, 'Luftkrieg im Raum München', pp. 321–41.

50 If and when Hitler made this remark cannot be established.

51 A locality at the southern end of Cherbourg town where a command post had been engineered into a mountain, and where Hennecke and Schlieben were captured.

52 Robert Reiter, CO, Art.Reg.1709, 709.Inf.Div.

53 On 8.8.1918 the British 4th Army (including the Canadian and Australian Corps), flanked by French 1st Army, attacked the trenches of German 2.Armee south-east of Amiens using over 500 tanks. Within a few hours the attackers had forced a great breach in the front, taken 29,000 prisoners and captured 400 guns. Ludwig stigmatised this as 'the black day of the German Army' because of the great losses in material and the only brief resistance offered by whole units before surrendering. Between 8 and 11 August around Amiens the Germans lost 74,000 men, the Allies 22,000. But neither Neuffer nor Reimann was there. Bose, 'Katastrophe des 8. August 1918'. For a general view from the British perspective see Harris, 'Amiens to the Armistice'.

54 Hitler's frequent amateurish meddling no doubt proved of benefit to the Allied cause. The generals used it to deflect attention from their own errors and heaped blame on Hitler alone for the disasters in the second half of the war. Wegner, 'Erschriebene Siege'. For Hitler's role as supreme leader see Klaus Schmider's study 'Warlord Hitler', Sutton, 2007.

55 Hennecke was very pessimistic about the military situation following the collapse of Army Group Centre after the surrender at Minsk on 11.7.1944. Contrary to his fears, however, the front was repaired and the Russian drive into Germany repealed. Evacuations were only achieved from Memel, which the Russians had encircled in mid-October 1944.

56 During the Spanish Civil War there were numerous cases of the children of Republicans being taken to the Soviet Union. Kowalsky, 'La Unión Soviética y la Guerra Civil española', pp. 96–121.

57 Until 1.3.1945 Turkey resisted pressure from the Western Allies to enter the war. Diplomatic relations with Berlin were broken off on 2.8.1944.

58 As Chief of the Army General Staff, Kurt Zeitzler had been agitating since June 1944 for Hitler to pull out of the Baltic states in order to strengthen the central sector of the Eastern Front. Hitler declined this and the request of C-in-C, Army Group North, Generaloberst Friessner, for permission to pull back a few weeks later. Hitler's main preoccupation was the possibility that he would lose Finland from the Axis. Only after Helsinki had departed the coalition on 2.9.1944, and a major Soviet offensive began 14 days later, did Hitler approve the withdrawal of units around Riga. Meier-Welcker, 'Abwehrkämpfe am Nordflügel der Ostfront'. For coalition politics see Salewski, 'Staatsräson und Waffenbrüderschaft'.

58a Vizeadmiral Hans-Erich Voss (30.10.1897–18.11.1969), from 1.3.1943 permanent representative of C-in-C, Kriegsmarine at FHQ.

59 Meant here is Generalleutnant Graf Max von Montgelas (1860–1938), great-grandson of the Bavarian president and son of Bavarian diplomat Ludwig von Montgelas. 1879 entered Bavarian Army; 1900 Battalion Cdr, East Asiatic Expeditionary Corps; 1901–3 Military Attaché, Peking. 1910–12 Senior QM, Kaiser's General Staff; 1912–15 CO, 4.Bavarian Inf.Div. After the war he worked for Foreign Ministry on publication of 'Deutsche Dokumente zum Kriegsausbruch' (German documents relating to the outbreak of war). He was a convinced opponent of the Versailles Treaty and the 'German War Guilt' clause.

60 Recent research on Großadmiral Erich Raeder (24.4.1876–6.11.1960), C-in-C, Kriegsmarine, prove his strong affinity to National Socialism. Jörg Hillmann, 'Erich Raeder', University of the Bundeswehr, Hamburg, in preparation.

61 La Glacerie, a village a few miles south of Cherbourg.

62 Generalfeldmarschall Walther von Brauchitsch and Generalfeldmarschall Fedor von Bock (3.12.1880–4.5.1945) never contradicted Hitler in personal conversation, but as C-in-C Army Group South in 1942, Bock was very critical of the operational leadership during the summer offensive and was relieved of command on 15.7.1942. Janssen, 'Walther von Brauchitsch'. For Bock, see Mühleisen, 'Fedor von Bock'.

63 Schaefer took a similarly gloomy view in SRGG 273, 16–19.3.1945, TNA WO 208/4177. On 10.4.1951 the generals were eventually granted a pension corresponding to their rank. Meyer, 'Führungsschicht', p. 648f.

64 See note 38 above.

65 Charles de Gaulle (22.11.1890–9.11.1970), addressing the Comité de Défense Nationale in Algiers on 12.8.1944, demanded the French occupation of the Rhineland without limit of time, the international control of the Ruhr and the prevention of a German central government. Young, 'France', p. 9.

66 Alfred Rosenberg (12.1.1893–16.10.1946), from 17.6.1941 to 30.4.1945 Reich Minister for the Eastern Territories. For his life see Ernst Piper, 'Rosenberg'.

67 Chief of the Army Personnel Bureau, Generalleutnant (1.11.1944 General der Infanterie) Wilhelm Burgdorf (15.2.1895–1.5.1945) addressed the course for senior adjutants on 3.8.1944 regarding the events of 20 July 1944. 'Tätigkeitsbericht Schmundt', p. 192.

68 At Goering's initiative the Wehrmacht introduced the Hitler salute on 21.7.1944.

69 Choltitz gives more details of his conversation with Hitler here than in his memoirs, but both accounts say much the same thing. Choltitz, 'Soldat unter Soldaten', p. 222f. and 'Brennt Paris?', pp. 6–11.

70 For Choltitz's commands in this period see his short biography.

71 General der Infanterie Hermann Reinecke (14.2.1888–10.10.1973), 1938 Chief of Bureaux, General Wehrmacht Affairs, from which the General Wehrmacht Bureau was created in 1939, and of which he remained head to the war's end. From 1.1.1944 he was also Chief of the National Socialist Command Staff at OKW. 28.10.1948 sentenced to life imprisonment at Nuremberg, October 1954 released. Streit, 'Reinecke'. For his activity in the field of military education see Förster, 'Geistige Kriegführung'.

72 General der Infanterie Rudolf Schmundt (13.8.1896–1.10.1944) was Chief Wehrmacht adjutant to Hitler, 28.1.1938 to his death and from 1.10.1942 head of the Army Personnel Bureau.

73 Generalfeldmarschall Erich von Lewinski known as von Manstein (24.11.1887–10.6.1973) was C-in-C, Army Group South in January 1944.

74 Generaloberst Karl Adolf Hollidt (24.4.1891–1.6.1973) was C-in-C, 6.Armee in January 1944.

75 No itinerary for senior commanders of all Wehrmacht branches at Posen exists, either as a detailed programme or as a list of those attending. It probably lasted two, and not the four days suggested by Choltitz. On 26.1.1944 Himmler addressed the assembled generals on the extermination of the Jews. If the memoirs of Freiherr von Gersdorff are believed, Choltitz was one of the few present who understood the enormity of Himmler's words. The conference at FHQ Rastenburg followed on 27.1.1944. Förster, 'Geistige Kriegführung'; Gersdorff, 'Soldat im Untergang', p. 145. Graf Rothkirch was also present at the Posen session. See his account, especially Hitler's address at SRGG 1135(c), 9.3.1945, TNA WO 208/4169, and also the version of Generalleutnant Richard Veith at SRGG 1149, 24.4.1945, TNA WO 208/4169.

76 See note 65 above.

77 For a concise summary of the protests by Johannes Blaskowitz (10.7.1883–5.2.1948) against crimes by SS and police units in Poland, see Clark, 'Blaskowitz'. Because of his criticisms, Blaskowitz never made Feldmarschall and received only second-class appointments. In a letter dated 6.2.1940 as C-in-C East he wrote, 'The feelings of the Army towards the SS and Polizei vary between abhorrence and loathing, and every soldier feels disgusted and revolted by their crimes. In this

connection one must not forget, however, that the Wehrmacht was also involved in the crimes in Poland'. Böhler, 'Tragische Verstrickung'.

78 Generalfeldmarschall Wilhelm Ritter von Leeb (5.9.1886–29.4.1956), from September 1939 to 16.1.1942 C-in-C, Army Group C, North.

79 Generalleutnant Kurt von Schleicher, influential Secretary of State at the Reichswehr Ministry involved in the fall of Reich Chancellor Hermann Müller and the installation of the presidential Cabinet. In December 1932 Reich Chancellor, failed in his attempt to find a broad social basis for his labour-creation methods. His attempt to break up the NSDAP by hiving off the Strasser wing also failed, forcing him into isolation in January 1933, when he stepped down. He was murdered with his wife on 30.6.1934, as part of the Röhm putsch. Plehwe, 'Schleicher'.

80 The pre-war concentration camps differed from the wartime variety. The first wave of arrivals in 1933 consisted of political opponents. From the autumn other groups such as beggars, recidivists and vagrants were incarcerated. The average stay at a camp pre-war was 12 months. In August 1939 the six camps at Buchenwald, Dachau, Flossenbürg, Mauthausen, Ravensbrück and Sachsenhausen had a total of 21,400 inmates, of whom 13,000 were convicted criminals at the end of 1938. Wachsmann, 'From Indefinite Confinement to Extermination', p. 177. The total number of deaths between 1936 and 1939 in all camps was 4,171. Müller-Römer's estimate of the situation is therefore incorrect. Drobisch/Wieland, 'System der Konzentrationslager', pp. 288, 303, 339.

81 Eberbach was thinking here of the new Type XXI and XXIII Elektroboote (E-boat) whose mass production had begun and which could have changed the fortunes of the U-boat Arm if put into service earlier. The same goes for the Me262 jet, due for supply to operational squadrons shortly after this conversation took place. See Neitzel, 'Bedeutungswandel der Kriegsmarine', p. 264ff; Blair, 'U-boot Krieg', Vol. 2, p. 824f.; Schabel, 'Wenn Wunder den Sieg bringen sollen'.

82 Choltitz was promoted faster than Bassenge, three years his junior. He rose in two years from Oberst to Generalleutnant, while Bassenge took three and a half years to rise from Oberst to Generalmajor. Choltitz's later ascent was presumably due to his having been the commander of units that had proven their worth well in Holland and Russia.

83 Oberst Andreas von Aulock (23.3.1893–23.6.1968) put up a stubborn defence of St Malo between 5 and 17.8.1944. At 1400hrs on the last day he sent a final signal, 'Mein Führer! The battle for St Malo will end today or tomorrow. Under the heaviest bombardment one defensive position after another has been reduced to rubble. If we go under, it will only have been after a fight to the bitter end. God protect you with his hand. Long live the Führer!' Ose, 'Entscheidung im Westen', p. 251f. See also Neitzel, 'Kampf um die deutschen Atlantik- und Kanalfestungen', p. 396f. Aulock was at Trent Park from 22 to 28.8.1944. On the day of his arrival he described the battle for St Malo at great length. He regretted having had to take 1,500 civilians into consideration, 'I would rather have let them die and held the town'. (GRGG 177, 22.8.1944, TNA WO 208/4363). The defence of St Malo so impressed Hitler that at Army Group B on 7 September 1944 he asked 'which people had been appointed as new commanders to fortifications and defence zones along the Channel coast, and if they had the commitment to defend it as at St Malo' (OKW/WFSt/Op. West Nr 7733260/44 gKdos, Chiefs, 7.9.1944, BA/MA, RH 19-IX/5, p. 88).

84 Generalleutnant Alfred Gerstenberg (6.4.1893–1.1.1959) Luftwaffe Cdr in Rumania is probably meant here. After the arrest of the Rumanian Head of State Ion Antonescu on 23.8.1944 by the Rumanian opposition, he had tried unsuccessfully to prevent the new Rumanian Government from changing sides. Gerstenberg failed to bring Bucharest and its troops under control. On 28.8.1944 he was captured by the Soviets.

85 On the night of 18.9.1944, 206 RAF Lancaster bombers and six Mosquitos attacked Bremerhaven, inflicting heavy damage on the city centre and docks; 618 people were killed, 1193 injured. Middlebrook/ Everitt, 'Bomber Command War Diaries', p. 586.

86 On the night of 11.9.1944, 226 RAF Lancaster bombers and nine Mosquitos attacked Darmstadt. A fire-storm ensued in which 11,000–12,000 persons were killed and 52.4 per cent of the city destroyed. See Engels, 'Deutschlands Zerstörung aus der Luft'.

87 In March 1945 around three million people lived in Germany west of the Rhine, about half the number there in 1939. The exodus was the result of a planned evacuation and privately organised flights. Henke, 'Besetzung Deutschlands', p. 351f.

88 Oberst Claus Graf Schenk von Stauffenberg.

89 Generalfeldmarschall Erwin Rommel (15.11.1891–14.10.1944), 15.1.1944 C-in-C Army Group B, France; seriously wounded 17.7.1944 when his car was attacked by low-flying aircraft.

90 See note 81 above.

91 Oberstgruppenführer Sepp Dietrich (28.5.1892–21.4.1966); from March 1933 Chief, Stabswache, Reich Chancellery (from September 1933 Leibstandarte *Adolf Hitler*). Dietrich was involved in the Röhm putsch murders, later became CO, SS-Div. Leibstandarte *Adolf Hitler* as career officer; 27.7.1943 CO, 1.Pz.Korps, which also fought in Normandy; 5.11.1944 CO, 6.SS.Pz.Armee; 6.8.1944 awarded Diamonds. See Clark, 'Josef Sepp Dietrich', see also Document 159.

92 According to Manfred Rommel, his father was convinced that Sepp Dietrich would follow him if there were an armistice in the West. Fraser, 'Knight's Cross', p. 541. Dietrich is alleged to have told Rommel, 'You are my superior officer, and therefore I will obey all your orders'. Gersdorff, 'Soldat im Untergang', p. 165. G. Meyer, 'Auswirkungen des 20.Juli 1944', p. 475f.

93 As regards Waffen-SS war crimes in the Soviet Union there is to date little reliable information. The same applies to atrocities committed to SS-Division Leibstandarte *Adolf Hitler* (LAH). Andrei Angrick indicates that the Division assisted Sonderkommando 10a in the murder of Jews at Taganrog, although he gives no closer details. Angrick, 'Besatzungspolitik und Massenmord', p. 315f, see also p. 311. According to Stein, 'Geschichte der Waffen-SS', p. 245, at the beginning of 1942 the LAH murdered 4,000 Red Army prisoners.

94 For the alleged military 'failure' of the coalition partners at Stalingrad and the political consequences see Kehrig, 'Stalingrad', pp. 45–217; Förster, 'Stalingrad'.

95 Franz von Papen (29.10.1879–2.5.1969) belonged to the conservative wing of the Centre; 1921–32 Member of Reichstag, 1.6.1932–17.11.1932 Reich Chancellor, until mid-1934 Vice-Chancellor in Hitler's first Cabinet, then envoy in Vienna and from April 1939 ambassador to Turkey.

96 On 19 April 1919 Rudolf von Sebottendorf obtained approval to form a Freikorps from members of the Thule Society and other volunteers. Its

purpose was to put down the revolutionary republic in Munich. By the
end of the month Freikorps *Oberland* was 250 strong and after reaching
Munich quickly swelled to battalion size. Hagen Schulze, 'Freikorps
und Republik', p. 96. The Freikorps made its name as a military force for
its role in the storming of the Annaberg monastery in Silesia in May
1921, and as a political force for its nationalist, anti-democratic and to
some extent anti-Jewish attitude. The successor organisation *Bund
Oberland* contributed to the destabilisation and eventual break-up of
the Weimar Republic. See Barth, 'Dolchstosslegende'; Fenske, 'Konservatismus'; Lohalm, 'Völkischer Radikalismus'. The 'Iron Division' –
not to be confused with the Kiel Iron Brigade' founded at Kiel in January
1919 – was formed on 18.1.1919 from remnants of the German 8.Armee
and with Allied approval. Its purpose was to impose law and order in the
Eastern Baltic. Sauer, 'Vom Mythos eines ewigen Soldatentums'. After
the Allies and German Government withdrew support from the unit,
the Iron Division kept fighting in the Baltic states until December 1919,
latterly alongside the Russian Western Army under Prince Avaloff-
Bermondt. After its disbandment, its former members worked to
undermine the Weimar Republic, as did most Freikorps men from the
region. See also Liulevicius, 'Kriegsland im Osten'; Nagel, 'Fememord'.
97 The defence of Brest tied down three US divisions and denied the Allies
access to a large natural harbour. The Allied advance, though delayed,
was not decisively hampered. Neitzel, 'Kampf um die deutschen
Atlantik – und Kanalfestungen', pp. 397–405.
98 Operation 'Market Garden' was begun on 17.9.1944 with the objective
of clearing the way into Germany. Three parachute divisions were
dropped behind the German lines to capture the bridges at Eindhoven,
Nijmegen and Arnhem. The British First Airborne Division failed to
take the bridge at Arnhem crucial to the advance and sustained heavy
losses. Detlev Vogel, 'Deutsche und Aliierte Kriegführung im Westen',
pp. 606–11.
99 Choltitz is referring here to Churchill's speech of 28.9.1944 in the House
of Commons, reproduced in Churchill, 'Speeches', pp. 6990–7007.
Churchill, who barely mentioned the Arnhem debacle, mentioned in his
address the Jewish Brigade fighting the Germans in Italy and which was
to take part in the eventual occupation of Germany; one cannot say of
the speech that it was especially hate-filled. The Jewish Brigade was
formed in September 1944 from Palestinian Jews and fought only in
Italy. It was disbanded in 1946. Beckman, 'The Jewish Brigade'.
100 Fregattenkapitän Karl Palmgreen (2.9.1891–16.9.1970) CO, 38.Mine-
sweeping Flotilla, was awarded the Oak Leaves to his Knight's Cross on
11.7.1944. He was not at Le Havre between 31.7.1944 and 14.8.1944 to
receive the decoration. On 24 August the flotilla returned to the Baltic
via Dieppe, Boulogne and Dunkirk, and so Palmgreen avoided capture.
War Diary, 38.Minesw.Flot., 16.7.1944–28.2.1945, BA/MA, RM69/236.
101 This is the classic conservative doctrine of the intent to encircle
Germany. It is interesting to note that Ramcke refrains from
expounding this theory in his 1943 book 'Vom Schiffsjungen zum
Fallschirmjäger-General', in which the basically non-political text
presents him as a very brave soldier originating from humble circum-
stances. At the end of October 1944 he said, 'Whatever is said about
Hitler and the Kaiser before him, the fact remains that all the wars in
Europe in the last 300 years were engineered exclusively by Great
Britain and simply for their notorious *balance of power*. Individual

British people are very charming, but the British as a whole are swine.'
GRGG 214, 20–3.10.1944, TNA WO 208/4363. See also GRGG 233,
12–16.12.1944, GRGG 238, 23–6.12.1944, TNA WO 208/4364.

102 The idea espoused here by Ramcke that the Waffen-SS recruited
extensively from within the nobility – an opinion also occasionally put
forward after the war – has no basis in fact. Only 10 per cent of Waffen-
SS generals were nobles, and the proportion amongst the Sturmbann-
führer grades was only 1.9 per cent, both clearly less than the Army
officer corps (1943 all active officers 6.5 per cent; May 1944, all generals,
about 20 per cent), Wegner, 'Hitler's Politische Soldaten', p. 224.

103 The blockade remained in force until 12.7.1919. The Allies used this as
an additional instrument to pressurise the Germans into signing the
Treaty of Versailles.

104 The number of people who starved to death as the result of the blockade
after the Armistice is unknown. Berger, 'Germany after the Armistice',
p. 207 puts the figure of deaths per day at 800. There are no official
statistics. See Vincent, 'The Politics of Hunger', p. 145. Berger's figure
for the first half of 1919 is clearly an overestimate. The latest research
on the subject had provided no fresh data. Osborne, 'Britain's Economic
Blockade of Germany'.

105 After the death of Heydrich in early June 1942, as a reprisal for his
assassination 198 persons were executed at the village of Lidice west of
Prague on 9.6.1942, and the locality razed to the ground. Karl Vogel,
'Lidice'.

106 Hitler refused to have an arsenal of biological weapons for offensive use
despite the reports of his leading military advisers on such weapons of
mass destruction in Allied hands, for example the British anthrax
bombs.* See Rolf-Dieter Müller, 'Albert Speer und die Rüstungspolitik
im Totalen Krieg', pp. 716–27.

107 Bassenge is probably referring to Himmler's speech of 26.7.1944 to
545.Volksgrenadier-Div. at Bitsch. In his long discourse he gave advice
on how the officer corps should handle the men under its command.
Himmler, 'Geheimreden', pp. 215–37, esp. p. 225.

108 'Die Lagerpost. Nachrichten aus der Heimat und aller Welt für die
deutschen Kriegsgefangenen in England' was a weekly information
sheet in simple format appearing for the first time in May 1942. It
provided comparatively sober news reports together with themes for
discussion and puzzles. Edition No. 74 of 7.10.1943 is at TNA WO
208/3467.

109 Von Brauchitsch received no gifts of property from Hitler, but in
common with others of Generaloberst rank and above enjoyed a
'function supplement' of RM4,000 monthly. Rumours circulated that
Hitler had made him a gift of between RM80,000 and 250,000. Janssen,
'Brauchitsch', p. 86.

110 Generalfeldmarschall Walther von Reichenau (8.10.1884–17.1.1942).
The ambitious Reichenau was keen to succeed Fristch as C-in-C Army
in February 1938, and was actually recommended by Hitler for the post,
but ran into determined opposition from prominent Army generals,
amongst them von Rundstedt. Reichenau remained to the forefront but
died in January 1942 while C-in-C Army Group South as the result of a
heart attack. Simms, 'Reichenau'; Richter, 'Walther von Reichenau'.

111 The described visit took place at the beginning of February 1944. For

---

* *Translator's note.* Germany had a large store of nerve gases however.

Karinhall and the court he held there see Knopf/Martens, 'Görings Reich'.

112 Feldmarschall Erhard Milch (30.3.1892–25.1.1972), from 1938 to 7.1.1945 Luftwaffe Inspector-General; 19.11.1941–20.6.1944 General in charge of aircraft production.

113 On the night of 16 May 1943, a special unit of 617 Squadron, RAF Bomber Command, attacked the Möhne, Sorpe and Eder dams in the Ruhr. Organisation 'Todt' put thousands of men to repair the damage, and all dams were restored by October 1943.

114 Generaloberst Bruno Loerzer (22.1.1891–22.8.1960), WWI fighter ace (44 kills, Pour le Merite). Goering flew as his observer in 1914/1915 before both were assigned to other units. 25.10.1939–22.2.1943 Commdg Gen. II.Fliegerkorps; from 23.2.1944 Head of Luftwaffe Personnel Bureau, Head of Personnel Equipment and National Socialist Leadership of Luftwaffe and Reich Air Ministry (RLM); 20.12.1944 Führer-Reserve.

115 This can only be Goering's daughter Edda (b. 2.6.1938).

116 Taormina, a town on the east coast of Sicily between Catania and Messina where II.Fliegerkorps Staff had its HQ for some months.

117 Even in captivity, Eberding did not understand that the purpose of the war was not simply to repeal the Versailles Treaty, but pursued far more wide-reaching aims. He had also not read 'Mein Kampf', where Hitler had condemned the 1914 frontiers as completely inadequate. For the Treaty of Versailles and its application between the wars see e.g. Krumeich, 'Versailles 1919'.

118 Wilhelm Frick (12.3.1977–16.10.1946), founding National Socialist, involved in Hitler putsch, 8/9.11.1923; 30.1.1933–24.8.1943 Reich Interior Minister.

119 The Hitler myth received its first substantial blow with the defeat at Stalingrad. Up to immediately before the invasion – Meyer is speaking here of May 1944 – the hope was still widespread that a decisive turn in the war was imminent and that Hitler would then quickly usher in 'Endsieg'. Even Meyer's assessment that the German people still 'believed in' Hitler is plausible on the basis of numerous other sources, but is not capable of empirical proof. The final break with Hitler did not occur until the spring of 1945. Kershaw, 'Hitler Mythos'.

120 Meyer refers here to the political-ideological assimilation of Army and Waffen-SS in 1944. This process has not been researched conclusively. The early premise has been that only sections of the three Wehrmacht services and the Waffen-SS felt especially bound to Hitler. An exact quantification cannot be made on the basis of what was known at the time. An interesting indication is provided by Peter Leeb in his dissertation 'Das Deutsche Westheer', where he states that while the Waffen-SS in the West kept fighting even when a situation was hopeless, Army units had already surrendered earlier. Förster, 'Geistige Krieg-führung'.

121 The Army C-in-Cs were not implicated in the coup attempt of 20.7.1944. In the run-up there were consultations that confirmed the conspirators in their belief that if successful they could count on the support of field marshals Rommel and von Kluge. Heinemann, 'Der militärische Widerstand', pp. 863–71. On 17.7.1944 Stauffenberg learned of a rumour that FHQ would be blown up in the next few days. This was 'a leak from his closest circle'. Ibid., p. 832.

122 After the withdrawal of German forces from Greece, the Greek Government in exile took over the running of affairs. The Communist

EAM left the government on 1.12.1944. In December 1944 and January 1945 heavy fighting occurred with British forces. After three years of civil war, in 1949 the pro-monarchists gained control of Greece. Tim Jones, 'British Army'; Smith, 'Victory of a Sort'.

123 During the Ardennes offensive from 16.12.1944 to 24.12.1944 US forces lost 8,497 dead, 46,170 wounded, 15,000 prisoners and 5,900 missing. 'Das Deutsche Reich und der Zweite Weltkrieg', Vol. 9/1, p. 632.

124 Choltitz refers here to his talk with Hitler on 7.8.1944. See Document 32.

125 There are no documents relating to Meyer's visits to Hitler. In his memoirs he only mentions receiving the Oak Leaves from Hitler at FHQ Winniza, Ukraine, at the end of February 1943. Kurt Meyer, 'Grenadiere', p. 185f.

126 The text of Goebbels's speech of 31.12.1944 has not survived. In his diary he mentions it only briefly, 'I recorded my end-of-year speech at midday. It is of a basically different character to my Christmas speech. In it I mention political problems and can therefore step out of myself more. It is not a good thing if I always deliver my speeches like a sermon. They must have some polemic again.' Goebbels, 'Diaries', Vol. 14, p. 500f. Hitler's speech of 1.1.1945 is reproduced in Domarus, 'Hitler', Vol. 2, pp. 2179–85.

127 This officer cannot be identified. According to some accounts, on 11.12.1944 Schaefer was in Nancy with an American diplomat and an intelligence officer, possibly General Robert A. McClure, Chief of the Psychological Warfare Division at SHAEF. Schaefer was unable to suggest any method of convincing the Germans to lay down their arms. He had described the fortifications at Zweibrücken to the Americans two days before in order to spare the town. BA/MA, Msg 2/79.

128 Chiang Kai-shek (31.10.1887–5.4.1975), from 1927 Head of the Chinese National Government of the Chinese People's Party (Kuomintang) was far stronger in 1945 than his civil war opponent Mao Tse-tung (26.12.1893–9.9.1976). He had gained a status with the Allies during World War II and participated in the Cairo Conference of 26.11.1943. In 1945 he was one of the 'Big Four' statesmen. The main actor in the struggle against Japan, he received substantially more military aid from the USA than Mao. On 14.8.1945 in a 'Treaty of Friendship', Stalin guaranteed the National Government large-scale concessions in northern China. With that the politics of expansion, which had terminated abruptly in 1905, began to roll again. Chen, 'China in 1945'.

129 Ramcke shows himself here as favouring the anti-Jewish and anti-Bolshevist core ideas of Nazi ideology. Volkmann, 'Russlandbild im Dritten Reich'. For Ramcke's thoughts on Jewish Bolshevism, see Förster, 'Russlandbild'. For an overview of the ideological alignment of the German military, see Förster, 'Geistige Kriegführung'. For the repeated claims of strong Jewish influence behind Bolshevism, see Slezkine, 'Jewish Century'.

130 The number of Germans wounded in World War II is 52.4 million.

131 Felbert served on the Eastern Front in WWI. It is known, however, that as Feldkommandant he had at least 17 insurgents executed. See note 354 below.

132 Hitler's speech of 30.1.1945 is reproduced in Domarus, 'Hitler', Vol. 2, pp. 2195–8. The generals were concerned particularly at the following passages, 'The horrifying fate unfolding today in the East, and which is killing tens and hundreds of thousands in village and province, in the

countryside and in cities will, despite all setbacks and tribulations, be beaten back and overcome by us in the end . . . Providence had it in her hand on 20 July to extinguish my life and put an end to my life's work by the bomb that exploded within a metre and a half of me. I see it as a confirmation of the mission entrusted to me that the Almighty protected me that day. In the coming years I will therefore pursue the path of uncompromising representation of the interests of my people, undeterred by any emergency and danger, and permeated by the holy conviction that ultimately the Almighty will not abandon him who in all his life never wanted anything but to save his people from a fate which, by its size and significance, it never deserved.'

133 He means here the youngest of the three sons, Götz Eberbach, born 1930.

134 General der Panzertruppen Leo Reichsfreiherr Geyr von Schweppenburg (2.3.1886–27.1.1974), 1.4.1933–12.10.1937 Military Attaché in London, then CO, 3.Pz.Div.; from 15.2.1940 Cmmdg Gen., XXIV.Pz.Korps; 26.6.1942 of XXXX.Pz.Korps and 1.10.1942 of LVIII.Pz.Korps, from which Pz.Gr. West was formed. On 3.7.1944 he was relieved for pessimistic assessment of situation, replaced by Eberbach; until the end of the war he was Inspekteur der Panzertruppen. Geyr was critical of the regime, and Hitler called him 'defeatist' and 'pessimist' frequently after his time as military attaché. He had therefore to take a back seat at the Army Personnel Bureau. Although a proven commander at the front, he was never promoted to Generaloberst. He was unwilling to commit himself to active resistance to the regime and declined Stauffenberg's approach in September 1942. Ose, 'Entscheidung im Westen', pp. 55, 151ff.; Peter Hoffman, 'Stauffenberg', p. 253. For Geyr and his influence on German rearmament, see Searle, 'Wehrmacht Generals', esp. p. 32ff.

135 The 'Revenge for Sadova' was a contemporary expression of French sensitivity at the shift in the European balance of power following the Prussian victory on 3.7.1866 at Königgrätz – this battle being named by the French after the nearby town of Sadova. This victory not only decided the war, but as a result Prussia rose from being a junior power to a major power of equal status to the France of Napoleon III.

136 The exact number of all German war dead is unknown. To the 5.3 million Wehrmacht and Waffen-SS dead must be added 400,000 dead by Allied bombing and 500,000 dead in expulsions and deportations. To these must also be added the civilian victims of the Nazi regime and the final battles of 1945, so that the final tally must lie somewhere between seven and eight million. Overmans, 'Verluste'.

137 The shooting of prisoners by *Grossdeutschland* Division mentioned by Broich must have occurred in July 1942 during the advance on Voronezh when the unit was close to Broich's 24.Pz.Div. It is the first mention of this war crime known to research.

138 The 'Sunday Times' article referred to by Eberbach remains unidentified. The four editions of January 1945 contain no mention of such reports by the Russians.

139 Schulz, 'Der deutsche Napoleon'.

140 Generalleutnant Wolfgang Thomale (25.2.1900–20.10.1978). From 1.6.1938–14.5.1941 Staff, OKH Inspekteur der Panzertruppen; 15.5.1941 CO, III.Pz.Reg.25; 5.8.1941, CO, Pz.Reg.27; 1.4.1942 OKH liaison officer between Chief of Army Ordnance and CO, Ersatzheer, Generaloberst Friedrich Fromm and Armaments Minister Speer; 1.3.1943 Chief of Staff, Insp. Gen. der Panzertruppen.

141 Generaloberst Heinz Guderian (17.6.1888–14.5.1954) was the founder of
the German panzer force and a highly successful commander of panzer
formations in Poland, France and Russia. He was highly decorated
(Knight's Cross, 27.10.1939, Oak Leaves 17.7.1941), Hitler relieved him
of command on 26.12.1941, and he was not re-employed until 1.3.1943,
as Insp. Gen der Panzertruppen. After the coup attempt of 20.7.1944
Hitler made him chargé d'affaires for the Chief of the Army General
Staff. After violent arguments with Hitler he was retired on 28.3.1945
and spent the period from 10.5.1945 to 17.6.1948 in US captivity. In
recent publications his role, particularly as Chief of the Army General
Staff, has been viewed critically. Wilhelm, 'Guderian'.
142 See note 63 above.
143 None of the German generals at Trent Park was handed over to the
Soviets. As a rule the Western Allies tried in their own tribunals those
generals accused of war crimes committed in the East. The only
exceptions were field marshals von Kleist and Schörner, who were in
British and US captivity respectively at the war's end, and were given
over to the Soviets.
144 Generalmajor Rudolph-Christoff Freiherr von Gersdorff (27.3.1905–
26.1.1980). Eberbach was apparently unaware that Gersdorff had been
part of Henning von Tresckow's resistance group and active in the coup
plans while at Army Group Centre (20.4.1941–1.2.1944). Gersdorff is
said to have rigged a bomb inside his uniform to kill Hitler and himself
at a Berlin exhibition on 21.3.1943. From 29.7.1944 he was Chief of
Staff, 7.Armee, of which Eberbach was C-in-C. Gersdorff, 'Soldat im
Untergang'.
145 For crimes committed by French troops during the occupation of the
Ruhr from 11.1.1923 see Jeannesson, 'Übergriffe'.
146 A connection between Ramcke and a Leutnant Hamm cannot be
confirmed. Ramcke does not mention this officer in his memoirs.
147 For art theft by the Nazis see Heuss, 'Kunst- und Kulturraub', and Kurz,
'Kunstraub in Europa', where France is treated comprehensively (pp.
119–250).
148 After the spring and summer offensives of 1918 had brought no pene-
trative successes, morale in the Germany Western Army plunged
perceptibly. Behind the front, thousands of soldiers milled around, lacking
the will to gamble their lives for a lost cause. Wilhelm Deist has coined
this as a 'covert military strike'. Estimates range from 750,000 to a million
'quitters' in the last months of the war. Deist, 'Verdeckter Militärstreik'.
149 The US 10th Armoured Division took Trier on 1–2.3.1945. Whereas the
Neue Brücke over the Moselle was destroyed by explosives towards
1900hrs on 1 March, the Römer Brücke fell into American hands
undamaged early the next morning. Christoffel, 'Krieg am Westwall', p.
478f.
150 The Kyll is a tributary of the Moselle. Its source is found on the Belgian
frontier, it flows south through the Eifel and empties into the Moselle at
Trier.
151 Rothkirch was acting commander of various corps from 1.1.1944 before
he reformed 3.Armeekorps at Trier on 3.11.1944. There are no details of
a deployment on the Eastern Front during 1944.
152 In his capacity as Cdr Ersatzheer from mid-September 1944, Himmler
planned 'the expansion of the Resistance in the border territories'. He
first used the term 'Werewolf' in a speech on 28.10.1944. Chief of the
planned Werewolf organisation, 'Inspector-General for Special Defence

at Reichsführer-SS′ was SS-Obergruppenführer and General der Waffen-SS Hans Prützmann (31.8.1901–21.5.1945), former HSSPF Ukraine/Russia South (November 1941–September 1944). He supervised the training of small commando units to operate against Allied occupation forces on German territory. Their major achievement was the assassination of Oberbürgermeister Franz Oppenhoff (18.8.1902–25.3.1945) of Aachen. After this 'success', Goebbels set the organisation along a new path with his 'Werewolf Proclamation' at the beginning of April 1945 in which he exhorted the German population as a whole to take up arms against the invader. Even if the Werewolf never achieved the importance that the National Socialist leadership hoped for it, and had no influence on the course of the war or the postwar period, its potency should not be underestimated. Biddiscombe, 'Werwolf!'; also Henke, 'Besetzung Deutschlands', pp. 160–8, 943–53.

153 On 26.2.1945, 2.Pz.Div. had one battleworthy Panther and two half tracks. The heavily battered 79 and 352.Volksgrenadier-Divisions also formed part of LIII.Korps. War Diary, 53.Armeekorps, Ia, BA/MA RH 24-53/130.

154 See note 152 above.

155 Units of the US 89th Infantry Division took Eisenach on 6.4.1945 without a fight. The heavy damage to the town was the result of five air raids between February 1944 and February 1945. Brunner, 'Bewegte Zeiten', p. 65f.

156 For the fighting for Wesel, during which Josef Ross was taken prisoner, see Berkel, 'Krieg vor der Haustür'.

157 After a short fight, Wertheim fell to 1st and 2nd Battalions, Reg.222, US 42nd Inf.Div. on 1.4.1945. The town received mortar and artillery fire on several occasions that day, the first before noon after a brief exchange with German resistance and again in the afternoon to convince Major Hermann Dürr to hoist the white flag. The road bridge over the Tauber, damaged by explosives set by German pioneers, was re-opened to traffic after a few hours. Contrary to Pfuhlstein's allegation, the artillery damage was negligible. No deaths were reported amongst the civilian population. Ehmer, 'Kampf um Nassig'.

158 On 11 and 12.12.1944 at FHQ Adlerhorst near Bad Nauheim, Hitler addressed between 20 to 30 generals. A part of his speech has survived. Domarus, 'Hitler', Vol. 2, p. 2171f. Viebig was present at Bad Nauheim in his capacity as CO, 277.Volksgrenadier-Division.

159 Generaloberst Hans-Georg Reinhardt (1.3.1887–22.11.1953) was C-in-C, Army Group Centre from 16.8.1944, relieved by Hitler for insubordination, 26.1.1945. On 16.12.1944 he noted in his diary, 'Counter-attack in the West is beginning. Marvellous.' (BA/MA N245/3) Reinhardt was a gifted and courageous panzer general who, despite many doubts over Nazi aggression, knuckled down and expressed no open criticism of Hitler to his face until January 1945. By doing so Reinhardt rose above the mass of German generals who followed Hitler's orders to the end either through cowardice, self-deception or fanaticism. Clasen, 'Reinhardt'.

160 The Chief of 7.Armee General Staff was Generalmajor Rudolph Christoff Freiherr von Gersdorff (27.3.1905–26.1.1980).

161 Generalleutnant Dr (Dentistry) Rudolf Hübner (29.4.1897–1965) was an infantry officer who distinguished himself (Knight's Cross) as a regimental commander. September 1943–January 1945, Head Section P2, Army Personnel Bureau, then CO, 303.Inf.Div., Döberitz. On

9.3.1945 Hitler ordered the setting up of a 'Flying Court Martial' under Hübner's command. In this capacity he answered to the Führer directly and received his orders from him personally. The Flying Court Martial was competent to try all charges involving members of the Wehrmacht and Waffen-SS, and could carry out its sentences immediately. The first victims of these mobile murder squads were four officers held responsible for the loss of the bridge at Remagen on 7.3.1945. The enabling order appears at Müller/Ueberschar, 'Kriegsende 1945', p. 163f.

162 Generalleutnant Willibald Utz (20.1.1893–1954), CO, 2.Gebirgs-Div. from 9.2.1945.

163 See note 161 above.

164 For the speech by Frederick the Great to his generals and regimental commanders on 4.12.1757, the eve of the Battle of Leuthen, see Kroener, 'Nun danket alle Gott'.

165 General der Infanterie Gustav Höhne (17.2.1893–1.7.1951), from 1.12.1944 Cmmdg Gen. LXXXIX.Pz.Korps.

166 In a radio broadcast on the late evening of 1 May 1945, Grossadmiral Dönitz announced the 'hero's death' of Adolf Hitler and issued a proclamation to the armed forces in the following terms, 'German Wehrmacht! My comrades! The Führer has fallen. Loyal to his grand concept to save the people of Europe from Bolshevism, he has sacrificed his life and found a hero's death. One of the greatest heroes in German history has left us. In proud veneration and mourning we lower our flags before him. The Führer has named me as his successor as Supreme Commander of the Wehrmacht and Head of State. I assume supreme command of all services of the German Wehrmacht with the intention of continuing the struggle against the Bolshevists until such time as the fighting forces and the hundreds of thousands of families in the German East have been saved from slavery and extermination. I am compelled to fight on against the British and Americans insofar as, and as long as, they hinder me in the execution of the struggle against Bolshevism. From you, who have already performed such great historical deeds and who now long for an end to the war, the situation demands further unconditional service. Only by carrying out my orders without reservation can chaos and defeat be avoided. That man is a coward and traitor who precisely now abandons his duty and by so doing leaves German women and children to die or become slaves. The oath of loyalty sworn to the Führer is still valid henceforth for each one of you without anything further from me as the successor appointed by the Führer.' The complete text of the proclamation is reproduced in Domarus, 'Hitler', Vol. 2, p. 2250f. For Dönitz's role as Hitler's successor see Hillmann, 'Reichsregierung in Flensburg'. For other reactions to the speech see SRGG 1177(c), 2.5.1945, TNA WO 208/4169.

167 Generalfeldmarschall Ernst Busch (6.7.1885–17.7.1945) was C-in-C, North-West from March 1945. On 1.5.1945 Dönitz nominated him C-in-C, North, with the task of leading the struggle in the North outside Norway and Denmark. Short biography at Mitcham, 'Busch'. Contrary to the statement in the protocol. he was not a signatory to the partial capitulation in northern Germany. OKW War Diary, Vol. 8, p. 1670f.

168 Franz appears to have forgotten that Hitler became Reich Chancellor *under* President Hindenburg and succeeded in seizing power in the land subsequently.

169 Heim had a surprisingly perceptive view that coincides with modern research ideas. Many generals such as Manstein could not, or would not,

see that the defeat of the German Reich was inevitable. Overy was right in saying, however, that the Allied first had to win the war. Overy, 'Why the Allies Won'.

170 There is no prominent statement by Frederick the Great from which one might infer that he admired Russian soldiers. On the contrary, the Prussian monarch spoke frequently of them in adverse vein. Kunisch, 'Friedrich der Grosse'.

171 For the operational efficiency of the Red Army see Mawdsley, 'Thunder in the East' together with Russian literature.

172 Despite the great operational successes of the Red Army from the winter of 1942 onwards, one should not overlook the fact that in its offensives it received repeated bitter setbacks to inspire caution. Tank corps which pushed too far forward were wiped out between the Donetz and Dnieper in February 1943, at Warsaw in August 1944 and at Grosswardeien in September 1944. For the superiority of the Wehrmacht over the Red Army in armoured tactics see Karl-Heinz Frieser, 'Das Deutsche Reich und der Zweite Weltkrieg', Vol. 8.

173 The plan for the French campaign was an idea of Generalleutnant Manstein. Hitler realised that it fitted in with his own concept and adopted it. Frieser, 'Blitzkrieg-Legende', pp. 71–116.

174 Heim is right if he doubts that the Blitzkrieg experience in France was transposed on Russia. It was hoped to break the backbone of the Red Army by means of great encirclements near the border. The German military leadership vastly underestimated the enormous resources and will to resist of the Soviets. 'Das Deutsche Reich und der Zweite Weltkrieg', Vol. 4.

175 In all, 62 different types of lorry of German manufacture were used by the Wehrmacht. Oswald, 'Kraftfahrzeuge und Panzer', p. 169f. The Army in the East was chronically short of lorries from the summer of 1941 onwards so that captured vehicles were increasingly pressed into service, which augmented the varieties. Although Armaments Minister Speer decided in 1942 to concentrate on producing only three weight classes of lorry, the problem of the variety of types remained unresolved. In the spring of 1943 on the Eastern Front there were 110 types of lorry identified with one particular division. Rolf-Dieter Müller, 'Albert Speer', p. 633f.

176 The Red Army had only two standard lorries, the GAZ-AA and ZIS-5. Most of the Lend-Lease vehicles were Studebaker US-6s.

177 To make up for the enormous losses in manpower due to the huge areas of territory falling under German occupation, the remainder of the workforce was obliged to perform compulsory overtime. An 11-hour day was required, all holidays were discontinued, many concerns went over to 24-hour production. Concerns vital to the war effort increased the workforce by employing women and teenage children and by taking workers away from non-essential occupations. Zverev, 'Ekonomika Vajuscich Derzav', p. 316. For the construction of bunkers and fire-fighting duties etc., a local Air Raid Precaution (MPO) was formed, run by the NKVD (see note 213 below), which mobilised all local residents aged between 16 and 60 for civil defence. If the military situation demanded it, MPO would also assemble a Home Army (Narodnoe Opolocenie). Its members would frequently be volunteers, although occasionally press-gang methods would be employed. Löwe, 'USSR', p. 1228. Also Barber/Harrison, 'Soviet Home Front'.

178 See note 205 below.

179 Between June 1940 and June 1941, 950 T-34/76As were built. These were succeeded by 9,290 T-34/76Bs between January 1941 and mid-June 1942. Deployed at the front in August 1941 for the first time, the production figures prove that by 1942 it had become the standard Soviet tank. Zalogal/Grandsen, 'Soviet Tanks'.

180 As a result of the German advance, by the autumn, significant centres of industry fell under German control. Production from iron ores fell in 1942 by between 32 and 38 per cent in comparison to pre-war levels, cast iron by 32 to 49 percent, steel 26 to 35 per cent. More than 80 per cent of all armaments factories, including 94 per cent of all aircraft factories, were close to the areas of war interest or not far from the front. In the regions east of the Urals a total of 3,500 major industrial projects were commenced and running in the 1941–45 period. Zverev, 'Ekonomika', p. 315ff. In the third quarter of 1941, 1,360 major concerns, mostly armaments, were evacuated east of the Urals. By the end of the year the number had risen to 1,523, by mid-1942 more then 1,200 were in operation at the new locations. Hildermeier, 'Geschichte der Sowjetunion', p. 634f.

181 The Geman 3.7-cm PAK36 anti-tank gun was the standard weapon of the Army from 1936 to 1941; 20,000 were built before production was halted in March 1942. In France in 1940 it was observed that the round did not penetrate the armour of British and French heavy tanks, and the gun was also found to be ineffective against Soviet tanks of the types T-34, KW-1 and KW-2. It was replaced during 1942 by the 5-cm and eventually 7.5-cm PAK40, delivered from February 1942. Hogg, 'Deutsche Artilleriewaffen', pp. 289–305; Hahn, 'Waffen', pp. 99–103. In the summer of 1941 the Soviet Army introduced the 5.7-cm ZIS-2 anti-tank gun, which in its various further developments remained in service to the end of the war.

182 Heim is probably referring here to the skilfully disguised push by the Red Army against Army Group Centre under the codename 'Operation Bagration', commencing 22.6.1944. The German assessment of the enemy situation before the assault was contradictory. Although the Department of Foreign Armies East had identified the focal point of the Soviet attack, they were surprised by its strength. Hitler and the Army Group Centre commanders were both deceived by the Soviet intention. Rolf-Dieter Müller, 'Der Zweite Weltkrieg', pp. 322–4.

183 The population of the Soviet Union at the beginning of 1940 was 194 million. Zverev, 'Ekonomika', p. 314. The mention of millions of Chinese coolies reflects the growing fears in the United States and Europe at the end of the nineteenth century that Russia could make use of this reservoir of Chinese people. Neitzel, 'Weltmacht oder Untergang', pp. 113–17, 240–5, 278f.

184 During the October Revolution and civil war the social layer of intelligentsia diminished from an estimated 2 million (1917) to barely 1 million (1923), but then rose again to 5.9 millions by 1939. Melville/Steffens, 'Bevölkerung', p. 1188f. Against that the Russian upper classes had been destroyed at the latest by the Stalinist industrialisation. Ibid., p. 1174.

185 This quote relates to losses amongst front-line troops. By the end of 1944, the Red Army had lost 26,579,242 officers and men of which 10,472,209 were classified as total losses (killed, died of natural causes, dead by accident, missing and PoW). Of the latter, 5.7 million were PoWs according to German statistics. Krivoseev, 'Grif sekretnosti snjat',

p. 143f. By the end of 1944 the Wehrmacht and Waffen-SS had 2,743,000 dead on the Eastern Front (Overmans, 'Verluste', p. 279) and 955,000 had been taken prisoner (Böhme, 'Die deutschen Kriegsgefangenen in sowjetischer Hand', p. 49), therefore 3,698,000 men. The ratio of total losses including PoWs is therefore 1:2.83, losses alone 1:1.74.

186 The strength of a Soviet rifle division was between 9,300 and 10,000 men.

187 For the partisan movement in the Ukraine, Berkhoff, 'Harvest of Despair', pp. 275–8.

188 Only twice did the Red Army deploy large military formations behind the German lines. After the Moscow counter-offensive in the winter of 1941, 250th Airborne Reg. and two battalions, 201st Airborne Brigade, in all around 1,640 men, were landed 40 kilometres south of Viasma near Znamenka and Zhelanye. H. Reinhardt, 'Luftlandungen'. On 24.9.1943, 4th and 5th Airborne Brigades were set down about 40 kilometres behind the German front at Krementshug south-east of Kiev for the purpose of setting up bridgeheads over the Dnieper. The operation was poorly coordinated and the troops were soon overwhelmed by German forces. Glanz, 'The Soviet Airborne Experience', pp. 91–112, Zaloga, 'Inside the Blue Berets', pp. 95–116. See also Karl-Heinz Frieser in 'Das Deutsche Reich und der Zweite Weltkrieg', Vol. 8. The Soviets also dropped a large number of well-trained agents in small platoons to collaborate with partisans. The total number is disputed. According to Thomas, 'Foreign Armies East', p. 274, there were more than 130,000 agents. This seems doubtful, for the number of active partisans in the summer of 1944, the height of their activity, did not exceed 280,000. Bonwetsch, 'Der Grosse Vaterländische Krieg', p. 944, note 2.

189 No detailed work exists on the deployment of Wehrmacht and SS forces against partisans on the Eastern Front.

190 For convoys of partisan plunder see Edition Musial, 'Sowjetische Partisanen' which though rich in material is neither comprehensive nor impartial. Also see dissertation by Alexander Brakel, 'Baronowicze 1939–1944'.

191 No adequate academic study on partisan anti-railway warfare using both German and Russian original sources has been made. It would seem that its influence on military developments at the front were slight because partisans failed to interrupt the German supply lines for any considerable period of time. Berkhoff, 'Harvest of Despair', p. 278f.

192 Meant here is Lt-Gen. Mikhail Popatov (1902–65), C-in-C, Soviet 5th Army. He entered the Red Army in 1920 and took part in the closing stages of the civil war. A Party member from 1926, he fought with success against the Japanese in 1939 and in 1941 took command of 5th Army at Kiev. On 21.9.1941 he was captured by the Germans; 1958–65 Chief of Military District, Odessa. His last rank was Col-General. Maslov, 'Captured Soviet Generals', p. 54ff.

193 General der Kavallerie Ernst Köstring (20.6.1876–20.11.1953) was born of German parents in Moscow and served as military attaché there from 1935 to 1941. In May 1941 German ambassador Werner Graf von Schulenburg authored a memorandum signed by Köstring and embassy advisers Gustav Hilger and Kurt von Tippelskirch in which they declared themselves opposed to the war. Gorodetsky, 'Täuschung', p. 262.

194 Thoma informed Crüwell of a conversation with Hitler after his return

from the Spanish Civil War in which Hitler had said, 'Look, I never go for intellect, I go only for intuition'. SRM 114, 24.11.1942, TNA WO 208/4136.

195 Heim is probably speaking of Churchill's radio broadcast on 13.5.1945 in which he said, 'And if you hold out alone long enough, there always comes a time when the tyrant makes some ghastly mistake. On June 22nd 1941 Hitler . . . hurled himself on Russia and came face to face with Marshal Stalin and the numberless millions of the Russian people.' Churchill, 'Speeches', Vol. VII, p. 7160.

196 See note 200 below.

197 Between 90 and 95 per cent of German soldiers in Red Army captivity in 1941 failed to survive. Probably most were murdered fairly soon after capture. Böhme, 'Die deutschen Kriegsgefangenen in sowjetischer Hand', p. 110. Atrocities against German prisoners occurred in the jurisdiction of 6.Armee, where Ferdinand Heim was Chief of Staff, particularly at the outset of the campaign. In the appendices to 6.Armee War Diary, Ia, some cases of crimes against German prisoners are documented in detail, some with an autopsy report and photographs. This material does not substantiate claims of 'innumerable cases'. Evidence of Soviet breaches of international law occur for example in the following files: -LI Armeekorps, Ic, Activity Report No. 1, 19.6.1941–31.7.1941 (BA/MA RH 24-51/54) (mutilated German corpses at Skomorochy, also mentioned at BA/MA RH 20-6, AOK 6, Ic/03, evening report, 1.7.1941, folio 41); 56.Inf.Div., Ic, Activity Report, 22.6.1941–1.8.1941 (BA/MA RH26-56/18) (Report on 'Bitterness' at Soviet war crimes); 99.(Light) Inf.Div., Ic, to Gen.Kdo XVII.Armeekorps, Ic, Breaches of international law by Red troops, 2.7.1941 (BA/MA RH26-99/21) (Reprisals ordered in response to Soviet war crimes); and 168.Inf.Div., Ic, Activity Report, 22–30.6.1941 (BA/MA RH26-168/40) (from 24.6.1941 several cases of serious mistreatment of German soldiers behind their own lines, responsibility not unequivocally clear).

198 6.Armee Staff was never at Kiev, a fact that Heim was at pains to emphasise after the war to support his assertion that he knew nothing about the mass murder at Babi Yar. The Army Staff was at Zhitomir to 13.9.1941 and moved from Ivankov to Prjevejasslav and Lubny to Poltava on 19.10.1941, where it remained until the spring of 1942. Details at BA/MA RH20-6/711.

199 Thoma presumably refers here to an OKH instruction at the end of August 1941 to execute not only the Commissars, but also the political leaders (Politruks) competent from regimental level downwards. A special order regarding 'Regiment-Kommissars' of November/December 1941 is unknown. See 'Das Deutsche Reich und Der Zweite Weltkrieg', Vol. 4, p. 1067f. The Army soon recognised that the Commissar Order bolstered the resistance of the Red Army. See also ibid., p. 1068.

200 Michail Tuchatshevsky (16.2.1893–11.6.1937) was Chief of the Red Army General Staff from 1925 to 1928, and from 1931 Head of Ordnance. In connection with the collaboration over armaments there had been bilateral visits to field manoeuvres and tours of inspection from 1925. Thus in 1928/29 five Soviet commanders of the third Assistant Commanding Officers' course stayed in Berlin for up to a year. Zeidler, 'Reichswehr und Rote Armee', pp. 224–7, Gorlow, 'Geheimsache Moskau-Berlin', p. 156.

201 Major-General Pawel Below commanded a 20,000-strong battle group formed from elements of 1.Guard-Cavalry Corps, airborne troops and

partisans, which became encircled behind the German lines in the Smolensk/Kirov area during the Soviet winter offensive. Thoma's 2.Pz.Div. set about wiping out this battle group from March 1942 onwards, and had succeeded by the beginning of June 1942. The partisan units were assembled in independent 'divisions' of which the unknown colonel mentioned here was apparently the partisans' liaison man to Below's staff. 'Das deutsche Reich und der Zweite Weltkrieg', Vol. 6, p. 865f. For the organisation of Below's units, see Armstrong, 'Soviet Partisans', p. 177f; Hinze, 'Hitze', pp. 124–8.

202 From the summer of 1941 numerous Russian so-called 'volunteers' were attached to German units and performed valuable service, particularly in supply. In May 1943 they numbered about 600,000. J. Hoffmann, 'Wlassow-Armee', p. 14.

203 The Commissar Order itself was not likely to have fallen into Red Army hands since the document was only circulated at Armee command level. It is quite possible that the Russians captured files that had been compiled at divisional level and which made reference to the Commissar Order. 'Das deutsche Reich und der Zweite Weltkrieg', Vol. 4, p. 438.

204 A placename resembling 'Vlasitchi' cannot be found in a gazeteer of Russian localities.

205 Brauchitsch and Halder definitely did not refuse the Commissar Order. After Hitler's address to the generals on 30.3.1941, Halder even ordered the first draft prepared. This was then passed from OKH to OKW, where it was put into its final textual form ready for signature. Brauchitsch's explanatory notes of 8.6.1941 did not attempt to transform the order in any way, but merely aimed to prevent Army units from committing excesses. That some Army commanders watered down the Commissar Order, or ignored it, is documented. The extent to which the order was enforced has given rise to controversy in the past. Felix Römer's Kiel dissertation 'Besondere Massnahmen' was based on a review of all available German archive material and proved that in more than 80 per cent of all German divisions commissars were liquidated, although the final total of commissars and politruks executed cannot be determined exactly because of the poor documentation on hand. Römer estimates it at 'a high four-digit figure', but 'never 10,000'. 'Das deutsche Reich und der Zweite Weltkrieg', Vol. 4, pp. 435–40, 1069f; Rohde, 'Politishe Indoktrination', Hartmann, 'Halder' pp. 241–54.

206 As General der Schnellen Truppen, von Thoma rarely left OKH HQ at Zossen until July 1941, and then only for short tours of inspection. He may therefore have been party to the internal debates about the Commissar Order, although his pocket diary has no entries to that effect. BA/MA N2/2.

207 To which OKW order von Thoma is referring here is unknown. Not until the structural change in the officer corps in the autumn of 1942 did it become obligatory for generals commanding troop units to endorse whole-heartedly 'the National Socialist worldview'. Thoma, taken prisoner in North Africa at the beginning of November 1942, may not have been aware of this change. Förster, 'Führerheer', p. 318.

208 General der Panzertruppe Walther Nehring (15.8.1892–20.4.1983), from 26.10.1940 CO, 18.Pz.Div.; 9.3.1942 Cmmdg Gen., Deutsches Afrika Korps; 15.11.1942 appointed Cdr, German forces in Tunisia; 9.12.1942 Führer-Reserve; 10.2.1943 C-in-C, XXIV.Pz.Korps; 21.4.1945 C-in-C, 1.Pz.Armee.

209 No such order by Nehring has been found in the War Diary, 18.Pz.Div.,

which deployed alongside Thoma's 17.Pz.Div. in the summer of 1941, nor in the Deutsches Afrika Korps War Diary.

210 Brauchitsch and Halder not only tolerated SS atrocities in Poland in 1939/1940, but became deeply inveigled in a war of extermination against the USSR in 1941 from an anti-Bolshevist standpoint. Hartmann, 'Halder'.

211 The report to OKW to which Thoma refers here is unidentified. On 31.12.1941 he maintained that amongst other things he had written, 'For a decent German soldier it is a disgrace and a scandal that he is being trained in this manner, in a way that is unworthy of a German soldier.' He received no reply to this letter. SRX 1442, 31.12.1944, TNA WO 208/4162. 24,000 Jews were murdered in Minsk in August and November 1941. Thoma can have had only indirect knowledge of these massacres because his division stood several hundred kilometres east of the city; on a tour of the front he was in the Minsk area on 1.7.1941 and 17.7.1941. When he took command of 17.Pz.Div.on 21.7.1941, this was already south-east of Smolensk. Accordingly it is more probable that he was referring to smaller-scale murders from the beginning of July 1941. Gerlach, 'Kalkulierte Morde', p. 549, 'Enzyklopädie des Holocaust', Vol. II, p. 950f, and see Thoma, diary entries 1, 17, 21.7.1941, BA/MA 2/2. A locality called Pskip cannot be found in the Russian gazeteer of placenames.

212 Crüwell was attempting here to justify the German mass murders behind the front as a reaction to illegal partisan warfare. This allowed him to knowingly skirt the fact that the Wehrmacht – independent of the danger that actually existed to some extent from dispersed Red Army units – proceeded with mindless brutality against the civilian population, Army units murdering tens of thousands of civilians under the pretext of combating partisans. This is not to mention the 700,000 to 750,000 victims of the SD-Einsatzgruppen in the period to the spring of 1942, which Crüwell also plays down valiantly. 'Das deutsche Reich und der Zweite Weltkrieg', pp. 1030–78; Krausnick/Wilhelm, 'Die Truppe des Weltanschauungskrieges', p. 620. It is also interesting that Thoma apparently knew that all Jews in the occupied territories were to be liquidated. For the mass murder of the Jewish civilian population in the Soviet Union, see Longerich, 'Politik der Vernichtung', pp. 293–418.

213 OGPU, Soviet secret service, 1922–24. At the time of World War II it was known as NKVD. For the alleged NKVD shootings in Poland see Musiel, 'Konterrevolutionäre Elemente'.

214 Ludowice is about 30 kilometres north-east of Thorn in Poland (formerly West Prussia), but Neuffer is probably thinking of another, White Russian locality of similar name near Minsk. Neuffer became Chief of Staff, Luftgaukommando Moskau on 1.12.1941 and would not have been aware of the murder of 7,000 Jews at Minsk on 20.11.1941. His account refers most probably to executions in March 1942 when 5,000 Jews were murdered. Neuffer was transferred out of Russia in April 1942. 'Enzyklopädie des Holocaust', Vol. II, p. 951.

215 For the involvement of Lithuanian auxiliaries in the mass shootings on the Eastern Front, see Dean, 'Collaboration'; Stang, 'Hilfspolizisten'.

216 From April to November 1942 Neuffer was CO, 5.Flak.Div. at Darmstadt. At this time there were seven large-scale deportations of Jews from Frankfurt am Main that had apparently not escaped Neuffer's notice. 'Dokumente zur Geschichte der Frankfurter Juden', p. 532f.

217 In the spring of 1943, German troops 20 kilometres west of Smolensk in

the Katyn Forest discovered the mass graves of 4,363 Polish officers murdered by the Red Army in 1940. Nazi propaganda made the best possible use of this opportunity. Goebbels, 'Diaries', Vol. 8, entries for 16, 17, 18, 19, 20, 23, 24 and 28.4.1943.

218 Oberst Johannes Heym (6.10.1894–?) was commandant of several airfields during the war. He was captured in Tunisia and arrived at Trent Park in mid-May 1943. On 21.8.1943 he was transferred to the United States.

219 During the invasion of Belgium in the summer and autumn of 1914, there spread amongst German troops an irrational fear of snipers, as a result of which they weighed in with great brutality against the civilian population, killing 6,500 persons and laying waste to 20,000 dwellings. The beginning of trench warfare quickly put an end to this madness. Horne/Kramer, 'German Atrocities'.

220 From June 1941 to June 1942 Liebenstein was Chief of Staff, Pz.Gr.2. The number of Soviet prisoners killed by this army has not yet been established. An approximate figure is expected from Römer's 'Besondere Massnahmen'. So far it is only certain that by the end of August 1941, 141 Commissars had been shot. 'Germany and the Second World War', Vol. 4, p. 567.

221 Until 15.8.1941 Ludwig Crüwell was CO, 11.Pz.Div., which acted in concert with Pz.Gr.1, Army Group South. A report by Ic, 11.Pz.Div. states that 10 Commissars were shot dead on 14.7.1941. Ic Report, 11.Pz.Div. to XXXXVIII.Armeekorps, BA/MA RH 4-48/198, Appx 29.

222 See additionally Streit, 'Keine Kameraden', p. 128.

223 Hitler expressed his distrust of Army generals on numerous occasions, as for example on 5.11.1939 when he threatened Brauchitsch that he would 'exorcise the spirit of Zossen'. One of the greatest crises occurred in the winter of 1941 and autumn of 1942 when the generals were not in a position to carry out Hitler's unrealistic orders. See e.g. Kershaw, 'Hitler, 1936–1945', pp. 369f, 605–11, 693–701, Hartmann, 'Halder', p. 331ff. One of Hitler's typical outbursts of rage against generals of the nobility fell on Karl-Wilhelm von Schlieben after he surrendered his Cherbourg command post on 26.6.1944. 'Hitlers Lagebesprechungen', p. 261, note 345.

224 See note 244 below for other references to German war crimes in Greece.

225 Generalleutnant Fritz Bayerlein (14.1.1899–31.1.1970) is meant here. From 25.2.1940 to 29.8.1941 Ia, Pz.Gr.2; from 5.10.1941 to 6.5.1943, Staff, North Africa. He was then flown out of Tunisia. Pz.Gr.2 was stationed in Warsaw for several weeks prior to the attack on Russia, and in this period Bayerlein would have been in the immediate vicinity of the ghetto created in November 1940. Szarota, 'Warschau unter dem Hakenkreuz'; Guderian, 'Erinnerungen eines Soldaten', p. 139. Thoma mentioned that a doctor assigned to his division 'was always going on about Völkisch matters, in racial stories'. It was from this doctor that he had learned of the dreadful conditions in the Warsaw ghetto. From the protocols it is not certain whether Thoma ever went through the ghetto himself. SRXX 1577, 11.2.1943, TNA WO 208/4162.

226 This is a reference to the mass murder of 33,771 Jews at Babi Yar near Kiev between 29 and 30.9.1941. See Rüss, 'Babij Jar', pp. 483–508.

227 See note 202 above.

228 Albert Leo Schlageter (12.8.1894–26.5.1923) attempted to blow up a stretch of the Duisburg–Düsseldorf railway track during the Ruhr disturbances. Arrested by the French, he was condemned to death on

8.5.1923 and executed on 26.5.1923. The Schlageter case caused an
uproar, although he was by no means the only victim of French and
Belgian repressive methods in the Ruhr. Up to 1.8.1924 141 Germans
had been killed there. Franke, 'Der erste Soldat', p. 33; Zwicker,
'Nationale Märtyrer'.

229 The speaker refers here to the 16 men killed during the Hitler putsch of
9 November 1923.

230 This is a reference to Hitler's conviction that only he could lead
Germany to 'greatness' in a war. Kershaw, 'Hitler, 1936–1945', p. 320;
Heer, 'Glaube des Adolf Hitler', pp. 293, 319.

231 The speaker alludes here to the German–Soviet Non-Aggression Pact of
23.8.1939, a relationship that brought Germany major economic
benefits in the period to 21.6.1941. Ahmann, 'Hitler-Stalin-Pakt';
Weinberg, 'Eine Welt in Waffen', pp. 222–7.

232 The following passage identifies the speaker as Generalleutnant von
Broich. He had been in Russia in 1941 as CO, Reiter-Reg.22 and 1, and
in this capacity would probably not have been shown the Commissar
Order. See note 242 below.

233 The opinion given here that the killing of hostages is covered by
international law is misleading. The 1907 Hague Convention relating to
land warfare contained no binding regulations, and it was left to
individual states to interpret how each would react in warfare to illegal
resistance. See in this connection the dissertation (in preparation) of
Andreas Toppe, 'Wehrmacht und Völkerrecht', also 'Zwischen Hammer
und Sichel – Bewaffneter Widerstand der Bevölkerung in Ostmittel-
europa während des Zweiten Weltkriegs und die Reaktion der
deustchen und sowjetischen Besatzungsmacht' in AHF No. 72,
8.11.2001.

234 Arnim probably means the great uprising by Indian nationalists against
the British Raj that shocked the nation in August 1942 and was put
down by force of arms. Hutchins, 'India's Revolution'.

235 Details of the involvement of the Army Weapons Office chemists in the
gassings are not known to exist.

236 In Berditschev, Ukraine, on 4.9.1941 1,500 Jews, on 15.9.1941 18,600,
and on 3.11.1941 another 2,000 were shot dead by German and
Ukrainian police. In Zhitomir, these police shot dead 5,000 Jews in July
and August 1941, and on 18.9.1941 another 3,145 Jews. 'Enzyklopädie
des Holocaust', Vol. 1, p. 185, Vol. 3., p. 1308. The identity of the senior
police official mentioned here is unknown. All that can be confirmed is
that the last Jewish survivors of Berditschev were executed in July 1942
by the local Sipo head, Alois Hülsdünker; Mazov, 'Berditschew'. During
his captivity Reimann spoke out about his front experiences in Russia
mainly to stress the enormous losses suffered by German units during
the 1941 advance. SRGG 736, 3.1.1944, SRGG 745, 6.1.1944, both TNA
WO 208/4167, and SRGG 820, 7.2.1944, TNA WO 208/4168.

237 Most recorded texts of the BBC German Service were destroyed after the
war. Therefore the material broadcast on the evening of 19.12.1943
cannot be reconstructed. Balfour, 'Der deutsche Dienst der BBC', p. 141.
BBC News brought daily reports about the war crimes trial in Kharkov.
BBC Written Archive Centre, letter dated 24.10.2002 to this author.

238 The first trial of German military personnel was held at Kharkov
between 15 and 18.12.1943. Hauptmann Wilhelm Langheld (Military
Abwehr), SS-Untersturmführer Hans Ritz, Reinhard Retzlaff (Secret
Field Police) and a Russian collaborator were accused of the murder of

Russian prisoners and civilians by the use of a mobile gassing truck. The accused were all condemned to death and hanged publicly. The trial was public, film cameras being allowed and a stenographed transcript was made available in several languages. Zeidler, 'Stalinjustiz contra NS-Verbrechen', p. 25ff; Streim, 'Behandlung', p. 251ff.

239 Hans-Jürgen von Arnim.

240 General der Artillerie Walther von Seydlitz Kurzbach (22.8.1888–28.4.1976) was Chairman of the anti-Nazi 'Bund Deutscher Offiziere' and Vice-President, 'Nationalkomitee Freies Deutschland'. Captured at Stalingrad 31.1.1943 as Commdg Gen. LI.Armeekorps, he pleaded for Hitler to be overthrown and an end to the war. Ueberschar, 'National-komitee'; older material, Frieser, 'Krieg hinter Stacheldraht'. On Seydlitz, see Reschin, 'General zwischen den Fronten'; Carnes, 'General zwischen Hitler und Stalin'.

241 Nothing is known of shootings by the SS-Leibstandarte in Greece in 1941. The exact circumstances in which Thoma and Dietrich knew each other from the 1920s is also unknown. From 1920 Thoma was active in 7.Bavarian (mot.)/7.Bav.Reichswehr-Div.; Dietrich was a member of Reichsbund Oberland and claimed to have taken part in the Hitler putsch, and so they were both in Bavaria. The conversation between Thoma and Dietrich can only have been held on 3.5.1941: Thoma was on an inspection tour in Greece from 28.4.1941 to 8.5.1941 and took part in the victory parade in Athens on 3.5.1941. Sepp Dietrich led the SS-Leibstandarte in the same parade. See Thoma Diary, 3.5.1941, BA/MA N2/2; Lehmann, 'Die Leibstandarte', Vol. 1, p. 425f. It also seems that Thoma and Dietrich met just after the French campaign. Thoma reported of this reunion, 'I can only repeat what Sepp Dietrich said to me towards the end of the French campaign in Normandy, "Look here, Herr General – you know what I was; I am an able soldier, I won't let anyone deny that, but a leader – that I am not."' SRGG 953, 11.7.1944, TNA WO 208/4168.

242 What Thoma says is incorrect. The Commissar Order of 6.6.1941 was an OKW guideline signed by Warlimont by virtue of his office. It had come from OKH and been given two additional paragraphs of limitations. It was distributed in this form to the Army Groups and Armies. Hitler never signed any order regarding Commissars. Transmission of the Order below Army Group/Army level was never envisaged. The Commissar Order is reproduced in Streim, 'Behandlung', p. 350f; see also 'Das deutsche Reich im Zweiten Weltkrieg', Vol. 4, p. 437f. The inspiration for the Order came from Hitler and was adopted willingly by both OKH and OKW. Although the extent to which it was enforced is not known in detail because of the paucity of source material, it was the rule rather than the exception to carry it out. See Römer, 'Besondere Massnahmen', and 'Das deutsche Reich im Zeiten Weltkrieg', Vol. 4, pp. 440–7. Even if the idea and the instructions to exterminate European Jewry did not originate with the Wehrmacht, it was in many ways implicated in the extermination programme. German soldiers had not only guilty knowledge of the acts but were also involved as active partners. Besides the mass murders in Russia in this connection, attention is drawn to the murder of the Jewish male population of Serbia. For the Wehrmacht involvement in National Socialist State crimes see R-D. Müller/Volkmann, 'Die Wehrmacht', pp. 739–966; and Manoschek, 'Serbien ist judenfrei'.

243 It is not known when and where Broich had these friendly troops shot,

neither in the files of Kav.Reg.21, 22 and 1, nor 1.Kav.Div., 24.Pz.Div. and 10.Pz.Div. It is also not known if Broich ever took part in shooting Commissars. 1.Kav.Div. War Diary records the shooting of a single Commissar on 16.7.1941, the exact circumstances and the names of those involved are omitted. BA/MA RH 29-1/4.

244 Krause refers in his account to German reprisals in October 1941 when units of Inf.Reg.382 of 164.Inf.Div. burnt down the villages of Kato and Ano Kerzilion and murdered over 200 civilians after partisans had sabotaged the Saloniki–Serres railway line. In October 1941 a total of 488 Greek civilians were murdered by German soldiers. The harsh reprisals led to the premature collapse of the partisan movement here, as had occurred in Serbia. Mazower, 'Inside Hitler's Greece', p. 87f; Fleischer, 'Im Kreuzschatten der Mächte', p. 130; and 'Schuld ohne Sühne'. Fritz Krause was Artillery Cdr 142 in Greece from 15.12.1941 to 31.8.1942 and knew Oberst Helmuth Beukemann (9.5.1894–13.7.1981), CO, Inf.Reg.382 there, who informed him of the massacres. Beukemann commanded the regiment from 13.1.1941 to 18.8.1942, and as CO, 75.Inf.Div., which fought on the southern sector of the Eastern Front, rose to the rank of Generalleutnant. He was transferred to OKH Personnel-Reserve on 10.7.1944 and not used again.

245 Neuffer's version has a few inaccuracies. The leading German private stud farm at Schlenderhan was founded by Eduard Oppenheim (1831–1909) in 1869 and passed later into the possession of the Jewish banking family. Simon Alfred Oppenheim (1864–1932) ran the racetrack. His wife Florence 'Flossy' née Mathews Hutchins was – as Neuffer says – not Jewish and attended school at Frankfurt am Main. Since Simon Oppenheim died in 1932, he was not the person mishandled. His two sons Waldemar (1894–1952) and Friedrich Carl (1900–78) were classified 'Mixed Race, 2nd Degree', by the Gestapo and were merely monitored until their arrest following 20.7.1944. As the name Oppenheim was common in Frankfurt, Neuffer confused the events told to him by Broich as pertaining to Simon Alfred Oppenheim. Stürmer et al., 'Wiegen und Wägen'.

246 See note 214 above.

247 General der Flieger Veit Fischer (18.5.1890–30.10.1966), 23.10.1941– 31.3.1943 Cmmdg Gen. and CO, Luftgau Moskau; 1941–45 Luftwaffe Cdr, May 1945–7.10.1955 Soviet PoW.

248 Imperial Germany of World War I was guilty of numerous breaches of international law although the scale obviously did not approach that of WWII. Neitzel, 'Kriegsausbruch'; also Henkel, 'Deutsche Kriegs-verbrechen'.

249 Oberst Hauck, 362.Inf.Div., PoW in Italy from 24.5.1944, expressed the same sentiment. 'The worst ranks are the officers from Leutnant to Hauptmann inclusive. I used not to converse with my Leutnants because there was such a gap that no basis existed at all.' GRGG 147, 16/17.6.1944, TNA WO 208/4363.

250 Unfortunately none of the files of Schützen-Reg.108/14.Pz.Div., commanded by Schlieben in Yugoslavia and at the beginning of the Russian campaign, which could throw light on his political and military outlook, have survived.

251 Generaloberst Johannes Blaskowitz (see note 77 above), October 1939–May 1940 C-in-C East, and in this capacity protested vociferously against SS murders. In the Polish campaign, Sattler was CO, Inf.Reg.176/61.Inf.Div., which remained in Poland as occupation troops

until November 1939 when transferred to the West. He probably had only hearsay knowledge of Blaskowitz's protests. Clark, 'Blaskowitz'. The later Feldmarschall Georg von Küchler (30.5.1881–25.5.1968) commanded 3.Armee in Poland and complained frequently at the mistreatment of Polish civilians. When a court martial sentenced a private of the SS-Verfügungstruppe Artillerie Reg. who had been involved in the murder of 50 Jews, to one year's imprisonment, he refused to confirm the sentence on the grounds that it was too mild. This led to a violent quarrel with the Gauleiter of East Prussia and Himmler. Küchler could do nothing to prevent the sentence being quashed altogether when the Waffen-SS received its own rules of justice in October 1939. Despite his own feelings, however, in July 1940 in the West he prohibited any criticism by his own 18.Armee soldiers of the brutal repressive measures against civilians in occupied Poland, '. . . I emphasise the need to ensure that all soldiers of the Army, especially the officers, withhold all criticism of the struggle against the population in the General-Gouvernement, for example the treatment of the Polish minority, the Jews and Church affairs. The final racial solution to this struggle, which has raged for centuries on the eastern borders [of the Reich] demands particularly strong measures. Certain units of Party and State are entrusted with the carrying out of the racial struggle in the east. The soldier must stay clear of these duties of other units. This means that he must not criticise that operation.' McCannon, 'Küchler'; Stein, 'Geschichte der Waffen-SS', p. 244.

252 Generalmajor Joachim Lemelsen (26.6.1888–30.3.1954) had SS-Obermusikmeister Müller-Jon of the SS-Leibstandarte arrested for the murder of 15 Jewish civilians and demanded that he be tried by Army Group. See Thun-Hohenstein, 'Verschwörer', p. 184. Between 21 and 28.9.1939 the LAH fought alongside 29.Inf.Div./XV.Armeekorps under General Hoth north of Warsaw around the Modlin fortifications. Sponeck was Hoth's Ia, and his account therefore has a high degree of plausibility. For the general context see Cüppers, '. . . auf eine so saubere und anständige SS-mässige Art: Die Waffen-SS in Polen, 1939–1941'.

253 There is no record of such an order.

254 Vyasma/Viasma.

255 Nothing else is known about the engagement of partisans by Spang's 266.Inf.Div. See Introduction, note 223.

256 Up to December 1941, 2,365 Jews were murdered at Gomel, and buried at Letshshinez on the road to Rechiza. 'Enzykloädie des Holocaust', Vol. 1, p. 552.

257 From 16 to 31.10.1943 (personnel file says 30.11.1943), Menny led 123.Inf.Div. defending the Dnieper island of Chortiza, where he sustained heavy losses. Menny remained on the island constantly and led his units successfully in the defence and counter-attack. It is certain that this division was not transferred to the Eastern Front from Norway. Possibly the event involved 333.Inf.Div., which Menny commanded from 7.6.1943 to 15.10.1943, and which came to Russia from *France*, being wiped out in October around Zaporoshye on the Dnieper. BA/MA Pers 6/750.

258 Zaporoshye.

259 It is not known to which camp Broich was referring.

260 Meant here is the later Generalleutnant Hans von Graevenitz (14.7.1894–9.12.1963), 1.8.1938–31.3.1943 Chief of OKW Assistance and Supply. The meeting between Broich and Graevenitz must have

taken place before the latter's promotion to Generalmajor on 1.2.1942.

261 During World War II around 5.7 million Russian prisoners passed through German hands. The exact number of those failing to survive captivity is estimated by Streit ('Keine Kamaraden', pp. 244–9) at 3.3 million, by Streim ('Behandlung', p. 246) at 2.53 million. The numbers for August 1944, when this conversation was recorded, were not much lower.

262 Nothing has been found in the archives regarding this incident. For the general context see Lappenküper, 'Der Schlächter von Paris'.

263 Meant here is the steel magnate Albert Vögler (8.2.1877–14.4.1945), Chairman of the Board, Vereinigte Stahlwerke (United Steelworks), Düsseldorf. During the war he served the Armaments Ministry as General Plenipotentiary for the Ruhr.

264 Eberbach is probably referring here to Himmler's speech to Wehrmacht generals at Sonthofen on 5.5.1944 on 'The Final Solution to the Jewish Question', in which he said, 'Had we not excluded the Jews from Germany, it would not have been possible to have endured the bomber offensive.' On 24.5.1944 Himmler addressed the generals at Sonthofen on the same theme. He could have spoken to Eberbach on this occasion. Himmler, 'Geheimreden', p. 202. For the Sonthofen speeches, see Förster, 'Geistige Kriegführung', p. 606f.

265 It is not known where Choltitz carried out these shootings of Jews. Presumably they occurred in his time as regimental commander in the Crimea, 1941/42, see note 285 below.

266 There are no court-martial papers for 20.Pz.Div. at the Bundesarchiv Kornelimünster, and so this case cannot be examined.

267 Later he admitted to having carried out only three death sentences on German soldiers. GRGG 228, 24–26.11.1944, TNA WO 208/4364. Nothing is known about these executions, and Ramcke did not mention them in a comprehensive signal describing the situation on taking over the fortifications, see 1.Skl.27479/44 gKdos 5.9.1944 BA/MA RM7/149, nor were executions mentioned in a long report from Oberleutnant (Naval Artillery) Jenne, AII to the Naval Commandant, Brittany, who escaped to Lorient on 10.9.1944 aboard a KFK, nor in a report by Naval Commandant Konteradmiral Kähler to the Lorient harbour commander. 'Kampf um Brest, Bericht Oberlt.(MA) Jenne, AII Seekommandant Bretagne', BA/MA RM 35II/68.

268 Meant here is Gzhatsk (or Gshask) 200 kilometres east of Smolensk on the main highway to Moscow.

269 Seyffardt refers here to the transportation of about 673,000 PoWs from the battles at Viasma and Briansk in October 1941 in which he was involved as CO, Inf.Reg.111/35.Inf.Div./3.Pz.Armee. The prisoners were force-marched cross-country as the crow flies for 150–250 kilometres to Smolensk before being entrained for PoW camps in the 'Reich Commissariat Ostland'. The death rate was very high, exact numbers are not known. Streit, 'Keine Kamaraden', pp. 162–71, Gerlach, 'Kalkulierte Morde', pp. 843–8.

270 Heyking was probably talking here of Himmler's speech to the generals at Sonthofen on 5.5.1944 in which he said, 'You may imagine how heavy a burden it was for me to carry out this order, which I obeyed and executed from obedience and utter conviction', Himmler, 'Geheim-reden', p. 202.

271 From the surviving files at BA/MA it is not apparent if Inf.Reg.16, commanded by Choltitz, enforced the Commissar Order or not.

272 Army C-in-C Brauchitsch, Chief of the Army General Staff Halder, C-in-C Army Group A von Rundstedt, Army Group B von Bock and Army Group C von Leeb all spoke out strongly against the early attack on France demanded by Hitler. Frieser, 'Blitzkrieg-Legende', pp. 110–15. For an introduction to the associated coup plans see Peter Hoffmann, 'Staatsstriech', pp. 165–86.

273 Even Eberbach remarked that Ramcke had systematically destroyed Brest. GRGG 214, 20–23.10.1944, TNA WO 208/4363. Oberleutnant Jenne (see note 267 above) wrote in his report from Brest, 'To clear the bomb damage, parties were assembled from Organisation Todt and railwaymen from the beginning. Their primary job was to keep the main supply routes open and carry out repairs. The Fortification Commandant decided later to burn down the area along the arterial road and blow up the walls to collapse inwards upon themselves. This was to avoid undesirable masses of rubble falling on the supply route in later air raids.' 'Kampf um Brest, Bericht Oberlt.(MA) Jenne, AII Seekommandant Bretagne', BA/MA RM 35II/68.

274 In the French Revolution, the city of Toulon placed itself voluntarily under the protection of Admiral Hood, who then seized a major part of the French war fleet. The British, their allies and French royalists were unable to beat off the attack of the Revolutionary Army and fled the city. It is not true to say that Hood destroyed it. Blanning, 'French Revolutionary Wars', p. 200.

275 In the gorge at Babi Yar, SD-Sonderkommando.4a and two parties from Polizei-Reg. Süd executed 33,771 Jews between 29 and 30.9.1941. A platoon of engineers from 6.Armee blew in the sides of the gorge to conceal the traces of the massacre. The name of the pioneer battalion commander involved is not known. Why Oberst Otto Elfeldt was at Kiev in September 1941 as Chief of Staff to the General of Artillery is likewise unknown. See Arnold, 'Eroberung und Behandlung der Stadt Kiew'; Rüss, 'Wer war verantwortlich für das Massaker von Babij Jar?'; and Wiehn, 'Die Schoah von Babij Jar'.

276 The shooting of a Scharführer of SS-Div. *Hitlerjugend* at Caen described here by Kurt Meyer is not documented in the German archives.

277 Eberbach meant here the 'Gerichtsbarkeitserlass' of 13.5.1941, which lifted the obligation to prosecute German soldiers who committed crimes against Soviet civilians, although rape was excluded. The total number of prosecutions fell sharply upon its introduction into the field. Meyer and Eberbach may have had knowledge of this document. A special order from Hitler in 1941 regarding punishment for rape is not known. Beck, 'Wehrmacht und sexuelle Gewalt'.

278 Hitler to the Reichstag, 30.1.1939. The speech is reproduced in Domarus, 'Hitler', Vol. 2, pp. 1047–67, here p. 1058.

279 SS-Brigade-führer and Generalmajor der Polizei Anton Dunckern (29.6.1905–19.12.1985), SD and finally SS and police chief of Metz, where he was taken PoW by the Americans in November 1944. He was interrogated at another centre and taken to the USA in April 1945. Sentenced to 20 years' imprisonment by a French military court in 1951, he was released in 1954 and became a lawyer in Munich. For his interrogation reports see SRGG 1120-1124, 11–23.1.1945, TNA WO 208/4169.

280 A thorough investigation of which war crimes Meyer may have had knowledge has not been made. Since he served with the SS from 1931 (SS-LAH from 1934), and the Waffen-SS must always be considered as

integral to the SS, it is hardly likely that he had no idea of the scale of Nazi war crimes. Against him personally, however, there lies only the shooting of Canadian PoWs in Normandy. Margolian, 'Conduct Unbecoming'; Nassua, 'Ahndung'.

281 Meyer was captured on 7.9.1944 near Namur. After ridding himself of his soldier's paybook and bloodied camouflage smock he assumed the identity of an Oberst of 2.Pz.Div. After a short spell in hospital he was transferred to a PoW camp where he was recognised on 8.11.1944 and flown to England. His memoirs deal with this episode at length. Kurt Meyer, 'Grenadiere', pp. 313–32.

282 The list of dead at IfZ has 83 names, 50 of them SA people. Gritschneider gives 90 names, Gritschneider, 'Der Führer hat sie zum Tode verurteilt', p. 60ff. The total number of those murdered is put at between 150 and 200. Longerich, 'Die braunen Bataillone', p. 219. Sepp Dietrich appeared at Stadelheim prison in company with a group of SS men with orders to kill SA leaders Hans-Peter von Heydebreck, August Schneidlhuber, Wilhelm Schmidt, Hans Erwin Graf von Spretti, Edmund Heines and Hans Hayn detained there. It cannot be determined reliably whether Dietrich was one of the shooters. The murderers of Röhm were Theodor Eicke (17.10.1892–16.2.1943) and Michael Lippert (14.4.1897–1.9.1969). Gritschneider, 'Der Führer hat sie zum Tode verurteilt', pp. 32–6.

283 Nothing is known regarding material support for those bereaved by the murders of 30.6.1934.

284 Meyer refers here to the liberation of Maidanek death camp at Lublin by the Red Army on 24.7.1944.

285 The major mass shooting of Jews in the Crimea took place at Simferopol between 13 and 15.12.1941, when units of Einsatzgruppen D shot 10,000 to 11,000 people in the city park. Inf.Reg.16 commanded by Choltitz was at Sevastopol at this time. What massacre was observed by the regimental officer is unknown. The total number of victims of genocide in the Crimea is estimated at about 40,000. 'Enzyklopädie des Holocaust', Vol. 2, p. 821f. For the involvement of local military field offices in the Holocaust see Oldenburg, 'Ideologie und militärisches Kalkül', pp. 159–224.

286 For euthanasia and its development in the eugenics of the Kaiserreich and Weimar republic see Klee, 'Euthenasie'.

287 On Hitler's order on 2.8.1944, Keitel summoned a session of the Wehrmacht Honour Court under the presidency of von Rundstedt. The other judges were Guderian, General der Infanterie Walter Schroth (3.6.1892–6.10.1944), General der Infanterie Karl Kriebel (26.2.1888–28.11.1961) and Generalleutnant Karl-Wilhelm Specht (22.5.1894–3.12.1953). The latter, who had won the Oak Leaves on the Eastern Front as CO, Inf.Reg.55 in 1941, was Insp.-Gen., Führer-Youth Movement. Generalmajor Ernst Maisel (16.9.1896–16.12.1978) prepared the protocols. Generalleutnant Heinrich Kirchheim deputised for Guderian at two sessions and at the special session for Speidel. The Honour Court was required to decide if officers suspected of complicity in the conspiracy were to be discharged from the Wehrmacht so that they could be tried in the People's Court, or simply released. It heard no legal argument and relied solely on evidence presented by the RSHA and Gestapo. At the first session on 4.8.1944, 22 principal conspirators involved in the 20.7.1944 coup attempt were expelled from the Wehrmacht, including Generalfeldmarshall von Witzleben and Generaloberst Ludwig Beck. At the four sittings of 4,

14, 24.8.1944 and 14.9.1944, 55 Army officers were discharged from
the Wehrmacht and another 29 released on the recommendation of the
Honour Court (including Hans Cramer on 24.8.1944 and Alexander
von Pfuhlstein on 14.9.1944). Charges against 19 other officers were
dropped. At a special session on 4.10.1944, by majority decision
Speidel was not dismissed from the Wehrmacht, and his superior
officer Rommel was implicated accordingly. Keitel and Specht voted
against Speidel. For the Honour Court, see Ueberschär, 'Stauffenberg',
p. 150f; Reuth, 'Rommel', p. 238ff; Domarus, 'Hitler', Vol. 2, p. 2137f;
and '20 Juli 1944', p. 195ff.

288 Elfeldt was Chief of Staff to General der Artillerie at OKH in the spring
of 1942. It is not known when he spoke to Graevenitz, who was head
of the OKW PoW office. For camp commandants who interceded for
their Soviet prisoners see Hartmann, 'Massensterben oder Massenvernichtung?'.

289 Makejewka, town in the Donetz basin. Kittel was commandant of
nearby Stalino (today Donezk) from 15.5.1942 to 19.9.1942.

290 See note 305 below.

291 Mezciems, today a suburb of Daugavapil (Dvinsk).

292 Here meaning SS-Gruppenführer and Generalleutnant der Polizei Paul
Hennicke (31.1.1883–25.7.1967), Police President of Weimar, April
1938–October 1942.

293 In Document 125 Kittel states that he met Hennicke in Rostov.

294 Kittel means the concentration camp at Cracow-Plaszow that was built
in 1942 as a forced-labour camp and was turned into a death camp in
1944. Between 22,000 and 24,000 were interned there that summer.
About 8,000 were murdered there. 'Enzykloädie des Holocaust', Vol. 2,
p. 118f. Kittel was commandant of Cracow city on 8.8.1944.

295 SS-Brigadeführer and Generalmajor der Polizei (8.11.1944) Dr (Law)
Walter Bierkamp (17.12.1901–16.4.1945), Sipo and SD Cdr, Cracow,
June 1943–February 1945.

296 Hans Frank (23.5.1903–16.10.1945) from 12.10.1939 General Governor
of Poland. Housden, 'Hans Frank'.

297 SS-Obergruppenführer Wilhelm Koppe (15.6.1896–2.7.1975) HSSPF
(Higher SS Police Chief). For the wrangling over jurisdiction between
Hans Frank and the HSSPF in Poland see Birn, 'Die Höheren SS und
Polizeiführer', pp. 197–206.

298 SS-Obergruppenführer Friedrich Wilhelm Krüger (8.5.1894–10.5.1945),
4.10.1939–9.11.1943 HSSPF East.

299 For Rostov see note 305 below, for Lublin note 326 below. Schaefer had
already heard of mass killings, including those of women and children,
at Maidanek. Kittel confirmed that it had been going on there for several
years. SRGG 1089(c), 27.12.1944, TNA WO 208/4169.

300 Kittel meant the death camp at Auschwitz in Polish Upper Silesia.

301 For gifts to generals see note 394 below.

302 See note 77 above.

303 There is no document proving the shooting of Commissars by Wahle's
Inf.Reg.267/94.Inf.Div. for November 1941. See Activity Report by Ic,
94.Inf.Div, 29.6.1941–12.12.1941. The only such incident within the
Division's jurisdiction is a liquidation on 2.9.1941, Ic morning report,
Gruppe Schwedler (IV.Armeekorps) to 17.Armee, 2.9.1941, BA/MA
RH20-17/278.

304 Prtemovsk near Bachmut, between Rostov and Kharkov.

305 Kittel apparently came to Dvinsk in his capacity as Oberst, Army Group

North Führer-Reserve, and witnessed the murder of Jews there. Around 14,000 Jews were killed at Dvinsk in three phases in July, August and November 1941. In Document 119, Kittel himself reports having protested against the time and place of the shootings, but not against the deed. 'Enzyklopädie des Holocaust, Vol. 1, p. 375.' The 3,000 or so Jews living in Stalino were murdered between December 1941 and April 1942. After that, numerous Jews from outlying communities were brought to the city and murdered. Kittel was city commandant from 15.5.1942 to 20.9.1942. The 2,000 Jews remaining behind in Rostov were killed off between 11 and 12.8.1942, a date before Kittel's appointment as commandant of Rostov on 20.9.1942. For the murder of Jews there see Angrick, 'Besatzungspolitik', pp. 320–2, 560–4. Later Kittel admitted having signed a death warrant at Rostov condemning five persons to be shot under martial law. 'One death sentence which I carried out I still regret today because it was a Russian who had shot at two Rumanian soldiers stealing his chickens.' SRGG 1089, 27.12.1944, TNA WO 208/4169.

306 Wildermuth was never a Feldkommandant. Possibly his service as a regimental commander in Serbia or as fortress commandant at Le Havre is meant, or he is being confused with Generalmajor Felbert.

307 Edwin Graf Rothkirch und Trach commanded 330.Inf.Div. from 5.1.1942. It was deployed the following month at Demidov, north of Smolensk, and also north of the Dnieper during the Soviet winter offensive.

308 In the Reich Commissariat Ukraine, on whose territory Rothkirch's Oberfeldkommandantur 365 had its HQ at Lvov, total power was vested in the hands of the HSSPF Russia South, Hans-Adolf Prützmann. In the 'Wagner–Heydrich Agreement' of 28.4.1941, the Wehrmacht had given the SS a free hand to root out 'anti-State and anti-Reich movements'. Ueberschär/Wette, 'Überfall', p. 249f. Nothing is known of a special local arrangement between Rothkirch as Oberfeldkommandant 365 or as CO, 330.Inf.Div., and the police.

309 See note 296 above.

310 See note 297above.

311 Here meaning SS-Gruppenführer and Generalleutnant der Polizei Paul Hennicke (31.1.1883–25.7.1967), Police President of Weimar, April 1938–October 1942. No details are known regarding the murder of civilian convicts by the SD.

312 See also Document 119.

313 Rothkirch had been at HQ, Commdg Gen. Security Forces, Army Group Centre, since 8.10.1943 and was appointed Cdr, White Russia. Following a positive appraisal by Feldmarschall Busch he was promoted to General der Kavallerie on 1.1.1944.

314 Up to January 1942 in Lvov alone about 11,000 Jews were killed. For the extermination of Jews in the Eastern Galician region of Oberfeld-kommandantur 365 see Pohl, 'National-Sozialistische Judenverfolgung'. In this post, Rothkirch apparently had a rather reserved attitude towards the SS. Alongside the civilian administration and the SS apparatus within the General-Gouvernement, as Wehrmacht representative Rothkirch had only a subordinate role in the region. Ibid., p. 93. For the role of the Oberfeldkommandantur see Krannhals, 'Die Judenver-nichtung in Polen'.

315 In July and August at Zhitomir, 5,000 Jews were murdered. Those not caught up in the first massacres were killed on 18 September 1941 when 3,145 Jews were executed 10 kilometres outside the city. Broich was

probably referring to this occurrence. Why he came to Zhitomir as CO, Reiter-Reg.22./1.Kav.Div. subordinated to Pz.Gr.2, Army Group Centre, is not known. Between 12 and 20.9.1941 while the division was out of the line to rest and repair, Broich apparently took the opportunity to visit Zhitomir. War Diary, 1.Kav.Div., BA/MA RH29/1-4. There is no trace of an Oberst von Monich in the Army List.

316 Choltitz flew to Berlin on 4.7.1942 to deliver a radio broadcast on the fighting at Sevastopol; a facsimile of the speech is published by Timo von Choltitz at www.choltitz.de. The Chief of Staff referred to here is Oberst Freidrich Schulz (15.10.1897–30.11.1976) who was Chief of Staff, 11.Armee between 12.5.1942 and 27.11.1942. In his memoirs, Choltitz did not mention the shooting of Jews in the vicinity of Simferopol airfield. Choltitz, 'Soldat unter Soldaten', p. 217. A total of about 40,000 Jews and Crimean hussars were murdered in the Crimea. 'Enzyklopädie des Holocaust', Vol. 2, p. 822.

317 See Document 133 and note 329 below.

318 Karl Röver (12.2.1889–15.5.1942) was Gauleiter of Weser-Ems from 1.10.1928 until his unexpected death.

319 For the general context see Heuzeroth, 'Verfolgte aus religiösen Gründen' and Pohlschneider, 'Der NS-Kirchenkampf in Oldenburg'.

320 The Janovska camp was at Lvov. It had no gas chambers but estimates range from 10,000 to 200,000 persons murdered there. 'Enzyklopädie des Holocaust', Vol. 2, p. 657ff. The nearest gas chambers were at Belzec camp, about 70 kilometres north-west of Lvov, where 600,000 Jews, Gypsies and Poles were murdered between mid-March and December 1942. For the murder of Jews in Galicia see Sandkühler, 'Endlösung in Galizien'.

321 What knowledge Ramcke had of the Holocaust can no longer be ascertained. Since he spent only four weeks from February 1944 on the Eastern Front in Ukraine it is possible that he knew little of it.

322 Dr Karl Lasch (29.12.1904–3.6.1942), Governor, Galicia district of General-Gouvernement with his seat at Lvov, 1.8.1941–24.1.1942. Lasch was recalled peremptorily on 14.1.1942 and executed on 3.6.1942 for corruption. For Lasch see Sandkühler, 'Endlösung in Galizien', esp. p. 447f; and Pohl, 'NS-Judenverfolgung' esp. p. 76f.

323 Rothkirch also mentions this in SRGG 1133(C), 9.3.1945, TNA, WO 208/4169. Under the cover name 'Aktion 1005' from June 1943 the SS began removing the evidence of mass murders in the East by opening the graves and burning the corpses. Spector, 'Aktion 1005'.

324 At Kutno, captured by German troops on 15.9.1939, the Jewish population was corralled into a ghetto in June 1940 where they lived under the most appalling circumstances. During March and April 1942 the ghetto was gradually emptied, the inhabitants being taken to Kulmhof camp for extermination. Nothing is known of the mass shootings of Jews at Kutno.

325 In 'Weltwoche: Unabhängige Schweizerische Umschau 13', (1945), No. 585, p. 3 (26.1.1945), accompanying an article 'Kann sich Hitler noch auf die SS verlassen?' ('Can Hitler Still Rely on the SS?'), a photograph was published above a caption indicating that it portrayed Polish civilians unearthing mass graves containing the corpses of their murdered countrymen. It shows two SS men, a number of civilians with shovels, and some corpses in civilian clothes. In the article an anonymous SS man speaks of events at Zhitomir in the winter of 1942 in which tens of thousands were murdered and interred in mass graves.

326 At Lublin-Maidanek death camp approximately 250,000 people were murdered by gassings and mass shootings between October 1941 and July 1944. The only large concentration camp in Czechoslovakia was at Theresienstadt (today Terezin), a ghetto-like complex 60 kilometres north-west of Prague. Between 24.11.1941 and 20.4.1945, 140,000 Jews were brought there from western and central Europe; 33,000 died of starvation and the poor hygiene conditions in the overcrowded camp; 88,000 went to the death camps in the east. 'Enzyklopädie des Holocaust', Vol. 3, pp. 1403–7.

327 General der Artillerie Alfred von Vollard-Bockelberg (18.6.1874– disappeared 1945), 6.9.1939 Military Cdr, Posen; 26.10.1939 C-in-C, Border Region Centre; 5.11.1939–14.5.1940 CO, Wehrkreis I, Königsberg. At this time Rothkirch was Ia, XXXIV.Armeekorps stationed in the General-Gouvernement and probably met Vollard-Bockelberg in October 1939.

328 Between 25.12.1942 and 10.6.1943, Wilhelm Daser was CO, Oberfeldkommandantur 670 at Lille, one of nine districts under the Military Cdr, Belgium and Northern France, General Alexander von Falkenhausen. Between 27.11.1942 and 10.7.1944, Falkenhausen had 240 hostages shot in 18 separate incidents; 30 persons were shot during Daser's period in office, 10 of whom were executed in Brussels on 16.1.1943 for attacks on Wehrmacht personnel in Oberfeldkommandantur 670 district. Daser authorised the seizure of hostages as a reaction to the attacks, but the death sentences were handed down by Falkenhausen. Weber, 'Die innere Sicherheit', esp. p. 139ff; Warmbrunn, 'Occupation of Belgium'.

329 Wildermuth refers here to the massacre at Kralievo in the nine days from 15.10.1941, in which 4,000 to 5,000 civilians were shot dead as a reprisal by units of 717.Inf.Div. After the town was attacked by Chetniks on 5.10.1941, the Dornier aircraft factory was closed the following day for the alleged unreliability of the workforce. These employees were then held in a workshop of railway coachmakers together with workshop and railroad staff. On 11.10.1941 the Chetniks launched a second attack on Kralievo that lasted until 16.10.1941. The attacks had had artillery support while Wehrmacht troops came under fire from the civilian population. On 15 and 16.10.1941 between 300 and 1,755 hostages were shot, including the Dornier employees. That a German factory supervisor was shot as a hostage is not confirmed by the archive. The Kralievo district commandant, Oberleutnant Alfons Matziowicz, had issued an instruction on 15.10.1941 that 100 Serbs were to be shot for every dead German. This was authorised under Keitel's order of 16.9.1941 that the death of a German was to be expiated by the killing of 50 to 100 Serbs; OKW War Diary, Vol. 1, p. 1068. There is scarcely any evidence of Wildermuth's involvement in the shootings. The 717.Inf.Div. files do not indicate when and on whose orders any particular batch of hostages were shot, although most were carried out by elements of Inf.Reg.749 under Major Desch, senior officer at Kralievo. This unit was guilty of other massacres in the Kralievo area after 16.10.1941. The activity report of Wildermuth's Inf.Reg.737 for September 1941 does prove, however, that atrocities were committed in his direct area of jurisdiction before the October incident. The report states, '140 to 150 enemy dead, 6 wounded, 92 prisoners, *32 prisoners shot*, 98 houses, 8 dwellings, 2 villages set alight and destroyed. 39 own forces killed, 47 wounded.' BA/MA RH26-117/3. The Commdg Gen.

Serbia, Franz Böhme (15.4.1885–29.5.1947) expressed harsh criticism at the unleashing of reprisals. 'The shooting of our agents, Croats and the workforce of German armaments factories are errors that cannot be made good.' Plenipotentiary Commdg Gen. Serbia, Chief Mil. V./QuNo 3208/41. 25.10.1941 BA/MA RH26/342-14. In Wildermuth's comprehensive fund of documents the only mention of hostages being shot is a diary entry for 18.10.1941, 'Kralievo has become a dead city. The viciousness of our reprisals was fearsome', BA/MA NL251-100. His biographer does not speak of the events at Kralievo. Kohlhaas, 'Eberhard Wildermuth', p. 99f. See also Manoschek, 'Serbien ist judenfrei', pp. 155–8. A concise arrangement of the crimes in the context of the partisan war appears in Schmider, 'Auf Umwegen zum Vernichtungskrieg?'.

330 In World War I, 48 German soldiers were executed for desertion, cowardice, etc. The British executed 291 of their own soldiers, To these must be added the executions of more than 750 Italian, 18 Belgian and 35 US soldiers (between April 1917 and June 1919). In France the courts martial handed down 2,400 death sentences to Army personnel of which about 500 were carried out. Beckett, 'The Great War', p. 227f; Bach, 'Fusillés pour l'exemple'.

331 The protest of General der Artillerie Paul Bader (20.7.1883–28.2.1971), Cmmdg Gen. of Higher Command LXV, Belgrade cannot be found in the archives.

332 On 18.10.1942 Hitler ordered that all commandos were to be executed without exception even if they wore uniform. This was as a reprisal for the British commando raid on the Channel Island of Sark on 4.10.1942 when German prisoners had been bound in such a way that they strangled themselves if they attempted to struggle free. No pardons were to be allowed. Individual commandos were to be handed over to the SD. The Order was first enforced on 11.12.1942 when two 'Cockleshell Heroes', members of an SBS canoe operation to attack shipping at Bordeaux, were executed. The original of the Order is at BA/MA RW41/v.606. For the application of the Order, see Friedrich, 'Das Gesetz des Krieges', pp. 295–306; Messerschmitt, 'Kommandobefehl und Völkerrechtsdenken'.

333 On 14.6.1944 a force of 243 RAF bombers attacked Le Havre, sinking numerous German warships and destroying large areas of the town and its docks. French casualties at 75 dead and 150 injured were light as the result of the dock area having been evacuated. For the attack see Hümmelchen, 'Die deutschen Schnellboote', p. 175f; and Tent, 'E-boat Alert', pp. 146–82.

334 By the end of 1937, 13,260 inmates had been registered at Dachau concentration camp. That year the camp had an average population of 2,535. This figure increased to 5,068 persons in 1938 after the camp was enlarged. That year 18,681 new prisoners passed through its gates. Kimmel, 'Konzentrationslager Dachau', p. 371; Drobisch/Wieland, 'System der Konzentrationslager', pp. 288, 303.

335 Commandant of Dachau camp in 1937 was SS-Oberführer Hans Loritz (12.12.1895–13.1.1946).

336 It is uncertain which person named Hasse is meant here. Possibly Broich was speaking of the later General der Infanterie Wilhelm Hasse (24.11.1895–13.1.1946) who, like Broich, was an Oberstleutnant in 1937. For Josias Erbprinz zu Waldeck und Pyrmont see note 356 below. Thoma, a native of Dachau, also visited Dachau camp before the war.

SRXX 1580, 12.2.1943, TNA WO 208/4162.
337 Oberst Franz August Maria Lex, from 1944 CO, Art.Reg.170; PoW
7.11.1944 Middelburg, Walcheren (Netherlands); Trent Park from
7.12.1944.
338 Werner Altemeyer, Head of Mayor's Staff, Riga.
339 Skirotava near Riga.
340 On 30.11.1944, 1,035 Berlin Jews were executed on the edge of woodland
near Rumbula. On 1.8.1941 and 9.12.1941 25,000–28,000 Jews, the
entire population of the Riga ghetto, were murdered at Rumbula.
'Enzyklopädie des Holocaust', Vol. 2, p. 1230. For the massacres and
Bruns's statement see also Jersak, 'Entscheidungen zu Mord und Lüge',
pp. 333–7.
341 General der Pioniere Alfred Jacob (1.4.1883–13.11.1963), from 1938
Inspector of Army Engineers and Fortifications.
342 Oberst (later Generalmajor) Erich Abberger (6.4.1895–3.5.1988), from
1.10.1939–1.9.1942 Chief of Staff to General Jacob, see note 341 above.
343 Hauptmann (Reserve) Dr Otto Schulz du Bois.
344 Admiral Wilhelm Canaris (1.1.1887–9.4.1945), from 1.1.1935 Head of
Military Abwehr at OKW; 23.7.1944 arrested on grounds of his close
contacts to military conspirators; 8.4.1945 admitted to treason in
kangaroo court at Flossenbürg concentration camp; 9.4.1945 executed
by hanging.
345 Bruns spoke out on 18.12.1948 in the OKW trials at Nuremberg as a
witness against Feldmarschall Wilhelm Ritter von Leeb. See also
Friedrich, 'Das Gesetz des Krieges', pp. 416–19.
346 About 99,000 Jews were murdered at Odessa, mostly by Rumanian
forces. 'Enzyklopädie des Holocaust', Vol. 2, p. 1058f.
347 See note 217 above.
348 For the night of the Reich Pogrom in Vienna see Ganglmair,
'Novemberpogrom 1938'; Rosenkranz, 'Reichskristallnacht'.
349 Dr Irmfried Eberl (8.9.1910–16.2.1948) is probably indicated here. At the
beginning of 1940 he took over as head of the Brandenburg-Havel
Euthanasia Institute and in the autumn of 1940 the institute at
Bernburg/Saale. A total of at least 18,000 persons were murdered at both
places under his directorship. Eberl was commandant at Treblinka death
camp in 1942. He was conscripted into the Wehrmacht on 31.1.1944.
After the war he practised as a doctor at Blaubeuren, where he was
arrested in January 1948 and committed suicide the following month.
He was not a lawyer, he had studied medicine at Innsbruck. Schulze,
'Euthenasie in Bernburg', pp. 155–7; Gehler, 'Heilen durch Töten', pp.
361–82.
350 By September 1941 the planned euthanasia programme had claimed
70,273 victims. Although organised euthanasia was halted after massive
protests, another 20,000 persons were killed in 'wildcat' actions. Klee,
'Euthanasie im NS-Staat'.
351 Up to February 1942, about two million Russian PoWs had died in
German captivity, 500,000 of them in the period from November 1941.
Streit, 'Keine Kamaraden', p. 128.
352 Between 3.4.1940 and 13.5.1940 the NKVD murdered 14,587 Polish
officers and police in Soviet captivity, of which 4,404 were killed at
Katyn near Smolensk, 3,896 at Kharkov and 6,287 at Kalinin. Misial,
'Das Schlachtfeld zweier totalitärer Systeme', p. 24f.
353 In 1944 Generalstabsintendant Friedrich Pauer was Departmental Head
V2 at OKH Army Admin.

354 A source documenting Felbert's activities as Feldkommandant
Besançon in detail is not known. The Feldkommandantur 560 War
Diary (BA/MA RH36-206) is not very enlightening, but mentions in
passing that its war court condemned 18 terrorists to death on
18.9.1943, of which 17 were shot 'without incident' on 26.9.1943. 40
death warrants signed by Felbert therefore seems a realistic figure. In his
memoirs written in captivity at the end of 1945 he says, '. . . As
Feldkommandant I tried to relieve the civilian population of the burden
that is always so heavy under foreign occupation. I saved many people
from the death penalty, preserved many from long prison sentences and
prevented many acts of violence by subordinate officers. But one could
not be everywhere and one did not get to hear everything, and so certain
things happened which should not have happened.' 'Memoirs', p. 57.
This statement was supported by French eyewitnesses in the court
proceedings and also by official documents. Felbert, Wehrmacht
Commander, North-Eastern France, pointed out on 4.2.1944 that the
Feldkommandant was not king in his kingdom and one had to get used
to the fact that the SD was not subordinate to him, and it was of great
importance to cooperate with this service office.

355 Himmler ordered the setting-up of the concentration camp at
Auschwitz on 27.4.1940. At this time Otto Elfeldt was Staff Officer,
Artillery, Army Group A in the West. There is nothing to indicate his
having visited Poland, and his knowledge of events there is therefore
noteworthy.

356 Josias Erbprinz zu Waldeck-Pyrmont (13.5.1896–30.11.1967), 6.10.1938
to the capitulation HSSPF Fulda-Werra. Sentenced to life imprisonment,
Buchenwald trials, 14.8.1947, released 1.12.1950.

357 Kurt Dittmar, Pionierführer 1.Armee, was in France in the summer of
1940 and took over 169.Inf.Div. in February 1941, at that time in the
process of formation in the Reich. There is no evidence that he might
have come to Paris, or even France, later, and so one assumes that
Dittmar knew of the existence of Auschwitz by the early summer of
1940.

358 Between 29.10.1942 and 1.11.1942, the 20,000 Jews inhabiting the
ghetto at Pinsk were shot ('Enzyklopädie des Holocaust', Vol. 3, p.
1113f.). If Feuchtinger was ever there is not known. From October 1941
to August 1942 he commanded Art.Reg.227/227.Inf.Div., which fought
on the northern sector of the Eastern Front, a great distance from Pinsk.
Subsequently he served with OKH Führer-Reserve and after April 1943
was exclusively in France.

359 General der Infanterie Edgar Röhricht (16.6.1892–11.2.1967) arrived
Trent Park 7.6.1945. The exact number of the dead at Dresden resulting
from the air raid on the night of 13.2.1945 is now estimated at between
25,000 and 40,000. The most recent study is Taylor, 'Dresden'.

360 Eberbach's statement was used against Kurt Meyer at his trial for war
crimes before a Canadian tribunal beginning 10.12.1945 at Aurich.
Meyer was sentenced to death on 28.12.1945, the sentence being
commuted to life imprisonment. Meyer was released in 1956. See note
280 above.

361 CO, Kradschützen (Motor-cycle Rifle) Battalion 34/4.Pz.Div. was Major
Erich von Stegmann (6.4.1896–?), succeeded on 9.1.1942 by Rittmeister
Bradel. Neumann, 'Die 4.Panzer Division', p. 444.

362 See note 375 below.

363 On 20.12.1941 during a five-hour talk with Hitler, Guderian attempted

to convince him to rescind his order of 16.12.1941 to halt. On 25.12.1941 Guderian was relieved of command after retreating without authority. Reinhardt, 'Die Wende vor Mosakau', pp. 225, 228. In his memoirs Guderian provided a much less dramatic version of the conversation than Thoma does here. Guderian, 'Erinnerungen eines Soldaten', pp. 240–6. Thoma stayed in Berlin from 1 to 7.8.1942 to accept his promotion to Generalleutnant, and visited Guderian on the morning of 5.8.1942. Diary 1942, BA/MA N2/2 and note 393 below.

364 General der Infanterie Rudolf Schmundt (13.8.1896–1.10.1944) had been Chief Wehrmacht Adjutant to Hitler from 28.1.1938, and from 1.10.1942 Head of the Army Personnel Bureau. He saw it as his mission to bind the Army to Hitler and National Socialism. Schmundt was not free of idealism and spared no effort to assist the commanders at the front. As an ardent admirer of Hitler he would not allow any kind of criticism of the Führer. See Stumpf, 'Rudolf Schmundt', and also short biography in 'Tätigkeitsbericht Schmundt', pp. 15–22.

365 Also Peter Hoffmann, 'Die Sicherheit des Diktators'; Seidler/Zeigert, 'Führerhauptquartiere', pp. 97–110, provide an overview of Hitler's burgeoning self-protective measures.

366 See note 49 above.

367 These names were not mentioned in the radio bulletins. The first report broadcast by German radio was an official announcement of the attempted assassination and stated only that Hitler had survived a bomb attempt unscathed and had received Mussolini for a long conference. The text is reproduced in Domarus, 'Hitler', Vol. 2, p. 2127. See also Peter Hoffmann, 'Staatsstreich', p. 540.

368 Hitler's radio address towards midnight on 20.7.1944 appears at Domarus, 'Hitler'. According to this transcript Hitler's concluding words were, 'In this I see a finger of Providence indicating that I must continue my work, and therefore I shall!'

369 It is not known in what capacity Reimann was involved with the NSDAP in the 1930s.

370 On 21.7.1944 a communiqué was issued regarding the introduction of the 'Hitler salute' throughout the Wehrmacht as advocated by Dönitz, Goering and Keitel. The Army was not mentioned in the text. In his address on the evening of 20.7.1944 Hitler did speak about the obedience to orders of the German Army. Domarus, 'Hitler', Vol. 2, pp. 2129–31.

371 For the reactions of Thoma and Bassenge to the assassination attempt see SRGG 961, 21.7.1944, TNA WO 208/4168. Both believed initially in the possibility of a simulated attempt as a pretext for a purge. Thoma's first reaction was, 'Now it has begun internally. I always told you . . . I know Stauffenberg very well. I was with him, Graf Stauffenberg, at HQ and he was always quite frank with his opinion, which was also mine'.

372 Oberst Claus Schenk Graf von Stauffenberg (15.11.1907–20.7.1944), 1938–May 1940 Staff Officer Ib, 1.Light-Div.; May 1940–February 1943 OKH Organisations-Abt.; February–April 1943 Staff Officer Ia, 10.Pz.Div.; 7.4.1943 seriously wounded, low-level air attack. Lost an eye, his right hand and two fingers of left hand; 1.10.1943 Chief of Staff, General Army office; 1.7.1944 Chief of Staff, C-in-C, Ersatzheer (Replacement Army). Peter Hoffmann, 'Stauffenberg'.

373 This protocol confirms the details that Broich made in 1962 about his conversations and attitude towards Stauffenberg. See ibid., p. 273f. For his visits to commanders at the front see note 387 below.

374 Heinrich Himmler became C-in-C, Ersatzheer and Heinz Guderian

Chief of Army General Staff. Presumably Sponeck had listened to Hitler's radio broadcast on the night of 20.7.1944 and misheard. In his speech Hitler stated that he had appointed Himmler C-in-C of the Heimat (i.e. Homeland) Army. See note 367 above for the speech.

375 Generaloberst Hans Jürgen Stumpff (15.6.1888–9.3.1968). At this time Stumpff was C-in-C, Luftflotte Reich. His jurisdiction was not affected by 20 July, nor was he mentioned in Hitler's speech. Since it is unlikely that Sponeck and Stumpff met in the war, having regard to their respective military duties, Sponeck had probably been influenced by Bassenge. The latter was Stumpff's Chief of General Staff at Luftflotte 5 between 1.8.1940 and 4.10.1940, and had said of his superior on 21.7.1944, 'Stumpff is the biggest twit you can imagine. I was his Chief of Staff. So, I was glad, I mean really glad, when I got away from him. Appalling.' SRGG 961, 21.7.1944, TNA WO 208/4168.

376 Nina Schenk Gräfin von Stauffenberg, née Freiin von Lerchenfeld (27.8.1913–02.04.2006).

377 At his death he was 37.

378 The bomb exploded during the midday situation conference at FHQ Wolfsschanze, Rastenburg, in East Prussia. Stauffenberg took part in this conference in his capacity as Chief of Ersatzheer Staff reporting on the formation of the Volksgrenadier-Divisions.

379 Stauffenberg had brought with him two explosive charges, but armed only one and left it in an attaché-case below the map table. Therefore the explosive effect was less than expected and killed only four of the 24 persons present, sparing Hitler. See note 389 below.

380 Radio broadcast by Hitler. Domarus, 'Hitler', Vol. 2, p. 2127ff.

381 Generalfeldmarschall Gerd von Rundstedt (12.12.1875–24.2.1953) was relieved of command as C-in-C West on 2.7.1944 and transferred to Führer-Reserve. He was not involved in the coup and later proved his loyalty to Hitler. Recalled to his former post on 5.9.1944, in August and September he was President of the Wehrmacht Honour Court (Ehrenhof), the purpose of whose sittings was to expel from the Wehrmacht those officers involved in the plot in order that they could be brought before the People's Court. Ziemke, 'Gerd von Rundstedt'; Messenger, 'The Last Prussian'; Huber, 'Gerd von Rundstedt'. The British officer, most probably 'Lord Aberfeldy' made most of his references to generals Hoepner, von Witzleben and Beck, who were all discharged from the Wehrmacht, having been involved in the plot.

382 Generaloberst Friedrich Dollmann (2.2.1882–28.6.1944), from 25.10.1939 C-in-C 7.Armee, which had been dislodged from Normandy in June 1944. On 28 June he suffered a heart attack at his command post. According to a report by Generalmajor Max Pemsel, Chief of Staff, 7.Armee, Dollmann committed suicide because he felt culpable for the defeat of his force. Ose, 'Entscheidung im Westen', p. 152, note 305.

383 General der Artillerie Erich Marcks (6.6.1891–12.6.1944), Cmmdg Gen., LXXXIV.Armeekorps, lost his life to a low-level air attack while visiting the front north of St Lo.

384 Stauffenberg's wife Nina (see note 376 above) was arrested at Schloss Lautingen near Ebingen where she had been staying since 18.7.1944. The family had owned the property since the early seventeenth century. Peter Hoffmann, 'Stauffenberg', pp. 15, 422, 447.

385 Alfred Schenk Graf von Stauffenberg (27.6.1860–20.1.1936) had been Major-at-Readiness between 1908 and 1918 and Senior Marshal at the Court of the King of Württemberg.

386 If both charges had been detonated, the blast would probably have been
    sufficient to kill all present in the barrack hut. See note 379 above.
387 In September 1942, Stauffenberg visited General der Infanterie Georg
    von Sodenstern (15.11.1889–20.7.1955), Chief of General Staff, Army
    Group B, and the Cmmdg Gen. XXXX.Pz.Korps, Leo Freiherr Geyr von
    Schweppenburg, and attempted without success to recruit them for the
    planned assassination of Hitler. On 26.1.1943 he attempted to persuade
    Generalfeldmarschall Erich von Manstein to head a coup d'état, which
    he declined. One cannot simply say that Manstein was the only field
    marshal 'who had not gone along with it'. Broich repeats here Stauffen-
    berg's impressions on the field marshals as a whole. Stauffenberg could
    only infer from Henning von Tresckow's soundings that Feldmarschall
    von Kluge was not opposed to a conspiracy but did not want to be part
    of it. At that time Stauffenberg could only have been certain of the
    support of von Witzleben. After the conversation with von Manstein,
    Stauffenberg remarked, 'These guys are either shitting their pants or
    have straw heads, and don't want it.' Peter Hoffmann, 'Stauffenberg', pp.
    250, 252f, 262f, 265–8. Broich was of the opinion in October 1943, from
    a conversation with Bassenge, 'that all had said they were ready', but
    none wanted to lead it. 'Manstein is the only one who said . . . the time
    is not yet ripe, and he rejected it absolutely, and it is madness.' SRGG
    506, 24.10.1943, TNA, WO 208/4166.
388 General der Infanterie Kurt Zeitzler (9.6.1895–25.9.1963) was Chief of
    the Army General Staff from 24.9.1942 to 20.7.1944. He applied to be
    relieved on four occasions and was only successful finally by reporting
    sick on 10.7.1944. Stahl, 'Zeitzler'.
389 Four persons lost their lives when the bomb exploded: stenographer Dr
    Heinz Berger died the same afternoon; Oberst Heinz Brandt, Ia Staff;
    Operations-Abt. and General der Flieger Günther Korten, Chief of the
    Luftwaffe General Staff died on 22.7.1944; Generalleutnant Rudolf
    Schmuundt, Hitler's Senior Wehrmacht Adjutant and Head of the Army
    personnel Office on 1.10.1944. Peter Hoffmann, 'Staatsstreich', p. 496.
390 The proclamations by Grossadmiral Dönitz are reproduced in, *inter alia*,
    Padfield, 'Dönitz', pp. 431, 434. The telgram of loyalty from Erhard
    Milch is reproduced in Irving, 'Tragödie der deutschen Luftwaffe', p.
    365.
391 Should read *Kurt* Zeitzler.
392 See note 141 above.
393 In February 1944, Guderian was assigned the Polish estate Deipenhof in
    the Reichsgau Wartheland for the equivalent of RM1.24 million. The
    German Reich dispossessed the Polish owners. Ueberschär/Vogel,
    'Dienen und Verdienen', pp. 169–72.
394 Generalfeldmarschall Ritter von Leeb (5.9.1876–29.4.1956) received
    from Hitler in 1941 and 1943 two monetary gifts totalling RM888,000,
    which he used in August 1944 to acquire a woodland property of 214
    hectares situated north of Passau. It is therefore incorrect to say that he
    turned down donations. Ueberschär/Vogel, 'Dienen und Verdienen', pp.
    151–7. Leeb commanded Army Group North during the Russian
    campaign in 1941. Relieved by Hitler on 6.1.1942, he was not used again.
    Leeb was firmly opposed to the invasion of France, and was the only
    Army Group commander prepared to participate in a coup under Halder.
    When Halder was surprised by Hitler's change of mind on 5.11.1939 and
    cancelled the coup preparations, Leeb lost interest and obeyed Hitler's
    orders to prepare the attack. Subsequently he had no further contact

with the opposition. Peter Hoffmann, 'Staatsstreich', pp. 161–5, 175, 179–83, 188f, also Leeb, 'Tagebuchaufzeichnungen', esp. pp. 50–4.

395 Here Sponeck had figured out the motivation of the conspirators, to go through with the coup despite its poor prospects in order to prove that the German resistance movement 'had dared to take the decisive gamble' as Henning von Trescow put it. It was not the intention to whitewash the Army morally or the officer corps as a whole, only the conspirators. Fest, 'Staatsreich', p. 240.

396 British propaganda called the Elser attempted assassination 'a second Reichstag fire'. Haasis, 'Georg Elser', p. 56. The 'Germany reports' of the SPD exiles show that immediately after the attempt there were suspicions that either Hitler himself, or certain NSDAP circles, were the string-pullers. This was based on the fact that it would not otherwise have been possible to have planned and carried out the action without the Gestapo and SS having known about it (ibid.). The SS came across rumours at a Fulda clerical seminar that attributed the attempt to the Party. The clergymen obtained their information from a Strasbourg transmitter (ibid., p. 61). A few days after the attempt Heinrich Müller assumed that Strasser and the Schwarze Front were behind Elser (ibid., p. 210), a theory advanced by the 'St Galler Tageblatt' on 24.11.1939 in an article probably inspired from Germany. Ernst Eggert, a stool pigeon at Sachsenhausen, circulated the rumour at the beginning of 1940 that Elser was an SS man and the attempt had been staged. His reasoning for this was that Elser was receiving such good treatment in custody that he could not possibly be a 'real' assassin and at the least had a good relationship with the SS. From his cell at Sachsenhausen Martin Niemöller also espoused this theory; he had heard the rumour before Elser arrived at the camp and maintained the assertion after the war (ibid., p. 214ff). One of Elser's guards, SS man Walter Usslepp, alleged that Hitler and Himmler had put Elser up to it personally (ibid., p. 222). Many corresponding witness accounts occur in the IfZ archive ZS/A.17.

397 Ley said in his speech, 'Degenerate to the marrow, blue-bloodied into idiocy, corruptible to the point of tribulation and cowardly as all low creatures, that is the nobility which the Jew sends forth against National Socialism, puts a bomb in their hands and turns them into murderers and criminals . . . if reactionaries believed they could raise their heads again, now they will have finally understood that their time has gone for ever. We will make up for that which had previously, perhaps consciously, been overlooked. This scum must be eliminated, exterminated root and branch. It is not sufficient just to seize the culprits and bring them ruthlessly to account – the whole brood must be wiped out. This goes above all for the traitors in Moscow, London and New York. Every German must be made aware that if he sets himself up against Germany at war, in print or by the spoken word, or incites treason by his act, then he and his family must die . . . whoever betrays us will be exterminated.' Robert Ley, 'Gott schütze den Führer', in 'Der Angriff', No. 180, 23.7.1944. Short extracts are reproduced in Conze, 'Adel und Adeligkeit in Widerstand', p. 269.

398 Generalleutnant Hans Graf von Sponeck (12.2.1888–23.7.1944), a cousin of Theodor Graf von Sponeck; CO, 22.Inf.Div., Poland, France and USSR; 22.10.1941 Leader, XXXXII.Armeekorps. Without reference to FHQ, on 29.12.1941 he abandoned the Kertsch Peninsula in the Crimea and was relieved of command two days later. Condemned to death by court martial on 23.1.1942 for 'negligent disobedience in the field', the

sentence was commuted on 22.2.1942 to six years' stockade at
Germersheim. A petition for remission of the sentence by von Manstein
on 20.6.1943 was refused by Hitler. Following 20.7.1944, he was
murdered on Himmler's order.

399 Reimann was confusing the twin older brothers of Stauffenberg,
Alexander and Berthold. The former (15.3.1905–27.1.1964) graduated in
Ancient History in 1931 and was Professor Extraordinary at Würzburg
from 1936. He was Ordinarius in Ancient History at Strasbourg for a
short while in 1942 before his recall to the front. On 20.7.1944 he was
serving in Athens as Leutnant (Reserve) with LXVIII.Armeekorps. He had
no knowledge of his brother's activities. Taken into *Sippenhaft*
(detention as a close relative of a traitor) on 30.7.1944, he was shunted
between various concentration camps and prisons until the end of the
war. His twin brother Marineoberstabsrichter Berthold Graf Schenk von
Stauffenberg (15.3.1905–10.8.1944), a Navy judge, was implicated in the
plot and hanged. He was one of only three naval officers actively involved
in the resistance. The standard work on the Stauffenberg brothers is Peter
Hoffmann, 'Stauffenberg'. See also Hillmann, 'Der 20 Juli 1944'.

400 Hitler spoke on 4.8.1944 at FHQ Wolfsschanze to a gathering of
Reichsleiters and Gauleiters. The official communiqué of 5.8.1944
stated that the traitors had not only been active in sabotaging the efforts
and struggles of the nation since 1941, but since the very seizure of
power itself. Domarus, 'Hitler', Vol. 2, p. 2138. The text of the speech by
Reichs-Commissar in Norway Josef Terboven (23.5.1898–11.5.1945) is
not recorded.

401 Generalleutnant Rudolf Stegmann (6.8.1894–18.6.1944) fell at
Briebeque, Normandy as CO, 77.Inf.Div., which he had led since
1.5.1944.

402 Regarding the Honour Court presided over by von Rundstedt see note
287 above.

403 From 1794 in the French Revolution three marshals were guillotined:
Augustin-Joseph de Mailly (b. 1708), Philippe de Noailles, Duc de
Mouchy (b. 1715) and Nicolas Luckner (b. 1722), a native of the
Oberpfalz.

404 See notes 407 and 479 below.

405 Julius Streicher (12.2.1885–16.10.1946) was one of the earliest NSDAP
members and founded the violently anti-Jewish weekly newspaper 'Der
Stürmer' in 1923. From 1929 he was Gauleiter of Central Franconia
(Mittelfranken). His rise to riches led to a Party inquiry that deprived
him of his offices in 1940. He continued to publish the newspaper. He
was condemned to death at Nuremberg and hanged.

406 Generalfeldmarschall Erwin von Witzleben (4.2.1881–8.8.1944), from
2.10.1938 C-in-C, Gruppenkommando, Frankfurt am Main; 1.9.1939 C-
in-C, 1.Armee; 26.10.1940–28.2.1942 C-in-C West. Steinbach,
'Zwischen Gefolgschaft, Gehorsam und Widerstand'.

407 On 8.8.1944 the following eight officers involved in the 20 July plot were
hanged at Berlin Plötzensee prison: Robert Bernardis, Albrecht von
Hagen, Paul von Hase, Erich Hoepner, Friedrich Karl Klausing,
Hellmuth Stieff, Erwin von Witzleben, Peter Graf Yorck von
Wartenburg. Fest, 'Staatsstreich', pp. 300–4.

408 From 1.4.1939 Spang was CO, Lower Rhine Fortifications and as such
was subordinate to von Witzleben (see note 406 above). Between 16.9
and 15.11.1940 Spang was Chief of Staff, 1.Armee and worked alongside
von Witzleben.

409 Generaloberst Ludwig von Beck (29.6.1880–20.7.1944), from 1.7.1935 to 8.8.1938 Chief of the Army General Staff.

410 Between 1925 and 1934 Spang served with Artillery Reg.5, of which Ludwig Beck was CO from 1.2.1929 to 1.10.1931.

411 Lieutenants Hanns Ludin and Richard Scheringer, and Oberleutnant Hans Friedrich Werdt established contacts with the NSDAP in 1929 for the purpose of forming National Socialist cells within the Reichswehr, and published a broadsheet calling for a 'national revolution'. The three officers were arrested on 10/11.3.1930 and charged with preparing an act of high treason. The Reich Court at Leipzig sentenced them to 18 months' military prison on 4.10.1930. As Regimental CO, Beck expressed to the court his understanding for the motives of the accused, which arose from a sense of national idealism, and condemned them only on disciplinary grounds. Bucher, 'Reichswehrprozess'; Klaus-Jürgen Müller, 'Beck', pp. 61f, 331–4.

412 Generalfeldmarschall Gerd von Rundstedt, 1.3.1942–2.7.1944 and 5.9.1944–10.3.1945 C-in-C West. He replaced Feldmarschall Erwin von Witzleben in this position.

413 Gerd von Rundstedt spoke excellent French and had a friendly correspondence with Marshal Pétain. The statement that he attempted to spare the French people appears more than dubious on the basis of contemporary research. 'Das deutsche Reich und der Zweite Weltkrieg, Vol. 5/2, pp. 174–81. See also Ziemke, 'Gerd von Rundstedt'. The affair is clarified in Peter Lieb's published dissertation 'Das deutsche Westheer in die Eskalation der Gewalt'.

414 Generaloberst Erich Hoepner (14.9.1886–8.8.1944) probably met Spang in World War I as a Staff Officer.

415 Hoepner proved himself a very able panzer leader in the Polish, French and Russian campaigns. After ordering 4.Pz.Armee to retreat from Moscow on 8.1.1942 he was relieved of command and discharged the Wehrmacht for cowardice and disobeying orders. He was also deprived of the right to wear uniform and decorations. Hitler was so enraged by other unauthorised retreats that he decided to make an example of Hoepner. In Berlin, Hoepner contacted Olbricht and took an active part in planning the coup d'état of 20 July. He was sentenced to death by the People's Court on 8.8.1944 and executed by hanging at Berlin-Plötzensee prison the same day.

416 Paul von Hase (24.7.1885–8–8–1944), from 15.11.1940 to 20.3.1944 City Commandant, Berlin and a leading figure in the attempted coup. October 1905 joined Kaiser-Alexander-Garde-Grenadier-Reg.1; 1921 married a Latvian from Mitan, Margarethe Freiin von Funck. Hase had four children (Alexander, Ina, Maria and Friedrich-Wilhelm). Kopp, 'Paul von Hase'.

417 At 1600hrs on 20.7.1944, Keitel passed the following order to all Wehrkreis commanders by telephone or signal, 'All orders from the Bendler-Strasse bearing the signatures of Generaloberst Hoepner, Feldmarschall von Witzleben, Gen.d.Inf. Olbricht or Gen.Oberst Fromm are invalid. These generals are to be considered mutineers. Oberst Graf von Stauffenberg carried out the attempt on the Führer's life. Henceforth only the orders of the Reichsführer-SS and the Chief of the OKW are to be obeyed. All measures "Walküre" are to be cancelled. Closest liaison is to be maintained with the Gauleiters, senior SS and police chiefs.' Since this order was also passed by telephone, there may be minor differences between the various texts. A mention of Halder in

this connection is unproven and probably the result of an error of memory. The order is reproduced in, *inter alia*, 'Tätigkeitsbericht Schmundt', p. 165.

418 SA-Obergruppenführer and General der Polizei Wolf Heinrich Graf von Helldorf (14.10.1896–15.8.1944); 1926 joined NSDAP; 1932 SA-Führer, Berlin-Brandenburg; 1932 Member Prussian Parliament; 1933 Member Reichstag; July 1935 Police President of Berlin. Despite his Nazi past and involvement in wrongdoings of the regime, from 1938 he was involved in the resistance, consorting with Goerdeler's circle, and was involved in the coup plot of 20 July 1944.

419 Close contact between Stauffenberg and Choltitz is not confirmed by research.

420 It is not known with which SS-Oberführer Choltitz spoke *immediately* after the attempt. LXXXIV.Armeekorps, which he commanded at that time, was subordinate to 17.SS-Pz.Grenadier-Div. 'Götz von Berlichingen' under SS-Brigade-Führer Otto Baum. What contact Choltitz had with Baum is unknown. In his memoirs, he mentioned only a conversation with his own Chief of Staff about the assassination attempt. During the train journey from FHQ Wolfsschanze to Berlin on the night of 7.8.1944, Choltitz talked with Reichsleiter Robert Ley, whom he did not know, and who explained to him the new Sippenhaft Law, which allowed the arrest of a traitor's kith and kin. Choltitz, 'Brennt Paris?' p. 13f, on Sippenhaft see, for example, Hett/Tuchel, 'Die Reaktionen des NS-Staates', pp. 383–8.

421 Generalleutnant Friedrich Brieth (25.5.1892–9.7.1982) commanded from 5.4.1943 to 24.5.1944 Artillery School I in Berlin. It trained artillery and regimental commanders.

422 Probably meant here is Burkhart Freiherr Loeffelholz von Colberg (6.5.1913–30.10.2000), who served in North Africa, latterly as Ia, 334.Inf.Div. He was flown out of Tunisia, then occupied various Staff positions, ended the war as Oberstleutnant and served with the Bundeswehr until 30.9.1971, retiring in the rank of Oberst.

423 Generalmajor Martin Lattmann (10.2.1896–11.8.1976) was captured at Stalingrad as CO, 14.Pz.Div. From 25.8.1940 to 15.4.1942 he was CO, Training Staff, Artillery School Jüterbog (from 26.1.1942 Artillery School II) and as such was responsible for the weapons training courses for young officers and applicants for the officer-reserve. Lattmann was decried as a 'wild Nazi general' but went through an ideological *volte-face* in captivity, joined the anti-Nazi Bund Deutscher Offiziere and took up a position on its left wing. After the war he served as a Generalmajor of the Volkspolizei at the DDR Interior Ministry and was active for various economic commissions. Frieser, 'Krieg hinter Stacheldraht', pp. 193, 371.

424 Between 8.2.1942 and 28.4.1942 at Demyansk, around 100,000 German soldiers remained encircled until 16.Armee opened a corridor for them; the then Generalleutnant Walther von Seydlitz-Kurzbach commanded the relief units from X.Armeekorps. 'Das deutsche Reich und der Zweite Weltkrieg', Vol. 4, pp. 639–41.

425 Tschugujew, city on the Severny Donetz.

426 Kharkov in the Ukraine.

427 Meant here is Oberst Hans Lattmann (b. 24.12.1894), summer 1944, Artillery Staff Officer, Army Group B. Lattmann was once assessed by Rommel as a 'convinced National Socialist' and so the statement he made to Beck is all the more interesting.

428 For Dietrich see note 91 above.

429 Generalleutnant Hans Speidel (28.10.1897–28.11.1984), from 14.4.1944–5.9.1944 Chief of Staff, Army Group B in France. He had prior knowledge of the 20 July plot and was arrested on 5.9.1944, but skilfully avoided incriminating himself and remained in detention until the war ended.

430 Oberst Hans-Jürgen Dingler (b. 30.3.1904), from 12.2.1944 to 4.1945 Chief of Staff, LVIII.Res.Pz.Korps. Postwar with West German Intelligence Gehlen/BND.

431 General der Panzertruppe Walter Krüger (23.3.1892–11.7.1973), Cmmdg Gen. LVIII.Res.Pz.Korps, was a highly decorated panzer leader who probably from his time as regimental commander in 1937 onwards had gained general ideas from Beck. It is not proven that they were any closer than this.

432 For Bayerlein see note 225 above. Fritz Bayerlein was awarded the Swords to his Knight's Cross on 20.7.1944. With his Pz.Lehr.Div. he had fought off numerous American attacks west of St Lo from 11 July. This may explain why he was in such good spirits at that point. A few days later the American Great Offensive crushed his unit. On 27.7.1944 he reported that his division had been wiped out. Ritgen, 'Panzer Lehr Division', pp. 155–70.

433 The date of these talks is unknown. Ritter mentions in his biography of Goerdeler that Choltitz spoke with him in March 1944. At the time Choltitz was a corps commander in Italy, therefore it is more likely that the meeting occurred between 16.4.1944 and 13.6.1944, when Choltitz was in the OKH Führer-Reserve. The detailed knowledge that Choltitz possessed of the course of the event is astonishing. Probably he had obtained the information from his Staff in Paris, who were in on the secret. Another source alleges that before the attempt in July 1944, Choltitz already knew everything about it. Oberleutnant Curt Vogel reported on a conversation between Choltitz and Generalmajor Eugen König, CO, 91.Luftlande-Div. (BA/MA MSg 1/647 and 2579).

434 General der Infanterie Friedrich Olbricht (4.10.1888–20.7.1944), from 15.2.1940 Chief of Army General Bureau.

435 Carl Goerdeler (31.7.1884–2.2.1945), 1930–37 Oberbürgermeister, Leipzig. Envisaged as Reich Chancellor in the event of a successful coup.

436 General der Nachrichtentruppe Erich Fellgiebel (4.10.1886–4.9.1944), from August 1938 Chief of Army Signals and Chief of Wehrmacht Signals Links at OKW, an early recruit to the Resistance. His task on 20.7.1944 was to cut off the signals systems at FHQ. He was arrested the next evening.

437 After 20.7.1944 Zeitzler was not sought out despite many lingering suspicions. Stahl, 'Zeitzler', p. 289.

438 See Document 32.

439 Meant here is lawyer Hans-Bernd von Haeften (15.12.1905–15.8.1944), from 1934 diplomatic service; 1940 Deputy Leader, Cultural Political Dept, Foreign Ministry. He was a member of the Kreisau circle and was earmarked for State Secretary at the Foreign Ministry should the coup have been successful. Arrested 20.7.1944, executed Berlin-Plötzensee prison.

440 Estimates of the numbers executed in the wake of 20 July vary. Hoffmann writes of between 600 and 700 persons arrested, about 200 tried and executed. There were in addition to these an unknown number of semi-official and unofficial executions. Hoffmann, 'Staatsstreich', p. 652.

441 Generaloberst Erwin Jaenecke (22.4.1890–3.7.1960), from 1.6.1943 C-in-
    C 17.Armee (Caucasus and latterly Crimea), advised Hitler on 29.4.1944
    in two verbal reports to abandon Sebastopol and allow his reduced Army
    the opportunity to retreat. He had the full agreement of Zeitzler, Chief
    of Army General Staff, and Heusinger, Chief of Operations Division, for
    his plan. Jaenecke described the catastrophic situation in an emotional
    manner and hammered the map table repeatedly. The second conference
    in the evening was even more tense. While returning to the Crimea he
    received the report that Hitler had relieved him of command and
    replaced him with his former Chief of Staff, Allmendinger. Jaenecke was
    expressly forbidden to return to the Crimea. A pre-court-martial
    investigation came to nothing. On 31.1.1945 he was discharged the
    Wehrmacht. KTB note on journey, C-in-C to FHQ, BA/MA RH20/17-
    270. Meanwhile Goerdeler had attempted to recruit Jaenecke for a
    conspiracy involving front commanders and the General Staff. Jaenecke
    supported the plan but contributed nothing. During their investigations
    of 20 July plot, the Gestapo came across his name on numerous
    occasions, and he was interrogated for eight hours in September 1944,
    RSHA concluding that he was not involved. Ritter, 'Goerdeler', p. 383;
    Jaenecke to Xylander, 4.11.1944, BA/MA N761/4. The few letters in his
    literary bequest leave no impression of an especially realistic appraisal
    of the strategic situation, nor of an even peripheral supportive stance for
    the opposition. On 24.2.1944 he wrote to his former commanding
    officer, Generaloberst Blaskowitz, 'I still cannot imagine that the British
    and Americans are so stupid that they will do the Russians' work for
    them and give the Bolshevists in Europe a leg-up into the saddle. On the
    other hand the Jews' hatred is probably so great that all reasonable
    considerations take a back seat', BA/MA N761/4. Pfuhlstein reported at
    Trent Park that at Olbricht's instigation he had spoken to Heusinger and
    Zeitzler's adjutant in order to gauge the extent of Zeitzler's disillusion
    with Hitler. He had bene told that Zeitzler was not yet 'ripe' to be
    indulged regarding the plans for a coup. GRGG 285, TNA, WO
    208/4177.
442 Goerdeler made numerous attempts to obtain an interview with
    Zeitzler. Beck and Stauffenberg considered these efforts useless.
    Choltitz, to whom Goerdeler had been introduced in the autumn of
    1943 through the mediation of Choltitz's cousin Baron Palombini,
    apparently promised to arrange that Goerdeler and Zeitzler should meet
    but then decided against it. Ritter, 'Goerdeler', p. 383.
443 Generaloberst Friedrich Fromm (8.10.1888–12.3.1945), Chief of Army
    Armaments and C-in-C Ersatzheer from the outbreak of war, knew of
    the coup plot by his Chief of Staff, Stauffenberg, but refused any
    involvement once he knew that Hitler had survived the assassination
    attempt. On the early morning of 21.7.1944 he had the four conspirators
    Stauffenberg, von Haeften, Olbricht and von Quirnheim shot in the
    Bendler-Strasse courtyard. Fromm himself was executed by shooting at
    Brandenburg-Görden Penitentiary on 12.3.1945. There is a very recent,
    monumental biography on Fromm: Kroener, 'Fromm'.
444 After the failure of the coup, Fromm gave Beck the oportunity to kill
    himself. Beck made two attempts, both of which failed. Fromm then
    ordered that he be 'put out of his misery', which was probably carried
    out by a Feldwebel. Kroener, 'Fromm', pp. 702–8.
445 Himmler, nominated Fromm's successor on 20.7.1944, made his
    appearance at the Bendler Block for the first time on 22.7.1944.

Choltitz's account must have been obtained from one of two other SS-Führer. Just after midnight on 21.7.1944 SS-Sturmbannführer Otto Skorzeny (12.6.1908–5.7.1975) arrived at the Bendler Block with a company of SS to support the Wachbataillon under Major Ernst-Otto Remer (8.8.1912–5.10.1997). SS-Obergruppenführer and General der Polizei Dr Ernst Kaltenbrunner (4.10.1903–15.10.1946), from 30.1.1943 Chief of RSHA and SD, had arrived there shortly before. Kroener, 'Fromm', p. 708f.

446 Manstein was certainly an independent thinker, but he had never been prepared to become involved politically against Hitler and had developed no major political ideology. He satisfied himself with the hope of achieving a 'stand-off' with the Russians on the Eastern Front. There is no academic biography. For general reading see Syring, 'Erich von Manstein'.

447 The poorly prepared Kapp putsch of 13–17.3.1920 cannot be compared to the coup attempt of 20.7.1944 because of the difference in the prevailing conditions. There is comprehensive documentation on the former, 'Der Kapp-Lüttwitz-Ludendorff Putsch. Dokumente'. From the older existing literature, the best account is Erger, 'Kapp-Lüttwitz Putsch'.

448 There is no doubt that the conspirators attempted to isolate the communications at FHQ Wolfsschanze, but this was frustrated by the complexity of the installation. The failure to shut down the distribution network run by the Reichspost was caused mainly by the refusal of Telegraphy Senior Inspector Senor to cooperate. Peter Hoffmann, 'Staatsstreich', pp. 415–28, 504, 508–11.

449 Eberbach was referring here to the brief conversation he had on 17.7.1944 at HQ, Pz.Gr. West shortly before Rommel was seriously wounded.

450 Genertalleutnant Alfred Gause (14.2.1896–30.9.1967) was from September 1941 to 7.5.1943 (with a short break) Chief of Staff, Pz.Gr./Pz.Armee/Heeresgr.Afrika, from 15.6.1944–10.9.1944 Chief of Staff, Pz.Gr. West and 5.Pz.Armee.

451 Meant here is Oberstleutnant (from 1.8.1944 Oberst) Franz Herber, Chief, Abt.Ib, General Army Bureau, who towards 2100hrs appointed himself leader of the counter-coup at the Bendler Block and, together with other officers of the General Army Bureau, helped put down the Stauffenberg putsch and released Fromm. Kroener, 'Fromm', p. 697.

452 The meeting of Geyr, Eberbach and Stauffenberg probably took place in mid-July 1941 when Stauffenberg visited the XXIV.Pz.Korps advanced command post in the area between Orsha and Smolensk. At that time Eberbach was CO, 5.Pz.Brigade/4.Pz.Div./XXIV.Pz.Korps. Leo Reichsfreiherr Geyr von Schweppenburg (2.3.1896–27.1.1974) was a friend of the Stauffenberg family. From 1922 to 1925 he had been Chief, 4.Squadron/18.Reiter-Reg.at Bad Cannstadt, and Claus's eldest brother Alexander von Stauffenberg served under him there. Peter Hoffmann, 'Stauffenberg', pp. 49, 135f, 223. For Stauffenberg's later attempts to recruit Geyr to the Resistance see note 387 above.

453 Eberbach was confusing two events here – possibly on the basis of misleading National Socialist press reporting in which the conspirators were blamed for the destruction of Army Group Centre. One event concerns General der Artillerie Fritz Lindemann (11.4.1894–22.9.1944), from 1.10.1943 General der Artillerie at Chief of Army Armaments and CO, Ersatzheer. He was involved in planning the coup, was arrested on

3.9.1944 and died 22.9.1944 as the result of a bullet wound to the stomach inflicted during his arrest. Mühlen, 'Sie gaben ihr Leben'. The second event concerned Generalmajor Gerhard Lindemann (2.8.1896–28.4.1894), from end May 1944 CO, 361.Inf.Div., captured by Soviets 22.7.1944 on central section of Eastern Front. Together with Generalleutnant Eberhard von Kurowski (10.9.1985–11.9.1957) – from 1.6.1943 CO, 110.Inf.Div., also captured by Soviets in July 1944 – on 14.8.1944 he broadcast on the radio station 'Freies Deutschland' a message inciting troops of Army Group Centre to lay down their arms. 'Tätigkeitsbericht Schmundt', p. 201. Lindeman and Kurowski also signed the declaration of the 50 generals of 8.12.1944.

454 Major Joachim Kuhn (b. 2.8.1913), under Stieff at Organisations-Abt., Army General Staff, was active in procuring explosives for an assassination attempt in 1943. From 22.6.1944 he was 1a, 28.Jäger-Div. A few days after 20.7.1944, his divisional commander Gustav Hostermann von Ziehlberg (10.12.1898–2.2.1945) received orders to place Kuhn under arrest and bring him to Berlin. Von Ziehlberg advised him of this and offered Kuhn the oportunity to avoid arrest by shooting himself. Instead, Kuhn crossed the Soviet line on 27 July. Von Ziehlberg was then court-martialled and sentenced to nine months' detention to be served at the front. Following a finding of guilt in a second trial in which he was charged with 'premeditated disobedience to an order in the face of the enemy', he was sentenced to death and executed by firing squad on 2.2.1945 at Berlin-Spandau. For Kuhn see esp. 'Neue Quellen zur Geschichte des 20.7.1944' and 'Tätigskeitsbericht Schmundt', pp. 181, 184, 287 and 297.

455 Generaladmiral Otto Schniewind (14.12.1897–26.3.1964) was not implicated in the plot, and he never held a minor role. From March 1943, C-in-C Naval Group Command North, he entered Führer-Reserve 31.7.1944. For the involvement of the Kriegsmarine see Hillmann, 'Der 20 Juli und die Marine'.

456 Eberbach vastly overestimates the extent of the support for the coup attempt. The basic problem of the plotters was that only the odd general supported it. The refusal of von Manstein was the rule, not the exception.

457 Why Hitler appointed Guderian to act as Chief of the Army General Staff on the evening of 20.7.1944 because of suspicions about Zeitzler has never been properly addressed by research. The plotters had recruited Guderian to gauge the depth of support amongst the Army generals. Subsequently Guderian indulged in homage to Hitler and his orders then bore evidence of a ruthless fanaticism in the sense of a 'fight to the last shell'. Wilhelm, 'Guderian'.

458 On Thomale see note 140 above. He was not implicated in the 20 July plot. What Eberbach meant by his observation that Thomale had been courageous in Berlin is unknown.

459 For Hitler's daily itinerary see Seidler/Zeigert, 'Führerhauptquartiere', pp. 110–14; Neumärker, 'Wolfsschanze', pp. 74–7.

460 General der Artillerie Eduard Wagner (1.4.1894–23.7.1944), from 1.8.1940 Army QM-General, joined the Opposition circle around Halder in 1939 but then immersed himself in his duties until 1942 and was thus implicated in the brutal policies in the war in the east. A long-term waverer, by the summer of 1944 he had become a leading advocate of the need to assassinate Hitler. He eluded his pursuers by suicide. Peter, 'Eduard Wagner'.

461 Oberst Eberhard Finckh (7.11.1899–30.8.1944), friendly with Stauffenberg from 1936, implicated in plot in Paris as Senior QM to Military Cdr, France. Arrested 26.7.1944, condemned to death by People's Court 30.8.1944 and executed same day at Berlin-Plötzensee.

462 General der Infanterie Walter Buhle (26.10.1894–27.12.1959), 1.9.1939 Chief, Organisations-Abt. at OKH; from 15.2.1942 Chief of OKW Army Staff; 1.2.1945 Chief of Army Ordnance. He suffered minor injuries in the 20 July blast.

463 Eberbach means Oberst Joachim Meichssner (4.4.1906–29.9.1944). At OKH from 1937, Olbricht recruited him to the conspiracy. Temporarily active with Buhle at OKW Army Staff, he was then appointed Chief of the Organisations-Abt., Wehrmacht Command Staff, where he had access to the Führer's situation conferences but did not want to be the assassin. Arrested end of July 1944, sentenced to death by the People's Court 29.9.1944 and executed same day at Berlin-Plötzensee.

464 On 10.7.1944 Hitler ordered the C-in-C Ersatzheer and Chief of Army Ordnance to set up 15 new 'Sperr-Divisionen' (barrier divisions) (29.Welle) as soon as possible. The intention was originally that they should protect the Reich borders in the East with effect from 1.9.1944. On 13.7.1944 the units were redesignated 'Grenadier Divisions', and by the beginning of October 1944 the 17 divisions of 29.Welle were now renamed 'Volksgrenadier Divisions'. Equipped only with anti-tank guns, artillery and transport, they were used mainly in the east from August 1944. It is not known if Hitler's idea for the barrier divisions influenced the conspirators to act at a particular time. Kroener, 'Fromm', esp. p. 667.

465 The former Battle Commandant of Aachen, Oberst Wilck, expressed the opinion on 28.10.1944 that the Army was 40 per cent Nazi and 60 per cent 'against'. If the Führer held on to the reins of power and that was the split, then the war would go on until Berlin fell and Germany was destroyed, Wilck prophesied. SRGG 1067, 28.10.1944, TNA, WO 208/4169.

466 Generalleutnant Paul Gerhard (20.4.1881–12.10.1953), from 1.8.1940 to 19.1.1945 Wehrersatz-Inspecteur, Allenstein. He had been CO, Inf.Reg.7 in 1931.

467 Freidrich Werner Graf von der Schulenburg (20.11.1875–10.11.1944), from 1934 to 1941 German ambassador to Moscow, joined the Goerdeler circle of resistance workers and was to have been Foreign Secretary had the coup been successful. Executed at Berlin-Plötzensee.

468 In a 1953 report, Pfuhlstein stated that Canaris had also been present, 'Canaris and Oster were standing together naked at the washbasin, Oster with a toothbrush in his mouth, completely numbed, gazing at me with a look of total horror. Canaris, who seemed a broken man physically, also stared at me in horror. He was holding the washbasin with both hands so as not to sink to his knees.' Quoted from Höhne, 'Canaris', p. 548. Generalmajor Hans Oster (9.8.1888–9.4.1945), from 1939 Head of OKW Abwehr Overseas Office at HQ, was one of the leading figures of the resistance movement; expelled from the Wehrmacht, 16.3.1943. The conspirators planned for him to be President of the Reich Military Court in the event of a successful coup. Found guilty of treason by SS tribunal at Flossenbürg concentration camp 8.4.1945 and executed illegally the following day. The Gestapo found a letter on Oster addressed to Canaris in which Pfuhlstein was described as a reliable man 'for the envisaged task'. GRGG 285(c), TNA,

WO 208/4177. In his interrogation by the British, Pfuhlstein was very critical of Admiral Canaris, calling him a 'desk general'. Höhne, 'Canaris', pp. 547–51; 'Spiegelbild einer Verschwörung: Die Kaltenbrunner-Bericht' pp. 370f, 405–8.

469 At Küstrin, Pfuhlstein met the following: General der Panzertruppe von Esebeck, Chief of Wehrkreis Command XVII (Vienna); Generalleutnant Sinzinger, City Commandant, Vienna; Generalmajor Siegfried von Stülpnagel, City Commandant, Stettin; Generalleutnant Speidel, Chief of Staff, Army Group B; Major Johann von Hassel, son of ambassador Ulrich von Hassel; Oberstleutnant von Kluge, son of the field marshal; Major Hoepner, son of Generaloberst Erich Hoepner; Major Fellgiebel, brother of General Erich Fellgiebel; Kriegerichtsrat Dr Kayser; Hauptmann Paulus, son of the field marshal; and Oberst von Cannstein, formerly of the Kavallerie-Schule, Blomberg. GRGG 285(c), TNA, WO 208/4177.

470 General der Infanterie Joachim von Stülpnagel (5.3.1880–15.7.1968), ended World War I as head of OHL Organisations-Abt. Between the wars he was a close colleague of General Hans von Seeckt. Pensioned-off 31.12.1931. After 20.7.1944 arrested as a 'politically unreliable' general and held for several months, including a stay at Ravensbrück concentration camp. Siegfried von Stülpnagel was a brother of Joachim and was detained between 5.8.1944 and 22.4.1945.

471 Ernst August Prinz von Hannover (1914–87) during the Russian campaign an Oberleutnant on Staff, Pz.Gr.4 (Generaloberst Hoepner). Severely wounded at Kharkov in the spring of 1943, he was arrested after 20 July and spent a few weeks at Gestapo HQ.

472 Bad Kösen an der Saale, situated between Halle and Weimar.

473 Hjalmar Schacht (22.1.1877–3.6.1970), 1933–39 President, Reichbank; 1934–37 Reich Economy Minister; 1935–37 General Plenipotentiary for the War Economy; until 1944 Reich Minister without Portfolio. He was in touch with the conspiracy from 1938. Arrested 23.7.1944 and taken directly to Ravensbrück; 31.8.1944 transferred to Gestapo HQ where according to his own testimony he remained four months before being sent to Flossenbürg. Schacht, 'Abrechnung mit Hitler'.

474 Franz Halder was arrested at Aschau, 21.7.1944 and delivered to Ravensbrück three days later. He spent the period 7.10.1944–7.2.1945 in the Gestapo HQ dungeons. Schall-Riaucour, 'Aufstand und Gehorsam', pp. 329–32.

475 Revin, town in northern France where the US Army had an interrogation camp for a short while.

476 Which Generalmajor commanded a panzer korps in the spring of 1945 is not known. The details are too general to identify whom Kirchheim meant here.

477 Kirchheim was speaking of the trials of: Oberstleutnant Bernhard Klamroth, Major (Reserve) Hans-Georg Klamroth, Major Egbert Hayessen, Legationsrat Adam Trott zu Solz, Legationsrat Bernd von Haeften and SA-Gruppenführer Wolf Graf von Helldorf before the People's Court on 15.8.1944. All six accused were sentenced to death. Adam von Trott zu Solz (9.8.1909–26.9.1944) worked in the information section at the Foreign Ministry and acted as an intermediary between the conspiracy and overseas. He was arrested 26.7.1944. Execution of his sentence of death was delayed for over a month. For the trials of 15.8.1944 see Wagner, 'Volksgerichtshof, pp. 601–67; Würmling, 'Adam Trott zu Solz'.

478 Roland Freisler (30.10.1893–3.2.1945), 1933 Secretary of State, Reich Justice Ministry, from 1942, President, People's Court.
479 For Hoepner see notes 414 and 415 above.
480 For Helldorf see note 418 above. The Major of the Reserve mentioned here is Hans-Georg Klamroth.
481 For the Honour Court see note 287 above. Ernst Kaltenbrunner, from 30.1.1943 Head RSHA, Chief of Sipo and SD.
482 SS-Gruppenführer Heinrich Müller (28.4.1900–disappeared 29.4.1945), Head of Gestapo.
483 In its session of 4.10.1944 the Honour Court had to decide whether Speidel should answer before the People's Court. This protocol supports the affidavit sworn by Guderian and Kirchheim in 1946 regarding the hearing. Both defended Speidel against Keitel and Kaltenbrunner on the basis that Speidel had reported the attempted assassination of Hitler to Rommel, and thus had done all that duty required of him. The acquittal of Speidel now implicated Rommel. For more see Reuth, 'Rommel', p. 238ff.
484 Kirchheim also spoke briefly about the Honour Court hearing in SRGG 1180(c), 1.5.1945, TNA WO 208/4169. Kirchheim was obliged to justify himself to his fellow prisoners because shortly after his capture he had made an appeal to Keitel on Radio Luxembourg to lay down arms, having recently been a judge of the Honour Court. Von Thoma called him 'scum' amd would not forget how he had delivered comrades to the gallows. GRGG 288, 24–26.4.1945, TNA WO 208/4177.
485 See note 477 above.
486 Meant here are Oberstleutnant Bernhard Klamroth (20.11.1910–15.8.1944) and his elder cousin and father-in-law Major (Reserve) Johannes Georg Klamroth (12.10.1898–26.8.1944).
487 The fragmentary remains of the recording tapes do not support the idea that Freisler behaved himself any better in the third session of the People's Court on 15.8.1944. 'Also in this principal trial he was unrestrained and tyrannical.' Wagner, 'Volksgerichtshof', p. 684.
488 Pfuhlstein reported in captivity that he had shared a ticklish situation with Kaltenbrunner when Hungarian soldiers attempted to take them both prisoner. It was only Pfuhlstein's determined reaction that avoided their being shot. This must have occurred on 19.3.1944 upon the German occupation of Hungary. GRGG 286, 19–21.4.1945, TNA, WO 208/4177. Black, 'Ernst Kaltenbrunner', does not mention the affair.

LIST OF DOCUMENTS

I. Politics, Strategy and the Different Camps at Trent Park

Document 1 (SRX 1140, 8.10.42): Crüwell · Krause
Document 2 (SRX 1160, 12.10.42): Crüwell · Krause
Document 3 (SRX 1167, 15.10.42): Crüwell · Krause
Document 4 (SRX 1230, 21.10.42): Crüwell · Krause
Document 5 (SRX 1537, 26.01.43): Thoma · Burckhardt
Document 6 (SRX 1587, 15.2.1943): Thoma
Document 7 (SRX 1603, 18.2.43): Crüwell · Thoma
Document 8 (SRGG 5, 16.5.43): Crüwell · Cramer
Document 9 (SRGG 126, 11.6.43): Broich
Document 10 (SRGG 156, 26.6.43): Crüwell · Hülsen
Document 11 (SRGG 161, 27.6.43): Frantz
Document 12 (SRGG 204, 9.7.43): Arnim
Document 13 (SRGG 342, 12.8.43): Crüwell
Document 14 (SRGG 399, 12.9.43): Thoma · Buhse
Document 15 (SRGG 615, 4.12.1943): Boes · Bühler
Document 16 (SRGG 748, 7.1.44): Boes
Document 17 (GRGG 139, 3.6.44): Neuffer · Kreipe
Document 18 (GRGG 140, 1–3.6.44): Kreipe
Document 19 (GRGG 149, 22–7.6.44): Broich; Krug
Document 20 (GRGG 153, 3.7.44): Bassenge · Hermann; Hennecke · Sattler
· Köhn
Document 21 (GRGG 154, 4.7.44): Hennecke · Bassenge · Thoma
Document 22 (GRGG 156, 8–10.7.44): Köhn · Hennecke
Document 24 (GRGG 159, 15/16.7.44): Hennecke · Krug · Rohrbach;
Neuffer · Reimann
Document 25 (GRGG 160, 15/16.7.44): Schlieben · Thoma; Köhn ·
Hennecke
Document 26 (GRGG 162, 19–22.7.44): Schlieben · Sattler
Document 27 (GRGG 164, 23/24.7.44): Hennecke · Krug · Köhn
Document 28 (GRGG 172, 8–12.8.44): Kessler · Reimann; Mundorff · Köhn
·?Hennecke
Document 29 (GRGG 173, 13/14.8.44): Spang · Krug
Document 30 (GRGG 176, 19–21.8.44): Klenk · Hellwig
Document 31 (GRGG 180, 25/26.8.44): Elfeldt · Menny · Badinsky
Document 32 (GRGG 183, 29.8.44): Menny; Schlieben · Choltitz; Choltitz ·
Bassenge · Thoma; Choltitz · Thoma
Document 33 (GRGG 185, 31.8–3.9.44): Müller-Römer · Hennecke
Document 34 (SRGG 1026(c), 3.9.44): Gutknecht · Eberbach
Document 35 (GRGG 186, 4/5.9.44): Bassenge · Thoma

Document 36 (GRGG 195, 16./17.9.44): Choltitz · Sponeck
Document 37 (GRGG 197, 20./21.9.44): Heinz Eberbach · Heinz Eugen
   Eberbach
Document 38 (GRGG 201(c), end September 44): Ramcke; Elster · Heyking
   · Heim
Document 39 (GRGG 203, 26/27.9.44): Thoma · Heyking · Ramcke
Document 40 (GRGG 204, 27–9.10.44): Reimann · Choltitz · Neuffer ·
   Schlieben
Document 41 (GRGG 206, 6.10.44): Schlieben · Elfeldt · Broich
Document 42 (GRGG 209, 7–10.10.44): Tresckow · Wülfingen; Ramcke
Document 43 (GRGG 210, 11/12.10.44): Choltitz · Schlieben; Bassenge ·
   Wahle; Choltitz; Mosel · Kaehler · Ramcke
Document 44 (GRGG 211, 14–17.10.44): Choltitz · Schlieben
Document 45 (SRGG 1065, 16.10.44): Broich · Bassenge · Schlieben ·
   Choltitz · Ramcke · Heim
Document 46 (GRGG 219, 4.–6.11.44): Choltitz · Bassenge; Bassenge
Document 47 (GRGG 222, 13–14.11.44): Reimann · Elfeldt
Document 48 (GRGG 225, 18/19.11.44): Eberding
Document 49 (GRGG 226, 20/21.11.44): Meyer · Bassenge
Document 50 (GRGG 231, 6/7.11.44): Wildermuth · Wilck
Document 51 (GRGG 233, 12–16.12.44): Meyer · Wildermuth · Heyking
Document 52 (GRGG 234, 18.12.44): Broich
Document 53 (GRGG 235, 21/22.12.44): Heim · Eberbach; Meyer ·
   Eberbach; Ramcke
Document 54 (GRGG 237, 21/22.12.44): (f) Meyer · Choltitz
Document 55 (GRGG 242, 31.12.44/1.1.45): Thoma · Bassenge · Wahle;
   Wilck · Wildermuth; Wahle; Choltitz · Ramcke; Bruhn · Felbert;
   Vaterrodt · Bruhn
Document 56 (Extract from SR Draft No.85, 1.1.45): Bruhn
Document 57 (Extract from SR Draft No.87, 1.1.45): Schaefer · Thoma
Document 58 (GRGG 247, 10–14.1.45): Kittel · Heyking
Document 59 (GRGG 248, 15–17.1.45): Schlieben · Elfeldt
Document 60 (GRGG 249, 18.1.45): Felbert
Document 61 (GRGG 253, 26/27.1.45): Schlieben · Ramcke; Felbert ·
   Bruhn; Neuffer · Thoma
Document 62 (GRGG 254, 28–31.1.45): Bruhn · Felbert; Wahle · Bassenge;
   Choltitz · Schlieben; Schlieben · Wahle; Ullersperger; Eberbach · Heim
   · Wildermuth; Broich · Eberbach; Eberbach · Heim
Document 63 (GRGG 259, 11–13.2.45): Choltitz · Vaterrodt
Document 64 (GRGG 260, 14/15.2.45): Broich; Wahle · Eberbach
Document 65 (GRGG 262, 18–20.2.45): Choltitz; Meyer · Ullersperger
Document 66 (GRGG 267, 2/3.3.45): Choltitz · Elfeldt; Bruhn; Choltitz ·
   Ramcke
Document 67 (GRGG 270, 9.3.45): Bassenge · Rothkirch · Thoma;
   Rothkirch · Choltitz; Rothkirch · Heim · Heydte · Bassenge
Document 68 (GRGG 273, 16–19.3.45): Rothkirch · Choltitz; Bassenge
Document 69 (GRGG 276, 25–27.3.45): Heim · Schlieben
Document 70 (GRGG 278, 30.3–2.4.45): Heim · Wildermuth
Document 71 (GRGG 280, 7.4.45): Heyking · Jösting
Document 72 (GRGG 282, 10–13.4.45): Ross · Bruhn; Daser · Ross · Bruhn
Document 73 (GRGG 284, 16.–18.4.45): Fischer · Bruhn
Document 74 (GRGG 286, 19.–21.4.45): Heim · Pfuhlstein
Document 75 (GRGG 289, 27./28.4.45): Heim · Viebig · Eberbach ·
   Bassenge · Rothkirch

II. 'We Have Tried to Exterminate Whole Communities.' War Crimes in Trent Park Conversations

Document 120 (SRGG 1093 (c), 28.12.44): Schaefer · Kittel
Document 121 (GRGG 245, 5–7.1.45): Wildermuth
Document 122 (GRGG 254, 28.–31.1.45): Kittel · Ramcke
Document 123 (GRGG 256, 3–5.2.45): Bruhn · Felbert
Document 124 (GRGG 260, 14/15.2.45): Wahle · Elfeldt
Document 125 (GRGG 264, 24–26.2.45): Kittel · Eberbach
Document 126 (GRGG 265, 27.2–1.3.45): Bruhn · Schlieben
Document 127 (GRGG 270, 9.3.45): Rothkirch · Choltitz
Document 128 (GRGG 271, 10–12.3.45): Bruhn; Broich · Choltitz ·
    Rothkirch
Document 129 (GRGG 272, 13.–16.3.45): Rothkirch · Ramcke
Document 130 (GRGG 273, 16.–19.3.45): Heydte · Wildermuth
Document 131 (GRGG 275, 24.3.45): Rothkirch
Document 132 (GRGG 276, 25–27.3.45): Daser · Thoma
Document 133 (GRGG 277, 28/29.3.45): Wildermuth · Heim · Heydte
Document 134 (GRGG 278, 30.3–2.4.45): Broich · Bruhn; Reimann
Document 135 (SRGG 1158 (c), 25.4.45): Bruns
Document 136 (GRGG 281, 8/9.4.45): Jösting
Document 137 (GRGG 286, 19–21.4.45): Wildermuth · Broich · Wahle ·
    Elfeldt
Document 138 (GRGG 288, 24–26.4.45): Heilmann · Fischer
Document 139 (SRGG 1203(c), 6.5.45): Siry
Document 140 (GRGG 300, 16/17.5.45): Habermehl
Document 141 (GRGG 301, 18/19.5.45): Dittmar · Schlieben · Broich ·
    Elfeldt · Holste; Dittmar · Thoma
Document 142 (GRGG 312, 1–6.6.45): Feuchtinger
Document 143 (GRGG 314, 7–30.6.45): [1.] Schlieben · Felbert; [2.] Oriola ·
    Siewert; [3.] Dittmar · Holste; [4.] Heim · Dittmar · Fink
Document 144 (GRGG 363, 24.9–9.10.45): [1.] Eberbach; [2.] Eberbach ·
    Wildermuth · Heydte; [3.] Eberbach · Heydte; [4.] Heydte · Eberbach ·
    Wildermuth; [5.] Heydte · Elfeldt · Heim

III. The Insurrection of Conscience. Reactions to 20 July 1944

Document 145 (GRGG 161, 20/21.7.44): Sponeck · Thoma; Bassenge;
    Thoma · Krug · Sattler; Hennecke · Krug · Köhn; Reimann · Broich ·
    Krug; Borcherdt · Reimann; Reimann · Krug; Bassenge
Document 146 (SRGG 962, 21.7.44): Broich · Sponeck · Thoma
Document 147 (GRGG 162, 19–22.7.44): Thoma · Bassenge; Broich; Broich ·
    Schlieben; Bassenge; Krug · Reimann; Schlieben · Broich
Document 148 (GRGG 171, 5–8.8.44): Broich · Sattler · Bassenge ·
    Borcherdt; Krug · Köhn; Krug · Reimann; Thoma; Rohrbach ·
    Herrmann; Sponeck · Thoma · Broich · Sattler; Schlieben
Document 149 (SRGG 969, 10.8.44): Spang
Document 150 (GRGG 180, 25/26.8.44): Liebenstein · Menny; Elfeldt ·
    Badinsky · Menny; Elfeldt · Menny
Document 151 (GRGG 181, end August 44): Choltitz
Document 152 (SRM 837, 26.8.44): Viebig · Beck
Document 153 (GRGG 183, 29.8.44): Bassenge · Choltitz · Elfeldt · Sponeck
    · Thoma · Schlieben · Neuffer
Document 154 (GRGG 186, 4/5.9.44): Choltitz · Badinski
Document 155 (GRGG 187, early September 44): Eberbach
Document 156 (SRGG 1087(c), 2.9.44): Eberbach · Gutknecht
Document 157 (GRGG 195, 16/17.9.44): Choltitz · Eberbach

SOURCES AND BIBLIOGRAPHY

I. ARCHIVE SOURCES

Bundesarchiv/Militärarchiv, Freiburg i. Br.

RH 10	Generalinspekteur der Panzertruppen
RH 19	Heeresgruppen
RH 20	Armeen
RH 24	Armeekorps
RH 26	Infanteriedivisionen
RH 27	Panzerdivisionen
RH 29	Kavalleriedivisionen
RH 36	Kommandanturen der Militärverwaltungen
RH 49	Kriegsgefangeneinrichtungen

RM 7	Seekriegsleitung
RM 35 II	Marinegruppenkommando West
RM 69	Minensuchflottillen
RW 41	Territoriale Befehlshaber in der Sowjetunion

MSg 1, MSg 2	Militärgeschichtliche Sammlungen

N 2	Private papers of Wilhelm Ritter von Thoma
N 61	Private papers of Hans-Jürgen von Arnim
N 245	Private papers of Hans-Georg Reinhardt
NL 251	Private papers of Eberhard Wildermuth
N 267	Private papers of Erwin Menny

Haus & Hof- und Staatsarchiv, Vienna

B 1544/8	Paul Meixner

The National Archives, Public Record Office, London

DEFE 1	Postal and Telegraph censorship Department, Ministry of Defence
FO 954	Foreign Office: Private Office Papers of Sir Anthony Eden, Earl of Avon, Secretary of State for Foreign Affairs1935–1946
PREM 3	Prime Minister's Office: Operational Correspondence and Papers 1937–1946

WO 193   War Office: Directorate of Military Operations and Plans, later
         Directorate of Military Operations: Files concerning Military
         Planning, Intelligence and Statistics (Collation Files) 1934–1958
WO 208   War Office: Directorate of Military Operations and Intelligence,
         and Directorate of Military Intelligence; Ministry of Defence,
         Defence Intelligence Staff: Files 1917–1974

National Archives, Washington

T-501,   Film 214 German Field Commands, Rear Areas
RG 319   Records of the Army Staff

Politisches Archiv des Auswärtigen Amtes, Berlin

R 41141

II. PRIVATE COLLECTIONS
Ludwig Crüwell
Hans Cramer
Ludwig Crüwell
Paul von Felbert
Peter Lex
Georg Neuffer

III. PRINTED SOURCES
20. Juli 1944, edited by Bundeszentrale für Heimatdienst, Bonn 1960
Ahmann, Rolf, 'Der Hitler-Stalin-Pakt. Eine Bewertung der Interpretationen
    sowjetischer Außenpolitik mit neuen Fragen und neuen Forschungen',
    in: Wolfgang Michalka (ed.), Der Zweite Weltkrieg. Analysen,
    Grundzüge, Forschungsbilanz, 2nd edn, Munich, Zurich 1990, pp.
    93–107
Angrick, Andrej, Besatzungspolitik und Massenmord. Die Einsatzgruppe D
    in der südlichen Sowjetunion 1941–1943, Hamburg 2003
Applebaum, Anne, Der Gulag, Berlin 2003. [Originally published in English
    as Gulag: A History of the Soviet Camps, London 2003]
Armstrong, John A. (ed.), Soviet Partisans in World War II, Madison 1964
Arnold, Klaus Jochen, 'Die Eroberung und Behandlung der Stadt Kiew durch
    die Wehrmacht im September 1941: Zur Radikalisierung der
    Besatzungspolitik', in: MGM 58 (1999), pp. 23–63
Bach, André, Fusillés pour l'exemple 1914–1915, Paris 2003
Balfour, Michael, 'Der deutsche Dienst der BBC und die britische
    Deutschlandpolitik. Zum Verhältnis von britischer Regierung und
    Propagandainstitutionen im Zweiten Weltkrieg', in: Klaus-Jürgen
    Müller, and David N. Dilks (eds), Großbritannien und der deutsche
    Widerstand 1933–1944, Paderborn 1994, pp. 139–60
Barber, John, and Mark Harrison, The Soviet Home Front, 1941–1945. A
    Social and Economic History of the USSR in World War II, London 1991
Barth, Boris, Dolchstoßlegende und politische Desintegration. Das Trauma
    der deutschen Niederlage im Ersten Weltkrieg 1914–1933, Düsseldorf
    2003
Beck, Birgit, Wehrmacht und sexuelle Gewalt. Sexualverbrechen vor
    deutschen Militärgerichten 1939–1945, Paderborn 2004

Beckett, Ian F.W., *The Great War 1914–1918*, Harlow 2001

Beckman, Morris, *The Jewish Brigade. An army with Two Masters, 1944–1945*, Staplehurst 1998

Berger, Maurice, *Germany after the Armistice*, New York 1920

Berkel, Alexander, *Krieg vor der Haustür. Rheinübergang und Luftlandung am Niederrhein 1945*, Wesel 2004

Berkhoff, Karel C., *Harvest of Despair. Life and Death in Ukraine under Nazi Rule*, Cambridge, MA, London 2004

Bernikov, Nikolaj N., 'Die propagandistische Tätigkeit des NKFD und des BDO sowie deren Zusammenarbeit mit den Politorganen der Roten Armee während des Krieges 1943–1945', in: Ueberschär (ed.), *Nationalkomitee*, op. cit., pp. 112–20

Biddiscombe, Perry, *Werwolf! The History of the National Socialist Guerilla Movement 1944–1946*, Cardiff 1998

Birn, Ruth Bettina, *Die Höheren SS- und Polizeiführer. Himmlers Vertreter im Reich und in den besetzten Gebieten*, Düsseldorf 1986

Black, Peter, *Ernst Kaltenbrunner. Vasall Himmlers: Eine SS-Karriere*, Paderborn 1991

Blair, Clay, *Der U-Boot-Krieg, Vol. 2, Die Gejagten 1942–1945*, Munich 1999

Blanning, Timothy C.W., *The French Revolutionary Wars 1787–1802*, London 1996

Böhler, Jochen, '"Tragische Verstrickung" oder Auftakt zum Vernichtungs-krieg? Die Wehrmacht in Polen 1939', in: Klaus-Michael Mallmann and Bogdan Musial (eds), *Genesis des Genozids. Polen 1939–1941*, Darmstadt 2004, pp. 36–56

Böhme, Kurt W., *Die deutschen Kriegsgefangenen in sowjetischer Hand. Eine Bilanz*, Munich 1966 (also published in Erich Maschke (ed.), *Zur Geschichte der deutschen Kriegsgefangenen des Zweiten Weltkrieges*, vol. VII)

Bonwetsch, Bernd, 'Der "Große Vaterländische Krieg": Vom deutschen Einfall bis zum sowjetischen Sieg (1941–1945)', in: Gottfried Schramm (ed.), *Handbuch der Geschichte Rußlands, Vol. 3, Von den autokratischen Reformen zum Sowjetstaat 1856–1945*, Stuttgart 1983

Boog, Horst, *Die deutsche Luftwaffenführung 1935–1945*, Stuttgart 1982

Bose, Thilo von, *Die Katastrophe des 8. August 1918*, Oldenburg 1930

Brakel, Alexander, 'Baranovici. Eine weißrussische Region unter deutscher und sowjetischer Besatzung 1939–1944', PhD dissertation, Mainz

Brunner, Reinhold, *Bewegte Zeiten. Eisenach zwischen 1919 und 1945*, Gudensberg-Gleichen 1994

Bucher, Peter, *Der Reichswehrprozeß. Der Hochverrat der Ulmer Reichswehroffiziere 1929/30*, Boppard 1967

Bungert, Heike, *Das Nationalkomitee und der Westen. Die Reaktion der Westalliierten auf das NKFD und die Freien Deutschen Bewegungen 1943–1948* (Transatlantische historische Studien, Vol. 8), Stuttgart 1997

Butler, David Gareth, *British Political Facts 1900–1985*, 6th edn, London 1986

Carnes, James Donald, *General zwischen Hitler und Stalin. Das Schicksal des Walther von Seydlitz*, Düsseldorf 1980

Chen, Jian, 'China in 1945', in: Gerhard Krebs (ed.), *1945 in Europe and Asia. Reconsidering the End of World War II and the Change of the World Order*, Munich 1997, pp. 213–34

Choltitz, Dietrich von, *Brennt Paris? Ein Tatsachenbericht des letzten deutschen Befehlshabers in Paris*, Mannheim 1950

—, *Soldat unter Soldaten*, Konstanz 1951

Christoffel, Edgar, *Krieg am Westwall 1944/45*, Trier 1989

Churchill, Winston S., *Complete Speeches*, edited by Robert Rhodes James, Vol. VII, 1943–1949, New York, London 1974

Clark, Christopher, 'Johannes Blaskowitz. Der christliche General', in: Smelser/Syring (eds), *Militärelite*, op. cit., pp. 28–49

—, 'Josef "Sepp" Dietrich. Landsknecht im Dienste Hitlers', in: Ronald Smelser and Enrico Syring (eds), *Die SS. Elite unter dem Totenkopf*, Paderborn 2000, pp. 119–133

Clasen, Christoph, *Generaloberst Hans-Georg Reinhardt*, Stuttgart 1996

Clausewitz, Carl von, *Vom Kriege*, Munich 2003

Conze, Eckart, 'Adel und Adeligkeit im Widerstand des 20. Juli 1944', in: Heinz Reif (ed.), *Adel und Bürgertum, Vol. 2, Entwicklungslinien und Wendepunkte im 20. Jahrhundert*, Berlin 2001

Cüppers, Martin, '"... auf eine so saubere und anständige SS-mäßige Art". Die Waffen-SS in Polen 1939–1941', in: Klaus-Michael Mallmann and Bogdan Musial (eds), *Genesis des Genozids. Polen 1939–1941*, Darmstadt 2004, pp. 90–110

Das Deutsche Reich und der Zweite Weltkrieg, Vol. 3, Der Mittelmeerraum und Südosteuropa, Stuttgart 1984

—, *Vol. 4: Der Angriff auf die Sowjetunion*, 2nd edn, Stuttgart 1987

—, *Vol. 5/2: Organisation und Mobilisierung des deutschen Machtbereichs. Kriegsverwaltung, Wirtschaft und personelle Ressourcen 1942–1944/45*, Stuttgart 1999

—, *Vol. 6: Der Globale Krieg. Die Ausweitung zum Weltkrieg und der Wechsel der Initiative 1941–1943*, Stuttgart 1990

—, *Vol. 8* (in preparation)

—, *Vol. 9/1: Die deutsche Kriegsgesellschaft 1939 bis 1945, Politisierung, Vernichtung, Überleben*, Stuttgart 2004

—, *Vol .9/2: Die deutsche Kriegsgesellschaft 1939 bis 1945. Ausbeutung, Deutungen, Ausgrenzung*, Stuttgart 2005

Dean, Martin, *Collaboration and the Holocaust. Crimes of the local Police in Belorussia and Ukraine, 1941–1944*, New York 2000

Deist, Wilhelm, 'Verdeckter Militärstreik', in: Wolfram Wette (ed.), *Der Krieg des kleinen Mannes*, 2nd edn, Munich 1995, pp. 146–67

Der Kapp-Lüttwitz-Ludendorff-Putsch, documents, edited by Erwin Könnemann, Gerhard Schulze, Munich 2002

Dobson, Alan P., *Anglo-American Relations in the Twentieth Century. Of Friendship, Conflict and the Rise and Decline of Superpowers*, London, New York 1995

Documente zur Geschichte der Frankfurter Juden: 1933–1945, edited by Kommission zur Erforschung der Geschichte der Frankfurter Juden, Frankfurt am Main 1963

Domarus, Max, *Hitler. Reden und Proklamationen 1932–1945*, Vol. 2, Würzburg 1963

Drobisch, Klaus, and Günther Wieland, *Das System der Konzentrations-lager 1933–1939*, Berlin 1993

Eckert, Astrid M., *Der Kampf um die Akten. Die Westalliierten und die Rück-gabe von deutschem Archivgut nach dem Zweiten Weltkrieg*, Berlin 2004

Ehmer, Hermann, 'Der Kampf um Nassig am 30./31. März und die Beset-zung Wertheims am 1. April 1945', in: *Wertheimer Jahrbuch 1984/85*, Wertheim 1985, pp. 195–216

Engels, Peter, 'Darmstadts Zerstörung aus der Luft', in: Fritz Deppert, Peter Engels, *Feuersturm und Widerstand. Darmstadt 1944*, Darmstadt 2004, pp. 57–88

Enzyklopädie des Holocaust. Die Verfolgung der europäischen Juden, edited by Israel Gutman, Eberhard Jäckel, Peter Longerich, Julius H. Schoeps, 3 vols, 2nd edn, Zürich, Munich 1998

Erger, Johannes, *Der Kapp-Lüttwitz-Putsch. Ein Beitrag zur deutschen Innenpolitik 1919/20*, Düsseldorf 1967

Eubank, Keith, *Summit at Teheran*, New York 1985

Fallois, Immo von, *Kalkül und Illusion: Der Machtkampf zwischen Reichswehr und SA während der Röhm-Krise 1934*, Berlin 1994

Fedorowich, Kent, 'Axis Prisoners of War as Sources for British Military Intelligence, 1939–42', in: *Intelligence and National Security*, 14, 1999, pp. 156–178

Fenske, Hans, *Konservatismus und Rechtsradikalismus in Bayern nach 1918*, Bad Homburg 1969

Fest, Joachim, *Staatsstreich. Der lange Weg zum 20. Juli*, Berlin 1994 [Trans. Bruce Little, *Plotting Hitler's death: the German resistance to Hitler, 1933–1945*, London 1996

Fischer, Alexander, 'Die Bewegung "Freies Deutschland‹ in der Sowjetunion: Widerstand hinter Stacheldraht?", in: *Aufstand des Gewissens. Der militärische Widerstand gegen Hitler und das NS-Regime 1933–1945*, 3rd edn, Herford 1987, pp. 439–63

Fleischer, Hagen, *Im Kreuzschatten der Mächte. Griechenland 1941–1944 (Okkupation – Resistance – Kollaboration)*, Frankfurt am Main 1986

—, 'Schuld ohne Sühne: Kriegsverbrechen in Griechenland', in: Wolfram Wette and Gerd R. Ueberschär (eds), *Kriegsverbrechen im 20. Jahrhundert*, Darmstadt 2001, pp. 208–21

Foltmann, Josef, and Hanns Möller-Witten, *Opfergang der Generale. Die Verluste der Generale und Admirale und der im gleichen Dienstrang stehenden sonstigen Offiziere und Beamten im Zweiten Weltkrieg*, 4th edn, Berlin 1959

Förster, Jürgen, *Stalingrad. Risse im Bündnis 1942/43*, Freiburg 1975

—, 'The Dynamics of Volksgemeinschaft: The Effectiveness of the German Military Establishment in the Second World War', in: Allan R. Millet and Williamson Murray (eds), *Military Effectiveness, Vol. III, The Second World War*, London 1988, pp. 180–220

—, 'Vom Führerheer der Republik zur Nationalsozialistischen Volksarmee. Zum Strukturwandel der Wehrmacht 1935–1945', in: Jost Dülffer, Bernd Martin and Günter Wollstein (eds), *Deutschland in Europa. Kontinuität und Bruch*, Frankfurt am Main, Berlin 1990, pp. 311–28.

—, 'Geistige Kriegführung in Deutschland', in: *Das Deutsche Reich und der Zweite Weltkrieg*, Vol. 9/1, op. cit., pp. 469–640

—, Zum Rußlandbild der Militärs 1941–1945', in: Hans-erich Volkmann (ed.), *Das Rußlandbild im Dritten Reich*, Köln, 1994, p. 311–328

Franke, Manfred, *Albert Leo Schlageter; Der erste Soldat des 3. Reiches. Die Entmythologisierung eines Helden*, Cologne 1980

Fraser, David, *Knight's Cross. A Life of Field Marshal Erwin Rommel*, London 1993

Friedrich, Jörg, *Das Gesetz des Krieges. Das deutsche Heer in Rußland. Der Prozeß gegen das Oberkommando der Wehrmacht*, 2nd edn, Munich 1996

Frieser, Karl-Heinz, *Blitzkrieg-Legende*, Munich 1995

—, *Die deutschen Kriegsgefangenen in der Sowjetunion und das Nationalkomitee Freies Deutschland*, Mainz 1981

Ganglmair, Siegwald (ed.), *Der Novemberpogrom 1938. Die Reichs - kristallnacht in Wien*, Vienna 1988

Gannon, Michael, *Black May*, New York 1998 (German edition: Berlin 1999)

Gehler, Michael, '"Heilen durch Töten" oder "Gott und Welt vergasen" – Vom Medizinstudent zum Massenmörder: Biographische Annäherungen zu Dr. Irmfried Eberl 1910–1948, in: Rolf Steininger (ed.), *Tirol und Vorarlberg in der NS-Zeit*, pp. 361–82

General Ernst Köstring. Der militärische Mittler zwischen dem Deutschen Reich und der Sowjetunion 1921–1941, edited by H. Teske, Frankfurt am Main 1966

Generaloberst Halder. Kriegstagebuch, edited by Hans-Adolf Jacobsen, Vol. 3, Stuttgart 1964

Gerlach, Christian, *Kalkulierte Morde. Die deutsche Wirtschafts- und Vernichtungspolitik in Weißrußland 1941–1944*, Hamburg 1999

Germany and the Second World War, edited by Militärgeschichtlichen Forschungsamt, Vol. 4, *The Attack on the Soviet Union*, Oxford 1998

Gersdorff, Rudolf-Christoph Freiherr von, *Soldat im Untergang*, Frankfurt am Main 1977

Glanz, David, *The Soviet Airborne Experience* (Combat Studies Institute, Research Survey No. 4), Ford Leavenworth, Kansas 1984

Goebbels, Joseph, *Die Tagebücher. Sämtliche Fragmente*, edited by Elke Fröhlich, *Part II, Diktate 1941–1945*, Vols 8, 11, 13, 14, Munich 1993–96

Gorlow, Sergej A., 'Geheimsache Moskau-Berlin. Die militärpolitische Zusammenarbeit zwischen der Sowjetunion und dem Deutschen Reich 1920–1933', in: *VfZG* 44 (1996), pp. 133–65

Gorodetsky, Gabriel, *Die große Täuschung. Hitler, Stalin und das Unternehmen Barbarossa*, Berlin 2001

Gritschneder, Otto, *'Der Führer hat sie zum Tode verurteilt'. Hitlers 'Röhm-Putsch'-Morde vor Gericht*, Munich 1993

Guderian, Heinz, *Erinnerungen eines Soldaten*, Heidelberg 1951 [Trans. Constantine FitzGibbon, *Panzer Leader*, London 1952]

Haasis, Hellmut G., *'Den Hitler jag' ich in die Luft'. Der Attentäter Georg Elser. Eine Biographie*, Berlin 1999

Hahn, Fritz, *Waffen und Geheimwaffen des deutschen Heeres 1933–1945*, Vol. 1, Koblenz 1986, Vol. 2, Koblenz 1987

Harnier, Wilhelm von, *Artillerie im Küstenkampf*, Munich 1969

Harris, J.P., *Amiens to the Armistice: The BEF in the Hundred Days' Campaign, 8 August–11 November 1918*, London 1998

Hart, Stephen Ashley, 'The Forgotten Liberator: The 1939–1945 Military Carrerr of General Sir Andrew Thorne', in: *Journal of the Society for Army Historical Research* 79 (2001), pp. 233–49

Hartmann, Christian, *Halder. Generalstabschef Hitlers 1938–1942*, Paderborn 1991

—, 'Massensterben oder Massenvernichtung? Sowjetische Kriegsgefangene im Unternehmen "Barbarossa". Aus dem Tagebuch eines Lagerkommandanten', in: *VfZG* 49 (2001) 1, pp. 97–158

Hathaway, Robert M., *Great Britain and the United States. Special Relations Since World War II*, Boston 1990

Häufele Günther, 'Zwangsumsiedlungen in Polen 1939–1941. Zum Vergleich sowjetischer und deutscher Besatzungspolitik', in: Dittmar Dahlmann and Gerhard Hirschfeld (eds), *Lager, Zwangsarbeit, Vertreibung und Deportation. Dimensionen der Massenverbrechen in der Sowjetunion und in Deutschland 1933 bis 1945*, Essen 1999, pp. 515–34

Heer, Friedrich, *Der Glaube des Adolf Hitler. Anatomie einer politischen Religiosität*, Munich, Esslingen 1968

Heiber, Helmut, *Goebbels-Reden, Vol. 2, 1939–1945*, Düsseldorf 1972

Heinemann, Winfried, 'Der militärische Widerstand und der Krieg', in: *Das Deutsche Reich und der Zweite Weltkrieg, Vol. 9/1*, op. cit., pp. 743–892

Henke, Klaus-Dietmar, *Die amerikanische Besetzung Deutschlands*, Munich 1995

Henkel, Gerd, 'Deutsche Kriegsverbrechen des Weltkrieges 1914–18 vor deutschen Gerichten', in: Wolfram Wette, Gerd R. Ueberschär (eds), *Kriegsverbrechen im 20. Jahrhundert*, Darmstadt 2001, pp. 85–98.

Hett, Ulrike, and Johannes Tuchel, 'Die Reaktionen des NS-Staates auf den Umsturzversuch vom 20. Juli 1944', in: Peter Steinbach, Johannes Tuchel (eds), *Widerstand gegen den Nationalsozialismus*, Berlin 1994, pp. 383–8

Heuss, Anja, *Kunst- und Kulturraub. Eine vergleichende Studie zur Besatzungspolitik der Nationalsozialisten in Frankreich und der Sowjetunion*, Heidelberg 2000

Heuzeroth, Günter (ed.), *Verfolgte aus religiösen Gründen. Dargestellt an Ereignissen im Oldenburger Land*, Oldenburg 1985

Heydte, Friedrich August Freiherr von der, *'Muß ich sterben – will ich fallen ...'. Ein Zeitzeuge erinnert sich*, Berg am See 1987

Hildebrand, Klaus, *Das vergangene Reich. Deutsche Außenpolitik von Bismarck bis Hitler*, Stuttgart 1995

Hildermeier, *Geschichte der Sowjetunion 1917–1991. Entstehung und Niedergang des ersten sozialistischen Staates*, Munich 1998

Hillmann, Jörg, 'Die "Reichsregierung" in Flensburg', in: Hillmann/ Zimmermann (eds), *Kriegsende 1945 in Deutschland*, op. cit., pp. 35–65

—, *Der 20. Juli 1944 und die Marine. Ein Beitrag zu Ereignis und Rezeption*, Bochum 2004

— and John Zimmermann (eds), *Kriegsende 1945 in Deutschland*, Munich 2002

Himmler, Heinrich, *Geheimreden 1933 bis 1945 und andere Ansprachen*, edited by Bradley F. Smith et al., Frankfurt am Main, Berlin, Vienna 1974

Hinsley, Francis H., *British Intelligence in the Second World War*, 5 vols, London 1979–90

Hinze, Rolf, *Hitze, Frost und Pulverdampf. Der Schicksalsweg der 20. Panzer-Division*, Bochum 1981

Hitlers Lagebesprechungen. Die Protokollfragmente seiner militärischen Konferenzen, edited by Helmut Heiber, Stuttgart 1962

Hitler's Uranium Club: The Secret Recordings at Farm Hall, annotated by Jeremy Bernstein, 2nd edn, New York 2001

Hoffmann, Dieter (ed.), *Operation Epsilon: Die Farm-Hall-Protokolle oder Die Angst der Alliierten vor der deutschen Atombombe*, Berlin 1993

Hoffmann, Joachim, *Die Geschichte der Wlassow-Armee*, Freiburg 1984

Hoffmann, Peter, *Die Sicherheit des Diktators – Hitlers Leibwachen, Schutzmaßnahmen, Residenzen, Hauptquartiere*, Munich, Zürich 1975

—, *Staatsstreich, Widerstand, Attentat. Der Kampf der Opposition gegen Hitler*, 4th edn, Munich, Zürich 1985

—, *Claus Schenk Graf von Stauffenberg und seine Brüder*, 2nd edn, Stuttgart 1992

Hogg, Ian, *Deutsche Artilleriewaffen im Zweiten Weltkrieg*, Stuttgart 1978 [Originally published in English as *German Artillery of World War Two*, London 1975]

Höhne, Heinz, *Canaris. Patriot im Zwielicht*, Munich 1976

Hölsken, Heinz Dieter, *Die V-Waffen. Entstehung, Propaganda, Krieg - seinsatz*, Stuttgart 1984

Hoppe, Hans-Joachim, *Bulgarien – Hitlers eigenwilliger Verbündeter*, Stuttgart 1979

Horne, John and Alan Kramer, *German Atrocities. A History of Denial*, New Haven, London 2001

Housden, Martryn, *Hans Frank. Lebensraum and Holocaust*, Basingstoke 2003

Huber, Rudolf Günter, *Gerd von Rundstedt. Sein Leben und Wirken im Spannungsfeld gesellschaftlicher Einflüsse und persönlicher Standort - bestimmung*, Frankfurt am Main 2004

Hümmelchen, Gerhard, *Die deutschen Schnellboote im Zweiten Weltkrieg*, Hamburg 1996

Hürter, Johannes, 'Auf dem Weg zur Militäropposition. Tresckow, Gersdorff, der Vernichtungskrieg und der Judenmord', in: *VfZG* 52 (2004) 3, pp. 527–62

—, *Die deutschen Oberbefehlshaber an der Ostfront 1941/42* (In preparation)

—, *Ein deutscher General an der Ostfront. Die Briefe und Tagebücher des Gotthard Heinrici 1941/42*, Erfurt 2001

Hutchins, Francis G., *India's Revolution. Gandhi and the Quit India Movement*, Cambridge 1973

Irving, David, *Die Tragödie der deutschen Luftwaffe. Aus den Akten und Erinnerungen von Feldmarschall Milch*, Frankfurt am Main, Berlin 1970 [Published in English as *The Rise and Fall of the Luftwaffe: The Life of Luftwaffe Marshal Erhard Milch*, London 1973]

—, *Rommel*, Hamburg 1978

—, *Führer und Reichskanzler. Adolf Hitler 1933–1945*, Munich 1989

Janssen, Karl-Heinz, 'Walther von Brauchitsch – Der überforderte Feldherr', in: Smelser/Syring, *Militärelite*, op. cit., pp. 83–98

—, and Fritz Tobias, *Der Sturz der Generäle. Hitler und die Blomberg-Fritsch-Krise 1938*, Munich 1994

Jeannesson, Stanislas, 'Übergriffe der französischen Besatzungsmacht und deutsche Beschwerden', in: Gerd Krumeich and Joachim Schröder (eds), *Der Schatten des Weltkriegs. Die Ruhrbesetzung 1923*, Essen 2004, pp. 207–31

Jersak, Tobias, 'Entscheidungen zu Mord und Lüge. Die deutsche Kriegsgesellschaft und der Holocaust', in: *Das Deutsche Reich und der Zweite Weltkrieg, Vol. 9/1*, op. cit., pp. 273–356

Jones, Kevin, 'From the Horse's Mouth: Luftwaffe POWs as Source for Air Ministry Intelligence During the Battle of Britain', in: *Intelligence and National Security*, 15 (2000) 4, pp. 60–80

Jones, Tim, 'The British Army and Counter-Guerrilla Warfare in Greece, 1945–49', in: *Small Wars & Insurgencies* 8 (1997), pp. 88–106

Kehrig, Manfred, *Stalingrad. Analyse und Documentation einer Schlacht*, Stuttgart 1974

Kershaw, Ian, *Der Hitler-Mythos. Führerkult und Volksmeinung*, Stuttgart 1999

—, *Hitler. 1936–1945*, Stuttgart 2000

Kimmel, Günther, 'Das Konzentrationslager Dachau', in: Martin Broszat and Elke Fröhlich (eds), *Bayern in der NS-Zeit II. Herrschaft und Gesellschaft im Konflikt*, Part A, Munich, Vienna 1979

Klee, Ernst, *'Euthanasie' im NS-Staat*, Frankfurt am Main 1993

Klink, Ernst, *Das Gesetz des Handelns. Die Operation 'Zitadelle' 1943*, Stuttgart 1966

Knopf, Volker, and Stefan Martens, *Görings Reich. Selbstinszenierungen in Carinhall*, 2nd edn, Berlin 1999

Kohlhaas, Wilhelm, *Eberhard Wildermuth. Ein aufrechter Bürger*, Bonn 1960
Koller, Karl, *Der letzte Monat: 14. April bis 27. Mai 1945. Tagebuch - aufzeichnungen des ehemaligen Chefs des Generalstabs der deutschen Luftwaffe*, Frankfurt, Berlin 1995
Kopp, Roland, *Paul von Hase. Von der Alexander-Kaserne nach Plötzensee. Eine deutsche Soldatenbiographie 1885–1944*, Münster 2001
Kowalsky, Daniel, *La Unión Soviética y la Guerra Civil española. Una revisión crítica*, Barcelona 2003
Krammer, Arnold, 'American Treatment of German Generals during World War II', in: *Journal of Military History* 54 (1990) 1, pp. 27–46
Krannhals, Hanns von, 'Die Judenvernichtung in Polen und die "Wehrmachtö', in: *WWR* 15 (1965), pp. 570–81
Kraus, Herbert, 'Karl Dönitz und das Ende des Dritten Reiches', in: Hans-Erich Volkmann (ed.), *Ende des Dritten Reiches – Ende des Zweiten Weltkrieges. Eine perspektivische Rückschau*, Munich, Zürich 1995, pp. 1–23
Krausnick, Helmut, and Hans-Heinrich Wilhelm, *Die Truppe des Weltanschauungskrieges. Die Einsatzgruppen der Sicherheitspolizei und des SD 1938–1942*, Stuttgart 1981
Krecker, Lothar, *Deutschland und die Türkei im Zweiten Weltkrieg*, Frankfurt am Main 1964
Kriegstagebuch des Oberkommandos der Wehrmacht, compiled by Helmuth Greiner and Percy Ernst Schramm (Auftrag des Arbeitskreises für Wehrforschung, edited by Percy Ernst Schramm, Vol. 1), Munich 1982
Kriegstagebuch des Oberkommandos der Wehrmacht, edited by Percy Ernst Schramm, Vols 7, and 8, Munich 1982
Krivošeev G.F., *Grif sekretnosti snjat. Poteri vooružennych sil SSSR v vojnach, boevych dejstvijach i voennych konfliktach. Statističeskoe issledovanie*, Moscow 1993
Kroener, Bernhard R., '*Der starke Mann im Heimatkriegsgebiet'. Generaloberst Friedrich Fromm. Eine Biographie*, Paderborn 2005
—, '"Nun danket alle Gott". Der Choral von Leuthen und Friedrich der Große als protestantischer Held. Die Produktion politischer Mythen im 19. und 20. Jahrhundert', in: Gerd Krumeich and Hartmut Lehmann (eds), '*Gott mit uns'. Nation, Religion und Gewalt im 19. und frühen 20. Jahrhundert*, Göttingen 2000, pp. 105–34
—, 'Strukturelle Veränderungen in der militärischen Gesellschaft des Dritten Reiches', in: Michael Prinz and Rainer Zitelmann (eds), *Nationalsozialismus und Modernisierung*, Darmstadt 1991, pp. 267–96
Krumeich, Gerd (ed.), *Versailles 1919: Ziele, Wirkung*, Wahrnehmung, Essen 2001
Kunisch, Johannes, *Friedrich der Große*, Munich 2005
Kunz, Andreas, *Wehrmacht und Niederlage. Die bewaffnete Macht in der Endphase der nationalsozialistischen Herrschaft 1944 bis 1945*, Munich 2005
Kurz, Jakob, *Kunstraub in Europa 1938–1945*, Hamburg 1989
Laar, Mart, 'Estland und der Kommunismus', in: Stéphane Courtois et al., *Das Schwarzbuch des Kommunismus 2*, Munich, Zürich 2005, pp. 268–82
Lappenküper, Ulrich, 'Der "Schlächter von Paris": Carl-Albrecht Oberg als Höherer SS- und Polizeiführer in Frankreich 1942–1944', in: Stefan Martens and Maurice Vaïsse (eds), *Frankreich und Deutschland im*

Krieg (November 1942–Herbst 1944). Okkupation, Kollaboration, Résistance, Bonn 2000, pp. 129–43.

Leeb, Generalfeldmarschall Wilhelm Ritter von, *Tagebuchaufzeichnungen und Lagebeurteilungen aus zwei Weltkriegen*, edited by Georg Meyer, Stuttgart 1976

Lehmann, Rudolf, *Die Leibstandarte, Bd. 1*, Osnabrück, 1984

Liddell Hart, Basil Henry, *Deutsche Generale des Zweiten Weltkrieges. Aussagen, Aufzeichnungen, Gespräche*, Munich 1965 [Originally published in English as The German Generals Talk, New York 1948]

Lieb, Peter, 'Das deutsche Westheer und die Eskalation der Gewalt. Kriegführung und Besatzungspolitik in Frankreich 1943/44', PhD dissertation, Munich 2004 (forthcoming).

Liulevicius, Vejas Gabriel, *Kriegsland im Osten. Eroberung, Kolo–nisierung und Militärherrschaft im Ersten Weltkrieg*, Hamburg 2002

Lohalm, Uwe, *Völkischer Radikalismus. Die Geschichte des Deutsch - völkischen Schutz- und Trutzbundes 1919–1923*, Hamburg 1970

Longerich, Peter, *Politik der Vernichtung. Eine Gesamtdarstellung der nationalsozialistischen Judenverfolgung*, Munich, Zürich 1998

—, *Die braunen Bataillone. Geschichte der SA*, Munich 1989

Löwe, Heinz-Dietrich, 'USSR. Defence Forces and Civil Defence', in: *The Oxford Companion to the Second World War*, Oxford, 1995, p. 1228

Ludewig, Joachim, *Der deutsche Rückzug aus Frankreich 1944*, Freiburg 1994

Lukacs, John, *Churchill und Hitler. Der Zweikampf*, Munich, Zürich 1995 [Originally published in English as *The Duel: Hitler vs. Churchill, 10 May–31 July 1940*, London 1990]

McCannon, John, 'Generalfeldmarschall Georg von Küchler', in: Überschär, *Hitlers militärische Elite*, op. cit., Vol. 1, pp. 138–45

Manoschek, Walter, *'Serbien ist judenfrei'. Militärische Besatzungspolitik und Judenvernichtung in Serbien 1941/42*, Munich 1993

Margolian, Howard, *Conduct Unbecoming: The Story of the Murder of Canadian Prisoners of War in Normandy*, Toronto 1998

Martin, Bernd, *Deutsch-sowjetische Sondierungen über einen separaten Friedensschluß im Zweiten Weltkrieg*, Freiburg 1985

Maslov, Aleksander A., *Captured Soviet Generals. The Fate of Soviet Generals captured by the Germans, 1941–1945*, London, Portland 2001

Mawdsley, Even, *Thunder in the East: The Nazi Soviet War, 1941–1945*, London 2005

Mazor, Michel, 'La fin de Berditschew', in: *Monde Juif* 25 (1969) 55, pp. 21–5

Mazower, Mark, *Inside Hitler's Greece. The Experience of Occupation, 1941–44*, New Haven, London 1993

Meier-Welcker, Hans (ed.), *Abwehrkämpfe am Nordflügel der Ostfront 1944–1945*, Stuttgart 1963

Melville Ralph and Thomas Steffens, 'Die Bevölkerung', in: *Handbuch der Geschichte Rußlands*, Vol. 3/II, Stuttgart 1983, pp. 1009–191

Messenger, Charles, *The Last Prussian. A Biography of Field Marshal Gerd von Rundstedt 1875–1953*, London 1991

Messerschmitt, Manfred, 'Kommandobefehl und Völkerrechtsdenken', in: Ursula von Gersdorff (ed.), *Geschichte und Militärgeschichte. Wege der Forschung*, Frankfurt am Main 1974, pp. 211–31

Meyer, Georg, *Adolf Heusinger: Dienst eines deutschen Soldaten 1916 bis 1964*, Hamburg 2001

—, 'Auswirkungen des 20. Juli 1944 auf das innere Gefüge der Wehrmacht bis Kriegsende und auf das soldatische Selbstverständnis im Vorfeld des

westdeutschen Verteidigungsbeitrages bis 1950/51', in: *Aufstand des Gewissens. Der militärische Widerstand gegen Hitler und das NS-Regime 1933–1945*, 3rd edn, Herford 1987, pp. 465–500
—, 'Zur Situation der deutschen militärischen Führungsschicht im Vorfeld des westdeutschen Verteidigungsbeitrages 1945–1950/51', in: *Anfänge westdeutscher Sicherheitspolitik, Vol. 1, Von der Kapitulation bis zum Pleven-Plan*, Munich 1982, pp. 577–775
Meyer, Kurt, *Grenadiere*, 9th edn, Munich 1994
Middlebrook, Martin, and Chris Everitt, *The Bomber Command War Diaries. An Operational Reference Book*, Harmondsworth 1985
Mitcham, Samuel W., 'Generalfeldmarschall Ernst Busch', in: Ueberschär (ed.), *Hitlers militärische Elite*, op. cit., Vol. 2, pp. 20–6
Mueller, Gene, 'Wilhelm Keitel – Der gehorsame Soldat', in: Smelser/ Syring, *Militärelite*, op. cit, pp.. 251–69
Mühleisen, Horst, 'Fedor von Bock – Soldat ohne Fortune', in: Smelser/ Syring, *Militärelite*, op. cit, pp. 66–82
—, 'Generaloberst Werner Freiherr von Fritsch', in: Ueberschär (ed.), *Hitlers militärische Elite*, op. cit., Vol. 1, pp. 61–70
Müller, Klaus-Jürgen, *General Ludwig Beck. Studien und Documente zur politisch-militärischen Vorstellungswelt und Tätigkeit des Generalstabschefs des deutschen Heeres 1933–1938*, Boppard 1980
Müller, Rolf-Dieter, *Der Zweite Weltkrieg*, Stuttgart 2004
—, 'Albert Speer und die Rüstungspolitik im Totalen Krieg', in: *Das Deutsche Reich und der Zweite Weltkrieg, Vol. 5/2*, op. cit.
—, and Gerd R. Ueberschär, *Kriegsende 1945*, Frankfurt am Main 1994
—, and Hans-Erich Volkmann (ed.), *Die Wehrmacht. Mythos und Realität*, Munich 1999
Muñoz, Antonio J., and Oleg V. Romanko, *Hitler's White Russians, Collaboration Extermination and Anti-Partisan Warfare in Byelorussia 1941–1944*, New York 2003
Musial, Bogdan, *'Konterrevolutionäre Elemente sind zu erschießen'. Die Brutalisierung des deutsch-sowjetischen Krieges im Sommer 1941*, Berlin, Munich 2000
—, 'Das Schlachtfeld zweier totalitärer Systeme. Polen unter deutscher und sowjetischer Herrschaft 1939–1941', in: Klaus-Michael Mallmann and Bogdan Musial (eds), *Genesis des Genozids. Polen 1939–1941*, Darmstadt 2004, pp. 13–35
— (ed.), *Sowjetische Partisanen in Weißrußland: Innenansichten aus dem Gebiet Baranovici 1941–1944. Eine Documentation*, Munich 2004
Nagel, Irmela, *Fememord und Fememordprozesse in der Weimarer Republik*, Cologne, Vienna 1991
Nassua, Rudolf, *Ahndung. Ermordung kanadischer Kriegsgefangener 1944 in der Normandie vor einem kanadischen Militärgericht 1945 in Aurich*, Aurich 2001
Neitzel, Sönke, *Weltmacht oder Untergang. Die Weltreichslehre im Zeitalter des Imperialismus*, Paderborn 2000
—, *Kriegsausbruch: Der Weg in den Ersten Weltkrieg*, Zürich, Munich 2002
—, 'Der Kampf um die deutschen Atlantik- und Kanalfestungen und sein Einfluß auf den alliierten Nachschub während der Befreiung Frankreichs 1944/45', in: *MGM 55* (1996), pp. 381–430
—, 'Der Bedeutungswandel der Kriegsmarine im Zweiten Weltkrieg', in: Rolf-Dieter Müller and Hans-Erich Volkmann (eds), *Die Wehrmacht. Mythos und Realität*, Munich 1999, pp. 245–66
—, 'Des Forschens noch wert? Anmerkungen zur Operationsgeschichte der

Waffen-SS', in: *MGZ* 61 (2002) 2, pp. 403–29

—, 'Deutsche Generäle in britischer Kriegsgefangenschaft 1942–1945. Eine Auswahledition der Abhörprotokolle des Combined Services Detailed Interrogation Centre UK', in: *VfZG* 52 (2004) 2, pp. 289–348

'Neue Quellen zur Geschichte des 20. Juli 1944 aus dem Archiv des Föderalen Sicherheitsdienstes der Russischen Föderation (FSB): "Eigenhändige Aussagen" von Major i.G. Joachim Kuhn', with a commentary by Boris Chavkin and Alexandr Kalganov, in: *Forum für osteuropäische Ideen- und Zeitgeschichte* 5 (2001) 2, pp. 355–402

Neumann, Joachim, *Die 4. Panzerdivision 1938–1943*, 2nd edn, Bonn 1989

Neumärker, Uwe, Robert Conrad, Cord Woywodt, *Wolfsschwanze. Hitler's Machtzentrale im Zweiten Weltkrieg*, Berlin 2007

Oldenburg, Manfred, *Ideologie und militärisches Kalkül. Die Besatzungspolitik der Wehrmacht in der Sowjetunion 1942*, Cologne 2004

Osborne, Eric W., *Britain's Economic Blockade of Germany, 1914–1919*, London, New York 2004

Ose, Dieter, *Entscheidung im Westen 1944. Der Oberbefehlshaber West und die Abwehr der alliierten Invasion*, Stuttgart 1982

Oswald, Werner, *Kraftfahrzeuge und Panzer der Reichswehr, Wehrmacht und Bundeswehr*, Stuttgart 1971

Ovendale, Ritchie, *Anglo-American Relations in the Twentieth-Century*, Basingstoke, London 1998

Overmans, Rüdiger, *Deutsche militärische Verluste im Zweiten Weltkrieg*, Munich 1999

Overy, Richard, *Why the Allies Won*, London 1995

—, *Verhöre: die NS-Elite in den Händen der Alliierten 1945*, Berlin 2002

Padfield, Peter, *Dönitz. Des Teufels Admiral*, Frankfurt am Main 1984 [Originally published in English as *Dönitz: the Last Führer. Portrait of a Nazi War Leader*, London 1984]

Permooser, Irmtraud, 'Der Luftkrieg im Raum München 1942–1945', PhD dissertation, 1993

Peter, Roland, 'General der Artillerie Eduard Wagner', in: Ueberschär (ed), *Hitlers militärische Elite*, op. cit., Vol. 1, pp. 263–9

Piper, Ernst, *Alfred Rosenberg. Hitlers Chefideologe*, Berlin 2005

Plehwe, Friedrich-Karl von, *Reichskanzler Kurt von Schleicher. Weimars letzte Chance gegen Hitler*, Berlin 1990

Pohl, Dieter, *Nationalsozialistische Judenverfolgung in Ostgalizien 1941–1944. Organisation und Durchführung eines staatlichen Massenverbrechens*, Munich 1996

Pohlschneider, Johannes, *Der nationalsozialistische Kirchenkampf in Oldenburg. Erinnerungen und Documente*, Kevelaer 1978

Ramcke, Bernhard, *Vom Schiffsjungen zum Fallschirmjägergeneral*, Berlin 1943

—, *Fallschirmjäger. Damals und danach*, Frankfurt am Main 1951

Reinhardt, H., 'Die russischen Luftlandungen im Bereich der Heeresgruppe Mitte in den ersten Monaten des Jahres 1942', in: *WWR* 8 (1958) 7, pp. 372–88

Reinhardt, Klaus, *Die Wende vor Moskau. Das Scheitern der Strategie Hitlers im Winter 1941/42*, Stuttgart 1972

Remy, Maurice Philipp, *Mythos Rommel*, Munich 2002

Reschin (Rešin), Leonid, *Feldmarschall im Kreuzverhör. Friedrich Paulus in sowjetischer Gefangenschaft 1943–1953*, Berlin 1996

—, 'General v. Seydlitz, der BdO und die Frage einer deutschen

Befreiungsarmee unter Stalin', in: Ueberschär (ed.), *Das National - komitee*, op. cit., pp. 225–38

Reuth, Ralf Georg, *Rommel. Das Ende einer Legende*, Munich, Zürich 2004

Richter, Tim, 'Walter von Reichenau (1884–1942). Eine Verortung im Spannungsfeld von Militär, Politik und Gesellschaft', PhD dissertation, Münster i. V.

Ringshausen, Gerhard, 'Der Aussagewert von Paraphen und der Handlungsspielraum des militärischen Widerstandes. Zu Johannes Hürter: Auf dem Weg zur Militäropposition', in: *VfZG* 53 (2005) 1, pp. 141–8

Ritgen, Helmut, *Die Geschichte der Panzer-Lehr-Division, 1944–1945*, Stuttgart 1979

Ritter, Gerhard, *Carl Goerdeler und die deutsche Widerstandsbewegung*, Stuttgart 1954 [Trans. and abridged by R.T. Clark. The German Resistance: Carl Goerdeler's Struggle against Tyranny, London 1958]

Rohde, Horst, 'Politische Indoktrination in höheren Stäben und in der Truppe – untersucht am Beispiel des Kommissarbefehls', in: Hans Poeppel et al. (eds), *Die Soldaten der Wehrmacht*, Munich 1998, pp. 124–58

Römer, Felix, 'Besondere Maßnahmen'. Weitergabe, Ausführung und Akzeptanz des Kommissarbefehls im Ostheer 1941/42', PhD dissertation, Kiel i.V. (in prepartion)

Rosenkranz, Herbert, *Reichskristallnacht. 9. November 1938 in Österreich*, Vienna 1968

Ruschenbusch, Eberhard, 'Dönitz, die Konzentrationslager und der Mord an den Juden', in: *Schiff und Zeit* 52 (2000), pp. 20–6

Rüss, Hartmut, 'Wer war verantwortlich für das Massaker von Babij Jar?', in: *MGM* 57 (1998) 2, pp. 483–508

Russisches Geographisches Namenbuch, edited by Max Vasmer and Herbert Bräuer, 11 vols, Wiesbaden 1964–88

Salewski, Michael, 'Staatsräson und Waffenbrüderschaft. Probleme der deutsch-finnischen Politik 1941–1944', in: *VfZG* 27 (1979), pp. 370–91

—, 'Die Abwehr der Invasion als Schlüssel zum "Endsieg"?', in: R-D. Müller/Volkmann (eds), *Die Wehrmacht*, op. cit., pp. 210–23

Sandkühler, Thomas, *'Endlösung' in Galizien. Der Judenmord in Ostpolen und die Rettungsinitiativen von Berthold Beitz 1941–1944*, Bonn 1996

Sauer, Bernhard, 'Vom ›Mythos eines ewigen Soldatentums‹. Der Feldzug deutscher Freikorps im Baltikum im Jahre 1919', in: *ZfG* 43 (1995), pp. 869–902

Schabel, Ralf, 'Wenn Wunder den Sieg bringen sollen. Wehrmacht und Waffentechnik im Luftkrieg', in: R-D. Müller/Volkmann (eds), *Die Wehrmacht*, op. cit., pp. 385–404

Schacht, Hjalmar, *Abrechnung mit Hitler*, Berlin, Frankfurt 1949

Schall-Riaucour, Heidemarie Gräfin, *Aufstand und Gehorsam. Offiziers–tum und Generalstab im Umbruch. Leben und Wirken von Generaloberst Franz Halder, Generalstabschef 1938–1942*, Wiesbaden 1972

Schmider, Klaus, *Partisanenkrieg in Jugoslawien 1941–1944*, Hamburg 2002

—, 'Auf Umwegen zum Vernichtungskrieg? Der Partisanenkrieg in Jugoslawien 1941–1944', in: R-D. Müller/Volkmann (eds), *Die Wehrmacht*, op. cit., pp. 901–22

Schmidt, Rainer F., *Rudolf Heß. Botengang eines Toren? Der Flug nach Großbritannien vom 10. Mai 1941*, Düsseldorf 1997

Schulz, Andreas, 'Der "deutsche" Napoleon – charismatisches Vorbild der

Nationalbewegung?', in: Frank Möller (ed.), *Charismatische Führer der deutschen Nation*, Munich 2004, pp. 19–41

Schulze, Dietmar, *'Euthanasie' in Bernburg. Die Landes-Heil- und Pflegeanstalt Bernburg/Anhaltinische Nervenklinik in der Zeit des Nationalsozialismus*, Essen 1999

Schulze, Hagen, *Freikorps und Republik 1918–1920*, Boppard/Rhein 1969

Schwendemann, Heinrich, '"Deutsche Menschen vor der Vernichtung durch den Bolschewismus retten". Das Programm der Regierung Dönitz und der Beginn einer Legendenbildung', in: Hillmann/Zimmermann (eds), *Kriegsende 1945 in Deutschland*, op. cit., pp. 9–33

Searle, Alaric, *Wehrmacht Generals, West German Society, and the Debate on Rearmament 1949–1959*, Westport 2003

Seidler, Franz W., and Dieter Ziegert, *Die Führerhauptquartiere. Anlagen und Planungen im Zweiten Weltkrieg*, Munich 2000

Seidt, Hans-Ulrich, *Berlin, Kabul, Moskau. Oskar Ritter von Niedermayer und Deutschlands Geopolitik*, Munich 2002

Sfikas, Thanasis D., *The British Labour Government and the Greek Civil War 1945–1949. The Imperialism of 'Non-Intervention'*, Keele 1994

Siewert, Curt, *Schuldig? Die Generale unter Hitler. Stellung und Einfluß der hohen militärischen Führer im nationalsozialistischen Staat. Das Maß ihrer Verantwortung und Schuld*, Bad Nauheim 1968

Simms, Brendan, 'Walther von Reichenau – Der politische General', in: Smelser/Syring (eds), *Militärelite*, op. cit., pp. 423–45

Slezkine, Yuri, *The Jewish Century*, Princeton 2004

Smelser, Enrico, and Ronald Syring (eds), *Die Militärelite des Dritten Reiches*, Berlin 1995

Smith, Eric D., *Victory of a Sort. The British in Greece, 1941–1946*, London 1988

Spector, Shmuel, '"Action 1005" – Effacing the Murder of Millions', in: *Holocaust and Genocide Studies* 5 (1990), pp. 157–73

Spiegelbild einer Verschwörung. Die Kaltenbrunner-Berichte an Bormann und Hitler über das Attentat vom 20. Juli 1944. Geheime Documente aus dem ehemaligen Reichssicherheitshauptamt, edited by Archiv Peter für Historische und Zeitgeschichtliche Documentation, Stuttgart 1961

Spielberger, Walter J., *Der Panzerkampfwagen Panther und seine Abarten*, Stuttgart 1978

Sponeck, Theodor Graf von, *Meine Erinnerungen*, Bächingen an der Brenz 1976 (privately published)

Stahl, Friedrich-Christian, 'Generaloberst Kurt Zeitzler', in: Ueberschär (ed.), *Hitlers militärische Elite*, op. cit., Vol. 2, pp. 283–92

Stang, Knut, 'Hilfspolizisten und Soldaten. Das 2./12. litauische Schutzmannschaftsbataillon in Kaunas und Weißrußland', in: R-D. Müller/Volkmann (eds), *Die Wehrmacht*, op. cit., pp. 858–78

Stansky, Peter, *Sassoon. The World of Philip and Sybil*, New Haven 2003

Stein, George H., *Geschichte der Waffen-SS*, Düsseldorf 1967

Steinbach, Peter, 'Zwischen Gefolgschaft, Gehorsam und Widerstand', in: Ueberschär (ed.), *Hitlers militärische Elite*, op. cit., Vol. 1, pp. 272–85

Streim, Alfred, *Die Behandlung sowjetischer Kriegsgefangener im 'Fall Barbarossa'*, Heidelberg, Karlsruhe 1981

Streit, Christian, *Keine Kameraden. Die Wehrmacht und die sowjetischen Kriegsgefangenen 1941–1945*, Stuttgart 1978

—, 'General der Infanterie Hermann Reinecke', in: Ueberschär (ed.), *Hitlers militärische Elite*, op. cit., Vol. 1, pp. 203–9

Stürmer, Michael, Gabriele Teichmann and Wilhelm Treue, *Wiegen und Wägen. Sal. Oppenheim jr. & Cie. Geschichte einer Bank und einer Familie*, Munich, Zürich 1994

Stumpf, Reinhard, *Die Wehrmacht-Elite. Rang- und Herkunftsstruktur der deutschen Generale und Admirale 1933–1945*, Boppard 1982

—, 'General der Infanterie Rudolf Schmundt', in: Ueberschär (ed.), *Hitlers militärische Elite*, op. cit., Vol. 2, pp. 226–35

Sullivan, Matthew Barry, *Auf der Schwelle zum Frieden. Deutsche Kriegsgefangene in Großbritannien*, Vienna, Hamburg 1981

Syring, Enrico, 'Erich von Manstein – Das operative Genie', in: Syring/Smelser (eds), *Militärelite*, op. cit., pp. 325–48

Szarota, Tomasz, *Warschau unter dem Hakenkreuz. Leben und Alltag im besetzten Warschau, 1.10.1939–31.7.1944*, Paderborn 1985

Tätigkeitsbericht des Chefs des Heerespersonalamtes General der Infanterie Rudolf Schmundt 1.10.1942–29.10.1944, edited by Dermont Bradley and Richard Schulze-Kossens, Osnabrück 1984

Taylor, Frederick, *Dresden. Tuesday 13 February 1945*, London 2004

Tent, James Foster, *E-Boat Alert. Defending the Normandy Invasion Fleet*, Annapolis 1996

Thomas, David, 'Foreign Armies East and German Military Intelligence in Russia 1941–1945', in: *Journal of Contemporary History* (1987), pp. 261–301

Thun-Hohenstein, Romedio Galeazzo Graf von, *Die Verschwörer. General Oster und die Militäropposition*, Munich 1984

Toliver, Raymond F., and Trevor J. Constable, *Adolf Galland*, Munich, Berlin 1992

Ueberschär, Gerd R., *Stauffenberg. Der 20. Juli 1944*, 2nd edn, Frankfurt am Main 2004

—, (ed.), *Das Nationalkomitee 'Freies Deutschland' und der Bund Deutscher Offiziere*, Frankfurt am Main 1995

—, (ed.), *Hitlers militärische Elite*, 2 vols, Darmstadt 1998

—, and Wolfram Wette (eds), *Der deutsche Überfall auf die Sowjetunion. 'Unternehmen Barbarossa' 1941*, Frankfurt and Main 1997

—, and Winfried Vogel, *Dienen und Verdienen. Hitlers Geschenke an seine Eliten*, Frankfurt am Main 1999

—, 'Das NKFD und der BDO im Kampf gegen Hitler 1943–1945', in: Gerd R. Ueberschär (ed.), *Das Nationalkomitee*, op. cit, pp. 31–51

Vincent, Charles Paul, *The Politics of Hunger. The Allied Blockade of Germany, 1915–1919*, Ohio 1985

Vogel, Detlev, 'Deutsche und Alliierte Kriegführung im Westen', in: *Das Deutsche Reich und der Zweite Weltkrieg, Vol. 7*, op. cit, pp. 419–639

Vogel, Karl, *Lidice. Ein Dorf in Böhmen. Rekonstruktion eines Verbrechens*, Berlin 1989

Volkmann, Hans-Erich (ed.), *Das Rußlandbild im Dritten Reich*, 2nd edn, Cologne 1994

Wachsmann, Nikolaus, 'From Indefinite Confinement to Extermination. "Habitual Criminals" in the Third Reich', in: Robert Gellately (ed.), *Social Outsiders in Nazi Germany*, Princeton 2001, pp. 165–91

Wagner, Walter, *Der Volksgerichtshof im nationalsozialistischen Staat*, Stuttgart 1974

Warmbrunn, Werner, *The German Occupation of Belgium 1940–1944*, New York 1993

Weber, Wolfram, *Die innere Sicherheit im besetzten Belgien und Nordfrankreich 1940–44*, Düsseldorf 1978

Wegner, Bernd, *Hitlers Politische Soldaten. Die Waffen-SS*, 6th edn, Paderborn 1999

—, 'Erschriebene Siege. Franz Halder, die "Historical Divisionö und die Rekonstruktion des Zweiten Weltkrieges im Geiste des deutschen Generalstabes', in: Ernst-Willi Hansen, Gerhard Schreiber and Bernd Wegner (eds) *Politischer Wandel, organisierte Gewalt und natio--nale Sicherheit. Beiträge zur neueren Geschichte Deutschlands und Frankreichs. Festschrift für Klaus-Jürgen Müller*, Munich 1995, pp. 287–302

Weinberg, Gerhard L., *Eine Welt in Waffen. Die globale Geschichte des Zweiten Weltkrieges*, Stuttgart 1995

Wiehn, Erhard Roy, *Die Schoah von Babij Jar. Das Massaker deutscher Sonderkommandos an der jüdischen Bevölkerung von Kiew 1941 fünfzig Jahre danach zum Gedenken*, Konstanz 1991

Wilhelm, Hans-Heinrich, 'Heinz Guderian – "Panzerpapst" und Generalstabschef', in: Smelser/Syring (eds), *Militärelite*, op. cit., pp. 187–208

Wolff, Helmut, *Die deutschen Kriegsgefangenen in britischer Hand. Ein Überblick (Zur Geschichte der deutschen Kriegsgefangenen des Zweiten Weltkrieges*, Vol. XI/1, edited by Erich Maschke), Munich 1974

Würmling, Henric L., *'Doppelspiel'. Adam Trott zu Solz im Widerstand gegen Hitler*, Munich 2004

Young, John W., *France, the Cold War and the Western Alliance 1944–1949. French Foreign Policy and Post-War Europe*, Leicester, London 1990

Zaloga, Steven J., *Inside the Blue Berets. A Combat History of Soviet and Russian Airborne Forces, 1930–1995*, Novato, CA 1995

Zaloga, Steven J., and James Grandsen, *Soviet Tanks and Combat Vehicles*, London 1984

Zeidler, Manfred, *Reichswehr und Rote Armee 1920–1933. Wege und Stationen einer ungewöhnlichen Zusammenarbeit*, Munich 1993

—, *Stalinjustiz contra NS-Verbrechen. Die Kriegsverbrecherprozesse gegen deutsche Kriegsgefangene in der UdSSR in den Jahren 1943–1952*, Dresden 1996

Ziemke, Earl F., 'Gerd von Rundstedt – Des ›Führers‹ gehorsamer Diener', in: Smelser/Syring (eds), *Militärelite*, op. cit., pp. 476–96

Zur Mühlen, Bengt von (ed.), *Sie gaben ihr Leben. Unbekannte Opfer des 20. Juli 1944. General Fritz Lindemann und seine Fluchthelfer*, Berlin 1995

Zverev, B.I.: 'E'konomika vojujuščich deržav. Sovetskij Sojuz', in: L.V. Pozdeev and E.N. Kul'kov (eds) *Mirovye vojny XX veka, Kniga 3, Vtoraja mirovaja vojna. Istoričeskij očerk*, Moscow 2002

Zwicker, Stefan, 'Nationale Märtyrer: Albert Leo Schlageter und Julius Fučik. Studien zu Heldenverehrung und Propaganda', PhD dissertation, Mainz 2005

Acknowledgments

It is probably one of the most pleasant duties of an author after completing his assignment to thank those of his friends and colleagues who supported him in his often laborious task.

First of all I would like to express my gratitude to my friend Dr Klaus Schmider for directing my attention to the transcripts and assisting me subsequently during the course of the work.

I should also like to offer special thanks to Herrn Felix Römer. He allowed me access to his partially-complete dissertation on the Commissar Order and helped me greatly to evaluate the written material bequeathed by General Ludwig Crüwell. I thank Dr Bernd Crüwell for placing his father's notes at my disposal.

Tim Richter and Jörn Hasenclever were generous enough to make available important sources. Drs. Alexander Brakel and Matthias Spreger provided me with many useful references to obscure literary sources. Marcus A König rendered sterling support in my research for the commentary. The typescript was prepared in her usual reliable manner by Frau Gertraud Tinelli.

I am obliged to Professor Rolf-Dieter Müller for his critical reading of the manuscript, and also to my friend Dr Jürgen Förster, with whom I had many conversations about the Trent Park generals. His impressive knowledge of the sources proved very valuable during my research.

I should also like to thank Oberstleutnant Michael Poppe at the Bundesarchiv/Militärarchiv who throughout gave me unstinting help.

I am most grateful to the Propyläen publishing house, particularly to Herrn Christian Seeger, for accepting my manuscript into the publishing programme, and for their outstanding collaboration.

Finally I thank Dr Gundula Bavendamm for her many-sided support and the unwavering understanding she had for me during the work. It cannot have been easy to deal with somebody more mentally present at Trent Park than elsewhere. To her I dedicate this book in gratitude.

INDEX